THE PLAYS OF EURIPIDES

SELECTED FRAGMENTARY PLAYS: I

General Editor
Professor Christopher Collard

Aris & Phillips Classical Texts

EURIPIDES

Selected Fragmentary Plays, Vol. 1

Telephus, Cretans, Stheneboea, Bellerophon, Cresphontes, rectheus, Phaethon, Wise Melanippe, Captive Melanippe

edited with introductions, translations and commentaries by

C. Collard, M. J. Cropp amd K. H. Lee

Aris & Phillips is an imprint of Oxbow Books

First published in the United Kingdom in 1995, reprinted with corrections 1997, reprinted
with corrections and addenda 2009 by
OXBOW BOOKS
10 Hythe Bridge Street, Oxford OX1 2EW

and in the United States by
OXBOW BOOKS
908 Darby Road, Havertown, PA 19083

© The authors C. Collard, M. J. Cropp and K. H. Lee

Paperback Edition: ISBN 978-0-85668-619-1

A CIP record for this book is available from the British Library

For a complete list of Aris & Phillips titles, please contact:

UNITED KINGDOM
Oxbow Books
Telephone (01865) 241249
Fax (01865) 794449
Email: oxbow@oxbowbooks.com
www.oxbowbooks.com

UNITED STATES OF AMERICA
Oxbow Books
Telephone (800) 791-9354
Fax (610) 853-9146
Email: queries@casemateacademic.com
www.casemateacademic.com/oxbow

Oxbow Books is part of the Casemate Group

CONTENTS OF VOLUME ONE

GENERAL EDITOR'S FOREWORD

In the earlier volumes of this Series I have begun my Foreword with the argument that Euripides' remarkable variety of subjects, ideas and methods challenges each generation of readers, and audiences, to a fresh appraisal. The complete plays, eighteen in number, are challenge enough; but there are about as many fragmentary plays which it is possible to reconstruct in outline and which increase and diversify the challenge still more. The Preface and General Introduction to this volume assert the great interest of these plays in their own right, and describe the ways in which they illuminate the complete plays while depending on them for their own illumination.

This volume, and a second which will complete the selection, appear to be the first of their kind for Euripides. While they are in the general style of the Aris and Phillips' Classical Texts, the fragmentary material on which they draw has sometimes to be presented and discussed on a fuller scale, and is offered to a rather wider readership. Not just school, college or university students and their teachers but also professional scholars will, we hope, be served by these volumes. For each play there is an editor's introduction which attempts reconstruction and appreciation, discussing context, plot, poetic resources and meaning. The Greek text is faced by an English prose translation — for many of the plays the first complete such translation to be published. The commentaries privilege interpretation and appreciation as far as possible over philological discussion; but the needs of fragmentary texts make the latter inseparable from the former.

The content and nature of this volume and its companion explain the omission of the General Introduction to the Series and of the General Bibliography which are found in other volumes. Instead, a General Introduction to the fragmentary tragedies is offered, including a section which reviews the special features and problems of these plays; and there is a Bibliography of works especially important to them.

University of Wales, Swansea
March 1995

Christopher Collard

PREFACE

This edition is directed at the need which has long been apparent to make some at least of Euripides' fragmentary plays more easily accessible in English to specialists and non-specialists alike. We hope too that it will encourage attention to some fascinating texts which are often of considerable importance to the critical appreciation of the poet. English readers have for long been frustrated for access to the majority of the fragmentary plays unless they command not only Greek but also either Latin or some of the modern languages.[1] Many of the fragments, and discussions of them, are in widely scattered publications; in our edition we try to bring together much of this work, especially of the 20th Century, for the benefit of readers of English, including those who have no Greek at all.

Our selection is of the most important and interesting plays, defined as those for which there is sufficient primary text and secondary evidence to permit at least an outline reconstruction and location of the fragments. Some readers will inevitably be disappointed that we have not included more plays; but a wider selection would have reduced the room for introduction and commentary to a scarcely useful minimum. Inevitably, too, some very fragmentary and uncertainly read texts have demanded more technical discussion than is usual for this Series.

Our discussions of most of the papyrus fragments, including all of those in Volume I, are based on previously published (or in one case about-to-be-published) editions of the papyri.

The second volume will include *Alexandros, Palamedes* and *Sisyphus* (the three plays which accompanied *Trojan Women* in the production of 415 B.C.),

---

[1] We record here some noteworthy publications in English. G. Murray, *Euripides* (transl. of *Hippolytus*, etc.: London, 1915[6]), 313-52 ('Appendix on Lost Plays') and W. N. Bates, *Euripides: A Student of Human Nature* (Philadelphia, 1930), 202-303 (ch. 5, 'The Lost Plays') give summary accounts of many plays (Bates gives 57); Page, *GLP* has an edition with brief introduction and translation of a few longer papyrus texts. There are excellent editions and commentaries, but without translations, in *Euripides' Kresphontes and Archelaos* by A. Harder (Leiden, 1985), *Euripides: Hypsipyle* by G. W. Bond (Oxford, 1963), *Euripides: Phaethon* by J. Diggle (Cambridge, 1970), and E. W. Handley and J. Rea, *The Telephus of Euripides* (London, 1957). T. B. L. Webster performed a great service to the fragmentary plays when he emphasized them in *The Tragedies of Euripides* (London, 1967).

vii

fragments of Euripides' first *Hippolytus* will be found with Michael Halleran's edition of the complete play in this Series. An *Index* to both volumes will be printed at the end of the second.

That we have been able to undertake this selective edition at a manageable price is due to the interest and support of our publishers Aris and Phillips; we are confident that our readers will share our gratitude to them.

In preparing our volumes, each of us took the first and also final responsibility for individual plays; our initials are put against them on the contents-page. All three of us have however read and annotated one another's successive drafts. It has been a great benefit and pleasure for us to hold discussions face to face, if usually in pairs, in all three of our home countries. For helping to make such collaboration possible we owe further gratitude to Aris and Phillips in Britain and to the research funds of our respective universities. We have been helped too by the initial encouragement and subsequently the comments of friends and colleagues. We particularly thank Michael Dewar, Pat Easterling, Robert Fowler, Eric Handley, Michael Halleran, Richard Hamilton, Richard Kannicht, Ludwig Koenen, Jim Neville, Stefan Radt, and Richard Seaford. Our greatest debt is to James Diggle, who has read almost the whole volume in draft and provided detailed comments and suggestions; we indicate some of these with his initials 'JD'.

Preparation of drafts and final copy was undertaken by Martin Cropp with the assistance of Lillian Kogawa in Calgary. Christopher Collard and Kevin Lee record their warmest thanks to both.

C. C. (Swansea)
M. J. C. (Calgary)
K. H. L. (Sydney)

March 1995

This revised edition was prepared for publication in April 2007. It incorporates corrections (we thank John Porter for bringing many of these to our attention) and some improvements in formatting. The fragment numbering of R. Kannicht in *TrGF 5*, superseding Nauck's, is now used throughout (see further p. 11 below). The *Addenda to Volume 1* first printed at the end of Volume 2 (2004) are now given at the end of this volume with some revisions and further additions (see note on p. 281).

C. C. (Oxford)
M. J. C. (Calgary)

March 2009

GENERAL INTRODUCTION

I. Some Categories of Evidence for the Fragmentary Plays

(i) Euripides' own words, the primary evidence, survive in (1) papyrus or parchment fragments of single plays or of collected 'editions' of the plays, which range in date from the 3ʳᵈ Century B.C. (*Erectheus*, for example) to the 5ᵗʰ or early 6ᵗʰ Century A.D. (*Phaethon*, for example); with these belong texts which were never complete but have survived as excerpts in now fragmentary anthologies (Pasiphae's speech in *Cretans*, for example, or the rebuttal of misogyny in *Captive Melanippe*); and in (2) the 'book fragments' — excerpts or quotations or references made by other ancient authors, anthologists, lexicographers and so on, almost all of them with their own manuscript traditions like that of Euripides' surviving and complete plays. The earliest such quotations are by the comic dramatist Aristophanes, Euripides' own contemporary; the latest are by Byzantine scholars, their sources often no longer identifiable. Some of the texts of the ancient writers who excerpt or annotate Euripides are themselves fragmentary, either because they are themselves excerpted in other writers or because their texts are carried in fragmentary manuscripts; in such cases we are even further from Euripides' own words.

For both (1) and (2) many of the texts or quotations come with incomplete details of authorship and ascription (or with none at all); some are attributed just to 'Euripides', some just to a play, no dramatist being named. In such cases attribution to poet and particular play is a question of scholarly judgement after consideration of such internal evidence or external pointers as can be found. There are inevitably many texts of disputed attribution: large papyrus fragments like those of a *Theseus* (P. Oxy. 2452: both Sophocles and Euripides are possible), quotations of a few lines or words, even single words. In our edition we cite the authority for attribution, ancient or modern, and review the disputable fragments as dispassionately as we can.

(ii) For Euripides the secondary evidence — official records, scholarly information, description, allusion, anecdote and the like — is much more extensive than for the other tragedians, and in one respect above all. Because his plays enjoyed greater popularity after his death than during his life — both in the theatre and on the page — there survive numerous 'hypotheses', of two kinds. The first are summary introductions to the plays, including information drawn from performance records, chiefly Athenian (*didascaliae: TrGF* I pp. 3–52); these go back to Aristophanes of Byzantium's edition of Tragedy about 200 B.C.; some of them were utilised and expanded by later scholars, both ancient

1

and Byzantine. The second kind are narrative plot summaries of disputed origin which were copied, modified or imitated from antiquity into the Byzantine period. The more complete of the hypotheses, of both kinds, are attached to the surviving plays in the main manuscript tradition; but for many of both the surviving and the fragmentary plays there are narrative summaries preserved either complete or in part both on papyrus and copied in later authors. Where they are complete or largely intact, they can aid reconstruction very considerably (as in *Alexandros*, *Wise Melanippe*, *Stheneboea*); where they are fragmentary they are at best suggestive (e.g. *Oedipus*, *Phaethon*), at worst of no benefit (e.g. *Bellerophon*, *Telephus*).[1]

(iii) Some of the book fragments are embedded in references to their plays which fill out the content or nature of both play and fragment, and allow the fragment to be located in the plot or assigned to an individual character. Such information is invaluable to reconstruction, but the caution necessary in using the less informative citations is not always heeded: scraps of information, and inferences from small hints, can seldom be brought convincingly together into large signposts. Many book fragments come without any information whatever concerning context, and even the primary meaning of the Greek may therefore be in doubt, particularly when they are moral generalisations. An extreme example of all these uncertainties is *Bellerophon*, for which there are over thirty book fragments but no sure path to their overall arrangement; a fragmentary hypothesis has not helped at all. Speculative reconstruction of such plays is wholly justifiable, indeed an almost irresistible challenge, and each attempt either narrows the possibilities or adds new ones; speculation however it must remain. Even the acquisition in this century of large new fragments can leave a play still no more than a broken outline, like *Cretans*; yet our hold on others has occasionally been enormously strengthened if not secured through gradual accretions (e.g. *Erectheus*, *Telephus* and, the best instance, *Alexandros*). The accidents of rediscovery bring surprising frustrations as well as large advances.

---

[1] Hypotheses: for the 'Aristophanic' kind see the bibl. in *Euripides: Hecuba*, ed. C. Collard (Warminster, 1991), 129, now to be supplemented from D. J. Mastronarde, *Euripides: Phoenissae* (Cambridge, 1994), 168 n. 2. Scholars are in general agreed that the narrative kind stem ultimately from a Euripidean collection composed in the 1st or 2nd Century A.D. but ascribed in order to acquire respectability to Aristotle's 4th Century B.C. pupil Dicaearchus: J. Rusten, *GRBS* 23 (1982), 357–67; R. Kassel in *ΣΧΟΛΙΑ: Studies...Holwerda* (Groningen, 1985), 53–9; W. Luppe in *Aristoteles: Werk und Wirkung* (Berlin, 1985), 610–2 — all three against M. W. Haslam, *GRBS* 16 (1975), 152–5. Considerable fragments of the Euripidean collection survive in papyri: see Austin (below, n. 3); W. Luppe, *Acta Antiqua* 33 (1992), 39–44 (on the 'hypotheses').

(iv) One category of secondary evidence — tertiary, rather — is of most uncertain, indeed strongly disputed, value to the reconstruction of fragmentary plays, not least because it is at the same time the most tangible: artistic representations, chiefly painting on pottery or walls and relief sculpture. Despite the caution of earlier scholars, Séchan's long study of 1926 induced many reconstructors to turn to vase-paintings, especially those from Athens itself earlier than or contemporary with the plays, with too strong a belief in their reliability. If vases pictured figures at rest or in activity suggestive of a mythical incident, they were adduced as probable reflections of a dramatic moment and identified with this or that play. In recent years recognition has grown that any painted scene, even where the painter has named the figures, is not inevitably to be associated with any particular play by any particular poet, still less with any single moment within it; and the greater the gap between the dramatist's lifetime and the datable painting or sculpture, the less is its direct usefulness. Even where it seems likely that a particular scene from Euripides is reflected in a vase-painting, it may appear that the painter has included additional elements and characters: for a good example see pp. 241–2 on *Wise Melanippe*. T. B. L. Webster, who in 1967 in his *The Tragedies of Euripides* pressed the evidence of art sometimes imaginatively far, wrote in 1970 'These pictures...are seldom completely accurate realistic representations of a stage scene, but it would be foolish to reject them because they are the records of an intelligent artist rather than of a stupid camera'. Since that was written, caution has increased. O. Taplin has recently (1993) traced the scholarly argument in terms of a "polarisation between 'text-driven' philologist-iconographers and 'autonom-ous' iconologists". Taplin contends that the many vases from southern Italy made in the period 425–325 B.C. (which constitute the great majority of those applied to the reconstruction of plays) are not 'scene-specific' in the way they reflect mythic incident, even if they are "*somehow* [his italics] related to Tragedy;" " . . . they do not 'expose' the inspiration for the myth by alluding openly to its tragic presentation".[2] Our attitude towards artistic representations

---

[2] Séchan, *Études*. Quotations from T. B. L. Webster, *Greek Theatre Production* (London, 1970[2]), xvi–xvii; O. Taplin, *Comic Angels* (Oxford, 1993), successively 21, 27, 26. The whole argument is documented by J. R. Green, *GRBS* 32 (1991), 15–50, esp. 38–44 (cf. Green, *Theatre* 22ff., 51ff.) and Taplin 21–9 (ch. 3 'Tragedy and Iconography'), cf. 6–8. See also Trendall-Webster, *Illustrations*, Introduction; A. D. Trendall, *The Red-Figure Vases of S. Italy and Sicily* (London, 1989), 262–4, and in T. Rasmussen, N. Spivey (eds.), *Looking at Greek Vases* (Cambridge, 1991), 151–3; B. A. Sparkes, *Greek Art* ('Greece and Rome' New Surveys in the Classics, 21: Oxford, 1991), 63–77; J. R. Green, E. W. Handley, *Images of the Greek Theatre* (London: British Museum Press, 1995), 12–13, 40–8, 63–4.

as guide to reconstruction of Euripides' plays is accordingly very cautious; but we recognise that such works may usefully prompt a reader's general imagination, just as they were themselves the product of artistic imagination.

II. Modern Study of the Fragmentary Plays

(i) The first scholarly collectors of Tragic fragments, from the middle 16th to the early 19th Centuries, could assemble material only from the book fragments, which for Euripides were more numerous and extensive than for Aeschylus and Sophocles. Since the early 19th Century these have been continually supplemented by further discoveries, above all of fragmentary ancient texts and hypotheses, and by the accretion of many artistic representations of mythic incident, chiefly paintings and relief sculpture, which have been studied and applied with the recent greater caution to the reconstruction of lost plays. For Euripides the new texts and secondary evidence have again greatly exceeded those for Aeschylus and Sophocles.[3]

The new texts and evidence have inevitably been published piecemeal as soon as possible after discovery, and in a great variety of places and languages. It is now over a century since A. Nauck in 1889 revised his famous one-volume edition of all the Tragic fragments then known. Nauck printed the Greek texts and ancient *testimonia* (sources, informatory references and the like) with a critical *apparatus* in Latin, but without synoptic reconstruction or commentary for any play (except *Phaethon*). The book was reprinted in 1964 with a Supplement by B. Snell which contained only book fragments discovered since

---

3   For accounts of the collecting and editing of Tragic fragments see: H. van Looy, *AC* 32 (1963), 170–84, an historical treatment forming part of his invaluable bibliographic surveys of the Euripidean fragments *ibid.* 162–99, 60 (1991), 295–311 and 61 (1992), 280–95; Austin, *NFE* 5–7: T.B.L. Webster, *Greek Tragedy* ('Greece and Rome' New Surveys in the Classics, No. 5, Oxford, 1971), 28–30; S. L. Radt in *TrGF* III pp. 9–10, IV pp. 9–13; R. Kassel in Hofmann and Harder, *Fragmenta Dramatica*, 243–53. All these accounts except Radt's and Kassel's omit the first systematic collection of Greek poetic, especially dramatic, fragments which did not rely entirely on ancient anthologists like Stobaeus. It was made by D. Canter (1545–1617), younger brother of W. Canter (1542–75) the first great modern editor of the tragedians; it was begun probably in partnership and before 1570. Parts of the original 7-volume manuscript collection survive in Paris and Oxford; the Bodleian Library has under the call-mark Ms. d'Orville 121 the complete Euripides volume, of some 600 pages. An account of the manuscripts, their failure to be published, their use by early scholars and subsequent history, especially their neglect after the middle of the 18th century, is given by J. A. Gruys, *The Early Printed Editions of Aeschylus, 1518–1664* (The Hague, 1981), 297–309, 342–6. C. Collard evaluates the Euripides volume in *AC* 64 (1995), 243–51.

Nauck; most of the papyrus texts new since Nauck were published in differing collections by H. von Arnim (1913: in German), D. L. Page (1941: in English) and, after Snell, by C. Austin (1968: in Latin). Papyri subsequently discovered have once more been published as soon as possible and individually. Between 1967 and 1985 the German scholar H.J. Mette twice documented both old and new texts, but reproduced or edited only a very few of them. Elaborate editions of individual fragmentary plays appear at intervals: see the introductory bibliographies, and e.g. p. vii n. 1 above. Translations of this or that fragmentary text or play have regularly appeared in learned journals all over the world, but there have so far been few translated collections, and none into English. At the time of writing this Introduction, in 1994, we still await publication of R. Kannicht's Euripides volume in the new *Tragicorum Graecorum Fragmenta* ('*Fragments of the Greek Tragedians*'), the magnificent successor-edition in five parts to Nauck's single volume. The long wait for publication attests the complexity of Kannicht's huge task. When his *Euripides* appears, it will offer all the known texts and *testimonia* with an *apparatus criticus* in Latin.

(ii) Imagine our notion of Shakespeare's art and thought without the text of *Hamlet* or *The Tempest*. The loss suffered by Euripides is even more serious, since of some 90 plays only 18 have come down to us intact.[4] Even on the basis of the extant plays we can determine that Euripides' *oeuvre* was of remarkable versatility, and so no serious study of Euripides can afford to ignore the additional information about the poet's dramatic technique and ideas which the fragments provide. So, for example, we cannot now fully appreciate why Aristophanes selected *Andromeda* as the tragedy which filled Dionysus in the *Frogs* (52ff.) with a deep yearning for the dead poet. But a study of the play's fragments gives us at least some idea of its remarkable features which prompted the scholiast on the same passage to name it 'one of the finest' of Euripides' dramas. Again, it must be remembered that while Euripides' first production was in 455 and his first victory in 441, only two extant plays, *Alcestis* and *Medea*, can be dated before 430. So the substantial fragments of *Telephus* (438), of *Cretans* (around 438?) and of *Stheneboea* (before 429?) are important for supplementing our knowledge of the poet's earlier work. This brief survey is intended to show how the fragmentary plays can broaden our knowledge of the material and structure of Euripides' plots, of his character drawing, dramaturgy and style.

---

[4] For the number of plays known to antiquity see the anonymous life of Euripides, most recently printed in D. Kovacs, *Euripidea*, Leiden 1994, 4f. Despite the rigorous defence of its authenticity by W. Ritchie (1964), the *Rhesus* is now generally regarded as spurious.

An important lacuna which the fragments fill concerns the myths on which Euripides drew for material. Twenty-eight of the plays whose titles we know were based on Trojan or Attic myth.[5] Of the extant plays the majority (thirteen) belong to this group, while only five (*Alcestis, Medea, Heracles, Phoenissae, Bacchae*) represent the forty-nine which have as their source other myths. Happily, this small sample is augmented by the fifteen or so examples which are to be treated in these volumes.[6]

Our knowledge of Euripides' wide range of dramatic motifs is broadened significantly by the fragmentary plays. These will be examined in detail in the Introductions to the individual plays; an overview is given here. The motif of the lost child recovering his past, familiar from the Oedipus story[7] and treated with interesting adjuncts in *Ion*, is a key element of *Captive Melanippe, Hypsipyle* and *Antiope*. These plays end with the children's foreshadowed glory, and further interest is created in the role of the bereft mothers, threatened by malicious outsiders and eventually rescued by their sons. Even from the fragments we can discern the imaginative variety with which Euripides has structured plots based on the same motif. Melanippe is in dire straits, imprisoned and possibly blinded. She is rescued by the twins she bore to Poseidon after they themselves have escaped an ambush planned by their jealous stepmother. Hypsipyle, once Jason's concubine, now serves in Nemea as nurse to the king's baby. She accidentally causes the death of the child and is saved from execution by the seer Amphiaraus and then from imprisonment by her two sons, who reveal their inherited nobility at funeral games. *Antiope* combines the rescue of Antiope with the punishment of her assailants by her twin sons, Amphion and Zethus.

The varied amalgam of the motifs of recognition, intrigue, and escape which are central to *Iphigenia in Tauris, Helen* and *Electra* are anticipated in yet another variation in *Cresphontes*, where the death of the true villain is preceded by the narrow escape of Cresphontes from Merope, who thinks he is her son's killer. A mother's attack on her unrecognised son, familiar from Creusa's plot against Ion, is also an element of the plot of *Alexandros* in which Hecuba is determined to kill Paris, taken for an upstart shepherd who outdid her sons in athletic prowess.

---

5   For lists see S. Radt in Hofmann and Harder, *Fragmenta Dramatica* 87 n.17 and 88 n. 20.

6   In Vol. I *Telephus* is Trojan, *Erectheus* Attic; in Vol. II *Philoctetes, Alexandros* and *Palamedes* are Trojan.

7   Incidentally, it is interesting to see from the few fragments of *Oedipus* how different Euripides' treatment of the story is from Sophocles'. Oedipus, whose misfortunes are revealed by Creon, not himself, is blinded by servants. Jocasta is presented not as a passive figure but with considerable force.

The luring of a victim to death was a motif which could gratify the audience, as in *Heracles*, or could be tinged with ambiguity, as in the Euripidean *Electra*. Lycus seems to have gone to a deserved death in *Antiope* when he is lured into the house to confront the murderous hands of the twins. But he is saved by Hermes and finally sees the error of his ways. In *Archelaus* the perfidious Thracian king Cisseus is taken off stage, it seems, by a mixture of guile and force, and is himself made to fall into the fiery pit he had prepared for the innocent Archelaus. In *Cresphontes* we are told how the villain Polyphontes falls victim to the combined strategy of mother and son. Merope feigns a reconciliation which prompts the villain to proceed to a sacrifice where, like Aegisthus in *Electra*, he is despatched by Cresphontes.

Ion's brilliant use of 'mirror scenes' involving repetition of both verbal and visual elements was seen earlier in *Stheneboea*. This tragedy is based on the 'Joseph and Potiphar's wife' story of Bellerophon and the wife of Proetus, king of Tiryns, who gives the play its name. The attempted seduction resisted by Bellerophon and two unsuccessful attempts on his life are followed by the seductress's death, thrown from the flying horse Pegasus.

That Euripides could write a single tragedy with an astonishing richness of theme and action is clear from extant plays like *Helen* and *Orestes*, and the fragments of *Telephus, Hypsipyle* and *Stheneboea*. What might he have done with a trilogy like the *Oresteia*? We know enough of the plays of 415 to say that they may have made a coherent trilogy, a structure which allowed more scope for the progressive development of theme and character and which cannot readily be discerned among other plays. The distraught Hecuba of *Troades* must be viewed against the backdrop of the *Alexandros* which showed the proud queen determined to kill her unrecognised son Paris. In that play too we hear the first sounds of Cassandra's prophetic voice which were to be echoed in *Troades*, in her lyric travesty of the marriage song and her sober forecast of the deaths awaiting Agamemnon and herself. Even the themes of unjustified punishment and the false categorisation of slave and free which are explored in *Troades* seem to have been foreshadowed in the two previous tragedies. After a debate on the nature of slavery Paris is threatened by his brother and mother partly because of his supposed lowly status; and Palamedes, described as 'the all wise, harmless nightingale of the Muses' (*Palamedes* F 588), is wrongly killed by the Greeks.

The fragmentary plays add significantly to the list of Euripides' striking characters. The hero of *Bellerophon* seems to have been developed into a figure opposed to the gods, a *theomachos* like Pentheus in *Bacchae*. He cannot abide the gods' injustice and so attempts to scale heaven mounted on Pegasus. To the list of the poet's engaging female characters like Creusa in *Ion* we can add the charming figure of Hypsipyle, who combines genteel decorum with an almost fussy concern for the baby she carries when she enters to confront her as yet unrecognised sons. More strident and provocative are Stheneboea the seductress who, like Phaedra, is challenged by a chaste young man, and Pasiphae in *Cretans* whose fluent tongue provokes Minos to exclaim before ordering her removal, 'has she had her tongue sharpened?' (F 472e.44). Cleverness rather than passion marks out Melanippe whose defence of her sex against misogynists (F 494) bears comparison with Medea's famous speech.

In organising his material for the stage Euripides had a sure eye for the theatrically effective. The fragmentary plays contribute to our appreciation of his use of costume, stage machinery and impressive tableaux. The ragged appearance of heroes like Telephus and Bellerophon became part of theatrical folklore and was repeatedly a source of Aristophanic fun. It is likely that Menelaus's sea-weedy appearance on his entrance in the *Helen* harks back to such costume and shows that Euripides could capitalize on a joke at his own expense. Another example of striking dress may have been seen in *Wise Melanippe* when, we are told in the hypothesis, Melanippe was ordered by her father to prepare her children for death by dressing them in funerary clothes. This probably led to a striking entry such as we find in *Heracles* when Megara leads out Heracles' children clad for death at the hands of Lycus.

Such entries bring to mind Euripides' imaginative use of group entrances to generate a variety of emotions. A solemn procession, like that accompanying the child Astyanax's corpse in *Troades* or Pentheus's remains in *Bacchae*, is likely to have brought the dead baby Opheltes onto the stage in *Hypsipyle*. The drowned Stheneboea is brought all the way from Melos to Tiryns by fishermen who, it is likely, added interest to the cortège by their characteristic dress and manner. In *Phaethon* (227ff.) a secondary chorus of girls enters to sing a wedding song, accompanied no doubt with much festive colour and movement. This offsets perfectly the horror of Phaethon's death expressed in the lyrics of the main chorus soon after (270ff.).

The fragments give us several examples of what was obviously a favourite motif: the timely entrance of a rescuer. Like Peleus in *Andromache*, and the Pythia in *Ion*, Amphiaraus arrives unexpectedly to rescue Hypsipyle who is threatened by Eurydice, the outraged mother of the dead Opheltes. Even more dramatic is the intervention of a god. Athena appears at the end of *Erectheus* and compels Poseidon to stop the earthquake by which he vents his rage against the victors over his son, and, like Apollo preventing the death of Hermione at the end of *Orestes*, Hermes stops the killing of Lycus in *Antiope*. But the most exciting instance of the motif is found in *Cresphontes*, when the unrecognised prince is saved from his axe-wielding mother by the last-minute intervention of an old retainer.

Euripides' use of stage machinery can be posited in several fragmentary plays. The ekkyklema, probably employed for the revelation of indoor scenes in *Heracles* and *Hippolytus*, may have been used to present the tableau showing the threatened maiden tied to her rock at the beginning of *Andromeda*. There are few certain instances of the use of the mechane or crane in the extant plays, but it is very likely to have been used for Bellerophon's flights on Pegasus in *Bellerophon* and *Stheneboea* and for Perseus's aerial entry in *Andromeda*. It would be typically Euripidean to employ the crane for the spectacular flight of unusually equipped mortals. Such a technique would most naturally have suggested the Aristophanic parody in *Peace*, where Pegasus is converted into a well-fed dung beetle.

Our knowledge of the breadth and colour of Euripides' style benefits materially from a study of the fragments. Several speeches contain telling thoughts neatly expressed. In *Oedipus* (F 556) there is reference to the 'tuneful reed which the river Melas grows, the gifted nightingale of sweet-breathing flutes'. Melanippe denies in striking language the idea that justice is meted out by Zeus in terms of a ledger which he keeps on high: the whole of heaven could not hold the account of men's sins (F 506). In *Stheneboea* (F 670) the purple-fisher's hard life is described in words which express affectionate distaste: '. . . his table is on the shore. The sea is a watery mother, no nurse where feet may walk; she is our plough-land, from her our living comes home by means of lines and traps.' *Andromeda* (F 136) contains an emotional address to Eros which, after stressing the god's universal power, ends with what seems a heart-broken threat.

Alongside these striking utterances we find, because of the nature of our sources, a disproportionately large number of gnomic statements, the content and phrasing of which are often predictable. The context may well have lent life and vigour to these maxims, as we see in the remarkable collection of them which *Erectheus* passes on, in testamentary manner, to his heir (F 362).

Patriotic rhetoric, reminiscent of Iphigenia's speech in *Iphigenia at Aulis*, pervades the long speech from *Erectheus* in which Praxithea declares her willingness to sacrifice her daughter to save the city (F 360). The speech contains two remarkable similes: Athens is autochthonous, but other cities are like scattered board-game pieces; a newcomer to a city must remain an alien, like an ill-fitting dowel in a plank of wood. The adversarial tone suggests that the speech was part of a debate over the issue of the claims of the state on the individual. We have enough of the debate between the twins in *Antiope* to understand why it was to be quoted from Plato down to the emperor Julian. This rhetorical *tour de force* juxtaposed the virtues of the active life with those of the quiet life of contemplation.

Feisty rhetoric is seen at its best in Pasiphae's speech of defence in *Cretans*. Her claim that, far from being at fault, she deserves pity for what she has suffered through 'the onslaught of a god' (F 472e.9) reminds one of Helen's defence in *Troades* and of other evasions of responsibility like the Nurse's in *Hippolytus*. But a feature of this speech is its blending of deep passion with the wit seen in the argument from 'likelihood' used to deny any voluntary attachment to the beast. With effective irony Pasiphae asks: 'Was he so handsome a sight in his clothes, and did his red hair, and his eyes, shine with such brilliance, and was his chin dark in contrast, like a ripening grape?'(F 472.13ff).

Vivid description and evocative writing are found in several fragmentary speeches. For example, the Messenger's graphic report of the failed attack on Melanippe's sons in *Captive Melanippe* (F 495) is comparable with the reports we hear in *Bacchae*, especially in its evocation of a rural setting. The unusual anapaestic opening of *Andromeda* is powerfully expressive of the maiden's terror, alone in the dark of the night.

Our appreciation of Euripides' lyric art is enriched by some remarkable songs among the fragments. One could single out the heartfelt appeal to Peace in *Cresphontes* (F 453), and the prayer for a restful old age in *Erectheus* (F 369) with its vivid image of a spear covered with cobwebs, which is picked up in the reference to a hoary head draped with garlands. At the end of the play lyrics shared by Praxithea and the Chorus move deftly from sobbing lament to a terrified reaction to the earthquake which makes the land 'dance with a rolling movement' (F 370.48). *Phaethon* includes a gem of Euripidean poetry in its Parodos (63ff.). The Chorus enters to sing of its own hopes and those of its masters for the coming wedding. But first it greets the arrival of the happy day with a panorama of the sights and sounds of early morning. The detail is precise, the transitions are smooth, and the selection of activities for mention gives evidence of a sure touch.

We conclude this survey with repeated emphasis on Euripides' versatility. It is generally agreed that he stretched Tragedy to its formal and thematic limits, and even from its fragments we can recover enough of a play's dramatic texture to discern something of Euripides' restless variety. The collection of fragmentary plays treated in these volumes affords a sweeping view of his wide-ranging material and imaginative techniques, and presents further, perhaps unexpected, evidence of the poet's remarkable ability to combine startling innovation with traditions which he himself helped to create.

III. Form and Content of this Edition

We present each play as follows: *First*, a summary Bibliography arranged under Texts and Testimonia, Myth (sources and analytic discussion), Illustrations (vase-paintings, frescos, sculpture etc.), Main Scholarly Discussions. *Second*, an Introduction discussing as appropriate the Plot (including the fitting of the fragments into an outline reconstruction and the use of *testimonia* and illustrations), the Myth and its history, Themes and Characterisation, Staging, Date, and Other Dramatisations and Later Influence. *Third*, Greek text with a critical apparatus in English, and on the facing page an English prose translation. *Fourth*, a Commentary in which lemmata are taken from the English translation. Text-critical discussion, also inseparable from fragmentary texts, is where possible segregated within square brackets, normally at the end of line-numbered sections.

The plays are printed in approximate chronological order. In this corrected edition of Volume I the fragments are presented with the numbering of the new *Tragicorum Graecorum Fragmenta (TrGF) Vol. 5*, which follows for the most part the numbering of Nauck–Snell. The numerical order of *TrGF* is also maintained, except in *Telephus* and in a few instances elsewhere (indicated by cross-references in Text and Translation) where considerations of reconstruction required a change. *TrGF* numbers identical with Nauck's are given in the Greek text and translation as (e.g.) **696**; those added by Snell or Kannicht are given as (e.g.) **705a**, and fragments renumbered by Kannicht in *TrGF* are given as (e.g.) **304a (68 N)**. All other references use the *TrGF* number only. An asterisk (*) marks fragments of Euripides assigned to a particular play by conjecture, a double asterisk (**) those attributed to Euripides himself by conjecture. Those numbers of Mette that we previously used for a few fragments are now replaced by their *TrGF* numbers, but Mette's numbers remain in the apparatus along with fragment-numbers from some important older editions such as C. Austin's *Nova Fragmenta Euripidea* (1968); we have not been able to add the numbers of the new Budé edition, J. Diggle's *Tragicorum Graecorum Fragmenta Selecta* (1998), or other recent editions of individual plays. Details of the first publications and other important editions of papyrus fragments are given in the play bibliographies and/or apparatus for the relevant fragment.

Spans of papyrus text which are heavily mutilated and yield only an intermittent idea of form and content are presented as succinctly as possible, often with a bare English description, e.g. 'ten damaged lyric lines of which only . . . is certainly legible'.

The Greek Text uses the following editorial signals:

[ ] in papyrus texts enclose supplements of textual matter conjectured to have stood there before physical loss;

⌊ ⌋ enclose matter deficient in a papyrus but extant elsewhere, usually in a book-fragment;

α (etc.) Subscript dots accompany letters uncertainly read in a papyrus. Under a blank space a dot stands for one letter reckoned to be missing;

| indicates a line-end in a papyrus where the printed colometry differs;

< > in texts other than papyrus enclose supplements of matter which the text did not contain but which Euripides is conjectured to have written; such brackets may contain three dots to indicate a brief loss which cannot be filled with confidence, or may be left empty to indicate a more extensive loss;

{ } in both papyrus and other texts enclose matter which stood in those texts but is judged inauthentic;

† † *Obeli* ('daggers') enclose matter judged incurably corrupt;

( ) enclose *(a)* speaker-identifications not supplied in the sources, or *(b)* parentheses within the text;

— A *paragraphus* at the left margin of the Greek text or Translation denotes an unidentified speaker;

The English Translation reproduces < >, { }, † † and ( ) as closely as possible from the Greek text, except that < > enclose translations of *all* conjectured supplements. In addition, all words judged uncertain and all supplements are italicized. Where possible, text-fragments are accompanied in the Translation by an indication of their probable location in the play. Line-numbers inserted into the Translation indicate as nearly as possible the end of the corresponding Greek verse-line.

The critical Apparatus contains only information essential to understanding the problems of identifying, constituting and interpreting primary texts or book-fragments (which are often physically damaged or deficient, or otherwise corrupt and uncertain). Only the principal text-sources are named. Most matters of orthography, word-division, accentuation and punctuation are omitted, and obvious corrections of obvious minor errors are not recorded. Editorial conjectures are mentioned in the Apparatus only if judged worthy of discussion in the Commentary.

BIBLIOGRAPHY AND ABBREVIATIONS

This edition is part of the Aris and Phillips Euripides Series. Most users will have ready access to at least one of the volumes containing the complete plays, all of which include the General Bibliography to the Series. We do not repeat it here, since the many works which we cite from it by abbreviated title will be easily identifiable. The largely supplementary bibliography below is confined to works of special and constant importance to the fragmentary plays, along with a few other recent items. The majority are in languages other than English, a reflection of where most study of the fragmentary plays has been carried out. Reference is made to these works, and to those in the General Bibliography, by author's name, abbreviated title and/or date, and page numbers.

R. Aélion, *Euripide héritier d'Eschyle* (2 vols., Paris, 1983)

R. Aélion, *Quelques grands mythes héroiques dans l'oeuvre d'Euripide* (Paris, 1986)

F. Brommer, *Denkmälerlisten zur griechischen Heldensage* (Marburg, 1971–6)

J. Diggle, *Euripidea* (Oxford, 1994)

J. R. Green, *Theatre in Ancient Greek Society* (London, 1994)

E. Hall, *Inventing the Barbarian* (Oxford, 1989)

H. Hofmann and A. Harder (eds.), *Fragmenta Dramatica* (Göttingen, 1991)

M. Hose, *Studien zum Chor bei Euripides*, I (Stuttgart, 1990), II (Stuttgart, 1991)

I. J. F de Jong, *Narrative in Drama: the Art of the Euripidean Messenger-Speech* (Leiden, 1991)

F. Jouan, *Euripide et les légendes des chants cypriens* (Paris, 1966)

M. Lloyd, *The Agon in Euripides* (Oxford, 1992)

H. van Looy, *Zes verloren Tragedies van Euripides* (Brussels, 1964)

M. Pohlenz, *Die griechische Tragödie*, 2nd ed. (Göttingen, 1954)

J. U. Powell (ed.), *New Chapters in the History of Greek Literature, Third Series* (Oxford, 1933)

P. Rau, *Paratragodia* (Munich, 1967)

K. Schefold, F. Jung, *Die Urkönige, Perseus, Bellerophon, Herakles und Theseus in der klassischen und hellenistischen Kunst* (Munich, 1988)

W. Schmid, *Geschichte der griechischen Literatur, III* (Munich, 1940)

L. Séchan, *Études sur la tragédie grecque dans ses rapports avec la céramique* (Paris, 1926)

A. D. Trendall, T. B. L. Webster, *Illustrations of Greek Drama* (London, 1971)

T. B. L.Webster, *Monuments illustrating Tragedy and Satyr-Play*, 2nd ed. (*BICS* Suppl. 20, London, 1967)

T. B. L. Webster, *The Tragedies of Euripides* (London, 1967)

M. L. West, *The Hesiodic Catalogue of Women* (Oxford, 1985)

U. von Wilamowitz-Moellendorff, *Analecta Euripidea* (Berlin, 1875)

U. von Wilamowitz-Moellendorff, *Der Glaube der Hellenen*, 3rd ed. (Darmstadt, 1959)

U. von Wilamowitz-Moellendorff, *Griechische Verskunst* (Berlin, 1921)

U. von Wilamowitz-Moellendorff, *Kleine Schriften, I–VI* (Berlin, 1935–72: reprinted papers containing in their footnotes many marginal corrections made by Wilamowitz in his copies of their first publications)

Abbreviations

(a) Standard Works of Reference

Brunn–Koerte   H. Brunn, G. Koerte, *I rilievi delle urne Etrusche* (Berlin, 1870–1916)

Burkert   W. Burkert, *Greek Religion* (trans. J. Raffan, Oxford, 1985)

CAH   *The Cambridge Ancient History*, 2nd/3rd ed. (Cambridge, 1972–2005)

Cairns, *Aidos*   D. Cairns, *Aidos* (Oxford, 1993)

Cropp–Fick   M. Cropp and G. Fick, *Resolutions and Chronology in Euripides* (London, 1985)

Dale, *LM*   A. M. Dale, *The Lyric Metres of Greek Drama*, 2nd ed. (Cambridge, 1968)

Denniston, *GP*   J. D. Denniston, *The Greek Particles*, 2nd ed. by K.J. Dover (Oxford, 1954)

Dover, *GPM*   K. J. Dover, *Greek Popular Morality in the time of Plato and Aristotle* (Oxford, 1974)

Gantz   T. Gantz, *Early Greek Myth: a Guide to Literary and Artistic Sources* (Baltimore and London, 1993)

Garland, *Death*   R. Garland, *The Greek Way of Death* (London, 1985)

Garland, *Life*   R. Garland, *The Greek Way of Life* (London, 1990)

Gildersleeve   B. L. Gildersleeve, *Syntax of Classical Greek* (2 vols., New York, 1900–11)

Goodwin   W. W. Goodwin, *Syntax of the Moods and Tenses of the Greek Verb* (London, 1889)

Graf, *Nordion. Kulte*   F. Graf, *Nordionische Kulte* (Rome, 1985)

Guthrie, *HGPh*   W. K. C. Guthrie, *History of Greek Philosophy* (Cambridge, 1962–1980)

KG   R. Kühner, *Ausführliche Grammatik der griechischen Sprache*, 2er. Teil, rev. B. Gerth (Hanover, 1898–1904)

Kranz, *Stasimon*   W. Kranz, *Stasimon* (Berlin, 1933)

Lacey, *Family*   W. K. P. Lacey, *The Family in Classical Greece* (London, 1968)

LIMC   *Lexicon Iconographicum Mythologiae Classicae* (Zurich, 1981– 99)

LSJ   H. G. Liddell, R. Scott, *A Greek English Lexicon* (with *Supplement*), 9th. ed., rev. H. Stuart-Jones etc. (Oxford, 1968)

Moorhouse, *Syntax*   A. C. Moorhouse, *The Syntax of Sophocles* (Leiden, 1982)

Nilsson, *GGR*   M. P. Nilsson, *Geschichte der griechischen Religion*, 3rd ed. (Berlin, 2 vols, 1967)

OCD   *Oxford Classical Dictionary*, 2nd ed. (Oxford, 1970)

OGCMA   *Oxford Guide to Classical Mythology in the Arts, 1300–1990s* (Oxford, 2 vols., 1993)

Parker, *Miasma*   R. Parker, *Miasma* (Oxford, 1983)

Preller–Robert	L. Preller, C. Robert, *Griechische Mythologie* (Berlin, 1894[1]–1921[4])
Pritchard, *ANET*	J. B. Pritchard (ed.), *Ancient Near Eastern Texts relating to the Old Testament*, 3rd ed. (Princeton, 1969)
Pritchett, *War*	W. K. Pritchett, *The Greek State at War* (Berkeley, 1971–1991)
RAC	*Reallexikon für Antike und Christentum* (Stuttgart, 1950–)
RE	*Real-Encyclopädie der classischen Altertumswissenschaft* (Stuttgart–Munich, 1893–1980)
Roscher	W. H. Roscher etc., *Griechische und Römische Mythologie* (Berlin, 1884–1937)
Smyth	H. W. Smyth, *Greek Grammar*, rev. G.M. Messing (Cambridge, Mass., 1956)
Stevens, *CE*	P. T. Stevens, *Colloquial Expressions in Euripides* (Wiesbaden, 1976)
Thompson, *Motif Index*	Thompson, Stith, *Motif Index of Folk Literature* (Copenhagen, 1955–8)
West, *Metre*	M. L. West, *Greek Metre* (Oxford, 1982)

(b) Editions of Fragmentary Texts

A/Austin/*NFE*	C. Austin, *Nova Fragmenta Euripidea in Papyris Reperta* (Berlin, 1968)
von Arnim	H. von Arnim, *Supplementum Euripideum* (Bonn, 1913)
BKT	W. Schubart, U. von Wilamowitz-Moellendorff, *Berliner Klassiker Texte* V.2 (Berlin, 1907)
CGFP	C. Austin, *Comicorum Graecorum Fragmenta in Papyris Reperta* (Berlin and New York, 1973)
DK	H. Diels, W. Kranz, *Die Fragmente der Vorsokratiker*, 6 ed., (Berlin, 1951–2)
EGF	M. Davies, *Epicorum Graecorum Fragmenta* (Göttingen, 1988)
FGH	F. Jacoby, *Fragmente der griechischen Historiker* (Berlin, 1923–58)
IEG	M. L. West, *Iambi et Elegi Graeci*, 2nd ed. (Oxford, 1989–91)
Jocelyn, *Ennius*	H. D. Jocelyn, *The Tragedies of Ennius* (Cambridge, 1967)
Kock	T. Kock, *Comicorum Atticorum Fragmenta* (Leipzig, 1880–7)
Koerte	A. Koerte, *Menandri Reliquiae* (Leipzig, Vol. II, 1959[2])
M/Mette	H. J. Mette, *Euripides: die Bruchstücke, Lustrum* 23/4 (1982); 25 (1983), 5–14: 27 (1985), 23–6
N/Nauck	A. Nauck, *Tragicorum Graecorum Fragmenta* , 2nd ed. (Leipzig, 1889), repr. with *Supplementum* by B. Snell (Hildesheim, 1964)
Page, *GLP*	D. L. Page, *Select Papyri, III: Literary Papyri, Poetry* (London and Cambridge, Mass., 1941)
PCG	R. Kassel, C. Austin, *Poetae Comici Graeci* (Berlin–New York, 1983– 2001)
PMG	D. L. Page, *Poetae Melici Graeci* (Oxford, 1962)

PMGF   M. Davies, *Poetarum Melicorum Graecorum Fragmenta* I (Oxford, 1991)
Stob.   C. Wachsmuth, O. Hense, *Ioannis Stobaei Anthologiae* (Berlin,
          1884–1923)
TrGF   *Tragicorum Graecorum Fragmenta* (Göttingen, 1971–2004):
          I. *Poetae Minores*, ed. B. Snell (1971, rev. R. Kannicht, 1981);
          II. *Adespota*, ed. R. Kannicht, B. Snell (1981); III. Aeschylus, ed. S.
          Radt (1985); IV. Sophocles, ed. S. Radt (1977); V. Euripides, ed. R.
          Kannicht, 2004
          Note. All *TrGF* volumes continue Nauck's numbering of the
          fragments, except that Vol. IV continues that of A.C. Pearson, *The
          Fragments of Sophocles* (Cambridge, 1917)

(c) Ancient Authors, Scholia, Papyri

The currently standard editions are used (Oxford Classical Texts, Bibliotheca
Teubneriana, Collection Budé, *The Oxyrhynchus Papyri*, etc.); these and other
standard editions are cited with the name of the editor when needed. For mythological
matters note especially:

Apollod. [Apollodorus], *The Library*, ed. and trans. J.G. Frazer, (Loeb
          Classical Library: London and Cambridge, Mass., 1921)
Hygin. *Fab.* *Hygini Fabulae*, ed. H.J. Rose, 3rd ed. (Leiden, 1963)

(d) Titles of Euripides' Plays (* = fragmentary play)

Alc. Alcestis   *Alcm.Cor.* *Alcmaeon in Corinth*   *Alcm.Ps.* *Alcmaeon in Psophis*
Alcmaeon Alcm.Cor. or Alcm.Ps. (assignment uncertain)   *And.* Andromache
Androm. *Andromeda*   *Antig.* *Antigone*   *Arch.* *Archelaus*   *Bacc.* Bacchae
Bell. *Bellerophon*   *Chrys.* *Chrysippus*   *Cresph.* *Cresphontes*   *Cret.*
Cretans   *Cret.W.* *Cretan Women*   *Cyc.* Cyclops   *El.* Electra   *Erec.*
Erectheus   *Hec.* Hecuba   *Hel.* Helen   *Hcld.* Heraclidae ('Children of
Heracles')   *HF* Hercules Furens ('Hercules Mad')   *Hipp.* Hippolytus
(*Stephanephoros*, 'Garlanded')   *Hipp.Cal.* *Hippolytus Calyptomenos* ('Veiled')
Hyps. *Hypsipyle*   *IA* Iphigenia at Aulis   *IT* Iphigenia in Tauris   *Med.* Medea
Mel.D. *Melanippe Desmotis* ('Captive Melanippe')   *Mel.S.* *Melanippe Sophe*
('Wise Melanippe')   *Mel.* Mel.D. or Mel.S. (assignment uncertain)   *Oed.* *Oedipus*
Or. Orestes   *Palam.* *Palamedes*   *Pha.* *Phaethon*   *Phil.* *Philoctetes*
Pho. Phoenissae ('Phoenician Women')   *Pir.* *Pirithous* (not certainly
Euripidean)   *Prot.* *Protesilaus*   *Rhad.* *Rhadamanthys* (not certainly
Euripidean)   *Rhes.* Rhesus (spurious)   *Sthen.* *Stheneboea*   *Supp.*
Suppliant Women   *Tel.* *Telephus*   *Tem.* *Temenus*   *Temenid.* *Temenidae*
('Children of Temenus')   *Tro.* Trojan Women

All other play titles, both of the complete *Ion* and of the fragmentary plays including
Tennes (not certainly Euripidean) and the two *Phrixus* plays ('A' and 'B'), are given in
full.

TELEPHUS

Texts, testimonia. P. Oxy. 2455 fr. 12 (= *TrGF* test. *iiib: Hypothesis?); Ar. *Ach.* Hypoth. I (see *TrGF* F 702a), Schol. *Ach.* 332 (see *TrGF* test. v.a); Ar. *Clouds* 921–4 with various Schol. (*TrGF* test. iiia); P. Berl. 9908; P. Milan 1; P. Rylands 482 (doubtful ascription); P. Oxy. 2460; *TrGF* F 696–727, 705a, 708a, 712a, 727a–c; Austin, *NFE* frs. 102–49; Mette Nos. 929–89; E. W. Handley and J. Rea, *The Telephus of Euripides* (London, 1957). See also Apparatus to F 696, 727a, 727b, 727c.

Myth. *Cypria* (Proclus), *EGF* p. 32; Hygin. *Fab.* 101 (= *TrGF* test. *iiic); Apollod. *Epit.* 3.17–20 (cf. Schol. A Hom. *Il.* 1.59, p. 16 Dindorf); Schol. rec. Ar. *Clouds* 919 (cf. *TrGF* test. iiia); Schol. Dem. 18.72; Dictys Cret. 2.10–12. Roscher V.274–308 (older bibl., 274); Preller-Robert II.3.1138–60 (esp. 1152–60); *RE* V.A (1934), 362–9; Bauchhenss-Thüriedl (below), 1–13; Gantz 428–31, 576–80; Strauss (below).

Illustrations. Séchan 509–12; Webster, *Euripides* (1967), 302; Trendall-Webster III.3.47–9; Chr. Bauchhenss-Thüriedl, *Der Mythos von Telephos in der antiken Bildkunst* (Würzburg, 1971); Schefold-Jung, *Urkönige* 214–5, Pl. 264–5; E. Csapo, *QUCC* 63 (1990), 41–52; *LIMC* I, 'Agamemnon', nos. 11–28; *LIMC* VII, 'Telephos' (M. Strauss, cf. his forthcoming *Studien zu Ikonographie und Geschichte des Mythos von Telephos*).

Main discussions. Wilamowitz, *BKT* V.2 (1907), 64–72; Séchan 503–18; A. Rostagni, *Scritti Minori* II.1 (1956), 134–52 = *RFIC* 5 (1927), 312–30; C. Brizi, *Atene e Roma* 9 (1928), 129–45; A. Buchwald, *Studien zur Chronologie der attischen Tragödie 455 bis 431* (diss. Königsberg, 1939), 24–33; Schmid 352–3; H.W. Miller, *CP* 43 (1948), 174–83; H. Metzger, *Mélanges...C. Picard* (Paris, 1949), II.746–51; H. Erbse, *Eranos* 52 (1954), 96–9; Handley and Rea (above) and review by H. Strohm, *Gnomon* 32 (1960), 600–5; H. J. Mette, *Der verlorene Aischylos* (Berlin, 1963), 81–94; Jouan 222–55 (bibl.); Webster, *Euripides* (1967), 43–8; Rau 19–50; M. Cavallone, *Boll.Class.* 3a Ser. I (1980), 93–107; G. Mengano Cavalli, *AAP* 31 (1982), 315–37; Aélion (1983), I.31–40 (bibl.); M. T. Ditifeci, *Prometheus* 10 (1984), 210–20; M. Heath, *CQ* 37 (1987), 272–80.

One of Euripides' most famous, or notorious, earlier plays, but one for which the mythographic and artistic evidence and the distorting filter of Aristophanes leave many uncertainties.

Telephus is the son of Heracles and Auge, who was banished from Tegea by her father king Aleos and became the wife of king Teuthras in Mysia near the Troad. Telephus became Teuthras's heir and led the Mysian forces resisting a mistaken attack by the Achaeans during their abortive first expedition to Troy. Wounded by Achilles, he was directed by an oracle to Argos to be healed by him and become the Achaeans' destined guide to Troy. His wounding and healing were apparently told in the *Cypria*; bare essentials of this account survive in Proclus and Apollodorus. Hygin. *Fab.* 101 shows dramatic influence without exactly reflecting Euripides: Telephus learns from Apollo (F 700 n.) that he can only be healed 'by the same spear that wounded him' (but this should be cryptic, 'the one that wounded you will heal you', as in Apollod. etc.). He comes to

17

Agamemnon and 'on Clytemnestra's advice' seizes Orestes from his cradle threatening to kill him if the Achaeans will not treat his wound. They have received an oracle that they cannot take Troy 'without Telephus' leadership' (in Euripides perhaps 'without the leadership of a native Greek': cf. F 727c.7–10; Webster [1938], 546 and [1967], 47); so they ask Achilles to heal him. Achilles replies that he is ignorant of medicine, but Odysseus perceives that the destined healer is the spear itself. Telephus is cured with its filings (F 724 n.). He refuses to help them in sacking Troy because he is Priam's son-in-law, but consents to guide them and after doing so returns to his homeland. Hyg. says nothing of Telephus' disguise as a beggar (clearly a main feature of Euripides' play), and Euripides' order of events at the end was different, for in F 727c Telephus has agreed conditionally to guide the fleet *before* Achilles arrives from Scyros.

For the play, some groups of fragments seem to suggest distinct scenes: a Prologue speech of Telephus explaining his situation, disguise and intentions (F 696, 697, 698, ?705a); an argument between Agamemnon and Menelaus about continuing the Trojan war (F 722, 723, ?713); Telephus in disguise addressing the Achaeans (F 703, 708–711), and other lines of his probably associated with this part of the play (F 705, 706, 707); some hostile reaction (F 712, 712a, ?715); a search somehow connected with his discovery (F 727a frs. 1, 5, 6, ?12; ?700, ?721). The climactic moment when he threatens Orestes at the altar is captured in vase-paintings. The fragments in turn suggest his help to the expedition and his healing (F 727a frs. 9, 10, F 727b(?), F 727c.1–10) and Achilles arriving and being persuaded to help him (F 727c.11–25, 716, 718, 724).

This rough and perhaps incomplete outline suggests the ordering of most of the fragments adopted in this edition; it remains in part speculative, especially for the dramatic sequence between Prologue and crisis. Additional clues come mainly from Aristophanes, who not only mocked *Tel.* incidentally for its outrageous introduction of a prince masquerading as a beggar (*Clouds* 921–4, *Frogs* 840–55) and generally lampooned Euripides' disabled heroes (e.g. *Ach.* 411ff., 1190ff., *Peace* 146–8, *Thesm.* 23–4), but twice parodied *Tel.* extensively:

In *Ach.* 204–625 (425 B.C.) Dicaeopolis is set upon by a Chorus hostile to his private truce with Sparta; he offers to defend himself with his head on a block (cf. F 706) and forces the Chorus to listen by seizing and threatening to kill a 'hostage' which is actually a charcoal basket (Schol. *Ach.* 332 says this mimics Aeschylus's Telephus who 'took and held Or. for his safety amongst the Greeks', but the original of this confused note very probably referred to Eur. as well). Before speaking Dic. visits Eur. to borrow the beggar's garb and equipment of 'Mysian Telephus' (430: F 704), explaining his purpose in Tel.'s words (440–1: F 698). His speech (496–556) is described in a hypothesis to *Ach.* as a parody of Tel.'s famous speech, and its beginning and main argument are adapted from it (497–8, 540–3, 555–6: F 703, 708–10). The Chorus's reaction is half indignant and half sympathetic; the general Lamachus arrives and the complaints made to and by him echo *Tel.* (577, 577b: F 712, 712a); attention is then diverted to the weaknesses of Lamachus (who himself seems to take on some traits of the wounded Telephus at the end of *Ach.*, 1204–26: cf. *Ach.* 1188 = *Tel.* F 705a; A. M. Bowie, *Aristophanes* (Cambridge, 1993), 30–1).

In *Thesm.* 466–764 (411 B.C.) a kinsman of Eur. has entered a women's meeting in disguise to defend Eur.'s representations of women in his plays. He argues that Eur. has only told (a small part of) the truth about women, who have therefore suffered nothing in excess of what they have done (518–9: F 711). As they react angrily, Cleisthenes arrives with a rumour of the kinsman's infiltration, and the latter is exposed. A search for other intruders begins, but he seizes a 'baby' and takes refuge at the altar, threatening to kill it (*Thesm.* 694–5). The scene takes another direction as the 'baby' turns out to be a wineskin.

Aristophanes' purposes in these paratragic sequences must be left unexplored here (on *Ach.* see Rostagni 134–52; H.P. Foley, *JHS* 108 [1988], 33–47; Bowie [above], 27–30 and on *Thesm.*, 217–27). As Handley 23–4 emphasised and Rau demonstrated in detail, his inventiveness and kaleidoscopic paratragic technique make it impossible to infer tragic models directly from them. The ancient commentaries on Aristophanes guarantee only Telephus' disguise and a speech. But from the considerable coincidences between comic texts, tragic fragments and vase-paintings most commentators reasonably infer that the comic sequence in *Thesm.* (debate, speech by disguised hero, hostile reaction, search for intruder, exposure of hero, hostage-taking) reflects in whole or part a similar sequence in *Tel.* A demand by Telephus for a hearing is then inferred from Dicaeopolis's insistence in *Ach.* on speaking in a just cause, even with his head on a block. (Erbse adopts *Ach.*'s sequence of search, exposure, hostage-taking, speech, but this seems incompatible with Telephus' speaking as a beggar in F 703, 712a. Mette's variant has no particular virtue: search, exposure, speech, hostage-taking.) The quarrel of Agamemnon and Menelaus about renewing the war is inserted either in the initial debate or (Webster, Handley and tentatively Rau) after Telephus has spoken; some earlier scholars placed it after his exposure.

So far, so good. But besides matters of detail some major questions remain:

(1) A supposed preliminary scene following the Prologue speech and showing Telephus rudely received by a servant (cf. Rostagni 140 n. 2, Jouan 229, Handley 31) rests almost entirely on unreliable inference from comparable scenes in Ar. *Ach.* 395ff., *Thesm.* 39ff. Possibly relevant is a report in Schol. Ar. *Clouds* 922 (and Tzetzes on 920) that Euripides presented Telephus as a beggar 'having with difficulty become the gatekeeper of Agamemnon's court' (cf. Handley 31–2, Webster, Mette). But this may only mean that he set himself up as a beggar at the door like Odysseus (Hom. *Od.* 17. 413, 466; 18. 10, 17, etc.).

(2) A role for Clytemnestra is suggested by Hyginus, by 'Mistress' in F 699 (see Comm.), arguably by F 727 and Ennius fr. 145, and by those illustrations in which she appears. Most commentators infer that Telephus gained her sponsorship in the Prologue scene, and that she was present at the hostage-taking (see esp. Séchan 505–8, Handley 30–1, and for doubts e.g. Wilamowitz 69–70, Strohm 605. Ditifeci would postpone the suggestion about Orestes until the crisis; cf. Brizi 133–7, 143–4). Her involvement would echo the story in Thuc. 1.136 (probably adopted by Aeschylus in his *Tel.*) that Themistocles in his flight from Greece successfully supplicated an old adversary, the Molossian king Admetus, on the queen's advice, taking his son and sitting at his hearth.

(On women's assistance to suppliants in Greek literature and in Mediterranean culture see J.N. Bremmer, *Mnem.* 33 [1980], 366–8.) Only some ambiguous wording in Hyginus suggests that Euripides' Clytemnestra might have acted malevolently because of the sacrifice of Iphigeneia (so Séchan, Rostagni 140–1, Jouan 230, Mengano Cavalli 325–6, Ditifeci. Of the ancient sources only the late Dictys Cret. 1.22 places her sacrifice before the expedition to Mysia. The *Cypria*, which Euripides probably followed, had Telephus healed and appointed as guide at Argos, then the gathering at Aulis and staying of the winds.)

(3) Three identities for the Chorus have been suggested (cf. Handley 32, Rau 21). Achaean leaders are unlikely, and contradicted by Achilles' enquiry after 'our comrades' in F 727c.12. For ordinary Achaean soldiers there is no positive argument. Argive elders are by far the most likely, being suitable addressees of F 712, 713 and (in part) F 703, and appropriately gathered before the palace at Argos which is surely the scene of the action.

(4) Telephus' strategy before the crisis is unclear. He probably presented himself as a Greek man down on his luck after being wounded during a landing in Mysia. But did he want to get healed *incognito*, or merely to get to a position where he could safely reveal his identity and supplicate Achilles? The latter seems plausible, and it may be that he was advised by Clytemnestra to use Orestes for supplication (as in Aeschylus), was threatened with premature recognition after intervening in arguments about the war against Troy, then abandoned his disguise and seized Orestes in self-protection.

(5) We know little of the content of Telephus' address(es) to the Achaeans. F 703 and 706 seem to be two speech openings, and F 710 and 711 are the conclusions of either two speeches or two arguments in one speech. Aristophanes' use of Telephus' arguments to criticise the Athenians' insistence on war against Sparta suggests these at least included a criticism of the Achaeans' insistence on war against Troy. Other possible topics are Telephus' own need for healing and a justification of the Mysians' attack on the Achaeans. Scholars have varied widely in accommodating the topics in one or two speeches and in placing the speech(es) within a dramatic sequence. If two speeches are rightly supposed, they may have occurred within a single debate scene, or in adjacent ones (cf. Teucer with Menelaus, then Agamemnon in Soph. *Ajax*).

(6) Strohm rejects the idea of an alert and search for an intruder (as in *Thesm.*) and suggests that Telephus betrayed himself directly in debate (cf. also Séchan, Rau). But F 727a fr. 1 more likely than not indicates an alert, or perhaps better a general alarm *after* the exposure as in *Thesm.* 655ff.

(7) Handley and Webster argue that the hostage-taking was not enacted but reported in a messenger speech: see further under *Staging* below.

(8) As to the dénouement, F 727c has the end of a choral ode anticipating Telephus' guiding the fleet to Troy, then the arrival of Achilles who must be persuaded by Odysseus to heal Telephus; and F 727b, if it belongs in this play, has the end of the preceding scene. F 716 strongly suggests that Achilles was not persuaded without supplication by Telephus himself (the supplication, recalled by Hor. *Epod.* 17.8–10, *Anth. Lat.* 184.9–10 Riese, no doubt originated with

Aeschylus if not earlier). Nothing indicates that the healing was shown, and the play may have ended with Achilles' promise secured, though Jouan 244, for example, follows Wilamowitz 70 in supposing that a Messenger reported the healing, and suggests a final celebration and departure (cf. Heath 279–80).

Other ascriptions. Many lines of Aristophanes have been speculatively identified as quotations or adaptations from *Tel.* Most occur in the scenes of *Ach.* and *Thesm.* derived from *Tel.*; some are ascribed by Schol. Ar. to Eur. or to Tragedy. A few other fragments of Eur. have been assigned. The list below includes *(a)* strong possibilities, and *(b)* other suggestions (for yet more see esp. Rostagni and Miller). See also *TrGF* 5.686–7.

(a) Ar. *Ach.* 384/436 (*Tel.* 946 M; Mette adds *Ach.* 435 = adesp. F 43), 'to equip myself to be as pitiful as possible'; plausibly ascribed to the Prologue in view of the repetition in Ar. Eur. *Oineus* F 568 = Ar. *Ach.* 472 (*Tel.* 139 A, 748/937 M), 'troublesome, not reckoning that I am hated by the kings'; the Schol. say, 'Symmachus says that it also comes from *Tel.*' Eur. F 918 (*Tel.* 136 A, 956 M; cf. Ar. *Ach.* 659–64), 'In response to this let him scheme as he will and use all his devices against me. Good is on my side, and right will be my ally; in no way shall I be caught acting ignobly'. Content, anapaestic metre, and the fact that it must be earlier than *Ach.* suggest this may belong with F 722 and 723 in the Atreids' quarrel (rather than the Achilles scene as Jouan suggests). Eur. F 975 (*Tel.* 137 A, Eur. 1371 M), anapaests, 'brotherly quarrels are difficult': perhaps a Choral comment on the Atreids' quarrel, but Eur. had quarrelling brothers in other plays such as *Antiope*. Ar. *Thesm.* 694–5 (*Tel.* 143 A, 966A M), 'struck by this dagger in his blood-filled veins he shall stain the altar': the kinsman's climactic threat to the baby/wineskin may well echo Eur. *Tel.*; the preceding phrase, 'But here upon the (sacrificial) thigh-bones', could be included (Rau 49). Eur. F 1066 (*Tel.* 138 A, 974 M), 'If I have been abandoned by my possessions, yet my good birth and nobility remain': attributed to *Tel.* by Hartung and many subsequently as the original of Accius, *Tel.* fr. VI Ribbeck, 'For if Fortune has been able to steal from me my kingdom and possessions, yet she has not been able to steal my virtue.' Some doubt must remain because F 1066 lacks two striking elements of Accius's lines, 'Fortune' and 'my kingdom', and the sentiment is in itself generic; 'my kingdom' would be spoken by Telephus without disguise, in his Prologue speech (Webster) or in his plea to Achilles (Handley).

(b) Eur. F 898a (*Tel.* 146 A, 959 M; cf. Ar. *Ach.* 203), 'And I am going to flee, now that I am free.' Ar. *Ach.* 449 (*Tel.* 141 A, 948.1 M), 'Depart from this stone-built abode'; Mette adds Ar. *Ach.* 450, 'O my heart — for you see how I am repelled from the house . . .'. Ar. *Ach.* 456 (*Tel.* 142 A, 950 M), 'Know that you are troublesome; get away from this house.' Eur. F 1003 (cf. Ar. *Ach.* 479), 'Release the barriers of the house'. *Tel.* 144 A (*Tel.* 966B M; cf. Ar. *Thesm.* 76–7), 'In this day it will be decided whether <*Telephus?*> still lives or is no more.' adesp. F 57 = Ar. *Lys.* 707 (*Lys.* 706 = *Tel.* F 699), 'Why, tell me, have you exited from the house thus scowling?' Eur. F 883 = Ar. *Lys.* 713 (*Tel.* 964 M), 'Shameful it is to speak, yet burdensome to keep silent.' Eur. F 885 (cf. Ar. *Frogs* 840), 'Is it so, son of the sea-dwelling goddess?' (i.e. Achilles). Eur. F 888 = Ar. *Frogs* 1400 (*Tel.* 140 A, 967 M), 'Achilles has thrown two ones and a four': in *Frogs* Dionysus ascribes this to Eur., but Alexandrian scholars could not locate it in any Euripidean text (see Schol. Ar. and cf. Eupolis F 372 *PCG*).

Illustrations. Two vase-paintings of Telephus at the altar precede Euripides' play: an Attic cup in Boston (c. 470 B.C.) with Telephus alone and threatened by Achilles; and an Attic pitcher in the British Museum (c. 450 B.C.) with Telephus calmly holding Orestes and Agamemnon calmly approaching to address him. The first seems to reflect an epic source, the second Aeschylus's dramatisation in which Telephus like Themistocles used Orestes for his supplication but did not threaten him (so most recently Csapo; for the linking of the first vase with Aeschylus, Bauchhenss-Thüriedl 18–25). Some sixteen vases of the 4ᵗʰ C. showing Telephus threatening Orestes with a sword while Agamemnon threateningly intervenes seem to reflect Euripides' play. Aristophanes' parodies also suggest that the threatening was Euripides' striking innovation, and the altar scene in *Thesm.* has in turn been identified by Csapo and Taplin on an Apulian vase of the 370s (see now Taplin, *Comic Angels* [Oxford, 1993], 36–40 with Pl. 11.4). Several of the vases include Clytemnestra restraining Agamemnon as if to protect Orestes. The scene is repeated and elaborated in a number of Etruscan cinerary urn reliefs (the relevant relief from the 2ⁿᵈ C. Telephus frieze at Pergamum is too damaged to be of help.) On a few vases, esp. an Attic krater in Berlin, and an elaborate Faliscan krater in Boston, Apollo observes the crisis from an upper level (prompted on the Faliscan krater by other divine observers), reminding us that his oracles about Telephus will be fulfilled. The presence of Clytemnestra and Apollo in these scenes raises questions about staging to be discussed below.

Myth. A Mysian king with Greek ancestry and loyalties divided between Greeks and Trojans belongs to the development of epic after the Aeolian Greeks' settlements in the Troy region. Telephus' story looks like a pastiche derived from other more central episodes of the Troy saga, perhaps developed as late as the 7ᵗʰ C. (cf. West, *Catalogue* 155). Neither Telephus nor his son Eurypylus is mentioned in the *Iliad* (though Mysians are amongst Troy's allies: *Il.* 2.858, 10.430, 14.512). The *Cypria* included the Achaean invasion of Mysia and Telephus' wounding, healing and guidance of the Greek fleet. In the *Little Iliad* Eurypylus came to Troy's aid and was killed by Neoptolemus (*EGF* p. 52 [Proclus] with F 6 and 7, also Hom. *Od.* 11. 520 [with Schol. = Acusilaus *FGH* 2 F 40]). Some archaic epic added an intervention by Telephus at Troy itself (see Robert 1126–7), but Telephus was chiefly known as Achilles' great adversary in Mysia (so Hes. fr. 165; Pind. *Ol.* 9.70–2, *Isthm.* 5.41–2, 8.49–52). As for his birth, the prevailing versions of the myth (unlike Hes. fr. 165) placed it in or near Tegea, whence Auge was transported to Mysia; Telephus either went with her or later found her there (cf. F 696.4–8 n.). For the episode at Argos the key factors — Telephus' Greek ancestry, heroic stature and achievements, rivalry with Achilles, unhealing wound, and destiny as the guide to Troy — were long established when Aeschylus appropriated the story for Tragedy.

Themes and characters. Sanctuary and supplication are a staple of Tragic plot construction (cf. Aesch. *Supp.*, *Eum.*, Soph. *OC*, Eur. *Hcld.*, *And.*, *Supp.*, *HF*, *Hcld.*). Aeschylus's *Tel.* and *Supp.* both dramatised the supplication of Greeks by aliens of Greek descent. Euripides, it seems, added Telephus' adoption of a disguise and his threat to Orestes, which allowed a melodramatic crisis comparable with the later hostage scenes *And.* 309ff. (Andromache's son), *Or.* 1323ff. (Hermione: cf. also Soph. *OC* 818ff.) and the threats of violence to suppliants in *HF* 238ff., *Ion* 1250ff. — although only *Tel.* cleverly combines threats both to and by the suppliant.

Telephus' disguise allows a typically Euripidean display of paradoxical and subversive rhetoric, the 'beggar' challenging the motives of the heroic campaign against Troy just as Melanippe in *Mel.S.* challenges orthodoxies while concealing her relationship with the babies she defends, only to be exposed in the end. Telephus was probably the first of Euripides' disabled and ragged heroes, and is certainly the most notorious thanks to Aristophanes' parodies. The list in Ar. *Ach.* 414–34 includes the deposed Oeneus, the blinded Phoenix, the crippled and abandoned Philoctetes, the outcasts Bellerophon and Thyestes, and the captive Ino; and it continues after 425 with such figures as the peasant Electra. Telephus differs from the other heroes in voluntarily adopting his rags without the heroic justifications allowed to Odysseus in the *Odyssey*; but it is not clear that this made the play controversial or unpopular as (e.g.) G. Paduano, *SCO* 16 (1967), 330–43 infers from Aristophanes. The comedian probably chose to dwell on mockery of Telephus because of the play's striking plot and situations. In *Ach.* 425–30 Aristophanes characterises Telephus and Bellerophon together as wretched, beggarly, importunate and rhetorically skilful. This comically one-sided formulation omits the moral and emotional dimensions inherent in their situations. Telephus has fallen into misfortune from a royal and heroic position. He appears as an outsider and victim of disillusionment, not unlike Bellerophon (cf. *Bell.* Introd., p. 101 below). He suffers like Philoctetes from an incurable wound, and his fate is meshed with the fates of Troy and of the Greeks in Asia. Euripides' development of these Tragic aspects is discernible to some extent in the fragments themselves.

In his disguise and rhetorical skill Telephus resembles Odysseus. His threat to Orestes recalls the threat to Telemachus which in the *Cypria* exposed Odysseus's pretence of madness (cf. Jouan, 251). The disguised Telephus in Argos recalls Odysseus disguised as a refugee slave in Troy and as a beggar in his own palace. Did Euripides portray Telephus negatively, like Odysseus in other plays, as 'a crafty Athenian politician, a cunning fellow thriving on stratagem and deceit' (Page, *GLP* 130–1), thus undermining his Aeschylean dignity (Jouan 253, Aélion I.40)? The displacement of Aeschylean grandeur by Euripidean realism is obvious; but the impression of a morally debased Telephus comes almost entirely from Aristophanes. Euripides' plot led to Telephus' recognition as a Greek, reconciliation with his enemies, supplication of Achilles, healing, and acceptance of his role as guide. The play foreshadowed *IA* in several ways including, not the sacrifice itself, but a delayed departure for Troy, a challenge to the campaign's legitimacy, the Atreidae in conflict, Achilles as a naive man of action, a 'political' Odysseus, and a resolution allowing the war to proceed. Whether it also anticipated *IA*'s disturbing portrayal of moral instability under political and ideological pressure, or the brutalities of *Tro.*, can only be guessed.

A particular concern in the play was Telephus' barbarian background (F 696.1–3, 14; F 719; F 727b.8–11?; F 727c.7–8). The epic story had asserted Greek colonial claims by creating a Mysian king born from Heracles and a Greek princess. The implications of such legends were sharpened for 5th C. Greece by the Persian empire's pressure on Greek colonies and its invasions of the Greek mainland. A consequent heightening of Greek ethnocentricity is widely reflected in the ideology of Athenian Tragedy, including no doubt the Telephus plays of both Aeschylus and Euripides: cf. Hall, *Inventing the Barbarian*, esp. 174–6, 221–3. Hall also sees a reflection of Pericles' Athenian citizenship law in the issue of Telephus' Greekness, but nothing known about the play supports her suggestion (p. 175) that Telephus was put on trial by Euripides like an Athenian defending himself against charges of foreign parentage; it was rather the Achaeans who were anxious to claim Telephus as a Greek.

Staging. We know too little about the theatrical conventions to say just how realistically Telephus' beggarly clothes and equipment were represented. Those of Ar. *Ach.* 407ff. are no doubt comically exaggerated, but Handley 29 is probably too conservative in supposing merely 'a king not dressed as a king, who described himself as wearing pauper's rags'. What Athena gives Odysseus in Hom. *Od.* 13.434–9 – a ragged chiton and outer garment, worn deerskin coat, staff, and tattered shoulder-bag – would seem a reasonable approximation.

Euripides' *Alcestis* (produced with *Tel.* in 438) and *Medea* (431) have no three-actor scenes, but these are not unlikely in a play such as *Tel.* with its epiodes of supplication and debate (cf. e.g. Aesch. *Eum.* 566ff., Eur. *Hcld.* 120ff., 474ff., 630ff., *And.* 547ff.). Whether the play's action included the altar scene has been disputed, but Aristophanes' vivid parodies make it overwhelmingly likely that it did (cf. Jouan 236–7, Rau 25, Heath 275–6). Two alternatives have been proposed: *(a)* as Metzger observed, the presence of Apollo with indications of a sanctuary on the Berlin vase (cf. now the Boston vase) and Telephus' appeal to Apollo Lykios (F 700) suggest that the hostage crisis was placed in the Argive sanctuary of Apollo Lyk(e)ios. Webster inferred that this action was reported in a messenger speech, but the inference is unnecessary since Apollo's sanctuary was in the centre of Argos (Paus. 2.19.4) and could be defined for dramatic purposes as a gathering-place in front of the royal palace (in Soph. *El.* 9 we hear of it as the 'Lykeian agora'); Telephus would then take refuge at the theatre's altar, defined in this play as Apollo's (cf. Jouan 226 n. 5). *(b)* Handley 36–7 preferred an altar scene reported from inside the palace, and J.P. Gould, *JHS* 93 (1973), 102–3 argues that a supplication such as Telephus' should have taken place in private and at the palace hearth. This is likely for Aeschylus's play, but the assumption that Euripides' Telephus followed the conventional procedure does not fit with what we know of his play. The threat of a killing before the audience can be compared with *Cresph.* F 456, *Ion* 1250ff., *Antiope* F 223.59ff., *Or.* 1503ff., 1567ff., and probably *Alexandros*. The mechanics of the seizure remain unclear, but there is no need to suppose with E. Csapo, *Phoenix* 40 (1986), 384 n. 13, that the scene itself had by now shifted to the interior court of the palace (as apparently at Aesch. *Cho.* 875ff.). Telephus may have been pursued from within the palace, carrying Orestes; or (since some vase-paintings include sacrificial implements fallen to the ground) he may have snatched Orestes from a sacrificial procession as it left or returned to the palace (cf. the staged funeral processions in *Alc.*; Hermione seized as she returns from making an offering, *Or.* 1323ff.; Electra inventing a sacrificial ceremony for her fictitious baby, *El.* 1124ff.). There is no direct evidence for Orestes' age in this play, and the vase-paintings suggest varying ages; he could have been not the infant of Hyginus's summary and the parody in Ar. *Thesm.* but a boy of three or four like Orestes at Aulis in *IA* 1241–8 and Andromache's son in *And.*

Date. 438 B.C. according to Hypoth. II *Alc.*: Sophocles won first prize (plays unrecorded), Euripides second with *Cret.W.*, *Alcm.Ps.*, *Tel.* and the extant *Alc.* The plays are unrelated in subject, and very little survives from the first two.

Other dramatisations; influence. Aeschylus treated Telephus' wounding and healing in *Mysians* (F 143–5) and *Telephus* (discussed above: F 238–40). We know little about either; they may have formed a narrative trilogy with (e.g.) *Iphigeneia*. For Sophocles a 4th C. inscription seems to record a *Telepheia*. This would probably have included *Aleadai* (a variant on Telephus' early life in which he incurred exile from Tegea by killing his uncles: F 77–91) and *Mysians* (probably about his arrival in Mysia and reunion with Auge: F 409–418). *Telephus* (F 727, one word!), *Assembly of the Achaeans* (F 143–8) and *Eurypylus* (F 206–222b) are candidates for the third tragedy, and *Telephus* on unreliable grounds for the satyr-play; but we know nothing of its plot, nor (now that F 727c is ascribed to our play) of anything connecting Telephus with *Assembly of the Achaeans*. For a summation of the problems and bibl. see Radt, *TrGF* IV, pp. 163, 434.

Almost nothing is known of the *Telephus* tragedies by Sophocles' son Iophon, by Agathon (late 5th C.), Cleophon (4th C.) and Moschion (3rd C.: see *TrGF* I 22 F 2c, 39 F 4, 77 F 11, 97 F 2), nor of the comic versions by Deinolochus (5th C.) and Rhinthon (3rd C.). Ennius's Latin *Telephus* (late 3rd/early 2nd C.) seems to have been modelled on Euripides', but its seven brief fragments add nothing reliable (for some resonances with Euripides see Jocelyn's commentary, especially on Enn. fr. 142 (cf. Eur. F 703), fr. 143 (F 697), fr. 146 (F 720); Ennius fr. 145 might perhaps help to confirm Clytemnestra's role as Telephus' sponsor as Handley 30–1 and Webster 146 suggest, but Jocelyn thinks it corrupt at the crucial point). Fifteen interesting fragments of Accius's *Telephus* (later 2nd C.) again suggest a play modelled on Euripides rather than Aeschylus (see esp. Handley 26 and throughout 28–39, also Webster and Jouan; for Aeschylus as model, Aélion 33 n. 12): frs. III–V and X Ribbeck suggest a disguised Telephus, and frs. VI, VIII, XI and XIII can be associated with Eur. F 1066 (cf. p. 21 above), 718, 727c.18 and 705 respectively. No ancient dramatic tradition is known after Accius, and *OGCMA* lists nothing from more recent times.

ΤΗΛΕΦΟΣ

test. *iiib Hypothesis? P. Oxy. 2455 fr. 12

```
. . . . . . . . . ]τασιν τῶν[
. . . . . . . . . ]ς· καὶ συμ [  ]ε . [
. . . . . . . . πέ]μψα[ι] περὶ τῆ[ς] τ[ .]λ̣[
. . . . . . ]ω [ . ἐ]πὶ τ[ὸ]ν χρησμὸν[
ἀπέσ]τειλεν· μαθὼν δ[ε] του[                    5
. . . ] . ὅτι τὸν [ ]αρξ[ . . . ]να[
. . ἡγ]εμόνα δεῖ ποιῆσ[αι κ]αὶ [
. . . . ]μ̣ λ[ . . ] καὶ πλ[ὴν] ε[
. . . . . . . . . . ]ιν· ἐπαν[
```

696 P. Milan 1 *Beginning of the Prologue speech:*

(ΤΗΛΕΦΟΣ)   ʾΩ γαῖα πατρὶς͵ ἣν Πέλοψ ὁρίζεται,
χαῖρ᾽, ὅς τε πέτραν Ἀρκάδων δυσχείμερον
Πὰν ἐμβατεύεις, ἔνθεν εὔχομαι γένος·
Αὔγη γὰρ Ἀλέου παῖς με τῶι Τιρυνθίωι
τίκτει λαθραίως Ἡρακλεῖ· σύνοιδ᾽ ὄρος   5
Παρθένιον, ἔνθα μητέρ᾽ ὠδίνων ἐμὴν
ἔλυσεν Εἰλείθυια, γίγνομαι δ᾽ ἐγώ.
καὶ πόλλ᾽ ἐμόχθησ᾽, ἀλλὰ συντεμῶ λόγον·
ἦλθον δὲ Μυσῶν πεδίον, ἔνθ᾽ ε⟨ὑ⟩ρὼν ἐμὴν
μητέρα κατοικῶ, καὶ δίδωσί μοι κράτη   10
Τεύθρας ὁ Μυσός, Τήλεφον δ᾽ ἐπώνυμον
καλοῦσί μ᾽ ἀστοὶ Μυσίαν κατὰ χθόνα·
τηλοῦ γὰρ οἰκῶν βίοτον ἐξιδρυσάμην.
Ἕλλην δὲ βαρβαροῖσιν ἦρχον ἐκπονῶν
πολλοῖς σὺν ὅπλοις πρίν ⟨γ᾽⟩ Ἀχαϊκὸς μολὼν   15
στρατὸς τὰ Μυσῶ[ν πε]δί᾽ ἐπ[ι]στρωφᾶι ποδί.

test. iiib Hypothesis? (p. 67 A; No. 931 M) P. Oxy. 2455 fr. 12 ed. Turner (1962). Original length of lines uncertain. Supplements by Turner.   1 perhaps ἐξέ]τασιν Turner   2 συμβ[ουλ]εύ[σαντος (e.g.) Turner   3 Τ[η]λ̣[έφου (e.g.) Turner   4 perhaps ἰάσε]ως Turner   5 or κου[6 [ ] perhaps nothing lost : Turner   or]ειξ[: Turner   7 or ποιήσ[ασθ]αι : Turner

26

TELEPHUS

test. *iiib Hypothesis?

. . . of the . . . and . . . *to send* . . . concerning *the* . . . for the prophecy . . . *he dispatched.* And learning[5] . . . that it was necessary . . . *to make* the . . . *leader and* . . . and *except* . . .

696 P. Milan *Beginning of the Prologue speech:*

Telephus. Greetings, ancestral land, which Pelops marked out as his own — and you, Pan, who haunt Arcadia's stormy crag whence I claim descent. Aleos's daughter Auge bore me secretly to Heracles of Tiryns; my witness is Mount[5] Parthenion, where Eileithyia released my mother from her labour and I was born. My hardships were many, but I shall cut short the story. I reached the Mysians' plain and found my mother; I have settled there, and Teuthras the Mysian has passed on his powers to me.[10] The people throughout the Mysian country call me Telephus after my origin; for I was living 'far off' when I established my life here. Although a Greek I led barbarians, fighting for victory in mighty armaments — till the Achaean host came[15] roaming over the Mysians' plain.

696 (102 A, 932 M) P. ˊMilan 1 (2ⁿᵈ C. B.C.) ed. A. Calderini, *Aegyptus* 15 (1935), 239–45, re-ed. M. Norsa, *La Scrittura Letteraria Greca* (Milan, 1939) 9, with Plate 4; cf. R. Goossens, *Chronique d'Égypte* 11 (1936), 511–6; Page, *GLP* 130–3; Handley 18. Corrections etc. by Calderini except where stated (P has many misspellings and grammatical errors)   1–7 (Εἰλείθυια) Dionys. Hal. *On Arrangement of Words* 26 (p. 139 Usener–Radermacher), attrib. Eur.   1 partly preserved in test. iiib (see above)   13 Schol. Ar. *Clouds* 138, attrib. Eur. (= F 884 N)   2 ωστε P (which often has ω for ο) ὥστε Dionys. (corr. there by R. Stephanus)   δυχιμερον P δυσχειμέρων Ἀρκάδων Dionys. (transposed there by Sylburg, -ρον Musgrave)   3 Πὰν om. Dionys. (supplied there by Scaliger)   4 αὐτὴ Dionys. (corr. there by Leopardus)   8 συνδεμων[λεγ]λογον P   9 Goossens 14 ηρχετεκτονων P   ἐκπονῶν Grégoire   ἠρχιτεκτόνουν Mette   15 πολλοισινενβλοισιν P 16 τὰ corr. from τε P read by Turner (see Handley)   Μυσῶ[ν πε]δί' Goossens μυσω͜ διον P ἐπ[ι]στρωφᾶι Handley επ[ ]στροφην P ἐπ[ε]στράφη Goossens ἐπ[ε]στρώφα Koerte   ποδί Goossens παγ[P   P has four more lines probably not from the same text.

27

705a   (Τη.)   ληιστὰς ἐλαύνων καὶ κατασπέρχων δορί

697   (Τη.)   πτώχ' ἀμφίβλητα σώματος λαβὼν ῥάκη
                    ἀλκτήρια †τύχης†

698   (Τη.)   δεῖ γάρ με δόξαι πτωχὸν ⟨   ⟩
                    εἶναι μὲν ὅσπερ εἰμί, φαίνεσθαι δὲ μή.

699   ἄνασσα πράγους τοῦδε καὶ βουλεύματος

722   ('Αγαμέμνων)   ἴθ' ὅποι χρήιζεις· οὐκ ἀπολοῦμαι
                    τῆς σῆς Ἑλένης οὕνεκα.

723   ('Αγ.)   Σπάρτην ἔλαχες, κείνην κόσμει·
                    τὰς δὲ Μυκήνας ἡμεῖς ἰδίαι.

713   ὦ πόλις "Αργους, κλύεθ' οἷα λέγει;

705   Τη.   κώπης ἀνάσσων κἀποβὰς εἰς Μυσίαν
                    ἐτραυματίσθην πολεμίωι βραχίονι.

707   καλῶς ἔχοι μοι, Τηλέφωι δ' ἀγὼ φρονῶ.

705a (112 A, 934 M) Ar. *Ach.* 1188, attrib. Eur. *Tel.* by Schol.   **697** (103 A, 935 M) ps.-
Diogenes, *Letter* 34.2 (*Epistol. Gr.* p. 248 Hercher), with ref. to Tel. arriving at Argos in Tragedy
1 ἀμφίβληστρα Burges   λαβόντα (for context) ps.-Diog.   **698** (104 A, 936 M) Ar. *Ach.* 440–1
with εἶναι τήμερον 'to be... today' at end of 1, attrib. Eur. *Tel.* by Schol.   1 ⟨ἐν τῆιδ' ἡμέραι⟩
Ditifeci   **699** (105 A, 963 M) Ar. *Lys.* 706, attrib. Eur. *Tel.* (at least the first two words) by
Schol.   Valckenaer added *Lys.* 707 ('why, tell me, have you exited from the house thus scowling?')
722 (130 A, 938 M) Schol. and Tzetzes on Ar. *Clouds* 891, attrib. Eur. *Tel.*; attrib. Agam. by
Bakhuyzen   **723** (131 A, 939 M) Stob. 3.39.9, attrib. Eur. *Tel.*   1 widely used and paraphrased as
a proverb, e.g. Cic. *Att.* 4.6.2 (cf. 1.20.3), Plut. *Mor.* 472e, 602b; see Nauck   **713** (121 A, 960 M)
Ar. *Knights* 813 where Schol. attrib. ὦ... "Αργους to Eur. *Tel.*, κλύεθ'... λέγει to Eur. *Med.* (=
Med. 168); also Ar. *Wealth* 601, where Schol. and Tzetzes attrib. ὦ... "Αργους to Eur. *Tel.* and

TELEPHUS 29

705a *(Tel.)* ... harrying the raiders and scattering them with my spear.

Telephus probably tells of his valour against the Achaeans.

697 *(Tel.)* ... taking beggarly rags cast about my body as protections †from fortune†

Telephus explains his disguise in the Prologue speech.

698 *(Tel.)* For I must seem ... beggar < >, to be the man I am but not appear so.

Probably more from the Prologue speech.

699 Mistress of this transaction and strategy ...

Probably Telephus adopting Clytemnestra's advice.

F 722–3 and probably 713 are from Agamemnon's quarrel with Menelaus (early in the play?)

722 *(Agamemnon)* Go where you want — I'll not die for your Helen's sake!

723 *(Ag.)* Sparta was your portion — govern her! I inherited Mycenae for myself.

713 O City of Argos, do you hear what he is saying?

705 *Tel.* Captaining an oar I disembarked into Mysia, and there was wounded by an enemy's arm.

Telephus, disguised, falsely explains his wound.

707 May it go well for me — and as I want it for Telephus.

Probably the disguised Telephus cryptically wishing himself well.

note Eur. *Pho.* 613 (ὦ πόλις). κλύεθ᾽ ... λέγει attrib. also to Eur. *Tel.* by Elmsley **705** (111 A, 933 M) 1 Aristot. *Rhet.* 1405a29, attrib. Tel. in Eur. *Tel.* (κώπας ἀνάσσειν some mss.); κώπης ἀνάσσων and ἀποβὰς εἰς Μυσίαν Steph. on *Rhet.* 1405a29, *Comm. Aristot. Gr.* XXI.2, pp. 313, 315 Rabe ἀποβὰς ... βραχίονι (and κώπης ... ἀνάσσειν in preceding paraphrase) Anon. Comm. on *Rhet.* 1405a29, *Comm. Aristot. Gr.* XXI.2, p. 169 Rabe 2 ἐτραυματίσθην πολεμίωι Nauck –θη –μω Anon. Comm. **707** (114 A, 947 M) Schol. Ar. *Ach.* 446, attrib. Eur. *Tel.*; paraphrased by Ar. and (unattrib.) Ath. 5.2, 186c ἔχοι μοι Dobree ἔχοιμι Schol. perhaps ἔχει μοι Nauck

30 EURIPIDES

703 (Τη.) μή μοι φθονήσητ', ἄνδρες Ἑλλήνων ἄκροι,
εἰ πτωχὸς ὢν τέτληκ' ἐν ἐσθλοῖσιν λέγειν.

708 (Τη.) ἐρεῖ τις, οὐ χρῆν.

**708a (Τη.) φέρ' εἰ ⟨ ⟩ ἐκπλεύσας σκάφει

709 (Τη.) καθῆσθ' ἂν ἐν δόμοισιν; ἢ πολλοῦ γε δεῖ.

710 Τη. τὸν δὲ Τήλεφον
οὐκ οἰόμεσθα;

711 (Τη.) εἶτα δὴ θυμούμεθα
παθόντες οὐδὲν μᾶλλον ἢ δεδρακότες;

712 ἅπασαν ἡμῶν τὴν πόλιν κακορροθεῖ.

**712a οὗτος σὺ τολμᾷς πτωχὸς ὢν λέγειν τάδε;

706 (Τη.) Ἀγάμεμνον, οὐδ' εἰ πέλεκυν ἐν χεροῖν ἔχων
μέλλοι τις εἰς τράχηλον ἐμβαλεῖν ἐμόν,
σιγήσομαι δίκαιά γ' ἀντειπεῖν ἔχων.

715 οὗ τἄρ' Ὀδυσσεύς ἐστιν αἱμύλος μόνος·
χρεία διδάσκει, κἂν βραδύς τις ᾖ, σοφόν.

703 (109 A, 951 M) Schol. Ar. *Ach*. 497, attrib. Eur. *Tel*.; line 1 recurs in Alexis fr. 63.7
708 (115 A, 952 M) Ar. *Ach*. 540, attrib. Eur. *Tel*. by Schol. 708a (116 A, 953 M) Ar. *Ach*.
541, attrib. Eur. *Tel*. by Wilamowitz 709 (117 A, 954 M) Ar. *Ach*. 543, attrib. (at least ἢ . . . δεῖ)
Eur. *Tel*. by Schol. 710 (118 A, 955 M) Ar. *Ach*. 555–6, attrib. (at least τὸν δὲ Τήλεφον) Eur.
Tel. by Schol.; paraphrased by Aristid. 2.59, p. 162 Behr, attrib. 'Tel. refuting Odysseus' by Schol.
Aristid., p. 375–6 Dindorf 711 (119 A, 965 M) Schol. Ar. *Thesm*. 518–9, attrib. Eur. *Tel*.
1 εἶτα δὴ (as Ar.'s text) Matthiae εἰ δὴ Schol. 2 μᾶλλον Schol. μεῖζον (as Ar.'s text) Nauck

Telephus disguised delivers a speech including the next five or six frs.:

703 *(Tel.)* Do not begrudge it me, foremost men of the Greeks, if I, a beggar, dare to speak amongst my betters.

708 *(Tel.)* Someone will say, 'it was not right'.

**708a *(Tel.)* Come now, suppose <   > had sailed out in a bark . . .

709 *(Tel.)* Would you have sat quiet at home? Nay, far from it!

710 *Tel.* . . . and do we think that Telephus (should) not (have done it)?

711 *(Tel.)* And then do we feel anger, when we have been no more victims than perpetrators?

Two reactions to Tel.'s speech:

712 He is vilifying our whole city.

**712a You — do you, a beggar, dare to say these things?

Telephus begins a further argument:

706 *(Tel.)* Agamemnon, even were someone holding an axe in his hands and ready to strike it on my neck, not even then will I keep silent; for I have a just reply to make.

715 Odysseus is not unrivalled as a wheedler, so it seems. Need teaches a man to be clever, even one who is slow to learn.

A comment on Telephus' persuasiveness.

---

712 (120 A, 957 M) Ar. *Ach.* 577, attrib. (at least κακορροθεῖ) Eur. *Tel.* by Schol.   Mette thinks of including *Ach.* 576 οὐ γὰρ οὗτος ἄνθρωπος πάλαι... 'Has not this fellow long since (been vilifying etc.)'   **712a** (145 A, — M; cf. p. 580 N) Ar. *Ach.* 577b   **706** (113 A, 969 M) Stob. 3.13. 3, attrib. Eur. *Tel.* 2 τις Gesner τε Stob.   **715** (123 A, 972 M) Stob. 3.29.55, attrib. Eur. *Tel.* 1 Plut. *Lysand.* 20.5, unattrib. 2 paraphrased as a proverb Suidas χ 465 (χρεία) = Menand. fr. inc. 229 K.–T. (cf. *Sthen.* F 663)   1 οὔ τἄρ' Porson οὐκ ἄρα Plut. οὐ γὰρ Stob. μόνον Plut.

32   EURIPIDES

727a P. Oxy. 2460

fr. 1   *Top of a column with centres of iambic trimeters 1–6,*
            ends of anapaestic dimeters 7–11:

1   ] . παντλεῖν εἰτι[7   ]πρ[ό]τερον πάντες τ . . [
2   ]τοί[ν]υν πάντες[8   ] . πόλιν μαστεύωμ[εν
3   ]εν κατ' ἄστυ· μη[9   ] . ις; τί δοκεῖ; πῶ[ς ἂν
4   ] . . [ ] . μηδεν . . [10] . ἐσαιμεν ἄρισ[τον
5   ]δοντες δ' αὐτὸν ενφ[11]μασ[τ]εύειν χρή·
6   ]μᾶς οἷς μέλει τ[

fr. 5   *Beginnings of ten anapaestic lines including:*

3   φήσομ[εν   6   κ[αίτοι τ]ί λέγω;[
4   -λ' οὐδὲν ἀληθές[7   ]φανεῖσθαι τ[
5   ἀλλ' ἤ με μάτην[

fr. 6   *Near-ends(?) of five iambic trimeters from top of the*
            fourth column after fr. 1, including:

1   πτω]χὸς ὢν οὐ πτω[χ-   3   φ]ράσας· τί προσμ[
2   ] . . . ν φράσειε[4   ]νου μέτ'εστι μ[

fr. 12   *Middles of thirteen iambic trimeters(?) including:*

2   ]σι συμμάχου[5   ]ἡμᾶς ὦ πρ[7   ]επαγηι πτω[χ
4   ] . οις Τηλεφο . [6   ]υκὼς εἴ τις ε[

            (F 727a continues below)

721   κακός τίς ἐστι προξένωι σοὶ χρώμενος.

700   (Τη.)   ὦ Φοῖβ' Ἄπολλον Λύκιε, τί ποτέ μ' ἐργάσηι;

727a (147 A; 940–4, 977–8 and 980–7 M) P. Oxy. 2460 (1st C. A.D.) ed. Rea in Handley and Rea
(1957) and with minimal revisions in *Oxy. Pap.* XXVII (1962); corrections and supplements in first
ed. except where noted; many speculative supplements in Mette (1963)   **fr. 1** 1]ἀπ- or]ἐπ- Rea
2]οι [σ]υνπαντες (= σύμπαντες) possible, Rea 5 perhaps ἰ]δόντες Austin 6 ὑ]μᾶς or ἡ]μᾶς
Rea 10 τε]λέσαιμεν Snell   **fr. 5** 3–4 ἀλ]ιλ' Snell   **fr. 6** 3 προσμ[ένεις; or -μ[ενῶ; Snell
4 P has the accent and apostrophe]ν οὖ μέτ(α) ἐστι or κεί]νου μέτ(α) ἐστι (not μέτεστι) Handley

727a P. Oxy.

fr. 1   *end of a speech calling for a search (1–6), then self-exhortation by the Chorus to pursue it?*

1 . . . *to get rid of* (?). . .   2 . . . *now then,* all . . .
3 . . . throughout the town . . .   4 . . . *nothing?* (or
nobody?) . . .   5 . . . and . . . –ing him . . .   6 . . . *you/us*
whose concern it is . . .

7–8   . . . previously(?) let us all . . . search the city
9–10   . . . What seems best? *How might we best* . . .
11 . . . must search . . .

fr. 5   *from the continuation of fr. 1.7–11?*

3 we shall say . . .   4–5 . . . nothing true; but either . . .
me vainly . . .   6 *And yet what* am I saying? . . .
7 . . . about to become evident . . .

fr. 6   *iambics (dialogue?), four columns later than fr. 1:*

1 . . . though a *beggar,* not *beggar(ly?)* . . .   2 . . . might
indicate . . .   3 . . . *indicating;* why (*or* what) . . . ?
4 . . . with(?) . . . is . . .

fr. 12   *possibly close to fr. 6:*

2 . . . <*of/from?*> an ally . . .   4 . . . Telephus . . .
5 . . . us, O . . .   6 . . . if someone . . .   7 . . . may lead
against . . . *beggar?* . . .

(F 727a continues below)

721   Some bad man is treating you as a guest-friend.

Suspicion about Telephus expressed to Agamemnon.

700   *(Tel.)* O Lycian Phoebus Apollo, whatever are you going to do
to me?

Telephus, probably during his exposure.

---

fr. 12 6 πεφ]υκὼς (e.g.) Rea   **721** (129 A, 976 M) Ammonius, *On similar and different
words,* No. 411 (πρόξενος, p. 106 Nickau), attrib. Eur. *Tel.* (whence *Etym. Gud.* p. 481, 29 Sturz)
700 (106 A, 961 M) Ar. *Knights* 1240, attrib. Eur. *Tel.* by Schol.

727 ἀπέπτυσ' ἐχθροῦ φωτὸς ἔχθιστον τέκος.

(**727a**, *cont'd*)

fr. 9 *Near-beginnings of nine iambic trimeters including:*

4 — εἶ]ἐν· τί δή σοι χρησ[6 π]ότερά σ' ἔτρωσαν [

5 χ]ωλὸν βολαίας τη[7] ις φανεῖ τοῦδ' ἀπα[

fr. 10 *Beginnings of twenty-one trimeters (speaker changes probably*
to be supplied where not visible) including:

2 — τί οὖν σ' ἀπείργε[ι 11 — 'Αγαμεμνον[

3 — τὸ μὴ προδοῦναι[12 (–?) βλ[ά]πτειν τὸ κο[ινόν

4 — [ο]ὔ [π]ού τις ἐχ[θ]ρῶν[13 — [ο]ὐκ οἶσθ' 'Οδυσσ[

5 — [ο]ὐκ οἶδα· δει[μ]αιν[14 (–?)]ἐν χρόνω[ι]ν αισ[

6 — κλαίω[ν] πλανήσει [16 (–?)] ω[ ]ἀκοῦσαι καιρός[

7 (–) α[ ]σεμνος [17 (–?)] ἀ[γ]ρίου του φωτός[

9 — ἀλλα ασι[γ]ᾶι[ ]ε[18 (–?)] [ ]εχετ[ ]λαμπρ[

10 — ἧσσόν γ' ἂν οὖν[

fr. 25 *Remnants of five lines including:*

2] 'Αχαιοισ[3 πέπ]οιθ' 'Οδυσσ[4] τι δοκεισ [

(*F 727a continues below*)

727 (135 A, 962 M) Schol. Ar. *Peace* 528, attrib. Eur. *Tel.* 'or *Tlepolemus*' (not a play of Eur.)
727a (cont'd) **fr. 9** 4 *paragraphus* marks change of speaker 6 or σε τρωσαντ[Rea **fr. 10** *paragraphi* for speaker changes visible at 2–6, 9–11, 13 4 χ[θ]ρω doubtful for space: Handley 5 δει[μ]αίν[ω δὲ Mette, Snell 7 κ]α[ὶ] σεμνός Diggle 9 perhaps ἄλλαις Rea ἀλλ' αἶσα σι[γ]ᾶν (e.g.) Snell 12 κο[ινόν M. Treu (see Strohm, *Gnomon* 32.603) **fr. 25** 2 'Αχαιοῖς[or 'Αχαιοι σ[Rea 4 τί δοκεῖ σ [Austin

727   I repudiate the most hateful child of a hateful father.

Probably Telephus rejecting pleas to spare the young Orestes.

(**727a**, *cont'd*)

fr. 9   *iambic line-beginnings: Agamemnon(?) addressing Tele-*
             phus after his exposure:

             4 *Very well*; what, then . . . to you . . .   5 *lamed* . . .
             <*from*/*of?*> . . . netted . . .   6 Did . . . wound you . . .
             7 . . . will reveal . . . of this . . .

fr. 10   *iambic dialogue perhaps between (a) Agamemnon and (b)*
             Telephus, including:

a.	So what is preventing you . . . ?	2
b.	Not to betray . . .	3
a.	Surely none of *our enemies* . . . ?	4
b.	I do not know; . . . *fear* . . .	5
a.	<*You*> will wander . . . weeping . . .	6
(b.)	. . . arrogant . . .	7
b.	But . . . *keep silent* . . .	9
a	. . . would . . . less, no doubt, in that case.	10
b	Agamemnon . . .	11
(a?)	To harm the *alliance* . . .	12
b?	Do you not know . . . Odysseus . . . ?	13
(a?)	. . . in time . . .	14
(a?)	. . . a proper time to listen . . .	16
(b?)	. . . <*from*/*of?*> some savage man . . .	17
(a?)	< > . . . *brilliant* . . .	18

fr. 25   *possibly more of the same scene:*

             2 . . . Achaeans . . .   3 *I have* (or . . . *has*) *confidence* (in?,
             that?) *Odysseus* . . .   4 . . . you think (*or* seem, *or* it
             seems) . . .

             (F 727a continues below)

727b   P. Rylands 482

Latter parts of iambic trimeters (1–15), then anapaests (16–19). The trimeters appear to be largely from a single speech (Odysseus?) with perhaps a response in 13–15 (Telephus?); then probably Chorus. Interpretation and ascription to Eur. Tel. are quite uncertain:

one line almost entirely lost

<table>
<tr><td>('Οδυσσεύς?)</td><td>]κοιν[   ]ἔρχεται[ι</td><td>2</td></tr>
<tr><td></td><td>]ς Τήλε[φ]ͺς τὰ πε[</td><td></td></tr>
<tr><td></td><td>]να[   ]ις καὶ κ[υ]βερνή[τ-</td><td></td></tr>
<tr><td></td><td>]αρω[ ] ἐκ νυκ[τό]ς· εἶτα σ[</td><td>5</td></tr>
<tr><td></td><td>]μεν [σύ]μβουλο[ς] ἐλθὲ τῶι [</td><td></td></tr>
<tr><td></td><td>] γὰρ ἡμῶν ὡς ὁ [μῦ]θος εστα[</td><td></td></tr>
<tr><td></td><td>]ρωτα καὶ νόμ[ο]ις Ἑλληνι[κοῖς</td><td></td></tr>
<tr><td></td><td>]υσι χρῆσθαι, τ[ῆ]ς τύχης αμ[ ] [</td><td></td></tr>
<tr><td></td><td>]οισιν ἐμπε[σ]εῖν· ἀστὸς γὰ[ρ] ὣς</td><td>10</td></tr>
<tr><td></td><td>] κηρύκειον ο[ ] δάκνει πλέον·</td><td></td></tr>
<tr><td></td><td>] οισαν τῆσδ' ἀφ' ἑσπέρας γνάθο[</td><td></td></tr>
<tr><td>(Τηλ.??)</td><td>] ην ε⟨ὖ⟩ θώμεθ' [ἀ]μνηστεῖν σε χρὴ</td><td></td></tr>
<tr><td></td><td>]τα· σοὶ δ' ὑπεξελεῖν πάρα</td><td></td></tr>
<tr><td></td><td>] μὴ πρόσχο[ρδ]ον, ὡς ἀνὴρ μόληι.</td><td>15</td></tr>
<tr><td>(Χορός?)</td><td>]υν τούτοις τ[ῶ]ι μὲν ξείνωι</td><td></td></tr>
<tr><td></td><td>]ιν πομπού[ς] παρατασσέσθω·</td><td></td></tr>
<tr><td></td><td>να]ύαρχος τίς [ἀν]ὴρ ἔσται;</td><td></td></tr>
<tr><td></td><td>] ἐκ τούτω[ν αὐ]τὸς ἐγὼ πᾶν</td><td></td></tr>
</table>

727c   P. Berlin 9908 (with P. Oxy. 2460 frs. 17–20)

Choral lyrics, then iambic dialogue between Achilles (newly arriving) and Odysseus:

col. i   *Only a few ends of choral lines are visible including:*

2 π]αρέστα   9 φυγάδες

727b (148 A, 979 M) P. Rylands 482 (2ⁿᵈ C. B.C.) ed. C. H. Roberts (with D. L. Page), *Catalogue of Gr. and Lat. Papyri in the John Rylands Library* (1938), 91–4 with Plate 4; cf. B. Snell, *Gnomon* 15 (1939), 538–40; Page, *GLP* 140–5. Attribution to Eur. *Tel.* uncertain. Supplements Roberts–Page except where noted. For speculative supplements see esp. Page in Roberts–Page; Webster, *Bull. Ryl. Libr.* 22 (1938), 543–9; Mette (1963)   2]κειν[Snell   3 Τήλε[φ] ἐς Rob.– Page Τήλε[φ]ο̣ς

727b P. Rylands

Not certainly from this play; possibly Odysseus advises
Telephus on becoming the Greeks' guide (1–12), Telephus
responds (13–15), the Chorus and/or Odysseus call for
action (16–19):

(Odysseus?) . . . common(?) . . . goes <   > Telephus . . .
the <   > sailor(s)? and captain(s?) <   > a t
night; then < [5]   > go (as?) counsellor for the
<   >. For (of/from?) us, as the report (or talk, or
saying) . . . <   > . . . and . . . to use Greek
laws . . . fortune . . . <   > to fall upon . . . ; for as a
member of the community[10] <   > herald's . . .
afflicts more; <   > from this evening . . . jaw(s?).
(Tel.??) <   > . . . we may settle . . . rightly, you should
(not?) be forgetful <   > and it is up to you to
remove <   > not in harmony, so that the man
may come.[15]
(Chorus?) <   > (for? with?) these . . . (for?) the
foreigner <   > let him appoint escorts. <   >
what man will be (the) naval commander? <   >
after this I myself . . . every . . .

727c P. Berlin (with P. Oxy.)

end of a Choral stasimon and beginning of a scene with
dialogue between Achilles (newly arriving) and Odysseus:

col. i   Choral line-ends including 2 stood beside 9 fugitives

---

Snell perhaps πέ[ργαμα Rob.–Page 4 σήμαινε] να[ύτα]ις καὶ κ[υ]βερνή[ταις τάδε (but να[ύτ]ης
possible) Rob.–Page end πόρον Webster 6 σὺ] μὲν Rob.–Page ἐλθέτω (e.g.) Snell 10 P has
the punctuation 11 ο[ὺ] or possibly ε[ἰ] Rob.–Page P has the punctuation 12]κ Rob.–Page
(hesitantly) οὐ . . . δά]κοι σ' ἄν . . . γνάθο[ς (e.g.) Snell (οὐκέτι . . . Koerte) γνάθο[ις Collard
13–15 spoken by Tel.? Webster (14–15 Snell, 12–15 Mette) 13 οὐ γάρ, τάδ'] ἦν Rob.–Page
14 τῶν εἰσέπει]τα Rob.-Page P has the punctuation 15 τῶνδ' εἴ τι] Rob.–Page (τοῖσδ' Snell)
16 ἄγε σ]ύν Rob.-Page 17 συμπλε]ῖν Rob.-Page 18 ὁ δὲ να]ύαρχος τίς . . . ; Snell εἰ
να]ύαρχός τις . . . Webster (-ός τις Rob.-Page) P has colon at end **727c** (149 A, 983 M) P.
Berlin 9908 (2ⁿᵈ C. A.D.) ed. Schubart and Wilamowitz, BKT V.2 (1907) 64–72 as from Soph. Assembly of the Achaeans; cf. Pearson, Fragments of Soph. (Cambridge, 1917), fr. 142; Page, GLP
12–15. Identified with Tel. by Handley and Rea (1957) editing P. Oxy. 2460 (cf. F 727a above); this

38   EURIPIDES

col. ii   (Χο.)   ἢ νότ[ου ἢ] ζεφύροιο δίνα
πέμψ[ει Τ]ρωιάδας ἀκτάς,
σύ τε π[ηδ]αλίωι παρεδρεύω[ν
φράσει[ς τ]ῶι κατὰ πρῶιραν
εὐθὺς Ἰλ[ίο]υ πόρον   5
Ἀτρείδα[ις] ἰδέσιθαμ.
σὲ γὰρ Τε[γ]εᾶμτις ἡμῖν,
Ἑλλάς, οὐχὶ Μυσία,ͺ τίκτει
ναύταν σύν τινιͺ δὴ θειῶν
καὶ πεμπτῆρ' ἀͺλίων ιἐͺρμετμῶν.   10

ΑΧΙΛΛΕΥΣ   μῶν καὶ σὺ καινὸς ποντίαͺς ἀπὸ χιθονὸς
ἥκεις, Ὀδυσσεῦ; ποῦ 'στι σύͺλλογος φι[ί]λων;
τί μέλλετ'; οὐ χρῆν ἥσυχοͺν κεῖσθαι ιπ[ό]δα.
'Οδ.   δοκεῖ στρατεύειν καὶ μέλειͺ τοῖς ἐν τέιλει
τάδ'· ἐν δέοντι δ' ἦλθες, ὦͺ παῖ Πηλέως.   15
'Αχ.   οὐ μὴν ἐπ' ἀκταῖς γ' ἐστὶ κωπήρͺημͺς στρατός,
οὔτ' οὖν ὁπλίτης ἐξετάζεται παρών.
'Οδ.   ἀλλ' αὐτίκα· σπεύδειν γὰρ ἐν καιρῶι χρεών.
'Αχ.   αἰεί ποτ' ἐστὲ νωχελεͺῖς καὶ μέͺλλετε,
ῥήσεις θ' ἕκαστος μυρίαςͺ καθήμιενος   20
λέγει, τὸ δ' ἔργον [ο]ὐδαμοῦͺ περαίνͺεται.
κἀͺ[γ]ὼ μέν, ὡς ὁρᾶ[τ]ε, δρᾶνͺ ἔͺτͺοιμοςͺ ὢν
ἥͺκͺω, στρατός τε Μ[υρ]μιδͺών, καὶ πλεύσ[ομαι
τὰ ιͺ[τ]ῶν Ἀτρειδ[ῶν οὐ μένων]ͺι μελλͺήμͺ[ατα.

col. iii   Only some speaker-notations Ἀχιλλ., Ὀδ. are visible.

719   Ἕλληνες ὄντες βαρβάροις δουλεύσομεν;

716 (partly in P. Oxy. 2460 fr. 32)
(Τη.?)   σὺ δ' εἶκ' ἀνάγκηι καὶ θεοῖσι μὴ μάχου·
τόλμα δὲ πͺρͺιοσβλέπειν με καὶ φρονήματος
χάλα. τά τοͺι μέͺγιστα πολλάκις θεὸς
ταπείν' ἔͺθͺηκͺε καὶ συνέστειλεν πάλιν.

traces of two more lines in the papyrus

has a few letters each from near the ends of 6–10 (fr. 18), 10–16 (fr. 19), 19–24 (fr. 20), and probably the first two letters each of 22–4 (fr. 17)   1 δίνα Murray δεινα P. Berl.   6 Barrett -δ[ᾶν Pearson 21]περαιν[P. Oxy. πορευεται P. Berl.   22 ὁρᾶ[τ]ε Hunt ὁραι[ ]ε P. Berl.   24 Page (cf. IA 818)

col. ii (Cho.) . . . gust of *southerly or* westerly breeze will bring . . .
to the shores of Troy; and you, stationed at the steering-oar,
will instruct the prow-man to observe a course direct for
Troy[5] *for* the Atreidae. For a Tegean mother, Greece not
Mysia, gave you birth to be — with a god's influence,
surely — a sailor and guide of our sea-going ships.[10]

Achilles.   Not, surely, fresh from your sea-bound land like me,
    Odysseus? Where is our comrades' gathering? Why the
    delay? There was no call for you to be cooling your heels!
Od.   The expedition is resolved on; the commanders have it in
    hand. You have come just when you were needed, son of
    Peleus.[15]
Ach.   And yet our army of rowers is not on the shore—nor, in fact,
    is our armoured host present and being reviewed.
Od.   It will be soon enough; one should hasten when the moment
    is ripe.
Ach.   You people are always sluggish, always delaying; each of
    you sits and delivers a thousand speeches,[20] and the
    business in hand is not the least bit finished! Well, I as you
    see have come here ready for action, I and my Myrmidon
    force, and I shall sail *<without waiting on>* the delays of the
    Atreidae.

Traces in col. iii of the papyrus show that this dialogue continued.

719   Are we who are Greeks going to be slaves to barbarians?

    *Achilles objecting to Telephus' leadership — or Menelaus
    urging the war on Troy?*

716 (with P. Oxy.)

    (Tel.?)   But you should yield to necessity and not fight against the
    gods. Consent to look on me, relax your pride! Often god
    makes the mightiest humble and brings them down from
    their height.

    Telephus begs Achilles to heal him?

beg. τα[P. Oxy.]ων P. Berl.   **719** (127 A, 977 M) Clem. Alex. *Strom.* 6.2.16, attrib. Eur. *Tel.*;
adapted by Thrasymachus 85 B 2 DK, ps.-Callisth. rec. β 1.25; the first three letters possibly in P.
Oxy. 2460 (F 727a) fr. 11.2   **716** (124 A, 985 M) 1–4 Stob. 3.22.32, attrib. Eur. *Tel.* in ms. S
2–6 (fragments) P. Oxy. 2460 (F 727a) fr. 32

718   ὥρα σε θυμοῦ κρείσσονα γνώμην ἔχειν.

724   πριστοῖσι λόγχης θέλγεται ῥινήμασιν.

(727a, cont'd)

fr. 13   *Beginnings of eight iambic trimeters including:*

    2 — τ]έχνηι γεμ[6 στ]είχοντί νυ[ν
    3 ὅ]μως δ' ονη [7 ἰδ]ού· πορευο[
    4 οὐ]κ ἀξιώσω[8 φρ]ουρεῖτέ νυ[ν
    5 — ὦ] φίλτατ', ὦ [

    (F 727a continues below)

Unplaced Fragments

701   μοχθεῖν ἀνάγκη τοὺς θέλοντας εὐτυχεῖν.

702   τόλμα σὺ κἄν τι τραχὺ νείμωσιν θεοί.

704   Μυσὸν Τήλεφον

714   (Τη.?)   τί γάρ με πλοῦτος ὠφελεῖ {νόσον};
                σμίκρ' ἂν θέλοιμι καὶ καθ' ἡμέραν ἔχων
                ἄλυπος οἰκεῖν μᾶλλον ἢ πλουτῶν νοσεῖν.

717   τί δ' ὦ τάλας σοι τῶιδε πείθεσθαι μέλει;

720   κακῶς ὄλοιτ' ἄν· ἄξιον γὰρ Ἑλλάδι.

718 (126 A, 970 M) Stob. 3.20.36, attrib. Eur. *Tel.*   **724** (132 A, 968 M) Plut. *Mor.* 46f, attrib. Eur. with ref. to Tel.'s wound   **727a** (cont'd) **fr. 13** *paragraphi* for speaker changes visible at 2, 5 6 -οντί νυ[ν so accented P   **701** (107 A, 971 M) Stob. 3.29.10, attrib. Eur. *Tel.*; also subjoined to Soph. F 397 in Stob. 3.29.25; unattrib. in several anthologies (all, or first two words which are also in *Aeolus* F 37.1)   **702** (108 A, 973 M) Stob. 4.10.10, attrib. Eur. *Tel.* in mss. MA (grouped with *Arch.* F 240, 244 in ms. S)   τόλμα σὺ Nauck τόλμ' ἀεὶ Stob. mss. SM τόλμης ἀεὶ ms. A τραχὺ νείμωσιν Bothe τρηχὺ νέμωσι(ν) Stob.   **704** (110 A, 945 M) Olympiodorus on Plat. *Gorg.* 521b 1 (p. 235 Westerink), attrib. Eur. *Tel.*; the phrase occurs in Ar. *Ach.* 430; cf. *Clouds* 922   **714** (122 A, 975 M) Sext. Emp., *Against the Professors* 11.56 (II, p. 388 Mutschmann, quoting Crantor F 13 Kayser), unattrib. 2–3 Stob. 4.31.64 and 4.33.11, both attrib. Eur. *Tel.* 1 {νόσον} Wilamowitz, *KS* I.288 n.1 νοσοῦντά γε Fabricius Handley 25 suspects

718   It is time for you to let your mind rule your temper.

Probably Odysseus persuading Achilles.

724   It is soothed by filings shaved from the spearhead.

The cure for Telephus' wound, perhaps described by Odysseus.

(727a, cont'd)

fr. 13   dialogue from near the end of the play?

2 – By skill . . .   3 But nevertheless . . .   4 I shall not
think fit . . .   5 – <O> dearest one, O . . .   6 . . . (for him?)
as he goes, now . . .   7 *Look* . . . go . . .   8 Keep watch
now . . .

(F 727a continues below)

Unplaced Fragments

701   Toil is required of those who want to prosper.

702   Show endurance, even if the gods deal out some harshness.

704   Mysian Telephus

714   *(Tel.?)*What does wealth avail me {in ill health}? I would
rather live pain-free with modest daily means than be
wealthy and suffering ill health.

Probably Telephus; several contexts are possible.

717   Stubborn man — why are you concerned to heed him?

Probably 'him' is Telephus; several contexts are possible.

720   He (*or* she) would perish miserably; that would be valuable
for Greece.

the whole line   2 μίκρ' ἄν Trincavelli (σ)μικρὰν Sext., Stob.   θέλοιμ' ἄν Stob. 4.31.64
2–3 ἔχων. . . μᾶλλον: ἄλυπον ἔχων οἰκεῖν βιοτὴν Sext. (ἔχων ἄλυπον . . . βίοτον Fabricius)
3 τροφὴν ἐνοικεῖν Stob. 4.31.64   **717** (125 A, 949 M) Schol. Ar. *Ach.* 454, attrib. Eur. *Tel.*
σοι . . . μέλει Schol. Lh σὺ . . . μέλλεις Schol. ΕΓ   **720** (128 A, 958 M) Schol. Ar. *Ach.* 8, attrib.
Eur. *Tel.*   ἄξιον . . . Ἑλλάδι Suidas π 715 Adler (παρωιδία), attrib. Eur. and Ar.

725   λοχαῖον σῖτον

726   ψυκτήρ

(727a, *cont'd)* Frs. *2–4, 7, 8, 11, 14–24, 26–51 include only a scattered handful of recognisable words. F 727c.5–24 includes frs. 17–20; F 716.2–6 includes fr. 32; F 719 may include fr. 11.2.*

725 (133 A, 988 M) *Etym. Gen.* λ 141 Alpers (λοχαῖον σῖτον), attrib. Eur. *Tel.*; Hesych. λ 1303 Latte (λοχαῖος), unattrib.; Phot. I.395.6 Naber (λοχαῖος σῖτος), unattrib.; and other lexicaa
726 (134 A, 989 M) Schol. Pl. *Symp.* 213e, attrib. Eur. *Tel.*; Hesych. ψ 264 Schmidt (ψυκτήρ), unattrib.

Commentary on *Telephus*

test. *iiib Hypothesis? The ascription to *Tel.* is tentative, *Tem.* also possible (Turner 58, 60–1; A. Harder in Hofmann and Harder, *Fragmenta Dramatica* 119 n. 7). [Text: for Turner's ἐξέ]τασιν *'review'* in 1 cf. F 727c.17. His other suggestions are 2 *'on the advice of . . .'* and 3–4 *'Tel<ephus's healing>'*.]

696. About a third of the Prologue speech, organised in a typically Euripidean way to reveal locale (1–3), Telephus' birth and parentage (3–7), and his more recent history (7–15) leading into a more detailed narrative of the events causing his present predicament. This narrative probably included F 705a and will have been followed by an explanation of his current strategy (like *Hec.* 45ff., *El.* 87ff.) including F 697–8.

1. Greetings, ancestral land: similar openings by a returning expatriate in *Oineus* F 558 (Diomedes), Aesch. *Mysians* F 143 (Telephus' servant); such invocations are frequent throughout Attic drama (Fraenkel on Aesch. *Ag.* 503). Other addresses to the locale *Alc.* 1, *El.* 1.   **marked out:** metaphorically bounding it with ownership markers (*horoi*): LSJ ὁρίζω IV.1. Present tense for a past action whose effect continues (KG I.137d), frequent esp. in prologues (5, 7, 10–12 etc.).

3. Pan: Hermes' son, traditionally born in Arcadia where his worship originated, typically a mountain-roamer: cf. *Hom.Hymn.* 19.1–15, 30–7. Telephus greets the god of the **stormy crag** where he was born, Mt. Parthenion (6).   **I claim descent:** cf. Epic γένος εὔχομαι (εἶναι) 'I claim my descent (to be)'; Heubeck on Hom. *Od.* 14.199.

4. Auge: usually she gives birth to Telephus in or near Tegea (Introd., p. 22). Aleos discovered this and either put them both in a chest which floated to Mysia (Hecataeus *FGH* 1 F 29), or gave Auge to Nauplius to drown or sell (and she came eventually to Teuthras in Mysia) and exposed Telephus on Parthenion where he was suckled by a doe (Apollod. 2.7.4, 3.9.1; cf. Moses Choren. *Progymn.* 3.3 and the plot of Euripides' late *Auge* where Heracles protected them, Webster, *Euripides* [1967], 238–41). Alternatively Auge, given to Nauplius to be drowned, bears Telephus on Parthenion (cf. 5–7), leaves him there where the doe suckles him, and is sold by Nauplius (Diod. 4. 33, consistently with Euripides here; Alcidamas *Odyss.* 13–17 has both mother and

725   corn concealing an ambush

726   a wine-cooler

(**727a**, *cont'd: see note opposite on remaining fragments.*)

child given to Teuthras). Both main outlines were heard at Tegea by Pausanias (8.48.7). **Tiryns**: the kingdom (not differentiated from Mycenae by the tragedians) which Heracles tried to regain from Eurystheus by performing his Labours.

5. **My witness is . . . :** lit. '(P.) shares in knowing' (LSJ σύνοιδα I); this semi-technical phrasing in Euripides also *El.* 43, *HF* 368.

6. **Parthenion:** modern Partheni, NE of Tegea, separating Arcadia from the Argolid. Pausanias (8.54.6) saw there a sanctuary of Telephus (cf. also Apollod. 1.8.6) near the place where Philippides encountered Pan before the battle of Marathon.

7. **Eileithuia:** Paus. 8.48.7 mentions a temple and statue of 'Eileithuia Auge on her knees' in Tegea where Auge was sometimes supposed to have given birth.

8. **I shall cut short . . . :** cf. Melanippe in her Prologue *Mel.S.* F 481.11, Electra in *Or.* 14. Telephus skirts his exposure, upbringing by herdsmen and search for his mother directed by the Delphic oracle (Diod. 4.33.11, Apollod. 3.9.1).

9–10. δέ renewing narrative after 'I shall cut short . . .': Denniston, *GP* 170.ii(b).

10. **passed on . . . powers:** like Cadmus, *Bacc.* 213; cf. *Pha.* 160–2 n.

11. **Teuthras:** Teuthrania lay around the R. Caicus (Strabo 12.8.1–2, 13.1.69, Hdt. 2.10.1, Xen. *Hell.* 3.1.6).

13. **'far off':** 'Telephus' is here linked with τηλοῦ, elsewhere with the 'teat' (θήλη) of the 'deer' (ἔλαφος), e.g. Apollod. 2.1.4, 3.9.1.

14. **Greek . . . barbarians:** a thematic contrast in this play: see Introd., p. 24. **fighting for victory:** *Or.* 653, *Hel.* 735, *Supp.* 319 (where see Collard) all have this verb for 'striving' in military contexts. [Text: P substitutes 3rd Pers. for 1st. Grégoire's conjecture is close to P's meaningless εκτονων; Mette's is clever but unconvincing in sense, 'I was supervisor'.]

16. **[roaming over:** lit. 'frequents on foot'; for the phrasing as restored cf. Phrynichus *TrGF* I 3 F 5, Eur. *Med.* 666. For historic Pres. tense in this construction (rare in general: Goodwin §633) cf. *Med.* 1173, *Hec.* 132.]

705a. Placed near F 705 by e.g. Buchwald, but better in the Prologue speech, Telephus describing his real exploits as defender rather than raider (e.g. Handley); hardly describing *Achilles'* exploits as Webster suggests. **raiders:** the Achaeans 'plunder' Mysia in the *Cypria* summary, Apollod. *Epit.* 3.17 etc.

697. [1. Text: *Hel.* 1079 (ms.) has ἀμφίβληστρα (normally 'garments') in a very similar phrase, but the adj. ἀμφίβλητα **cast about** seems needed there (see Kannicht) and here where it is the transmitted reading. ἀμφίβλητος is not found elsewhere; cf. ἔκβλητος *Hec.* 699, πρόβλητος Soph. *Aj.* 830, ὑπόβλητος Soph. *Aj.* 481, *OC* 794. **2. protections:** for ἀλκτήρια see, besides LSJ, Pfeiffer on Callim. fr. 346. †**from fortune†**: metre requires ἀλκτήρι' and a vowel starting the next word (unless the phrase originated as a line-ending καὶ τύχης ἀλκτήρια '. . . and protections from fortune': JD).]

698. Schol. Ar. *Ach.* 440–1 gives 'these two lines' to *Tel.*, but the last two words of 440 are unmetrical and unidiomatic for Tragedy. [Text: Ditifeci's 'during this day' is the best of several similar suggestions, but an infin. with δόξαι **seem** . . . and a connection with 441 would be preferable, unless the lines were not sequential in Euripides.] **2. be the man I am:** i.e. retain my real, noble nature (*physis*): for the contrast cf. esp. Aesch. *Sept.* 592.

699. At Ar. *Lys.* 706 this line is spoken by the Chorus-leader to Lysistrata as she enters in distress, and some of the subsequent lines are paratragic (see Introd., p. 21). The inclusion of *Lys.* 707 in the *Tel.* fr. (see App.) and Miller's inference (178 n. 21) that the whole passage in *Lys.* resembles an original in *Tel.* are misplaced. But it is not very likely that the Fem. ἄνασσα 'Mistress' is due to Ar. rather than Euripides (as Wilamowitz 70 suspected), nor that the punctuation and syntax of the line were different in *Tel.* ('Mistress, of this transaction . . .': so Nauck, cf. Handley 23, Heath 276 n. 16). **Mistress** means 'supervisor' (cf. LSJ ἄναξ IV, ἀνάσσω II, F 705 below). This can hardly be Telephus' own heart (Wecklein) or a deity such as Athena (Buchwald; Telephus is under Apollo's guidance: F 700; vases, p. 22 above). So it is probably Clytemnestra sponsoring Telephus' use of supplication with Orestes (see Introd. pp. 19–20).

722, 723. *Metre:* recitative anapaests, probably exchanged with Menelaus after a quarrelsome iambic dialogue; cf. *Med.* 1389–1404. **722.** Agam.'s contempt for the motive for the war recalls Achilles at Hom. *Il.* 9. 337–9; his refusal to die for it contrasts with his fear for Menelaus's death, *Il.* 4. 169–74.; cf. *IA* 382–4. (For Helen as bringer of death cf. *Il.* 2.161–2, 177–8, Aesch. *Ag.* 447–8, 681–98, etc.) **723.** Teucer rebukes Menelaus in similar terms, Soph. *Aj.* 1102–8 (see Stanford's Comm.), as does Peleus in Eur. *And.* 582, reflecting Athenian resentment of Spartan influence in the Greek world.

713. A call to witness (cf. *Supp.* 808 with Collard, *Med.* 168 etc.), perhaps from the Chorus reacting to Telephus' speech (Séchan) but more probably from Agamemnon against Menelaus like the other anapaests F 722, 723, ?918 (Handley 40, and others). In Ar. *Knights* the Sausage-seller is appealing against the Paphlagonian. [Text: Elmsley's inclusion of the whole line in the fr. is widely accepted but questioned by Handley; Schol. Ar. cites another source for its second half.]

705. Telephus falsely explains his wound to Clytemnestra (Handley, Heath) or the Achaean leaders (Séchan, Jouan). His story seems to have inverted his actual experience. Cf. also Odysseus's false story of a disastrous raid, Hom. *Od.* 14.258–72 =

17.427–41. **captaining an oar:** i.e. being in a ship's crew; 'oar' here is not a synecdoche for 'ship' (as in F 727c.10): cf. *Cyc.* 86 ('oar-lords' = 'rowers'), Broadhead on Aesch. *Pers.* 378. Aristotle (App.) cites the phrase as inappropriate terminology. [Text: the Anon. Comm.'s 'he was wounded' cannot be right if Telephus is the speaker as Aristotle says.]

707. Probably Telephus pretending to wish himself ill (so e.g. Séchan) rather than e.g. Odysseus wishing him ill (Webster); this exploits the euphemistic ambiguity of **as I want it** (cf. e.g. *HF* 748 with Bond) [Text: 'may I flourish' (Schol.) does not cohere with what follows. Dobree's **may it go well for me** is more consistent with the paraphrases mentioned in App. than Nauck's 'it is going well for me'.]

703. The model for the beginning of Dicaeopolis's speech dressed as Telephus, Ar. *Ach.* 496–556 (cf. Ar. *Ach.* Hypoth.; Introd., pp. 18–19).

708, 708a, 709, 710. Dicaeopolis's speech justifies Sparta's reaction to Athens's Megarian decrees of 431 B.C. with: 'Someone will say, "they shouldn't have" — but tell me, what should they have done?'[540] Come now, suppose some Spartan had sailed out in a bark[541] and denounced a little Seriphian dog as contraband and sold it off,[542] would you have sat quiet at home? Nay, far from it![543] On the contrary, you would have launched three hundred ships[544] *[then ten comic lines on naval preparations]*. I know that this is what you would have done — and then do we think[555] that Tel. should not have? In that case we are lacking in good sense!'[556] **708.** *Ach.* 540 must all be close to Tel.'s argument but the second half is probably too loosely phrased for Euripides' early play (Buchwald and Jouan 234 n. 7 defend it with *Or.* 665). Similar anticipations of an objection (*procatalepsis*) *Or.* 665, *Bacc.* 204; cf. Hom. *Il.* 6.459; Lloyd, *Agon* 30–1. **708a.** Wilamowitz identified this fr. (questioned by Ditifeci 218) through its incongruous topic and the Tragic word σκάφος 'bark' (targeted in Ar. *Thesm.* 877, *Lys.* 139 etc.). **709.** Schol. Ar. quotes only **nay, far from it** but the whole line is generally given to *Tel.*; cf. *And.* 670, 'Would you have sat in silence? I think not!' (in a similar argument; also *Hcld.* 1005–8). **710.** The attribution to 'Tel. refuting Odysseus' (see App.) is difficult if the scene involved Tel., Agamemnon and Menelaus. Probably the Schol. is mistaken (e.g. Handley 34), though Webster places F 710 in a separate scene.

711. Conclusion of an argument, probably associated with F 703, 708–10 (or with F 706?). [2. Text: Nauck's 'greater' is widely accepted but the Schol.'s text is more intelligible, 'having no more suffered than done' (οὐδέν adverbial). For the legalistic senses of the participles cf. Denniston on *El.* 1045).]

712. Probably an appeal to the Chorus by Agamemnon (cf. Menelaus, *Or.* 1623) or the Chorus-leader (cf. *HF* 252ff.), rather than Odysseus intervening to discredit Telephus (Handley 36) or Menelaus meaning by πόλιν Greece as a whole (Webster). **vilifying:** cf. *Sthen.* F 661.29 n.

712a. In Ar. *Ach.* Lamachus is responding to F 712 — even though in that context he does not know what Dicaeopolis has said. This and the similar parodies at *Ach.* 558

and 593 support the attribution to *Tel*. **You—**: οὗτος pointing 'a surprised or indignant question' (Stevens, *CE* 37).

706. Probably the start of a separate debate speech. On such sympathy-raising opening ploys see Lloyd, *Agon* 26–7. Telephus' hypothesis (which has a certain resonance when addressed to Agamemnon) becomes a reality for Dicaeopolis in *Ach.* (317–8, 359–67 etc.: see Rau 27 on Ar.'s parodic technique here).

715. The speaker might be the Chorus-leader (so e.g. Buchwald). **1. so it seems** (τἄρ' = τοι ἄρα): Denniston, *GP* 555. **wheedler**: αἱμύλος (or -ιος) in Euripides here and the lexicographic F 1095; cf. *Rhes.* 498, 709, Soph. *Ajax* 839 (all Odysseus), Soph. F 816. **2. teaches a man to be wise**: cf. *Hcld.* 574, *El.* 376. Phrasing: cf. *Sthen.* F 663.

727a. P. Oxy. is identified with *Tel.* through F 716. Its publication in 1957 also identified P. Berl. (F 727c) with *Tel.* The relative positions of P. Oxy. frs. 1 and 6 are known from column numbers in the document on its other side. The distance between can only be roughly estimated since the column heights are unknown. Otherwise the fragment placings depend on content. See Handley 35–9 and Webster for analysis. **fr. 1.** A search for an intruder or intruders (Introd., pp. 19, 20)? Lines 1–6 seem to belong to a speech rather than dialogue. **1. to get rid of**: ἀπαντλεῖν *Or.* 1641, [Aesch.] *PV* 84; ἐπαντλεῖν 'to pour over' is less apt (and in Tragedy only Eur. F 899.4). **2. now then, all**: or perhaps (App.) 'all *together*'. **5.** ἱ]δόντες '*seeing*' (Austin) gives better phrasing than δόντες 'giving'. **10.** Snell suggests '*how might* we best *<fulfil>* . . .'.

fr. 5. Content and anapaestic metre suggest a connection with fr. 1, though not immediately after it (Handley 36). The Chorus debates, or perhaps (Ditifeci) Telephus debates with himself. [Text, 3–4: the indented line continues the preceding line, paroemiac following dimeter; hence Snell '*<but>* **nothing** . . .'.]

fr. 6. This fr. is 4 columns or c. 120–160 lines later than fr. 1. Line 1 surely contrasts Telephus' appearance with his behaviour (Handley 36); several forms of πτωχός or πτωχικός 'beggar(ly)' would fit at the end. [The text probably contains near lineends; Snell is probably right in 3 with 'why *<are you waiting>*' or 'why *<shall I wait>*?' **4.** Handley suggests 'with whom' or 'with him', understanding P's μέτ'ἐστι as showing that μέτ(α) is the Prep. governing a preceding pronoun as in *El.* 574 σοῦ μέθ' 'with you', *IA* 967 ὧν μέτ' 'with whom'. But we may yet have the line-ending μέτεστί μ[οι 'I have a share in', with P's apostrophe marking off the prefix of the compound verb.]

fr. 12. Perhaps close to fr. 6 if a *beggar* is still being discussed (cf. Handley 36). [Text, 6: Rea's supplement would probably give 'if someone *<born>*....']

721. Presumably a warning about Telephus during his exposure or the hostage-taking. **guest-friend**: πρόξενος is normally an official sponsor, here for ordinary ξένος (Ammonius, App.).

700. In *Knights* the Paphlagonian is learning that an oracle has identified the Sausage-seller as his destined conqueror. Here Telephus is probably about to be recognised and feeling that Apollo's advice about his healing has put him at the mercy of the Greeks. Cf. esp. Soph. *OT* 738 and (phrasing) Eur. *Bacc.* 492. **Lycian:** on the possible relevance in the play of the Argive Apollo Lykeios see Introd., p. 24. By Euripides' time Apollo's ancient title Lykeios ('wolf-god'? On origins and cult see Burkert 144–5; M. Jameson, *Archaiognosia* 1 (1980), 213–36; Graf, *Nordion. Kulte* 220–5) was being artificially interpreted amongst other things as 'Lycian'; and Telephus was supposed at least in later legend (Menaechmus *FGH* 131 F 11, Paus. 9.41.1; cf. Robert 1152 n. 1) to have consulted Apollo's oracle at Patara in Lycia (mentioned by e.g. Hdt. 1.182). The many, originally Anatolian, cults of Apollo as healer and prophet (listed by Nilsson, *GGR* I.545–6) included one at Gryneion near the mouth of the Caicus in Tel.'s homeland (cf. Hecataeus *FGH* 1 F 225, Hdt. 1.149, Strabo 13.3.5); one would expect Tel. to have consulted Apollo here originally, though sources do not mention this and its mythical founder was Tel.'s grandson Grynos (Servius on Verg. *Ecl.* 6.72). [Text: Wilamowitz, *Glaube* I.144 n. 2 (cf. *KS* I.288 n. 1) eliminated the second half of the line from *Tel.* on metrical grounds which are insubstantial: see Cropp-Fick 30.]

727. The parody Ar. *Peace* 528 gives no clue about Euripides' context or speaker. The fr. is often attributed to Clytemnestra advising Telephus in the Prologue to use Orestes as a hostage (e.g. Séchan 507, 514, Rau 20); the hatred is then explained by the fact or the anticipation of the sacrifice of Iphigeneia. This is far-fetched, and inconsistent with the vase-painters' depiction of Clytemnestra's role in the hostage-taking (see Introd., p. 22). The sacrifice at Aulis normally *follows* the Telephus episode (Dictys 1.19ff. is an exception). Euripides never elsewhere portrays Clytemnestra as hating her son, even when he gives her reasons for hating Agamemnon from the moment of their marriage (*IA* 1148–56). It is far more likely that the words are spoken by Telephus as he threatens Orestes (so Handley 37, Webster, Jouan 239, Heath 286), probably after becoming unexpectedly hostile to him. **repudiate:** lit. 'I spat away' ('instantaneous' aorist), expressing revulsion or repudiation (e.g. *IA* 509, 874; without object e.g. *Hipp.* 614, *Hec.* 1276); originally a ritual action to avert evil (cf. Gow on Theocr. 6.39).

727a fr. 9. 4–6. Very well (etc.): Rea notes the possibilities of (4) χρησ[τό- or χρήσ[ιμο- 'useful', χρησ[μό- 'oracle', χρὴ σ['is necessary . . .', and (4–6) a speech-opening with questions structured like *Hec.* 313–6; so Handley 37 suggests e.g. 'Very well. Then what is *good* to help you, lamed . . . Were you wounded by . . . ?' The placing before fr. 10 is only a possibility. **5. netted:** this seems to be the meaning of βολαῖος in its only other known occurrence, *TrGF* II adesp. F 391 referring to a netted tunny-fish: see E. Fraenkel, *Glotta* 37 (1959), 285–7. Tel. is compared with a speared fish?

fr. 10. Telephus is clearly one speaker. It seems likely (Strohm, Austin) that **11 Agamemnon** is Voc. case and Agam. the other speaker (though Handley 37 prefers **13 Odysseus** as the Voc.). Agam. will be trying to bully Telephus into agreement, to be followed later by Odysseus using negotiation; cf. Soph. *Aj.* 1226ff. **2–6.** Probably Telephus offers reasons for hesitating to help the Achaeans and Agam. turns from persuasion (2, 4) to threat (6). **5.** Collard suggests '<but I> fear . .'. **6.** <You> will **wander . . . weeping:** 'you'll do *x* weeping' or 'you'll weep if you do *x*' are colloquial forms of threat (e.g. *Hcld.* 270, *And.* 758; Stevens, *CE* 15–16, LSJ κλαίω I.2); either, then, 'you'll suffer for it if you wander (i.e. stray from my plan? persist in your uncertainty?)', or 'you'll wander, regretting it, if (you do not join us?)'. **wander:** perhaps metaphorical 'be in doubt' (LSJ πλανάω I.5), Telephus having pleaded fear and doubt in 5. **7.** Diggle suggests '*<And>*' at the start. **10. no doubt:** ironic, cf. γε ... οὖν in *Med.* 504, ?588; Denniston, *GP* 449. **11–12.** Telephus pleads for consideration, Agam. insists on the importance of the common cause? **17. savage man:** probably Achilles, famously ἄγριος at e.g. Hom. *Il.* 9.629, 24.41. [Text: **9.** Snell's 'But *<your lot is>* to keep silent' is hardly possible; Euripides uses αἶσα rarely and in the strong sense 'god-sent destiny' (*And.* 1203, *Supp.* 625). Rea's ἄλλαις ('other', Dat.) would imply ἃ σι[γ]ᾶι[, '(about) which ... *keep(s) silent*'. Perhaps ἀλλ᾽ ἃ[ρ]α (Collard: Denniston, *GP* 50 lists a few prose examples).]

fr. 25. [Text: **4.** Austin's '*<What do>* you think' is far from certain.]

727b. Nothing in the content or style of this fr. proves its ascription to Euripides or *Tel.* The vocabulary includes five words which would be unique in Euripides, but all are specialised and naturally rare throughout Tragedy (11 κηρυκεῖον Soph. once, adjectively; 13 ἀμνηστεῖν Soph. once (conjectured by Diggle, *IA* 667); 18 ναύαρχος Aesch. twice, Soph. once; 15 πρόσχορδος and 17 παρατάσσομαι Middle, not in Tragedy). Relevance is suggested by the mentions (not all secure) of 'Telephus' (3), sailors and captain(s) (4), a 'counsellor' (6), Greek laws and citizenship (8–10), an affliction (11), the need for a certain man to come (15), escorts and a naval commander (16–18). Roberts–Page argued (and reconstructed) for a context early in a play about Telephus, thinking of Sophocles' *Gathering of the Achaeans* to which F 727c (P. Berl.) was then thought to belong. Webster argued more persuasively (cf. Snell; Koerte, *APF* 14 [1939], 116) for a moment when Telephus' Greek descent is established, his future as guide to the Greek fleet anticipated, and his healing yet to be negotiated with Achilles, i.e. shortly before F 727c. The publication of P. Oxy. in 1957 brought P. Ryl. along with P. Berl. into consideration for Eur. *Tel.* It may yet be from a different play about Telephus. In supplementing and interpreting P. Ryl. the risks of circular argument and building error on error are considerable. A conservative text is printed here (cf. Snell) with a limited commentary mainly on the text; the more speculative supplements of Page, Webster and Mette (see start of App.) are not considered in detail. Besides Roberts, Page and Webster see esp. Handley 21–2, 38 and Jouan 240–1 on the problems of context and ascription, and on the text Snell, Handley 20–1.

　　　Lines 1ff. are the end of a speech giving instructions (by Odysseus the diplomat?); Telephus perhaps responds in 13–15. Then anapaests accompany the transition from talk to action, as often in play-closures and sometimes at other scene-ends (Soph. *Ant.* 929ff., Eur. *Cyc.* 483ff., *Tro.* 782ff.). Thus P. Ryl. could be placed shortly before the Stasimon which ends in F 727c (as Webster suggested), with the anapaests 16ff. delivered by the Chorus or an actor, or split (16–18 Chorus, 19 Odysseus?).

2. Text: *common:* or '*that*', if Snell's reading is right.]

3. Telephus: there seems to be no other plausible supplement, Telephus being either addressed in the Voc. case (Roberts–Page) or subject in the Nom. (Snell). [Text: τὰ πέ[ργαμα (App.) would mean 'Troy' ('to Troy', Roberts-Page) as at Soph. *Phil.*

347, 1334, cf. 353, 611, all with ref. to prophecies about the taking of Troy; cf. LSJ
Πέργαμος, Stesich. fr. 192.3 *PMGF*, Eur. *Tro.* 556, 851.]

4. [Text: Page suggests '<*indicate these things to the*> **sailors and captains**', Webster
'<*indicate the way (to Troy)*> . . .'. But Nom. sing. να[ύτ]ης is possible (App.), or e.g.
καὶ κ[υ]βερνή[της γενοῦ '. . . and become the steersman' (cf. F 727c col. ii.3–4,
9–10).]

5. **at night:** ἐκ νυκτός or -ῶν Xen. *Cyr.* 1.4.2 (cf. Soph. *El.* 780), Hom. *Od.* 12.286, etc.

6. [Text: σὺ] μὲν '<*you*> for your part **go** . . .', Roberts–Page; Snell ἐλθέτω 'let him
go'.]

7. **as the report (*or* talk, *or* saying)** . . . : for meanings of μῦθος see LSJ. 'Talk' or
'report' might fit the deliberation suggested by the previous line.   [Text: ὡς ὁ μῦθος
may be self-contained, 'as the saying/report has it'; comparable expressions occur with
and without 'is' (Collard on *Supp.* 655). Roberts–Page consider ὡς ὁ μῦθός ἐστ(ι) ('as
the/ your report/story goes'); Webster's ὡς ὁ μῦθος ἔστα[ται could mean 'as the
story/report stands (cf. Soph. *El.* 50) but hardly his 'as the decree runs'.]

8–10. **use Greek laws . . . member of the community:** the topic here may be the
acceptance of Telephus by the Greeks as a fellow Greek (so Webster); cf. Introd., p. 24
on the importance of Telephus' being Greek rather than barbarian. ἀστός (10) suggests
'not ξένος', 'not foreign' (cf. *Ion* 290, *Med.* 224, *El.* 795).

11. **herald's:** κηρύκειον is often 'a herald's staff' but also known as an adj. (Soph.
F 784); here taken questionably by Page and Webster as a prohibition on foreigners
leading the Achaeans against Troy.   **afflicts:** lit. 'bites', but with no evident relation to
the 'jaw(s)' of the next line. [Text: the suggestions in App. give '<*does not*> afflict' or
'<*if*> (it?) afflicts'; also possible are οὗ 'where' and several forms of the rel. pron.
more: in degree or amount, not time as Webster's 'harms you no more' supposes.

12. Snell's and Koerte's '. . . jaw <*will no longer*> *afflict you* **from this evening**' may
be on the right lines (for the self-contained first-foot dactyl cf. F 696.10); Collard's
'. . . afflict you *with its* **jaws**' improves this. 'Jaw(s)' would be metaphorical for the
suppuration of Telephus' wound, cf. *Med.* 1201, the princess's flesh torn away 'by the
poison's invisible jaws'.

13–15. Page suggested '<*For*> if **we may settle** <*these things*> **rightly, you should**
<*not*> **be forgetful** <*of what comes next*>', assuming the speech continues. But
(Webster) this might be Telephus responding with a slightly different opening; 14–15
would suit Telephus reminding Odysseus to secure Achilles' help.

15. Perhaps '<*any of these things that is* > **not in harmony**' (Page) or '**anything** <*that
is*> **not in harmony** <*with these things*>' (Snell). πρόσχορδος does not elsewhere
have this metaphorical sense.

16–17. Roberts–Page suggest '<*Come now,*> *with* **these let him appoint escorts** *for the*
foreigner <*to sail along with him*>'.

18. ναύαρχος is normally the commander of a fleet (LSJ); not a suitable word for
Telephus as guide.   [Text: Snell's '<*and*> **what man** . . .' is more likely than
Webster's '<*if*> any man . . .' (enclitic τις bridging the mid-line diaeresis of the
anapaestic dimeter would be unusual).]

19. **after this:** ἐκ τούτων as in *Med.* 1103, *Bacc.* 639.

727c. The few traces of col. 1 indicate a Choral stasimon which continues in col. 2 as the Chorus look forward to Telephus' guiding the fleet; then a scene begins with Achilles arriving from Scyros and met by Odysseus who will negotiate the healing with him. Speaker notations in col. 3 indicate a continued dialogue between them.

1–10. An *envoi* for those setting sail, like *IT* 1123–37, *Hel.* 1451–64; cf. the retrospective *El.* 432–41, and *Pha.* 79–86 (with Comm. below, p. 228, on epic models etc.). Here the Chorus, imagining the fleet under sail, adopt some epic mannerisms: 1 Gen. ζεφύροιο; 2 Τρωιάδας ἀκτάς 'terminal Acc.'; 5 εὐθὺς Ἰλίου (see n. below). *Metre.* Aeolochoriambic, with trochaics in 5 and 8. Pauses in rhythm and sense after 2 and 6.

1. gust: δίνα can denote movements 'to and fro' (Willink on *Or.* 982–4), here probably the rising and falling of the wind.   [Text: P's δεινὰ 'terrible' would agree with a lost preceding noun denoting wind (Wilamowitz), and hardly suits this context (despite Ditifeci 217).]

3–6. Telephus at the stern will instruct the prow-man (with a better view ahead) to pick out a course. Wilamowitz cites an exact description, Plut. *Agis* 1.   **5–6. to observe:** ἰδέσθαι Mid. for 'getting a good look at' (cf. προορώμενοι, Plut. *Agis* 1; Kannicht on *Hel.* 122).   **direct for Troy:** Wilamowitz rightly took εὐθὺς Ἰλίου as an adjectival phrase like *Hipp.* 1197 τὴν εὐθὺς Ἄργους . . . ὁδόν 'the road direct to Argos' (a mild epicism: Barrett).   **6.** [Text: *for* the Atreidae: better than Pearson's '(course) of the Atreidae'.]

8.   Greece not Mysia: cf. F 696.4 n., Introd. p. 24.   **gave:** Greek Pres. tense (F 696.1 n.).

10.   ships: lit. 'oars', part of ship denoting whole (synecdoche); cf. *And.* 855, *IT* 140, *Hel.* 192 etc.; Breitenbach 174.   **guide:** πεμπτήρ uniquely here; cf. LSJ πέμπω III.

11–24. Achilles arrives from Scyros. In the Epic Cycle he had been separated from the Achaean fleet by a storm after the attack on Mysia, and landed at Scyros where he married the king's daughter Deidameia (*Cypria* summary; *Little Iliad* fr. 4; on his connection with Scyros see M. Davies, *The Epic Cycle* [Bristol, 1989], 44–5; Robert 1156–60). He enters brusquely, unannounced as in *IA* 801–18 where he is also unaware of the crisis and impatient of delay. Odysseus seems to be expecting him, and his response is typical of his traditional diplomatic character.

11.   sea-bound land: for Odysseus Ithaca, for Achilles Scyros (see above).

13.   There was no call: χρῆν Imperf. of present situation; cf. *Cresph.* F 449.3 n.   **to be cooling your heels:** lit. 'for your foot to lie quiet'; 'a quiet foot' denotes idleness *Med.* 217, *Bacc.* 647, quiet progress in the suspect verse *Or.* 136.

16.   And yet . . . not . . . : for οὐ μὴν . . . γε cf. e.g. *Hipp.* 885, 914; Denniston, *GP* 335.   **of rowers:** κωπήρης is lit. 'oar-equipped', whether of rowers (here, *Tro.* 160) or ships (Eur. *Hel.* 1381, Aesch. *Pers.* 416).

17.   nor, in fact: οὔτε following οὐ . . . adds an afterthought (Denniston, *GP* 420); οὖν added to οὔτε stresses this addition (Denniston 509–10.).

18.   one should hasten (etc.): Pearson compares Soph. *Phil.* 637 καίριος σπουδή ('good speed in good season', Jebb), Eur. *Hel.* 718 'hastening as he did he gained nothing'; cf. also *Mel.* F 501.

19.   sluggish: νωχελής is Ionic, used by Euripides of Orestes' fevered limbs (*Or.* 800), its abstract in Hom. *Il.* 19.411, Achilles' horse addressing him; etymology uncertain, νω- probably containing a negative prefix (cf. νωθής of similar meaning).

21. [Text: **is . . . finished:** P. Oxy.'s verb is exactly right (e.g. *Pho.* 1703, *Ion* 1569; LSJ περαίνω I.1). P. Berl.'s 'makes progress' is not attested in this metaphorical sense before the 4ᵗʰ C.]

22–4. Achilles' words recall his and Diomedes' criticisms of Agamemnon's hesitancy in the *Iliad* (1.225–8, 9.38–49), and Achilles' desire that he and Patroclus alone might take Troy (16.97–100). For Agamemnon's hesitancy and differences with Menelaus in this play cf. F 722, 723.

24. The line as restored by Page (confirmed in part by P. Oxy.) is almost identical with *IA* 818 where Achilles cites the impatient Myrmidons (Diggle in his new Oxford Text doubts that Euripides composed that speech). Aeschin. 3.72 quotes Demosthenes as paraphrasing it in a debate on the Macedonian threat.

719. Probably Achilles speaks (Welcker), but possibly Menelaus earlier (Wecklein). Greeks naturally superior to servile Asiatics, *And.* 665–6 (see Stevens there), *IA* 1400, *Med.* 536–8, *Hel.* 273–6 (Egyptians), Aristot. *Pol.* 1252b9. Cf. Introd. p. 24 on Greek *vs.* barbarian in this play.

716. Plausibly assigned to Telephus pleading with Achilles. **4. makes . . . brings:** Greek Aorists. συστέλλω (LSJ I.3) as *HF* 1417, *Tro.* 108, *Androm.* F 150(?).

718. Perhaps Telephus or (more likely) Odysseus is persuading Achilles (and his celebrated **temper**), but Webster places the fr. in the Atreids' quarrel. **It is time:** ὥρα (ἐστί) as *Hcld.* 288, *Pho.* 1584, etc.; LSJ (C) B.I.3. **let your mind rule:** lit. 'have a mind stronger than . . .' cf. *Med.* 1079 ('temper stronger than my planning'), Theognis 631 'mind stronger than temper', Pind. *Pyth.* 5.107 'mind stronger than injustice', Callim. fr. 384.56 'mind stronger than good fortune'.

724. Usually ascribed to Odysseus (but by some to a Messenger reporting Telephus' healing: Introd., p. 21). Carefully balanced wording, with hyperbaton in πριστοῖσι . . . ῥινήμασι, **filings shaved**, stresses the information. **soothed**, or 'charmed', suggests a magical quality in the cure (θέλγειν usually describes magical incantations, sleep or love). Achilles' bronze-tipped ash spear was given to his father by Cheiron (Hom. *Il.* 16.143 = 19.390). Its rust is Telephus' cure in Apollod. *Epit.* 3.20 and was so depicted in a famous painting of Parrhasios (late 5ᵗʰ C.) according to Plin. *NH* 25.42, 34.152, cf. 35.71; this may have reflected Euripides' play, and may be recalled in an Etruscan mirror-decoration (see e.g. Roscher V.307, Bauchhenss-Thüriedl 33–4). Ditifeci 219 however suggests that rust was the cure in the *Cypria* while metal-filings and Achilles' ignorance of medicine (Hyginus) were dramatic innovations of Euripides. The real medical use of bronze-filings is mentioned by Hippocr. *Gynaec.* 1.78 (ῥινήματα), iron-rust and iron-scale by Plin. *NH* 34.152–4. Frazer on Apollod. *Epit.* 3.20 lists folk-beliefs about cures by the weapon that wounded, hair of the dog that bit, etc. Still, the divine instrumentality of the spear seems to have been its important feature in our play.

727a fr. 13. *Paragraphi* and phrasing suggest stichomythia, Telephus expressing obligation (3, 5) and preparing to depart (7), Achilles instructing (6, 8). Cf. Handley 39. [Text: **3. ονη** .[: probably from verb ὀνίνημι or noun ὄνησις 'benefit'. **7. go:** πορεύο[μαι (metrically awkward), πορευό[μεσθα 'I/we am going', or πορεύο[υ 'go!']

701. A common thought, e.g. Hes. *WD* 306–313, *Hel.* 756, *Erec.* F 364, *Arch.* F 233, F 236–40; cf. Denniston on *El.* 80–1, Collard on *Supp.* 323b. F 701 and 702 might be (e.g.) Clytemnestra exhorting Telephus, or Menelaus exhorting Agamemnon.

702. Another commonplace: see e.g. Bond on *HF* 1228.   [Text: the adjustments eliminate the Ionic form τρηχὺ and give iambic rhythm.]

704. Olympiodorus (App.) indicates that 'call him a Mysian if you like' was proverbial for 'call him what you will', and that 'Mysian Telephus' was said by someone asking about Telephus; perhaps, then, Odysseus exposing Telephus' identity (e.g. Handley, Rau, Webster), or Telephus referring to himself when in disguise (Séchan, Jouan, Heath).   [Text: there are no real grounds for including all of Ar. *Ach.* 430 in the fr. Attempts to extend it with elements of Olympiod.'s obscure explanation (e.g. Nauck) were dismissed by Wilamowitz, *KS* I.288 n. 1.]

714. Possibly Telephus in the Prologue speech (e.g. Jouan, Heath) or to Clytemnestra (Handley, Webster). Health without wealth better than wealth without health: [Pl.] *Eryxias* 393b6ff.; similarly good fortune *vs.* wealth, Hdt. 1.32.5–6. Health the supreme good, e.g. Simonides *PMG* 604, Ariphron *PMG* 813, Anon. *PMG* 890. **2. daily:** καθ' ἡμέραν of essential livelihood, e.g. *El.* 235, *Bell.* F 286.9, Soph. *OC* 1364, Thuc. 1.2, and in expressions of limited needs *Hec.* 317–8 (very similar phrasing to our line 2), *Alc.* 788–9; cf. *Pho.* 401.   [Text: **1.** νόσον 'sickness' barely makes sense as a second object of 'avails'; deletion is preferable to a weak emendation anticipating the point of the next two lines ('when I am sick', Fabricius); or a word like πολύς or μέγας ('<great> wealth') might have been displaced. **2–3.** Stob. 4.33.11 gives good sense with the minor adjustment of σμικρὰν which has led to confusion in the other sources (Sext. 'Might I consent to live with a small and daily livelihood than . . .'; Stob. 4.31. 64 'Might I consent to inhabit with a small and daily nourishment rather than . . .')]

717. A hostile comment concerning Telephus, for which several contexts are obviously possible.   **stubborn** (τάλας): see *Cresph.* F 448a.85 n.   [Text: unmetrical σὺ . . . μέλλεις 'are you going to . . .' is an easy corruption of σοι . . . μέλει 'is it of interest to you to . . .']

720. A ref to Telephus or Paris or Helen.   [Text: the similar Ennius *Tel.* fr. 146 is a curse, but speculative conjectures such as Dobree's Epic/Ionic Plur. ὀλοίατ(ο), which Nauck printed, are not needed.]

725. The sources explain this as 'leaning (corn), in which one can lie in ambush' (*Etym. Gen.*), or 'corn leaning because of its ripeness' (Hesych.), or 'deep, or leaning because of rain' (Phot.). λοχαῖος in *Alc.* 846 probably describes a place 'of ambush' (cf. λόχος 'ambush'; verb λοχάω). We may infer mention in *Tel.* of a field of ripe corn enabling an ambush, perhaps in connection with the battle in which Telephus was wounded.

726. a wine-cooler: a word not found elsewhere before Pl. *Symp.* 213e2, where a Schol. records its use in *Tel.* A context can hardly be guessed: perhaps in simile or metaphor.

CRETANS

Texts, testimonia. P. Berlin 13217; P. Oxy. 2461; *TrGF* F 471a, 472, 472a–g, and (?)988; Page, *GLP* 70–7; R. Cantarella, *I Cretesi* (Milan, 1964); Austin, *NFE* frs. 78–82; Mette Nos. 633–641A.

Myth. Hes. fr. 145; Bacchyl. *Dithyr.* 26; Eur. *Hipp.* 337–8 and Schol. on 887; Ovid, *Ars Am.* 1.289–326; Diod. Sic. 4.77; Hygin. *Fab.* 40; Apollod. 3.1.3–4, 3.15.8; Plut. *Thes.* 16; Zenobius 4.92. *The myth in Euripides' play:* Ar. *Frogs* 849–50, 1356, 1359 and Schol.; Plut. *Thes.* 15.2; Libanius, *Or.* 44.73, *Decl.* 1.177; John Malalas, *Chronogr.* p. 31.6–8, 85.22–86.11 Dindorf (see *TrGF* test. iib) and (?) p. 359.15–18 (= *TrGF* F *471a). *Pasiphae: RE* XVIII.4 (1949), 2069–82; F. Frontisi-Ducroux, *Dédale* (Paris, 1975), 137–140; Gantz 260–1. *Daedalus and Icarus:* Roscher I.934–7; Preller–Robert II.1.364–9; G. Becatti, *MDAI*(R) 60/61 (1953/4), 22–36; Frontisi-Ducroux (above), 151–90; *LIMC* III, 'Daidalos'; Gantz 273–5.

Illustrations. Webster, *Euripides* (1967) 299. *Pasiphae and Daedalus:* K. Schefold, *Die Wände Pompejis* (Berlin, 1957), Index; Cantarella (above), 37–42 and Pls. i–ix. *Daedalus and Icarus:* Schefold and Jung, *Urkönige* 56–62, Pl. 52–9 and (best bibl.) Notes 124–46; M. Kokolakis, *Actes 12. Congr. Int. d'Arch. 1983* II (1988), 115–20; *LIMC* (above).

Main discussions. Wilamowitz, *BKT* V.2, 76–9; A. Kappelmacher in *Wiener Eranos* (Graz, 1909), 26–37 (older bibl.); M. Croiset, *REG* 28 (1915), 217–33; Schmid 410–2; Pohlenz I.249–51, II.102; A. Rivier, *Etudes de littérature grecque,* ed. F. Lasserre, J. Sulliger (Genève, 1975), 43–60 (= *Mélanges A. Bonnard* [Neuchâtel, 1958], 51–74); Cantarella (above) and reviews by D. W. Lucas, *Gnomon* 37 (1965), 454–7 and C. Corbato, *RFIC* 93 (1965), 193–9; Webster, *Euripides* (1967), 87–92; K. J. Reckford, *TAPA* 104 (1974), 307–28; C. Dolfi, *Prometheus* 10 (1984), 121–38 esp. on frs. 472 N, 81 and 82 A (F 472, 472b–c and 472e below).

The play is a shadow, mysterious and frustrating.

    The fragments are very few, and remarkable in two ways. First, despite their fewness, they include two quite extensive primary texts written in the 2nd Century A.D. Second, the play has left no mark whatever on the gnomological tradition from which so many Tragic book fragments come. In this respect *Cret.* is unique among Euripides' tragedies, for such lack of representation is character-istic of satyric drama. The lack must be simple accident, for the plot is not less likely to have generated sententious words than other plays about immoral women like *Cret.W.* and *Hipp.*, for example (indeed, *Cret.* F 472e.10, 27–8 and 40–1 are very probable targets for any anthologist). It is however possible that the union of Pasiphae and the bull was found too offensive for ordinary educ-

ational reading. The paucity of secondary evidence for the content and character of
the play is also striking; and there is no fragment as yet of a hypothesis.

The premiss of the mythical plot is contained within F 472e.23–6: in order
to secure his rule over Crete Minos prayed to Poseidon for a confirmatory
portent, a bull, one of the god's frequent manifestations; he vowed to sacrifice it
to the god in return. When the animal appeared, however, Minos kept it for his
own herd and sacrificed another in its place; to punish him Poseidon visited his
wife Pasiphae with a sexual infatuation for the god's bull. The rest of the myth
is given in part by Apollod. 3.1.3–4: the supreme carpenter-builder Daedalus
helped Pasiphae achieve her passion by making an artificial cow inside which
she concealed herself and received the bull (cf. Bacchyl. *Dithyr.* 26). She later
gave birth to the Minotaur, half man, half bull (F 472b.29, cf. Hes. fr. 145),
which Minos upon oracular guidance shut in a labyrinth built by Daedalus. This
story is told more succinctly but also continued by Hygin. *Fab.* 40 (cf. Schol.
on Eur. *Hipp.* 887): Minos discovered Daedalus's help to Pasiphae and put him
in chains. Pasiphae freed him and he then made wings for himself and his son
Icarus with which to escape; but the boy flew too near the sun, his wings
disintegrated in its heat and he fell to his death in the sea. Daedalus continued his
flight to reach King Cocalus in Sicily (cf. Zenob. 4.92; Diod. 4.77.7–9).

Until the 20th C. only two fragments were certainly known. The first,
F 472f, is a brief lyric greeting to the Chorus of Cretan priests of Zeus; it is
made by Minos, probably, who is on stage when the Chorus enter and recite the
second fragment, F 472, the beginning of their Parodos, which is addressed to
him (but F 472f is put late in the play by Kannicht: see Comm.). It had already
been presumed from several sources that the play dealt with Pasiphae's union
(from e.g. Timachidas in Schol. Ar. *Frogs* 850; Plut. *Thes.* 15); then in 1907
the Berlin Parchment yielded an excerpt from a scene where Pasiphae defends
herself cleverly but uselessly against Minos's retribution: his imprisonment of
her, and her intended death like that of e.g. Sophocles' *Antigone*, are Euripides'
innovation in the myth; this is F 472e. In 1962 came the Oxyrhynchus Papyrus
(F 472b–c) to fill out the action between F 472 and F 472e. One fragment gives
the end of a lyric passage, probably choral, invoking the gods to avert disaster,
another offers scraps of a stichomythic interrogation about the Minotaur, a third
has the start of a following episode; the stichomythia includes the line fr. 997 N
(= F 472b.29) and makes likely the location earlier in the play also of F 472a
(= fr. 996 N), a one-line description of the Minotaur.

These fragments have been readily located within the outline of a plot. After
a divine Prologue speech, probably from Aphrodite as the agent of Pasiphae's
passion (Webster 87, cf. Comm. on F 472b–c.49), Minos's anxiety at news of a
portentous birth makes him summon the Chorus of priests to advise him; the
heart of the action is his progressive discovery of Pasiphae's behaviour and of

the Minotaur, and his punishment of her; the ending is perhaps a messenger's report of Pasiphae's miraculous release by a god (Schmid 412), who then comes to explain: Poseidon or Athena are usually suggested. For a complete action this appears rather thin, however, unless Euripides allowed Pasiphae to review her conduct and her plans to escape detection (with her Nurse? — that would predate and preempt Phaedra in *Hipp.*: see below). It is therefore attractive to extend the plot to the escape of Daedalus and Icarus, in accordance with the statement by Schol. on Ar. *Frogs* 849 (= *TrGF* F 472g) that Icarus had a 'rather bold role' and a monody in *Cret.* (see below and Comm. on F 472f). This will make Hyginus' narrative almost coextensive with the play, giving room for Minos's arrest and imprisonment of Daedalus and Icarus and then their escape (even if it will be unclear how Pasiphae herself escaped and helped to free them; perhaps both escapes were reported by a messenger). Icarus would have sung 'boldly' before flying and his fall have been reported (or forecast?) by the god: so approximately Webster 87ff. The action too would be as full of incident as in *Sthen.*, for example (see pp. 79–80), another play about a woman's sinful love but without the full analysis of its nature which distinguishes the later *Hipp.*

Accordingly F 988 has been brought into the play as a one-line accusation of Daedalus by Minos that he made things outside his usual work of carpentry. That would be a reference to the artificial cow; while Pasiphae alludes to it at F 472e.17–18, there is nevertheless no other mention of Daedalus or Icarus in the surviving fragments. (F 988 is not included by Kannicht.)

In the text of Ar. *Frogs* 849 Aeschylus accuses Euripides of 'collecting Cretan monodies and bringing unholy marriages into his art'. This has been taken by some to indicate not only that *Cret.* contained the monody of Icarus mentioned by the Schol. but that this early song was distinctive enough to typify and to lend lasting notoriety to Euripides' monodic style; others have seen in 'unholy marriages' an allusion to Pasiphae's union with the bull (cf. her own ironic reference to it as a marriage at F 472e.16–20). The second claim may be true, although it is better related to Cretan Aerope's improper union with a serv-ant in *Cret.W.* mentioned by the Schol. (*TrGF Cret.W.* test. iiib, F 460), to Pasiphae's daughter Phaedra (*Hipp.* 337–8) in her love for her stepson, or even to the sibling incest of Canace in *Aeolus* (P.Oxy. 2457.18ff. = *TrGF Aeolus* test. ii). The first claim is judiciously handled by Dover (Comm. on *Frogs* 849): 'The association between Crete and dancing (Pind. fr. 107b, Soph. *Aj.* 699), in combination with Euripides' fondness for monodies and his use of Cretan myths, is quite enough to account for 'Cretan monodies'; cf. also Wilamowitz 78 n. 2.

Other ascriptions. Sometimes canvassed for *Cret.* are: 912 N (No. 636f M; F 10 Cant), a prayer to Zeus to accept an unburnt offering of fruit and grain; comparable with F 472, the Chorus's description of their ritual abstinences, and attrib. by Valckenaer;

1004 N (No. 636A /1404 M; F 11 Cant), a supposed reference by Euripides to 'blood flowing in all living animals'; similarly comparable with F 472 and attributed by Wilamowitz 77 n. 1, *KS* I.191;   *TrGF* II adesp. 34 (No. 634f M; T 4 Cant), an unconfidently restored trimeter describing a labyrinth;   *TrGF* II adesp. 60 (*Sthen.* No. 880c M; *Cret.* F inc 7 Cant), a fear that 'someone may fall into the sea', referred by Schol. Ar. *Peace* 141b to the flight of Icarus or of Stheneboea: cf. *Sthen.*, Introd. p. 81.   F 943, 1009, 1023 (with 225 = *TrGF Antiope* F 182a) and Soph. F 14, all attributed by Hartung, are universally rejected.

Illustrations. The myth was very popular with dramatists (see below), so that it is more than usually risky to appeal in reconstructing Euripides' play to works of art for the most part later, some much later, in date; Webster 87ff. made the most use, but Trendall–Webster has no entry for *Cret.* For example, two or three vase paintings from S. Italy (415–320 B.C.: Webster 299) show either Daedalus affixing wings to Icarus or Daedalus supplicating Minos (along with Pasiphae, e.g. Cantarella Pl. I, Schefold–Jung Pl. 54: note the almost certain discrepancy from Euripides). Hellenistic urns and Pompeian frescos have a range of scenes, including the making of the artificial cow; this is depicted too on a Roman sarcophagus now in the Louvre (all in Webster 299, cf. Cantarella Pl. II, Schefold–Jung Pls. 53, 59, 52). This bizarre story belonged as much to literature, both poetry and prose, as to the stage; both inspired artists, for whom the subject became a commonplace. Supplication of Minos and the off-stage affixing of wings might have occurred in a tragedy, but not the making of the cow; we simply do not know whether they appeared in Euripides' play.

Themes and characters. Euripides' tragedies about 'bad and unhappy' women (Webster, *Euripides* [1967], 240, cf. e.g. 31, 86) often portray improper sexual attractions or unions. The resulting babies lead to threats to the mothers, e.g. Auge after her rape (F 271b) or Canace in *Aeolus* who concealed her incestuous child (*TrGF Aeolus* test. ii) as Pasiphae concealed the Minotaur, or to both mother and child, e.g. in *Mel.S.* (see p. 240), again after an attempt at concealment. In that play Melanippe defends her exposure of her babies from fear of her father; F 485 is compared with our F 472e by e.g. Schmid 412, Webster 148, Vysoky. The interrogation of Pasiphae's Nurse by Minos (F 472b) may have a counterpart in the later *Alope*, where Alope gave her Nurse her rape-child to expose (so Webster 94 — but interrogation of servants is not rare in Euripides, e.g. *Phaethon* 317ff.).

Pasiphae however is distinctive amid these repeatedly used plots. First, her illicit passion is for an animal (and the resulting baby monstrous). Second, this same abnormality, and Pasiphae's ascription of it to divine cause (F 472e.9), make it unlikely that Euripides afforded her any long analysis of her human weakness comparable with Phaedra's in *Hipp.* A problem in understanding the portrayal of her passion was set out by Pohlenz I. 250 and discussed most helpfully by Rivier: her defence that, because a god maddened her, her sin was therefore not voluntary (F 472e.10, cf. 20–6), continues with an immediate appeal afterwards (11–20) to purely human — and contemporarily fashionable — argument from probability; moreover, the involuntariness of wrongdoing was equally a frequent defence in the lawcourts of Euripides' Athens (Rivier 57–9, 60; cf. Dolfi 129–33). Did Euripides use the myth for its literal meaning, that Pasiphae is an innocent sufferer helpless against external and divine cause (Rivier 59), or to provide mere background for the misery of her passion (Croiset 225–6) and an exciting action of discovery, punishment and escape? Or did he expose the myth to criticism as an account of human suffering under heaven, wanting rather to examine the irrationality and autonomy of Pasiphae's passion (Pohlenz)? Rivier rightly warned (60) that these questions are prompted largely because Pasiphae's one long speech in F 472e affords us our only hold upon the play's nature, and that our answers will be precarious as long as we know nothing further about the extent of her role or the whole play's direction and tone. Reckford's conclusion (322) in a comparison of Phaedra and Pasiphae, that Pasiphae is 'morally inferior' and in part responsible for her sin, shows the danger of building a wider interpretation upon that one speech. There is in any case the considerable possibility that the speech is deliberately self-contained, a typical Euripidean exercise in rhetorical exploitation of the dramatic circumstance.

Against the idea that the play may be critical of myth and divine explanation stands the apparent significance, even in our few fragments, of the Chorus of priests, whose sanctity is stressed in the long fragment of their Parodos (472); who pray for divine aid (F 472b.1–8); who emphasize divine causation to Minos after Pasiphae pleads it in defence (F 472e.42) — and who give the play its name (cf. Page, *GLP*, p. 73). Although Minos calls the priests to his aid (F 472f), he could not have been portrayed as himself an initiate and pure[1] — not because he had sacrificed an animal in the past (so e.g. Croiset 232–3, against Wilamowitz 78 who thought of the play as Euripides' attack on ascetic mysticism), but because he had broken his vow to Poseidon (F 472e.23–6). Moreover, F 472e shows us a Minos who is angry, quick and hard (1, 43–52), and Pasiphae accuses him of bloodthirstiness (36–9: see below under 'Other Dramatisations', and Comm.). In her recriminatory spirit there she again resembles Phaedra in *Hipp.* (cf. 728–31, 1310–2), just as the instantly repressive Minos resembles Theseus (*Hipp.* 882–90, 893–8).

---

[1] It is not certainly relevant to *Cret.* that Ephorus 70 F 143 *FGH* relates how Minos (a son of Zeus) would go every nine years to Zeus's cave on Mt. Ida and return (Moses-like) with instructions from the god.

In sum: our lack of information leaves us frustrated about both the compass and the general character of the play.

Staging. The fragments suggest no unusual effects. The baby Minotaur would not have been shown in a tragedy. If Icarus had a monody before his flight, it is possible that he was lifted from sight on the machine; that, and perhaps the mere fact that he was a boy or boasted he would fly very high, could have caused the description of his role as 'rather bold' by the Schol. on Ar. *Frogs* 849.

Date. Two metrical features suggest an early date. An anapaestic start to the Choral Parodos (F 472) is found only in the earliest plays, near *Alc.* of 438 (Rivier 44). The complete absence of resolution in the fifty or so dialogue trimeters which survive, the majority in F 472e, is consistent with the rhythmic strictness found in complete plays down to *Hipp.* of 428 (Webster 4 and Cropp–Fick 70, 82, who place *Cret.* anywhere between 455 and 428). A date earlier than either Hippolytus play is suggested by the possible back-reference to Pasiphae in *Cret.* at *Hipp.* 337–8 (Webster 86). It is tempting to follow Pohlenz I. 250 and put *Cret.* near *Cret.W.* of 438, for in that play Aerope like Pasiphae has sinned before the action starts and is similarly detected and condemned; Aerope is finally saved by human compassion (Schol. on Soph. *Aj.* 1297 = *TrGF Cressae* test. iiia), as Pasiphae perhaps was by divine (above).

ΚΡΗΤΕΣ

*471a　　　See App. on F 472.3 below.

472f (471 N) ΜΙΝΩΣ ὦ Κρῆτες, Ἴδας τέκνα . . .

472　　　　ΧΟΡΟΣ Φοινικογενοῦς τέκνον Εὐρώπης
　　　　　　　　καὶ τοῦ μεγάλου Ζηνός, ἀνάσσων
　　　　　　　　Κρήτης ἑκατομπτολιέθρου·
　　　　　　　　ἥκω ζαθέους ναοὺς προλιπών,
　　　　　　　　οὓς αὐθιγενὴς στεγανοὺς παρέχει　　　　5
　　　　　　　　τμηθεῖσα δοκοὺς Χαλύβωι πελέκει
　　　　　　　　καὶ ταυροδέτωι κόλληι κραθεῖσ'
　　　　　　　　ἀτρεκεῖς ἁρμοὺς κυπάρισσος.
　　　　　　　　ἁγνὸν δὲ βίον τείνομεν ἐξ οὗ
　　　　　　　　Διὸς Ἰδαίου μύστης γενόμην　　　　　　10

472f (471 N, F 5.2 Cant, 78 A, 640a M) Ar. *Frogs* 1356, attrib. by Schol. to Eur. *Cret.* ἀλλ' ὦ Ar. ἀλλ' del. Austin Ἴδης Nauck　　　**472** (F 3 Cant, 79 A, 635 M) Porphyry, *On Abstinence* 4.19: '. . . Eur.) says that Zeus's prophets in Crete were abstinent . . . Those in the Chorus address Minos (F 472)'; cf. Jerome, *Against Jovinian* 14: 'Eur. records that in Crete the prophets of Zeus abstained not only from meat but also from cooked food' (see 19–20).　　　**3** may be paraphrased by

Other dramatisations. The myths of Minos were favourites with the tragedians. Aeschylus's *Cretan Women*, Sophocles' *Manteis* (*'Seers'*) and Euripides' *Polyidus* may all have dealt with the recovery after oracular guidance of the missing Glaucus, son of Minos and Pasiphae. Sophocles' *Camici* (inhabitants of a town in Sicily where Minos pursued the escaped Daedalus) was parodied in Aristophanes' *Cocalus*; Sophocles wrote also a *Daedalus* and *Minos* of unknown content. All these plays, as well as Pasiphae's accusation of Minos as bloodthirsty in our F 472e.36–9, may lie behind ancient comment that the tragedians often portrayed Minos as harsh or tyrannical (Strabo 10.4.8 speaks of 'the old writers', after quotation of Ephorus *FGH* 70 F 143, cf. [Plato], *Minos* 318d; both = *TrGF Cret.* test. iv). Comedy also liked the myth. Alcaeus wrote a *Pasiphae* about 400 B.C. Aristophanes about the same time wrote a *Daedalus* (as did three later poets); in his play the carpenter makes Zeus an artificial swan in which to seduce Leda (see *PCG* III.2, p. 116). The Pasiphae episode, and the potentially farcical Minotaur, were evidently a constant source of fun. Roman adaptations are known, e.g. Accius's *Minos* (or *Minotaur*). For the rich medieval and subsequent treatment of the myth in art see *OGCMA* II.666–9 (Minos and Minotaur), 842–4 (Pasiphae).

CRETANS

*471a   *See App. on F 472.3 below.*

472f **(471 N)**

    (Minos) Cretans, children of Ida . . . !

    Minos greets the Chorus at their entry (F 472).

472   *Beginning of the Chorus's Parodos:*

    Chorus. Child of Europa born to Phoenix and of great Zeus, lord over Crete of the hundred cities! To come here I have left the most holy temple, its roof furnished by cypress grown on the very site[5] and cut with Chalybean axe into beams and brought together with bonding ox-glue into exact joints. Pure is the life I have maintained since I became an initiate of Idaean Zeus[10]

John Malalas, *Chronogr.* p. 359.17 Dindorf (= F *471a: see Comm.) 4–8 ἥκω...ἁρμούς cited by Erotian, *Hippocr. Gloss.*, ἀτρεκέως (p. 11.16–22 Nachmanson), attrib. Eur. *Cret.* 12–15 = P. Oxy. 2461 fr. 4 12 Hesychius Ω 218 (IV.324–9 Schmidt) has ὠμοφάγους δαίτας, unattrib. 1 Φο. παῖ τῆς Τυρίας τεκ. Εὐρ. Porph. παῖ τῆς Τυρ. del. Bothe τεκ. Εὐρ. del. Merkelbach, *RhM* 97 (1954), 373–5 5–6 δοκοὺς Erot. δορὸς Porph. word-order von Arnim, Austin τμηθεῖσα δ. στ. παρ. Porph., Erot. Χαλ. πελ. τμη. δοκ. Wilamowitz 7 κόλληι κραθεῖσ' Hermann κολληθεὶς Erot. κρηθεῖσ' Porph. κόλληι ⟨ζευχ⟩θεῖσ' Wilamowitz κόλληι ⟨πηχ⟩θεῖσ' Austin 8 κυπάρισσος Bentley –ου Porph.

60 EURIPIDES

καὶ νυκτιπόλου Ζαγρέως βούτης
τὰς ὠμοφάγους δαῖτας τελέσας,
μητρί τ' ὀρείαι δᾶιδας ἀνασχὼν
μετὰ Κουρήτων
βάκχος ἐκλήθην ὁσιωθείς.   15
πάλλευκα δ' ἔχων εἵματα φεύγω
γένεσίν τε βροτῶν καὶ νεκροθήκας
οὐ χριμπτόμενος,
τήν τ' ἐμψύχων
βρῶσιν ἐδεστῶν πεφύλαγμαι.   20

472a   σύμμεικτον εἶδος κἀποφώλιον βρέφος

472b–c P. Oxy. 2461

fr. 2 col. i   *ends of eight lyric lines, metre uncertain*

1]εσις ὅτ' ἐπιπνεῖ   5]. α μέλπων   1–8
2]ος Λυκίας ἄπο   6]. ψ. ασε μέγαν
3 Λα]τώιε παῖ   7]φοις
4]λ[.]ν ὦναξ   8 εὐ]πάτειρα

at least twenty-six lines missing

fr. 2 col. ii   *beginnings of seven lines (metre unclear) with no indi-*   9–17
cation of speaker, then two lines each preserving only
a marginal note of the speaker, 16 Χο, 17 Μι

fr. 1   *words from near the centres of eleven dialogue trimeters*   18–28
including 25 θ]εοῖσι προσβ[ολ]ὴν[*then:*

(Τροφός) ταύ]ρου μέμεικται καὶ βροτοῖυ διπλῆι φύσει.
(Μίνως) ἥκ]ουσα καὶ πρίν· πῶς δ' ο[30

11 βούτης Wilamowitz (–ας Diels) βροντὰς Porph.   12 τὰς Bergk τάς τ' Porph. [P.Oxy.]
δαῖτας Hartung δαίτας Porph., Hesych. [P.Oxy.]   13 ὁριοδᾶδας Porph., corr. Scaliger   14
μετὰ Wilamowitz καὶ P.Oxy., Porph. καὶ Κουρήτων ⟨ἐνόπλοισι χοροῖς⟩ (e.g.) M. L. West,
The Orphic Poems (Oxford, 1983), 153 n. 141   17–18 cola divided by Diggle   17 ⟨ψυχῆς τε
λύσιν⟩ after βροτῶν (e.g.) Wilamowitz (1907) 77 n.1, but lacuna doubted, *Glaube* II.183 n. 2
νεκροθήκας Wecklein –ης Porph. –αις Wilamowitz   18 ⟨τοῖσιν μυσαροῖς⟩ οὐ χρ. (e.g.)
Diggle   19 τ' del. Wilamowitz   **472a** (996 N, F inc 6 Cant, 80 A, 637b M) Plut. *Thes.* 15.2,
attrib. Eur., immediately before citation (unattrib.) of F 997 N = 472b.29; Plut. *Mor.* 520c, unattrib.
(996, 997 assigned to *Cret.* by G. Koerte in *Aufsätze…E. Curtius* [Berlin, 1884], 205)   κἀποφύλ-
ιον Housman, *Classical Papers* 1255   βρέφος Plut. *Thes.* τέρας Plut. *Mor.* (altered for context)

and a herdsman of nocturnal Zagreus, after performing feasts of raw
flesh; and holding aloft torches to the mountain mother among the
Curetes I was named a celebrant after consecration.[15] In clothing all
of white I shun both the birth of mortals and the laying-places of
the dead, which I do not approach; and I have guarded myself
against the eating of living food.[20]

472a   . . . an infant of mixed form, without purpose . . .

An early description of the Minotaur; speaker unidentifiable.

472b–c P. Oxy. *fragments from Minos's anxious inquiry into the
                Minotaur's origin:*

fr. 2 col. i 1 . . . when *?retribution* blasts 5 . . . singing
         2 . . . from Lycia   6 *(nothing*
         3 . . . son of Leto   7   *intelligible)*
         4 . . . , lord!   8 . . . daughter of a great father

Lyric appeal (?Chorus) to Apollo to avert disaster.

at least twenty-six lines missing

fr. 2 col. ii *fragmentary lines, the last two with a marginal note*   9–17
           of the speaker: 16 *Cho(rus)*   17 *Mi(nos)*

fr. 1   *fragmentary trimeters including:*   18–28
        25 *(? with the gods)* onslaught

(Nurse) Two natures are mingled in it, bull and man.
(Minos) I have heard that before, in fact; but how . . . ?   30

472b–c (F 2 Cant, 81 A, 637o M) P. Oxy. 2461 (2nd C. A.D.) ed. Turner (1962), partly re-ed.
H. Lloyd-Jones, *Gnomon* 35 (1963), 447–9. Turner stated that the fibre-structure would 'permit but
not require' the placing of the end of fr. 2 col. ii to provide the beginnings of the first lines in fr. 1;
this placing is approved by Lloyd-Jones and Austin. Identified for *Cretans* by H. J. Mette, *Hermes*
91 (1961), 256: fr. 4 = F 472.12–15 (see there and on 29 below). Fr. 5 (= F 472d K, 2f Cant, — A,
No. 639 M) is exiguous. 1 νέμ]εσις Cantarella 2 ἄπο Parsons 3 Lloyd-Jones 6 ? με
τὰν Austin 29, 31 etc. (Τρ)οφός, 30, 32 etc. (Μί)νως Cantarella (Τρ), (Χο)ρός D.L. Page,
PCPhS 13 (1967), 33 (Μι), (Χο) Lloyd-Jones, Austin 29 = F 997 N (Plut. *Thes.* 15.2, attrib.
Eur.), cf. on F 472a μεμῖχθαι Plut. (altered for context) 30 Webster

(Τρ.) στέ]ρνοις ἔφεδρον κρᾶτα τ[αύρειον φέρει.

(Μι.) τετρ]ασκελὴς γὰρ ἢ δίβαμ[ος ἔρχεται;

(Τρ.) δίπ]ους [μ]ελαίνηι δασκ[

(Μι.) ἦ κ]αί τι πρὸς τοῖσδ᾽ ἄλλο[

(Τρ.) μύ]ωπος οἴστρου κέρκον[35

(Μι.) ten letters]υ γῆρυν[

(Τρ.) eleven letters]φορβάδος[

(Μι.) μ]αστ[ὸς] δὲ μ[η]τρὸς ἢ βοὸς σ[

(Τρ.) τρ]έφ[ου]σιν οἱ τεκόντες ου [

scraps of four more (stichomythic?) trimeters including   40–43

40 δωμάτων   41 τοῖς τεκο[ῦσι

fr. 3 = F 472c *traces of three lines ending a lyric passage (metre*   44–45

unclear), the last line beginning ἀπείρου μι[46

then the start of a dialogue episode:

(—) Κρήτης απα[47

φόβος τὰ θεῖα τοῖσι σώφροσιν βροτῶν

πολλὴ γὰρ [

ἐμοι [50

472e P. Berlin 13217

(Μι.) οὐ γάρ τιν᾽ ἄλλην φημὶ τολμῆσαι τάδε.

(Χο.) σὺ †δ᾽ ἐκ κακῶν†, ἄναξ,

φρόντισον εὖ καλύψαι.

Πασιφάη ἀρνουμένη μὲν οὐκέτ᾽ ἂν πίθοιμί σε·

πάντως γὰρ ἤδη δῆλον ὡς ἔχει τάδε.   5

ἐγ[ὼ] γὰρ εἰ μὲν ἀνδρὶ προύβαλον δέμας

τοὐμὸν λαθραίαν ἐμπολωμένη Κύπριν,

ὀρθῶς ἂν ἤδη μάχ[λο]ς οὖσ᾽ ἐφαινόμην·

νῦν δ᾽, ἐκ θεοῦ γὰρ προσβολῆς ἐμηνάμην,

31 beg. Barrett   33 δίπ]ους Lloyd-Jones ('διπ]λους an error in P. Oxy.')   34 beg. Barrett
]ντι Turner νέο]ν τι (e.g.) Austin   end [σημαίνειν ἔχεις (e.g.) Barrett   35 οἴστρου Barrett
ε . . . ου others   37 end [μόσχου δίκην (e.g.) Page   38 beg. Page   end σ[φ᾽ ἐθήλασεν;
(e.g.) Page   σ[μικρὸν τρέφει; (e.g.) Collard   40 Page].ιλωμάτων (]γ or]τ Austin) P. Oxy.
47 ἀπά[σης (e.g.) Barrett   48 = TrGF adesp. 356, placed here by Barrett (= F 2d.5 Cant, No. 638
M: Plut. *Mor.* 34a, Stob. 3.3.30); this identification entertained by Austin, not admitted by Kannicht

(Nu.) *<It has a bull's>* head resting on its breast.
(Mi.) So *<does it go>* on *four* legs or walk on two?
(Nu.) On *two* feet, dark (?) with black . . .
(Mi.) And is there anything further . . . ?
(Nu.) *<Against>* the gadfly's *sting ?it has* a . . . tail.   35
(Mi.)   . . . voice . . .
(Nu.)   . . . *of a* grazing . . .
(Mi.) And *?does* a mother's breast or a cow's . . . ?
(Nu.) Its parents nurse *?it* . . .

40 . . . of the house . . .   41 . . . to its parents . . .   40–43

fr. 3 = F 472c *end of a lyric passage:*   44, 45
       . . . inexperienced . . . (*or* limitless *or* mainland)   46
       then start of a dialogue episode:
       . . . of Crete . . .   47
       The divine brings fear to the wise among mankind;
       for great *? is* . . .
       to me . . .   50

       Speaker of 47–50 unidentifiable (?Minos, ?Pasiphae).

472e P. Berlin *Pasiphae defends herself unavailingly against Minos:*

(Mi.) No other woman I think had the audacity for this.

(Cho.) You, my lord, †after (these) horrors†, must think to conceal them well.

Pasiphae. If I went on denying it I should not persuade you; for it is wholly clear already how these things stand.[5] Now, if I had thrown myself at a man and tried to sell my body for sex in secret, I would already and rightly be revealed as libidinous. As it is, because a god's onslaught made me mad, I suffer; but my

---

472e (F 4 Cant, 82 A, 641 M) P. Berl. 13217 (a single page of parchment, 2nd C. A.D.; vv. 1–26 on *recto*, 27–52 on *verso*; now lost) ed. Schubart and Wilamowitz, *BKT* V.2 (1907), 73–9; re-ed. (among others) von Arnim (1913), Page, *GLP* (1941), Cantarella (1964), Austin (1968). Text and supplements Wilamowitz unless indicated.   1 Minos, 2–3 Chorus: Koerte 1–3 Chorus: others   2 σὺ δ⟨ὲ κακὸν⟩ ἐκ κακῶν (e.g.) Wilamowitz δ⟨ὲ κάκ'⟩ Cropp δὲ κ⟨άκιστα⟩ Diggle   3 φρονησον P. Berl.   7 and 12 reflected in Eubulus *PCG* fr. 67.8–9 (= *TrGF* II adesp. 154) καὶ μὴ λαθραίαν Κύπριν, αἰσχίστην νόσον (Meineke: ὅσων mss. νόσων Hunter) | πασῶν, διώκειν   8 Hunt

ἀλγῶ μέν, ἐστὶ δ' οὐχ ἑκο[ύσ]ιον κακόν.　　　　　10
ἔχει γὰρ οὐδὲν εἰκός· ἐς τί γὰρ βοὸς
βλέψασ' ἐδήχθην θυμὸν αἰσχίστηι νόσωι;
ὡς εὐπρεπὴς μὲν ἐν πέπλοισιν ἦν ἰδεῖν,
πυρσῆς δὲ χαίτης καὶ παρ' ὀμμάτων σέλας
οἰνωπὸν ἐξέλαμπε περ[καί]νων γένυν;　　　　　15
οὐ μὴν δέμας γ' εὔρ[υθμον　　　　ν]υμφίου·
τοιῶνδε λέκτρω[ν οὕνεκ' εἰς] πεδοστιβῆ
ῥινὸν καθισ . . . [　　　　　　　]ται;
ἀλλ' οὐδὲ παίδων . [　　　　　] πόσιν
θέσθαι. τί δῆτα τῆι[δ' ἐμαι]νόμην νόσωι;　　　20
δαίμων ὁ τοῦδε κἄμ' ἐ[νέπλησεν κα]κῶν,
μάλιστα δ' οὗτος οισε[　　　　　]ων·
ταῦρον γὰρ οὐκ ἔσφαξ[εν ὅν γ' ἐπηύ]ξατο
ἐλθόντα θύσειν φάσμα [πο]ντίω[ι θε]ῶι.
ἐκ τῶνδέ τοί σ' ὑπῆλθ[ε κἀ]πετείσ[ατο　　　25
δίκην Ποσειδῶν, ἐς δ' ἔμ' ἔσκηψ[εν νόσον.
κἄπειτ' αὐτεῖς καὶ σὺ μαρτύρηι θεοὺς
αὐτὸς τάδ' ἔρξας καὶ καταισχύνας ἐμέ;
κἀγὼ μὲν ἡ τεκοῦσα κοὐδὲν αἰτία
ἔκρυψα πληγὴν δαίμονος θεήλατον,　　　　　30
σὺ δ', εὐπρεπῆ γὰρ κἀπιδείξασθαι καλά,
τῆς σῆς γυναικός, ὦ κάκιστ' ἀνδρῶν φρονῶν,
ὡς οὐ μεθέξων πᾶσι κηρύσσεις τάδε.
σύ τοί μ' ἀπόλλυς, σὴ γὰρ ἡ 'ξ[αμ]αρτία,
ἐκ σοῦ νοσοῦμεν.
　　　　　πρὸς τάδ' εἴτε ποντίαν　　　35
κτείνειν δοκεῖ σοι, κτε[ῖ]ν'· ἐπίστασαι δέ τοι
μιαιφόν' ἔργα καὶ σφαγὰς ἀνδροκτόνους·
εἴτ' ὠμοσίτου τῆς ἐμῆς ἐρᾶις φαγεῖν
σαρκός, πάρεστι· μὴ 'λλίπηις θοινώμενος.
ἐλεύθεροι γὰρ κοὐδὲν ἠδικηκότες　　　　　40
τῆς σῆς ἕκατι ζημ[ία]ς θανούμεθα.

---

15 end: question-mark, Schmid　　16 ἦν τοῦ ν]υμφίου Croiset　　ὧδε ν]υμφίου Page
ὥστε ν]υμφίου Cropp and (doubtfully) Diggle　　18 the letters after καθ were barely legible
through permeation of ink from the *verso*; καθισ . . . . read by Wilamowitz, supplementing (e.g.)

sin is not voluntary.[10] Why, it has no likelihood! What was there I saw in a bull to eat at my heart, in such shameful affliction? Was he so handsome a sight in his clothes, and did his red hair, and his eyes, shine with such brilliance, and was his chin dark in contrast, like a ripening grape?[15] My bridegroom's body <?was> certainly not graceful! <For> such a marriage <   > into an animal's hide? Not <?for> children either <   > to make (him) my husband. Why indeed was I *mad* with this affliction?[20]

It is this man's destiny <has filled> me too with *misery*, and this man here most of all <   >; for he did not slaughter the bull <which> he *vowed* he would sacrifice to the *sea-<god>* when its manifestation came. This is the reason, let me tell you, why Poseidon has trapped you and exacted[25] his justice; but he launched <the affliction> at me. And then you cry aloud and call the gods to witness — you! — when you did these things yourself and brought shame down on me? Furthermore, I myself, the mother, the wholly innocent, I hid the god's blow, sent from heaven;[30] but you — fine and proper things to put on show! — you proclaim them to everybody about your wife, you husband with the most evil of minds, as if you will have no part in them. You! You are my destroyer, for yours is the real sin, yours the cause of my affliction!

So then, if you have decided[35] to kill me in the sea, go on, kill me! — you understand bloody deeds and cut-throat murders well enough — or if you are longing to feed on my flesh raw, here it is: do not go short on your banquet! Free, and wholly innocent of wrong,[40] we shall be dying where the penalty should be yours.

καθείσ[ηι σῶμα Κύπρις ἄχθε]ται   σῶμ' ὅδ' ἐξοργίζε]ται; Page καθέρξασθα[ί με σῶμ' ὅδ' οἴε]ται; read in facsimile of P. Berl. and supplemented by von Arnim καθεῖν[αι σῶμά μ' οὗτος οἴε]ται; Collard   19 φ[ύτορ' εἰκὸς ἦν] read (insecurely) and supplemented (e.g.) by Wilamowitz ο[ὔνεκ' εἰκὸς ἦν] (e.g.) Collard ἐ[ς σποράν ἔδει] Cropp   20 δηταν P. Berl. 21 ἐ[πλήρωσεν or ἐ[μέστωσεν J. Diggle, ICS 6 (1981), 98 = Euripidea 215   22 οἷς ἔ[δρασ' ἄναγνος] ὤν (e.g.) Wilamowitz οἷς ἐ[χρῆν οὐ πιστὸς] ὤν Austin   23 ὄν (Page) γ ἐπηύ]ξατο Austin ὡς κατηύ]ξατο Wilamowitz   26 νόσον Collard νόσος Austin 27 κἀπιμαρτύρηι Wilamowitz 28 as question Diggle, Euripidea 498 39 'λλίπηις Murray, Schmid λιπηις P. Berl. 41]σονουμεθα P. Berl., marking end of speech

66   EURIPIDES

(Χο.)   πολλοῖσι δῆλον [ὡς θεήλατον] κακὸν
        τόδ' ἐστίν· ὀργη[   ] ͜ς, ἄναξ;

(Μι.)   ἀρ' ἐστόμωται; μ[   ] βοᾶι.
        χωρεῖτε, λόγχη[   ]υμενη,   45
        λάζυσθε τὴν πανο[ῦργον, ὡ]ς κακῶς θάνηι,
        καὶ τὴν ξυνεργὸν [τήνδε, δ]ωμάτων δ' ἔσω
        ἄγο]ντες αὐτὰς ἔρ[ξατ' ἐς κρυπτ]ήριον,
        ὡς μ]ηκέτ' εἰσίδ[ωσιν ἡλίου κ]ύκλον.

(Χο.)   ἄ]ναξ, ἐπίσχ[ες· φρο]ντί[δος] γὰρ ἄξιον   50
        τὸ πρ[ᾶγ]μα· [. .]ης δ' ο[ὕτις] εὔβουλος βροτῶν.

(Μι.)   κ[αὶ δὴ] δ[έδοκται] μὴ ἀναβάλλεσθαι δίκην.

472f (471 N)   See above before F 472.

472g   See above, Introduction, p. 55.

*988   (Μι.)   τέκτων γὰρ ὢν ἔπρασσες οὐ ξυλουργικά.

42 (Χο.) Hunt   43 ὀργῆ[ς ἐξάνες δειν]ῆς Austin ~ τῆς σ]ῆς Collard ὀργῆ[ι μὴ λίαν εἴξη]ις (e.g.) Wilamowitz   44 margin Μιν[ως read by Wilamowitz, βασιλ[ευς by Schubart end: ͜ς above βοαι P. Berl. (= βοαῖς? = βοᾶις Austin)   45 λόγχη[ι δ' ἡδ' ἴτω φρουρο]υμένη Page end κρατο]υμένη von Arnim   46 κακῶς Wilamowitz (but expressly deprecated by him) καλῶς P. Berl.   47 [τῆσδε Cantarella   48 κρυπτ]ήριον Herwerden   49 P. Berl. marks

Commentary on *Cretans*

472f (471 N). Nauck and Austin reasonably print the fr. before the Chorus's Parodos, F 472; since Minos is addressed there, he is the probable speaker here. The formal style suits very well an initial greeting to priests who have been anxiously summoned. Because the words are part of Aristophanes' parodic monody *Frogs* 1331–64, however, Cantarella, Mette and now Kannicht believe that they derive from Icarus' monody mentioned by Schol. *Frogs* 849 (above, p. 55); but a boy speaking to priests would hardly address them as children. Some Schol. on 1359 (on Dictynna, a Cretan name for Artemis) say 'this is from Euripides, beside the words from *Cret.*', whence some editors infer that 1356–63 contain other phrases from *Cret.*: so e.g. F 5.2–7 Cant, No. 640b M; but see Wilamowitz 77 n. 1 and esp. Rau 134–6. **children of Ida**: the Cretans as devotees of the 'Great Mother', Rhea, whose son Zeus was nurtured in a cave on Mt. Ida, F 472.9–15 and n. [Text: ἀλλά, deleted by Austin, is unlikely to begin an initial greeting. Retention of Ἴδας (Austin) gives a lyric iambic greeting to the entering Chorus; *IT* 123/6 or *Tro.* 143/153 are comparable. Diggle would retain both as the start of a dochmiac line. Change to Ἴδης (Nauck, but he retained ἀλλά) gives part of a spoken trimeter; then *Hcld.* 69 is comparable.]

(Cho.) It is clear to many <*that*> this misery is <*sent from heaven.*
> anger, my lord.
Mi. Has she had her tongue sharpened? She is shouting <
>. Go, <   > my spear,[45] seize
the *evil creature*, so she may die miserably — and her
accomplice <*here; take*> them inside the house and <*shut
them in a*> dungeon, <*so*> they may look no longer on the
circle <*of the sun*>.
(Cho.) My lord, hold back: the matter deserves[50] *reflection; no one*
< . . . > is well-advised.
(Mi.) <*It is decided*>: no deferment of justice.

472f (471 N) *See above before F 472*

472g *See above, Introduction, p. 55.*

***988** (Mi.)* You are a builder, but you were not practising carpentry.
(If from Cret.*)* Minos *accuses* Daedalus *of building the
artificial cow.*

end of speech   50 (Xo.) Hunt, rest Schubart   51 P. Berl. marks end of speech   52 (Mι.) Hunt,
rest Roberts   **988** (F inc 9 Cant, 641 M; omitted by Austin and Kannicht) Plut. *Mor.* 812e, attrib.
Eur.; assigned to *Cretans* by Wilamowitz, *KS* I.192.

472. The Parodos of the Chorus of Cretan priests, in anapaestic metre; for their
address on entry to the already present Minos cf. e.g. *And.* 117, *Hec.* 98 and on
F 472f above.   This evocative and famous fragment is the subject of unending discussion. It is the earliest surviving description of an initiatory cult honouring Zeus at
his birthplace on Cretan Ida (see e.g. Burkert 48, 280); but it is a highly poetic
description and argument persists, in what sense Euripides' detail may be judged
accurate. The general opinion is that he is mingling elements of ritual from various
times and places, some poetic in provenance, some no doubt contemporary, in order
to engage and impress his audience, and to establish for the Chorus a religious authority from which they may comment on the actions of both Pasiphae and Minos, and
perhaps Daedalus: see F 472b–c.1–7, 48; 472e.42–3, 50–1. The literature is huge,
but see esp. Wilamowitz (1907), 77 n.1 and *KS* I.513 n.1 expanded in *Glaube* II.183–
4; A. J. Festugière, *Rev. Bibl.* 44 (1935), 372–4 (best analysis of the text);
W. Fauth, *RE* IXA.2 (1967), 2226–31, 2243–57; B. Gallistl, *WJA* 7 (1981), 235–47;
H. Verbruggen, *Le Zeus des Crétois* (Paris, 1981), 200–6; Burkert (above);
G. Casadio, *Didattica del Classico* 2 (1990), 278–310.

1–2. Europa has confused parentage. Hom. *Il.* 14.321, Hes. fr. 141–7 and others, like Euripides here, make her father Phoenix, brother of Theban Cadmus; other sources name Agenor, King of Tyre (see below) or even Cadmus. Zeus carried her off in the form of a bull, brought her to Crete and fathered Minos on her (with other sons). Phoenix gave up his search for her and instead established a people named after him as the Phoenicians (Eur. *Phrixus?B* F 819): so Europa is 'Phoenician' or 'Tyrian' whether her father was Phoenix or Agenor. The 'bull' in the whole myth is thus variously Zeus's manifestation to Europa, Poseidon's portent for Minos (F 472e. 23–4), to which Pasiphae was attracted (F 472e.9–18), and the resulting hybrid Minotaur (F 472b.29–38); cf. Reckford 320 n.16. [Text: Bothe rightly deleted 'daughter of the Tyrian (Europa)', a doublet of **child of Europa**, although they resemble a genuine phrase at *Hyps.* I.iii.20 Bond. To delete **child of Europa** (Merkelbach) removes one of the parental names formally coupled by the Chorus.]

3. Crete of the hundred cities: a 'formulaic' appellation found first at Hom. *Il.* 2.649. Archaeology has indeed uncovered about 100 sites active in the late 7th C.: J. Boardman, in *CAH* III^2.3.222ff. (225–6 on the Ida cave). P. Carrara, *ZPE* 69 (1987), 20–4, detects in John Malalas p. 359 a paraphrase of this line and perhaps a vestige of the play's opening lines, supposing an apostrophe of the scene like *And.* 1, *El.* 1 etc. Kannicht in *TrGF* F *471a follows Carrara in assigning the reference to Euripides but not certainly to *Cret.*; so too an allusion to Zeus's rape of Europa at Malalas p. 31.6–8 (F 820 (b)).

4–8. To come here (etc.): the wording implies a break of routine, but is also a formula registering the arrival of important characters, e.g. gods *Tro.* 1, *And.* 1232, or an entering chorus, *Pho.* 202 (see Mastronarde). **its roof . . . into exact joints**: translation destroys a complex and highly poetic sequence of words, the Greek subject **cypress** being reserved to the very end; see also on 9–15 below. Note the progression 4 temple, 5 roof, 6 beams. Significance often attaches to words thus postponed, and cypress was a common timber, and Crete famous for it: 'roofed with cypress' *Hyps.* P. Oxy. 852 fr. 58.10 Bond, and in a temple Pind. *Pyth.* 5.39; R. Meiggs, *Trees and Timber etc.* (Oxford, 1982), 200, 430f.; probably the ceiling is meant, cf. the Epidauros temple (below), A.T. Hodge, *The Woodwork of Greek Roofs* (Cambridge, 1960), 124. The word-order emphasizes the no less prominent leading adj. **grown on the very site**. **Chalybean:** i.e. 'steel'. The Chalybes were a people of the S.E. Black Sea lands famous for metal-working, esp. in iron. **ox-glue** was (and is) made from the hides: Ar. *Hist. Anim.* 3.11, Plin. *Nat. Hist.* 11.231; *Encyc. Britann.* 11th ed., XII (1910), 144. For glue in a building see Hodge (above) 126, A. Burford, *ABSA* 61 (1966), 331 (Index: the Epidaurus temple inscription of c. 360 B.C.), and *Craftsmen in Greek and Roman Society* (London, 1972), 99–100. The carpentry of roofs employed variously mortising, dowelling, nailing and glueing: Hodge 97, 126. [The text of these lines is insecure; the word-order of Porphyry and Erotian in 5–6 has been changed by editors for greater clarity. **its roof** translates οὓς . . . στεγανούς, the adj. going with the pronoun as in 'roofed house' *TrGF* II adesp.

115.2, *Cyc.* 324, cf. Fraenkel on *Ag.* 358. δοκούς is internal Acc. with τμηθεῖσα, 'cut *into* beams', for which see LSJ τέμνειν II.4.a, IV.1. **brought together with bonding ox-glue**: in Hermann's ingenious combination of the discrepant Porphyry and Erotian, κραθεῖσ', lit. 'mixed', expresses the idea of making separate things into a whole; cf. e.g. the verb used of alloying metals Dem. 24. 114, the metaphor συγκρατὸν ζεῦγος Eur. *And.* 495, lit. 'mingled yoke', describing the close embrace of mother and child. Distrusting Hermann's 'mixed' Wilamowitz conjectured 'yoked', i.e. 'joined', with ζευγνύναι as used of a pair of carpentered doors at Hom. *Il.* 18.276; Austin suggested 'fixed', with πηγνύναι as used of a carpentered joint (ἁρμός again) at *Erec.* F 360.12. In ταυροδέτωι the verbal part is Active, '**bonding**': for such adjs. in -δετος cf. *IT* 1043 χαλίνοις λινοδέτοις 'ropes of flax which bind (moor) ships', and the analysis by J. Diggle, *SIFC* 7 (1984), 197–8 = *Euripidea* 343; the Accus. ἁρμούς is 'internal' with a verb of similar meaning, *Hipp.* 253 φιλίας ἀνακίρνασθαι 'to compound friendships', Soph. *Trach.* 157, KG I.125.]

9–15. Pure . . . consecration: the translation preserves the conspicuous 'bracketing' of the whole intricate sentence by these two important words (interestingly repeating the same positioning of the less important 'grown on the very site... cypress' in 4–8). Festugière 372–3 shows that the structure of the dependent clause **since I became** etc. helps to integrate apparently separate cultic phenomena: there are two components each consisting of a main verb and dependent participle, **became . . . performing** 10–12 and **holding aloft . . . was named** 13–15. [Text: this structure is secured by the removal of the connective τε in 12; West tries to preserve the καί in 14, against Wilamowitz, by supplementing 'and <*in the armed dances*> of the Curetes'.]   The Chorus are successively (1) **initiate** of Zeus, (2) **herdsman of nocturnal Zagreus** and (3) **celebrant** of Zeus's **mother** Rhea. 'Initiate', 'nocturnal' and 'celebrant' are all terms for 'worshipper' at Heraclitus 22 B 14 DK (see e.g. A. Henrichs in Hofmann and Harder, *Fragmenta Dramatica* 190), cf. the vocabulary of Ar. *Frogs* 334–45 etc.; 'herdsman' has the same connotation: see below. (1) and (3) are linked in the **Curetes**, guardians of the *kouros* or boy-Zeus in the ritual re-enactment of the birth in the cave on Mt. Ida; but they are also in that capacity attendant on his mother (*Bacc.* 120, *Hyps.* I.iii.24 Bond, Strabo 3.19: Burkert 261–2). The word **celebrant**, βακχός, denotes primarily an ecstatic devotee of Dionysus-Bacchus, but Euripides associates the word in its fem. form 'Bacchant' with the Curetes and Cretan Rhea in the worship of Dionysus at *Bacc.* 120–9 and with that of Cybele in Asia Minor at *Bacc.* 78–88, 131–4 (see Dodds on 78–9, Burkert 177–9). The initiatory **feasts of raw flesh** by Zagreus's worshippers resemble those of Dionysus *Bacc.* 139 (Dodds xviff., cf. R. Seaford, *CQ* 31 [1981], 265f.); some have argued that **Zagreus** was known to Euripides as a Cretan cult-name of Dionysus, an identification made later by e.g. Callim. fr. 43.117 (most recently Gallistl, against e.g. Wilamowitz, Festugière and Burkert 298). For the association of the name Zagreus with Zeus himself see Verbruggen 123–5. The name Zagreus was etymologized in antiquity as ζα-αγρευς 'great hunter'; ἀγρεύς 'hunter' is applied to Dionysus at *Bacc.* 1192 (see Dodds). **herdsman**, lit. 'ox-herd': the word registers the open country as the scene of Zagreus's rites, but it connotes particularly the cult of Dionysus in his manifestation as a 'bull' (Dodds, *Bacchae* p. xviii): thus βουκόλος of the same meaning is a Dionysiac worshipper at *Antiope* F 203 = xxxvii Kambitsis (excellent n.); cf. Cratinus's comedy Βουκόλοι, *PCG* frs. 17–22. The word later connotes any god's worshipper: LSJ, inscriptional evidence. **nocturnal** also gives the idea of Dionysiac rites: Dodds on *Bacc.* 486, at Delphi *Ion* 718. Other details: **Pure**: for the idea cf. 16–20, Seaford on *Bacc.* 74, part of a cult-hymn with a similar emphasis; Casadio 282–3. **life I have maintained**: the verb τείνειν as *Med.* 670, *Ion* 625 etc. **performing**: the verb τελεῖν is the ritual term, *Bacc.* 73, 485, *El.* 863 etc. **holding aloft torches**: as in many gods' rites, Dionysus's at Delphi *Ion* 716, Hecate's at Ar. *Frogs* 1361, above all in the Eleusinian Mysteries *Frogs* 313–4 etc. **consecration**: 'for priestly service', Burkert 270. [Text: **feasts**: the Greek word is wrongly accented in Porphyry as 'dividers', i.e. 'butchers'; that is how Hesychius too misinterpreted it. **herdsman** is surely correct, but Casadio 288–90 has recently defended Porph.'s βροντάς, 'performing Zagreus's thunder and feasts': imitation of thunder and display of lightning-stones were parts of ritual.]

16–20. Of the ritual avoidances described here abstinence from **living food** characterizes particularly the Pythagorean and Orphic 'sects', e.g. *Hipp.* 952, Callim. fr. 191.61–2; Burkert 301–2; Dover on Ar. *Frogs* 1032; but their mention induced earlier scholars to apply some of the details in 10–15 also to these sects — this despite the apparent contradiction between 19–20 abstinence from meat and 12 feasts of raw flesh. The ritual phenomena of 10–15 and the ascetic practices of 16–20 are brought together quite artificially, and are nowhere attested for any one cult or sect: see e.g. Casadio 294–300. The avoidance of birth and death as polluting is common to much Greek religious practice, e.g. birth *IT* 381–3, death there and *Alc.* 22–3: Parker, *Miasma* 33 and 39; Burkert 78–9; Verbruggen 200–6. **clothing all of white**: expressly the converse of funereal black, *Alc.* 923; prescribed for celebrants e.g. (cited by Austin) Dittenberger, *Sylloge*[3] 736.16 (1ˢᵗ C. B.C.). [Text: Wecklein's small change in 17 restores an excellent sequence of ideas, first the avoidance of birth and death, a regular pairing emphasised by the enclosing word-order **shun ... not approach**, then the avoidance of meat. Before his second thoughts Wilamowitz had supplemented with 'both the birth of mortals <*and the setting free of their souls*> 'and associated the avoidance of birth with that of meat. **and not approaching ... I have guarded ... :** JD finds the partic. οὐ χριμπτόμενος otiose after φεύγω and suggests it once controlled a now missing Dat., e.g. 'not approaching <*the polluted*>'. **the laying-places of the dead**: the first occurrence of the compound noun νεκροθήκη for the common θήκη (νεκρῶν), e.g. Soph. *El.* 896, Hdt. 1.187.]

472a. Context: the reference to the Minotaur is certain; the similarity of this dialogue trimeter to 472b.29 suggests that it came from an earlier point in the play, perhaps a preliminary report of the birth. **form:** translated as Acc. of 'respect', *Alc.* 333, *Hec.* 269 etc. [Text: since **mixed form** suggests the infant's strangeness, it is better to keep transmitted ἀποφώλιον **without purpose,** which adds a different idea. The adj. describes a 'useless' person Hom. *Od.* 14.142, cf. 'barren' 11.249, where Schol. paraphrase with ἄγονος, the word used by Aristot. *Gen. An.* 746b15 to describe the sterility of mules, creatures cross-bred like the Minotaur. Housman conjectured ἀποφύλιον *'sui generis',* lit. 'not from a breed, kind, species', and cited Aesch. *Eum.* 57 'I have not seen this company's (the Furies') natural kind', their φῦλον. The two words are confused in the ancient lexicographers: see Radt on Aesch. F 287.]

472b–c. 1–8. If the supplement *retribution* in 1 is right, the Chorus are appealing to Apollo as **son of Leto** and **lord,** probably to avert or ameliorate the feared disaster; he is to come from **Lycia,** one of his favourite homes e.g. Pind. *Pyth.* 1.39, **singing** himself in response to the paean hymn addressed to him as Apollo Paion, 'Healer' (as the Cretans do at *Hom. Hymn. Ap.* 517, e.g.); cf. Burkert 145 etc. Apollo is often appealed to in company with his sister Artemis; it is tempting to see her name here in **daughter of a great father** (Zeus), one of her cult-titles Ap. Rhod. 1.570, cf. *Hipp.* 68. But Cantarella notes that the adj. may equally connote Pasiphae, daughter of the Sun at Ap. Rhod. 3.999. **blasts:** gods violently 'breathe' their power or will, e.g. Aphrodite *Hipp.* 563, Ares *Pho.* 789.

9–43. The placing of fr. 2 col. ii before fr. 1, and their overlap, are technical possibilities; the placing is logical dramatically, so that the Chorus's lyric anxiety precedes Minos's enquiry about the Minotaur. Also, the naming of the speakers in 16 and 17 as Chorus and Minos has implications for assigning the parts in the stichomythic dialogue filling almost all of fr. 1. Lloyd-Jones thought that Minos answered the questions of the Chorus. Page and Mette (*Lustrum* 23/24 [1981–2], 170) justly observed that Pasiphae's Nurse is much more likely to provide the information; then Minos rather than the Chorus asked the questions, esp. in a long stichomythia. With this attribution of the voice-parts in fr. 1, and if fr. 2 col. ii closely preceded it, there must have been room for the Nurse to be introduced. Perhaps she was already present; perhaps it was she who gave a brief preliminary account in F 472a to the Chorus, who then repeated it to Minos; at 30 here he says 'I have heard that before'. Minos would conduct only one interrogation, like Theseus at *Hipp.* 855ff. before his irreversible condemnation (cf. our F 472e.52) of Hippolytus, 882ff.

25. onslaught: cf. on F 472e.9 below.

29. Cf. F 472a. Hes. fr. 145.16–17 has a (mutilated) description of the Minotaur (cf. our 31, 33); for its **two natures** cf. Verg. *Aen.* 6.25–6, Sen. *Ph.* 691 etc.

32. [So . . . ? γάρ interrogative as *And.* 203, *Hec.* 688 etc.: Denniston, *GP* 82. *<does it go>*: verb of motion as *Rhes.* 215, the only other occurrence of the adj. δίβαμος **walk(ing) on** two (feet).]

33. dark(?): some form of δάσκιος 'shadowy, dark-coloured' stood here describing the Minotaur's hide (but at F 472e.14 it seems to be dark red).

34. One model for reconstruction is *Bacc.* 834 'And is there anything further you can add for me?'; '. . . <*you can state*>' Barrett; 'Is there anything else <*new*> . . .' Austin; cf. also (JD) *Alc.* 557, Aesch. *Pers.* 237.

35. Restoration of *sting* is not certain. While οἶστρος can have this sense (metaphorical, too, e.g. *Hipp.* 1300 of Phaedra's love), at e.g. Hom. *Od.* 22. 300 it is the cattle-fly itself, as μύωψ here and e.g. Aesch. *Supp.* 307. But the presence of **tail** suggests the creature's means of self-protection from flies; and in 37 the adj. 'grazing' seems to emphasize the Minotaur's animal part.

36. Probably a question, 'Is its **voice** human or animal?' (Page). Answer: the latter, 37.

37. '<*like*> a **grazing** <*calf*>', Page. The adj. occurs in P. Oxy. 2452 fr. 19 from a *Theseus* play; it may describe the Minotaur there;

38. [*does* (etc.): a Present tense is required, for the Minotaur is still dependent for its food, 39. Unlike Page's '<*did*> . . . <*suckle it*>?', Collard's '*does* . . . <*nurse (the) little (Minotaur)*>?' meets this need: for 'little' cf. σμικρός *Or.* 462, *Cresph.* F 448a.55 (but in both places with a part., 'being small', which JD would find necessary here).]

39. its parents: the Greek Plural (Masc.) is allusive: see on F 472e.41. Only Pasiphae (and perhaps the Nurse herself as her helper still) can be meant, but the Nurse is trying still to conceal that from Minos.

46. inexperienced: this seems the most suitable meaning; the Greek letters could yield any of the three given, but one cannot be determined without knowledge of context and metre.

47 ff. Perhaps the start of a major 'confiding' statement to the male Chorus by the male Minos (so Cropp, comparing e.g. *Hipp.* 372ff., Phaedra to female Chorus). 47 was complete in sense (? '*I speak as lord*> of *all* (Barrett) **Crete**', cf. F 472.2–3), for 48 too is self-contained, a truism provoked by the immediate catastrophe. Fear of godhead e.g. Aesch. *Supp.* 749 'Zeus brings fear among mankind'; cf. Eur. *El.* 473, *Supp.* 554. Barrett's restoration here of *TrGF* II F adesp. 356 is irresistible.

49. great: the adj. is applied to Aphrodite in her tyrannous power *Hipp.* 1, 443, *IA* 557, cf. Ar. *Frogs* 1046; most aptly here too, if the goddess was the Prologue speaker (Webster 87) and was angry at Pasiphae's neglect of her worship (Hygin. *Fab.* 40) or with any daughter of the Sun because he betrayed her adultery with Ares (Schol. Eur. *Hipp.* 47 etc.) — and announced that Poseidon had employed her to punish Minos through Pasiphae (F 472e.25–6), as Athene brings in Poseidon at *Tro.* 62, 73.

472e. The (now lost) single leaf of P. Berlin may well have been deliberately preserved from a complete text, as a rhetorical *tour de force* and model. Its main part is Pasiphae's attempted self-exculpation through incrimination of her accuser and judge — and husband — Minos (4–41n.), preceded by its dramatic introduction, the Chorus' advice to Minos to conceal the matter (1–3), and followed by their brief exchange which gives the outcome, immediate punishment (42–52). It is certain from the two lyric lines of the Chorus which directly precede Pasiphae's speech that it is not part of a symmetrical *agon* structure favoured by Euripides for so many of his persons 'on trial', such as Hippolytus in the scene *Hipp.* 932–1089 or Helen *Tro.* 895–1059 (see Collard on *Hec.* 216–443); cf. Lucas, *Gnomon* 35 (1965), 456; Lloyd, *Agon* 50. The Parchment had not a few bad scribal errors, so that conjectural supplement of its many gaps is both more hazardous and more justifiable than usual: see esp. on 18, 19.

1. No other woman: Minos points to Pasiphae rather than the Nurse her accomplice (who is present, 47; cf. on F 472b.9–43); he does not address her, and she remains '3rd Person' after her speech, 44, 46, 48–9.

2–3. Two lyric lines, the text corrupt in 2 and possibly in 3; together with the trimeter 1, spoken by Minos, they make the end of a probably brief 'epirrhematic' system as the excited prelude to Pasiphae's speech, like that preceding Iphis's monologue at *Supp.* 1072–9, 1080–1113 (see Collard's n.). [For his supplement in 2, '<horror> after (these) horrors', Wilamowitz compared Soph. *Ant.* 1281 'what still worse horror is there to follow horror?'; Cropp's <horrors> is technically superior. Similar expressions occur first Hom. *Il.* 19.290, e.g. *Pho.* 371. Believing only the one horror of Pasiphae's conduct to be at issue, JD suggests '<worst> of horrors', the grammatical expression like Soph. *OT* 334. **think to conceal:** nearest in Euripides to this use of φροντίζειν and bare Infin. is *Hcld.* 680; KG II.6f. give mostly prose illustrations; φρόνησον 'have a mind to conceal' in P. Berl. is equally doubtful for Euripides. The Chorus are advising Minos to conceal what he has already made public (33), what Pasiphae has tried to hide (30, cf. 48–9 n.).]

4–41. Euripides makes Pasiphae exploit the techniques adopted by a contemporary lawcourt defendant when the facts of the case are damningly incontrovertible (4–5) and all effort is directed to presenting them so that they can be evaluated quite differently (6–20); then the responsibility is thrown on to the plaintiff by 'counter-accusation' (ἀντικατηγορία, 21–35: cf. e.g. the equally skilful Helen against Hecuba *Tro.* 919ff.; Antiphon, *Tetralogy* III.2; the display piece Gorgias, *Palamedes*: Dolfi 130ff., Lloyd, *Agon* 102). The speech ends with defiance and denigration (35–41; compare e.g. Hecuba countering Helen, *Tro.* 1022ff.).

Details: in her first part Pasiphae trails an unreal hypothesis about her past sexual behaviour (6–8) before she pretends lack of motive for so improbable a liaison with a bull (11–20): at 11 and perhaps 19, she uses expressly the fashionable contemporary argument from likelihood or 'probability', τὸ εἰκός: cf. e.g. *Hipp.* 615, *Med.* 345, *Or.* 539 etc., implicitly *Hipp.* 962–70, 1007–15: Lloyd, *Agon* 29; lack of motive *Hipp.* 1009ff. again, *Tro.* 946–7; Gorgias, *Palamedes* 13ff. Throughout the speech she pleads the injury to herself (10, 30, 41) and her innocence (9–10, 29–40). With her claim at 10, 'my sin is not voluntary', cf. Phaedra at *Hipp.* 319; *Auge* F 265.2, *Dictys* F 339.4; the wording resembles the Socratic and Platonic contention e.g. *Prot.* 346d, *Meno* 78a: Guthrie, *HGPh* III. 459ff.; cf. Introd., above, p. 57. She imputes the blame rather to 'the god' (9, 21, 25–6, 30), cf. Helen at *Tro.* 948, Eurystheus *Hcld.* 989, *HF* 1393 (with Bond's n.), and e.g. Hom. *Il.* 19.86–7, Hdt. 1.45.2; or blames Minos himself (22–4, 27–8,

34–5, 41), like Helen blaming Hecuba *Tro*. 920, Orestes Clytemnestra *Or*. 586: Lloyd, *Agon* 124 n. 25. Pasiphae describes her passion as a 'disease' (transl. **affliction** 12, 20, ?26, 35), as Phaedra does hers (physically too) in *Hipp*. and as Bellerophon presents Stheneboea's: see *Sthen*. F 661.6 n.

4 . If I went on denying: cf. Antigone's defiant admission before she counterattacks, Soph. *Ant*. 443; and Orestes at Aesch. *Eum*. 463, 558, 661. **not persuade:** a defendant's fear, e.g. *Hipp*. 1062, F 1067.4. **went on . . . not** translates οὐκέτι in the idiom discussed by Dawe on Soph. *OT* 115 'he did not go on to return in the way he set out', cf. (JD) *Tro*. 846.

6 . thrown myself at a man: cf. *Hel*. 28 'Aphrodite offered (Paris) my body'.

6 – 7 . myself . . . my body translates the periphrasis τοὐμὸν δέμας, commonly meaning no more than 'me', e.g. *Hec*. 724, *Hel*. 383; cf. *El*. 1341 'wed Electra's body' and the similar sexual tone of *Alc*. 1133, *Supp*. 823, our 16.

7 . sell: like a prostitute, LSJ ἐμπολή III, καπηλεύω II.2 (both later Greek); conversely women 'buy' a husband with their dowry, *Med*. 233, *El*. 1090, cf. *Pha*. 159. **sex:** lit. 'Cypris', the goddess Aphrodite's name is depersonalised and often connotes illicit sex, e.g. *Hec*. 825, *Tro*. 988 etc.

7, 12. Eubulus (*app*.) means 'and not pursue sex in secret, the most shameful disease of all' (Meineke; 'of all diseases', Hunter).

8 . libidinous: μάχλος also Aesch. *Supp*. 636, F 325 in Tragedy; used esp. of wanton women Hes. *WD* 586, fr. 132; of effeminate Paris Hom. *Il*. 24.30.

9 . a god's onslaught: cf. F 472b.25, *Hipp*. 241; of love's affliction *Med*. 640.

1 0 . I suffer: ἀλγῶ 1ˢᵗ Person as in Electra's resentment *El*. 1118.

1 2 . shameful: adultery's shame e.g. *Hipp*. 331, 404, 1165, *Sthen*. F 661.5.

1 3 – 1 5 . Hippolytus similarly rejects the imputation that Phaedra was bodily attractive to him *Hipp*. 1009–10; cf. Helen's helpless beauty *Hel*. 27, 383. **eat at my heart:** passion's effect as at *Hipp*. 1303, *Med*. 8 etc., most famously Aesch. *Ag*. 742. **handsome . . . clothes:** cf. Paris's exotic dress supposedly alluring Helen *Tro*. 991. **red:** the adj. πυρσός suits both the bull's tawny hide and the implied human lover with his fine head of auburn hair; for hair's attraction see Dodds on *Bacc*. 235. **shine with such brilliance:** the root λαμπ- is applied to the physically splendid (English uses the Latin metaphor) *Autolycus* F 282.3, *Syleus* F 688.4; for the closer reference to the brilliant **eyes** of a lover cf. Aesch. F 243.1 (φλέγειν 'blaze, flash'), a young woman; for love in the eyes, a commonplace, see commentators on *Bacc*. 236, *Hipp*. 525–6, Aesch. *Ag*. 742, Sappho fr. 138 L.–P. (ἐκλάμπειν here with internal Acc. as Aesch. F 300.4.) **dark in contrast:** an attempt to translate the unique verb περκαίνειν, glossed by Hesych. π 1970 (III.323 Schmidt) with διαποικίλλεσθαι 'variegate'. The commoner form is περκάζειν, 'turn dark' (of ripening grapes etc.), applied in the same metaphor to a human beard Call. *Hymn*. 5.76; cf. 'wine-coloured', i.e. darkbearded, chin, *Pho*. 1160.

1 6 . bridegroom's body: see on 6–7 above. [Text, **graceful:** only the adj. εὔρυθμος suits the beginning ευρ[; of a youth Pl. *Prot*. 326b etc. **<?was>:** Croiset's supplement of a past tense seems inescapable, the article translating as

My. Cropp suggests 'graceful *<like a>* **bridegroom's**' (but Diggle doubts that Pasiphae should credit an unspecified bridegroom with grace); for comparative ὥστε cf. *Bacc.* 748–52; Denniston, *GP* 526–7.]

17–18. The probable sense is generally agreed to have been 'did I put myself inside an animal's hide to make such a marriage?' The reference to Daedalus's artificial cow (Introd., p. 54) is certain; the adj. πεδοστιβής, **animal's**, lit. 'treading the ground', describes quadrupeds Aesch. *Supp.* 1000, *Rhes.* 254. [Restoration of the text is made harder by the uncertainty of the letters after καθ in 18 and the ending of 18 in]ται, which is likely to be a Pres. Indic. Wilamowitz with '*<Aphrodite is offended at me for lowering my body into . . . >*' wrongly pre-empts the attribution of cause to the god Poseidon, 21ff. Page with '*<is this man* (Minos) *angry at me for . . .>*' and von Arnim with '*<does this man think I enclosed my body in>*' are much more likely; and '*think*' links the arguments from (im)probability in 13–16 with 19: so Collard suggests '*<does he think I lowered my body>*'. καθεῖναι with Acc. and εἰς with Acc. as *Cyc.* 457, *Ion* 435f. etc.]

19. The general sense is again clear, restoration again unconfident. [Wilamowitz, Kappelmacher and von Arnim disagreed about the vestigial letter following παίδων. Wilamowitz's supplement gives 'Nor *<was it likely>* I made him my husband *<to be father>* of my children', but is unmetrical (φύτορ' has first syllable short). Effective rhetoric would be maintained by repeating the phrase with οὕνεκα 'for . . .', i.e. 'to get' at the start of the successive improbable hypotheses in 17 and 19, 'Not *<for>* children either *<was it likely>* I made (him) my husband'. Cropp's supplement gives 'nor *<was there need>* either *<to make him>* my husband *<for the begetting>* of children', cf. *Med.* 718 'I shall make you beget children'. *Male* excuses for adultery in order to get children *Med.* 490–1, *Ion* 840. **not . . . either**: for ἀλλ' οὐδέ adding a less likely argument see Denniston, *GP* 22.]

21. **this man's destiny**: for this use of the noun δαίμων, personified and qualified by a possessive), see Stevens on *And.* 98, citing e.g. *Supp.* 591, Aesch. *Ag.* 1569. Minos's 'destiny' works through the god Poseidon, named in 24, 26; the idea does not conflict with the anonymous 'god' already blamed by Pasiphae in 9 and again in 30. V. Longo, *Maia* 18 (1966), 196–7, has strenuously advocated the interpretation 'this man's god', i.e. Poseidon, but then the explicit names of 24 and 26 are otiose. **this man**: i.e. 'you' the opponent, a lawcourt usage: ?22, Craik on *Pho.* 454, Lloyd, *Agon* 86 n. 59. *<filled>*: e.g. *Hel.* 769, *Pho.* 170 (joy); Diggle's supplements give the same sense.

22. [Textual supplements: Wilamowitz's *<impure in his actions>* or Austin's *<faithless to his duty>* are good, for 22 must name the fault which incurred Poseidon's retribution in 23–6.]

23–4. For Minos's falsity cf. Apollod. 3.1.3–4 and Introd. p. 54 above. For Poseidon's bull (from the sea; cf. *Hipp.* 1214) see on F 472.1–2. **when its manifestation came**: φάσμα is quasi-predicative to ταῦρον . . . ἐλθόντα, like the noun ὄναρ 'dream' after the same participle in *HF* 495 and perhaps like σκιά after ἐλθέ (Wilamowitz's punctuation) 494. φάσμα is used of corporeal apparitions at e.g. Aesch. *Ag.* 145, Pind. *Ol.* 8.43; cf. *El.* 565 'treasure' (i.e. Orestes) which the god is manifesting (φαίνει)'.

25–6. trapped: the verb ὑπέρχεσθαι, lit. 'go underneath', of unperceived or insidious destruction, *IA* 444 (a god's), *Hipp.* 992 (Theseus's of Hippolytus); cf. Collard on *Supp.* 138. **launched at me**: the verb σκήπτειν and compounds are more often transitive (Collard here, cf. *Med.* 1333 gods launch an avenger) than intrans. (Austin, 'struck me', cf. *Hipp.* 438 gods' anger). Pasiphae continues her emphasis on the **<*affliction*>** (4–41 n.).

27. And then: for κἄπειτα cf. *Supp.* 1058, *HF* 266 etc.; Denniston, *GP* 311; Diggle, *Euripidea* 498. **you!**: heavy emphasis, weakened by Wilamowitz's removal of the pronoun (the word-order is anomalous). Pasiphae particularly stresses that she, not Minos, is entitled to invoke the gods since he, not she, has offended them.

29–30. hid: cf. on 2–3, 48–9; so Phaedra tried to hide her own 'horror', *Hipp.* 333 τὸ δεινόν, 393 etc. **blow . . . from heaven**: 9, ?42; cf. on 4–41 above, (JD) the Sophoclean Phaedra at F 680.3 (νόσος, 'affliction'); divine blows *Pha.* 279, *Ion* 282 etc.

31–3. The translation reproduces as nearly as possible the sardonic sequence of the original: **put on show** contrasts with 30 'hid' (exactly as in *Cret.W.* F 460.2–3 of Aerope's seduction); **wife** and **husband** are pointedly juxtaposed; the purpose of **proclaim them to everybody** is negative, for Minos to be seen to **have no part** (in the responsibility: μετέχειν exactly as *And.* 499—but there may be ambiguity in the Greek order, i.e. 'to have no part in your wife'.). Greek construction: 31 the Inf. depends on the coordinated Accs. εὐπρεπῆ and καλά which are appositional to and resumed in terminal 33 τάδε; 32 γυναικός Gen. with κηρύσσειν τάδε 'proclaim this about', a Sophoclean idiom e.g. *El.* 317, cf. Denniston on Eur. *El.* 228 ('tell the world', πᾶσι: *And.* 436, *Cret.W.* F 460.3 etc.); 32 κάκιστ(α) Acc. controlled by φρονῶν but as Superl. itself controlling the partitive Gen. ἀνδρῶν, e.g. Thuc. 1.48.4 ταῖς ἄριστα τῶν νεῶν πλεούσαις, KG I 24 n. 1.

34–5. you . . . yours . . . yours: taking up the 2nd Pers. words of 31–2; the counter-accusation's climax is followed by the bitter taunts of 35–9.

35–9. Invitations to alternative executions *HF* 319–20, Soph. *OT* 1411–2.

35. So then: for the Greek phrase heralding an Imperative cf. *Ion* 685, 693 etc.; Diggle, *Studies* 38.

35–6. kill me in the sea: by throwing from a cliff *Cyc.* 166 or simple drowning *OT* 1411. Corbato 166 sees an allusion here to the attempted suicide of Britomartis when pursued by the lustful Minos, Call. *Hymn.* 3.190–7; rather, perhaps, to the attempted drowning of the disgraced Aerope by her father in *Cret.W.*, *TrGF Cressae* test. iiia (Schol. on *Aj.* 1295–7), or of Auge thrown by her father into the sea in a chest with her son Telephus (cf. Comm. on *Tel.* F 696.4). There may be no conscious irony that Minos may kill Pasiphae in the sea from which came the bull he failed to kill, 23–4. For the predicative adj. ποντίαν with κτείνειν cf. *Hec.* [797], *Cyc.* 300.

3 6 – 7. well enough: an attempt to translate τοι (sarcastic: see Denniston, *GP* 541). A long explanatory parenthesis interrupts the two **if**s 35, 38; for such interruptions see e.g. Collard on *Supp.* 634, Mastronarde on *Pho* 167; within a single clause *Alc.* 1085, *Ion* 699 etc. **cut-throat murders:** near-pleonasm in the Greek, like *Hec.* 571, *Hyps.* F 8/9.9 Bond etc.

3 7 – 9. feed on my flesh raw: as Andromache taunts the ruthless Greeks to cannibalise Astyanax after his execution *Tro.* 774f.; the model for such barbarism is Achilles' wish for Hector *Il.* 22.347, cf. Collard on *Hec.* 1072f. Cannibalism here and bloodthirstiness in 36–7 may also evoke Minos's annual sacrifice of Athenian boys and girls as prey for the Minotaur in the labyrinth (dramatised in Eur. *Theseus*, e.g. F 385/6). Wilamowitz 78 saw here a sardonic reference to the priests' abstinence from flesh (F 472.19–20); cf. Introd., p. 57; allusion to the ritual eating of such flesh (F 472.12) is also unlikely. **here it is:** as Polyxena offers her throat for knifing *Hec.* 565, Amphitryon *HF* 319. **banquet:** the same word evokes the Cyclops's horrid cannibalism, *Cyc.* 377, 550. [Text, **go short:** the compound verb ἐλλείπειν is required in this idiom with a participle: LSJ I.7.]

4 0 – 1. Free: in spirit, but Pasiphae hopes to avoid the physical repression which Minos at once imposes, 45–9. Similarly Euripides' self-sacrificing and innocent girls aspire to die 'free', but in the sense that this willing death absolves their killers of pollution: Wilkins on *Hcld.* 559, cf. Collard on *Hec.* 550. **we shall be dying etc.:** the threatened Helen *Tro.* 904 and Amphitryon *HF* 210 also voice moral outrage. Pasiphae uses the Masc. Plur. common to women in self-reference, usually 1ˢᵗ Pers., *Hipp.* 287, 389 etc.; KG I.83. Cf. on F 472b.39.

4 2 . clear: the Chorus pick up Pasiphae's 'wholly clear' in 5 above. **<sent from heaven>:** 30 n.

4 3 . E.g. '<*Relent from your terrible*> anger' Austin, cf. *Hipp.* 900 (with 901 cf. our 51 below); Collard's simpler '. . . <*your*> anger' emphasises human reaction to divine cause, 42; '<*Don't give way too much to*> anger' Wilamowitz, cf. *Hel.* 80.

4 4 . . . . her tongue sharpened? i.e. got that hard edge to it, as a weapon has a sharp 'mouth' (στόμα) e.g. *Supp.* 1206, Soph. *Aj.* 651; the verb στομοῦν as Ar. *Clouds* 1108, LSJ II.3; cf. the noun στόμωσις 'hardness of mouth', ·Soph. *OC* 794; also *Med.* 525 'busy hurtful mouth'. Minos's subsequent command to repress Pasiphae shows that the verb cannot mean 'Has she been muzzled?', like the 'false prophets' silenced at Hdt 4.69; cf. *Hec.*1283, *Licymnius* F 479. **is shouting:** P. Berl. had an apparent suprascript variant: perhaps 'with (her) shouts' rather than 'you shout' (Austin), since Pasiphae is still 3ʳᵈ Pers.

4 5 . The best supplement so far found is Page's '<*let her go guarded*> (?by) my *spearmen*'; for 'let *x* go' as an exit command cf. *El.* 500. *Tro.* 880–1 exemplifies two Imperatives in asyndeton in such a command, with intervening Voc.: so Wilamowitz's demand for a Voc. here is compelling (but he rightly rejected λόγχη, never so used in its collective sense). λόγχη[ι Dat. (Page) or λόγχη[ς Gen. seems likely, the latter perhaps controlled by a Voc. noun or participle.

4 6 . die miserably: κακῶς as in execution threats *Med.* 1386, *Hcld.* 958; Antigone of her own death Soph. *Ant.* 895, cf. 59. [Wilamowitz strongly wished to retain

78 EURIPIDES

καλῶς 'die her fine death', a sardonic riposte to Pasiphae's bravado 40–1; for καλῶς 'bravely' cf. *Hec.* 329, 'nobly' *IA* 1252 etc.]

47. her accomplice <*here*>: the Nurse's presence is a sure inference from the Fem. 'them', 48. Cantarella's τῆσδε gives just 'her accomplice', i.e. off-stage.

48–9. dungeon: Herwerden's supplement exactly meets Wilamowitz's demand (p. 76) for a windowless prison; cf. Antigone's subterranean death-prison, Soph. *Ant.* 774, 885–8, and on the Tragic theme of imprisoned women R. Seaford, *JHS* 110 (1990), 76–90. Both 48 and 49 ironically evoke a different 'concealment' for Pasiphae: Minos puts her away when he should have concealed her disgrace as she tried herself to do (29–30 n.) and as the Chorus advised him (2–3 n.). [The noun κρυπτήριον is unattested, but the adj. describes a cave in an oracle quoted by Paus. 8.42.6.] **look . . . on the circle <*of the sun*>**: i.e. live, *Hec.* 412; cf. the ending of Antigone's light, Soph. *Ant.* 879.

51. [Text: the supplement of an adj. meaning 'hasty' is needed; cf. e.g. Soph. *OT* 616–7 'hasty thought is not safe', Theogn. 329 (JD).]

52. <*It is decided*>: cf. Pasiphae at 36, 'if you have decided'; used of a death sentence Soph. *Ant.* 576 (again comparable with *Cret.*: cf. 4–41 n., 46 n.), a sentence of exile *Bacc.* 1350; cf. 'it is fixed' *And.* 255, *Or.* 1330. **justice**: Minos pronounces his own but undergoes Poseidon's, 26.

988. The attribution is probable: Minos accuses Daedalus of assisting Pasiphae with the artificial cow. Later mythographers (Hygin. *Fab.* 40; Apollod. 3.1.4) describe a real cow's hide stretched by Daedalus on a wooden frame, and it is pictured so on vase paintings and a Roman sarcophagus (cf. Introd. p. 56). The fr. does not make construction from wood impossible, for Minos may have only the outward appearance in mind: cf. F 472e.17–18. **builder**: somewhat awkwardly translates τέκτων, primarily a constructor in wood, of buildings e.g. *Ion* 1129, *Or.* 1570, and esp. of wooden images e.g. *Alc.* 348. Daedalus was the supreme τέκτων of myth (Bacchyl. *Dithyr.* 26.6) and his moving images were legendary (see Collard on *Hec.* 836–40, to be supplemented from this n.). For the mythic meaning of 'deceitful' artificial animals see Frontisi-Ducroux 140.

STHENEBOEA

Texts, testimonia. P. Oxy. 2455 and P. Strasb. 2676 (Hypothesis = *TrGF* test. iia); *TrGF* F 661–671, ?adesp. 292; Mette Nos. 879–891.

Myth. Hom. *Il.* 6.155–202 and Schol., esp. (from Schol. A on 155) Asclepiades, *FGH* 12 F 13; Hes. *Theog.* 319–25 and frs. 43.81–91, 129.16–24; Hygin. *Astron.* 2.18.1 and *Fab.* 57; Apollod. 2.3; Roscher IV.1506–22; Preller-Robert II.1.179–85; R. Peppmüller, *WS* 75 (1962), 13–21; Papamichael, *Dodone* (below); Aélion (1986), 185–7; Gantz 311–6.

Illustrations. Séchan 494–502; Webster, *Monuments*[2] (1967), 80, 163f.; *Euripides* (1967) 301f.; Trendall–Webster III.3.43–6 (bibl.); J. Moret, *AntK* 15 (1972), 95–106; N. Yalouris, *Pegasus: The Art of the Legend* (Westerham, 1977[2]), xviii–xix, xxiv, Plates 44, 45, 58, 70 (main story) and 6, 47 (Chimaera); Schefold and Jung, *Urkönige* 115–27 with Plates 139–54 and (best bibl.) Notes 269–300. Chimaera: P. Boulter, *Hesperia* 33 (1969), 133–40; *LIMC* III (1986), 'Chimaira'. For the main story *LIMC* promises an entry under 'Pegasos'. See also under *Bellerophon*, p. 98.

Main discussions. Wilamowitz, *KS* I.274–81 (= *CPh* 3 [1908], 225–32); A .W. Pickard-Cambridge in Powell (ed.), *New Chapters* III.131–7; Schmid 391–3; Page, *GLP* 126–9; Pohlenz I.275–6, II.115; B. Zühlke, *Phil.* 105 (1961), 1–15, 198–225; K. Vysoky, *ZJKF* 5 (1963), 73–80 (German résumé in *BCO* 9 (1964), 175); D. Korzeniewski, *Phil.* 108 (1964), 45–65; Hourmouziades 152–3; Webster, *Euripides* (1967), 80–4; A. M. Braet, *AC* 42 (1973), 82–112 (fullest bibl.); E. M. Papamichael, *Dodone* 12 (1983), 45–75, cf. 139–52; Aélion (1986), 187–91, 195–6. See also W. Luppe's papers in Comm. on Hypothesis below.

A play of remarkable content and effects. Although the fragments are few, they include most of the Prologue speech, preserved in a Byzantine writer together with a complete narrative hypothesis (test. iia). The unsuccessful seduction of Bellerophon by Stheneboea leads to two plots against him by her husband, Proetus King of Tiryns, to whom she secretly accuses Bellerophon of attempted rape. The first plot fails when Bellerophon, in ignorance of the accusation, takes a sealed letter from Proetus to Stheneboea's father, Iobates King of Lycia, with orders for Bellerophon's death; Iobates commits him to what is hoped to be a fatal battle with the monstrous Chimaera; but Bellerophon kills it with the aid of the winged horse Pegasus. The second plot fails when Bellerophon, returning to Tiryns and somehow forewarned of it, himself deceives Stheneboea into elopement with him on Pegasus, only to throw her off into the sea to drown. Bellerophon returns to Tiryns for triumphant explanation to Proetus, who has been brought Stheneboea's body by fishermen. Two — or even three — revenge plots, then, with the would-be victim becoming victor; two time gaps in the action, with Bellerophon's two absences; demonstrative theatricality with at least one appearance of the winged horse.

Even with a complete Hypothesis, it remains difficult to articulate this busy drama into an episodic structure and to place most of the book fragments convincingly within it. A first problem is whether Bellerophon exited after his Prologue speech (F 661) and was not seen again until his return from the Chimaera: Webster 80, 82 argued this, positing that Proetus in a soliloquy before the choral Parodos tells both of Stheneboea's accusation and of the letter already taken away by Bellerophon (Braet 107ff. broadly agrees, cf. Aélion 189). Another view is that Bellerophon was still present in Epis. 1 for Stheneboea's nurse to pursue the seduction (Schmid 391; Zühlke 216f.) and for Proetus to give him the letter (but as late as Epis. 2, Papamichael 55f.). An extreme solution to this first problem — indeed its sidestepping — was proposed by Zühlke, anxious not to reconstruct a stage action with two or more revenge plots and two absences by Bellerophon, and with a double offence against the so-called 'unity of time': he suggested that the Chimaera episode happened *before* the play and that Bellerophon narrated it in a now missing part of his Prologue speech (Zühlke 4f., 198ff.; supported by Korzeniewski 45, but anticipated by G. Murray, *Euripides* [p. vii n.1], 343). Vysoky, Webster 81 and esp. Braet 85–107 have convincingly rejected this stratagem, but it is favoured by Jouan 195–6. A first exit by Bellerophon in Epis. 1 seems most likely, after a scenically effective encounter with Proetus, if not also with Stheneboea present herself, for this is the moment most frequently pictured by vase-painters (see below). As to 'time', Wilamowitz 280 first compared the fluent handling of interrupted 'literal' time in other plays, e.g. Aesch. *Ag.* 39/350/503/810. For remarks on the 'semblance of continuity of time', i.e. 'dramatic' time, see Taplin (1977), 290–3. Pohlenz I. 276 (cf. Braet 111) emphasizes how Bellerophon's possession of the winged horse makes his absences credibly 'shorter'. Re-entries by one character are naturally frequent, e.g. Jason at *Med.* 446, 866, 1293; after a long 'literal' interval e.g. Theseus at *Supp.* 597/838 (then 1165). As to doubled intrigues and plots, cf. e.g. *And.*, and for Euripides' use of a letter *Hipp.*, *IT* and *IA.*

F 663–5 are usually given to the Nurse, but for each of these frs. it must remain uncertain whether she is generalising to the Chorus, arguing with Bellerophon, or encouraging Stheneboea — and when: either before Bellerophon first goes off (most scholars, e.g. Webster 80, 82) or after (Papamichael).

F 667 cannot be confidently located but seems to be Bellerophon's accusation of his treacherous host Proetus: see the Comm.

F 665a and 668 came probably from Bellerophon's own account of the Chimaera fight after his return (Epis. 2 or 3), 669 from his scene persuading Stheneboea to fly away with him (Hypoth. 12–13): this must be towards the end, in Epis. 3 or 4, before the Messenger's report of her death (F 670) in Epis. 4 or 5. These fragments do not help at all to clarify how Bellerophon learned of Proetus's second plot (Hypoth. 13–14), whether it was before or after he formed his own. The Hypothesis says that Bellerophon was told 'by him', i.e. Proetus, but that is nonsense. Rabe emended to 'by someone', which has found favour (not necessarily a stage character, and certainly not the Chorus if they were Tirynthian women naturally sympathetic to their queen: compare Phaedra, Nurse and Chorus in *Hipp.*). Wilamowitz emended to 'by her' — which is wrong if Hypoth. 19–20 is correct with 'Bellerophon twice the subject of plots by both (i.e. Proetus and Stheneboea)', but possible if Stheneboea had kept her passion for Bellerophon despite his rejection, or was remorseful and responded to his pretended seduction; it is very possibly right if Luppe's change of 19–20 is accepted (as here), to 'twice the subject of plots, he had exacted. . . penalty from both.'

Earlier scholars asked what Bellerophon does between killing Stheneboea and returning, and imported F 305 from *Bell.*, supposing it to recount his acquittal of her murder before a court at Argos, in a trial like that at *Or.* 866ff. (where the Scholia adduce the fragment). Such a detail is no more missed, or necessary, than e.g. Medea's actions between killing her children (*Med.* 1282, off-stage) and returning in the sky chariot (1317).

The last fragment, 671, is almost certainly part of Proetus's sad disillusion with his wife, when Bellerophon explains her whole story in the Exodos.

Other ascriptions. The inclusion of adesp. F 292 (a greeting to the King of Tiryns; assigned by Hartung) is a fair possibility. If F 666 belongs to this play and not *Bell.* (the latter, Stob.; Wilamowitz 277, Zühlke 244), Bellerophon is reproving either the Nurse (before he 'seduces' Stheneboea, Webster 83) or Stheneboea (Papamichael 62f.). Generally rejected are F 305 (above) and adesp. F 60 (= Ar. *Peace* 140, fear that someone may fall into the sea, referred loosely by Schol. 141b to the flight of Icarus in *Cretans* [see p. 56] or to Stheneboea's anxiety). Van Leeuwen and Henderson in their Commentaries on Ar. *Lys.* 865–9, a paratragic description of a cheerless house when its wife has left, have suggested that those lines may be modelled on Proetus's despair after Stheneboea has gone; the nearby 856–7 may reflect our play too: see Comm. on F 664.

Illustrations. About a dozen vase-paintings, most from S. Italy and the century or so after the play's composition, show Proetus giving the letter to Bellerophon But they vary in the number, behaviour and placing of these and other characters, Stheneboea, Nurse – and Pegasus. Some show simply Bellerophon with Pegasus leaving Proetus. J. Moret, *AntK* 15 (1972), 95–106 is extremely sceptical of their dependence on Euripides' play; see also J. R. Green, *Lustrum* 31 (1991), 56; above, General Introd. I.(iv). For a time one much discussed fragment (Würzburg M. 4696 + 4710; about 350 B.C.) was held to combine in one narrative

scene Bellerophon's first return, with Stheneboea and Nurse listening in door-
ways, and his final return, with Proetus raging helplessly against him like Jason
against Medea aloft at the end of her name-play: see Webster, *Euripides* 84;
Trendall-Webster III.3.43; but recent opinion sees in the figure of Bellerophon
on Pegasus only a decorative function, as the ornamental akroterion of a stage
building, and refers the main scene perhaps to Jason and Pelias in *Peliades*:
H. Bulle, cf. E. Simon, *The Ancient Theatre* (London, 1982), 24; S. Hiller,
AuA 19 (1973), 84; Schefold on Pl. 141. For *Sthen.* the paintings are chiefly an
important spur to our own imagination (salutary caution by Aélion 188–9).

There are pictures and sculpture of the off-stage incidents, Bellerophon
fighting the Chimaera (Boulter; *LIMC*) and (vase-paintings only) throwing
Stheneboea from Pegasus (e.g. Schefold Pl. 149).

Myth. Euripides derives the attempted seduction, letter and Chimaera fight from
Iliad 6 (which however does not include Pegasus); this is the only surviving
extensive account earlier than the play. Stheneboea is called Anteia there, and
still in Hygin. *Astron.* (but not in *Fab.*); but she has her name in Hesiod. Later
mythographers (e.g. Hyginus, but only in *Fab.*) wrote of Stheneboea's suicide
from shame, perhaps influenced by the powerful Phaedra-Hippolytus story.
Euripides either innovated with her murder by Bellerophon (known to us only
from the Hypothesis) or used an otherwise lost variant version; Hygin. *Astron.*
has a variant with Bellerophon fleeing before he is incriminated.

Staging. The winged horse seems to have made more impact in *Bell.* (see pp. 98,
101), but in *Sthen.* it may have appeared twice. Proetus's secret hope for
Bellerophon's death might be more credible if he did not yet possess the horse,
although Hygin. *Astron.* says he sent him to Iobates 'because he knew he had
the horse' (Hes. fr. 43.82 and Pind. *Ol.* 13.65ff. do not say when the gods gave
it to him, but their gift would fit their wish to save an innocent from the
Chimaera; cf. *Il.* 6.171). F 665a has been taken by some to show that Pegasus
was visible at Bellerophon's first return, and all agree that Bellerophon at the
play's end used him, acting half like a 'god from the machine'. It is probable
that Euripides would not weaken the final effect by using the 'machine'
beforehand, so that for any first appearance either a real horse with artificial
wings is suggested, led in and out (Wilamowitz 278, Pickard-Cambridge 137), or
perhaps a riderless horse symbolically on the 'machine' (Hourmouziades 152f.)
with the full effect reserved for the end, or even Pegasus off-stage with
Bellerophon's words 'Pegasus here' accompanying a gesture: see H.-J. Newiger,
WJA 16 (1990), 37 n. 22 and Comm. on F 665a. The vase-paintings are no
guide, for Pegasus appears in them largely as an iconographic pointer: see above
on the Würzburg fragment.

Themes and characters. Stheneboea in her sinful and then vindictive passion is recognisable in the character type of Phaedra in *Hippolytus* (Ar. *Frogs* 1044 couples them): this is the 'Potiphar's wife' motif, widespread in many cultures: the Phoenix story (Eur. F 803a–818) from Hom. *Il.* 9.448; the Peleus story (F 617–24) cf. Apollod. 3.13.12–13; Peppmüller 13–21 (Asiatic background to the Bellerophon story; cf. White, cited p. 98); Papamichael 139–52; Jouan 187–91, 206–8; Thompson, *Motif Index* IV.474, V.386. Similarly Bellerophon is in the style of the handsome but chaste youth, often a visitor (F 661.7; cf. Peleus again) or an 'outdoor type' (Hippolytus, cf. Melanion at Ar. *Lys.* 781–92), who unwittingly brings disaster to a man's household: F 661.31, cf. 19ff.; Bellerophon as a refugee murderer purified by his host Proetus (F 661.16–18) is like Peleus purified by Acastus, or Adrastus purified by Croesus (Hdt. 1.34–45). Hippolytus is chaste – asexual, indeed – devotional and plotted against; Aphrodite dooms him, but his obstinate integrity makes him seem self-destructive. Bellerophon here is chaste, controlling his sexuality but not denying it (F 661. 19–25; this difference from Hippolytus is stressed by Jouan 195); he is plotted against but retaliatory: clearly Euripides is widening the human range of this familiar theme. A Nurse is often the sexual intermediary in these plays (F 661. 11): cf. *Hippolytus* again, 490ff. (see e.g. Jouan 197); *Cretans*, pp. 55, 56; Sen. *Ph.* 271–3.

The fullness and theatricality of *Sthen.* suggest that Euripides had less room to examine the psychologies of Stheneboea and Bellerophon than of Phaedra and Hippolytus (*pace* Aélion 191), and that *Sthen.* was an exciting if intensely human play while the surviving Hippolytus play at least was more deliberately tragic. The same question arises about the portrayal of Pasiphae in *Cret.*: see p. 57. What we have of Bellerophon's Prologue gives no hint of his later capacity for vengeance, despite a previous killing (F 661.17), but Hippolytus's self-destruction is entirely credible after his brief first appearance.

Date. There is a reference to Stheneboea the wife of Proetus (but as king of Corinth, not Tiryns) in the fragmentary commentary on Eupolis's *Prospaltioi* of 429 B.C. (*PCG* fr. 259.126; P. Oxy. 2813). If the allusion is to Euripides' play, it gives a fixed point considerably earlier than the parodies of F 663 and 665 in Ar. *Wasps* of 422. The play is one of many about 'bad' or 'unhappy' women located as a thematic type before about 425 (Webster 31, 86). Its metrical practice puts it loosely in the period before 420 (Cropp–Fick 22, 70, 91). The similarities between Stheneboea and Phaedra, and of the prologue style to *Medea* of 431, also point to composition near our (revised) *Hippolytus* of 428 (see e.g. Zühlke 198f.).

Other dramatisations; influence. See also on *Bell.* below. The Stheneboea story was almost certainly not treated in Sophocles' *Iobates*, of which only a couple of lines survive (F 297–9); only the title is known of Astydamas the Younger's 4th C. *Bellerophon* (*TrGF* I 60 F 1g.). No Roman derivatives are known Later literature and art: *OGCMA* I.274–6.

ΣΘΕΝΕΒΟΙΑ

test. iia Hypothesis

... ἐν Σθενεβοίαι τῶι δράματι ... ἔστι δὲ ἡ ὑπόθεσις αὕτη. Προῖτος Ἄβαντος μὲν ἦν υἱός, Ἀκρισίου δὲ ἀδελφός, βασιλεὺς δὲ Τίρυνθος. Σθενεβοίαν δὲ γήμας ἐξ αὐτῆς ἐγέννησε παῖδας. Βελλεροφόντην δὲ φεύγοντα ἐκ Κορίνθου διὰ φόνον αὐτὸς μὲν ἥγνισε τοῦ μύσους, ἡ γυνὴ δὲ αὐτοῦ τὸν ξένον ἠγάπησε. τυχεῖν 5 δὲ οὐ δυναμένη τῶν ἐπιθυμηθέντων διέβαλεν ὡς ἐπιθέμενον ἑαυτῆι τὸν Βελλεροφόντην· πιστεύσας δὲ ἐκείνηι ὁ Προῖτος αὐτὸν εἰς Καρίαν ἐξέπεμψεν, ἵνα ἀπόληται· δέλτον γὰρ αὐτῶι δοὺς ἐκέλευσε πρὸς Ἰοβάτην διακομίζειν. ὁ δὲ τοῖς γεγραμ-μένοις ἀκόλουθα πράττων προσέταξεν αὐτῶι διακινδυνεῦσαι 10 πρὸς τὴν Χίμαιραν. ὁ δὲ ἀγωνισάμενος τὸ θηρίον ἀνεῖλε. πάλιν δὲ ἐπιστρέψας εἰς τὴν Τίρυνθα τὸν ⟨μὲν⟩ Προῖτον κατεμέμψα-το, ἀνέσεισε δὲ τὴν Σθενεβοίαν ὡς ⟨εἰς⟩ τὴν Καρίαν ἀπάξων. μαθὼν δὲ παρά του ἐκ Προίτου δευτέραν ἐπιβουλὴν φθάσας ἀνεχώρησεν. ἀναθέμενος δὲ ἐπὶ τὸν Πήγασον τὴν Σθενεβοίαν 15 μετέωρος ἐπὶ τὴν θάλασσαν ἤρθη· γενόμενος δὲ κατὰ Μῆλον τὴν νῆσον ἐκείνην ἀπέρριψεν· ταύτην μὲν οὖν ἀποθανοῦσαν ἁλιεῖς ἀναλαβόντες διεκόμισαν εἰς τὴν Τίρυνθα. πάλιν δὲ ἐπιστρέψας ὁ Βελλεροφόντης πρὸς τὸν Προῖτον αὐτὸς ὡμολόγησε πεπραχέναι ταῦτα· δὶς γὰρ ἐπιβουλευθείς, παρ' ἀμφοτέρων 20 δίκην εἰληφέναι τὴν πρέπουσαν, τῆς μὲν εἰς τὸ ζῆν, τοῦ δὲ εἰς τὸ λυπεῖσθαι.

test. iia Hypothesis (880a,b M) Ioannes Logothetes, *Comm.* on Hermogenes Περὶ μεθόδου δεινότητος 30 p. 447.14ff. Rabe, first publ. by H. Rabe, *RhM* 63 (1908), 146–7, mutilated in Gregory of Corinth, *Comm* . . . *Rhet. Gr.* 7.1321 Walz (whence Nauck² p. 567f.); frs. of 2 Προῖτος—8 Καρίαν and 16 κατὰ Μῆλον—22 in P. Oxy. 2455 frs. 5 and 6 (2ⁿᵈ C. A.D.) ed. Turner (1962) and scraps of 11–13 in frs. 24 and 95 acc. to W. Luppe, *ZPE* 49 (1982), 19–20, *Wiss. Z. Halle* 34.1 (1985), 99–102; scraps of 1–4 φεύγοντα in P. Strasb. 2676 fr. Bd (2ⁿᵈ C. A.D.), ed. Schwartz, *ZPE* 4 (1967), 44 acc. to W. Luppe, *ZPE* 55 (1984), 7–8. The word-order of P. Oxy. is preferred here, where determinable.   2 Ἄβαντος Nauck Ἀβάντου prob. P. Oxy. μὲν ἦν υἱός P. Oxy. Πρ. ἦν Ἀκάμαντος υἱός Ioann.   4 αὐτὸς Wilamowitz, Luppe (1985) αὐτὸν Ioann. [P. Oxy.]

STHENEBOEA

test. iia Hypothesis

. . . in his play *Stheneboea* . . . Its plot is this: Proetus was the son of Abas and brother of Acrisius, and king of Tiryns. He married Stheneboea and got children by her. When Bellerophon came in refuge from Corinth because of a murder, Proetus purified him of his pollution but his wife fell in love with their guest. Unable[5] to achieve her desires she traduced Bellerophon as having assaulted her. Proetus believed her and sent him away to Caria, to be killed: he gave him a letter and told him to take it to Iobates, who acted in accordance with what was written and ordered Bellerophon to risk his life[10] against the Chimaera; but he fought the beast and destroyed it. Returning to Tiryns he held Proetus to blame but excited Stheneboea with the pretence that he would take her off <to> Caria. Told by someone of a second plot from Proetus, he anticipated it by going away. He put Stheneboea up on Pegasus[15] and flew high in the air towards the sea. When he was near the island of Melos he threw her off. Fishermen recovered her after her death and brought her to Tiryns. Returning once more to Proetus Bellerophon confessed that he had done these things himself: since he had twice been the subject of plots,[20] he had exacted the appropriate penalty from both of them, her life from her and his misery from him.

6 ἐπιθυμηθέντων Ioann. ms. L., Greg. and prob. P. Oxy.   ἐπιθυμημάτων Ioann. ms. V
7 Βελλεροφόντην P. Oxy. Κορίνθιον Ioann.   πιστ[εύσας δὲ ἐκείνηι prob. P. Oxy. πεισθεὶς δὲ ὁ Πρ. Ioann.   9 γράμμασιν Greg.   12 ὑποστρέψας Greg. (also 18)   ⟨μὲν⟩ J. Diggle, *ZPE* 77 (1989), 6 = *Euripidea* 334   13 ⟨εἰς⟩ Wilamowitz   14 παρά του Rabe παρ᾽ αὐτοῦ Ioann. παρ᾽ αὐτῆς Wilamowitz [P. Oxy. and Greg.]   16 γενόμενος-18 Τίρυνθα Ioann., mutilated Greg.; P. Oxy. has only part-words and differing order   17 ἐκεί]νην P. Oxy. ταύτην Ioann. ταύτην Diggle (above) αὐτὴν Ioann. [P. Oxy.]   20 ἐπιβουλευθείς, παρ᾽ ἀμφοτέρων Luppe, *ZPE* 75 (1988), 49–50 ἐπιβουλευθεὶς ὑπ᾽ ἀμφοτέρων, Ioann. [P. Oxy.]

661   *from the Prologue speech:*

ΒΕΛΛΕΡΟΦΟΝΤΗΣ
οὐκ ἔστιν ὅστις πάντ' ἀνὴρ εὐδαιμονεῖ.
ἢ γὰρ πεφυκὼς ἐσθλὸς οὐκ ἔχει βίον,
ἢ δυσγενὴς ὢν πλουσίαν ἀροῖ πλάκα.
πολλοὺς δὲ πλούτωι καὶ γένει γαυρουμένους
γυνὴ κατήισχυν' ἐν δόμοισι νηπία.   5
τοιᾶιδε Προῖτος ⟨γῆς⟩ ἄναξ νόσωι νοσεῖ·
ξένον γὰρ ἱκέτην τῆσδ' ἔμ' ἐλθόντα στέγης   7
⟨   ⟩   7a
λόγοισι πείθει καὶ δόλωι θηρεύεται
κρυφαῖον εὐνῆς εἰς ὁμιλίαν πεσεῖν.
ἀεὶ γὰρ ἥπερ τῶιδ' ἐφέστηκεν λόγωι   10
τροφὸς γεραιὰ καὶ ξυνίστησιν λέχος,
ὑμνεῖ τὸν αὐτὸν μῦθον· '᾽Ω κακῶς φρονῶν,
πιθοῦ· τί μαίνηι; τλῆθι δεσποίνης ἐμῆς   13
⟨   ⟩   13a
κτήσηι δ' ἄνακτος δώμαθ' ἐν πεισθεὶς βραχύ.'
ἐγὼ δὲ θεσμοὺς Ζῆνά θ' ἱκέσιον σέβων   15
Προῖτόν τε τιμῶν, ὅς μ' ἐδέξατ' εἰς δόμους
λιπόντα γαῖαν Σισύφου φόνον τ' ἐμῆς
ἔνιψε χειρὸς αἷμ' ἐπισφάξας νέον,
οὐπώποτ' ἠθέλησα δέξασθαι λόγους,
οὐδ' εἰς νοσοῦντας ὑβρίσαι δόμους ξένος,   20
μισῶν ἔρωτα δεινόν, ὃς φθείρει βροτούς.
διπλοῖ γὰρ εἴσ' ἔρωτες ἔντροφοι χθονί·
ὁ μὲν γεγὼς ἔχθιστος εἰς Ἅιδην φέρει,
ὁ δ' εἰς τὸ σῶφρον ἐπ' ἀρετήν τ' ἄγων ἔρως
ζηλωτὸς ἀνθρώποισιν, ὧν εἴην ἐγώ.   25
†οὐκοῦν νομίζω καὶ θανεῖν γε σωφρονῶν.†
ἀλλ' εἰς ἀγρὸν γὰρ ἐξιὼν βουλεύσομαι·
οὐ γάρ με λύει τοῖσδ' ἐφημένον δόμοις

---

661 (880a, f–s M) Ioann. prefaces the Hypothesis (above) with a citation of lines 24–5
(= 672 N/880r, s M), stating that Eur. has those words in his *Sthen*. 'when he brings on Bell.
moralising'; then after the Hypoth. he has 'at any rate Bell. is brought on soliloquising (lines 1–31)'
1–3 = 661 N/880e²–p M (from Ar. *Frogs* 1217–9 and Schol. V Dindorf). 1 is given by P. Oxy.
2455 (Hypothesis above) and much cited or imitated, e.g. Menand. *Aspis* 407   4–5 = **662 N**/
880q M (from Stob. 4.22b.46)   4 γαυρουμένους Stob. τιμωμένους Ioann.   6 ⟨γῆς⟩ Buecheler
7 ἔμ' ἐλθόντα von Arnim ἐπελθόντα Ioann.   7a one line missing (after 6, Zühlke) or order

661 *from the Prologue speech:*

Bellerophon. There is no man who is completely fortunate: either he is well-born but lacks a living, or he is of low birth but ploughs rich acres. Many men proud of their wealth and birth are brought disgrace by a foolish wife in their home.[5] Such is the affliction of Proetus, <*the land's*> king; for when I came under his roof here as guest and suppliant < *Stheneboea*> uses guileful persuasion in pursuing me, to make me fall to joining her secretly in her bed. Her old nurse who is charged with this talk[10] and shares the attempt at our union, is always reciting the same story: 'You fool, be persuaded! Why this madness? Have the courage < > my mistress's < >: you'll get the king's palace if you are persuaded in this one small thing!' I have reverence however for Zeus the god of suppliants and his laws,[15] and honour for Proetus who received me in his house after I left Sisyphus's land, and who cleansed bloodshed from my hands with a sacrifice of fresh blood over them; I have never yet been willing to entertain that talk of hers, nor to violate a troubled household while I am its guest,[20] from my hatred of the dangerous love which destroys people. For there are two kinds of love native on earth: one is our worst enemy and leads to death, while the other, which tends to self-restraint and virtue, is the love coveted by men among whom I wish to belong myself.[25] †So I consider even death if I may keep my self-restraint(?)† Now I will go out into the country and deliberate. It is no good to me to sit here at this house and be loudly abused

7, 8, 11, 10, 12, 13, 9 Rabe; 7a contained the names of Bell. and Sthen. according to Korzeniewski   11 λόχον W. Luppe, *RhM* 133 (1990), 186–7; cf. on 13a   12–13 φρονῶν πιθοῦ Wilamowitz φρενῶν πείθει Ioann.   13a one line missing, Korzeniewski: M. Gronewald, *RhM* 131 (1988), 189–90 inserted F 889/No. 178 M πεσεῖν ἐς εὐνὴν καὶ γαμήλιον λέχος   14 κτήσηι Rabe κτῆσαι Ioann.   δώμαθ' ἐν πεισθεὶς Wilamowitz δῶμα πεισθείς τι Ioann.   15 θεσμοὺς Rabe θεοὺς Ioann.   17–18 φόνον τ' ἐμῆς ἔνιψε χειρὸς von Arnim and Wilamowitz φόνων τ' ἐμὰς ἔνιψε χεῖρας Ioann.   20 νοσοῦντας Brinkmann νοσοῦντος Ioann.   22 διπλοῖ γὰρ εἴσ' ἔρωτες ἔντροφοι Mekler διπλοῖ γὰρ ἔρωτες ἐν(σ)τρέφονται Ioann. ἐνστρέφουσ' ἔρωτες ⟨ἐν⟩ χθονί W. Luppe, *Phil.* 137 (1993), 139–42   22–23 del. Wilamowitz   24–5 = **672** N/ 880r, s M (from Aeschines 1.151; Stob. 1.9.2)   26 καὶ θανεῖν γε σωφρονῶν del. Wilamowitz; several lines missing after 26, Korzeniewski   27 ἐξιὼν βουλεύσομαι Wilamowitz and M. L. West, *BICS* 30 (1983), 76 ἐξιέναι βουλήσομαι Ioann.

κακορροθεῖσθαι μὴ θέλοντ᾽ εἶναι κακόν,
οὐδ᾽ αὖ κατειπεῖν καὶ γυναικὶ προσβαλεῖν   30
κηλῖδα Προίτου καὶ διασπάσαι δόμον ...

662 N   = F 661.4–5 above

663   ποιητὴν ἄρα
Ἔρως διδάσκει, κἂν ἄμουσος ἦι τὸ πρίν.

664   πεσὸν δέ νιν λέληθεν οὐδὲν ἐκ χερός,
ἀλλ᾽ εὐθὺς αὐδᾶι ᾽Τῶι Κορινθίωι ξένωι᾽.

665   τοιαῦτ᾽ ἀλύει· νουθετούμενος δ᾽ ἔρως
μᾶλλον πιέζει.

665a   (Βε.) παίω Χιμαίρας εἰς σφαγάς, πυρὸς δ᾽ ἀθὴρ
βάλλει με καὶ τοῦδ᾽ αἰθαλοῖ πυκνὸν πτέρον.

*666   ὦ παγκακίστη καὶ γυνή· τί γὰρ λέγων
μεῖζόν σε τοῦδ᾽ ὄνειδος ἐξείποι τις ἄν;

667   τίς ἄνδρα τιμᾶι ξεναπάτην;

668   ἄνευ τύχης γάρ, ὥσπερ ἡ παροιμία,
πόνος μονωθεὶς οὐκέτ᾽ †ἀλγύνει† βροτούς.

663 (882 M) 2b Ar. *Wasps* 1074 and, attrib. Eur. *Sthen.*, Schol. 1074a; 1–2 Plut. *Mor.* 762b, attrib. Eur., cf. *Mor.* 405f, 622c; there are other citations, adaptations and allusions: 2 is imitated by Menand. *Carthag.* fr. 7 Sandbach (= fr. 229 Koerte²), perhaps conflated with Eur. *Tel.* F 715.2. 1 ποιητὴν most witnesses μουσικήν Plut. 622c; other witnesses have variations acc. to context ⟨δ᾽⟩ ἄρα Nauck.   **664** (883 M) Athenaeus 10.30, 427e, ᾽Eur. says of Sthen. when she believes Bell. dead...᾽ 2b appears in Ar. *Thesm.* 404 attrib. to Eur. *Sthen.* by Schol. and in the same context as Athenaeus at Hesych. K 3629 Latte (Κορίνθιος ξένος), also attrib.; Cratinus *PCG* fr. 299.4 has an obscene travesty.   **665** (884 M) Ar. *Wasps* 111–2, attrib. Eur. *Sthen.* by Schol. 111; Plut. *Mor.* 71a, attrib. Eur.; Galen, *Opinions...Hippocr. etc.* 4.6.30 de Lacy, unattrib. 1–2 δ᾽ ἔρως ... πιέζει Plut., Galen δ᾽ ἀεὶ ... δικάζει Ar. (altered for context)   **665a** (885 M) Photius, *Lexicon* A 475 Theodoridis (ἀθήρ), attrib. Eur. *Sthen.*; A 469 where ἀθήρ) omits the fr. 1 (Βε.) Wilamowitz, *KS* IV.529 Χίμαιραν Wilamowitz   2 αἰθαλοῖ Wilamowitz - ἦ Photius   **666** (886 M) Stob. 4.22.168, attrib. Eur. *Bell.* (also = No. 382 M); attrib. *Sthen.* Meineke 1 καὶ] δὴ Blaydes   **667** (887 M) Photius, *Lexicon* I.455.8 Naber (ξεναπάτης) (= Antiatticist,

for refusing to do wrong; nor, furthermore, to denounce Proetus's
wife and bring[30] a stain on her, and tear this household apart . . .

662 N   = F 661.4–5 above

663   A poet in fact is taught by Love, even if he has no skill
                  before.

                  Probably the Nurse explaining Love's urgency.

664   Nothing fallen from a hand but she notices it and immed-
                  iately says 'To our guest from Corinth!'

                  *The sympathetic Nurse relates – to the Chorus? to Bellero-
                  phon at his first return? – Stheneboea's wishful gesture
                  towards the would-be lover she believes dead.*

665   Such is her frenzy; but when love is reproved, it is the more
                  oppressive.

                  Again the Nurse, perhaps to Bellerophon; possibly before F 664.

665a (*Bell.*) I strike into the Chimaera's throat, and a pointed flame
                  hits me and scorches the thick-plumed wing of Pegasus here.

                  *Bellerophon narrates his victory, perhaps to the Nurse (cf. F
                  666) or Proetus.*

*666   Utterly vile, and a woman! What word of greater reproach
                  for you could one voice than this?

                  If from this play, Bellerophon accusing (probably) the Nurse.

667   Who honours a man who deceives his guest?

                  *If the fr. comes this late in the play, Bellerophon accuses
                  Proetus – but to his face, or to someone else?*

668   Without luck, as the proverb goes, work on its own no
                  longer †distresses† men.

                  Context unknowable without further evidence.

Anecd. Gr. I.109.30 Bekker), attrib. Eur. *Sthen.*; Pollux 3.58 Bethe, attrib. Eur.   **668** (888 M)
Stob. 3.29.36, attrib. Eur. *Sthen.*   1 ἂν (? ἦν) εὐτυχῆις Badham   1–2 ἦν εὐτυχῆι . . .
πονηθεὶς Vitelli   2 ἀλδαίνει Musgrave

669 (?) πέλας δὲ ταύτης δεινὸς ἵδρυται Κράγος
ἔνθηρος, ἧι ληισταῖρσι φρουρεῖται ⟨πόρος⟩
κλύδωνι δεινῶι καὶ βαρυστόνωι βρέμων.
(Βε.) πτηνὸς πορεύσει…

670 βίος δὲ πορφυρέως θαλάσσιος
οὐκ εὐτράπεζος, ἀλλ' ἐπάκτιοι φάτναι.
ὑγρὰ δὲ μήτηρ, οὐ πεδοστιβὴς τροφὸς
θάλασσα· τήνδ' ἀροῦμεν, ἐκ ταύτης βίος
βρόχοισι καὶ πέδαισιν οἴκαδ' ἔρχεται.

671 κομίζετ' εἴσω τήνδε· πιστεύειν δὲ χρὴ
γυναικὶ μηδὲν ὅστις εὖ φρονεῖ βροτῶν.

672 N = F 661.24–5 above

669 (889 M) 4 = Ar. *Peace* 126, attrib. Eur. *Sthen.* by Schol. 126a citing 1–4; but Schol. also has 'some think 126 parodied from *Bell.*': cf. Comm. on *Bell.* F 306.   1–3 and 4 given to different voices by von Arnim   1 Κράγος Meineke κράτος written compendiously Schol.   2 ἧι ληιστ- ῆρσι Meineke ἢ ληστῆς Schol.   ⟨πόρος⟩ Meineke   3 βαρυστόνωι Dindorf βροτοστόνωι Schol.   βρέμων Meineke -ει Schol.   4 πτηνὸς πορεύσει πῶλος· οὐ ναυσθλώσομαι Ar. ('The winged horse shall carry me; I will not go by ship.')   670 (890 M) Athenaeus 10.18, 421f

,

Commentary on *Stheneboea*

test. iia Hypothesis. This text, like the Hypotheses to *Wise Melanippe* (p. 248 below) and *Pirithous* (*TrGF* I 43 [Critias] F 1) is known to us from the 11th C. A.D. Byzantine commentator Ioannes Logothetes and the derivative 12th C. Gregory of Corinth. For its provenance see General Introd. I.(ii).

2 . Son of Abas: for Proetus's ancestry and power at Tiryns (or Argos: *Il.* 6.159) see Apollod. 2.2.1, cf. Paus. 2.16.2, 25.7.

3 . children by her: three daughters, Hes. fr. 129.16–24; a son too, Apollod. 2.2.2. A numeral is perhaps lost from Ioann. (Cropp); cf. Wilamowitz on *HF* Hypoth. 2. The detail suggests the security of Stheneboea's marriage, which she imperils, cf. below on F 661.5.

4 . because of a murder: at F 661.17 Bellerophon does not say whose, but Apollod. 2.3.1 names his brother; Schol. *Il.* 6. 155 (Asclepiades) records that he is named Bellerophon because he killed a man 'Belleros'; *-phontes* in his Greek

669 *(?)* Near it is situated dreadful Cragus, full of beasts, where <*the passage*> is watched by robbers, roaring with dreadful waves and their deep groan.

(Bell.) The winged . . . shall carry . . .

Stheneboea protesting at the danger if she goes with Bellerophon?

670 A purple-fisher's living from the sea is not luxurious; his table is on the shore. The sea is a watery mother, no nurse where feet may walk; she is our ploughland, from her our living comes home by means of lines and traps.

A fisherman as 'messenger' reports the recovery of Stheneboea's body: see Hypothesis 17f.

671 Carry her inside. A sensible man should not put any trust in a woman.

Proetus at play-end orders the removal off-stage of his dead wife.

672 N = *F 661.24–5 above*

attrib. Eur. *Sthen.*; line 1 only Phryn. *Soph. Prep.* p. 53.4 von Borries, unattrib.   1 πορφυρέως Lobeck -οῦς Athen. [Phryn.] -εὺς Hermann   **671** (891 M) Stob. 4.28.6, attrib. Eur. *Sthen.*

name = 'killer'. J. A. White, *AJP* 103 (1987), 120ff., discusses more recent etymologies, himself linking 'Bell.-' with Eastern Baal, Greek Βῆλος 'Lord, Master'. Short-term exile was normal in classical Athens for involuntary homicides: see Parker, *Miasma* 114–8 and (more widespread in myth) 376–92. One-year exile for Apollo in *Alc.* 1–7, Theseus in *Hipp.* 34–7, Aeolus in *Mel.S.* Hypoth. 5.

5 . fell in love: *Il.* 6.160ff., Hygin. *Astron.* 2.18.1 (Anteia); Apollod. 2.3.1; etc.

8, 13. Caria: if Ioann. reflects Eur.'s own nomenclature, Eur. subsumed the mythical Lycia under it as in the loose grouping of S.W. Asia Minor mainland cities recorded as 'Caria' in the Athenian tribute lists until 438 B.C.: see commentators on Thuc. 2.9.4.   **letter etc.:** lit. 'tablet', folded and sealed: *Hipp.* 864, *IA* 155. The story at *Il.* 6.168f. is the earliest Greek literary reference to written communication; for its likely nature see Kirk's *Commentary*.

9 . Iobates: Stheneboea's father, cf. *Il.* 6.170.

11. Chimaera: *Il.* 6.180ff. describes it as 'a lion in front, a snake behind, a ram in the middle, breathing fire'; Hes. *Theog.* 320f. gives it the heads of the three animals; artistic representations vary. The fight is described at Hes. *Theog.* 319–25, (with other feats) *Il.* 6. 179ff., Pind. *Ol.* 13.70ff. See also Cropp on *El.* 474.

13. excited: ἀνασείειν usually describes physical shaking (e.g. hair, *Bacc.* 240, 930) or brandishing, but in Hellenistic Greek it becomes 'excite, stir up'. The manner of deceiving Stheneboea is reported also by Schol. Ar. *Peace* 140.

13–14. told by someone: the textual problem is discussed above, p. 81.

16. Melos: if this is the island lying about 160 km. S.W. of Tiryns, Eur.'s geography for once strains credulity: only local fishermen (F 670) would know to bring the body to Tiryns. The geographical problem might be explained by some aetiological connection between the island and the myth now lost to us.

19–20. twice . . . the subject of plots: both meaning and rhetorical balance support Luppe's conjecture (discussed above, p. 81).

661. Style and content, and the citation of line 1 in P. Oxy. 2455 immediately after the text of the Hypothesis, show that this is the Prologue speech, but it is incomplete. After 7 we miss the name of Stheneboea and perhaps of Bellerophon, in perhaps more than the one line desiderated by Korzeniewski; and after 13 we miss a little of the detail, how Bellerophon is to take up her advances (Rabe's rearrangement of the lines does not meet the first lack; Gronewald would supply the second, but with an unlikely repetition of 9 and 11 'union', by importing fr. 889 '*<to fall into>* **my mistress's** *<bed and marriage couch>*': then Luppe replaces 11 'at our union' with 'to ambush me'). Either 26 is corrupt or at least one line is missing after it to complete its sense, perhaps both. Korzeniewski 50–61 regards as many as 13 lines as missing in his wholesale reconstruction of the speech; both he and Zühlke usefully observe that the speech in Ioann. is well short of the average Euripidean prologue of well over 40 lines. A concluding indication of what evasive action Bellerophon may deliberate (compare e.g. Hippolytus, *Hipp.* 108–13) and an exit line perhaps anticipating someone's imminent entry (frequent, like *Hipp.* 51ff., *Hec.* 52ff.) are almost certainly missing.

The Prologue typically gives the audience the necessary background: the speaker's circumstance 4–20, 27–31 and reaction 15–26, his identity 7–7a, 16–18 and the mise-en-scène 6–7, 28. Its consistent moral tone is untypical of a prologue speech and develops from the opening aphorism like *Hcld.* 1–5 and *Or.* 1–3.

1–5. Lines 2–3 offer two mutually exclusive examples of the truth of 1; 4 reconciles them, but 5 immediately qualifies them with a particular example of the play's starting point, adultery.

1. No man . . . fortunate: a tragic cliché, *Supp.* 170, *Alex.* F 45, *Auge* F 273.3, cf. Solon to Croesus, Hdt. 1.32.4–5.

2–3. The relationship between birth, wealth, poverty and morality is one of Eur.'s constant preoccupations, thematic e.g. in *El.*, 37f., 253, 367–76 etc.; cf. e.g. *Arch.* F 249, *And.* 766ff. and in *Bell.* F 285.3–18.

5 . foolish: i.e. promiscuous, the connotation as *Hipp*. 398, 644, *Tro*. 989–91; such a wife destroys a house's stability *Dictys* F 340, *And*. 672ff., cf. *And*. 192ff.

6 . the land's: Tiryns, Hypoth. 2 etc.: between Argos and Nauplion, about 50 km. south of Corinth (17) by road.   **affliction:** lit. 'disease', metaphorical as often, e.g. 20, and thematic both literally and figuratively in e.g. *Hipp*. (Phaedra) and *Cret*. (Pasiphae), as perhaps in *Sthen*.: see *Cret*. F 472e.4–41 n.

7 . guest and suppliant: purified (16ff.) by the host but then destroying him: cf. Introd., p. 83.

7 a . Bellerophon's name is almost certainly missing here (Korzeniewski), for Eur. habitually identifies his prologue speakers early on, e.g. *Tel*. F 696.4, *Mel.S*. F 481.6, *Hec*. 1–3 etc. The line began perhaps τὸν (E.W. Handley) Βελλεροφόντην; for the prosody see Collard on *Supp*. 888 or (without τὸν) West, *Metre* 82.

8 . guileful persuasion: for 'erotic' persuasion in general see Buxton 31–46. Compare esp. *Il*. 14.208–9, in the scene of the seduction of Zeus by Hera which is the ancestor of all literary seductions.   **pursuing:** lit. 'hunting', a sexual metaphor *Bacc*. 459, 688, *Hipp.Cal*. F 428 etc.

9 . fall: the verb perhaps implies passion, e.g. Zeus and Hera again, *Hel*. 1093; cf. *Hec*. 926, (Oedipus and Jocasta) Soph. *OT* 1210. **secretly:** adulterously, *El*. 720, *HF* 1344 etc.

1 1 . nurse: see Introd., pp. 80, 83.

1 2 . reciting: lit. 'singing', this 'flat' use of ὑμνεῖν also Soph. *Aj*. 292, perhaps Eur. *Pho*. 438, Plato (LSJ II).

1 3 . Why this madness?: an idiom of incredulity, *Med*. 1129, *Hec*. 1280, *IT* 1300. **Have the courage etc.:** so the Nurse challenges Phaedra, *Hipp*. 476.

1 4 . the king's palace: the lure to the adulterous Aegisthus, *El*. 11–13, 321–2; cf. Candaules' wife to Gyges, Hdt. 1.11.2. This detail appears in Hygin. *Astron*. 2.18.1 as part of Stheneboea's own persuasion. Hippolytus imagines it to be part of his father's suspicion, *Hipp*. 1010–11.   [Text: **you'll get** translates Rabe's unprovable conjecture κτήσηι; the Imperative κτῆσαι in Ioann. may have been co-ordinated with 13 'have the courage', cf. *Hcld*. 174–6 'be persuaded . . . get'.]

1 5 . Zeus not only protects guests and suppliants (e.g. Aesch. *Supp*. 1, 428) but oversees their own behaviour (Aesch. *Ag*. 61 etc.: Paris!): see J. Gould, *JHS* 93 (1973), 90–4; J. Mikalson, *Honour Thy Gods* (Chapel Hill, 1991), 74 n. 28; cf. on F 667.

1 7 . Sisyphus's land: Bellerophon was grandson to Sisyphus, who founded Corinth (Ephyra): Hom. *Il*. 6.152f. **murder:** see on Hypoth. 4. The prologue speaker is a refugee murderer also in *HF* 16.

1 8 . fresh blood: the first, polluting bloodshed is cleansed by fresh blood over the killer's hands (*IT* 1223–4, Ap. Rhod. 4.702–17, cf. Heracl. 22 B5 DK) from a pure and properly consecrated animal victim (pig's blood, Aesch. *Eum*. 283): Burkert 80–2; Parker, *Miasma* 370ff. The ritual reproduces the literal requital of killing by killing, e.g. *Or*. 510, Soph. *O.T*. 100.

2 0 . violate: the verb ὑβρίζειν of adultery *IT* 13, Lys. 1.16 etc., rape *Hipp*. 1073; cf. on 31 'stain'.

22ff. two kinds of love etc.: cf. *IA* 547ff., one happy (and virtuous, 544: cf. 24 below), one bringing discord; *Oed.* F 547 good and bad gratifications; *Theseus* F 388 implicitly. Hes. *WD* 11–24 has two 'strifes', good and bad. Other such surprisingly deliberate analyses at *Hipp.* 385ff., the two 'shames'; cf. on *Bell.* F'285.3–5.

22. [Text: **native**: for the adj. in Mekler's correction cf. Soph. *Aj.* 622, *OC* 1362. Luppe's conjecture, technically less probable, means 'two kinds of love at large'.]

23f. leads ... tends: metaphors from roads 'leading', *Supp.* 295, *IT* 988 etc.

24. virtue: Bellerophon's virtue: 26, 29; *Il.* 6.162.

25. among whom (etc.): compare Phaedra's converse prayer, for moral dissociation, *Hipp.* 430. For the bare Gen. with the verb εἰμί cf. Ar. *Wealth* 345, LSJ C.II.c., Jebb on Soph. *El.* 199.

†26†. The translation is for convenience; it cannot be got from the Greek (despite Braet 103). [Text: καί . . . γε is always a connective or coordinate in Eur. (so Korzeniewski supposes a lacuna) and νομίζειν with Aor. Inf. of a future intention is very doubtful.]

27. Now I will go etc.: an exit formula, often with ἀλλά e.g. *Hec.* 1054, *IT* 636; often a reason is given, as with γάρ here, e.g. to avoid a new entrant *Hec.* 52, *Bacc.* 1143 — and here? **into the country**: like Hippolytus, *Hipp.* 110f., 659f. [Text: **deliberate**: conjectured independently by Wilamowitz and West; the latter compares esp. *Bacc.* 843 'go inside and . . .', Menand. *Georg.* 20, *Epitr.* 161–3. The (unmetrical) text of Ioann. means 'I shall wish to go out'.]

29. be loudly abused: a faint metaphor from crashing waves, *Hipp.* 340 etc. **wrong**: for κακός of sexual sin cf. *Mel.D.* F 493.4, *Mel.* F 497.4, *Hipp.* 1031, 1077 etc., *Oed.* F 547.2.

31. stain: sexual metaphor as Soph. *OT* 1384; cf. χραίνειν *Hipp.* 1266. **tear . . . apart**: vigorous image as *Alc.* 657, (cities) Pl. *Laws* 875a. **household**: i.e. its family base, δόμος as *HF* 1243, *Med.* 114, 794.

663. The Nurse (probably) is explaining Love's power; in the parody at *Wasps* 1074 Bdelycleon is confident of teaching manners to his boorish father, as Love teaches poetry to an inartistic lover. **no skill**: the adj. ἄμουσος as *Cyc.* 426, F 1020, cf. *Med.* 1089 and in Menand. fr. 229* Koerte² where the wording resembles *Tel.* F 715.2. Love makes a poet: esp. Pl. *Symp.* 196d8ff. (citing line 2b); Nicias in Schol. Theocr. 11.1 (Gow p. 209), a paraphrase of our fr.; 'love teaches me courage': Phaedra in *Hipp.Cal.* F 430. The fr. reflects the tireless ancient debate, whether poetic or any skill (and later, morality) must be inborn and developed, or can be acquired from nothing; Aristid. *Or.* 26.3 and 41.11 relate our line 2 to Dionysus's inspirational power to make a dancer. See e.g. D. A. Russell, *Criticism in Antiquity* (London, 1981), ch. 5. [Text: only the full context could confirm Nauck's connective particle; and the combination δ' ἄρα is very rare in Tragedy: Denniston, *GP* 33, 35.]

664. Stheneboea 'toasts' Bellerophon, believing him dead. Athenaeus cites the fr. in relation to the game of *kottabos* (see *OCD*, 'Games'), when drinkers sometimes threw their wine-drops with a toast 'Here's to/In memory of . . . ': see e.g. Xen. *Hell.* 2.3.56. The only other certain allusion to 'toasting' with table food is Ar. *Lys.* 853–7, which reverses the action for a sexual joke: a woman toasts a man she fancies while eating. Eur. could not depict a queen playing *kottabos*, and substitutes fallen table food for thrown wine. Schol. on Ar. *Thesm.* 404 says the parody there mocks the notorious Corinthian sexual laxity; in the coarse adaptation by Cratinus a woman (not a lady!) does throw wine and toasts 'My prick from Corinth!'

665. More on Love's power, F 663; cf. *Dictys* F 340.1–2, 'Love (Aphrodite) relaxes not at all when reproved; if you use violence, moreover, it usually becomes more intense'; *Hipp.* 443–6.

665a. The wording **Pegasus here** is generally thought to reveal the horse's presence on stage: see above, p. 82. O. Taplin, *The Stagecraft of Aeschylus* (Oxford, 1977), 261n. takes the pronoun ὅδε (transl. 'here') to indicate visibility, comparing Oceanus's mount (a griffin?) at *PV* 286; but the pronoun frequently refers to a person (or thing) whom the spectators are invited to imagine as only just out of view: see e.g. Stevens on *And.* 710, 735, Collard on *Supp.* 392. (Photius cites the verse to illustrate ἀθήρ 'the tip of a corn-ear' in metaphor as a **pointed flame**; the same usage at Aesch. F 154 from Hesychius A 1580 Latte; cf. *Phrixus* F 836 'a (pointed) beard of flame'. **throat:** σφαγαί Plur., lit. 'throat-wound', like Aesch. *Pers* 863, Thuc. 4.48.3; controlling a possessive Gen. like *Or.* 291 'drive your sword into your mother's throat!', where West's note gives the close anatomical location. Wilamowitz wanted 'I strike the Chimaera and wound it fatally', thinking the animal needed a thrust behind its shoulder (σφαγαί as at Xen. *Cyn.* 10.16, a boar); but our fr. shows that when Bellerophon struck, flame burst out, i.e. fiery breath from its cut throat. **thick-plumed wing:** an Homeric phrase, of birds *Il.* 11.454, *Od.* 5.53 etc.)

666. The accusation of an evil woman suits the plot of *Sthen.*, not *Bell.*; perhaps the speaker's name displaced the play's in the anthology. If this fr. occurs relatively late in the play, when Bellerophon already plans to seduce Stheneboea, he is probably accusing the Nurse rather than Stheneboea herself. **and a woman:** the bare noun as a second insult seems stylistically improbable (contrast 'utterly vile' alone, *Hipp.* 682, 'most supremely hateful woman' *Med.* 1323; hence Blaydes's emphatic, non-connective 'indeed', i.e. 'you vilest of women, indeed'). But cf. Carcinus *TrGF* I 70 F 3 'why should one spell out women's wickedness? It would suffice, just to say "woman" ', and the bare noun emphasized at *And.* 85, *Hipp.* 406, *Aeolus* F 36. **What word (etc.):** explaining an abusive term, *Med.* 465–6: Diggle, *Studies* 90.

667. who deceives his guest: if the fr. is correctly located, Bellerophon accuses Proetus after discovering his plot, Hypoth. 12. ξεναπάτης is not a rare word, but applied usually to one who deceives a *host*, e.g. *Tro.* 866, Ibycus *PMG* 282.10 = *PMGF* S 151.10, of Paris; *Med.* 1392 Jason. If the usual sense holds here too, the line will have to be located very early in the play, perhaps even in Bellerophon's Prologue, when he fears to outrage his host Proetus by accepting Stheneboea's advances. Jouan 203, translating with 'host', and reconstructing rather differently, thinks of an *agon* between Proetus and Bellerophon early in the play.

668. the proverb: for such quotations cf. *Licymnius* F 474, Aesch. *Ag.* 264, *Bell.* F 285.1 n. For the general idea cf. *Cret.W.* F 461, *Tel.* F 701; the idea here is generally expressed in reverse, 'no good fortune without work', *Cret.W.* F 461, *Tel.* F 701, Soph. *El.* 945.   [The text is contradictory; instead of **distresses** something like 'helps, benefits' is needed, e.g. ὠφελεῖ (Cropp), but the corruption is then difficult to explain. This change, like Musgrave's 'strengthens' or Badham's and Vitelli's bathetic 'successful work no longer distresses men', does not help to suggest a context. For the idiomatic tautology 'on its own without' cf. *Ion* 775, Collard on *Supp.* 190.]

669. The complete fr. stands in Schol. Ar. as a single speech, but *Peace* 126 (= line 4) is Trygaeus's answer to his daughter's question in 124–5 'What means will you have of journeying? No ship will take you on this journey'; the brisk asyndeton in 126 suits an answer (whence von Arnim's distribution). If our fr. is a single speech, Bellerophon continues his description of Lycia, based on his previous journey, with a reassurance to (?) Stheneboea; if our line 4 is Bellerophon's answer, he is talking to (?) Stheneboea, a native of Lycia, who is protesting at the danger if she goes with Bellerophon. Rau 94f. takes all of *Peace* 126 as Euripidean (indeed, ναυσθλοῦν 'go by ship' is unique to Eur.: Collard on *Supp.* 1037); but Schol. states that the line is parodic, and the curt tone may suit Trygaeus to his daughter but not Bellerophon to his doubting passenger.

1. it (Fem. in the Greek): reference unknowable.   **Cragus** (a palmary correction): Meineke adduced Strabo 14.3.5 who gives this seaside mountain as the haunt of the Chimaera; 'a mountain in Lycia' Hesych. K 3903 Latte and Alexand. Polyhistor *FGH* 273 F 58.

2. full of beasts: the adj. ἔνθηρος describes a mountain also Soph. *Ichneutae* F 314.216.   **robbers** — or pirates, always notorious in the Aegean, Hom. *Od.* 3. 73 etc., Thuc. 1. 5ff. For the rare Dative of a personal agent with a Present Passive cf. Soph. *Aj.* 539, KG I.422.

3. (the waves') **deep groan:** a common metaphor, *HF* 861, Soph. *Ant.* 1145 etc. [Text: Dindorf's conjecture is easier than Schol. 'which bring grief to men', a unique adj. perhaps defensible from the similarly formed Aesch. *Supp.* 665 βροτόλοιγος 'which brings plague to men'.]

6 7 0. The lines are remarkable for revealing much more of a messenger's occupation, and his characterful view of it, than is usual in Eur. (see de Jong 65–72), for their homely but precise detail, and for their antithetical manner, emphasized by asyndeton — unless this simple rhetoric also 'characterises' a simple man like the Guard in Soph. *Antigone*. The description of poor fishermen anticipates the self-pitying folk in New Comedy (Pl. *Rope* 290ff., 906ff.) and Hellenistic poetry (Gow on Theocr. 21.6–18); cf. Alciphron 1.1.2, 1.3.3 etc.; Webster 83f. Certainly much fish was cheap (Athenaeus' context) — and fishermen therefore poor — in Eur.'s Athens: Ar. *Wasps* 491, *Knights* 646, 672 etc. The messenger at *IT* 263 reports a seaside incident near a purple-fishers' cave.

1 . **purple-fisher:** the shellfish *murex* was both caught for food and sun-dried for its dye, esp. in the E. Mediterranean: W. D. Thompson, *Glossary of Greek Fishes* (Oxford, 1947), 209–19; cf. on 5 below. [Text: idiom requires the Gen. of the Greek noun (Lobeck) when it stands between and amplifies another noun and its adj., here 'living . . . from the sea', not its Nom. (Hermann) which would stand with 'living' alone, e.g. *Ion* 1373; Athen. has an Attic form of the Homeric adj. πορφύρεος, 'restless' (or 'livid': sense disputed), applied to the sea alone, e.g. *Il.* 1.482. The adj. θαλάσσιος, 'from the sea', is not otiose, for it anticipates the antithesis in 3–4: wet = harsh ‖ dry (= easier).]

2 . **luxurious:** εὐτράπεζος as in F 1052.3; for τράπεζα 'table' as the index of comfort cf. e.g. *Hipp.* 110, *Hel.* 296; a menial's 'table' *Alc.* 2. **table:** lit. 'manger'. The word φάτνη gives perhaps a slightly humorous tone, for it describes human fare in the satyric *Eurystheus* F 378.1 and occurs in proverbs (LSJ I.2); cf. perhaps English 'trough, nose-bag'.

3 . **watery:** ὑγρός is an Homeric 'formulaic' adj. for the sea, *Il.* 14.308 etc.; *IT* 948, *Hel.* 1209. **mother:** the land is naturally this to its dependants, so that the sea can be viewed the same way and 'ploughed', vs. 4 (see n.). **nurse** too is widely figurative (land, e.g. *Pho.* 686), and the noun τροφός follows the verb τρέφειν, e.g. *Hec.* 1181 'neither sea nor land nourishes etc.' **where feet may walk:** πεδοστιβής is a heavily poetic adj. (Aesch. *Supp.* 1000, Eur. *Med.* 1123, *Cret.* F 472e.17 etc., normally 'treading the ground'), discrepant in register with its context here.

4 . **plough-:** despite its naturalness, the metaphor seems new here; commonly ἀροῦν is 'cut, cleave' a course in the sea like a ploughed furrow, as τέμνειν: see Johansen–Whittle on Aesch. *Supp.* 1007 or Pfeiffer on Call. fr. 572. But cf. Theocr. fr. 3.2 'for one who gets his living from the sea, his nets are his plough-shares', cited by West on Hes. *Th.* 440 'work (ἐργάζεσθαι) the sea'.

5 . **lines:** βρόχος is a *looped* line, or net (e.g. for hunting, *Hel.* 1169). **traps:** πέδαι are lit. 'shackles'; but cf. πέζα 'fish-trap' at Opp. *Hal.* 3.83. Purple-fish were caught in wicker baskets strung on lines (Thompson, 204; Pearson on Soph. F 504); for fishermen's pots see Theocr. 21.11, Oppian above.

671. 'Do not trust a woman' is an age-old saw, Hom. *Od.* 11.456, Hes. *WD* 375; Page on *Med.* 421.

BELLEROPHON

Texts, testimonia. P.Oxy. 3651 (= *TrGF* test. iiia) and 4017 fr. 4 (= *TrGF* test. *iiib);
TrGF F 285–312; Mette Nos. 358–393.

Myth. Hom. *Il.* 6.192–205 and Schol. T on 200–5; Asclepiades, *FGH* I.12 F 13 (from
Schol. A on Hom. *Il.* 6.155); Pind. *Isthm.* 7.43–7, *Ol.* 13.91–2 and Schol.; Schol. Ar.
Peace 147a,b; Apollod. 2.3.2; Hygin. *Fab.* 57.4–5, cf. *Astron.* 2.18.1; (?)*Anth.Pal.*
3.15. Roscher I.772–3; Preller–Robert II.1.183–5; R. Peppmüller, *WS* 75 (1962),
13–21; J. A. White, *AJP* 103 (1987), 119–27; Gantz 314–6.

Illustrations. Brommer, *Denkmälerlisten* II.29–64 lists on 48 three 7th C. B.C.
Cretan reliefs of Bell. falling from Pegasus; cf. Webster, *Monuments* (1967) 156,
a 1st C. A.D. terracotta lamp. For Bell. in general see S. Hiller, *AuA* 19 (1973),
83–100 and bibl. for *Sthen.*, p. 79. *LIMC* promises an entry for Bell. under 'Pegasos'.

Main discussions. A. Caputi, *RAL* 18 (1909), 509–26 (older bibl.); Schmid 393–4;
Pohlenz I.290–3, II.115–6; K. Vysoky, *ZJKF* 5 (1963), 133–43 (German résumé in
BCO 9 [1964], 358); A. Carlini, *SCO* 14 (1965), 201–5; Webster, *Euripides* (1967),
109–11; Rau 89–97; L. di Gregorio, *CCC* 4 (1983), 159–213, 365–82; Aélion
(1986), 192–6; W. Luppe, *Eikasmos* 1 (1990), 171–7; C. Riedweg, *ICS* 15 (1990),
39–53. Cf. Comm. on F 289, 286b (= 292 N).

The gnomic character of nearly all the thirty or so book fragments, and scanti-
ness of secondary information, frustrate reconstruction. The very fragmentary
Hypothesis in P. Oxy. 3651 adds nothing definite, like the further, even more
disappointing fragment in P. Oxy. 4017; they do not appear to overlap. The few
works of art only attest but do not illuminate one of the few facts we have,
Bellerophon's fall from Pegasus. Caputi and di Gregorio before the publication
of P. Oxy. 3651 in 1984, and Luppe after it, squeezed the thin evidence and
applied conjecture well beyond Webster's justified caution. The play's loss is
particularly unfortunate, for the gnomic fragments suggest that it was one of
Euripides' most sustained treatments of man's disillusion with god: see esp.
Pohlenz 292–3, Aélion 194–5, Riedweg 41–8.

The high point, perhaps the climax of the action, was Bellerophon's attempt
to scale Heaven on Pegasus the winged horse, in order to confront the gods with
their apparent injustice. But Pegasus threw him off; he reappeared crippled by the
fall and in rags, and may have died at the play's end (perhaps comparably with
the wounded Hippolytus, *Hipp.* 1342, 1457). This much of the action can be
established from Pind. *Isthm.* 7.43–7, Schol Ar. *Peace* 147a,b and especially
Asclepiades; Hygin. *Astron.* 2.18.1 has Bellerophon fall from Pegasus for fear
of the height, but does not give his reason for the flight. The Pegasus-flight is

heavily parodied in Ar. *Peace* 58–176, esp. 135f., 146f. (see Rau), and the ragged cripple at *Ach.* 426f. Only F 306–12 (including 309a) of the book fragments come with information to locate them in this action.

Bellerophon is in Lycia, perhaps after some kind of reconciliation with King Iobates, whose daughter Stheneboea's disastrous attempt to seduce him was the plot of her name-play (pp. 79–81); but it is not known whether Euripides was 'completing' the story of Bellerophon her killer by showing him here humiliated by the gods for his inhumanity to her (suggested by Wilamowitz, *KS* I. 279, cf. perhaps Hom. *Il.* 6.200–1 below). Euripides innovated with Stheneboea's killing and in *Bell.* he may have used the version in which she took her own life from shame (e.g. Hygin. *Fab.* 57.5) – before the play began, for *Il.* 6.192ff. and later e.g. Hyginus and Apollod. 2.3.2 have it that Iobates married another daughter to Bellerophon and shared or bequeathed his kingdom. The central fact of the play for us is the Pegasus-flight, but accounts of the myth vary in giving Bellerophon's motive in seeking to reach the gods and remonstrate: despair at the death of his children, killed by the gods, which made him reclusive, Schol. T. on *Il.* 6.202a; disillusion that his triumphs with Pegasus (*Il.* 6.183–90 etc.) had turned to ashes, leading to melancholia, Aristot. *Probl.* 953a21ff.; or even arrogance which induced him to challenge the gods (which they thwarted by maddening Pegasus to throw him), Pindar *Isthm.* 7.44, Asclepiades. These motives could all or singly have led to the tragic flight; Caputi 519 saw Euripides' innovation in combining melancholia with arrogance. They leave small room and little cause for a revenge plot against Bellerophon by Stheneboea's son Megapenthes, least of all after he has fallen from Pegasus. Carlini and di Gregorio have again pressed this 19th C. suggestion after Caputi repeated it in 1909; it depends heavily on a difficult interpretation of F 305 (see Comm.), on the inclusion of F 304a (= 68 N: see Comm.), and on the belief that the textually corrupt epigram *Anth.Pal.* 3.15, which purports to describe a 2nd C. B.C. temple relief at Cyzicus depicting Bellerophon rescued from the plot by his son Glaucus, reflects Euripides' play. (On the epigrams in *Anth.Pal.* 3 see further under *Cresph.*, p. 122 below.) P. Waltz, *Anth. Pal.* (Budé ed.) I (1928), 83–90, 97 points out that this is the only allusion to such a plot, and that Glaucus is the name not of Bellerophon's son but of his father, *Il.* 6.197, or grandson, *ibid.* 119. The ground for arguing the inclusion in the play is in all very weak; Schmid and Vysoky also were rightly cautious; Webster ignores it. (*Sthen.* F 669 is sometimes ascribed to *Bell.*: see Comm. on F 306 below.)

Two sources, Asclepiades and Schol. Pind. *Ol.* 13.91–2, state that Bellerophon's wandering through Lycia in rags began after his fall, but *Il.* 6.200–1 puts his reclusive isolation simply on the Aleian Plain (etymologised as 'Wanderer's' Plain, Schol. A on *Il.* 6.201a) without saying whether it was before or after he became disillusioned with the gods, and why he was so. (White [1987], who compares with Bellerophon's wanderings those of Cain after killing Abel, *Genesis* 4.16, and Peppmüller [1962] discuss the Asiatic background to Bellerophon's story; cf. on *Sthen.*, p. 83 above.) Di Gregorio has Bellerophon wandering from the start of the play — but would he have Pegasus still? Both the wandering and the rags, both before and after his fall, are consistent with what little we can establish from the varying accounts, despite an ancient protest (Schol. T on *Il.* 6. 200–5) that he could not wander if crippled by his fall.

Who were the other characters? Not Stheneboea, unless she has avoided death and returned to her father, and unless F 666 belongs (see under *Sthen.*); her name is conjecturally restored in P. Oxy. 4017 but its context is irrecoverable. Her father Iobates, however, was almost certainly a play character. Whether Megapenthes was there or not, a son of Bellerophon probably was, either an unknown Glaucus or, conceivably, Isander who is hesitantly identified in the fragmentary Hypothesis P. Oxy. 3651.13 — but this is the son named by Hom. *Il.* 6.203 as killed by the god Ares, his death a cause of Bellerophon's misery. A messenger (rather than Bellerophon himself, or a son) would narrate the fall. Only a god at play-end could tell of Pegasus's new rôle serving Zeus's chariot (F 312). It is impossible on our present evidence to fill out the cast list. It is a reasonable assumption that the Chorus was formed by men of Lycia.

Most reconstructions are therefore content with putting a long examination of Bellerophon's distrust of the gods' justice (F 285, 286, 293) in the early episodes; an opposing position is taken in F 287, 291–2, 294, 301–2 — but is this in one scene only? who is the opponent? Iobates? someone addresses F 291 to 'my son'. F 288–90, 295–8 cannot be placed in any such argument, or elsewhere, without fuller evidence. Aélion 193 n. 24 nevertheless assigns F 286, 288–98, 301–4, including the lyric F 303–4, to a single *agon* scene between Bellerophon and Iobates. F 300 is Bellerophon's final despair before his flight. This is the best that can be done with F 285–302, the gnomic fragments from dialogue; and the Chorus moralise in two more, in agreement with Bellerophon's opponent, 303–4. Then comes Bellerophon's preparation for his flight, F 306–8; the narrative may have included F 309 and 309a. At the end Bellerophon tries to console himself for what virtues he had (F 310) before he is taken off-stage, probably dying (F 311); and the god speaks (F 312; perhaps also F 309, Aélion 193). F 305 is impossible to locate; it is assigned by some to *Sthen.* (p. 81). Mette lists also F 662 and 663 as his Nos. 381 and 382, but they belong to *Sthen.*; and F 324 from *Danae* as his No. 393, which Seneca, *Letters* 115.14 translates and incorrectly attributes to *Bell.*

In di Gregorio's extremely speculative reconstruction, Prologue and Parodos are blank; Bellerophon is weakened by disillusion and persecuted by Iobates, but comforted by Glaucus (Episode 1); then Megapenthes threatens him, with Glaucus dissuading his flight (Epis. 2); although Iobates tries to deter

Megapenthes, Bellerophon flies (Epis. 3); messenger scene (Epis. 4) and Exodos (with god) complete the play. Even more difficult is Luppe's supplementation of P. Oxy. 3651.2–5 to make Bellerophon in the first part of the play exact a 'fitting' revenge for a seduced daughter-in-law — an incident nowhere attested.

Themes and characters. Bellerophon's defiant doubt of the gods' justice has been compared with the more violent hostility of Prometheus (see esp. Schmid 394) or of Pentheus, his flight with the disastrous folly of Phaethon (F 781 = 214ff. Diggle; see pp. 199–200). Pohlenz 292 and others see him as a self-portrait by Euripides, searching fruitlessly for life's meaning. Aélion 195 agrees with the comparison, differentiating Bellerophon from Prometheus, Pentheus and Phaethon rather than comparing him, and emphasising the originality of his characterisation as a passionate world-weary man who hardens instead of yielding in trying to prove the unfairness of existence. There are some similarities too with Heracles, who survives the goddess Hera's enmity at huge cost. Webster 110 puts Bellerophon into the tradition of the great resisters, Prometheus again or Ajax; for Webster F 286b (= 292 N) encapsulates the whole play: 'the gods should behave like skilful doctors'. It seems certain that Euripides once again enlarged what is to us a shadowy if melodramatic incident into a profound study of human disquiet.

Staging. The parody in Ar. *Peace* (see Rau) concentrates on the preparations (1–153) for the flight and then the departure and arrival 'on the machine' (154–76: F 306–7, cf. Hourmouziades 151–2, Taplin 444). After his fall and return Bellerophon is lame (*Peace* 147, cf. *Ach.* 427) and ragged (*Ach.* 426) — ragged like the earlier Euripidean Telephus, much mocked by Aristophanes in *Ach.* 440, 497 etc. (F 698, 704: see pp. 18–19), and e.g. the later humiliated Electra, *El.* 185, or shipwrecked Menelaus, *Hel.* 421–3.

Date. Earlier than the parodies in Ar. *Ach.* of 425; the metrical evidence considered by Webster, *Euripides* 4 and Cropp–Fick 22, 70, 77 puts the play anywhere in the period 455–425. Probably later than *Sthen.* (before 429: see p. 83); the very different characterisation of Bellerophon makes it most unlikely that the two were produced together.

Other dramatisations; influence. Soph. *Iobates* (F 294–7) is too shadowy to permit comparison: see Pearson. Only the title is known of Astydamas the Younger's *Bell.*, *TGF* I 60 T 1, F 1g. Bellerophon (and Pegasus) in later art: *OGCMA* I.274–6.

ΒΕΛΛΕΡΟΦΟΝΤΗΣ

test. *iiib Hypothesis P. Oxy. 4017 fr. 4

Badly damaged centres of nine lines giving no continuous sense:

1 συ]μφορα [4]μετανεπ[ ]ων [6] Σθενεβο [ ] [
7]τοπουστου [ ] [8]λερ [ ]ν [

test. iiia *(perhaps later in the same)* **Hypothesis** P. Oxy. 3651

Top of a single column with beginnings (some very damaged) of thirty-four lines, of which 1–22 are the end of an hypothesis to Bell., *23–34 the start of one to the satyr-play* Busiris. *Sixteen or more letters are missing from the end of every line.*

1 διεγνωκότος [
2 σθαι προσελθὼ[ν
3 ἰδίου καὶ ἀδελφ[
4 Βελλεροφόντη[
5 τὴν πρέπουσα[ν
6 αὐ[τ]ὸς συνεπε[
7 θη · νεκρὸν [
8 πειν τὸν ἐχ [
9 ἀπὸ τῶν[σ] ταυρ[
10 σαντα ὑπολ[Βελ]

11 λερο]φόντην[
12 ...] δρυ [ποτα[μ
13 ...]νδρον εξε[
14, 15, 17 *only a few letters*
16] α τὴν χώ[ραν
18 τ]ὰς πηγὰς [
19]αι τὸν Βελλερ[οφόντην
20] [τ]ῆς Λυκία[ς
21 ...]τὴν ναῦν[
22] κ αν · διε[

285 (Βε.) ἐγὼ τὸ μὲν δὴ πανταχοῦ θρυλούμενον
κράτιστον εἶναι φημὶ μὴ φῦναι βροτῶι ·
τριῶν δὲ μοιρῶν ἐγκρινῶ νικᾶν μίαν,
πλούτου τε χώτωι σπέρμα γενναῖον προσῆι
πενίας τ' · ἀριθμὸν γὰρ τοσόνδε προυθέμην ·   5
ὁ μὲν ζάπλουτος, εἰς γένος δ' οὐκ εὐτυχής,
ἀλγεῖ μὲν ἀλγεῖ, παγκαλῶς δ' ἀλγύνεται
ὄλβου διοίγων θάλαμον ἥδιστον χερί ·
ἔξω δὲ βαίνων τοῦδε τὸν πάρος χρόνον
πλουτῶν ὑπ' ἄτης ζεῦγλαν ἀσχάλλει πεσών.   10
ὅστις δὲ γαῦρον σπέρμα γενναῖόν τ' ἔχων
βίου σπανίζει, τῶι γένει μὲν εὐτυχεῖ,
πενίαι δ' ἐλάσσων ἐστίν, †ἐν δ' ἀλγύνεται

102

BELLEROPHON

test. *iiib Hypothesis

1 *disaster* 4 ? 6 *Stheneboea* 7 ? 8 (?*Bellerophon*)

test. iiia Hypothesis

1 having determined . . . 2 to ( ) . . . going to . . . 3 (his)
own ( ) and brother (*or* sister) . . . 4 Bellerophon . . .
5 the fitting . . . 6 he himself . . . 7 . . . corpse . . . 8 ?
9 from the (?Taurus) . . . 10 ? 11 Bellerophon . . .
12 river *(written above the line)* 13 (*Isander* ?) . . . 14 ?
15 ? 16 . . . the *country* . . . 17 ? 18 the springs . . .
19 Bellerophon . . . 20 . . . of Lycia . . . 21 . . . the ship . . .
22 . . . *(punctuation)* . . .

285 *(Bellerophon)* I myself say — in fact it's a common refrain
everywhere — that it's best for a man not to have been born. He
has three estates, of which I shall be judging one superior; and they
are wealth, noble blood, and poverty: that's the complete count I
put forward.[5] The very wealthy man, but without the fortune of
birth, is miserable, yes, miserable — but it is a splendid misery
when his hand opens up his treasure-house for his delight; yet
when he goes outside it, despite his wealth during the time before,
he falls under folly's yoke and suffers hard.[10] Then, the man with
proud and noble blood who lacks a living, has the fortune of his
birth but poverty makes him inferior; †his thoughts inside are

test. iiib (– M) P. Oxy. 4017 fr. 4 ed. H. M. Cockle (1994) 4 also μετανοη[Cockle, comparing
μετανοήσας Hyp. *And.* 5, cf. -ησεν 12 7]τόπους τούτ[ου]ς Cockle 8 Βελ]λερο[φο]ντη[
Cockle **test. iiia** (— M) P. Oxy. 3651 ed. H. M. Cockle (1984); cf. Luppe, *Eikasmos.* 3 ἰ- of
ἰδίου added in margin 9 ? Ταυρ[ικῶν Cockle 13 ? Ἴσα]νδρον rather than Μαία]νδρον
Cockle 18 Luppe. τ]ὰς ποινὰς [Cockle **285** (367 M) 1–18 Stob. 4.33.16, attrib. Eur.
1–2 Stob. 4.34.38, attrib. Eur. *Bell.* 11–14 Stob. 4.32b.23, attrib. Eur. *Bell.* 15–20 Stob. 4.33.9a,
attrib. Eur. *Bell.* 20 Stob. 3.32.3, unattrib. 8 Plut. *Mor.* 1069b, unattrib. 3 ἐγκρινῶ
Gaisford (-ίνω Pierson) ἐν κρίνω Stob. 7 μέν, ἄλγει . . . ἀμύνεται Badham 9–10 text
doubtful 10 ζεύγλαν ἀ(ν)σχάλλει Salmasius ζεύς τ' ἀνασχάλλει Stob. ζεύγματ' Collard
13 πενίας Badham ἐστί· κεἰ βαρύνεται Ι φρενῶν (Stob. 33.9a and 16) . . . [δ'] Gomperz ἔνθ'
ἀλγύνεται Ι φέρων or ἐν δ' ἀλγήδοσι Ι φρενῶν . . . [δ'] Collard

φρονῶντ† ὑπ' αἰδοῦς δ' ἔργ' ἀπωθεῖται χερῶν.
ὁ δ' οὐδὲν οὐδείς, διὰ τέλους δὲ δυστυχῶν,   15
τοσῶιδε νικᾶι· τοῦ γὰρ εὖ τητώμενος
οὐκ οἶδεν, ἀεὶ δυστυχῶν κακῶς τ' ἔχων.
οὕτως ἄριστον μὴ πεπειρᾶσθαι καλῶν.
ἐκεῖνο γὰρ μεμνήμεθ', οἷος ἦ ποτε
κἀγὼ μετ' ἀνδρῶν ἡνίκ' ηὐτύχουν βίωι ...   20

286   (Βε.)   φησίν τις εἶναι δῆτ' ἐν οὐρανῶι θεούς;
οὐκ εἰσίν, οὐκ εἴσ', εἴ τις ἀνθρώπων θέλει
μὴ τῶι παλαιῶι μῶρος ὢν χρῆσθαι λόγωι.
σκέψασθε δ' αὐτοί, μὴ ἐπὶ τοῖς ἐμοῖς λόγοις
γνώμην ἔχοντες. φήμ' ἐγὼ τυραννίδα   5
κτείνειν τε πλείστους κτημάτων τ' ἀποστερεῖν
ὅρκους τε παραβαίνοντας ἐκπορθεῖν πόλεις·
καὶ ταῦτα δρῶντες μᾶλλόν εἰσ' εὐδαίμονες
τῶν εὐσεβούντων ἡσυχῆι καθ' ἡμέραν.
πόλεις τε μικρὰς οἶδα τιμώσας θεούς,   10
αἳ μειζόνων κλύουσι δυσσεβεστέρων
λόγχης ἀριθμῶι πλείονος κρατούμεναι.
οἶμαι δ' ἂν ὑμᾶς, εἴ τις ἀργὸς ὢν θεοῖς
εὔχοιτο καὶ μὴ χειρὶ συλλέγοι βίον
⟨   ⟩
τὰ θεῖα πυργοῦσ' αἱ κακαί τε συμφοραί ...   15

286a   Fragmentary start of a gnomology entry from Bell.; only the
            words οἱ θεοί are complete.

286b   (292 N)   πρὸς τὴν νόσον τοι καὶ τὸν ἰατρὸν χρεὼν
ἰδόντ' ἀκεῖσθαι, μὴ ἐπιτὰξ τὰ φάρμακα
διδόντ', ἐὰν μὴ ταῦτα τῆι νόσωι πρέπηι.
νόσοι δὲ θνητῶν αἱ μέν εἰσ' αὐθαίρετοι,
αἱ δ' ἐκ θεῶν πάρεισιν, ἀλλὰ τῶι νόμωι   5
ἰώμεθ' αὐτάς. ἀλλ', ὅ σοι λέξαι θέλω,
εἰ θεοί τι δρῶσιν αἰσχρόν, οὐκ εἰσὶν θεοί.

---

14 φρονῶν δ' ... [δ'] Stob. 32b   φρενῶν ... δ', γ' or [δ'] 33.9a and 16   18 ἄμεινον Stob.
33.9a   19 οἷον Nauck   20 βίωι] ποτέ (from 19) Stob. 33.9a.   **286** (385 M) Ps.-Justin,
Monarch. 5.6, attrib. (Eur.) Bell., following citation of F 286b.7   11 δυσσεβεστέρων Grotius -
ωι Ps.-Justin   14–15 lacuna marked by Grotius (of 3 lines, Riedweg 44–6), but 15 may be a
separate fragment:

misery† and shame makes him reject manual work. The absolute nobody however, in misfortune to the end,[15] is superior in as much as he is unaware that he lacks well-being, since he is always in misfortune and distress. So it is best not to have experienced good things. For that's what I remember, what I too once was like among men when my life was fortunate . . .[20]

From an early monologue of Bellerophon setting out his dissatisfactions.

286 *(Bell.)* Does someone say there are indeed gods in heaven? There are not, there are not, if a man is willing not to rely foolishly on the antiquated reasoning. Consider for yourselves, do not base your opinion on words of mine. I say myself that tyranny[5] kills very many men and deprives them of their possessions; and that tyrants break their oaths to ransack cities, and in doing this they are more prosperous under heaven than men who live quietly in reverence from day to day. I know too of small cities doing honour to the gods[10] which are subject to larger, more impious ones, because they are overcome by a more numerous army. I think that, if a man were lazy and prayed to the gods and did not go gathering his livelihood with his hand, you would <   > . . . fortify religion, and ill fortune . . .[15]

Bellerophon's attack on divine injustice, also early in the play.

286a   . . . the gods . . .

286b (292 N)

The doctor too should cure when he has looked at the disease and not give medicines summarily, in case these do not suit it. Men's diseases are some of them self-chosen, some of them visited by gods, but we treat them[5] according to our rule. But what I want to tell you is this: if gods do anything shameful, they are not gods.

Opposition (vs. 6–7) to Bell.'s condemnation of the gods, F 286.

cf. on F 293, 294, 296   **286a** (390 M) Gnomology, *PSI* 1476 fr. C. 13–15 (ed. Bartoletti, *Atti XI Congr. Int. Pap.*, Milan 1966, p. 12) = Austin, *NFE* fr. 155.   **286b** (292 N, 384 M) Stob. 4.36.7, attrib. Eur. *Bell.*; 1–3 *ibid.* 5, attrib. Eur.   7 Plut. *Mor.* 21a and 1049f, attrib. Eur.; Ps.-Justin, *Monarch.* 5.6, attrib. (Eur.) *Bell.*: cf. on F 286   2 ἰᾶσθαι Stob. mss. MA   ἐπιτάξ τὰ Nauck ἐπιτακτὰ Stob.   6 lacuna of 2 lines after αὐτάς C. W. Müller, *RhM* 136 (1993), 116–21 ἀλλ' ὅ M. L. West, *BICS* 30 (1983), 72 ἀλλὰ Stob. ἄλλο Gomperz   7 φαῦλον Plut. 21a, Ps.-Justin

287 τοῖς πράγμασιν γὰρ οὐχὶ θυμοῦσθαι χρεών·
μέλει γὰρ αὐτοῖς οὐδέν· ἀλλ᾽ οὑντυγχάνων
τὰ πράγματ᾽ ὀρθῶς ἢν τιθῆι, πράσσει καλῶς.

288 δόλοι δὲ καὶ σκοτεινὰ μηχανήματα
χρείας ἄνανδρα φάρμαχ᾽ ηὕρηται βροτοῖς.

289 νείκη γὰρ ἀνδρῶν φόνια καὶ μάχας χρεὼν
δόλοισι κλέπτειν· τῆς δ᾽ ἀληθείας ὁδὸς
φαύλη τίς ἐστι· ψεύδεσιν δ᾽ Ἄρης φίλος.

290 ἀεὶ γὰρ ἄνδρα σκαιὸν ἰσχυρὸν φύσει
ἧσσον δέδοικα τἀσθενοῦς τε καὶ σοφοῦ.

291 ὦ παῖ, νέων τοι δρᾶν μὲν ἔντονοι χέρες,
βουλαὶ δ᾽ ἀμείνους εἰσὶ τῶν γεραιτέρων·
ὁ γὰρ χρόνος δίδαγμα ποικιλώτατον.

292 N = F 286b above

293 τιμή σ᾽ ἐπαίρει τῶν πέλας μεῖζον φρονεῖν.

* * *

θνήισκοιμ᾽ ἄν· οὐ γὰρ ἄξιον λεύσσειν φάος
κακοὺς ὁρῶντας ἐκδίκως τιμωμένους.

294 φθονοῦσιν αὐτοὶ χείρονες πεφυκότες·
εἰς τἀπίσημα δ᾽ ὁ φθόνος πηδᾶν φιλεῖ.

295 ἤδη γὰρ εἶδον καὶ δίκης παραστάτας
ἐσθλοὺς πονηρῶι τῶι φθόνωι νικωμένους.

287 (379 M) Stob. 4.44.39, attrib. Eur. *Bell.*; 4.13.14b, separated by Hense from 13.14 = F 1053 N,
attrib. Eur.; Plut. *Mor.* 467a, unattrib.; [Plut.] *Life of Homer* ch. 153 (VII.424 Bernadakis), attrib.
Eur.; 1–2a M. Antonin. 7.38 and (1 only) 11.6, unattrib.   288 (374 M) Stob. 3.8.1, attrib. Eur. *Bell.*
2 ἄνανδρα Herwerden -ου Stob.   289 (380 M) Stob. 4.13.20, attrib. Eur. *Bell.* 1 χρεὼν
Meineke χερῶν Stob.   290 (378 M) Stob. 4.13.5, attrib. Eur. *Bell.*   291 (389 M) Stob. 4.50a.2,
attrib. Eur. *Bell.* 1–2; paraphrased by Cornutus, *Theol. Gr. comp.* 31; 2 = Menand. *Monostich.* 158
1 εὔτονοι preferred by Nauck (Cornutus has εὐτονώτεραι χέρες)   2 βουλαὶ Heimsoeth,
approved by Nauck, *Index Trag.* p. xxi γνῶμαι Stob. ψυχαὶ Cornutus   293 (387 M) Stob.
4.42.1, attrib. Eur. *Bell.*   1 μεῖζον Cobet μᾶλλον Stob.   2–3 are a different fr. (Meineke);
Matthiae assigns 1 and 2–3 to different speakers in a single fr.   3 ὁρῶντα μὴ ἐνδίκως Dobree
294 (376 M) Stob. 3.38.13 mss. MA, attrib. Eur. (ms. S joins the fr. with 12); 2 is repeated in ms. M

287   One should not get angry with affairs, for they show no
        concern; but if a man handles affairs correctly as he
        encounters them, he fares well.

Someone is consoling or countering Bellerophon; cf. F 301, 302.

288   Tricks and dark schemes are mankind's invention as
        cowardly remedies against need.

Context unidentifiable (above, p. 100).

289   One should accomplish men's bloody quarrels and fighting
        secretly, through guile. The way of truth is ineffectual; war
        is a friend to lies.

Context unidentifiable: see above on F 288.

290   I always fear a stupid if bodily powerful man less than one
        who is both weak and clever.

Context unidentifiable: see Comm. on F 288.

291   My son, young men's arms are indeed taut for action, but
        old men's counsels are better; for time teaches the most
        subtle lessons.

An older man — Iobates? Chorus? — advises Bellerophon?

292 N   = F 286b above

293   Honour is exciting you to be haughtier than those around you.

                            * * *

        I'd rather die. It is not worth living, if people see bad men
        unjustly honoured.

Context unidentifiable, but 2–3 suit Bellerophon's disillusion.

294   The naturally inferior become envious of their own accord;
        distinction usually has envy leap in its direction.

An opponent of Bellerophon.

295   In the past I have seen even virtuous supporters at a trial
        overcome by the evil which is envy.

Context: as F 294 — perhaps Bellerophon's cynical response.

after 38.18, attrib. Eur. *Bell.*   1 and 2 are separated as different frs. by Meineke, Hense
295 (377 M) Stob. 3.38.19, ms. S only, attrib. Eur. *Bell.*

108 EURIPIDES

296   ἀνὴρ δὲ χρηστὸς χρηστὸν οὐ μισεῖ ποτε,
κακὸς κακῶι δὲ συντέτηκεν ἡδονῆι·
φιλεῖ δὲ θοὐμόφυλον ἀνθρώπους ἄγειν.

297   ὡς ἔμφυτος μὲν πᾶσιν ἀνθρώποις κάκη·
ὅστις δὲ πλεῖστον μισθὸν εἰς χεῖρας λαβὼν
κακὸς γένηται, τῶιδε συγγνώμη μὲν οὔ,
πλείω δὲ μισθὸν μείζονος τόλμης ἔχων
τὸν τῶν ψεγόντων ῥᾶιον ἂν φέροι λόγον.   5

298   οὐκ ἂν γένοιτο τραῦμ', ἐάν τις ἐγξέσηι
θάμνοις ἐλείοις, οὐδ' ἂν ἐκ μητρὸς κακῆς
ἐσθλοὶ γένοιντο παῖδες εἰς ἀλκὴν δορός.

299   πρὸς τὴν ἀνάγκην πάντα τἄλλ' ἔστ' ἀσθενῆ.

300   οἴμοι· τί δ' οἴμοι; θνητά τοι πεπόνθαμεν.

301   ὁρᾶις δ' ἀέλπτους μυρίων ἀναστροφάς·
πολλοὶ μὲν οἶδμα διέφυγον θαλάσσιον,
πολλοὶ δὲ λόγχαις πολεμίων ἀμείνονες
ἥσσους γεγῶτες κρείσσον' ἦλθον εἰς τύχην.

302   θάρσος δὲ πρὸς τὰς συμφορὰς μέγα σθένει.

303 (Χορός)   οὐδέποτ' εὐτυχίαν κακοῦ ἀνδρὸς ὑπέρφρονά τ' ὄλβον
βέβαιον εἰκάσαι χρεών,
οὐδ' ἀδίκων γενεάν· ὁ γὰρ οὐδενὸς ἐκφὺς
χρόνος δικαίους ἐπάγων κανόνας
δείκνυσιν ἀνθρώπων κακότητας ὅμως.   5

296 (371 M) Stob. 2.33.2, attrib. Eur. Bell. 1 = Menand. Monost. 28 2 is loosely cited by Aristot. Eth.Eud. 1238a 34 and 1239b 22, cf. Eth.M. 1209b 36 2 κακὸς κακῶι Aristot. -ῶι -ὸς Stob. ἡδονῆι Aristot. 1238, 1239 -αῖς Stob. 3 separated as a different fr. by Hense 297 (375 M) Stob. 3.10.17, attrib. Eur. Bell. 2 πλεῖστον suspect μεῖστον Bücheler μικρὸν Heath 5 ψεγόντων … λόγον Jacobs λεγόντων … ψόγον Stob. 298 (383 M) Stob. 4.30.10, attrib. Eur. Bell. 1–2 text insecure τραῦμ' ἐάν Nauck τραῦμα εἰ Stob. τραύματ' ἦν Hense ἐγξέσηι Heath ἐγξύσηι Stob. θάμνους ἐλείους Salmasius θαλλοὺς ἐλ. Cropp θαλλοῖς ἐλαίας Housman, Class. Papers 1254 299 (370 M) Stob. 1.4.2b, attrib. Eur. Bell. 300 (366 M) Diog. Laert. 4.26, attrib. Eur. Bell.; Suidas O 101 Adler, attrib. Eur. Bell., Plut. Mor. 475c, attrib. Eur.; Synesius, Epist. 126 p. 215.1 Garzya, unattrib. 301 (388 M) Stob. 4.47.11, attrib. Eur. Bell. 1 ἀέλπτους Nauck -ων Stob. 2 lacuna following, Kannicht on Hel. 713–4

296   A good man never hates a good, but a bad happily blends with bad; affinity usually attracts men.

Context: unknowable.

297   All men have badness in their nature! The one who takes most pay into his hands, and proves bad, gets no pardon; but if he has more pay for greater audacity, he'll endure censorious talk more easily.[5]

Perhaps to be associated with F 296 and 298 in their general despair of morality.

298   A man won't produce a wound if he whittles in marshy thickets, nor a base mother produce sons excellent at spear-fighting.

Context: see on F 297.

299   Against necessity everything else is weak.

Perhaps Bellerophon, defiant in his intention?

300   My misery! But why 'My misery!'? My suffering is only human.

Probably Bellerophon's final defiance before his flight.

301   You see unexpected reversals for countless people: many escape the ocean's surge; many excellent men defeated by enemy spears come to better fortune.

Someone is trying to console or dissuade Bellerophon.

302   Courage is very powerful against misfortune.

Further consolation for Bellerophon?

303   (Chorus) One ought never to imagine the success of a bad man, and his proud wealth, as secure, nor the lineage of unjust men; for time, which was born from nothing, adduces standards which are just and shows the wickedness of men in spite of all.[5]

Probably after Bell.'s departure, perhaps with F 304 (see Comm.).

---

302 (373 M) Stob. 3.7.1, attrib. Eur. *Bell.*   **303** (372 M) Stob. 3.2.13, attrib. Eur. *Bell.*; Theophilus, *To Autolycus* 2.37, omitting 4 δικαίους . . . κανόνας and stopping at 5 κακότητας   1 τ' Gesner δ' Stob., om. Theoph.   5 ὅμως M. L. West, *BICS* 30 (1983), 72 ἐμοί Stob.

110 EURIPIDES

304 (Χο.) ποῦ δὴ τὸ σαφὲς θνατοῖς βιοτᾶς;
θοαῖσι μὲν ναυσὶ πόρον πνοαὶ κατὰ βένθος †ἅλιον†
ἰθύνουσι, τύχας δὲ θνατῶν τὸ μὲν μέγ' ἐς οὐδὲν
ὁ πολὺς χρόνος μεθίστησιν, τὸ δὲ μεῖον αὔξων . . .

304a (68 N) (Α.) μητέρα κατέκτα τὴν ἐμήν· βραχὺς λόγος.
(Β.) ἑκὼν ἑκοῦσαν ἢ ⟨οὐ⟩ θέλουσαν οὐχ ἑκών;

305 . . . καὶ ξεστὸν ὄχθον Δαναϊδῶν ἑδρασμάτων,
στὰς ἐν μέσοισιν εἶπε κηρύκων . . .

306 (Βε.) ἄγ', ὦ φίλον μοι Πηγάσου ταχὺ πτερόν.

307 (Βε.) ἴθι χρυσοχάλιν' αἴρων πτέρυγας.

**307a (Βε.) σπεῦδ', ὦ ψυχή . . .
308 πάρες, ὦ σκιερὰ φυλλάς, ὑπερβῶ
κρηναῖα νάπη· τὸν ὑπὲρ κεφαλῆς
αἰθέρ' ἰδέσθαι σπεύδω, τίν' ἔχει
στάσιν εὐοδίας. 5

309 ἔπτησσ' ὑπείκων μᾶλλον †εἰ μᾶλλον† θέλοι.

309a τῶι δ' ἐξ ὑδρηλῶν αἰθέρος προσφθεγμάτων . . .

310 (311 N) (Βε.) ἦσθ' εἰς θεοὺς μὲν εὐσεβής, ὅτ' ἦσθ', ἀεὶ
ξένοις τ' ἐπήρκεις οὐδ' ἔκαμνες εἰς φίλους.

304 (386 M) Stob. 4.42.12, attrib. Eur. *Bell.*, approx. as ed. by Wilamowitz, *KS* IV 480   2 βένθος
Grotius -ους Stob.   ἅλιαι Stob. ms. A   304a (68 N, 391 M) Aristot. *Eth.Nic.* 1136a13, attrib.
Eur.; Michael Ephes. (Comm. on *Eth.Nic.*) p. 56.20–3 Hayduck, attrib. Eur. *Bell.*; anon., *Comm.*
Aristot. Gr. XX, p. 240.29–31 Heylblut, attrib. Eur. *Bell.* Attrib. *Alcmaeon Psoph.* by Welcker,
reasserted for *Bell.* by A. Carlini, *SCO* 14 (1965), 201–5, cf. A. Tuilier, *REG* 78 (1965), 406; di
Gregorio 199–204; Riedweg 52. Division between two speakers: Welcker   1 κατέκταν
(following a Latin transl. of Aristotle) Boissonade   ⟨οὐ⟩ Grotius   ⟨οὐχ⟩ ἑκοῦσαν Blaydes
305 (392 M) Schol. Eur. *Or.* 872, attrib. *Bell.*; attrib. *Sthen.* by Wecklein (see p. 81)   1 κὰς
ξεστὸν . . . στάς, ἐν Ellis   306 (359 M) Schol. Ar. *Peace* 76b, attrib. Eur. *Bell.* (cf. *Peace* 135
ἐχρῆν σε Πηγάσου ξεῦξαι πτερόν, 'you ought to have yoked the winged Pegasus'); Suidas ε
1897 Adler (ἑώρημα), attrib. Eur. ταχὺ om. Schol.   307 (360 M) Schol. Ar. *Peace* 154d,
attrib. (Eur.) *Bell.*   307a, 308 (361 M) 1–2 Ar. *Wasps* 757 (σπεῦδ', ὦ ψυχή – ποῦ μοι ψυχή;
– πάρες, ὦ σκιερά)   2 πάρες—5 Schol. 757b, attrib. *Bell.* 1 σπεῦδ', ὦ ψυχή restored to fr.
by Wilamowitz, *KS* IV. 481f., cf. Rau 154   5 Εἰνοδία Heath, Rau   309 (362 M) Plut. *Mor.*
529e, attrib. Eur., with Pegasus 'submitting' to Bell.; 807e, with ref. to Eur.'s Pegasus   εἰ μᾶλλον

304 *(Cho.)* Where indeed is there sureness in man's life? For swift ships the winds drive a straight path on the †ocean† deep, but men's fortunes are changed by the largeness of time, their greatness to nothing, while with increase for the lesser . . .

Context: see on F 303.

304a (68 N) *(A.)* He killed my mother; it's briefly told.

   (B.) Willingly, with her will – or unwillingly, against her wish?

If this belongs to the play, Megapenthes is speaking of Bell. killing Stheneboea.

305 . . . and the high dressed-stone tribunal of the Danaids, he stood in the midst of the heralds and said . . .

Context wholly uncertain, perhaps not even from this play.

F 306–8 come from Bellerophon's preparation for his flight.

306 *(Bell.)* Come, my dear swift-winged Pegasus . . . !

307 Go, with your golden bit, lifting your wings . . . !

**307a, 308 Hasten, my soul . . . Let me pass, you shadowy foliage; let me cross the watery dells. I am in haste to see the heaven above my head, what state it has for a good journey.

309 (Pegasus) stooped, submitting more †if ever he was more† willing.

A messenger? Bellerophon's own narration?

309a For him, from heaven's watery salutations . . .

The messenger describes Bellerophon after his fall?

310 (311 N) You were reverent towards the gods while you lived, always, a help to strangers and untiring for your friends.

Bellerophon on the point of death addresses his own heart.

θέλοι Plut. 807e mss. GV (ἢ other mss.) ἢ (om. μᾶλλον) θέλοι Plut. 529e ἢι μ. θ. Munro, *JPh* 10 (1882) 237 ἤ τις ἂν θέλοι Mette **309a** (363 M) Herodian, Καθολικὴ προσωιδ. cod. Vindob. hist. Gr. 10.5, ed. H. Hunger, *JoeByzGes* 16 (1967), 22, attrib. Eur. *Bell.* ὑδρηλῶν Diggle -ρῶν Her. **310** (311 N, 368 M) Aelian, *Nature of Animals* 5.34, attrib. Eur. *Bell.*

311 (310 N)   κομίζετ᾽ εἴσω τόνδε τὸν δυσδαίμονα.

312   ὑφ᾽ ἅρματ᾽ ἐλθὼν Ζηνὸς ἀστραπηφορεῖ

311 (310 N, 369 M) Schol. Ar. *Knights* 1249a, attrib. Eur. *Bell.*   κυλίνδετ᾽ Ar. in 1249   **312**
(364 M) Schol. Ar. *Peace* 722, attrib. Eur. *Bell.*; Schol. Hes. *Theog.* 286, attrib. Eur. *Bell.*
ἀστραπὴν φέρει Schol. Hes.

Commentary on Bellerophon

Hypothesis (test. iiib). If P. Oxy. 4017 is from the same version as 3651, it almost certainly preceded it in the text: Stheneboea's name (6) would have appeared in the initial background narrative, to which *disaster* (1) belonged: that refers perhaps to Bellerophon's revenge upon her (see *Sthen.*, Introd. p. 79), of which he may have 'repented' (Cockle's hazardous conjecture in 4, comparing the verb's use in the hypothesis to *And.*). In 7 Cockle's probable conjecture *these places* may be as vague in reference as *country* (if correct) in 3651.16.

(test. iiia). The scrappy 3651 represents perhaps half the full text and summarises therefore perhaps the second half or more of the plot (cf. Luppe 172). It is as difficult to relate its wording as that of 4017 to the general reconstruction. There is nothing to suggest mention of the Pegasus-flight; and 21 **ship** is problematic in an inland plot! The Hypothesis is of the same kind as that to *Sthen.*: see pp. 1–2, 84–5.

1 . having determined: almost certainly Bellerophon.

5 . fitting <*penalty*> Luppe, as part of his very speculative reconstruction (above, pp. 98, 101); he compares *Sthen.* test. ii.21 (also Hypothesis).

7 . corpse begins the Greek sentence; unlikely to be one of Bellerophon's own slain children, Hom. *Il.* 6.203–5.

9 . Taurus: if correct, this is the mountain range N. of the Lycian (20) plain.

1 2 . river: a gloss, but the missing or damaged name it explains is 'not obvious' (Cockle); so Cockle prefers to restore the probable but rather distant name in 13 as **Isander**, a son of Bellerophon, rather than Meander, the Lycian river.

1 8 . springs: reading uncertain, but Luppe rejects Cockle's 'penalties'.

2 2 . Cockle adds the punctuation; if correctly, the last sentence was very brief.

285. The reflective, even rhetorical, manner of this disquisition suggests that it is the start (or near-start) of a monologue early in the play — but the style and length are not those of an orientatory prologue speech, *pace* Johansen, *General Reflection* 127f., despite similarities in topic to *Sthen.* F 661.1–3 (start of the Prologue) and in analytic method with F 661.22–5: see Comm. there.

311 (310 N) Take this ill-fated man inside.

The final scene, with Bellerophon near death.

312   ... (Pegasus) has gone to carry lightning alongside Zeus' chariot.

A god 'finishes the story' of Pegasus after he has thrown Bellerophon.

1 – 2. common refrain: this axiom occurs first at Theognis 425, most famously at Soph. *OC* 1225, cf. Eur. F 908.1; Alexis fr. 145.14–16 'the saying of the wise'. For the appeal to a 'proverb' see on *Sthen.* F 668.

3 – 5. three estates ... one superior: *wealth* (6–10), *noble blood* (11–14), and (best) *poverty* (15–17). For such evaluative categorisations in Eur. cf. esp. *El.* 367– 76 (373 'how ... distinguish and rate correctly?', Future as 3 here); politico-economic categorisation of citizens *Supp.* 238–45, *Ion* 595–606, *Aeolus* F 21 etc. **estates:** μοῖρα as *Supp.* 238, see Collard, or Page on *Med.* 430. **noble blood:** lit. 'whoever has noble breeding'; the Greek substantival clause between two nouns expresses the middle, different category: Aesch. *Sept.* 197, cf. Kannicht on *Hel.* 1137. **count:** ἀριθμός of a numbered 'category' *Ion* 1014, *Mel.D.* F 492.5. **put forward:** as a contention, an orator's word, *Hipp.* 382, *Pho.* 559.

7 . miserable, yes, miserable: such doubling is rare in dialogue, and heavily emphatic; the same verb *And.* 980; cf. F 286.2 below, Mastronarde on *Pho.* 584. **splendid misery:** extending but sardonically inverting the emphasis: oxymoron like *Tro.* 727 'Grieve nobly!', *Hipp.* 384, *Hel.* 1633 etc.

8 – 1 4. Commonplaces about wealth's joy (e.g. *Danae* F 324) or pain (e.g. *Danae* F 326), and its links with birth (see e.g. Cropp on *El.* 37). The high man less able to bear deprivation, e.g. *Hel.* 417–9, *HF* 1291–3; cf. Hdt. 1.32.5–6

8 – 1 0. despite his wealth ... before: i.e. his wealth itself predisposes him to folly, cf. e.g. *Hipp.* 774f., Diggle on *Pha.* 165.   [Text: **yoke:** the noun ζεῦγλα is not elsewhere used figuratively until Hellenistic Greek (LSJ); so perhaps ζεύγματα, *IA* 443 of 'fate'.]

11 – 1 2 . proud ... blood: *Alex.* F 52.9, 1040, cf. *Sthen.* F 661.4.

1 3 – 1 4 . inferior: for the social value in adjs. meaning 'less' cf. F 304.3–4 below, *Supp.* 437 (see Collard), *Erec.* F 361, Thuc. 1.76.2 etc.   **manual work:** beneath the dignity of a noble, as perhaps Hes. *WD* 311, 317 (see Cairns, *Aidos* 150 n. 9); *El.* 65, *Rhes.* 176, Ar. *Birds* 1432, Dem. 18.257.   [Text: †**his thoughts ... misery†:** the discrepancies between the two citations in Stob. only complicate the problems: (a) the compound verb ἐναλγύνεσθαι is unattested; Eur. does not use ἐν adverbially; (b) the participle φρονῶν gives weak sense (as translated); the noun φρενῶν will translate only with αἰδοῦς 'shame of mind makes', but this is against the idiom of unqualified ὑπ᾽ αἰδοῦς, e.g. *Erec.* F 362.33; so Gomperz's 'and if he is burdened by it, shame of mind makes ... (etc.)' is not likely. Perhaps ἔνθ᾽ ἀλγύνεται Ι φέρων 'thereupon he bears (cf. *Hec.* 376) it in misery, and shame makes...'; or ἐν δ᾽ ἀλγηδόσι Ι φρενῶν ... [δ᾽] 'and in his mind's misery (phrasing as *Oenomaus* F 573.3) shame makes ...'.]

15.absolute nobody: οὐδέν intensifies οὐδείς, juxtaposed negatives like *IT* 115, *Antigone* F 165. For οὐδείς 'a person of no account' cf. *And.* 700, *IA* 371, Ar. *Knights* 158. The Neut. οὐδέν is more usual with the article, e.g. *Pho.* 598; the idiom is examined by A. C. Moorhouse, *CQ* 15 (1965), 31–40.

16.is superior: the judgement promised in 3, but the conclusion is given rather in 18. This definition of superiority resembles *Tro.* 638–41, in the destitute Andromache's attempt at self-comfort; cf. *IT* 1117–22.

19. Bellerophon's reminiscence seems incomplete, and resembles Nestor's nostalgia for his past glory, Hom. *Il.* 1.269, 9.105 etc. [Text: **remember what I ...** was like: construction as e.g. *Hcld.* 741; Nauck's Neuter is not less idiomatic, e.g. *Med.* 889 ἐσμὲν οἷόν ἐσμεν, 'we are what kind we are'.]

286. Bellerophon attacks divine injustice, exemplified in his own undeserved misery, for he was a pious man, F 310. Complaints at the unfair prosperity of the irreligious (7, 11) at the expense of the pious (8–9) are a cliché: F 293.3 below, *Hipp.* 1102ff., *Scyrii* F 684, cf. Riedweg 41. They are often countered by trust in the gods', or time's, justice, as by the Chorus at F 303, 304 below, cf. *Alc.* 604–5, *Ion* 1621–2, and in reward for the worker *El.* 80–1 (very similar in wording), cf. *Tel.* F 701 n. The attack on tyranny's success (5–12) is also a commonplace (see 5 n.), but some reconstructions of the play read it as directed against Iobates: above p. 100.

3. antiquated reasoning: so old as to be superannuated; for this sense of παλαιός see commentators on *Hel.* 1056; ἀρχαῖος has the same nuance F 1088. 'Ancient reasoning' (in other contexts) is contested at e.g. Aesch. *Ag.* 750f., approved at e.g. *Pho.* 438, *Aeolus* F 25.

4. consider for yourselves: an orator's manoeuvre, appealing for confirmation but also persuading an audience that the speaker is only formulating their own beliefs, *Supp.* 476, *Hipp.* 943, *Tro.* 931 etc.; cf. Lloyd 45 and n. 24.

5. tyranny: its crimes are a commonplace, (Collard on) *Supp.* 429, 453, *Ion* 621ff.; 'tyranny, prosperous injustice', *Pho.* 549; cf. *TrGF* II adesp. 181. For the Greek congruence of Sing. noun and Plur. participle in 7 cf. e.g. *Hec.* 38–9, Soph. *Ant.* 1021; KG I.54.

9. from day to day: implicitly, without getting wealth: cf. *Tel.* F 714.2 n.

12. army: λόγχη, lit. 'spear', in synecdoche as often, *Pho.* 442 etc.

13–14 are clearly an uncompleted argument, approximately 'if you saw a lazy man rewarded for his prayers, you would <agree with me that the gods are not concerned to reward virtue, etc.>'. Cf. *El.* 80–1 'no lazy man could gather his livelihood without work.'

1 5 . This verse, while consistent with Bellerophon's atheism, has become attached in the anthological tradition to the major fragment; it may not even stem from *Bell*. Moreover, the position of connective τε shows that the verse is itself defective. Most of Riedweg's article is nevertheless devoted to arguing for its retention and to filling the lacuna plausibly.   **fortify:** metaph. as *Tro*. 612, *Med*. 526.

286b (292 N). The context is identified differently by A. M. Mesturini, *Ann. Fac...Genova* 1981, 35–56 (see *APh* 52 [1981],112), who places the lines in Bellerophon's own 'self-absolution' at the play's end.

1 . too: recovery of the context might show that καί means rather 'in fact': Denniston, *GP* 312. 'Look at the symptoms first': F 917, 1072; cf. Hippocr. *Airs etc*. 1 'study the local conditions first'.

2 . summarily: ἐπιτάξ as Com. adesp. 1296 Kock; LSJ II; W. Nestle, *Hermes* 7 3 (1935), 27n. and N. Collinge, *BICS* 9 (1962), 45. Another meaning is possible, 'continuously': Nauck here, cf. LSJ I and perhaps *TrGF* II adesp. 587. LSJ III give also 'according to prescription' for Call. fr. 178.9 (but that idea comes in our line 5), as if cognate with medical ἐπιτάσσειν, ἐπιτακτός (Stob. here) 'prescribe, prescribed'.

4ff. diseases . . . self-chosen: literal in 1 and 3, 'disease' now takes on its common half-metaphorical meaning for any human malcondition; cf. esp. F 1026 'most of men's troubles are self-chosen', and the famous *Hipp*. 358–9, 380–3 for troubles recognised but still embraced; Dover, *GPM* 146.   **visited by gods:** conventionally treated therefore by ritual purification: for the idea see Pearson o n Soph. F 650 'divine disease', Ar. *Wasps* 118; Parker, *Miasma* ch. 7, esp. 2 16–8. 5th C. medicine regarded such disease as outside a doctor's province: see the 'Hippocratic' passages, e.g. *Prognostic*, ch. 1 (Vol. 2.110–2) Littré = ch. I Jones ('Loeb'), cited by Müller (see our App.) 117 n. 4. See also *Mel.S*. F 481.17 n. Whether **treat them** refers to both diseases or only to the divine (so Nestle [n. o n 2 above] 27–8), Eur. seems to be rejecting any distinction for the doctor, like the 'Hippocratic' *Sacred Disease* ch. 18 (Vol. 6.394) Littré = ch. XXI Jones; and Eur.'s essential point in 1–3 holds, 'examine first, then treat'. This link makes against the otherwise tempting suggestion (Cropp) that 1–3, cited separately by Stob. 4.36.5, and 4–7 are separate frs.

But what does the medical analogy mean for Bellerophon? That some human afflictions are beyond human remedy because god-sent like his own misery, or that they may nevertheless be helped by normal diagnosis and treatment? And what i s the connection between 1–6a and 7 **if the gods do anything shameful, they are not gods** ('anything mean', Plut. 21a, Ps.-Justin, preferred by Müller 119)? Simply that the speaker does not believe the gods to be morally capable of visiting anything incurable upon men, and that Bellerophon therefore must take heart and find a cure? Müller thinks the connection incomplete, however, and would supplement ' . . . **to our rule.** <*The gods are indifferent to what they bring about, even if we entreat them.*> But . . .'.

6. [But what . . . : Text: West sought better idiom (but for Stob's 'But I tell you . . .' Müller cites *Hec.* 1232. Gomperz, with 'I want to tell you another thing', identified the same lack of connection as Müller).] **7.** For the incompatibility of god and evil cf. *El.* 583–4, *IT* 391, (commentators on) *HF* 1341ff.; Soph. F 247.4.

287. *Stob.* 4.44 has many quotations on 'pragmatism', e.g. *Hipp.* 203–7, *Aeolus* F 37; [Plut.] cites e.g. Eur. *Mel.* F 505, 965, Hom. *Il.* 16.404ff. **not get angry:** the philosophy of equanimity, *Antiope* F 196 etc. cited by Dodds on *Bacc.* 424–6. **affairs** (twice) . . . **fares:** reproducing the alliteration and assonance, if not the weak pun, in the Greek.

288. dark: of scheming, *Supp.* 324; cf. 'secret scheming' *Ion* 1116. **cowardly:** scheming is 'not manly' *And.* 446, *Med.* 412–3.

289. A. M. Mesturini, *Helikon* 20/21 (1980/1[1983]), 301–7 reviews interpretations of this fragment so difficult without its context, suggesting it may be part of Bellerophon's dying reflection on his life, cf. esp. F 310, also F 285.19–20, F 300. **1. accomplish:** κλέπτειν 'achieve, carry out by stealth' like Soph. *El.* 37 (a murder); cf. Jebb on *Aj.* 189.   [Text: explanatory γάρ necessitates Meineke's χρεών, providing a construction for the inf. κλέπτειν; Mesturini 305 keeps χερῶν at the cost of an unlikely imperatival Inf. (very rare: Diggle, *Studies* 10f.).] **2. truth is ineffectual:** this sense of the adj. φαῦλος is shown by the contrast with **war is a friend to lies**; cf. *Med.* 807, *And.* 379. The adj. is regularly coloured by its context: see Dodds on *Bacc.* 430–3, who takes it here as 'simple, straightforward', in conformity with the maxim at *Pho.* 469, Aesch. F 176. At *Hel.* 745 φαῦλος is equated with 'full of lies'.

290. For the thought cf. *Aeolus* F 27, Soph. F 939, *TrGF* II adesp. 540; brainless athletes: Cropp on *El.* 386–90.   Line 1 has two juxtaposed but contrasting adjs. in asyndeton; cf. Denniston on *El.* 253.

291. 1–2. For this contrast between young and old, earliest at Hom. *Il.* 4.322–4, Stob. cites e.g. *Pho.* 528–30, *Mel.(?)D.* F 508; cf. Hes. fr. 321 (proverbial) 'Deeds belong to the young, deliberation to the middle-aged, prayers to the old'.   **3. time** the teacher: *Hipp.* 252, *Supp.* 419–20, *Peleus* F 619.   **subtle:** meaning of ποικίλος as *Pho.* 470, cf. LSJ III.3.   [Text, **1 taut:** preferable to εὔτονοι 'well-toned', despite Nauck's appeal to Cornutus.]

293. It is hard to think who can be meant by 'you' in 1, unless it is Bellerophon himself rejecting the world; but then his 'honour' will be *amour propre* and it is impossible to find a necessary link between 'honour' in 1 (it has been attacked by conjecture) and 'honoured' in 3. Dobree's conjecture keeps the three lines as one fragment but makes the thought of 3 particular to the speaker on seeing the instance in 1:

' . . . not worth (my) living if I see . . . '. **1.** For the bad effects of ambition cf. *Pho.* 532, *IA* 527. **2.** Revulsion at prosperity of the wicked: F 286 n. above.

294. Envy in Eur.: esp. *Ino* F 403, *Oed.* F 551; cf. Carcinus *TrGF* I 70 F 8. **leap:** the image here implies hostility, cf. Bond on *HF* 66; instinctive quickness, e.g. *Or.* 896, *Mel.* F 506.1.

295. supporters at a trial: παραστάται is a synonym for συνήγοροι, the Athenian legal term (MacDowell on Ar. *Wasps* 482), which occurs in Tragedy at Aesch. *Ag.* 831; cf. σύνδικοι Aesch. *Eum.* 761, (verb) *Med.* 158. Anachronism is hardly felt in so compelling a comparison. An alternative but less vivid interpretation is 'supporters of justice'; cf. e.g. Soph. *El.* 529. **2 envy:** different from the natural envies of F 294; Bellerophon (if it is he) may be making just a 'debating point', or confirming that envy is all-corrupting.

296. Sympathy between similar moralities: *Aegeus* F 7, *Hyps.* F 759, *Phoenix* F 812, cf. *And.* 683f., *Or.* 805; Aristotle cited in the App. Friendship based on kinship (3 ὁμόφυλον) *HF* 1200.

297. Without the context it is impossible to fix the meaning of **1 badness** (κάκη) or the sequence of thought, or indeed to be confident of the text. 'Cowardice' (and 'proves a coward' in 3) is equally possible, esp. (Cropp) in the light of 4 'audacity' and (JD) if the speaker is being cynical as at e.g. *Pho.* 524–5. **in their nature:** for this idea cf. *Hipp.Cal.* F 444.2, F 1027.5. **2–4.** Venality: *Danae* F 325, Hes. *WD* 356–60; Pind. *Pyth.* 3.54f.; Soph. *OT* 387f. [Text: **2** most pay (or 'very much pay') produces an intelligible contrast with 4 'more pay (etc).'; Bücheler's 'least' (a form not attested for Eur.) or Heath's 'little' makes the contrast plain. **3. proves:** for the Greek Subjunctive see *Erec.* F 360.11 n.]

298. won't . . . nor: i.e. 'just as not . . . so not', so-called paratactic comparison, more common with 'both . . . and': *Pha.* 124–6 n., Denniston, *GP* 515. Both contentions here rest on proverbs: with 1–2a cf. *Hcld.* 684 'you don't see a wound without action', cf. Aesch. *Sept.* 398; with 2b–3 cf. *Dictys* F 333 'the old saying's got it right: a base father won't produce a good son', *Alcm.(?)Cor.* F 75, *Phoenix* F 810, all cited here by Stob. [Text and translation are insecure: Nauck and Heath tidied the errors in 1. ξε- is a short-vowel form of ξυ- 'plane, whittle', ξυστόν a Homeric spear, *Hec.* 920; for ξεστός ('made of dressed stone') see on F 305 below. The preverb 'in' in the (unique) compound ἐγξεῖν is otiose and the lack of an object harsh. Salmasius tried 'whittles sticks from marshes', i.e. to make spears, but θάμνοι are always 'thickets', not single pieces of wood. Cropp develops 'whittles marshy shoots', θάλλους, from Housman's 'whittles with shoots (of olive)': i.e. no wounds come from festal olive wreaths.] **2. marshy:** producing only sapwood, useless for weapons.

300. For the sentiment cf. *Cresph*. F 454, F 1075.1, *HF* 1227–8, 1314, *Ion* 969, Aesch. *Pers*. 706. For the question **But why** . . . cf. *IA* 460, *Pho*. 1726; Diggle, *Studies* 51; it is semi-colloquial (Stevens, *CE* 40), suggesting stress.

301. For the maxim in line 1 cf. *Ion* 1511, *Alcmena* F 100 and the tail-pieces to *And*., *Bacc*. etc. [Text: Kannicht on *Hel*. 713–4 translates 3 as 'many overcoming their enemies in war', and misses before it '<encountered much stormier weather>' as completion of a double antithesis in 1–2 to the double one of 3–4 (he compares the structure of *Scyrii* F 684). But ἀμείνονες cannot be 'stronger', for that is κρείσσονες (e.g. F 286.11–12 above, *Med*. 315.]

302. For the thought cf. esp. *Ino* F 416.

303. This fr. and the next are the strongest counter to B.'s criticism of the gods in F 286; so they may be associated with his departure (but see next note on *Metre*).

Metre: dactylo-epitrite (see West, *BICS*), whereas F 304 has different, mixed rhythms; the probability is they may not come from the same ode.

2. **secure**: adj. βέβαιος and axiom as *Erec*. F 354 etc.; Cropp on *El*. 940–4.

3. **time . . . born from nothing**: time is 'self-generated', αὐτοφυής *Pir*. F 593.1 N = *TrGF* I Critias 43 F 4.1, i.e. has no 'father' – but is itself a father of 'lifetimes' or 'days' *Hcld*. 900, *Supp*. 787, *Antiope* F 222: see J. de Romilly, *Time in Greek Tragedy* (Ithaca, 1968), 37 for the concept.

4–5. Time the revealer of truth (and therefore judge) *Hipp*. 430, 1051, *Alex*. F 60, *Antiope* F 202; de Romilly 51; time the changer of fortunes: see on F 304.3 below. **standards**: metaphor from a mason's measure, *Hec*. 602, *El*. 52 etc.

5. [**in spite of all**: West's conjecture explains the impossible 'to me' of Stob. as a copyist's error (examples of this confusion in Diggle, *Studies* 39).]

304. *Metre*: anapaestic dimeter in 1, followed remarkably by complex choriambic tetrameters in 2–4 according to Wilamowitz, *KS* IV. 480, cf. *Verskunst* 292; but the text may not be secure enough to scan confidently (JD suggests 2–4 are perhaps six aeolic dimeters). Cf. on F 303.

1. **sureness**: for the doubt cf. *Thyestes* F 391.2–3, *HF* 62; for the Greek articular expression *Or*. 397, *Hel*. 1149, *Bacc*. 877.

2–3. **drive a straight path**: with ἰθύνειν here compare εὐθύνειν of a ship, *Hec*. 39. [†oceant deep: usage indicates that the tautologous adj. ἅλιον goes with the noun for 'sea, deep etc.', e.g. *And*. 1012, and that κατά controls the Accus. (Grotius), e.g. *And*. 849; but the end of 2 is metrically at fault, despite Wilamowitz: see above.]

3–4. The instability of human life is a cliché, *Hcld*. 101–4, cf. on *Sthen*. F 661. 1–3; winds and waves are symbols (usually) of its mutability, *Supp*. 554, *Ion* 1507, *Tro*. 102–4, not, as here, a contrast with it; time is the agent of change *Hipp*. 1108ff., *HF* 506ff., *Or*. 976ff., cf. de Romilly (see F 303.3 n.) 120.   **the lesser**: for the 'value' adj. see on F 285.13. For the change from Fem. τύχας to subdivided Neuts. τὸ μέν . . . τὸ δέ ('construction according to sense') cf. *Pho.* 1460ff., *Bacc.* 1131ff.

304a (68 N). These lines are assigned to *Bell.* by those who believe it included a rôle for Megapenthes, attempting to revenge his mother Stheneboea's killing by Bellerophon: see pp. 99, 100. Others have assigned them to one of the *Alcmaeon*s, where Alcmaeon is a matricide (then κατέκταν 'I killed' is read in 1); van Looy, *Zes Tragedies* 97–8 finds the question insoluble. The lines are cited by Aristotle (and his two commentators) for the 'extraordinary' second verse; Eur. has similar gratuitous sophistries *Hipp.* 319, *Hcld.* 531, *IT* 512.

305. A 'trial' (of Bellerophon?) at Argos (city of the **Danaids**) is even more difficult to locate in this play (unless explained as part of a narrative from there) than it is in *Sthen.*, to which some transfer it (p. 81). Di Gregorio 204ff., followed by Riedweg 52, has it as part of Megapenthes' narrative, how the people of Argos voted to punish Bellerophon for killing Stheneboea. **dressed-stone:** the adj., a favourite of Eur., describes finished masonry, *Pha.* 222, *Tro.* 46, *Or.* 1388 etc. [Text: Schol. *Or.* quote the fr. to illustrate a high tribunal (871) postulated in Argos; the text can only be sound if line 1 completes a picture of someone ascending the tribunal, and 2, a main clause, introduces his words; compare perhaps *IT* 962, Orestes taking 'the stand' at Athens. The two lines are joined in the conjecture of Ellis 'he took his stand on the tribunal', but the prep. εἰς is then strained: contrast *IT* 962 'stood trial'. The heralds, also on the tribunal, control the speakers, *Or.* 885.]

306. Lit. 'dear swift wing of Pegasus', a form of solemn address common in Tragedy (Barrett on *Hipp.* 651) but derived from a periphrastic idiom of Epic (e.g. Hom. *Il.* 8.281 'Teucer, dear head'); here it suggests an heroic venture. Cf. Pegasus's 'thick-plumed wing', πυκνὸν πτερόν, *Sthen.* F 665a. As to Ar. *Peace* 135 (see App.), Rau 95 inclines to think that the word τραγικώτερος 'more tragic', beginning 136, suggests that 135 ζεῦξαι πτερόν 'yoke the wing' comes also from this context of *Bell.*: quite possibly. *Peace* 126 has 'the winged ... shall carry ...'; Schol. there attributes the line either to *Sthen.* where it is more at home (F 669.4 and Comm.) or to *Bell.*

307. For the quality of the parody in *Peace* 154, esp. of Eur. describing the noise of the bit, see Platnauer's n. **golden bit:** *IA* 219 'horses with elaborate mouth-pieces of gold'. *Metre:* anapaests, see on next fragment.

307a, 308. *Metre:* anapaests, suggesting steady movement: is B. now ascending?
1. my soul! Aristophanes mocks Eur.'s frequent self-address by his characters; at the start of monodies (here?) *IT* 882, *Ion* 859; cf. F 310, *Cresph.* F 448a.83–6 n.; Rau 37.
2–3. foliage . . . dells: Bellerophon is evidently in broken country before his flight, on the Aleian Plain (see Introd. p. 99) only after his fall. Eur. has many descriptions of wooded river-valleys, e.g. *Bacc.* 1051–2, 1094–5.

5. [**state ... for a good journey:** text explained by Wilamowitz, *KS* IV.480, repudiating his earlier acceptance of Heath's conjecture 'what position Einodia ('Way-goddess', i.e. Hecate) has'. An image of Hecate stood outside large houses; but as a goddess largely of the night, she has no standing at the door of the bright heaven.] The **heaven** (αἰθέρα, 4) shows the weather; στάσις, **state** or 'quarter', of a wind Alcaeus Z.2.1 L.–P., Hdt. 2.26.2, [Aesch.] *PV* 1087; the noun εὐοδία, **good journey**, Aesch. F 36, Ar. *Frogs* 1528 etc.

309. **stooped:** the verb πτήσσειν describes animals only when in fear, usually cowering birds, e.g. *HF* 974. But at Soph. F 659.9 a horse 'cowers' in shame for its cropped mane: if that is Pegasus's posture here expressing his reluctance to be mounted, 'if ... willing' is wrong. But Bellerophon wishes him to fly: so either Munro's 'in whatever way (Bellerophon) more wished' is attractive, or Mette's 'more than a man might wish'. [The text is hardly sound, but Plut. cites the line twice to illustrate excessive yielding to the appeals of others.]

309a. The closest analogy for the metaphor in **salutations** seems to be Soph. *OT* 1428 '(the polluted Oedipus) whom neither earth nor holy rain nor sunlight will welcome'. [Text: Diggle points to *Supp.* 206 for the confusion of ὑδρηλός and (very rare: LSJ) ὑδρηρός.]

310 (311 N). Aelian has 'Eur. praises Bellerophon too as having prepared himself heroically and proudly for death; at any rate he has made him address his own heart with "you were ... friends" and things on that theme'. It may be inferred that Bellerophon again addressed himself with ὦ ψυχή, 'My soul!', as in F 307a (n.). **while you lived:** cf. Bellerophon's allusion to his earlier prosperity, F 285.20 ('and piety', Riedweg 53). True to strangers, guests *Alc.* 855ff., *Hec.* 715 etc.; to friends *Hec.* 1226, *Or.* 1155.

311 (310 N). Aristophanes' substitution of κυλίνδετ', 'wheel (him) inside', for κομίζετ' suggests he intends parody of our play's final scene, with a crippled and dying hero wheeled off-stage on the *eccyclema* (was he therefore also brought on by it?). Neil, *Knights ad loc.* denies this, and wonders whether the Schol. is not misattributing the very similar line from the end of *Sthen.*, F 671. **ill-fated man:** perhaps a ref. to Bellerophon's hostility to the gods, cf. F 286.8 where he speaks of those 'more prosperous under heaven'. The dying Hippolytus uses the same word to describe himself, *Hipp.* 1387.

312. The god speaking here was most probably Athena who in some accounts helped Bellerophon master Pegasus at Pirene. Pegasus works apparently as a detached horse, and is not yoked (that would be ὑπό and Dat., 'under the chariot'). Pind. *Ol.* 13.92 has Pegasus stabled by Zeus on Olympus; Asclepiades (on Hom. *Il.* 6.155) has him given by Zeus to Dawn, to guarantee the safety of her chariot; Arat. *Phaenom.* 205ff. and Hygin. *Astron.* 2.18.1 have him turned into a star. For the rare verb ἀστραπηφορεῖν cf. the adj. in -φόρος *Bacc.* 3.

CRESPHONTES

Texts, testimonia. P. Oxy. 2458 with P. Mich. Inv. 6973 (see F 448a); P. Fayum (see F 449); *TrGF* F 448a–459; Austin, *NFE* frs. 66–77; Mette Nos. 599–616; O. Musso, *Euripide: Cresfonte* (Milan, 1974); A. Harder, *Euripides' Kresphontes and Archelaos* (Leiden, 1985).

Myth. Hygin. *Fab.* 137 and 184(b); Apollod. 2.8.4–5; *Anth.Pal.* 3.5. 'History' of the *Heraclids in Messenia*: Isocr. 6.22–5 and 31–3; Ephorus *FGH* 70 F 116 (= Strabo 8.4.7); Nicolaus Damasc. *FGH* 90 F 31 and 34; Pausanias 4.3.3–8 (cf. 2.18.7–19.2, 8.5.6–7). Preller–Robert II.2.671–5; L. Pearson, *Historia* 11 (1962), 397–426 (bibl.); Harder (above), 7–12; Gantz 735–6.

Illustrations. None extant.

Main discussions. T. von Wilamowitz-Moellendorff, *Die dramatische Technik des Sophokles* (Berlin, 1917), 251–6; Schmid 395–7; H. J. Mette, *Hermes* 92 (1964), 391–5 and *Lustrum* 9 (1964), 66–7; K. Matthiessen, *Elektra, Taurische Iphigenie und Helena* (1964), 111–4; S. Cengarle, *Dioniso* 40 (1966), 63–76; Webster, *Euripides* (1967), 136–43; Z. Vysoky, *Strahovská Knihovna* 5–6 (1970–1), 5–18 (German summary, 19–21); Burnett, *Catastrophe Survived* 18–21; Musso (above); Harder (above), and reviews by J. Wilkins, *CR* 38 (1988) 209–10, W. Luppe, *Mnemosyne* 42 (1989) 175–82.

The Cresphontes of our play is a great-great-great-grandson of Heracles and son of Cresphontes the legendary leader of the Dorian settlement of Messenia after the 'Return of the Heracleidae'. His story is known mainly from Hyginus, who probably reflects Euripides fairly closely in *Fab.* 184(b) (*Fab.* 137 is a brief summary):

> . . . Polyphontes seized the throne after killing Cresphontes. The infant son whom Merope had borne to Cresphontes she secretly entrusted to a family friend in Aetolia. Polyphontes sought this child with great effort, promising gold to whoever should kill him. On reaching puberty Cresphontes made a plan to avenge the death of his father and brothers. So he came to king Polyphontes to request the gold, saying that he had killed the son of Cresphontes and Merope, Telephontes. For the moment the king told him to stay in a guest-room so that he might enquire further about him. Cresphontes fell asleep through fatigue, and an old man who had been a messenger between mother and son came to Merope weeping, saying that he was not with the family friend and was nowhere to be found. Merope, believing the sleeping man to be her son's murderer, came into the room (?: see F 456 n.) with an axe, unwittingly intending to slay her own son. But the old man recognised him and restrained the mother from her crime. When Merope realised her enemy had given her the opportunity of avenging herself, she made things up with Polyphontes. As the joyful king was performing a religious ceremony his guest, falsely pretending to have killed the victim, killed him and regained his paternal kingdom.

121

Two differences from Hyginus appear in our fragments. Merope probably sent her infant son to her father (see F 448a.57), mentioned in Apollod. 2.8.5 and named by Pausanias and others as Cypselus of Arcadia. Also Hyginus suggests Euripides called the boy Telephontes, but nothing supports this; it could be a false name used by Cresphontes during the play, but more probably the name in Hyginus is corrupt or a summariser's aberration (Harder 52, Luppe 176–7).

Apollod. 2.8.5 concerning the Heracleidae ends with the elder Cresphontes killed after a short reign 'along with two of his sons' (cf. F 448a.51), Polyphontes ('also one of the Heracleidae': see under *Myth* below) seizing power and taking Merope against her will, and a third son Aepytus, 'whom she gave to her father to bring up' (see above, and again under *Myth* below), returning secretly to kill Polyphontes and regain the kingdom.

Anth. Pal. 3.5 is a late epigram designed as a 'caption' to one of the reliefs showing scenes of filial piety on the 2nd C. B.C. monument at Cyzicus to Apollonis, mother of the Pergamene rulers Attalus and Eumenes. (Other such epigrams are noticed in our Introductions to *Bell.*, *Mel.D.* and in Vol. 2 *Antiope* and *Hyps.*). In 3.5 Cresphontes is described as killing Polyphontes with a spear in the back while Merope attacks him with a staff. This probably reflects Euripides' play loosely, but Euripides will have put the killing in a report speech and is unlikely to have given Merope so active a role.

Other testimonia, apart from some citing the fragments themselves, do little to illuminate the play's substance (see Harder 27–9, 47–56). It opened with the arrival of Cresphontes, who probably spoke the Prologue speech giving the story so far and certainly (as P. Oxy. showed, F 448a) learned more of the local situation from perhaps a palace servant; he then delivered a monologue expressing doubt followed by determination to proceed with the assault on Polyphontes with his mother's help. The Parodos (as P. Mich. has lately revealed, also F 448a) introduced the Chorus of old Messenian men sympathetic to the legitimate royal house and to Merope, but no doubt subdued by the usurper. Hyginus's summary then requires *(a)* Polyphontes introduced and confronted by the disguised Cresphontes who claims the reward, is told to wait while further enquiries are made, and is shown to the guest quarters where he falls asleep (Epis. 1?); *(b)* the Old Man bringing news of Cresphontes' disappearance to Merope; they plan and initiate her attack on Cresphontes but the Old Man recognises him, and the three proceed to plot the attack on Polyphontes (Epis. 2 and 3?); *(c)* Merope offering reconciliation to Polyphontes who with guard lowered proceeds to a sacrifice where Cresphontes takes his opportunity to attack (presumably a report speech) and reclaims his kingdom (Epis. 4 and 5?). This makes a dramatic sequence comparable in obvious ways with Aesch. *Cho.*, Soph. *El.*, and especially Eur. *El.* (where the disguised Orestes receives hospitality, is recognised by his old tutor, plots with the tutor and Electra, and kills Aegisthus by surprise at a sacrifice). But several important features remain unclear: the precise strategy of Cresphontes and situation of Merope at the outset; how the first Episode was elaborated (a confrontation between Merope and Polyphontes has been hypothesised and would add some welcome complexity); when the Old Man arrived (before Cresphontes' rearrival, or after?); the staging of Merope's attack on Cresphontes (see F 456 n.); and the scenario for the killing of Polyphontes (more likely within or close to the palace than in the country as in *El.*). Little can be said about the closure of the play; there is not much to provide complications — possibly, however, some further political conflict (cf. F 453) which might bring a final intervention by a god (Heracles?) like Athena's bringing peace in Ithaca in the *Odyssey*: a divine confirmation that Cresphontes' hands were clean after the murder is surely needed.

Contexts are certain only for F 448a and F 456. Several other fragments may belong to the scene of Merope's pretended reconciliation with Polyphontes (F 449, 451, 452, and esp. 454, 455, 458) and F 459 to the celebration of his death, but all have alternatives (see Comm. in each case).

Other ascriptions. F 1083 (from a prologue, quoted by Strabo 8.5.6) has often been attributed to *Cresph.* (lately by Musso, and by Vysoky to a play of Euripides about the elder Cresphontes which he hypothesises on inadequate grounds); it belongs better with *Tem.* or *Temenid.* as known from P. Oxy. 2455 frs. 8–11, 107 and P. Mich. inv. 1319 (much discussed recently: see now A. Harder in *Fragmenta Dramatica*, 117–36). In an Appendix to her edition (275–80) Harder duly rejects the implausible attributions of *Erec.* F 362.18–20 (cf. F 362 App.), *Polyidus* F 645, and F 908, 908a, 908b, 953, 1058.

Myth. An elaborate but now poorly preserved tradition told how the descendants of Heracles 'returned' to the Peloponnese in the fourth generation after his death, overthrew the ruling dynasties, and established the Dorian kingdoms (Diod. Sic. 4.57–8, Apollod. 2.8; *LIMC* IV, 'Herakleidai'; convenient discussion in M. P. Nilsson, *Cults, Myths, Oracles and Politics in Ancient Greece* [repr. New York, 1972], 65–80; further refs. in Harder in *Fragmenta Dramatica*, 129 n. 29). These legends, even if not politico-aetiological inventions of the archaic period, were certainly subjected to constant variation and revision in connection with the internal and external politics of the Peloponnesian states and their neighbours; there was no standard version in Euripides' time. For Messenia the picture is further complicated by its subjugation to the Spartans from the late 8th C. until its liberation in 371 and the foundation of the city of Messene in 369. There are virtually no traces of a Messenian historical or literary record within this period; a history may have been largely invented at independence within the existing traditions of the more dominant Peloponnesian states (see Pearson under *Myth* above). This process may, however, have begun in the 5th C., e.g. after the Messenian rebellion of 465–56 when Athens settled Messenian refugees at Naupactus (E. Schwartz, *Hermes* 34 [1899], 449). Euripides' play, produced probably near the time when some of these Messenians returned to their own land to assist Athens in holding Pylos against the Spartans (425), may well have had a political thrust comparable with that of *Heracleidae*.

The elder Cresphontes was said to have won Messenia by trickery when the Heraclid leaders drew lots for Messenia, the Argolid and Laconia (Apollod. 2.8.4; cf. Soph. *Aj.* 1285–7). In Isocr. 6.22–5, 31–3 and Nicolaus F 31, 34 (probably following Ephorus) accounts of his career continue in a hostile vein: he precipitates a civil conflict which his youngest son Aepytus survives, but which persists until the Spartan subjugation. Pausanias 4.3.8 differs in making Aepytus a popular ruler, so that the royal family came to be called Aepytidae rather than Heracleidae. The name Aepytus is not recorded until after Euripides' time; it belonged to a long established Arcadian hero and to Cypselus's father, and its attachment to the Messenian royal house seems politically motivated: cf. Harder 54 with refs. Polyphontes — one of the Heracleidae in F 448a.43 and in Apollod. 2.8.5, erroneously a brother of the elder Cresphontes in Gellius's citation of F 451 — is nowhere to be seen in the 'historical' versions and may be regarded as Euripides' invention (see F 448a.43 n., Harder 9) along with the bulk of the dramatic plot, including the return *incognito* of the young hero, the predicament of the bereaved wife, the Old Man as go-between, Merope's attack on Cresphontes and the recognition, and the killing of the tyrant at a sacrifice.

Themes and characters. These plot motifs have much in common with the story of Orestes' return, especially in Aesch. *Cho.* Orestes too returns *incognito* from exile, impelled by the memory of his murdered father, announces his own death, has to deal with a mother married to the usurper (a relative), and takes the usurper by surprise to regain his kingdom. Clytemnestra is inverted in Merope, and the hard problem of matricide gives way to the excitement and pathos of the mother's unwitting attack on her son. (The old retainer's restraint of her axe-blow is itself derived from a long-standing feature of the Orestes story: cf. Burnett 20–1, Harder 17–18.) *Cresph.* also seems to foreshadow the dramatic developments of the Orestes myth in Soph. *El.* and Eur. *El.* which were probably produced in the few years after it (for the comparisons see esp. T. Wilamowitz, Harder 14–18); and more could be said about Merope as one of Euripides' many isolated women, about the mother's assault on an unrecognised son (e.g. Creusa in *Ion*, Hecuba in *Alex.*), and about *Cresph.*'s early place among the 'recognition and intrigue' plots which run through *El.* to *IT* and *Hel.* (see esp. Matthiessen).

Cresph. itself perhaps relied mainly on incident (understandably, given an invented plot and no foregoing literary tradition), although its full character may remain unrevealed by our largely moralistic fragments. If Euripides went further in exploring Merope's predicament as a woman or the implications of power gained through violent revenge, we cannot say how. Political conflict (*stasis*) seems to have received some attention, Polyphontes being comparable with the tyrants Aegisthus in the Orestes plays and Lycus in *HF* (Webster 141, Harder 102–3; cf. F 448a.124, F 453.10), but *HF* warns us against assuming that these features were necessarily thematic. There is little trace of a religious dimension, although Euripides could have given Heracles (and through him Zeus) some influence in the outcome, more probably from Olympus as *deus ex machina* (see above, p. 123) than from the underworld (cf. F 450 n.).

Staging. The scene is the royal palace, the known personnel a Chorus of aged Messenians, Cresphontes, Merope, Polyphontes, Old Man, and Cresphontes' informant in the Prologue. A 'messenger' and a god appearing at the end have been suggested above. That may be all: Eur. *El.* works with virtually the same distribution, and Soph. *El.* with six human characters. The only problem of staging concerns Merope's attack on Cresphontes: our witnesses make it hard to be sure whether this action was visible to the audience but may imply an action moving from behind the *skene* onto the stage (see Comm. on F 456).

Date. Not after 421, since F 453 was parodied in Ar. *Georgoi* (425–421: *Georg.* frs. 102, 111). If F 453 was quoted in summer 424 (see Comm.), this puts *Cresph.* not later than Dionysia 424. The weak case for dating after 428 on the metrical evidence (Cropp–Fick 81–2) is slightly strengthened by the additional iambic material in F 448a. Harder 4 suggests F 449 should be later than a supposed earliest publication date of 430 for Herodotus, but this is debatable. A possible connection with the Athenian occupation of Pylos in 425 has been mentioned above, p. 124. Musso xxvi–xxvii, cf. *SIFC* 36 (1964), 68–89, attempts to narrow the range to 425–422, preferring Dionysia 423.

Other dramatisations; influence. No other Greek tragedian is known to have treated this story, nor indeed those of Cresphontes' father, uncle and cousins which Euripides treated in *Tem.*, *Temenid.*, and *Arch.* The certain fragments of Ennius's Latin *Cresphontes* (frs. 54–9 Jocelyn) can be matched with Euripides' plot but do not illuminate it: see Jocelyn, *Ennius* 270–81; P. Frassinetti, *CCC* 2 (1981), 15–23; Harder 5–7. There is very little evidence for contemporary impact of *Cresph.* (though see F 453 n.), but the plot crisis at least was remembered and became an Aristotelian example of the best kind of tragic action, with unwitting kin murder narrowly avoided through a recognition (Aristot. *Poet.* 1454a5–7). The citations of F 450, 451, 454, 458 and esp. 456 suggest Merope and Cresphontes were familiar tragic characters in the heyday of the Roman Empire. Aristotle's notice and Hyginus's summary, along with the dramatic and political possibilities inherent in the near kin murder and tyrannicide, caused it to be much used from the late 16th C. The 18th C. saw tragedies by Zeno, Maffei, Voltaire and Alfieri, and over thirty operas. Note also Matthew Arnold's poetic tragedy *Merope* (1858). See *OGCMA* II.659–61; M. Petrovska, *Merope: the dramatic impact of a myth* (New York etc., 1984).

ΚΡΕΣΦΟΝΤΗΣ

448a P. Oxy. 2458 and P. Mich. Inv. 6973

P. Oxy. col. I *trimeter ends from top of column including:*   1–12

fr. 1.i   1].τειν δόλωι   2 τυρα]ννικῆς   5]πατήρ   12 τ]έκνα

   rest of column missing   13–39

P. Oxy. col. II *top of column:*

fr.1.ii   Κρεσφ.   μ[ῶν ἄδικο]ς οἴκων δε[σ]πότης περὶ ξένους;   40
   —   ὁ [ζῶν γ'], ὁ δ' οὐκ ὢν πᾶσι προσφιλέστατος.
   Κρ.   τ[ίς δ' ἔσ]τι; τὸν δὲ μηκέτ' ὄντ' αὖθις φράσον.   15
   —   ἀ[φ' Ἡ]ρ[α]κλειδῶν, ὄνομα Πολυφόντης, ξένε.
   Κρ.   [ὁ κα]τθανὼν δὲ δεσπότης τίς ἦν δόμων;
   —   ταὐτοῦ γένους τοῦδ' οἶσθα Κρεσφόντην κλύων;   45
   Κρ.   κτιστῆρά γ' ὄντα τῆσδε γῆς Μεσσηνία[ς.
   —   τοῦτον κατακτὰς δῶμα Πολυφόντης [ἔ]χει.   20
   Κρ.   πότερα βιαίως ἢ τύχαις ἀκουσίοις;
   —   βίαι δολώσας, ὡς τυραννεύοι χθονός.
   (Κρ.)   ἄπαιδά γ' ὄντα καὶ γυναικὸς ἄζυγα;   50
   (—)   οὔκ, ἀλλὰ δισσοὺς συγκ[ατέ]κτεινεν κόρους.
   Κρ.   ἦ πᾶσ' ὄλωλε δῆτα κα[ὶ] τέκνων σπορά;   25
   (Κρ.)   εἰς ἐστὶ παίδων λοιπ[ός], εἴπερ ἔστ' ἔτι.
   (Κρ.)   πῶς τόν γε θάνατο[ν καὶ] τύχας ὑπεκφυγών;
   —   μαστοῦ 'πὶ θηλῆς σμ[ικρ]ὸς ὢν ἔτ'[..] [55
   Κρ.   ἔκδημο[ς] ὢν τῆσ[δ' ἢ 'πιχ]ώριος χθ[ονός;
   —   μητρ[ὸ]ς [π]ατήρ νιν[30
   (Κρ.)   ἥξει [........].. [

448a (601–4 M, 66 A, 2A–F Musso) P. Oxy. 2458 (3rd C. A.D.), incl. lines 1–116, ed. Turner (1962), re-ed. Harder (1985), cf. S. Bonnycastle and L. Koenen (BK), forthcoming; P. Mich. Inv. 6973 (2nd C. B.C.), incl. lines 82–128, ed. BK. Text of 1–81 (P. Oxy. alone) Harder, text of 82–128 (P. Oxy. *plus* P. Mich.) BK, except as noted. Supplements by Turner in P. Oxy., by BK in P. Mich. except as noted. Line numbers BK (italic numbers P. Oxy. as in Harder). Speaker notations with *paragraphi* in P. Oxy.: ᾱ 40, 42, 44, 46, 48, 52, 56, 83; ȳ 41, 43, 45, 47, 49, 53, 55, 57; χ⁰ 110 (*paragr.* lost); *paragraphi* also 51, 54, 58. Photographs of P. Oxy. in Turner (1962) and of fr. 1 in Turner, *Greek Manuscripts of the Ancient World*, No. 32.   1 δόλωι read by Koenen δε[ ]ω Turner

CRESPHONTES

448a P. Oxy. and P. Mich.

fragments of the Prologue speech (probably Cresphontes):   1–12
    1 ... *by guile* ...   2 ... *roya l* ...   5 ... *father* ...
    12 ... children ...

dialogue between the disguised Cresphontes and (?)Servant:

Cresphontes. *<You> don't mean* the master of the house *<deals un-
    righteously>* with strangers?   40
Servant? The *<living one, yes,>* though the late one was most
    welcoming to all.
Cr. *<Who is he?>* Then tell me next of the one who is dead.
Se. *One of the Heraclids*; his name is Polyphontes, stranger.
Cr. And the master of the house who died — who then was he?
Se. You have heard of Cresphontes, one of this same family?   45
Cr. I have — the settler of this land of Messenia.
Se. This man Polyphontes slew, and possesses his house.
Cr. With violence, or through some involuntary misfortune?
Se. Through a violent plot, so that he might rule the land.
(Cr.) Was it a childless man he killed, unwedded to a wife?   50
(Se.) No; in addition he killed a pair of sons.
Cr. All of that family's seed has perished, then?
Se. One of the sons is left — if indeed he still is.
(Cr.) How did this one escape their death *<and>* misfortunes?
Se. Being still *small* at the breast's teat <   >   55
Cr. Abroad from *this country*, *<or>* residing here?
Se. His mother's father ... him <   >
(Cr.) ... *will come* <   >

(δ' ἐ[γ]ὼ? Harder)   2 Barrett (see Harder)   ῾Ελλ]ηνικῆς? Turner   40   μ[ῶν Austin   ἀ[ρα
ἄδικο]ς Turner   41 Dale (see Turner)   42 Turner and (δ') Barrett (see Austin)   55 σμ[ικρ]ὸς
Mette   ετ[ ]' i.e. ἔτ[ι] P. Oxy. read by Harder   ἔτ'[ἐ]ξ[έδυ Austin (ἔτ' ἐ[ξέδυ Görschen)   ἔτ' [ἐν]
τ[ροφαῖς Radt (see Harder)   ἔτ'[ἦν] τ[ροφοῦ Diggle   ]φ[or]ι[read by Koenen   56 Barrett (see
Austin)   57 [ἔτρεφεν 'Αρκάδων ἄναξ (e.g.) Barrett (see Harder)

128   EURIPIDES

estimated three lines missing, then near-   59–61
beginnings of trimeters from same column including: 62–68

fr. 3   62] παῖς οδε[66   ]ν' ἐχθρ [*32ῷ38*
           64] δὴ τί παῖς ομη[67   ο]ὐχὶ χρη[
           65 θ]ανόντος ταυτ[

probably no interval,
then trimeter ends from the rest of the same column: 69–78

fr. 2.i 71 δ]άμαρτ' ἔχειν   75] ας ἀντιτείσετα[ι
           72] πόσιν   76]ε ἂν γένοιτ' ἐμ[*39–47*
           73]η πάρος δέρην   77] ἑστίας ἴθι
           74]εις ἐχθροὺς ἔχει

no interval before top of next column (trimeters):

P. Oxy. col. III and P. Mich. col. I

Ox.1.iii   γυνὴ δε [79
                  πόσιν θ' ὑ[
                  ξέναι δ' ε [50
Ox.1.iii, Mi.1+2 κλαύ σασα· χαῖρε[   ]ατα
        Κρ.   αἰαῖ · τί δράσω π[   ]
                  πῶς δ' ἀθλίοισι   ε [   ] ς
                  δεῖ σ' ὦ τάλαινα καρδ[ία   ]η   85
                  ξίφος τε θηικτόν, ὦ ταλ[α-   ] α   55
                  ὦ νερ τέραι χθὼν [   ] ἄπο
                  "Αιδη θ' ὸς ἄρχει[ς] [   ] κάτω
                  ὃν εἰ μεν ἐχθρα[   ] [
Ox.1.iii, Mi.1   *traces of two lines*   90, 91
                  νῦν ει ποτ' ιε [60
                  ὑμεῖς τ' ἐάσιατ[
                  μνησ θέντ ες ει [
                  [πατρὸς] σφ [ ] [ ] [95
Ox.1.iii   ὦ φίλτατε [
                  traces of one line   65
                  κ]αὶ νῦν μ [
                  traces of one more line

                  estimated six lines missing   100–105

estimated three lines missing   59–61

more of the dialogue ?

62 ... son ...   64 then what ... boy ...   65 ... (off
from?) the one who died (?) ...   66 ... enemy (?)
... 67 ... not ...

probably no interval

end of dialogue and start of short speech by ?Servant;   69–78
line-ends, including:

71 ... to possess a (*or* as) wife   72 ... husband
73 previously ... throat   74 ... has enemies
75 ... will avenge   76 ... might happen ...
77 ... go ... hearth ...

end of ?Servant's speech and start of speech by   79–99
Cresphontes (line-beginnings):

79 ... woman (*or* wife) ...   80 and ... husband ...
81 and alien (*women?*) ...   82 ?having shed tears ...
farewell ...

Cr.   83 Alas, what shall I do ...   84 and how ... wretched
... 85 You ought, O unyielding *heart* ...   86 and ...
a sharpened sword, O *unyielding* ...   87 O land below
... from ...   88 and you, Hades, who rule ...
beneath ...   89 whom ... hatred (*or* hostile ...)
destroyed ...   92 now, if ever ...   93 and you,
permit ...   94 remembering ...   95 [father] ...
96 O dearest ...   98 now too ...

estimated six lines missing   100–105

59–61 see Comm. (coincidence of 62 with 58 is unlikely)   65–8 could coincide with 69–72
65 ταὐτ[P. Oxy. (i.e. prob. ταὐτό or ταὐτά)   71 identified by Mette with F 1060 ἐχθροῖσιν εἴη
πολεμίαν δάμαρτ' ἔχειν   76 ἂν γένοιτο corr. to ἀγγέλλοιτο (or -τε) with corr. deleted P. Oxy.
ἐμ[οί Mette   77 τῆσδ' ἀφ'] Koenen (ἀφ'] Harder)   80 ποσίντε'υ[P. Oxy. (accent due to following enclitic)   81 δ'εσ[BK   82–99, 108–9, text to left of] is in P. Oxy. only, to right of] in P.
Mich. only   82–9 this alignment of line-ends (P. Mich. fr. 2) not certain   82 [κλαύ]σασα P. Mich.
κλαίουσα P. Oxy.   χαιρε[P. Mich.   83 π[ῶς Slings (see BK)   84 ἀθλίοισιν ἐπ' ἔργο[ν? P. Mich.
85 καρδ[ία καὶ χεὶρ ἐμ]ή (e.g.) BK, cf. *Alc.* 837   88]θ':]τε P. Mich. δ[P. Oxy.   89 ὃν εἰλ[or
ὃν θ' εἰ[P. Oxy.   λεν ἐχθρα[P. Mich.   92 νῦν] εἴ or νῦν δ'] εἴ P. Mich. νυνϊ P. Oxy.

130　　　　　　EURIPIDES

P. Oxy. col. III (cont'd) and P. Mich. col. II

trimeters, then lyric Choral Parodos:

Mi.2　　　οὐκ ἔστι τό[λ]μης τῆσδ' ὅπως ἀφέξομ[αι]　　　106
　　　　　σὺν μητρὶ [τ]ὸν ἐμὸν ἐχθρὸν ὥστε μὴ [οὐ κτανεῖν.
Ox.2.ii, Mi.2　Ζεῦ, Ζεῦ, σύ γ' ἡμᾶς εὐτυχεστέρους πατ[ρὸς
　　　　　θὲς ἀλλ' ἐπειδὴ ιμονογενεῖς λελείμμε[θα.

ΧΟΡΟΣ
　　　　　αἰαῖ· φεῦ· ιῶ γεραιοί, πρόβατε τᾶιδει[　　　　　[στρ.?
　　　　　‖ βάρεα γοιυνάτων φέροντεςι ‖ πολυετ[έα　　　71-2 111
　　　　　ιμακροβίοται ‖ μέλεα. δίικε τὸ βάκτρ[
Ox.2.ii, Mi.2+3　ὑὲς οὐδας·ι ‖ ἔκλυον ιτάδε μέλαθρα *(space)*　　‖[
　　　　　 .] ... [.] . ι λωνι ‖ τυράννοιυ μόνα[.ι] . [
　　　　　μονου στερένται ‖ τοῦ πάλιαι ποτε[.ι] ... [　　75-6 115
　　　　　 .. ν .[.] . [.]ςι ‖ ὁ πολυδιάκρυτοςι ‖ ὅσιον α ιιατο[
Mi.2+3　　　εμαυ[ ]α[.]. φεῦ, φεῦ· ὦ γῆρας, ὦ παι δι .[
　　　　　τάλα[ι]να [.....] . μως πτεροῦ[σι]σα
　　　　　ἀειδο[.......] η φιλοπροσωιδ[ί]αι
　　　　　ἀλεαι [.......]στρεφει παρα[　　　　　120
　　　　　ζυγει[.......]ος οὗ πόθωι στ[έι]νεις
　　　　　δεινα[.......]αζε. συγγόνου δ' [όι]δ' ἀσθε[νέσι
　　　　　χερὶ σφ[........]ν τέκνοισι φονίω[ι ι
　　　　　ἅμ' αἰτ[........]δ' ἐμοὶ κακῶν ὤ[ν ι

　　　　　τότε [.........] πατρὸς τέκινων .[　　　　　[ἀντ.?
　　　　　 . ε . [.........]νοις δεοικ .ι . ηπ[　　　　　126
　　　　　 .. [.........] ηταδειπαφεθ[
　　　　　 .ω . [...... τυ]ράννων κυσίιν τε

P. Oxy. frr. 4, 5, 6 *unplaced scraps of six, two and one lines*　　　79–86

107 μὴ [οὐ (Slings) κτανεῖν BK　108 Ζευ Ζευ[σ]υγη[P. Oxy. read by Koenen　109 ἀλλ'
ἐπειδει P. Mich. ἐπειδε[or ἐπειδη[with τὰ ἄλλα inserted above then changed to τὰ δ' ἄλλα
P. Oxy. 110–6 ‖ indicates new line-beginnings in P. Oxy. (whose colometry differs from P. Mich.);
ι ι encloses text represented in P. Mich. only　111 πολυετ[P. Oxy. read by BK (π[Turner, Harder)
πολυ[P. Mich. or πολυετ[ῶν or πολυετ[εῖς BK　112 μακροβιωτα P. Mich. δ'ϊ[P. Oxy.
δίκε τὸ βάκτρ[ον BK (who consider correction to δίκετε but disfavour βάκτρ[α see Comm.)
113–28 ι marks the join between P. Mich. frs. 2 and 3　113 ἔκλωσα[P. Oxy.　114 end perhaps

end of Cresphontes' speech: 106–109
>There is no way I shall shirk this harsh enterprise and
>fail to kill my foe with my mother's aid. Zeus, Zeus,
>make me more fortunate than my father — now at least
>when I am left as his only son!

The Chorus enter, singing (Parodos): 110–128

Chorus. Alas! Woe!
(Strophe?) Old men, step forward this way . . .[115] bearing
the *years-old* weight which loads your knees, your
long-lived limbs. Set your staff(s?) to the ground.
I heard(?) (that?) these halls <   > deprived in
loneliness of their ruler's only(?) . . . the one who in
former times < . . .[120]. . . >. The much wept < . . . >. (It
is?) acceptable to the gods . . . for me . . . Alas, alas! O
old age, O . . . wretched < . . . > . . . feathered . . . sing-
< . . . > with love of harmony . . . < . . . > . . . < . . . >[120]
. . . < . . . > with yearning for whom you *moan* . . .
terrible < . . . >. But *this* man *with* bloody hand < . . . >
his brother's *frail* children, being also . . . of < . . . >
evils for me.

(Antistrophe?) At that time < . . . > father's children < . . .[125]
. . . > . . . <   > these . . . <   > of tyrants
and for dogs . . .

ⁱτέ[κνου or ⁱτέ[κνων BK   116 ἄφ‖ατο[ν BK, reading αφ[in P. Oxy., α[φ‖]ατο[in P. Mich. frs 2–3
117 ἔμ' αὐ[δ]ᾶ[ν] BK   117 ὦ πα‖δι [−122]αζε see Comm. on speculative restorations by BK
and others   117–8 Πα‖νδίο[νος] τάλαινα [παῖς or Πα‖νδιο[νὶς] τάλαινα Haslam   119 ἀείδο[υσ'
(e.g.: ἀειδε[less probable) BK   μέ]λη (e.g.) BK   120 ἀλεᾶι BK   [φωνᾶι τ' ἐπι]στρεφεῖ Haslam
παρά[φρων BK, Harder   120–1 [ἀπο]ⁱζυγεῖ[σα τοῦ παιδὸς BK (παιδ]ὸς Haslam, τοῦ Slings)
122 (ἐ)στέν]αζε (e.g.) BK   123 σφ[αγεὺς or σφ[αγὴν BK   124 αἴτ[ιος τοσῶν]δ' BK   ὤ[ν BK
perhaps κακῶν, ὤ· Collard   125 *paragraphus* in P. Mich. seems to denote antistrophe
126 perhaps δὲ οἶκτος BK   127]λη or]αη BK, who suggest μέ]λη τάδ' (or τὰ δ') ἐ]παφεθ[έντα

449 (partly in P. Fayum)

    traces of two lines in the papyrus, then:

    ἐχρῆν γὰρ ἡμᾶς σύλ̣λογον ̣ποιουμένους
    τὸν φύντα θρηνεῖν εἰ̣ς ὅσ̓ ἔρχεται κακά,
    τὸν δ̓ αὖ θανόντα καὶ̣ πόνων ̣πεπαυμένον   5
    χαίροντας εὐφημοῦ̣ν̣τας ἐ̣κπέμπειν δόμων.

    traces of three more lines in the papyrus

450   Κρ.   εἰ μὲν γὰρ οἰκεῖ νερτέρας ὑπὸ χθονὸς
              ἐν τοῖσιν οὐκέτ̓ οὖσιν, οὐδὲν ἂν σθένοι.

451   Μερόπη   εἰ γάρ σ̓ ἔμελλεν, ὡς σὺ φῄς, κτείνειν πόσις,
                   χρῆν καὶ σὲ μέλλειν, ὡς χρόνος παρήλυθεν.

452   ἐκεῖνο γὰρ πέπονθ̓ ὅπερ πάντες βροτοί·
            φιλῶν μάλιστ̓ ἐμαυτὸν οὐκ αἰσχύνομαι.

453   Χο.   Εἰρήνα βαθύπλουτε καὶ   *[στρ.*
            καλλίστα μακάρων θεῶν,
            ζῆλός μοι σέθεν ὡς χρονίζεις.
            δέδοικα δὲ μὴ πρὶν πόνοις
            ὑπερβάληι με γῆρας,   5
            πρὶν σὰν χαρίεσσαν προσιδεῖν ὥραν
            καὶ καλλιχόρους ἀοιδὰς

---

449 (615 M, 67 A, 5 Musso) 3–6 Sext. Emp. *Outlines of Pyrrhonism* 3.230, Clem. Alex. *Strom.*
3.3.15.2, Stob. 4.52.42, all attrib. Eur.; Schol. Hermogenes, ed. Walz, *Rhet. Gr.* VII.765, unattrib.;
Latin transl. Cic. *Tusc.* 1.115, attrib. Eur. *Cresph.*   4–6 Strabo 11.11.8, Menand. Rhet. 2.413
Russell–Wilson, both attrib. Eur. (these lines 'familiar to most people and well known', Menand.);
Plut. *Mor.* 36f, unattrib.   3–6 widely quoted elsewhere in whole or part, often unattrib.; some minor
differences in the citations not noted below. P. Fayum (1ˢᵗ–2ⁿᵈ C. B.C.), ed. R.A. Coles, *ZPE* 6
(1970) 247–8, has centres of 3–6 and perhaps (see Comm.) of the preceding two and following three
lines.   3 ἐχρῆν most witnesses (*decebat* Cic.) ἔδει Clem. and a few others   5 κακῶν Sext.
450 (607 M, 68 A, 3 Musso) [Plut.] *Mor.* 110b ('Cresph. – the one in Eur. – speaking about
Heracles')   **451** (605 M, 69 A, 9 Musso) Aul. Gell. 6.3.28, attrib. Eur. ('Merope rebutting Polyph.';

449 (with P. Fayum)

We would do better to assemble and bewail a newborn child for all the troubles he is entering — and when a man dies and has his rest from hardships,[5] to escort him from his home rejoicing with glad cries.

Context uncertain (close to F 454, 455?)

450   *Cr.* If he dwells below in the nether land amongst those who are no more, he can have no strength.

Cresphontes despairing(?) of help from his ancestor Heracles.

451   *Merope.* If, as you claim, my husband was 'waiting' to kill you, you should have 'waited' too, as time had passed.

Merope to Polyphontes, in an early confrontation or the 'reconciliation' scene.

452   My experience is the same as every man's: I feel no disgrace in loving myself above all.

Polyphontes to Merope, close to F 451?

453   *Beginning of one of the play's main Stasima:*

Cho. *(strophe)* Peace, with your depths of wealth, most beauteous of the blessed gods, I yearn for you as you delay your coming; I fear old age may overwhelm me with hardships[5] before I look upon your graceful beauty, your songs joined

of the older Gell. mss. only V cites the Greek).   2 χρῆν Casaubon χρὴ Gell.   ἕως Valckenaer παρήλυθεν Hertz παρηαλυθεν Gell.   **452** (606 M, 70 A, 8 Musso) 1–2 Schol. B Eur. *Med.* 84, attrib. Eur. *Cresph.*   2 Schol. A *Med.* 84, attrib. Eur. *Cresph.*; *Apophthegm. Vindob.* 139 Wachsmuth, attrib. Eur.   **453** (613 M, 71 A, 4 Musso) Stob. 4.14.1, attrib. Eur. *Cresph.* ('Chorus', ms. S)   1–8 Polyb. 12.26.5 (= Timaeus *FGH* 566 F 22), attrib. Eur.; 1–2 parod. Ar. *Georgoi* fr. 111 (Stob.'s next entry) Εἰρήνη βαθύπλουτε καὶ ζευγάριον βοεικόν... ('Peace, with your depths of wealth, and little team of oxen...').   1 καὶ om. Polyb.   4 πόνοις om. Polyb. πρὶν del. Hartung   6 σὰν Grotius (σὴν Gesner) ἂν Polyb. γὰρ Stob. (περ ms. A) προεῖδε Stob. (προιδεῖν ms. A)   χαρ. ὥραν προσ. L. Kayser προσ. χαρ. ὥραν Austin χαρ. ἰδεῖν ὥραν Page (see Austin)   7 καλλιχρόνους Stob. mss. SM

φιλοστεφάνους τε κώμους.
ἴθι μοι, πότνα, πόλιν·

τὰν δ᾽ ἐχθρὰν Στάσιν εἶργ᾽ ἀπ᾽ οἴ- [ἀντ.
κων τὰν μαινομέναν τ᾽ Ἔριν 11
θηκτῶι τερπομέναν σιδάρωι.

454 Με. τεθνᾶσι παῖδες οὐκ ἐμοὶ μόνηι βροτῶν
οὐδ᾽ ἀνδρὸς ἐστερήμεθ᾽, ἀλλὰ μυρίαι
τὸν αὐτὸν ἐξήντλησαν ὡς ἐγὼ βίον.

455 ... καὶ δὶς ἕπτ᾽ αὐτῆς τέκνα
Νιόβης θανόντα Λοξίου τοξεύμασιν.

456 Με. †ὠνητέραν† δὴ τήνδ᾽ ἐγὼ δίδωμί σοι
πληγήν.

457 αἰδὼς ἐν ὀφθαλμοῖσι γίγνεται, τέκνον.

458 Με. αἱ τύχαι δέ με
μισθὸν λαβοῦσαι τῶν ἐμῶν τὰ φίλτατα
σοφὴν ἔθηκαν.

459 κέρδη τοιαῦτα χρή τινα κτᾶσθαι βροτῶν,
ἐφ᾽ οἷσι μέλλει μήποθ᾽ ὕστερον στένειν.

9 πότνα Bergk πότνια Polyb., Stob. (ἴθ᾽) ἴθι μοι, πότνια, πόλιν Diggle in R. Pintaudi (ed.), *Miscellanea Papyrologica* (Florence, 1980), 59 and *CQ* 40 (1990), 116 n. 86 πάλιν Bergk 10–12 metrical responsion with 1–3 recognised by Bergk 454 (608 M, 72 A, 11 Musso) [Plut.] *Mor.* 110d ('Merope moves the theatre, producing manly words . . .'), assigned to Eur. *Cresph.* by Barnes 3 πότμον Nauck 455 (609 M, 73 A, 12 Musso) Schol. Eur. *Pho.* 159, attrib. Eur. *Cresph.* The number fourteen for Niobe's children also attrib. Eur. by Aul. Gell. 20.7.2 and prob. Schol. Bacchyl. fr. 20D.6 Snell–Maehler. αὐτῆς suspected by Nauck Νιόβη Bothe ἔφθ᾽ αὐτῆς . . . Νιόβην (sc. ἰδοῦσαν) Cropp ὁμοῦ for Νιόβης, with (e.g.) Νιόβης τε μόχθους preceding the fr., Wecklein (τὴν Τανταλείαν preceding, Barrett:

with fine dancing, your garland-loving revels. Come,
mistress, to my city.

(Antistrophe) Ban from our homes the hateful Discord,[10] and
the raging Strife who delights in sharpened iron . . .

454 *Mer..* Not I alone have had children who have died, nor lost my
husband; countless other women have drained the same
misery from life as I.

Merope pretending resignation in the 'reconciliation' scene?

455   . . . and the twice seven children of Niobe herself, those who
were killed by Loxias's shafts.

Context: probably as F 454.

456 *Mer.* † . . . † is this blow that I give to you!

'Merope . . . lifting the axe against her son . . .' (Plutarch)

457   Shame is born in the eyes, my child.

Context unclear.

458 *Mer.* My misfortunes have taught me wisdom, taking as their fee
the dearest of my loved ones.

Merope to Polyphontes in the 'reconciliation' scene?

459   The kind of profits a mortal should acquire are those he is
never going to lament later.

Context uncertain (in or after a report of Polyphontes' death?)

---

see Harder)   **456** (616 M, 74 A, 6 Musso) Plut. *Mor.* 998e ('And consider Merope in the tragedy, lifting
the axe against her very own son believing him to be her son's murderer . . .'), assigned to Eur. *Cresph.* by
Valckenaer   1 †ὡνητέραν†: ὁσιωτέραν Turnebus ὦ νέρτερ' "Αιδη Porson   2 πληγήν deleted by
Cobet   **457** (612 M, 75 A, 7 Musso) Stob. 3.31.15, attrib. Eur. *Cresph.*   **458** (610 M, 76 A,
10 Musso) Plut. *Mor.* 90a ('as Merope says . . .'), assigned to Eur. *Cresph.* by Barnes   **459** (614 M,
77 A, 13 Musso) Stob. 4.31.95, attrib. Eur. *Cresph.*, followed without new heading by a repetition of
4.31.57 (= *Dictys* F 341)

Commentary on *Cresphontes*

Note. Fuller discussion is available at almost every point in Annette Harder's 1985 edition. For the new Michigan papyrus we depend entirely on the draft publication of the papyrus by Bonnycastle and Koenen (forthcoming), while not necessarily following them in all matters of interpretation. The authoritative publication will provide much fuller information and discussion than the scope of this volume allows. Professor Koenen's courtesy in providing the draft and permitting its use is here gratefully acknowledged.

448a. In the reconstruction adopted by BK, the two papyri together span 128 lines from Prologue and Parodos. The positions of P. Oxy. fr. 3 (see 59–68 n.) and of P. Mich. fr. 2 (see App. for 82–9), and the joining of P. Mich. fr. 3 with fr. 2 (see Comm. on 110–28) are not entirely certain. BK plausibly suggest that P. Oxy. was preceded by one of its (probably 39/40-line) columns containing the beginning of the play, P. Mich. by five of its 23/24-line columns; so our line 110 (Chorus entry) is towards line 150 of the play. The speakers in 40–58 are marked as $\bar{\alpha}$ and $\bar{\gamma}$, i.e. First and Third Actors (cf. Harder 22–4 and refs. in E.G. Turner, *Greek Manuscripts of the Ancient World* [London, 1987²], 149 n. 63). $\bar{\alpha}$ also speaks the speech 83–109 and is obviously Cresphontes, who has asked his questions in the guise of a stranger, like Orestes with Electra, *El.* 215ff., and is now alone. The fact that $\bar{\gamma}$ discusses with a stranger the behaviour of the 'masters of the house' (40–3) and some intimate details of the family's history (esp. 53ff.) suggests that this is a person of lower rank attached to the household, probably not young, and perhaps female if 73–82 include details of Merope's private condition (so Burnett, Musso, BK; Webster and Harder are undecided). This servant probably had an expository role confined to this scene, for no one later in the play can have been aware of this encounter. (The servant cannot have recognised Cresphontes as Mette suggested: cf. Cengarle 69.)

Between 58 and 83 we have the close of the dialogue and a short speech by the Servant (77?–83), and before 40 presumably a Prologue speech with 1–12 falling near its end. Their remnants suit Cresphontes himself, and the audience should know his identity before the dialogue and his subsequent speech; so we probably have Cresphontes speaking the Prologue speech and the Servant responding to a request by him for admission (cf. *Hel.* 435ff.) or possibly going on some errand (cf. *El.* 102ff.). There are broadly similar schemes in *And.*, *Hel.* (twice) and *Or.* (cf. Burnett, Harder). For a Prologue speech by a returning exile cf. Aesch. *Choephori*. A more complex Prologue scheme as in Eur. *El.* (Orestes arriving after a Prologue monologue by the Peasant and a scene between the Peasant and Electra) cannot be entirely ruled out.

In the 'second Prologue' of *Helen* (386–514) the Old Woman answering Menelaus's knock tries to repel him, warns him of Theoclymenus's hostility to Greeks and suggests he should go to some other house. Cresphontes' question about hospitality (40), the possible 'go <*away from this*> house' (77), and 'Farewell' (82) may indicate a similar pattern (cf. Harder 57, BK). On the implied stage movements see 79–82 n., and on the motivation of the monologue 83–6 n.

136

1–12. Probably near the end of Cresphontes' Prologue monologue, reviewing Polyphontes' crimes and/or (cf. *Orestes* in *El.* 82–101, Soph. *El.* 32–66) Cresphontes' situation and plans. **1.** *by guile*: Koenen's reading ('*and I*', Harder); Cresphontes may well recall Polyphontes' use of guile and justify his own use of it, cf. 49 n., *El.* 88 (with Cropp's n.), *HF* 588–98. **2.** *royal*: Eur. has τυραννικός often of royal palaces or accoutrements, unpejoratively.

40–58. The Servant describes Polyphontes' coup and the younger Cresphontes' survival.
40. *<unrighteously>*: i.e. inhospitably; proper treatment of strangers was important and safeguarded by Zeus Xenios (see Burkert 130; for ἄδικος, δίκαιος etc., '(un)righteous' or '(un)just', in similar contexts see e.g. *Cyc.* 272, *Alc.* 1147–8, *Hec.* 715, 1235). Harder sees Polyphontes' attitude as partly motivated by the tyrant's typical fear of overthrow (cf. Collard, *Supplices*, II.212) and of Cresphontes' return (cf. Aegisthus in *El.*, esp. 614–7).

42. [next: LSJ αὖθις III. Harder explains μηκέτι (not οὐκέτι) as generic ('the speaker finds it *generally* more important to deal with living persons first . . .') rather than due to the imperative leading verb (so Turner; cf. KG 2. 201 n. 4, Smyth §2737). More probably it implies ignorance of the dead man's identity ('whoever it is who is no more') or is 'characterising' (stressing that the dead man is in a different category from the living one: cf. e.g. Soph. *OC* 77–9; Moorhouse, *Syntax* 326). Collard compares *Hel.* 1289 and suggests Cresphontes speaks guardedly or euphemistically.]

43. *Heraclids*: see p. 124 above. This explanation and the shape of the name suggest (cf. Harder 9) that Polyphontes was at least unfamiliar to Eur.'s audience if not invented by him, like Lycus in *HF* (31–2), Theoclymenus in *Helen* (9, 61–3). So does the similarity of 'Polyphontes' with 'Cresphontes', along with its possible interpretation as 'much murdering'; cf. Polymestor alongside Polydorus and Polyxena in *Hec.* (Collard, *Hecuba*, 34 n. 63), Theoclymenus and Theonoe in *Helen*. **stranger**: dramatic irony; cf. Electra in *El.* 247, 259 etc.; Hom. *Od.* 14.53–8 etc.

46. Not to be taken as a question; the affirmative γε (Denniston, *GP* 130ff.) is against this, and the pattern in 45–7 ('You know . . .?' — 'Yes . . .' — 'Well then . . .') is widespread in stichomythia (see Harder 64–5). **settler of . . . Messenia**: see p. 124 above.

49. *a violent plot*: guile joined to violence discredits the usurper: cf. *Bell.* F 288 n., Cropp on *El.* 9.

50. *childless*: sons should avenge their father's death; the murderer would be wise to kill them first: cf. Hom. *Od.* 3.196 etc., Cropp on *El.* 22–3.

51. *sons*: see p. 122 above.

52. *All . . . then?*: ἦ gives urgency to the question, δῆτα signals the inference from the preceding line: Denniston, *GP* 271. **seed**: lit. 'sowing/offspring (consisting of children'; cf. Soph. *Ant.* 1164 (same phrase), Eur. *Tro.* 503.

53. *if indeed he still is*: dramatic irony and pathos as e.g. *Hec.* 429 (where Hecuba's fear is sadly true), *El.* 557, Hom. *Od.* 14.44.

54–5. A similar question and answer in *Ion* 279–80.

54. *their death <and> misfortunes*: hendiadys, 'their sad death'; Harder compares e.g. 'avoiding death and the spirits of doom', Hom. *Od.* 2.352 etc.

55. [Text: σμ[ικρ]ὸς *small* remains uncertain (see Harder). Radt's line-end supplement gives 'in nurture'. A finite verb is more likely, bridging the participles in this and the next line. Görschen's 'escaped' is less attractive than Diggle's '. . . <he was> still at <his nurse's>breast's teat', but with the latter the repetition 'being . . . he was' (ὧν ἔτ᾽ ἦν) is a little awkward. Collard notes that ἐτ[ύγχανεν would be convincing if the traces allowed it ('he chanced to be . . . at the breast's teat').]

56. [<or> *residing*: Text: Barrett's is the only attractive supplement for contrast with ἔκδημος, **Abroad,** although ἐπιχώριος elsewhere means 'local' (LSJ).]

57. **His mother's father:** see p. 122 above. Barrett's supplement gives '<nurtured> him, <the king of the Arcadians>'.

58. *will come*: Harder's reading. This verb in the Future often refers to return from a long absence: either Indicative (cf. Aesch. *Ag.* 1280, Eur. *El.* 263, *HF* 75) or Infinitive (e.g. 'Is there hope that he will come?', cf. *HF* 296, Aesch. *Ag.* 679).

59–68. Three lines are missing (59–61) if P. Oxy. fr. 3 is rightly placed soon after fr. 1 col. ii. The words in 62–6 seem to be stichomythic and may (Harder following Barrett) contain questions and answers about the survivor's name. 58 and 62 can hardly be fitted together as the same line.

69–99. The start of Cresphontes' scene-closing monologue (83ff.) has a speaker-notation. A short speech by the Servant has begun perhaps at 77.

71. . . . **to possess a** (*or* as) **wife:** Mette identified this with F 1060 (see App.), 'may it be for my enemies to possess a hostile wife', but the same line-ending occurs in Eur. *Hcld.* 523, *IT* 696, similar ones elsewhere; this instance was hardly unique in the lost plays. F 1060 could fit as a gnomic reply by the Servant to a question from Cresphontes about Merope's attitude to Polyphontes (cf. e.g. *El.* 264–5: *Or.* 'Did Clytemnestra accept Aegisthus's mistreatment of you?' — *El.* 'Women are devoted to husbands, stranger, not children'), but the line need only have concerned Polyphontes' desire to make her his wife.

73. previously . . . throat: either suicide (contemplated) or mourning (prolonged) is a plausible topic, e.g. '<she would> sooner <twist the noose around her> throat' (than appease her new husband, cf. 72), or '<she tears with her nails (τέμνει δ᾽ ὄνυξιν, BK) her> previously <beautiful (εὐπρεπ]ῆ, Harder)> throat' (cf. *El.* 147). Wilkins (see bibl.) notes *Med.* 30, Medea turning her head away (στρέψασα . . . δέρην) in anguish.

75–6. will avenge . . . might happen: probably the Servant asks if the younger Cresphontes will avenge his father's death, and Cresphontes expresses his longing that this should happen. Very similar terminology in *Supp.* 1142–4 where the sons of the Seven cry out to their dead fathers ('shall I ever avenge . . .? If only it might happen!'). [Text, 76: the deleted correction in P. Oxy. gives 'might be reported' (with -o elided; less likely 'you might report', with -ε elided; in either case perhaps a wish). The gist was probably similar with either reading. Mette's '<to/for me>' is the best but not the only possibility at line-end.]

77. hearth: Gen., so an instruction to go '<from this> hearth' (Koenen following Harder) is likely, but '<close to>' (πέλας, ἐγγύς) also possible.

79–82. The Servant is probably describing the situation in the palace; then **woman** and **husband** are Merope and Polyphontes, and the female person **having shed tears**

(or 'shedding tears' in P. Oxy.) is Merope or possibly the Servant. **alien** (Fem. Plur.) might refer to things (e.g. 'alien lands' or [cf. *Tro.* 1038] 'alien beds') but more probably to people; BK suggest Merope's maids, the speaker being one of them. **farewell:** the Servant departs, either into the house or on an errand. [Text: BK's accentuation as 2nd Pers. Imper. is plausible though not inevitable.] Cresphontes after his closing speech presumably departs (like Orestes in Soph. *El.* 51ff.) or hides (like Orestes in Aesch. *Cho.* 20, Eur. *El.* 102ff.), to allow for the Chorus's entry.

83–109. Cresphontes in a soliloquy recognises the crisis (83–6), prays for aid (at least 87–98), avows his courage (at least 106–7), and makes a parting appeal to Zeus (108–9).

83–6. The recognition of crisis is formulaic, '**Alas, what shall I do ... and how ...**' (full analysis of the formula and its extensions: R. Fowler, *HSCP* 91 [1987], 5–38. Slings suggesting '<*How*> ... and how' compares *Alc.* 912–3, *Ion* 859–60, but obviously other question words would fit in 83). But what is the crisis? Perhaps simply the dangers involved in getting close to the tyrant (cf. *El.* 605, 615–7, *HF* 588–92, *Hel.* 479–82), although Harder suggests some feature of Merope's distress revealed by the Servant (cf. 73 n.), and Burnett and BK a revelation of the price on Cresphontes' head (but he should probably know of this already, like Orestes in *El.*). 85–6 more likely answer 83–4 than continue the question, since a continuation of the question leaves no room for an answer and a difficulty in coordinating 86 with 85. As an answer, 85–6 have little room for expression of what Cr. ought to do; this makes the suggestions of BK for 85 '**O unyielding heart** <*and arm of mine*>', and Slings for 86 '*O harsh* <*misfortune*>', a little unattractive. Perhaps ὦ τάλ[αινα χείρ should be the supplement in 86, e.g., '<*You should take courage,*> O unyielding heart, <*and you,*> O unyielding <*arm,*> a sharpened sword.' For similar self-exhortations towards a noble goal, reminiscent of Hom. *Od.* 20.13–24, cf. *Alc.* 837 (heart and arm), *Bell.* F 308.1 (soul: see Comm. there), Ar. *Ach.* 485 (heart: parody of Eur.); and with undesirable goal *Med.* 1056–7 (spirit, cf. Neophron *TrGF* 15 F 2.1–3), 1244 ('Come my unyielding hand, take the sword'), *IT* 344 (heart), *Or.* 466 (heart and soul). For this sense of τάλας (with which cf. τόλμης 'harsh enterprise', 106) see Denniston on *El.* 1171; J. R. Wilson, *AJP* 92 (1971), 292–300.

87–92. O land below (etc.): the first of two or three appeals for aid from Hades and the dead (starting at 87, 93?, 96) with elements familiar from *El.* 671–84, *HF* 490–6, *Or.* 1225–45, Aesch. *Pers.* 628ff., *Cho.* 306–509, Soph. *El.* 67–72, 110–20. The first seems to concentrate on the Underworld and Hades its ruler (87–8), perhaps Cresphontes' dead father (89ff., cf. on 96–8 below) and possibly other dead or spirits in 90–1, culminating in the request '**now, if ever** <*I have made offerings/ prayers to you*>' (or '... <*you have heard me in the past*>'). [Text: 87 cannot be identified with F 456 (see n. there). In 89 the antecedent of **whom** is unclear; BK suggest 'Father **below**' for the end of 88, judging ὃν εἱλ[, e.g. 'whom <*your kinsman's*> hatred *destroyed*', more likely than ὃν θ' εἱ[, 'and the one whom ...'. **hatred** is doubtful since Fem. forms of the adj. ἐχθρός are equally possible, e.g. ἐχθρᾷ[ι ... χερί (Collard) 'with hostile hand'.]

93–5. and you . . . : probably a new address (phrased like e.g. Soph. *El.* 69, Eur. *El.* 677) to a different group such as ancestral or local gods (Soph. *El.* 67–72 adds land and home), called on to remember the father's death or family's rights.   [Text: **〚father〛** (Gen.), written and deleted at the beginning of 95 in P. Oxy., perhaps originated in a related explanatory note.]

96–8. O dearest . . . (etc.): probably an appeal to his father (Musso, Harder, BK), repeated as in *El.* 677–84, *Or.* 1225–39, Aesch. *Cho.* 479ff.

106–9. After the gap (100–5), Cresphontes ends his monologue by declaring his resolve and demanding Zeus's help.   **There is no way I shall shirk:** a similar climactic declaration of resolve, *Erec.* F 360.52.   **my mother's aid:** taken for granted, like Electra's by Orestes, *El.* 100–1, though Merope's communication with Cresphontes *via* the Old Man may have been more regular until recently (see Hyginus, p. 121 above); now he does not foresee her reaction to his disguised arrival!   **Zeus:** similar and repeated appeals to Zeus for restoration by Orestes, Electra and allies, Aesch. *Cho.* 18–19 (similarly placed) etc., Eur. *El.* 135–9 (the appeal interjected), 672–4, *Or.* 1242–5. Zeus has a leading interest as patron of Justice, legitimate rulers, and inheritance rights (cf. Cropp on *El.* 671).   **more fortunate:** similar requests for success in such petitions, *Or.* 1243, Aesch. *Cho.* 785? (see Garvie); BK also note Soph. *Aj.* 550, 'My son, may you become more fortunate than your father (πατρὸς εὐτυχέστερος)'. **his only son:** stress on the orphanhood of the petitioners, Aesch. *Cho.* 246–54, 794–6; on their misery, *Cho.* 409, Eur. *El.* 135–6, 672; cf. *Supp.* 1123ff. The rare word μονογενεῖς (cf. Aesch. *Ag.* 898) stresses the heir's importance.   [Text: **now at least . . . :** P. Mich.'s reading is no more than a copying error. The variants in P. Oxy. are due to misunderstanding of 'apodotic' ἀλλά (see Denniston, *GP* 13), as BK point out rendering, 'Make me luckier than my father was, (if not for other reasons, then at least) because I am left behind as his only son'. The alternative suggested here is perhaps more pointed, '. . . (if not when he was alive, then at least) now that . . .'; for temporal ἐπειδή with Perfect tense, cf. ἐπεί at *Hec.* 312, *Hel.* 61, *Or.* 267.]

110–28. Parodos: the Chorus of Old Men enter, complaining of their infirmity and expressing sympathy for Merope and the sufferings of the legitimate royal family. Their coming may be motivated by something they have heard (see 113 n.). For their characterisation see 110–2 n., and on BK's suggestion that the Parodos is 'amoebaic' (Merope participating), 117–22 n.   The text raises some problems and uncertainties which can only be briefly mentioned below. (The joining of frs. 2 and 3 — 'all but certain', BK — may require caution over the resulting readings in 113–28). Readers are referred to the forthcoming publication of P. Mich. for full discussion of the details and conjectural restorations.

Metre. The colometries of the papyri differ (see Text and App.). BK argue that P. Mich., although early, does have a colometric arrangment as indicated by its uneven length of lines; they prefer this to P. Oxy.'s though modifying it in 114, 116–7, 120–2, and analyse both as combining dochmiac and iambic elements in 110–9 (110–6 in P. Oxy.; 121–4 in P. Mich are readily seen as iambic). JD suggests a cretic/trochaic/

iambic analysis of P. Oxy.'s colometry and is inclined to prefer this (one might compare *HF* 131–7).

110–2. Old men (etc.): the Chorus's opening complaints indicate extreme age: cf. e.g. Aesch. *Ag.* 72–82, Eur. *HF* 107–30, Ar. *Ach.* 204–32, *Wasps* 230–47. In *Ag.*, *HF* and *Cresph.* an emphatically aged Chorus represents helplessness in a political crisis (cf. Bond on *HF* 107–37). Other generic features: mutual encouragement (*HF*, *Ach.*, *Wasps*), complaints of weakness and slowness (all), use of staffs (*Ag.*, *HF*; cf. *Pho.* 1719 with Mastronarde's text and comm.). Such motifs are not confined to parodoi (cf. e.g. F 453 below) or to Choruses (cf. Cropp on *El.* 487–92). **step forward:** Plural in collective self-address like e.g. *HF* 119–23, 131–3. [Text: comparison with 125 suggests that at least one syllable is lost at the end of 110. **years-old weight:** alternative supplements (App.) would apply 'years-old' to 'knees' or 'old men'.]

112–3. Set: 'throw' is the normal sense of the poetic verb δικεῖν (on which see Mastronarde on *Pho.* 665), but actual throwing is incongruous here; the old men should be planting and leaning on their staffs at each step. Perhaps the verb suggests 'let fall' as βάλλω sometimes does (LSJ II.3; cf. esp. *El.* 1344, *Rhes.* 721). [Text: the change from Plur. 'step forward' to Sing. 'put your staff' is surprising, and (JD) the inclusion of τὸ (**your**) is stylistically awkward unless the text had a phrase such as τὸ βάκτρ[ων ἔρεισμ(α) 'the support (consisting) of your staffs'. Preferable would be δίκετε βάκτρ[α 'set (your) staffs' which BK consider while noting that βάκτρ(α) would not metrically match their restoration in 127.]

113. I heard (P. Mich.) is a common device motivating Chorus's arrivals (cf. e.g. *Hel.* 185 with Kannicht on *Hel.* 179–90; *Med.* 131); but metrical interpretation of ἐς οὖδας ἔκλυον is difficult, and what the Chorus might have heard is not obvious. P. Oxy.'s 'I wept' (along with P. Oxy.'s iambic colometry) may be preferable (JD); either, then, a true past tense or an 'instantaneous' Aorist like e.g. *Supp.* 1162, *Hel.* 663 (perhaps, 'I weep *<as I see>* this house . . .').

114. their ruler's only . . . : BK are unsure if the traces at line-end represent text; τέ[κνου or τέ[κνων would give either 'their ruler's only son' (i.e. Cresphontes: cf. 109) or 'their only ruler's son(s)'.

116–7. (It is?) acceptable (etc.): BK's reading gives a dubiously abrupt and contorted sentence, 'It is acceptable to the gods for me to voice an unspeakable thing'. (On the concept ὅσιον see Parker, *Miasma* 330; Burkert 269–70.)

117. O old age: a complaint as at *Supp.* 1108 (illustrated in Collard's n.), *Phoenix* F 805; cf. 110–2 n. and F 453.5. Old age is fully personified at *HF* 649ff. (see Bond's note there on iconography).

117–22. O . . . wretched (etc.): BK follow Haslam in thinking that this passage describes a singing bird, i.e. the nightingale into which Procne, daughter of the Athenian king Pandion, was transformed. Her husband Tereus seduced her sister Philomela, then cut out her tongue; Procne punished him by killing her own son Itys (a name representing the nightingale's song of endless grief) and became a stock poetic example of maternal mourning (cf. *Pha.* 67–70, Fraenkel on Aesch. *Ag.* 1144f.). The supplements of Haslam and BK (incompletely represented in the present App.) proceed as follows: '**O** *Pandion's* **wretched** *<daughter>* . . . **feathered, sing-***<ing . . . >* . . .

with *foolish* **love of harmony** *<and> modulating <voice>, crazed, separated <from that> child* **with yearning for whom you** *moan*, *cry* < . . . > **terrible** < . . . >'. The transitions in 117 ('O, old age — O Pandion's daughter') and 122 (introducing 'this man') are then very abrupt. To alleviate this BK suggest that the address to the nightingale, and perhaps the remainder of the strophe, is sung from within the palace by Merope. But an intrusion here by Merope would be very abrupt, and a complex lyric passage sung offstage without preparation or explanation is unparalleled in Tragedy. A Chorus can arrive bringing or seeking news, and even 'addressing' the main character, without any exchange during the Parodos: *Alc.* 77ff., *Hipp.* 121ff. etc. (BK note the possibility of a parody in Ar. *Birds* 202ff. and compare Chorus-actor exchanges in some metrically similar Parodoi, but these points do not carry much weight.) Perhaps a restoration in which the Chorus address Merope (cf. the Chorus's words to Heracles' family, *HF* 115–8) and compare her with Procne is to be sought.

119. **love of harmony:** the word φιλοπροσῳδία is not found elsewhere.

120. [Text: BK accent ἀλεᾶι as Dat. of ἀλεός (which Hesych. α 2737 Latte attributes to Aesch. [F 410] as Doric for epic/elegiac ἠλεός 'distraught') — questionably because of the word's rarity and (JD) the hiatus between it and the word it would qualify, φιλοπροσῳδίαι. There is no obvious help from ἀλέα 'escape' or 'warmth'. Perhaps ἀλᾶι or ἀλαί[νεις 'you wander' has been corrupted? For his conjecture ἐπι]στρεφεῖ 'modulating' applied to the nightingale's voice Haslam compares Aristot. *Hist. An.* 632b24.]

122. **But** *this* **man (etc.):** i.e. Polyphontes, compounding the murder of his brother by that of his two sons. BK suggest the supplements 'slaughterer' or 'slaughter' since the vocabulary of ritual slaughter (σφάζειν, σφαγεύς etc.) is often applied to tragic murder victims: cf. esp. *HF* 451.

123. [Text: *with bloody hand:* the line-end supplement fits the sense very well, but JD notes that it creates an unlikely hiatus before ἅμ' which makes Gen. φονίῳ[ν worth considering, or perhaps φο⟨ι⟩νίῳ[ν for more obvious iambic metre.]

124. BK's supplement gives '**being also** *the cause* **of** *<so many>* **evils for me**'. The evils are presumably political troubles: cf. F 453.10–12. Collard's 'O!' rather than the participle 'being' is possible.

125–8. These lines seem to dwell on the aftermath of Polyphontes' murders.

126. BK's tentative reading suggests 'and . . . lamentation (*or* pity)'.

127. BK take their restored line-end phrase as referring to 'limbs . . . thrown to the dogs', but ἐπαφίημι means 'discharge *at*' and there are many possibilities such as βέ]λη 'missiles' (JD).

449. The main part is sometimes cited simply as a philosophical warning against over-valuing life or procreation (Clement) or fearing death. In context the lines were probably consolatory, as in Menander's citation: Merope, then, is being consoled or consoling herself in one of the situations which are possible for F 454 (see n.), 455 and perhaps 458; more likely after the report of Cresphontes' death than before it.   [Text: on the exiguous P. Fayum see Harder 25–6, 98. A blank space in its line 2 suggests that this line may be a heading and the text an anthology.]

The pessimism in these lines is amply illustrated by Harder; some relevant passages are already collected with our fr. in its sources, e.g. Hom. *Il.* 17.446–7, Theognis 425–8. For death as acquittal or avoidance of the toils of life see also R. Kassel, *Untersuch. zur gr. und röm. Konsolationsliteratur* (Munich, 1958), 75–6; R. Lattimore, *Themes in Greek and Latin Epitaphs* (Urbana, 1962), 205–10, 259–60. The custom recommended here is recorded by Hdt. 5.4.2 as the practice of the Thracian Trausi (see Harder for comparable practices and anthropological intrepretation). Since the phrasings are so similar (see R. Browning, *CR* 75 [1961] 201–2), there may be a direct borrowing from Hdt. by Eur., as apparently by Soph. *Ant.* 908–12 (Hdt. 3.119), *OC* 337–41 (Hdt. 2.35, also foreign customs). **3. We would do better:** lit. 'it was appropriate' (but not so arranged). ἐχρῆν is preferable to ἔδει 'it was obligatory': see Barrett on *Hipp.* 41. Similarly phrased criticisms of human customs and propensities: F 908a (same sentiment), *Hipp.* 253–60, 645–50, *Theseus* F 388 etc.; of the divinely ordained natural or moral order, e.g. *Med.* 573–5, *Hipp.* 616–24, 925–31, *Ion* 1312–19. **4. bewail . . . for all . . . :** lit. 'bewail . . . into how many . . .': cf. F 453.3, Smyth §2687, KG II.370–1. **6. rejoicing with glad cries:** lit. 'rejoicing, crying joyfully'; asyndeton adding vigour: cf. Bond on *HF* 602. For εὐφημέω 'express joy at a festive occasion' (opp. δυσφημέω of mourning, e.g. *Hec.* 181) Harder compares Aesch. *Ag.* 596, Ar. *Plut.* 758 (also asyndeton), Diod. Sic. 5.49.1.

450. [Plut.] *Consol. Apollon.* cites this shortly before F 454. It is surely from our play, though some including Harder have contemplated a play involving the elder Cresphontes. The remark seems to emphasise the challenge to Cresphontes who cannot rely on help from his mighty ancestor: cf. *HF* 145–6, 296–7, 490–6 (Heracles), *Tro.* 752–4 (Hector). Plausible contexts include the Prologue speech, or a discussion of strategy after the recognition, or Cresphontes deceiving Polyphontes (and so not genuinely despairing: cf. *HF* 717–9). Webster 142 compares *El.* 677–84 and suggests that εἰ μὲν . . . means 'if on the one hand . . .', allowing a follow-up e.g. 'but if he is in heaven, he will see justice done'. **no strength:** like the Heracles of Hom. *Od.* 11.604–26, an insubstantial inhabitant of the underworld; cf. Hom. *Il.* 18.117–9. The belief that Heracles became an Olympian god after his death appears to have succeeded (early in the 6ᵗʰ C.) an earlier belief defining him as a 'hero', a spirit of the dead who might exercise powers from the underworld (alluded to by Megara in her appeal to him, *HF* 494–5). See West on Hes. *Theog.* 947–55 and esp. for art J. Boardman in *LIMC* VI.121–32; on the apotheosis T. C. W. Stinton in *JHS* Suppl. 15 (1987), 1–16 = *Coll. Papers on Greek Tragedy* (Oxford, 1990), 493–507. Eur. could still exploit the ambiguity, notably in *HF* where Heracles' aspirations to divinity are dashed by his madness and Theseus expects him to die and enter Hades (1331), and in *Hcld.* where his children's salvation is hailed as proof of his ascension (910–8). For Heracles' relevance to *Cresph.* see Introd., pp. 123–4, 125 above.

451. Cited by Gellius in a discussion of unreasonable argumentation. The context may be Merope's pretended reconciliation with Polyphontes rather than an earlier confrontation; a debating point of this kind suits a position of concealed superiority (like Electra's in *El.* 1060–96), her gist being, 'You were wrong to do it, but . . .' (so Musso). Gellius says that she 'outwitted' *(eluserit)* Polyphontes with this remark. **waiting . . . waited:** ἔμελλεν . . . μέλλειν puns on two possible nuances of μέλλειν, either 'intend' or 'hesitate, delay'; cf. *Ion* 1295, 1300–1, Dem. 6.15.　[Text: probably sound with the simple correction to παρήλυθεν.　**as time had passed:** with Harder's interpretation, since Cresphontes was allegedly *waiting*, then Polyphontes should have done the same. Valckenaer's ἕως 'until' for 'as' is plausible; Eur. does not elsewhere treat ἕως as a monosyllable, but cf. Soph. *Aj.* 1117 etc. and for the synizesis -εω- in Eur. Diggle, *Studies* 93, 120.]

452. Cited by Schol. *Med.* 85–8 where the Tutor notes a similar attitude in Jason. The speaker is much more likely Polyphontes (choices for context as F 451) than the disguised Cresphontes.　**1. My experience is the same (etc.):** similar wording in *Bell.* F 300.　**2. loving myself above all:** a crude egotism like Jason's (and sophistically justified as not being shameless: cf. Lycus, *HF* 165–6) rather than an acceptably balanced self-interest (e.g. Soph. *OC* 309, Eur. *Hel.* 999); for the distinction see Aristot. *Eth. Nic.* 1168a28ff.

453. The fr. is found in Stob.'s section 'On Peace', along with *Erec.* F 369 (see notes there and on F 370.5–10), Ar. *Georg.* fr. 111, Bacchyl. *Paean* 4.61–80, Eur. *Supp.* 481–93, etc.; cf. also Theocr. 16. 88–96. Dating of *Cresph.* is assisted by Ar.'s parody of 1–2, and perhaps by Timaeus's report (see App.) that Hermocrates quoted 1–8 at the Sicilian peace conference of Summer 424: see Introduction, p. 125. Comparable passages concern the ending of wars, but here the Chorus resent the internal discord, *stasis*, which has facilitated Polyphontes' coup (cf. *HF* 33–4, 588–91) and may have been a significant dimension of Eur.'s play (see p. 125). Their invocatory hymn (ὕμνος κλητικός) to Peace uses some of the standard elements of prayers for the presence and beneficence of a deity (see notes below: in general, Burkert 74–5; J. M. Bremer in H. S. Versnel (ed.), *Faith, Hope and Worship* [Leiden, 1981], 193–7, also 212–3 on hymns in drama; Ar. *Peace* 560–600, 974–1016 have comic prayers to Peace). The Aeolic metre is typical for this purpose. The prayer's formality and extent suggest it opened a Stasimon, but how the Stasimon developed is unclear. A Choral prayer or expression of need can direct the audience's anticipation and emotion at various dramatic moments: following a major exposition early in the play (e.g. *Hipp.* 525ff., *Ion* 452ff.), or at a pause after a central and crucial development (e.g. *HF* 637ff.), or before the crisis (e.g. *Ion* 1048ff., *IT* 1233ff., cf. Soph. *Ant.* 1115ff.).

1–2. O Peace (etc.): the deity is typically invoked by name and attributes (abundance, beauty). Hesiod defined 'flourishing' Peace as one of the three Horae (bringers of prosperity: cf. 1, 6–9) along with Order and Justice (Eunomia, Diké: contrast 10–12 here), their parents being Zeus and Themis (Right): see *Theog.* 901–2 with West's notes, *WD* 227–8 (Peace a *kourotrophos*, 'child nourisher', in a just and prosperous land); cf. Eur. *Supp.* 490–1.

3–6. I yearn ... I fear ... : an expression of anxiety presses the deity to respond (e.g. Sappho fr. 1.3–4 L.–P., Eur. *Or.* 180). Line 3 is lit. 'there is yearning for you in me (considering) how you are temporizing': see on F 449.4. ζῆλος includes regretful envy for those enjoying Peace: cf. Harder here, Willink on *Or.* 971–3. **old age ... hardships:** a motif resumed from the Parodos (F 448a.110–3 n.), as in *HF* 637ff. following 107–30, 268–9. They are not yet 'overwhelmed', being still active in thought and self-expression, esp. song and celebration (cf. *HF* 673–86). [Text: for 4–6 πρὶν ... πρὶν, 'sooner ... before', see LSJ πρίν B init. The first πρίν has often been deleted, but a false insertion is not easily explained; M. Chiara Martinelli, *SCO* 37 (1987), 165–74 defends the metre in Stob. and (cf. Dale, *LM*, 144) the word-order in 6.]

7–8. songs ... fine dancing: communal singing and dancing at religious and social celebrations, esp. weddings (cf. *Pha.* 227–44, 246–7 nn.); here connoting the gifts of Peace as e.g. *Erec.* F 369.3 (n.), F 370. 5–10, Ar. *Peace* 774–5, 976, Bacchyl. *Paean* 4.61–8.

9. Come ... : an explicit summons as e.g. Sappho fr. 1.5, 25; Soph. *Ant.* 1144; Eur. *Ion* 458, *Or.* 176, *Bacc.* 553, 583. [Text: for the form πότνα see Dodds on *Bacc.* 370, a verse of identical rhythm (also *HF* 679, 680); this is a simpler correction than Diggle's added <ἴθι>. Bergk's πάλιν would give 'Return, mistress, for me'.]

10–11. Discord ... Strife: Eris/Strife as a goddess is common in early epic (Hom. *Il.* 4. 440, 18.535 etc., Hes. *Theog.* 226, *WD* 11–20 (good and bad kinds), *Cypria* (Proclus) *EGF* p. 31) and in 6ᵗʰ C. art (see esp. Paus. 5.19.2, 10.26.6; *LIMC* III, 'Eris'). The idea acquired cosmological complexity in 5ᵗʰ C. cosmological thought which is sometimes reflected in Eur.: see Willink on *Or.* 12–14, 1001–2; J. R. Wilson, *G&R* 26 (1977), 7–20. 'Discord' is a secondary meaning of στάσις (LSJ III.2), the personification not found earlier than here except probably in Aesch. *Eum.* 977 (so Page, cf. Podlecki on 976ff.).

454. On the citation see F 450 n., and for similar sentiments *Bell.* F 300 n. The ascription to Merope suffices to identify Eur.'s play. The context is probably her pretence at reconciliation with Polyphontes rather than an earlier scene (e.g. Wecklein, Harder); a self-consolation in the extreme terms of this and F 455 suggests that all of Merope's children are supposed to be dead. **drained:** (ἐξ-, ἀπ-)αντλέω applies lit. to bilge-water and the like but in Tragedy often suggests 'drain to the dregs', 'endure all the wretchedness of', without any prospect of relief' (Dale on *Alc.* 354; cf. esp. *Hipp.* 898 = 1049). [Text: **3. life:** Nauck's πότμον gives '(drained the same) fortune', plausibly since (JD) the same substitution is found in mss. at Soph. *Ant.* 83 (cf. H. Lloyd-Jones and N. Wilson, *Sophoclea* [Oxford, 1990], 118; also conjectured at Eur. *Hec.* 1270).

455. Cited by Schol. *Pho.* 159 with ref. to Niobe's 'seven' daughters. Her variably numbered children were killed by Apollo and Artemis to punish her insulting comparison of her own maternal achievement with their mother Leto's: see esp. Hom. *Il.* 24.602–17. Her story became a traditional example of extreme grief in bereavement. The speaker is probably Merope: cf. F 454 n. and perhaps 449, 458; her loss is not so great as Niobe's, or she will not prolong her grief as Niobe did. **Loxias's:** on this name of Apollo see note on *Mel.D.* F 494.14; Artemis's share (killing the daughters) is absent through allusory brevity, or because the sentence is quoted incomplete. [Text: suspect because αὐτῆς 'herself' has no apparent purpose. With Νιόβης detached it will mean 'her' (e.g. Wecklein, 'and her twice seven children dying *together*'). Bothe made Niobe Nom. (*'and* Niobe *<saw>* . . .). Cropp suggests e.g. '*<I have heard that* . . . > and that Niobe *<saw>* her own twice seven children dying . . .'; this complexity would lead to confusion when part of the sentence was detached for quotation.]

456. Plut.'s citation (see App.) continues: 'What a stir does she (Merope) make in the theatre, making people rigid with fright, and there is fear lest she should anticipate the old man who is trying to grab her and should wound the lad'. This seems to describe a scene experienced by the audience, whereas Hyginus (see p. 121) suggests Merope went into an inner room or alcove (*chalcidicum*: for the word's possible senses see *Thes. Ling. Lat. Onomasticon* II.366; Hyginus is describing domestic, not scenic architecture). The key points of the two accounts are Cresphontes taken *inside* and *asleep* when attacked, and the audience *directly experiencing* the attack and seeing the crucial moment. These are preserved if Polyphontes takes Cresphontes inside to the guest quarters (cf. Aesch. *Cho.* 712ff., Eur. *Alc.* 546ff.), Merope and the Old Man plan the attack on stage and go inside to execute it, the Chorus hear and interpret cries from inside, then Cresphontes emerges pursued by his attackers and is recognised by the Old Man as Merope delivers this fr.; cf. Jahn, *Arch.Zeit.* 12 (1854), 228–9, summarised by Harder 116. Elements can be compared or contrasted with Aesch. *Cho.* 885ff. (Clytemnestra's call for an axe with which to confront the emerging Orestes), *Or.* 1369ff. and 1503ff. (the Phrygian fleeing from the slaughter in the palace, Orestes later emerging in pursuit), and Hecuba's attack on Paris in *Alex.* Hypoth. 29–30; Hose I.273–4 compares *Antiope* F 223.28ff. (where Lycus is lured into the hut, then brought out for the *coup de grâce* by Amphion, but Hermes intervenes). For less attractive alternatives (a purely narrative report speech; offstage action throughout with Choral commentary; use of the ekkyklema; Cresphontes sleeping and attacked in sight of the audience or on a concealed part of the stage) and discussion see Burnett, Musso xxi–xxii, Harder 114–7, Luppe 176–7, J. de Miguel Jover, *Minerva* 3 [1989], 143–59. [Text: for the meaningless †ὠνητέραν† Turnebus's ὁσιωτέραν gives 'a more lawful blow is this . . .' (than those which killed her husband and son); but the supposed corruption is quite extreme. Porson's ὦ νέρτερ' "Αιδη, 'O nether Hades . . .', cannot coexist with 'I give you this *blow*' but could be right if πληγήν 'blow' is the wrong word in the next line as some have thought; then cf. *Mel.D.* F 495.30 ἔδωκε νερτέροις 'delivered . . . to the powers below'. This fr. cannot coincide with F 448a.87–8 (now fixed in the Prologue).]

457. This thought was proverbial (Aristot. *Rhet.* 1384a33); a proper sense of shame will make one avert one's eyes from the person evoking it; e.g. *Hom. hymn.* 4.214–5 with Richardson's Comm., Hom. *Il.* 9.372–3, Eur. *IA* 994; Cairns, *Aidos* 158 and Index under '*aidos* . . . in the eyes'. **child:** not necessarily spoken by a parent; Cresphontes is the obvious candidate as addressee, with Merope or the Old Man as speaker.

458. Ascribed simply to Merope (cf. F 454, 456) by Plutarch *On gaining benefit from one's enemies*. Usually placed in the 'reconciliation' scene, Merope pretending a wise acceptance of her situation.   **taught me wisdom:** lit. 'made me wise'; Harder argues that in 5th C. moral terminology σοφήν should mean 'clever' rather than 'sensible'. That will be Merope's hidden meaning in misleading Polyphontes, but the explicit reference is to proper moral understanding and behaviour; cf. e.g. *Hcld.* 458, *And.* 1165 (see Stevens), *HF* 300, *El.* 295–6 (see Denniston, Cropp); moral self-awareness is the benefit to which Plut. refers.   **fee:** alluding to the charges (mentioned explicitly at *Hec.* 818) of the 'Sophists' or *sophia*-teachers of Eur.'s time; on their professional practices see Guthrie, *HGPh* III, 41–4. μισθός of human currency also *Hel.* 971, *IA* 1169.   **dearest of my loved ones:** i.e. her family.

459. The fr. is certainly limited to the first two lines of Stob. 4.31.95 (from the section *On Wealth*). Ill-gotten gains bring retribution: cf. Hes. *WD* 320–6, Solon fr. 13.7–13 etc. (Cropp on *El.* 940–4, where greed is a conventional trait of the 'tyrannical' usurper). The context is probably after Polyphontes' death, with the Chorus-leader, or a triumphant Cresphontes or Merope making a comment on where he went wrong. An earlier warning to Polyphontes or the disguised Cresphontes is much less likely.

ERECTHEUS

Texts, testimonia. P. Sorbonne 2328 (see App. for F 370); *TrGF* F 349–60, 360a, 361–9, 369a–d, 370 (= P. Sorb.); Austin, *NFE* frs. 39–65; Mette Nos. 448–476; A. Martínez Díez, *Euripides: Erecteo* (Madrid, 1976); P. Carrara, *Euripide: Eretteo* (Florence, 1977).

Myth. Eur. *Ion* 275–82; Lycurg. *Leocr.* 98–101; Dem. 60.8, 27; [Demaratus] *FGH* 42 F 4; Hygin. *Fab.* 46, 238.2; [Plut.] *Mor.* 310d; Apollod. 3.15.4; Ael. Aristid. 1.85–8 with Schol. p. 110 Dindorf; Schol. Arat. *Phaenom.* 172; Photius, 'παρθένοι' (II.64 Naber), citing Phanodemus *FGH* 325 F 4, Phrynichus *PCG* fr. 31.   E. Ermatinger, *Die attische Autochthonensage bis auf Euripides* (Berlin, 1897); *RE* 6 (1909), 404–10, 1117–20; M.A. Schwartz, *Erechtheus et Theseus apud Eur. et Atthidographos* (Leiden, 1917); Preller–Robert II.i.140–4; C. Picard, *Rev.Hist.* 166 (1931), 1–76; U. Kron, *Die zehn attischen Phylenheroen* (Berlin, 1976), 32–55; Carrara (above), 18–27; M. Lacore, *REA* 85 (1983), 215–34; R. Simms, *GRBS* 24 (1983), 197–208; R. Parker in J. N. Bremmer (ed.), *Interpretations of Greek Mythology* (London, 1986), 187–214; *LIMC* (below); E. Kearns, *The Heroes of Attica* (London, 1989), 113–5, 160; Gantz 233–5, 242–4.

Illustrations. Webster, *Monuments* 157; L. Weidauer, *Antike Kunst* 12 (1969), 91–3; Clairmont (below), 491–3; Kron (above), 76–7, 256; Schefold and Jung, *Urkönige* 70–2; *LIMC* IV.56–9 ('Eumolpos'), 923–51 ('Erechtheus', esp. 938–41, 949); J. Breton Connelly, *AIA Abstracts* (1992), 25 (cf. S. Peirce and A. Steiner, *BMCR* 5 [1994], 81).

Main discussions. Schwartz (above); J. Schmitt, *Freiwilliger Opfertod bei Eur.* (Giessen, 1921), 32–7, 63–9, 93–8; Schmid 428–30; Webster, *Euripides* (1967), 127–30; V. di Benedetto, *Euripide: teatro e società* (Turin, 1971), 145–53; W. Calder, *GRBS* 10 (1969), 147–56; J. C. Kamerbeek, *Mnem.* 23 (1970), 113–26, and in Hofmann and Harder (eds.), *Fragmenta Dramatica* 111–6; H. van Looy, *Hommages...M. Delcourt* (Brussels, 1970), 115–22; C. Clairmont, *GRBS* 12 (1971), 485–93; M. Treu, *Chiron* 1 (1971), 115–31; A. Martínez Díez, *Emerita* 43 (1975), 207–39 and 44 (1976), 1–20; U. Albini, *PP* 40 (1985), 354–60; Aélion (1986), 198–215; E. O'Connor-Visser, *Aspects of Human Sacrifice in the Tragedies of Euripides* (Amsterdam, 1987), 148–76; J. Wilkins in A. Powell (ed.), *Euripides, Women and Sexuality* (London, 1990), 177–94; R. E. Harder, *Die Frauenrolle bei Euripides* (Stuttgart, 1993), 172–6, 336–42.

Like Euripides' *Heraclidae* and *Supplices*, *Erectheus* dramatises a glorious but costly moment in the legendary history of Athens. Its tragic nature and solemnity lie in showing how individual life and happiness must be expended for the survival and destiny of the community.

The essence of Euripides' plot is given in the 4th C. speech of Lycurgus against Leocrates (*Leocr.* 98–101). Quoting Praxithea's renunciation speech (F 360), he explains that Eumolpus, son of Poseidon and Chione, attacked Attica with a Thracian host during the reign of Erectheus, who after consulting Delphi sacrificed his daughter to ensure victory. Ps.-Plut. *Mor.* 310d, also referring to

Euripides, mentions a consultation between Erectheus and his wife about the sacrifice, as does a similar (unattributed) summary from the *Stories from Tragedy* of ps.-Demaratus, *FGH* 42 F 4. Largely in agreement with these is a section of the Panathenaic speech of Aelius Aristides (1.85–8: 2nd C. A.D.). The architecture of the play can thus be determined: Erectheus returns from Delphi at or near the beginning. The typical rhythm of Euripides' dramatisations of voluntary sacrificial death (*Hcld.*, *Hec.*, *Pho.*, *IA*: cf. Schmitt, Wilkins) suggests that the sacrifice was resisted, then accepted after a decisive renunciation speech; F 360 will have been the culmination of this process, with Praxithea overruling a reluctant Erectheus (cf. F 360. 1–3, 36–7) and quite possibly her own initial revulsion (O'Connor-Visser 156–7). Battle preparations then proceed, and a pre-battle scene includes Erectheus's farewell speech (F 362) foreshadowing his death and advising his heir on political conduct. When the papyrus fragment from the ending of the play (F 370) begins, Praxithea and the Chorus of old men are anxiously awaiting the news which shortly comes: the attackers are defeated and Eumolpus dead, but Erectheus has also died, engulfed in a chasm created by Poseidon's trident blow (F 370.59–60 n.). A gap in the papyrus deprives us of most of the Messenger scene, and when this text resumes Praxithea is lamenting not only Erectheus and her sacrificed daughter but also her other daughters (whose deaths are omitted by the direct *testimonia*; they have presumably killed themselves so as to share in the sacrifice: cf. Apollod. 3.15.4, Hygin. *Fab.* 46, Schol. Aristid. 1.85). In a last assault Poseidon shatters the palace with an earthquake, but Athena appears and forbids further damage. She announces her final dispositions (F 370.63ff.): the daughters, once buried, will be deified and worshipped as the Hyacinthids; Erectheus will also receive a sanctuary and worship as 'Poseidon Erectheus'; Praxithea is to be Athena's priestess (i.e., the first priestess of Athena Polias). Zeus has determined (99ff.) the future of Eumolpus's descendants as priests at Eleusis, and (110–4) the catasterism of the Erectheids/Hyacinthids as the Hyades.

A few more points can be asserted with reasonable confidence. F 349 is generally assigned to a Prologue speech by Poseidon, who knows Eumolpus's life story (F 369a may belong with it: so e.g. Carrara); thus the divine adversaries dominate the beginning and end of the play as in *Hipp.* A ritual supplication of the gods for the safety of the city occurred at some point (F 350, 351: see Comm. there). The Stasimon including F 369 (the Chorus yearning for peace, as again in F 370.5–10) probably came shortly before the start of F 370, in the time gap containing the battle (though Schmid, Martínez and others suggest an earlier placing).

Other features have been speculatively proposed. Some (e.g. Schwartz 20) have inferred from F 367–8 that Erectheus consulted Dodona as well as Delphi, but this is unknown to the *testimonia* and the inference is not cogent (see Comm.

there). Still less likely is a consultation with Teiresias (cf. e.g. Webster 129; Martínez, *Emerita* 44 [1976], 5), who in *Pho.* 852–7 tells Creon that he has just returned from assisting Erectheus against Eumolpus; this is surely an *ad hoc* invention in *Pho.*, preparing for the human sacrifice which Teiresias will soon demand there.

F 352–4 are generally assigned (and some add F 355–6) to a scene in which Erectheus asserts the injustice of the invasion and his confidence of victory. This scene may well have been a confrontation, like those of *Hcld.* 120ff., *Supp.* 399ff., with a herald sent by Eumolpus to state his claim to Attica and demand its surrender (so e.g. Ermatinger 93–4, van Looy 120ff.); some dramatic indication of the forces threatening Athens was surely needed. Ermatinger and van Looy consider identifying the go-between as the Dodonaean seer Skiros who is said by Paus. 1.36.4 to have fallen in battle while assisting the Eleusinians against Athens. This is another way of accounting for F 367–8, but the argument for associating Skiros with Euripides' play is tenuous (for the varied traditions associating him with the war, the Skira festival and Athena Skiras see Kearns 197–8; Parker 204; W. Burkert, *Homo Necans* [Eng tr., Berkeley, 1983], 143–9). Nothing in the fragments suggests that Euripides connected the Eleusinians with Eumolpus's invasion (cf. *Myth* below).

Erectheus's daughters number three in F 357, F 360.36 (cf. Schol. Arat. *Phaen.* 172), and Euripides probably had the eldest sacrificed (ps.-Demaratus; the youngest, Apollod. 3.15.4). They are nameless in the fragments and direct *testimonia*, and probably also in the play like 'Macaria' in *Hcld.* (so e.g. Schmitt 98, O'Connor-Visser 167–8). The name Chthonia for the sacrificed daughter has sometimes been accepted from Hyginus's peculiar account (e.g. Schwartz 21, 24; Robert 143; Martínez, *Emerita* 43 [1975], 234–5), but this identification is probably artificial. (Apollod. 3.15.1–3 names Procris, Creusa, Chthonia and Oreithuia, all with their own life stories, quite separately from the unnamed daughters in the sacrifice story, 3.15.4. Photius, perhaps drawing the details from Phanodemus whom he later cites, names these four as the younger sisters of two who sacrificed themselves, Protogeneia and Pandora.) Ps.-Demaratus names Persephone as the goddess receiving the sacrifice, as in *Hcld.* (cf. Wilkins on *Hcld.* 408–9). It is not certain that the daughter spoke, or even appeared (Aélion doubts it); F 350 and 351 need have nothing to do with the human sacrifice (though some have thought they do: see Comm.). But F 358 encouraging 'children' to love their mother might best be placed in an early familial scene, before Erectheus reveals the oracle (cf. O'Connor-Visser 155–6). The daughters can hardly have been involved in the decision scene where Praxithea made the decisive speech (F 360). The idea that she then tricked her daughter into attending her own sacrifice (e.g. Schmitt 67 following Welcker and Hartung; cf. Kamerbeek [1990], 115) is groundless, being based in part on false analogy with the story of Iphigeneia and in part on a misinterpretation of Aristides 1.87, 'her mother brought her for the sacrifice after adorning her as if sending her to a festival'; this in its context obviously means that she sent her gladly rather than sadly (cf. *IA* 1437–48, Iphigeneia demanding gladness). A glad farewell scene thus remains possible, and even likely; in any case the play must have left the impression that the victim at least acquiesced in her death, as was necessary for a 'good' sacrifice (cf. *Hcld., Pho., IA*). Praxithea presumably stayed behind (like the mothers in *Hec.*, *IA*) and heard about the sacrifice at the beginning of the main battle report (cf. *Pho.* 1090–2; so e.g. Schmitt 67), or perhaps separately before Erectheus's departure (cf. *Hec.* 484ff.; Webster 128, Aélion 207, Carrara); it seems too central to have been elided altogether as in *Hcld.*

Apollod. 3.15.4 says that the sisters 'slaughtered' themselves after swearing ('in some accounts') that all should perish together. Hyginus mentioning a similar oath has them 'kill' (*Fab.* 46) or 'precipitate' (*Fab.* 238.2) themselves. Phanodemus (and, Photius's citation suggests, Phrynichus in his comedy *Monotropos*, 414 B.C.) recorded two daughters offering themselves for sacrifice on the Hyacinthus hill. The sisters in Euripides certainly swore an oath (cf. F 370.70) and probably killed themselves in such a way as to assist the sacrifice and the salvation of Athens; Schmitt's (68) suggestion that they might have done this without forewarning their parents, like Menoeceus in *Pho.* 977–1012, is attractive though purely hypothetical. If their deaths were quasi-sacrificial rather than suicides from grief, they presumably did not occur in the palace (as Treu 121 n. 25 suggests). If they occurred in conjunction with the actual sacrifice (cf. Apollod.), they were probably reported with it, but a self-precipitation from the cliffs (cf. Hygin. *Fab.* 238.2) told in a second post-battle report is attractive if their bodies, over which Praxithea laments at the end (F 370.68), were 'falling' (F 370.27?) and are 'bruised' (F 370.36–8?).

The identity of the son addressed by Erectheus in F 362 and the remark about adoption in F 359 are puzzling. F 362.1–4 and 32 show that Erectheus is speaking as father to son and heir. F 362.2–3 ('you are old enough now to understand . . .') and Erectheus's not taking him into battle show that he is not an adult, though quite possibly in late adolescence. Yet Praxithea in F 360.22–5 denies having sons, and Schwartz's (22) inference that she means only adult sons is invalidated by F 360.36–7 where she mentions only herself, Erectheus and the sisters as beneficiaries of her daughter's sacrifice. It has usually been inferred that F 362 is addressed to an adopted heir, and F 359 on the inferiority of adopted sons is probably relevant to this (rather than to the adoption of a substitute sacrificial victim: see Comm.). A plausible scenario for F 359 is that Praxithea is criticising Erectheus's reliance on an adopted heir because she thinks Erectheus can survive the battle and beget sons of his own, or that the succession will be passed on through the daughters whom she expects to survive; this would be a further, dramatically ironic display of her blindness to the impending obliteration of her family, contrasted with Erectheus's expectation of his own death. It may even be that Erectheus has decided on the adoption after his visit to Delphi and performs it during the play, between F 360 and F 362. The heir's identity (cf. Comm. on F 362) remains uncertain because of the extreme artificiality and fluidity of the traditions about the Athenian royal succession, which were only beginning to be formulated systematically in Euripides' time (for a survey see Gantz 233–49).

Other ascriptions. None merits discussion. F 981 is mistakenly combined in the text of Plutarch with F 360.7–10 (see App. to F 360). Snell's F 369c is really a *testimonium* rather than a fragment: a scrap of commentary on Thuc. 2.15.1 in P. Oxy. 853 mentions Eur. *Erec.* in some unidentifiable connection with Thuc.'s mention of the attack on Athens of the 'Eleusinians with Eumolpus' (see now *TrGF* test. v).

Myth. Erectheus is mentioned in Hom. *Il.* 2.546–9 (cf. *Od.* 7.80–1) as the autochthonous forebear of the Athenian people, protégé and associate of Athena herself. In Euripides' time Athenian mythology (e.g. *Ion* 267ff.) was tending to distinguish the heroic Erectheus from the primeval and semi-serpentine Ericthonius (as 'joint heirs to a single mythological inheritance', Parker 201 with notes 60–2). Whether they *originated* as separate figures later merged and re-separated, or Ericthonius is simply an offshoot of Erectheus, is debated. Euripides' play is the earliest record of the heroic Erectheus's only *geste*, the defence of Attica against Eumolpus. This must originally have been set in a conflict between Athens and Eleusis of the kind mentioned in Thuc. 2.15.1 as historical but in fact largely or entirely mythical. The priestly family of the Eumolpidae, hierophants of the Mysteries at Eleusis, claimed descent from the 'mighty Eumolpus' mentioned in the *Homeric Hymn to Demeter*, who at some point had come to be regarded as a son of Poseidon (see Comm. on F 370. 100–1). The Athenians will have fought Eumolpus and the Eleusinians for control of the Mysteries. But Euripides presents Eumolpus as invading Attica with a horde of Thracians to claim it in the name of his father Poseidon, who had himself unsuccessfully claimed it against Athena (see esp. F 360.46–9, F 369.4, F 370.13, 55–7; also Lycurgus, ps.-Demaratus and Aristides cited above as following Euripides, and e.g. Pl. *Menex.* 239a, Isocr. 4.68, 12.193). At the end of the play Athena seems to ordain a *future* connection of Eumolpus's descendants with Eleusis and the Mysteries (see Comm. on F 370.100ff.). Euripides, then, treated the war as a struggle between Greeks and barbarians (Ermatinger 104–6, Schwartz 14–19, Treu 116–7), in conformity with the ideology of imperial Athens and the circumstances of the Archidamian war of the 420s, while suppressing the tradition of internal conflict between Athens and Eleusis.

A Thracian background for the Eleusinian Mysteries and the Eumolpidae may have been already developed to associate the Thracian Orpheus with them (cf. Parker 203 with refs. n. 68); or Euripides might possibly have created the Thracian connection himself by 'barbarising' the Eleusinian war (cf. Hall, *Inventing the Barbarian* 105–6). In either case Euripides' barbaric Eumolpus had to be distinguished from, and was hence made an ancestor of, the Eumolpus who founded the Mysteries. Some post-Euripidean sources (cf. F 370.100–1 n.) do link the Thracian's invasion with the Athens–Eleusis war, and in another Athenian tradition (Paus. 1.5.2, 1.27.4, 1.38.2, 2.14.2) the Thracian Eumolpus helps the Eleusinians, survives the war (his son, the barbarously named Immarados, is killed by Erectheus) and administers the Mysteries after a negotiated peace. Such accounts could reflect either a pre-Euripidean 'Thracianising' tradition or a compromise with Euripides' own innovation.

Euripides' genealogy linking the barbarian Eumolpus with the priestly families of Eleusis is obscured by the incompleteness of the papyrus text (see Comm. on F 370.100–1, 113–4). A further network of aetiologies in the better preserved part of Athena's speech accounts for the cults of the Hyacinthids and of Poseidon Erectheus, and for the priestesshood of Athena Polias (F 370.67–97, Comm.).

Athenian mythology, with its emphasis on the perpetuation of the community, contains other stories of the saving of the city through the death of a king (Codrus) or the sacrifice or suicide of maidens (the daughters of Hyacinthus and of Leos, and in one account Aglauros daughter of Cecrops, who otherwise precipitated herself with her sister after opening the chest containing the baby Ericthonius: cf. Kearns 24–7, 55–63). The identification of the Erectheids with the Hyacinthids (or simply 'Maidens') is likely to have been invented close to Euripides' time (cf. Carrara 19–20, Aélion 203–4), Erectheus's sacrifice of his daughters and his own death in battle somewhat earlier (Parker 203 with n. 66; Eur. *Ion* 277–82 takes both for granted). The further identification of the Hyacinthids with the Hyads seems unique to Euripides (see on F 370.107–8).

Illustrations. No 'illustration' of a dramatic scene exists. Scenes from the myth which were reported in Euripides' play — the sacrifice of the Erectheid(s), Erectheus in battle — have been identified, questionably at best, amongst the sculptural decorations of several of Athens's most famous classical temples including the Parthenon and the Erectheum: Kron in *LIMC* 'Erechtheus' is sceptical, E. Simon in *LIMC* 'Chthonia' (concerning the sacrificial scenes) is less so. Pausanias (1.27.4) saw on the Acropolis a sculptural group of Erectheus and Eumolpus or Immarados which, if identical with the 'Erectheus' of Myron (cf. Paus. 9.30.1), would be earlier than Euripides' play. J. Breton Connelly's recent and revolutionary suggestion that the Parthenon Frieze shows the sacrifice of the Erectheids will be much debated (see e.g. the criticisms of E. Harrison reported by Peirce and Steiner). A Lucanian vase from the end of the 5ᵗʰ C. (*LIMC* 'Eumolpos', No. 19), as interpreted by Weidauer, shows Poseidon and Eumolpus (or the young Immarados?) riding into battle on one side, Athena confronting them in a chariot on the other; Clairmont identifies Athena's charioteer as the daughter of Erectheus, but it seems doubtful that the virgin just sacrificed and (in Euripides) about to become a Hyad could have been assigned this role in art.

Themes and characters. The fragments hardly allow easy conclusions about the tone of the play. Several features seem problematic at least to modern minds: human sacrifice is accepted and shown to be effective, at least in a mythical context; it is favoured, even with enthusiasm, by the victim's mother (probably through Euripides' invention); the two sisters die gratuitously (again probably Euripides' elaboration: should the ambivalent presentation of Evadne's gratuitous suicide in *Supp.* be compared?); Praxithea becomes pathetic and demoralised in the total loss of her family, symbolised in the ruin of the palace (though the extent of her remorse is regrettably unclear: cf. Comm. on F 370. 41–2); Athena's consolations at the end might seem emptily formal and impersonal. These sombre features have suggested to some critics that Euripides was ironically undercutting the play's surface political and religious values (e.g. di Benedetto; Vellacott, *Ironic Drama* 194–7; Michelini 90), so that the ruin of royal family and palace reflects the threat posed to the whole community by these values. For others, however, the play solemnly proclaims or even advocates the 'communal' ideology of imperial Athens, however questionably in modern eyes, through the example of the royal family's devotion to the city's survival, their acceptance of the costs, and their reward of commemoration in legend and cult (see recently Aélion, O'Connor-Visser, Wilkins; on the political relevance of Euripides' use of the sacrifice theme, J. de Romilly, *RPh* 39 [1965], 41–6). This is for the most part a convincing view; it is unlikely that Euripides shaped the events of the play with covert distaste, or that many if any of his audience felt such distaste. The plot is founded on a threat to the very survival of Athens as a centre of civilisation by an unprovoked barbarian invasion (to read the Chorus's yearnings for peace as criticisms of Athenian bellicosity is, then, naive). The crucial decision may be centred on Praxithea because renunciation of personal and family attachments in favour of the community's survival is best epitomised in the mother (as in the famously unmaternal mothers of Spartan warriors); her acceptance legitimises the sacrifice while also allowing the king a seemly reluctance. The sisters' voluntary deaths may have seemed to enhance the willingness of the one inevitable sacrifice. The compensations offered by Athena, the foundation of cults fundamental to the Athenian community, and the enforcement of Athena's and Zeus's order over Poseidon's disorder are in Athenian ideology outcomes of great value. Wilkins (189) rightly argues that *Erec.* and *Hcld.*, expressing (with *Supp.*) themes central to the Athenian patriotic canon, need to be distinguished from *Hec.*, *Pho.*, and *IA* which put their human sacrifices in a plainly (rather than ironically) ambivalent light, and do so outside the context of Athenian mythology. There remains nevertheless an impression that Euripides has made the mythical event uneasy and problematic, shading the public and historical imperatives of Athenian ideology with a recognition of their human cost to individuals, and in particular to Praxithea and her daughters as the public demands of the crisis impel them to action and suffering outside their normal private realm of female, family-based stability (cf. R. Harder 339–42). The play may have recognised these ethical problems without suggesting facile answers, and so achieved a tragic impact characteristic of Euripides.

Staging. The scene is set on the Acropolis, where Praxithea and the Chorus await news of the battle in F 370.3–4. For problems of staging in the final scene see Comm. on F 370.44–54 (the earthquake), 55–117 (Athena's appearance), and 68 (bodies on stage?).

Date. See esp. Calder, Carrara 13–17, Cropp–Fick 79. *Erec.* belongs near the end of the 420s or soon thereafter. It was quoted in Ar. *Lys.* and *Thesm.* of 411 (see F 363, 370) and possibly in the somewhat earlier *Horae* (see *Erec.* F 357, 366 with Comm.), though not obviously in the *Peace* of 421 (despite Calder's suggestion with ref. to *Erec.* F 369, *Peace* 437–8, 1127ff.). A literal interpretation of Plut. *Nic.* 9.5 places *Erec.* during the Athenian–Spartan truce of 423–2, i.e. at the Lenaea or more probably Dionysia of 422 (so e.g. Webster, Calder, Carrara); but Plutarch's chronological implications should not be pressed (so e.g. Cropp–Fick, Parker 212 n. 64; cf. C. Pelling, *JHS* 100 [1980], 127–9). The relationship between the production of the play and the building of the Erectheum (cf. F 370.90–1) is too uncertain in nature to be of help. The rate of resolutions in the numerous surviving trimeters suggested the range 421–411 to Cropp–Fick, and an adjustment in the text of F 370.117 (see Comm. there) brings 422 even closer to statistically founded 'plausibility'.

Other dramatisations; influence. Euripides' dramatisation, the only one in Attic Tragedy, must have contributed to establishing the myth in the Athenian ideological canon. This status promoted later recollection of the plot in the mythographic tradition, but F 360 from Lycurgus is the only book fragment suggesting a first-hand acquaintance with the text, all others being transmitted through anthologies, lexica, etc. The only papyrus is early (3rd C. B.C.). Ennius's *Erectheus* is the only ancient derivative; two of its three brief fragments look like versions of Euripides' lines (fr. 60 ~ F 370.44; fr. 61 ~ F 360.51–2; Jocelyn rightly rejects attributions to *Erec.* of several other Ennian fragments). Swinburne's *Erechtheus* (1876) stands alone in modern times.

ΕΡΕΧΘΕΥΣ

349 (Ποσειδῶν) Αἰθιοπίαν νιν ἐξέσωσ᾽ ἐπὶ χθόνα.

350   καί μοι, πολὺν γὰρ πελανὸν ἐκπέμπεις δόμων,
φράσον σελήνας τάσδε πυρίνου χλόης …

351   ὀλολύζετ᾽, ὦ γυναῖκες, ὡς ἔλθηι θεὰ
χρυσῆν ἔχουσα Γοργόν᾽ ἐπίκουρος πόλει.

352   ὡς σὺν θεοῖσι τοὺς σοφοὺς κινεῖν δόρυ
στρατηλάτας χρή, τῶν θεῶν δὲ μὴ βίαι.

353   οὐδεὶς στρατεύσας ἄδικα σῶς ἦλθεν πάλιν.

354   τὰς οὐσίας γὰρ μᾶλλον ἢ τὰς ἁρπαγὰς
τιμᾶν δίκαιον· οὔτε γὰρ πλοῦτός ποτε
βέβαιος ἄδικος …

355   ναῦς ἡ μεγίστη κρεῖσσον ἢ σμικρὸν σκάφος.

356   ⟨ἐσθλοὺς ἐγὼ⟩
ὀλίγους ἐπαινῶ μᾶλλον ἢ πολλοὺς κακούς.

---

349 (39 A, 451 M, 2 Car, 1 Mar) Steph. Byz. *Ethn.*, Αἰθίοψ (p. 47 Meineke), attrib. Eur. *Erec.*
ἐξέσωσ᾽ Lobeck -ας Steph.   **350** (40 A, 452 M, 11 Car, 17 Mar) Suidas α 2082 Adler
(ἀνάστατοι), attrib. Eur. *Erec.*; Suidas β 458 (βοῦς ἕβδομος) refers similarly to Eur. *Erec.* but
without quotation; several lexica give σελήνη 'moon' as a kind of cake, without source-citation
2 πυρίνου Kuster πυρίμου Suidas   **351** (41 A, 453 M, 12 Car, 15 Mar) Schol. Ar. *Peace* 97,
attrib. Eur. *Erec.*   1 ἔλθηι Seidler ἐλέχθη Schol.   2 χρυσῆν Seidler ἡ χρυσὸν Schol.
352 (42 A, 462 M, 5 Car, 5 Mar) Stob. 4.13.12, attrib. Eur. *Erec.*   **353** (43 A, 463 M, 6 Car,

156

ERECTHEUS

349 *(Poseidon)* I rescued him and took him to the Ethiopian land.

Poseidon in the Prologue recalls rescuing the infant Eumolpus.

350 And — since you are dispatching much sacred gruel from
the house — explain to me *<why/where you are taking?>*
these 'moons' made from young wheat . . .

Praxithea is asked about her preparation of supplicatory sacrifices?

351 Ululate, women, so the goddess may come with her golden
Gorgon to defend the city.

Praxithea leads the supplication of Athena.

352 Wise generals should mobilise in concord with the gods, not
in defiance of them.

Erectheus responds to Eumolpus's threats (delivered by a herald?)

353 No one campaigning unjustly returns in safety.

Context probably as F 352.

354 It is right to respect property rather than plunder. No wealth
is ever secure if wrongly acquired . . .

Context probably as F 352.

355 The biggest ship is superior to a little skiff.

Confidence in Thracian numbers, expressed by Eumolpus's herald?

356 I myself set store by a few *<brave>* men rather than a
multitude of inferior ones.

Probably a response from Erectheus to F 355.

---

6 Mar) Stob. 4.13.13, attrib. Eur. *Erec.*   **354** (44 A, 468 M, 7 Car, 7 Mar) Stob. 4.31.105, attrib.
Eur. *Erec.*   **355** (45 A, 465 M, 20 Car, 10 Mar) Stob. 4.17.13, attrib. Eur. *Erec.*   μικρὸν Stob.
356 (46 A, 461 M, 21 Car, 8 Mar) Stob. 4.10.19, attrib. Eur. *Erec.*   (ἐσθλοὺς ἐγὼ) Hense

158　　EURIPIDES

357　　ζεῦγος τριπάρθενον

358　　οὐκ ἔστι μητρὸς οὐδὲν ἥδιον τέκνοις·
　　　　ἐρᾶτε μητρός, παῖδες, ὡς οὐκ ἔστ' ἔρως
　　　　τοιοῦτος ἄλλος ὅστις ἡδίων ἐρᾶν.

359　　θετῶν δὲ παίδων ποῦ κράτος; τὰ φύντα γὰρ
　　　　κρείσσω νομίζειν τῶν δοκημάτων χρεών.

360　Πραξιθέα　τὰς χάριτας ὅστις εὐγενῶς χαρίζεται,
　　　　ἥδιον ἐν βροτοῖσιν· οἳ δὲ δρῶσι μέν,
　　　　χρόνωι δὲ δρῶσι, δυσγενέστερον ⟨τόδε⟩.
　　　　ἐγὼ δὲ δώσω παῖδα τὴν ἐμὴν κτανεῖν.
　　　　λογίζομαι δὲ πολλά· πρῶτα μὲν πόλιν　　　　　　5
　　　　οὐκ ἄν τιν' ἄλλην τῆσδε βελτίω λαβεῖν·
　　　　ἧι πρῶτα μὲν λεὼς οὐκ ἐπακτὸς ἄλλοθεν,
　　　　αὐτόχθονες δ' ἔφυμεν· αἱ δ' ἄλλαι πόλεις
　　　　πεσσῶν ὁμοίως διαφοραῖς ἐκτισμέναι
　　　　ἄλλαι παρ' ἄλλων εἰσὶν εἰσαγώγιμοι.　　　　　　10
　　　　ὅστις δ' ἀπ' ἄλλης πόλεος οἰκήσηι πόλιν,
　　　　ἁρμὸς πονηρὸς ὥσπερ ἐν ξύλωι παγείς,
　　　　λόγωι πολίτης ἐστί, τοῖς δ' ἔργοισιν οὔ.
　　　　ἔπειτα τέκνα τοῦδ' ἕκατι τίκτομεν,
　　　　ὡς θεῶν τε βωμοὺς πατρίδα τε ῥυώμεθα.　　　　15
　　　　πόλεως δ' ἁπάσης τοὔνομ' ἕν, πολλοὶ δέ νιν
　　　　ναίουσι· τούτους πῶς διαφθεῖραί με χρή,
　　　　ἐξὸν προπάντων μίαν ὕπερ δοῦναι θανεῖν;
　　　　εἴπερ γὰρ ἀριθμὸν οἶδα καὶ τοὐλάσσονος
　　　　τὸ μεῖζον, †ἑνὸς† οἶκος οὐ πλέον στένει　　　　20
　　　　πταίσας ἁπάσης πόλεος οὐδ' ἴσον φέρει.
　　　　εἰ δ' ἦν ἐν οἴκοις ἀντὶ θηλειῶν στάχυς
　　　　ἄρσην, πόλιν δὲ πολεμία κατεῖχε φλόξ,

357 (47 A, 472 M, 24 Car, Inc. sed. 4 Mar) Hesych. ζ 125 Latte, attrib. Eur. Erec.　　358 (48 A,
467 M, 13 Car, 16 Mar) Stob. 4.25.4, attrib. Eur. Erec.; Orion 8, attrib. Eur.　2–3 regarded as a
separate fr. by Kassel and others　1 ἔστιν οὐδὲν μητρὸς Stob.　3 οἷος Stob.　　359 (49 A, 466
M, 8 Car, 18 Mar) Stob. 4.24.28, attrib. Eur. Erec.　　360 (50 A, 456 M, 10 Car, 13 Mar) Lycurg.
In Leocr. 100, attrib. Eur. Erec.　7–10 Plut. Mor. 604d, with F 981 subjoined, attrib. Eur.
3 ⟨τόδε⟩ Kamerbeek ⟨λέγω⟩ Meineke ⟨τοῦτο⟩ δυσγεν. Gesner　4 Taylor τὴν ἐμὴν παῖδα Lycurg.

357   a team of three maidens

        A reference to Erectheus's daughters (close to F 358?)

358   Nothing is more delightful to children than a mother. Love
        your mother, children, for there is no other such love that is
        more delightful to give.

        Erectheus in a family scene early in the play?

359   Where is the advantage in adopted children? Natural things
        should be considered superior to suppositious ones.

        Probably Praxithea criticising Erectheus for adopting an heir.

360   *Praxithea volunteers her daughter for sacrifice:*

        Praxithea. When someone renders favours in the noble way,
        it is gratifying to others. When they act but do so slowly,
        <this is> ill-bred. I, then, shall give my daughter to be
        killed. I take many things into account, and first of all,[5] that
        I could not find any other city better than this. To begin
        with, we are an autochthonous people, not introduced from
        elsewhere; other communities, founded as it were through
        board-game moves, are imported, different ones from differ-
        ent places.[10] Now someone who settles in one city from
        another is like a peg ill-fitted in a piece of wood — a citizen
        in name, but not in his actions.

        Secondly, our very reason for bearing children is to
        safeguard the gods' altars and our homeland.[15] The city as a
        whole has just a single name, but its inhabitants are many;
        how can it be right for me to destroy them when I can give
        one girl to die for all? If I can count and distinguish larger
        from smaller, †one person's† family does not lament more[20]
        if it falls than a whole city, nor does it suffer an equal
        affliction.

        If our family included a crop of male children instead of
        females, and the flame of war was gripping our city, would I

9 ὁμοίως Lycurg. ed. Aldin., Plut. ὁμοίαις Lycurg.   διαφορηθεῖσαι βολαῖς Plut.   11 οἰκήσηι
Meineke (ᾤκησεν Dobree) οἰκίζει Lycurg.   14 ἕκατι Matthiae (ἕκητι Lycurg. ed. Aldin.) ἕνεκα
Lycurg.   16 ἕν (Scaliger), πολλοὶ Musgrave ἐν πολλοῖς Lycurg.   18 προπάντων . . . ὕπερ
Meineke (ὕπερ Matthiae)   πρὸ πάντων . . . ὑπερδοῦναι Lycurg.   19–21 condemned by Austin
20 οὐνὸς Emperius εἰς ἂν . . . σθένοι . . . φέροι Dobree   21 στένει Blass σθένει Lycurg.

160 EURIPIDES

οὐκ ἄν νιν ἐξέπεμπον εἰς μάχην δορός,
θάνατον προταρβοῦσ'· ἀλλ' ἔμοιγ' εἴη τέκνα   25
⟨ἃ⟩ καὶ μάχοιτο καὶ μετ' ἀνδράσιν πρέποι,
μὴ σχήματ' ἄλλως ἐν πόλει πεφυκότα.
τὰ μητέρων δὲ δάκρυ' ὅταν πέμπηι τέκνα,
πολλοὺς ἐθήλυν' εἰς μάχην ὁρμωμένους.
μισῶ γυναῖκας αἵτινες πρὸ τοῦ καλοῦ   30
ζῆν παῖδας εἵλοντ' ἢ παρήινεσαν κακά.
καὶ μὴν θανόντες γ' ἐν μάχηι πολλῶν μέτα
τύμβον τε κοινὸν ἔλαχον εὔκλειάν τ' ἴσην·
τῆμῆι δὲ παιδὶ στέφανος εἷς μιᾶι μόνηι
πόλεως θανούσηι τῆσδ' ὕπερ δοθήσεται,   35
καὶ τὴν τεκοῦσαν καὶ σὲ δύο θ' ὁμοσπόρω
σώσει· τί τούτων οὐχὶ δέξασθαι καλόν;
τὴν οὐκ ἐμὴν ⟨δὴ⟩ πλὴν φύσει δώσω κόρην
θῦσαι πρὸ γαίας. εἰ γὰρ αἱρεθήσεται
πόλις, τί παίδων τῶν ἐμῶν μέτεστί μοι;   40
οὔκουν ἅπαντα τοὐπ' ἐμοὶ σωθήσεται;
{ἄρξουσί τ' ἄλλοι, τήνδ' ἐγὼ σώσω πόλιν.}
ἐκεῖνο δ' οὗ ⟨τὸ⟩ πλεῖστον ἐν κοινῶι μέρος,
οὐκ ἔσθ' ἑκούσης τῆς ἐμῆς ψυχῆς †ἄτερτ†
προγόνων παλαι⟨ὰ⟩ θέσμι' ⟨ὅσ⟩τις ἐκβαλεῖ·   45
οὐδ' ἀντ' ἐλαίας χρυσέας τε Γοργόνος
τρίαιναν ὀρθὴν στᾶσαν ἐν πόλεως βάθροις
Εὔμολπος οὐδὲ Θρῆιξ ἀναστέψει λεὼς
στεφάνοισι, Παλλὰς δ' οὐδαμοῦ τιμήσεται.
χρῆσθ', ὦ πολῖται, τοῖς ἐμοῖς λοχεύμασιν,   50
σώιζεσθε, νικᾶτ'· ἀντὶ γὰρ ψυχῆς μιᾶς
οὐκ ἔσθ' ὅπως οὐ τήνδ' ἐγὼ σώσω πόλιν.
ὦ πατρίς, εἴθε πάντες οἳ ναίουσί σε
οὕτω φιλοῖεν ὡς ἐγώ· καὶ ῥαιδίως
οἰκοῖμεν ἄν σε κοὐδὲν ἂν πάσχοις κακόν.   55

24 νιν Matthiae μὴν Lycurg.   25 εἴη Lycurg. ed. Aldin. ἐστὶ Lycurg. ἔστω Hermann   26 ⟨ἃ⟩
Lycurg. ed. Aldin.   27 σχήματ' Scaliger σχήματα δ' Lycurg.   31 εἵλοντ' ἢ Matthiae -ντο καὶ
Lycurg.   34–5 εἷς μιᾶι μόνηι . . . θανούσηι Tyrwhitt ἡ μία μόνη . . . θανοῦσα Lycurg.
36 ὁμοσπόρω Bekker -ων Lycurg. (-ους some mss., ed. Aldin.)   37 σώσει· τί Melanchthon
ὡς εἴ τι Lycurg.   38 ⟨δὴ⟩ Nauck ⟨οὖν⟩ Nagel   41 ἅπαντα Reiske ἅπαντας Lycurg. τοὐπ'

be refusing to send them out to battle for fear of their deaths? No, give me sons[25] who would not only fight but stand out amongst the men and not be mere figures raised in the city to no use. When mothers' tears send children on their way, they soften many men as they leave for battle. I detest women who choose life rather than virtue[30] for their sons, or exhort them to cowardice. And sons, if they die in battle, earn a common tomb and equal glory shared with many others; my daughter, though, will be awarded one crown for herself alone when she dies for this city,[35] and will save her mother, and you, and her two sisters: which of these things is not a fine reward?

This girl, not mine in fact except through birth, I shall give to be sacrificed in defence of our land. If the city is captured, what share in my children have I then?[40] Shall not the whole then be saved, so far as is in my power? {And others will govern, I shall save this city.} And as for the matter in which the public has the greatest stake: there is none who shall with my consent † ... † cast out our ancestors' ancient institutions.[45] nor in place of the olive and the golden Gorgon shall Eumolpus or his Thracian folk plant the trident in the city's foundations and crown it with garlands, and Pallas be not at all honoured.

Citizens, make use of the offspring of my womb,[50] be saved, be victorious! To spare one life I shall surely not refuse to save our city. My home land, I wish that all your inhabitants loved you as I do: then we would dwell in you untroubled, and you would never be subjected to harm.[55]

Rehdantz γοῦν τ' Lycurg. τοῦν (Reiske) γ' Heinrich   42 deleted by Busche   ἄρξουσί τ' Lycurg. mss. NA ἄρξουσιν mss. MZ   43 Lycurg. ed. Aldin.   ἐκείνω δὲ οὐ πλ. Lycurg.   44 †ἄτερ†: ἄνερ Valckenaer ἀνήρ Bothe ποτε Austin   45 Lycurg. ed. Aldin. (παλαιὰ, ἐκβαλεῖ) and Reiske πάλαι θέσμιά τις ἐκβάλλει Lycurg.   46 ἀντ' ἐλαίας Boettiger (ἐλάας Dobree) ἂν τελείας Lycurg. 48 ἀναστέψει Musgrave ἀναστρέψει Lycurg.   51 σώιζεσθε, νικᾶτ' Lycurg. ed. Aldin. -σθε καὶ νικᾶτε Lycurg.   52 οὐ τήνδ' ἐγὼ Lycurg. ed. Aldin. ὑμῖν τήνδ' ἐγὼ οὐ Lycurg.

360a Πρ. φιλῶ τέκν’, ἀλλὰ πατρίδ’ ἐμὴν μᾶλλον φιλῶ.

361 N = F 370.21–2

362 (Ἐρεχθεύς) ὀρθῶς μ’ ἐπήρου· βούλομαι δέ σοι, τέκνον,
(φρονεῖς γὰρ ἤδη κἀποσώσαι’ ἂν πατρὸς
γνώμας φράσαντος, ἢν θάνω) παραινέσαι
κειμήλι’ ἐσθλὰ καὶ νέοισι χρήσιμα.
βραχεῖ δὲ μύθωι πολλὰ συλλαβὼν ἐρῶ.   5
πρῶτον φρένας μὲν ἠπίους ἔχειν χρεών·
τῶι πλουσίωι τε τῶι τε μὴ διδοὺς μέρος
ἴσον σεαυτὸν εὐσεβῆ πᾶσιν δίδου.
δυοῖν παρόντοιν πραγμάτοιν πρὸς θάτερον
γνώμην προσάπτων τὴν ἐναντίαν μέθες.   10
ἀδίκως δὲ μὴ κτῶ χρήματ’, ἢν βούληι πολὺν
χρόνον μελάθροις ἐμμένειν· τὰ γὰρ κακῶς
οἴκους ἐσελθόντ’ οὐκ ἔχει σωτηρίαν.
ἔχειν δὲ πειρῶ· τοῦτο γὰρ τό τ’ εὐγενὲς
καὶ τοὺς γάμους δίδωσι τοὺς πρώτους ἔχειν.   15
ἐν τῶι πένεσθαι δ’ ἐστὶν ἥ τ’ ἀδοξία,
κἂν ἦι σοφός τις, ἥ τ’ ἀτιμία βίου.
φίλους δὲ τοὺς μὲν μὴ χαλῶντας ἐν λόγοις
κέκτησο· τοὺς δὲ πρὸς χάριν σὺν ἡδονῆι
τῆι σῆι †πονηρούς† κλῆιθρον εἰργέτω στέγης.   20
ὁμιλίας δὲ τὰς γεραιτέρων φίλει,
ἀκόλαστ⟨α δ⟩’ ἤθη λαμπρὰ συγγελᾶν μόνον
μίσει· βραχεῖα τέρψις ἡδονῆς κακῆς.
ἐξουσίαι δὲ μήποτ’ ἐντρυφῶν, τέκνον,
αἰσχροὺς ἔρωτας δημοτῶν διωκαθεῖν·   25
ὃ καὶ σίδηρον ἀγχόνας τ’ ἐφέλκεται,
χρηστῶν πενήτων ἤν τις αἰσχύνηι τέκνα.

360a (adesp. 411 N, Eur. *Erec.* 51 A, 456d M, 9 Car, 14 Mar) Plut.*Mor.* 809d, attrib. Eur.; paraphr. by Lycurg. *Leocr.* 101 with ref. to Erec.’s wife in Eur. *Erec.*, and in part by Cic. *fam.* 12.14.7, unattrib.; attrib. Eur. *Erec.* by Porson   **362** (53 A, 458 M, 14 Car, 19 Mar) Stob. 3.3.18 (Trinc., Voss., unattrib.; omitted in ms. S; only 18–20 in mss. MA, attrib. Eur. *Erec.*)   Elsewhere in Stob. (all attrib. Eur. *Erec.*): 11–13 (4.31.97), 14–17 (4.31.25 and 36), 18–20 (3.14.3), 21–3 (4.50.3), 24–7 (3.17.6), 28–31 (4.2.4); several minor discrepancies amongst the Stob. citations are not noticed here.

360a   *Pr.* I love my children, but love my homeland more.

   Praxithea reaffirms her decision.

361 N   *= F 370.21–2*

362   *Erectheus bids farewell to his adopted son:*

   (Erectheus) You have enquired of me rightly; and I want, my son (for you have understanding now and will preserve your father's precepts once I have explained them, in case I die) to give you a store of advice that is edifying and valuable to the young. In a brief statement I shall sum up much.[5]

   First, you should maintain a kindly nature; to rich and poor alike give an equal share, and show yourself open and respectful to everyone.

   When two matters are before you, attach your opinion to one of them and dismiss the opposite opinion.[10]

   Do not acquire possessions unjustly if you want them to remain a long time in your dwelling; those that enter a house wrongly do not have permanence. Try, though, to have possessions; this bestows nobility and the means to make the best marriages.[15] With poverty comes low reputation, even if one is wise, and low esteem in one's life.

   Make friends of those who do not give way in discussions, and bar your door to those who †are worthless† for your gratification and pleasure.[20]

   Value the company of older men, and detest unbridled behaviour which is notable only for raising laughs: there's brief enjoyment in dishonourable pleasure.

   Never indulge your power, my son, and pursue disgraceful desires for commoners;[25] it is an invitation to stabbing or strangling, when someone shames the children of the worthy poor.

18–20 Plut. *Mor.* 63a, wrongly attrib. to 'the tragic Merope' (cf. *Cresph.* Introd., p. 123) 21 Menand. *Sentent.* 572, unattrib.   29–31 Plut. *Mor.* 337f, unattrib.   2 κἀποσώσαι(ο) Porson -αις Stob.   3 παραινέσαι Gesner -ας Stob.   8 εὐσεβῆ corr. in Stob. ms. B -εῖν others 10 προσάπτων Gesner -ειν Stob.   μέθες Salmasius μίσει Stob.   στύγει Boissonade πρόσαπτε ... μεθείς Madvig (μεθείς Musgrave)   20 †πονηροὺς†: λαλοῦντας Matthiae λέγοντας Herwerden τὴν σὴν ὀκνηροὺς Collard   21 τὰς γεραιτέρων Meineke τὰς -ρας Stob. 4.50.3, Menand. (most mss.) τὰς -ρους Stob. 3.3.18 τῶν –ρων Menand. ms. B   22 Gesner 24 ἐξουσίαν Stob. 3.3.18   ἐντρυφῶν Kock εὐτυχῶν Stob. 3.3.18 (-ὼν 3.17.6) ἐντυχών Wagner 25 διωκάθηις Cobet

164 EURIPIDES

καὶ τοὺς πονηροὺς μήποτ' αὔξαν' ἐν πόλει·
κακοὶ γὰρ ἐμπλησθέντες ἢ νομίσματος
ἢ πόλεος ἐμπεσόντες εἰς ἀρχήν τινα   30
σκιρτῶσιν, ἀδόκητ' εὐτυχησάντων δόμων.
ἀλλ' ὦ τέκνον μοι δὸς χέρ', ὡς θίγηι πατήρ,
καὶ χαῖρ'· ὑπ' αἰδοῦς δ' οὐ λίαν ⟨σ'⟩ ἀσπάζομαι·
γυναικόφρων γὰρ θυμὸς ἀνδρὸς οὐ σοφοῦ.

363   εἷς μὲν λόγος μοι δεῦρ' ἀεὶ περαίνεται.

364   ἐκ τῶν πόνων τοι τἀγάθ' αὔξεται βροτοῖς.

365   αἰδοῦς δὲ καὐτὸς δυσκρίτως ἔχω πέρι·
      καὶ δεῖ γὰρ αὐτῆς κἄστιν αὖ κακὸν μέγα.

366   τοὐνθένδ' ἀπίχθυς βαρβάρους οἰκεῖν δοκῶ.

367   ἐν ἀστρώτωι πέδωι
      εὕδουσι, πηγαῖς δ' οὐχ ὑγραίνουσιν πόδας.

368   μίασμα δρυός

369   (Χορός)   κείσθω δόρυ μοι μίτον ἀμφιπλέκειν ἀράχναις·
      μετὰ δ' ἡσυχίας πολιῶι γήραι συνοικῶν
      ἄιδοιμι κάρα στεφάνοις πολιὸν στεφανώσας,

28 αὔξαν' ἐν Bothe αὐξάνειν Stob. 3.3.18 αὔξειν ἐν Stob. 4.2.4   30 τιμάς τινας Plut.
31 ἀδίκως Stob. 3.3.18   33 ⟨σ'⟩ Heath   363 (54 A, 459 M, 16 Car, 9 Mar) Ar. Lys. 1135,
attrib. Eur. Erec. by a Schol. erroneously placed at 1131; Anecd. Bachmann I.191.29, attrib. Eur.
364 (55 A, 460 M, 19 Car, Inc. sed. 1 Mar) Stob. 3.29.9, attrib. Eur. Erec.; Stob. 3.29.22 combined
with Arch. F 239 (ὁ δ' ἡδὺς αἰὼν ἡ κακή τ' ἀνανδρία οὔτ' οἶκον οὔτε πόλιν ἀνορθώσειεν ἄν 'A
pleasant life and contemptible unmanliness will raise up neither family nor city'), attrib. Eur. Erec.;
Orion 7.2 again combined with F 239, attrib. Eur. Erec.; cited or paraphrased several times
elsewhere as proverbial, unattrib.   365 (56 A, 469 M, 15 Car, 12 Mar) Clem. Alex. Strom. 6.2.9,
attrib. Eur. Erec.   1 καὐτὸς H. Stephanus αὐτὸς Clem.   2 αὖ Badham οὐ Clem.   366 (57 A,
454 M, 25 Car, 2 Mar) Eustath. on Hom. Od. 12.252 (= Aristoph. Byz. fr. 48A Slater; cf. Aristoph.
Com., PCG fr. 586), attrib. confusedly to 'Aristoph. Erec.'   367 (58 A, 455 M, 3 Car, 3 Mar)

Never let villains prosper in the city. Bad men gorged with
money, or falling upon some office in the city,[30] become unruly
with their family's unexpected success.
And now, my son, give your hand to your father's touch.
Farewell! Modesty restrains me from embracing you excessively.
It's a foolish man who shows a womanly temper.

363   One of my arguments has been rehearsed so far.

        Context unknown.

364   The goods that mortals enjoy grow out of their hardships.

        Context unknown.

365   I too find it hard to decide about modesty. It is needed, but it
                is also a great evil.

        Context uncertain (speaker Erectheus?).

366   The area beyond that is inhabited, I believe, by barbarians
                who eat no fish.

        Context uncertain.

367   They sleep on uncovered ground and do not wet their feet
                with water.

        A reference to the priests at Dodona, context uncertain.

368   pollution of the oak

        A further reference to Dodona, context again uncertain.

369   *(Chorus.)* Let my spear lie idle for spiders to weave their webs on
                it. May I live in tranquillity, dwelling with grey old age, and
                crown my grey head with garlands and sing songs, after

Clem. Alex. *Strom.* 6.2.7, attrib. Eur. *Erec.*   2 πηγαῖς ... πόδας Eustath. on Hom. *Il.* 16.235,
attrib. Eur. *Erec.*   1–2 ἐν ... εὕδουσι Musgrave εὔδ. ἐν ἀστρ. πέδωι Clem.   **368** (59 A, 470
M, 4 Car, 4 Mar) Proverb. Append. 3.97, attrib. Eur. *Erec.*   **369** (60 A, 464 M, 17 Car, 11 Mar)
Stob. 4.14.4, attrib. Eur. *Erec.*   1 Plut. *Nic.* 9, unattrib.; paraphr. by Eustath. on Hom. *Od.* 16.35
1 κείσθω Plut. ἀρκείσθω Stob. (from χ^op. κείσθω: Hense)   ἀράχναις Plut. -αι Stob.
2 συνοικῶν Cropp -οίην Stob.   -ος Page   3 ἄιδοιμι (Valckenaer) κάρα στεφάνοις Page
ἀείδοιμι δὲ στεφάνοις κάρα Stob.

Θρηικίαν πέλταν πρὸς ᾿Αθάνας
περικίοσιν ἀγκρεμάσας θαλάμοις,					5
δελτῶν τ᾿ ἀναπτύσσοιμι γᾶ-
ρυν ᾇ σοφοὶ κλέονται.

369a			ἀνέγγυοι γάμοι

369b			ἀνέξοδον

369c Sn			See Introduction, p. 152; TrGF test. v.

369d (370 N)			᾿Ασιάδος κρούματα

370 P. Sorbonne 2328

col. i		Alternating song (1–2?, 5–10) and dialogue (3–4, 11):			1–11
(Χο.)		..]ωσι τάχα[about fifteen letters ἐ]ποίησε πᾶν
			..]ει Χάρων .. [

(—)		τί]ς ἂν πρὸς ἀγμοῖς Παλλάδος σταθεὶ⟨ς⟩ ποδὶ
			κ]ῆρυξ γένοιτ᾿ ἂν τῶν κατὰ στ⟨ρ⟩ατόν, φίλοι;

(Χο.)		ἦ ποτ᾿ ἀνὰ πόλιν ἀλαλαῖς ἰὴ παιὰν			5
			κ]αλλίνικον βοάσω μέλος ἀναλαβόμενος
			ἔρ]γον γεραιᾶς χερὸς Λίβυος ἀχοῦντος
			λω]τοῦ κιθάριδος βοαισ . . . . ε
			. .] . ι τροχαλὸς ἑπομέναις; ἆρα νέα γέρον-
			τι [κοι]νώσεται χοροῦ παρθένος;			10

4 Θρηικίαν Diggle (Blaydes) Θρή(ι)κιον Stob. πρὸς deleted by Page	5 περικίοσιν Grotius
περὶ κίοσιν Stob. (παρὰ ms. A)	7 ᾇ Austin ἂν Stob. (ἂν ms. M)	κλέονται Gaisford κλέωνται
Stob. (καλέσονται ms. A)			**369a** (61 A, 473 M, 1 Car, Inc. sed. 2 Mar) Photius α 1787
Theodoridis (ἀνέγγυοι γάμοι), attrib. Eur. Erec. γάμου M.L. West, BICS 30 (1983), 73	**369b**
(62 A, 474 M, 22 Car, Inc. sed. 3 Mar) Photius α 1849 Theodoridis, attrib. Eur. Erec.	**369d**
(370 N, 64 A, 471 M, 23 Car, Inc. sed. 5 Mar) Etym. Magn. 153.30–2 Gaisford, attrib. Ar. (cf. Ar.
Thesm. 120 κρούματα τ᾿ ᾿Ασιάδος) parodying Eur. Erec. (Etym. Gen. α 1365 Adler lacks the ref. to
Eur. Erec.)	**370** (— N, 65 A, 476 M, 18 Car, 20 Mar) P. Sorbonne 2328 (= P: 3ʳᵈ C. B.C.) ed.
C. Austin (with contributions from Barrett, Kassel, Lloyd-Jones, Page, Parsons, Reeve, Turner),
Rech. de Papyrolog. 4 (1967), 11–67 with French Transl. and Comm.; with minor changes NFE;

hanging a Thracian shield upon Athena's columned halls;[5]
and may I unfold the voice of the tablets through which the
wise are renowned.

From a Choral stasimon (after Erectheus's departure to battle?).

369a   unbetrothed union(s)

                 Poseidon refers to his union with Chione (Prologue)?

369b   exitless

                 Context unknown.

369c Sn   *See Introduction, p. 152;* TrGF *test. v.*

369d (370 N)   *(Aristophanes, parodying Eur.'s* Erectheus, *used the phrase)*

                 thrummings of the Asian (cithara)

                 Context unknown.

370 P. Sorbonne

    *The Chorus (and Praxithea?) await news of the battle; alternating
song (1–2?, 5–10) and dialogue (3–4, 11):*

    (Cho.) . . . quickly <   > did everything . . .

             Charon(?) <   >.

    (Chorus-leader or *Praxithea).* Who, friends, will stand by Pallas's
scarps and be our reporter of how the army fares?

    (Cho.) Shall I ever shout out through the city the glorious victory
song, '*alalaí ié paián*',[5] taking up the task of my aged hand,
(with?) the Libyan lotus pipe sounding < . . . > (with?) the
cithara's *noise* <   >, wheeling along (with?) <   >
following? Shall young girl share with aged man in the
dancing?[10]

Martínez Díez with Spanish Transl. and Comm.; Carrara with Comm. See also Kamerbeek (1970),
Diggle (1980), M. L. West, *BICS* 30 (1983), 73. Corr. and suppl. Austin except where noted.
Photographs of P in Austin (1967), Martínez Díez, Carrara   21–2 Stob. 4.53.16, attrib. Eur. *Erec.* (=
fr. 361 N, 52 A, 457 M), placed here by Kamerbeek   1–11 assigned to Cho. by Austin; 1–2, 5–11
Cho., 3–4 Prax. Martínez   1 ταχε[read by Martínez   κἀ]ποίησε Kamerbeek   2 perhaps Χάρωνι
Austin   perhaps e.g.]εἶχ' ἀρῶν (or ἄρ' ὦν) Kamerbeek   3 beg. Barrett   5]ἦ or ἄρ]α Lloyd-
Jones   6 ἀνα- read by Austin and others ἵνα Turner   7 ἀχοῦντος Austin ἀχάεντος P (confirmed
by Carrara)   8 perhaps βοαῖς κατα Austin βοᾶι συντε Martínez (συντ Carrara)   end perhaps
βαδε or βαλε Austin   9]ωι or]οι, e.g. ὁδ]ῶι Austin πο]δὶ Martínez   10 beg. Page

168 EURIPIDES

(—) ἀ]λλ᾽ εἰσορῶ γὰρ τόνδ᾽ ἀπὸ στρατοῦ πέλ[ας

about ten lines missing

col. ii   *end of Messenger's opening announcement and start of*   12–22
his ensuing dialogue with Praxithea:

("Αγγελος)   μη [. . . 'Ερεχθ]εὺς ὡς τροπαῖα[
ἔστη[σε χώρ]αι τῆιδε βαρβά[ρ
(Πρ.) καλῶ[ς ἔλεξ]ας· ἀλλὰ τίς γαρειθ[
("Αγ.) πέπτ[ωκε .]. . . . . π ρευ[15
(Πρ.) πόσις δ᾽ 'Ερεχθεύς ἐστί μοι σεσ[ωμένος;
("Αγ.) μακάριός ἐστι κεῖνος εὐδαίμων [τ᾽ ἀνήρ.
(Πρ.) εἰ ζῆι γε πόλεώς τ᾽ εὐτυχῆ νίκ[ην φέρει.
("Αγ.) ὥστ᾽ αὐτὰ ταῦτα σκῦλα λειφθ[ῆναι
(Πρ.) τί φήις; τέθνηκεν ἢ φάος βλέπε[ι τόδε;   20
("Αγ.) τέθνηκ᾽· ἐγὼ δὲ τοὺις καλῶς τεθνηκότας
ζιῆν φημὶ μ]ᾶλλοιν †τοῦ βλέπειν τοὺς μὴ καλῶς†.

traces of one more line, then about 100 lines missing

col. iii   *line-ends, some or all lyric; 25 and 28 at least delivered*   23–32
by Praxithea, including:

23   ]ε δυστήνου μόρον   28   ]νον δ᾽ ἀπύουσα
25   ]υσ᾽ ἐμὰς κόρας   30   ]πωσι δωμάτων
26   ]τεγην   31   ]λαιναι
· 27   ] επιπτετε   32   ]προσοψιν ει . . . . . [

about ten lines missing

12 μὴ σ[τένετ᾽ (or σ[τένε γ᾽) Carrara 'Ερεχθ]εὺς Page τροπαῖ᾽ α[ὐτῆι χερί (e.g.) Austin (better α[ὐτοῦ χερί Kamerbeek) τροπαῖα μυρίων (. . . βαρβά[ρων) Cropp   13 χώρ]αι or γαί]αι Austin βαρβά[ρων (Austin) Διί Collard βαρβά[ρου δορός or στρατοῦ (e.g.) Reeve   14–21 paragraphi show speaker-changes in P   14 τίς γ᾽ "Αρει 'θ[ανεν Austin (doubtfully: θ[ανών Martínez)   15 πέπτ[ωκε δ]ὴ or μὲ]ν Austin   πρὸς ἧπαρ Εὔ[μολπος τυπείς (e.g.) Page (ἧπαρ tentatively confirmed by Martínez, Carrara)   17 [τ᾽ ἀνήρ Diggle   [θ᾽ ἅμα Austin   18 φέρει Martínez

(Chorus-leader). But wait: I can see approaching here from
    our army . . .

about ten lines missing

end of Messenger's opening announcement and start of his   12–22
ensuing dialogue with Praxithea:

(Messenger) Do not(?) < . . . >; for *Erectheus* has set up a trophy
            < . . . > for this *land* over the barbarian(s?) < . . . >.
(Pr.) You have *spoken* well. But who . . . < . . . >?
(Me.) < . . . > *has fallen* . . . <   >.   15
(Pr.) And my husband Erectheus — has he survived?
(Me.) He is a blessed <*and*> a fortunate <*man*>.
(Pr.) He does if he is alive and <*bringing*> our city's successful
            victory.
(Me.) With luck enough for these very spoils to have been left
            < . . . >.
(Pr.) What are you saying? He is dead, or sees <*this*> light of day?   20
(Me.) Dead — yet those who have died nobly, I declare, are more
            alive than †those who have died ignobly are alive†.

about one hundred lines lost including Messenger's speech,
then line-ends of Praxithea (at least 25, 28) and perhaps
Chorus from a joint lyric lament, including: 23–32

23   wretched < . . . >'s fate   25   my daughters
26   *building* (or *land*)   27   you/he were/are/was falling
28   crying out (*or* calling on)   30   (they) may *be absent*
from (*or* may *leave* . . . of) the house   31   *wretched* (or
stone-built, or *black*)   32   countenance (*or* sight, *or* to . . .
sight)

about ten lines missing

tentatively, West   ἄγει Austin   19 end μόνον Austin   πόλει Kamerbeek   θεοῖς Cropp
22 ζ[. . . . . .] αλλο read in P by Carrara   κοὐ Diels   τ' οὐ Tucker   26 σ]τέγην Page   perhaps
]τε γῆν Austin   27 ἐπίπτετε or]ε πίπτετε or ἔπιπτέ τε Austin   30 ἀ]πῶσι Kassel (ἐκ)λί]πωσι
Austin   31 τά]λαιναι Page   perhaps]λαίναι Austin   perhaps μέ]λαιναι Cropp   32 πρόσοψιν or
πρὸς ὄψιν, then κεισ or κεκ (so πρόσοψιν εἰσορᾶν unlikely) Austin

col. iv   *end of a lyric exchange of lamentations between Praxithea*
          and Chorus, then (45) *lyric reaction to Poseidon's*
          earthquake and (55) *speech of Athena:*

(Χο.)   *one line with a few illegible traces*   33
         Δηοῦς κάρα· φερόμεθ' ἀγόμεθ' ἐπὶ δάκρυα·   34
         σὲ δ' αἰαῖ διῆλθέ σ', οἴμοι.

(Πρ.)   αἰαῖ·   35
         τίν' ἐπὶ | πρῶτον, ἢ σὲ τὰν πάτραν, ἢ σὲ τὰν
         φίλαν | παρθένων †δραμων† φρενομανεῖ τάφωι |
         τακερὰ μέλεα προσεῖδον, παπαῖ,
         ἢ τὸν | κάτω πόσιν ἐμὸν στένω .... |
         φόνια φυσήματ'; ἢ σὲ τὰν πρὸ πόλεως   40
         τὸν ἀνίερον ἀνίερον ⟨ἀν⟩όσιον ἀνόσιον
         καὶ κορυφὰν ἀπάται θ[
         οἱ]χόμεθ' οἰχόμεθ', ὦ π[
col. v   ὡς ἄδ]ακρύς τις ὠμόφρων ⟨θ'⟩ ὃς κακοῖς ἐμοῖς οὐ στένει.

(Χο.)   φεῦ φε]ῦ, ἰὼ Γᾶ, φεύγετε .... υ....   45
         πόνων] εἴ τί μοί ποτ' εἴη τελευτά.
         ]γετε χώρας χθόνιος μ ..... νοις
         ]ατας· ὀρχεῖται δὲ π[ό]λεος πέδον σάλωι·
         ] . ἐμβάλλει Ποσειδῶν πόλει
         ]ηπερ δυστανοτατα ..... εμοι   50
         ]ων πόνοι πάρεισι, συμπίπτει στέγη·
         ] ασεν στρατός, οἰχόμεθα ... πάσαις
         ] . υ ..... πα .... ραφε πάντα
         ἐν δώ]μασι⟨ν⟩ πάλαι βακχεύων.

('ΑΘΗΝΑ)   αὐδῶ τρία⟨ι⟩ναν τῆσδ' ἀπο⟨σ⟩τρέφειν χθονός,   55
             πόντιε Πόσειδον, μηδὲ γῆν ἀναστατοῦν

---

34 δηιους P   κόρα Diggle, Collard   35-9 | indicate P's line-ends   35 διῆλθεν Diggle
P shows speaker-change by space within line   37 δραμων read by Austin, conjecturing ἄθλι' ὦν
ατανων (hence Ἄταν ὦν) Kamerbeek   δράμω Collard   φρενομανεῖ Kamerbeek (earlier rejected by
Austin)   38 τακερὰ read doubtfully by Austin   τὰ κρυερὰ or δακρυτὰ Kamerbeek
41 ⟨ἀν⟩όσιον Turner   perhaps ἱερὸν ἀνίερον ὅσιον ἀνόσιον Diggle   42 κορυφὰν Austin -ην P
θ[εοῦ or θ[εόθεν (e.g.) Austin   43 π[ολιῆται or -ῖται Austin π[όλις or π[όλι Παλλάδος Diggle
44 beg. Kassel (ἄδ]ακρύς also Parsons)   ⟨θ'⟩ Cropp   dicolon at end (for division from adjacent
line, or change of speaker: Austin)   45-54 assigned to Praxithea by Martínez (cf. Austin [1967],

col. iv   *Praxithea's lament with the Chorus continues:*

(Cho.)   . . . Deo's head (?). We are carried, we are led, to tears.
          But you (alas!), you it has pierced (o me!).

(Pr.)   Alas![35] To whom first, to you our fatherland, or to you my
          daughters' dear † . . . † in (my?) crazed funeral rite I have
          looked upon your bruised limbs, a-aah!; *or* shall I lament
          my husband below <   > murderous blasts, or you, who
          in defence of the city[40] . . . that unholy, unholy,
          unhallowed, <*un*>hallowed — and the height . . . through
          deceit <   >? We are lost, lost, O <   . *H o w* >
          incapable of tears <*and*> cruel is anyone who does not
          lament my sufferings.

(Cho.)   Oh, Oh! O earth! Flee <   [45]   > if I might find in
          any way an ending of my troubles. <   > of/from the
          land < . . . > subterranean <   >. The city's ground is
          set dancing by the quake! Poseidon is hurling < . . . > on
          the city < . . . > . . . most miserabl(y?) < . . . > *for me(?).*[50]
          Here are troubles < . . . >; the roof is collapsing! Our
          army *has* < . . . >, we are lost . . . with/in all <   > every-
          thing with his bacchic dancing just now in the palace.

     The goddess Athena appears above

(Athena.)   I call on you, sea-god Poseidon, to turn your trident
          away from this region,[55] and not to uproot my land and

---

50), to Chorus tentatively by Carrara   45 beg. Page   after φεύγετε perhaps ταχαδ or ταχαα
Carrara (ταχα Austin)   end e.g. φευγετε Austin   46 πόνων] or κακῶν] Austin   perhaps τί⟨ς⟩
Austin   47 φεύ]γετε Austin   perhaps μαινομένοις Austin   47–8 (ἐκ)φεύ]γετε χώρας χθονίας
μαινομένοις [ποσὶν] (or -αις [φρεσὶν]) ἄτας Kamerbeek   49 ἄτα]ν (e.g.) Austin ὄλεθρο]ν
Carrara ἔνοσι]ν Diggle   50]ἥπερ (for ἅπερ?) δυστανοτάτα Austin   51 βάθρ]ων Austin ἐκ
πόν]ων Kamerbeek σεισμ]ῶν Diggle   52 ἐδά]μασεν (e.g.) Austin   53 ἀνατέτραφε may be too
long for space: Austin (-τέτροφε Kamerbeek)   πάντα or ταῦτα Austin   54 (ἀνατέτροφε πανθ')
οὺν δώ]μασι⟨ν⟩ Kamerbeek   55 asterisk in P's left margin probably marks new scene
56 ἀνάστατον Kamerbeek (suggested by Austin)

172　　　　　EURIPIDES

πόλιν τ' ἐρείπειν τὴν ἐμὴν ἐπήρατον·
μηδ' εὐτυχῇ σοι δοῖεν⟨......⟩οι·
οὐχ εἰς ἅδην σ' ἔπλησεν; οὐ κατὰ χθονὸς
κρύψας Ἐρεχθέα τῆς ἐμῆς ἤψω φρενός;　　　　60
κἄπε]ιτα μέλλεις ταῦτα δὴ τελεσφόρα
...ν]ερτεροι[*about thirteen letters*]˙σεν θεά;

col. vi
σὺ δ',] ὦ χθονὸς [σώτειρα Κηφισοῦ] κόρη,
ἄκου' Ἀθάνας τῆς ἀμήτορο[ς λό]γους·
καὶ πρῶτα μέν σοι σημανῶ παι[δὸς] πέρι　　　　65
ἣν τῆσδε χώρας σὸς προθύεται [πόσι]ς·
θάψον νιν οὗπερ ἐξέπνευσ' ο[ἰκτ]ρὸν βίον,
καὶ τάσδ' ἀδελφὰς ἐν τάφωι τ[αὐτ]ῶι χθονὸς
γενναιότητος οὕνεχ', αἵτιν[ες φί]λης
ὅρκους ἀδελφῆς οὐκ ἐτόλμησα[ν λι]πεῖν.　　　　70
ψυχαὶ μὲν οὖν τῶνδ' οὐ βεβᾶσ' ["Αιδ]ην πάρα,
εἰς δ' αἰθέρ' αὐτῶν πνεῦμ' ἐγὼ [κ]ατώικισα·
ὄνομα δὲ κλεινὸν θήσομαι κα[θ' Ἑλλ]άδα
Ὑακινθίδας βροτοῖσι κικλή[σκε]ιν θεάς.
ἔπει⟨......⟩κα˙οιχετητ[˙˙˙]μένη　　　　75
τοῦ συ⟨........⟩ὑακίν[θου γ]άνος
καὶ γῆν ἔσωσε, τοῖς ἐμοῖς ἀστο[ῖς λέγ]ω
ἐνιαυσίαις σφας μὴ λελησμ[ένους] χρόνωι
θυσίαισι τιμᾶν καὶ σφαγαῖσι [βουκ]τόνοις
κοσμοῦ[ντας ἱ]εροῖς παρθένων [χορεύ]μασιν·　　　　80
γνον[˙˙˙˙˙˙]χθρ˙εἰς μάχη[ν
κιν˙[˙˙˙˙˙]ας ἀσπίδα στρατ[

col. vii
πρώταισι θύειν πρότομα πολεμίου δορὸς
τῆς οἰνοποιοῦ μὴ θιγόντας ἀμπέλου
μηδ' εἰς πυρὰν σπένδοντας ἀλλὰ πολυπόνου　　　　85
καρπὸν μελίσσης ποταμίαις πηγαῖς ὁμοῦ·
ἄβατον δὲ τέμενος παισὶ ταῖσδ' εἶναι χρεών,
εἴργειν τε μή τις πολεμίων θύσηι λαθὼν
νίκην μὲν αὐτοῖς, γῆι δὲ τῆιδε πημονήν.

58 perhaps δοῖεν⟨......⟩θεοί Austin δοιενω read by Carrara　　59 οὐκ εἰς P　　61 κἄπε]ιτα
Page (ἔπε]ιτα Austin) τί δ]ῆτα Reeve　question-mark after μέλλεις Carrara　τολεσφορα(?) P
62 σὺν ν]ερτέροι[σ(ιν) Page σὺν ν]ερτέροι[ς δρᾶν Martínez τοῖς ν]ερτ. Cropp　perhaps]ησεν or
]κισεν Austin or]ωσεν Martínez p. 72　εἴ σ' ἐνί]κησεν θεά (e.g.) Martínez τῆ⟨ι⟩ 'ν ν]ερτέροι[σι

demolish my delightful city; and may < . . . > not *give* you (a?)
fortunate < . . . >. Has not one victim given you your fill? Have
you not gripped my heart by confining Erectheus below the
earth?[60] And after that you are going to < . . . > these fulfilments
(for?) the nether *powers* < . . . > goddess < . . . >?

<*And you, Cephisus'*> daughter, <*saviour*> of this land, hear
now the words of motherless Athena. First I shall instruct you
about your child[65] whom your husband has caused to be sacrificed
in defence of this country. Bury her at the place where she
breathed out her lamented life, and these sisters of hers with her in
the same earth-tomb because of their nobility, seeing that they did
not rashly abandon their pledges to their beloved sister.[70] Therefore
their souls have not descended to Hades' realm; I myself have
lodged their spirits in the heaven, and shall establish a renowned
name, 'divine Hyacinthids', for mortals to call them by throughout
all Greece. Because < . . . > . . . < . . . >-ing[75] . . . of the < . . . >
hyacinth's brightness and preserved the land, I instruct my citizens
to honour them, never forgetting over time, with annual sacrifices
and slaughterings of *oxen*, adorning the festivals with sacred
maiden-dances;[80] <*and*> *learn*-< . . . > . . . < . . . > into/for battle,
rous-< . . . > shield < . . . >, to offer first to them (the Hyacinthids)
the sacrifice preliminary to battle, not touching the wine-producing
vine nor pouring wine upon the altar but rather the industrious[85]
bee's produce together with stream-water. There shall be an untrodden sanctuary dedicated to these maidens; you must prevent
any of your enemies from secretly making offerings there so as to
bring victory to themselves and affliction to this land.

θύματ' ἐπιδ]ώσε⟨ι⟩ν θεᾶι (e.g.) Diggle   63 Barrett (σώτειρα Page)   75 perhaps ἐπεὶ δ'
ἀπαχθεῖσ' ὤιχετ' Kamerbeek   κἀπώιχεθ' ἡ τ[ιμω]μένη (or τ[ητω]μένη, or ἠτ[ιμασ]μένη)
Austin ἠμ[φιεσ]μένη or ἠπ[ατη]μένη Kamerbeek   76 τοῦ συ[μφέροντος οὕνεχ' Kamerbeek
78 ἐνιαυσίαις Barrett -ωι P   79 end Barrett, Page σφαγαῖσιν[P   81 ἐ]χθρὸς or ἐ]χθρα Austin
end εἰς μάχη[ν ὁρμώμενος (e.g.) Austin   γνόν[τας ἐ]χθρὸν . . . ὁρμώμενον (e.g.) Kamerbeek
γνόν[τας δ' ὅτ' ἐ]χθρὰ⟨ν⟩ Treu (ἐ]χθρὸς West) γνόν[τας . . .] . . . εἰς μάχη[ν ὅταν μολὼν (or εἰς
μάχη[ς ἀγῶν' ὅταν) ǀ κινῆ[ι etc. (e.g.) Diggle   82 κινῆ[ι πρὸς ὑμ]ᾶς . . . στρατ[ευμάτων or
στρατ[ηλατῶν (e.g.) Austin κινο[ῦντ' ἐφ' ὑμ]ᾶς ἀσπίδα στρατ[εύματος (e.g.) Kamerbeek

174 EURIPIDES

κινῇ[ι πρὸς ὑμ]ᾶς ... στρατ[ηλάτης (e.g.) Diggle

πόσει δὲ τῶι σῶι σηκὸν ἐν μέσηι πόλει 90
τεῦξαι κελεύω περιβόλοισι λαΐνοις·
κεκλήσεται δὲ τοῦ κτανόντος οὕνεκα
σεμνὸς Ποσειδῶν ὄνομ' ἐπωνομασμένος
ἀστοῖς Ἐρεχθεὺς ἐν φοναῖσι βουθύτοις.
σοὶ δ', ἢ πόλεως τῆσδ' ἐξανώρθωσας βάθρα, 95
δίδωμι βωμοῖς τοῖς ἐμοῖσιν ἔμπυρα
πόλει προθύειν ἱερέαν κεκλημένην.
ἃ μὲν κατ' αἶαν τήνδε ⟨δεῖ⟩ 'κπονεῖν κλύεις,
ἃ δ' αὖ δικάζει Ζεὺς πατὴρ ἐν οὐρανῶι
λέγοιμ' ἄν· Εὔμολπος γὰρ Εὐμόλπου γεγὼ[ς 100

col. viii   τοῦ κατθ[ανόντος 101

then line-beginnings from the rest of Athena's speech: 102–17

102 Δημητρ[110 ἄρρητά γε[
103 ὃν χρὴ γεν[έσθαι   111 πόνος τε . [
104 γήμαντ[112 σεμνῶν . [
105 μίαν δε [113 Ἑρμοῦ το[
106 καὶ τὴν τ[114 Κήρυκες[
107 Ὑάσιν δεμ . [115 ἀλλ' ἴσχε . [
108 ἄστρων λ [116 οἰκτρὰς αὐ[τ
109 Δηοῦς μι[117 καὶ ταπε[

Start of Praxithea's response: 118–9

118 (Πρ.) δέσποινα [119 ο]ἰκτροὶ με[

101 Parsons end τοῦδε πέμπτος ἔκγονος (e.g.) West   103 Page   105 δελ[or δεα[Austin   δ'
ἀ[δελφῶν (e.g.) Barrett   109 δηιους P   117 τὰ πε[ρὶ Austin τάπε[or τάπ'ε[(e.g. καὶ τάπ' ἐμῶν
ἔκπρασσε νῦν κηρυγμάτων) Cropp   τάπ' ἐκείνοις Collard   118 paragraphus marks speaker-
change

For your husband I command the building in mid-city of a precinct[90] with stone enclosure. In recollection of his killer the citizens, slaughtering sacrificial oxen, shall call him august Poseidon surnamed Erectheus.

To you, Praxithea, who have restored this city's foundations,[95] I grant the right to make burnt sacrifices for the city on my altars with the title of priestess.

You have heard what <*must be*> brought to pass in this land. Now I shall pronounce the judgement of Zeus my father in heaven. Eumolpus, born from the Eumolpus[100] who *has died* . . .

(only the beginnings of the remaining lines are preserved)

102	. . . Demeter . . .	110	(things) not to be uttered . . .
103	who is to *become* . . .	111	toil (*or* trouble) . . .
104	marrying . . .	112	of/from holy . . .
105	and one *(Fem.)* . . .	113	of/from Hermes . . .
106	and the *(Fem.)* . . .	114	Kerykes . . .
107	and to/for the Hyades . . .	115	But restrain . . .
108	stars . . .	116	piteous . . . *cry out* . . .
109	of/from Deo . . .	117	and the things . . .

Start of Praxithea's response:

118	*(Pr.)* Mistress . . .	119	piteous . . .

Commentary on *Erectheus*

349. These words are consistent with Apollod. 3.15.4 where Poseidon sires Eumolpus by Chione, 'Snow-maiden' (daughter of Boreas the North Wind and the Athenian princess Oreithuia at least in post-Euripidean tradition and perhaps for Eur. too: cf. Parker 212 n. 64); she conceals this from her father by throwing the baby into the sea, and Poseidon takes him to be raised by a sea-nymph in Ethiopia (on which country see *Pha.* Introd., pp. 200–1; S. West on Hom. *Od.* 1.22–4). Apollod.'s complicated narrative connecting Eumolpus with Thrace and Eleusis is of uncertain relevance to Eur.'s play. [Text: Steph.'s 'you saved' is unmetrical; Lobeck's 'I saved' (rather than -σ(ε) 'he saved') makes Poseidon the Prologue speaker; he would naturally know Eumolpus's life story.]

350. Probably addressed (by Erectheus on his return from Delphi?) to Praxithea as she prepared sacrifices for the city's protection. The scene perhaps prefigured her appointment as priestess of Athena Polias at the end of the play. Carrara and Martínez prefer to connect the fr. with preparations for the human sacrifice (cf. Kamerbeek [1970], 113–4); Carrara suggests the Chorus-leader as questioner.   **sacred gruel:** *pelanos* was a mixture of wheat-meal, oil and honey used for libations and sacrificial cakes (on the latter see A. Henrichs in *Atti del XVII Congr. Int. di Papirologia* [Naples, 1984], 258–61). *Pelanoi* were 'cakes' in local Athenian parlance (Paus. 8.2.3), as are **moons** here (large round cakes, the sources of the fr. explain). [Text: for πυρίνου cf. *Eurysth.* F 373; P. Maas, *Kl. Schr.* 205 n. 6 favours retaining the form πύρινος like e.g. ὕλιμος, *Mel.D.* F 495.34.]

351. Sometimes placed in a report speech (cf. Austin citing Snell); by Carrara in a report of the human sacrifice (but Athena can hardly have an interest in this, so comparison with *IA* 1467, 1492 is unhelpful). An early scene may well have *shown* Praxithea, like Hecuba in Hom. *Il.* 6.268ff., leading a subsidiary chorus of women in supplicating Athena (cf. *Hipp.* 58–60; Kamerbeek [1992], 111–2, 115); this would foreshadow the goddess's appearance at the end.   **Ululate:** the women's *ololugmos* is often mentioned in association with sacrifices (cf. Diggle, *Euripidea* 478), but also in contexts of prayer as by the Trojan women, Hom. *Il.* 6.301; cf. Aesch. *Sept.* 265–70. The **Gorgon** adorning Athena's protective aegis is **golden** as on the shield of Pheidias's statue in the Parthenon (cf. Calder 152–3).

352–6. Plausibly assigned to an early confrontation between Erectheus and a herald of Eumolpus (Introd., p. 150), though some of these frs. could be Erectheus stating his own policy. Divine will and a just cause are stressed in similar contexts, *Hcld.* 253–8, *Supp.* 594–7.   **352. Wise . . . with the gods:** similar language *Mel.D.* F 490 (cf. *Supp.* 155–61, Adrastus ruined by ignoring seers). **mobilise:** lit. 'activate the spear': cf. F 370.82 (below), *And.* 607.   **354.** Wrongly acquired possessions are insecure: a

176

fundamental tenet of Greek ethics, cf. F 362.11–13, *Bell.* F 303.1–2 and e.g. Hes. *WD* 320–6, Solon *IEG* fr. 13.7–13; Cropp on *El.* 940–4 (add *Ino* F 419).   **property:** a common meaning of οὐσία in prose and Comedy; cf. *HF* 337 (with Wilamowitz), *Hel.* 1253; Plur. for the generalising context and balance with **plunder**, here 'things seized' like *El.* 896, cf. LSJ II, rather than 'seizures' (e.g. *Hel.* 904, a similar injunction). **355.** A threat from the herald (cf. *Hcld.* 274–8), or an assertion of Athenian resources? For similar (proverbial) nautical terminology cf. Dem. 9.69–70. **356.** For the thought cf. *Arch.* F 243, 244 (all are in Stob.'s section 'Commendation of courage'). [Text, F 356: a supplement like Hense's is needed, to avoid 'I prefer a few bad men to many'! For ἐσθλοί/κακοί contrasted cf. *Temenid.* F 728, *Arch.* F 244 with Harder's Comm.]

357. Lit. 'a three-maiden yoke-team' (cf. *Pha.* 104 n.). Eur. often coins poetic compound number-adjectives (cf. Breitenbach 190). This phrase was parodied (the source says) in Ar. *Horae*, *PCG* fr. 580 ζεῦγος τρίδουλον 'three-slave yoke-team'.

358. A whole-hearted commendation of mother-love (contrast e.g. F 1064, *Mel.* F 498), probably spoken by Erectheus and contrasting pathetically with Praxithea's later willingness to see her daughter sacrificed. This fr. makes it likely that the royal daughters appeared in the play, but it could possibly have been proclaimed to children in general (see on Text below) in a conversation with Praxithea. Webster places it close to F 362, and Carrara suggests these are the victim's words from a reported sacrifice-scene; but Erectheus's arrival home from Delphi is at least as good a context, cf. the affectionate exchange of Agamemnon with the arriving Clytemnestra and Iphigeneia, *IA* 630–42 (Kamerbeek [1970], 114).   **Nothing is more delightful:** similar gnomic phrasing *Supp.* 1101, *Phoenix* F 817.3.   **Love:** strongly emphasised by the repetition and placing of ἐρᾶτε . . . ἔρως . . . ἐρᾶν. The Greek term normally connotes a desire *for* someone or something, here simply a strong emotional attachment like 'loving one's country', *Temenid.* F 729 (cf. Mastronarde on *Pho.* 359). [Text: 1–3 have a typical pattern of gnomic assertion capped by a general exhortation with 'paraenetic Imperative' (cf. e.g. *Peliad.* F 609, *And.* 621–3 [with Stevens' note], 944–53); so 2–3 should not be made a separate fr. Stob. has 'normalising' variants in 1 and 3.]

359. *Mel.D.* F 491 gives another argument against adoption; cf. also *Ion* 607–15, 657–60 (Creusa expected to be jealous of the adopted Ion). Adoption was a normal device for perpetuating the *oikos* in the absence of a natural heir, though adopted sons did not acquire absolute property rights for themselves (Lacey, *Family* 24–5, 146). The subject of the fr. is probably the adoption of the son whom Erectheus addresses in F 362 (see Introd., p. 151–2), though it has sometimes been assigned to the debate about the sacrifice of a child — Erectheus rejecting a proposal from Praxithea to adopt a son who can be sacrificed (Webster), or she rejecting his proposal to adopt a son (Aélion, Kamerbeek [1992], 114) or a daughter (Carrara).   **Where:** dismissive or at least sceptical: Stevens on *And.* 591, LSJ II.   **Natural things . . . supposititious ones:** those who *are* sons by nature (*physis*) are superior to those *deemed* (δοκεῖν) to be so by law or custom (*nomos*). The point is sophistically countered in Soph. F 86. δοκήματα = 'suppositions' or 'illusions', *HF* 111; cf. δοξάσματα = 'objects of supposition (δοξάζειν)', *Mel.D.* F 495.42 (similarly contrasting natural and supposititious).

360. Praxithea's great speech is addressed to Erectheus ('you', 36), countering his objections to the sacrifice (cf. Kamerbeek in Hofmann and Harder, *Fragmenta Dramatica* 114). See Introd., p. 154 on its character. It has a clear rhetorical organisation (cf. Carrara 64, differing slightly over the last dozen lines): 1–4 gnomic introduction, thematic statement; 5–13 first justification (autochthony); 14–49 second justification (children owed to the preservation of the community; 22–37 special reasons for allowing the sacrifice of a daughter); 50–5 conclusion and peroration. Traditional arguments for nobility and patriotism are adapted to the ideology of democratic Athens (see notes on 5–13, 14–21, 32–5, 38–49, 45) and to the unique sacrifice envisaged. There are many similarities with the speeches of others resigning themselves nobly to death (especially sacrifice) in Eur.: 'Macaria' in *Hcld.*, Polyxena in *Hec.*, Menoeceus (saviour of his city) in *Pho.*, Iphigeneia in *IA.* Schmitt 28–41 and Wilkins (1990) survey and compare the common motifs.

1–3. Praxithea appeals to an aristocratic rule of generosity (hence '**noble . . . ill-bred**'): Isocr. 1.39, Menand. *Sentent.* 824, *Anth. Pal.* 10.30 etc. (Kamerbeek [1970], 114); cf. *Rhes.* 411–2. [Text: **2–3.** Both Kamerbeek (1970) and Gesner give '<*this is*> illbred'; Meineke's '<*I call it*> ill-bred' is only loosely comparable with *Mel.D.* F 495.43. Neuter δυσγενέστερον and the Greek structure 'those who . . . , this is . . . ' are balanced against the same structure in 1–2, for which cf. e.g. *Pha.* 160–2 below, *Tro.* 648–9, *Hipp.* 426–7 with Barrett's Comm.]

4. **I, then:** ἐγὼ δὲ in transition from the gnomic introduction: Denniston, *GP* 170 cites *Pho.* 473 etc.

5–13. The claim that autochthony made the Athenians better or more 'noble' than other Greeks (and hence the *crème de la crème* of humanity) was a favourite topic of Athenian patriotic rhetoric, e.g. *Ion* 737, Hdt. 7.161.3, Isocr. 4.24, and in funeral speeches Thuc. 2.36.1, Lys. 2.17, etc.; cf. N. Loraux, *The Invention of Athens* (Eng. tr., Cambridge Mass., 1986), 148–50; Kearns 110–3.

8–13. Other states lack the stability and sense of community bestowed by autochthony: cf. Pl. *Menex.* 238e, Isocr. 12.121–4.

9. founded etc.: lit. 'founded similarly to the shifts of board-pieces'. *Pessoi* were the pieces used in board-games, here probably the game *Poleis* ('Cities') which involved isolating and capturing one's opponents pieces, an apt metaphor for political fragmentation (Pl. *Rep.* 422e8, Aristot. *Pol.* 1253a7). See R. G. Austin, 'Greek Board Games', *Antiquity* 14 (1940), 257–71, esp. 263–6; Collard on *Supp.* 409. [Text: Lycurg. ed. Aldin. corrects the awkwardness of Lycurg.'s 'founded through shifts similar (to those) of board-pieces' (where Dative πεσσοῖς 'to board-pieces' would be more natural: JD). Plut.'s 'dispersed similarly to the throws of board-pieces' makes worse sense (though C. Austin compares διαφορέω of population dispersal, Pl. *Laws* 693a).]

11. [Text: οἰκίζει would mean 'founds' or 'populates'. For Subj. οἰκήσηι (from οἰκέω) without ἄν after ὅστις cf. e.g. *Or.* 805, *Bell.* F 297.3; KG II 426 n. 1.]

12. peg ill-fitted: contrast the 'exact joints' of *Cret.* F 472.8 (see n. there on woodworking technicalities).

14–21. The claims of homeland and gods, and the priority of community over individual or family (to be restated conclusively in 38–41).

14. [Text: poetic ἕκατι was displaced by the equivalent but unmetrical ἕνεκα.]

15. gods' altars . . . homeland: di Benedetto 146 compares the war-cry at Salamis, Aesch. *Pers.* 403–4, 'Free your homeland; free your children, your wives, and the seats of your ancestral gods'.

16. [Lycurg.'s text is almost meaningless.]

18. one . . . for all: similar arguments by the heroines at *Hcld.* 579–80, *IA* 1390. [Text: the compound verb ὑπερδοῦναι would be unique. For the phrasing cf. 35 below, *El.* 1026 (J. Diggle in R. Pintaudi [ed.], *Miscellanea Papyrologica* [Florence, 1980], 57). Denniston on *El.* 574 studies postposition of prepositions in Tragic trimeters. Eur. uses intensive πρόπας in *Pho.* 624, 1504, *Or.* 972.]

19–21. If I can count etc.: a family's prosperity and failure are subordinate to the city's: cf. 39–40, Thuc. 2.60.2–4, Soph. *Ant.* 189–90, Xen. *Mem.* 3.7.9 (de Romilly [see Introd., p. 154], 42–3). **distinguish larger from smaller:** lit. 'know the (= what is) larger rather than smaller': cf. *Alcmaeon* F 79.1. [Text: Austin condemns 19–21 as 'pedantic and unsuitable' and repetitious after 16–18. They are better seen as complementary to 16–18 (cf. Thuc. cited above). The *oikos* is a new element in the argument and relevant to its development in 22ff. For similar mathematical pedantry cf. *Ion* 1137–9.]

20 [Text: †one person's†: οὐνὸς for ὁ ἐνὸς ('the one person's') is possible though not exactly paralleled (probable similar corruptions include *IT* 637, *IA* 522). ἁπλοῦς 'a single' might be considered (cf. e.g. *Pha.* 125). Dobree suggested 'one family would not . . .'. **does not lament:** similarly corrupted in *And.* 672 (Diggle [above, 18 n.], 57). The transmitted 'is not stronger' is a less apt metaphor here than in *Hec.* 294–5, 1188, *Hel.* 514.]

22–5. 'Others are willing/expected to face death': cf. *Hcld.* 503–6, *Pho.* 999–1005, *IA* 1387–90. On Erectheus's lack of male progeny see Introd., p. 151.

25–7. Honour in the city depends on willingness to fight in the front line: a motif of archaic martial poetry, e.g. Callinus *IEG* fr. 1.6–11, Tyrtaeus *IEG* fr. 12. [Text, 25: **give me:** lit. 'may there be for me', rather than transmitted 'there is' or Hermann's 'let there be'; Diggle (above, 18 n.), 57 compares *El.* 948–9.]

26. stand out etc.: μετ(ά) . . . πρέποι (not strictly in tmesis here) recalls epic μεταπρέπειν, Hom. *Il.* 2.579 etc. (in tmesis *Od.* 8.172 = Hes. *Theog.* 92).

28–31. Maternal sentiment subordinated to honour: cf. *HF* 290–4 (Megara), F 360a n. The Chorus at *Pho.* 1054–61 wish for sons like the self-sacrificing Menoeceus.

29. soften: lit. 'feminize'; cf. on F 362.33–4. The Greek verb (gnomic Aorist as in 31, 33) occurs in Tragedy only here and Soph. *Aj.* 651. **many men:** a few mothers weeping cause widespread demoralisation. Mothers insist on courage from sons, *Supp.* 320, 343–5; Iphigeneia rejects her mother's tears, *IA* 1433–5.

30–1. life rather than virtue: rejection of 'life-loving' (φιλοψυχία) is a commonplace in such situations: *Hcld.* 533–4, *Hec.* 347–8, 377–8, etc. Cf. on F 370.21–2 and (rejections of life with dishonour) Stob. 4.53. [Text: 'or' for 'and' restores metre.]

32–5. common tomb: common burial at the battle-site was a normal Greek practice. A civic funeral for those killed in a campaign was a special Athenian institution, famously described by Thuc. 2.34: see esp. Gomme's Comm. there and Loraux (above, 5–13 n.), 15–42.

34. crown: here metaphorical as e.g. *HF* 1334, *Tro.* 401, Thuc. 2.46. [Lycurg.'s text is syntactically incoherent. For εἷς μιᾶι 'one for one' cf. *El.* 337, where Denniston lists similar juxtapositions.]

36–7. will save . . . : a vain hope; Erectheus and all the daughters will be lost.

38–49. The implication of 14–21 is now stated: 'rights' in the family depend on the integrity of the polis (39–41). Then the idea of preserving communal institutions is elaborated (43–9: cf. 15).

38. not mine except through birth: cf. *IA* 1386, 'You gave me birth for all Greeks'. [Text, **in fact:** δὴ highlighting 'not mine' (cf. Denniston, *GP* 204–5) is better palaeographically and rhetorically than Nagel's 'therefore'.]

41. Shall not . . . then: οὔκουν in rhetorical questions, e.g. *Alc.* 794 (also capping an argument), *Hcld.* 112, *Pho.* 179 (see Mastronarde); Denniston, *GP* 431, 436. [Text: Lycurg.'s text requires the obvious change to Nom. 'all'. For the meaningless γοῦν τ' both τοῦν γ' and τοὔπ' will give 'in respect of what is in my power' (ἐν e.g. *IA* 1273–4 [similar context], *Hel.* 1425; ἕν γ' ἐμοί Soph. *OC* 153; ἐπὶ *Alc.* 455, *Hel.* 887), but (JD) τὸ ἐπ' ἐμοί Xen. *Cyr.* 5.4.11, cited by Rehdantz, supports τοὔπ' here.]

42. [Text: the line, abrupt and best suited to a man preferring to die for his city rather than rule it, may have intruded from a marginal comparison with 52, which ends identically.]

43. as for etc.: lit. 'as for that in which the largest share is (held) in common'; the city's political and religious institutions are a joint responsibility of its citizens. For ἐκεῖνο 'that (matter)' used in rhetorical organisation cf. e.g. *And.* 668, *IA* 1392. [Text: the complex syntax has been reduced to nonsense in transmission.]

44. [Text: †ἄτερ† turns **with my consent** (cf. e.g. *IA* 1361) ineptly into 'without my consent'. Valckenaer's '(O) husband' (cf. 36) makes the declaration too weak. For Bothe's '(there is no) man . . .' cf. *Sthen.* F 661.1, *Tro.* 1051; but 'man' is not required (*Alc.* 848, *Supp.* 412 etc.). Austin's simple 'ever' is plausible enough.]

45. our ancestors' ancient institutions: Athenian patriotic rhetoric often celebrates the establishment by 'our ancestors' of laws and a constitution embodying justice and fostering excellence in successive generations of Athenians: in funeral speeches Thuc. 2.36ff., Lys. 2.18 etc.; elsewhere e.g. Isocr. 2.39. Such praises of democracy have an aristocratic tone: Loraux (above, 5–13 n.) 172ff. [Text: corrected for sense and metre.]

46. olive: Athena's sacred olive had grown on the Acropolis from time immemorial (regenerating itself after the Persian sack, Hdt. 8.55) and was being incorporated in the Erectheum; the Parthenon's West pediment showed her giving it to the Athenians to win the patronage of Athens from Poseidon. **golden Gorgon:** see F 351 n. [Text: corrected for sense.]

47. trident: Poseidon's weapon and symbol already in Homer (*Il.* 12.27, *Od.* 4.506, 5.292). **city's foundations:** evoking the sacred integrity of the city: see notes on F 370.95, *Mel.D.* F 494. Poseidon will threaten them with his earthquake at the end of the play (see F 370.45–57).

48. [Text: corrected (from 'overturn') for sense.]

50–1. Make use . . . be saved etc.: Imperatives proclaim her conclusive determination as *Hcld.* 528–9, *IA* 1398. [Text: corrected for metre.]

51. a single life: cf. 18 above, *IA* 1390.

52. [Text: corrected for metre.]

53–5. Similar claims of virtue concluding speeches of renunciation: *Pho.* 1015–18 (also exhorting patriotism, but probably spurious), *Alc.* 323–5, *Hcld.* 531–4, *And.* 413–8. 'If all were as patriotic as I . . .', Lys. 25.15.

360a. Paraphrased by Lycurgus after quoting F 360, and probably part of a stichomythic argument with Erectheus after Praxithea's speech. **I love my children:** child-love (φιλοτεκνία) is similarly balanced against public interest (though to different effects in different circumstances) in *Hcld.* 410–5, *Pho.* 963–7, *IA* 1255– 8; cf. also Megara resigning her children to an inevitable death, *HF* 280–1.

362. The sources are uninformative, but this is clearly Erectheus addressing his young heir as he departs for battle (see Introd., p. 151). The heir has been identified as the younger Cecrops (Welcker; cf. e.g. Martínez, *Emerita* 43 [1975], 238–9), or Ion (so e.g. Wilamowitz, Schmid 430 n. 4, Carrara), or Xuthus (Owen, *Ion*, p. xv; Webster 129; van Looy 122). Cecrops emerges as Erectheus's natural son and heir in Apollod. 3.15.1 and 4, Paus. 1.5.3., 7.1.2, but nowhere as an adopted son. Ion sometimes leads the Athenians against Eumolpus and the Eleusinians, but in *Erec.* the heir is too young to fight, and Ion was known as the son of Erectheus's daughter Creusa (see Comm. on *Mel.S.* F 481.9–11), who in *Erec.* seems not to exist (*Ion* 277–80 makes her an infant at the relevant time). Xuthus, who traditionally is Creusa's imported husband, could hardly be adopted by Erectheus as an adolescent. (Carrara insists that F 362.2 'you have understanding' can only apply to an adult, comparing Aeschin. 1.139; but that highly tendentious passage gives no reliable guidance; it is surely an adolescent who is 'old enough to understand' and asked to 'preserve' a 'store of advice'.) We can only conclude that in this play Eur. devised an heir for Erectheus (perhaps Cecrops or Ion) in some idiosyncratic way.

As a bequest Erectheus offers ethical advice on public conduct, decision-making, counsel, acquiring wealth, choosing friends and associates, and avoiding sexual hybris and inappropriate political promotions. The advice is broadly aristocratic in tone, apt at some points for a future monarch, and consistent with the ethos of Periclean Athens. The speech reflects the Precept-poetry of Mesopotamia and Egypt (as early as the 3rd millennium) and archaic Greece (e.g. Hesiod's *Works and Days* and the gnomic collections of Phocylides and Theognis: see M.L. West, *Hesiod: Works and Days*

[Oxford, 1978], 3–25, a wide-ranging survey). Precept-poems are typically framed as advice from father to son or sage adviser to ruler or young noble. Isocrates 1 and 2 are rhetorical prose derivatives.

1. rightly . . . **I want:** these words in comparable speech-openings, *Pho.* 930 and *Supp.* 858 respectively. Erectheus accedes gladly to a request for ethical guidance.

2. have understanding . . . **will preserve:** similar terms and context, Aesch. *Supp.* 204–6. For Middle κἀποσώισαι(ο) 'remember, observe' cf. LSJ σώιζω I.4.

3. [Text: 'I want . . . to give . . .' rather than 'I want to . . . (by) giving . . .'.]

4. store: κειμήλια, 'things laid away', metaph. as *Hcld.* 591 etc. (cf. Diggle on *Pha.* 56).

5. In a brief statement etc.: cf. [Aesch.] *PV* 505, Thuc. 2.45.2 (before genuinely brief statements). Rhetorical claims to brevity in Eur.: *IA* 378, 400.

6. kindly nature: a merit in rulers, Hom. *Od.* 2.230–4 = 5.8–12, Isocr. 15.70.

7–8. an equal share: for this phrase cf. *El.* 888. Here the 'share' is in politics. In Athenian ideology the politically correct ruler has democratic sympathies and the poor participate; cf. *Supp.* 403–8, 434–5, *IA* 339–45, *Pleisthenes* F 626.1–2., Thuc. 2.37.1. [Text: the Inf. εὐσεβεῖν suggests 'and show yourself equal for all to respect'. Diggle (above, F 360.18 n.), 58 elucidates text and syntax.]

9–10. When two matters etc.: the point is essentially traditional: a (just) decision once made should be acted on, not subjected to dispute (cf. Hom. *Od.* 18.414–5 = 20.322–3; Soph. *El.* 466–7). But the terminology also suggests rejection of the sophistic claim that opposite opinions are equally valid on any question: Martínez compares *Antiope* F 189 'On every matter (πρᾶγμα) one could compose two (alternative) arguments if one were clever at speaking', *Supp.* 486–7 'Everyone knows the superior of two arguments, and what is good, what bad' (Collard collects other refs. to 'two arguments' in Eur.; see also Kells on Soph. *El.* 466–7). Treu 130 thinks Eur. is implicitly recommending concentration on one strategic objective at a time and discouraging Athenian *polypragmosyne* ('busy-bodiedness'), but this is not consistent with the idea of an **opposite opinion** (cf. *HF* 204–5) being dismissed. [Text, 10. Stob.'s 'to attach' cannot coexist with an Imperative at line-end, and μίσει 'detest' is unmetrical (the substitute στύγει is unlikely with an impersonal object). προσάπτων . . . μέθες 'attaching . . . dismiss' is slightly more apt than πρόσαπτε . . . μεθείς 'attach . . . dismissing'.]

11–13. Unjustly acquired possessions are insecure: see F 354 n.

14. Try . . . **to have possessions:** a proper goal, implicit throughout Hes. *WD*, explicit in Solon *IEG* fr. 13.7.

14–17. nobility . . . **best marriages etc.:** Soph. F 88 has a similar catalogue. Recognition and 'nobility' depend on wealth, e.g. *Pho.* 438–41, *El.* 37–8 with Cropp's n., Stob. 4.31 and 32 (and, regarding good marriages, *Thyestes* F 395); but wealth a poor indicator of moral nobility, *El.* 373–4 etc.

18–20. 'Value straight talkers, distrust panderers who will indulge and mislead you' is conventional advice to a ruler (cf. e.g. Pind. *Pyth.* 2.72–88, Isocr. 1.30, 2.28). The tyrant is generally hostile to the best and brightest around him as threats to his rule: e.g. Hdt. 3.80.4, *Supp.* 444–6 with Collard's note. The Athenian democracy valued freedom of speech as a mark of independence and self-reliance (see e.g. Mastronarde on *Pho.* 391–5). [Text: †are worthless†: sense and phrasing seem to require e.g.

'those speaking' (Matthiae, Herwerden; hardly Ferrari's πονοῦντας '(those) exerting themselves', *SIFC* 50 [1978], 234). Kamerbeek (1970) 118 shows that πονηρούς aptly describes the people referred to here (cf. 28), but not that it fits in this sentence. Collard's suggestion gives 'those who gladly are timid for your gratification'.]

21–3. company: a formative influence, e.g. *And.* 684–5; Cropp on *El.* 384–5; cf. Isocr. 1.5., 2.27. **older men** have the wisdom of experience (cf. *Bell.* F 291.1–2 n.); the rash advice of the young can be disastrous (e.g. *Supp.* 160 with Collard's n., 232–4).

22. unbridled behaviour . . . laughs: cf. *Mel.D.* F 492, Isocr. 1.15.

23. dishonourable pleasure: similarly Isocr. 1.16.

24–7. Sexual abuse of young citizens (and wives), an occupational vice of tyrants, invites revenge killings: *Supp.* 452–5, Thuc. 6.54–8, Isocr. 3.36, Aristot. *Pol.* 1314b 23–7; (wives) *El.* 947 with Cropp's n. **commoners . . . poor:** Carrara compares Xen. *Mem.* 1.2.58. Erectheus's speech tends to polarise rulers and humble people. For 'worthy poor' cf. *And.* 640, *El.* 253 (with Denniston), *Or.* 870, Thuc. 2.40.1. **It is etc.:** the rel. pron. with καί adds 'dangerous' to 'disgraceful': cf. Denniston, *GP* 294–5. **strangling:** ἀγχόνη usually refers to suicide by hanging, esp. of women, but violent killing *Bacc.* 246 (see Dodds). [Text, 24. Stob.'s 'being fortunate as to power' is implausible, Wagner's 'chancing upon power' unsuited to Erectheus's heir (but Carrara and Martínez retain it). Kock's ἐντρυφῶν 'indulging/luxuriating in' is apt (cf. LSJ); Eur. has the compound only at *Cyc.* 588 in a slightly different usage, but the simple verb several times (cf. Collard on *Supp.* 214, 552). In 25, διωκαθεῖν **pursue** is an imperatival infinitive; cf. *Tro.* 422, *Or.* 624 and perhaps a few others in Eur.: Diggle, *Studies* 10–11; Wilkins on *Hcld.* 313–4, 751. Cobet's Aor. Subj. is not likely in a general prohibition. For refs. on verbs in -αθ- (διωκαθ- is only here in Eur.) see Mastronarde on *Pho.* 1175.]

28. villains: for this political/moral connotation of πονηροί (like that of κακοί **bad men,** 29) cf. *Supp.* 423–5, Ar. *Knights* 186, [Xen.] *Ath. Pol.* 1.5 etc.; πονηροί are natural associates of tyrants, e.g. *Ion* 627, Aristot. *Pol.* 5.11.12. It can hardly be inferred that Eur. is attacking democratic politics (di Benedetto 149–50) or Cleon (Treu 130).

31. become unruly: lit. 'leap about' (horses *Pho.* 1125, maenads *Bacc.* 169, 446); they will cause political disruption by pursuing wealth and power, even tyranny, for themselves: cf. *Pleisthenes* F 626.4–7, *HF* 588–92. [Text: 'unjustly' (Stob. 3.3.18) is a banal substitute, as is Plut.'s 'some honours' in 30.]

33–4. Modesty . . . womanly temper: Erectheus meets Praxithea's standards for departures into battle, F 360.28–9. Heracles is called 'womanly' by Theseus for wanting to gaze on his dead sons and embrace his father before departing, *HF* 1406f. Highly emotional partings of mothers from children in extreme predicaments: *Hec.* 409f., 438–40, *HF* 485–9, *Tro.* 757–63. [Text, 33: Heath supplied 'you'; ἀσπάζομαι lacks an object in e.g. Hom. *Il.* 10.542, but never in Eur.]

363. In Ar. the line ends the lengthy first section of a speech by Lysistrata. **so far:** for δεῦρ' ἀεί, lit. 'to this point continuously', cf. Mastronarde on *Pho.* 1209; Aesch. *Eum.* 596; ending a speech, *TrGF* II adesp. F 183. [Text: *Lys.* 1131– 4 are not part of the fr.]

364. A common thought: see on *Tel.* F 701. [The lines identical with *Arch.* F 239 attached to our fr. in two citations are best confined to *Arch.*: see Harder there.]

365. *Aidos* (**modesty**, sense of shame) may inhibit desirable self-expression: Hom. *Il.* 24.45 (if the line belongs there), Hes. *WD* 318 (see West's Comm.); cf. *Ion* 336–7, *IA* 900–2, 1341–4, and the difficult *Hipp.* 385–6; Cairns, *Aidos* 324. The speaker is male (καὐτὸς), probably Erectheus (so Austin; Kamerbeek [1992], 114 suggests he is broaching the topic of the sacrifice). Carrara thinks of someone responding to Erectheus's ref. to *aidos* in F 362.33.   [Text: Stephanus corrected for metre, Badham for sense.]

366. ἄπιχθυς, lit. 'fishless', is recorded (through Aristoph. Byz.) only here and in Ar. *Horae* fr. 586 *PCG* 'unfishly fish', possibly a parody of Eur.   **area:** presumably in or beyond Eumolpus's Thrace.

367. Clement cites the fr. for its similarity with Achilles' description of the 'foot-unwashed, ground-sleeping' Helloi or Selloi, Zeus's interpreters at Dodona (Hom. *Il.* 16.233–5; the conditions were due to priestly taboos); cf. Soph. *Trach.* 1166– 8, Callim. *Hymn.* 4.284–5. Some have seen here a ref. to Erectheus consulting Dodona, others to the Dodonaean seer Skiros assisting the invaders (see Introd., pp. 149–50; Carrara notes that the Selloi are described as Thracian in Schol. Callim. fr. 23.3). It may simply be that Erectheus considered Dodona as a possible sanctuary for his daughter, as Creon sends his son into refuge *via* Delphi and Dodona, *Pho.* 976–83. [Text: Musgrave restored metre.]

368. The source claims (probably falsely) that Eur. alluded in this fr. to the sacrilege of the Thebans who had killed a misbehaving prophetess at Dodona (for her story see Zenob. 2.84, Ephorus *FGH* 70 F 119 = Strabo 9.2.4, Heraclid. Pont. fr. 14a Wehrli = Diog. Laert. 5.9, etc.). For the idea of polluting the sacred see Parker, *Miasma* 145–6 comparing Aesch. *Ag.* 1645, Eur. *Hcld.* 264 etc., Pl. *Laws* 917b.

369. Stob.'s section 'On Peace' also has *Cresph.* F 453 (see Comm. there), Ar. *Georg.* fr. 111, Bacchyl. *Paean* 4.61–80, Eur. *Supp.* 481–93 etc., which share generic similarities. On the fr.'s use in dating the play see Introd., p. 155.
    Metre. Dactylic ('enoplian') in 1–3, 5 (on 4 see below); iambic close in 6–7.
1. **spiders . . . webs:** for the image cf. Hom. *Od.* 16.35. In Bacchyl. *Paean* 4.69–72 spiders are to weave on shields, rust to consume swords; cf. Theocr. 16.96–7, perhaps Soph. F 286 (see Radt's App.).   [Text: Stob. has 'let it suffice' in an unexampled Middle form (perhaps misreading and incorporating the Greek heading 'Chor(us)': Hense), and at the end 'a spider'.]
2–3. Song and garlands characterise peace: Bacchyl. *Paean* 4. 63, *Cresph.* F 453.7– 8, *Supp.* 489, *Pho.* 786–8. Old men join songs of celebration: F 370.5–10 and (with garlands) *HF* 677–8.   [Text: Page (resisted by di Benedetto 149 n. 12) improved metre while retaining Stob.'s sense. In 2 he changed 'may I dwell with' to 'as a co-

dweller with', comparing Ariphron *PMG* fr. 1.2 for the corruption. Cropp's 'dwelling with' retains a verb-form often used by Eur. στεφανωθείς ('my grey head garlanded . . .'), printed without comment by Wilamowitz, *Gr. Verskunst* 388, would be an attractive reading (JD).]

4–5. hanging a Thracian shield etc.: arms dedicated in Greek temples were either a defeated enemy's or one's own 'retired' after a military career. Here the two motifs are poetically combined to evoke both relief from war and entry into a tranquil old age. On arms dedications see Pritchett, *War* III.240–95; A. Jackson in V. Hanson (ed.), *Hoplites* (London, 1991), 228–49. [Text: Page deleted πρὸς, but (Martínez, Carrara) the similar phrase *Bacc.* 1239–40 includes it; Diggle (F 360. 18 n.), 58 also retains it and makes the Greek adj. 'Thracian' trisyllabic as elsewhere in Eur., comparing Soph. *Aj.* 181, *Ant.* 782, *OC* 1079 for metre (a trochaic–dactylic colon); he now prefers the normal Fem. ending and adds *Alc.* 595/604.]

5. columned: the adj. περικίων is known only through restorations here and *IT* 404. Cf. *Ion* 185 'fine-columned (εὐκίονες) courts', Soph. *Ant.* 285–6 'columned (ἀμφικίονας) temples'.

6–7. The Chorus will devote their leisure to acquiring wisdom (cf. the female Chorus of *Med.*, 1081ff.), consulting the books (**unfold . . . tablets**: cf. *Mel.* F 506.2 n.) containing the **voice** (i.e. words) of the **wise** men of old. This wisdom, characterised as somewhat arcane, would include the past (epic poetry), prophecy, natural science and medicine etc. In *Alc.* 962–72 the Chorus have searched many traditions including 'tablets' transmitting the 'voice' of Orpheus. In *IA* 798 'tablets' convey myths. Austin compares Xen. *Mem.* 1.6.14, Socrates 'unrolling the treasures of the wise men of old which they wrote in books . . .'.

369a. unbetrothed: i.e. illegitimate.   **union(s):** Plural γάμοι often has a Singular reference. Kamerbeek (1970), 118 takes this as a ref. to Poseidon 's union with Eumolpus's mother Chione. Carrara, agreeing, places the fr. in Poseidon's Prologue-speech. [Text: West prefers 'unbetrothed of marriage' (referring to Erectheus's unmarried daughters?) since Photius explains the phrase as 'those not united in marriage'; but that explanation may be loosely phrased. ἀνέγγυος can describe illegitimate children or unions, or unbetrothed women (LSJ).]

369b. exitless: the earliest instance of the word. Its context cannot be guessed.

369d (370 N). The source indicates that the phrase 'thrummings of the Asian' (i.e., Asian cithara) in Ar. *Thesm.* 120 was parodied from Eur. *Erec.*; so Eur.'s phrase was Ἀσιάδος κρούματα (so e.g. Austin) or something like it. Martínez limits it to a form of Ἀσιάς, since κροῦμα is not known as a Tragic word; but it might be its inappropriateness that invited the parody. For 'Asian cithara' in full cf. e.g. *Hyps.* fr. 64.101, *Cyc.* 443. The cithara was associated with Asia Minor and adjacent Greek settlements such as Lesbos, home of the great early citharists Terpander and Arion (Douris *FGH* 76 F 81 with Jacoby's n., Plut. *Mor.* 1133c).

370. Austin's excellent edition (1967) is fundamental for study of the papyrus, which preserves in part a span of some 240 lines reaching nearly to the end of the play: end of an agitated lyric scene as the Chorus await the outcome of the battle (1–11), a messenger's arrival (12–22) and speech (missing), lamentation of Praxithea with Chorus (23–44), an earthquake caused by Poseidon (Choral commentary, 45–54), and Athena's intervention and speech pronouncing outcomes (55–119).

1–11. The Chorus awaits news of the crisis in a scene like *Supp.* 598–632, *El.* 746–60. Lines 5–10 are sung iambics and dochmiacs; 3–4 are probably spoken by the Chorus-leader like 11 (Praxithea can easily enter to confront the arriving messenger after 11, despite Carrara's doubt); 1–2 are probably Choral lyric (metre undeterminable), though Austin and Carrara suggest trimeters.

2. Charon (possibly Dat. case, Austin) is hard to explain in this context, other word-divisions not impossible (e.g. 'about to raise' or 'being, then': Kamerbeek). Eur. names the ferryman of the dead in *Alc.* 254, 361, *HF* 432.

3–4. friends: equally apt for the Chorus-leader (e.g. *El.* 747) or Praxithea (e.g. *El.* 751). **Pallas's scarps:** the cliffs and ravines of the Acropolis; for rare ἀγμός (ἀγ- 'break') cf. *IT* 263, *Bacc.* 1094.   **reporter:** preparing the messenger's arrival (cf. Cropp on *El.* 759).

5–6. shall I (etc.): similar expectant choral questions *Bacc.* 862ff., *Rhes.* 360ff. **victory song:** on the chants *kallinikos* and *alalai ié paián* cf. *HF* 180 with Bond's note, Ar. *Lys.* 1291; together, Ar. *Birds* 1763–4. The paean was used in pleas for, or celebrations of, deliverance; cf. Burkert 74, 145, LSJ Παιάν.

6. [Text, **taking up:** Middle ἀναλαμβάνομαι is not found elsewhere in Tragedy, but its participle fits the context better than ἵνα λαβόμενος 'so that, grasping . . .' (needing a Gen. object: Kamerbeek).]

7. task of my aged hand: song and dance inspire choristers despite weakness: F 369.1–3, *HF* 673–86, Aesch. *Ag.* 104–6.

7–8. Libyan lotus pipe: cf. *Tro.* 544, *Hel.* 170, *HF* 674 etc. On the aulos, often made from the wood of the Libyan lotus tree, see Cropp on *El.* 716; M.L. West, *Ancient Greek Music* (Oxford, 1992), 81–107.   [Text, **sounding:** the adj. ἠχήεις/ἀχάεις (whence P's ἀχάεντος) is not Tragic (doubtfully Aesch. *Sept.* 915). Austin's Gen. abs. part. is preferable, and provides clear dochmiac rhythm.]

8. *noise:* lit. 'shout(s)': Austin compares *Hyps.* fr. I.iii.9–10 'the cithara shouted', Pind. *Ol.* 3.8, *Pyth.* 10.38.   [Text: probably Dat. Sing. or Plur. βοαῖ(ς) was governed by a part. agreeing with λωτοῦ or a prep. such as ὁμοῦ '<*along with*>' (Kamerbeek) or σύν (Carrara, Martínez: perhaps σύν τ[ε 'and with' (σύν taken 'in common' with both preceding and following phrase: cf. e.g. *IT* 886; Breitenbach 211–2); or βοαῖσίν τ(ε) (Collard); hence e.g. '<*with*> cithara's *noise and* <*maidens* . . . > **following.**']

9. wheeling along: τροχαλός 'running', hence 'rolling' (e.g. a wagon, *IA* 146), describes an old man hurrying before the North wind, Hes. *WD* 518–9. Austin would add 'on the pathway', Martínez 'on foot'.   **following** (see 8 n.): ἑπομέναις agreeing with βοαῖς (Austin) offers difficult word-order and poor sense.

9–10. young maiden . . . aged man: a wistful juxtaposition (cf. *HF* 687–94, Alcman *PMGF* fr. 26) suggesting general celebration (cf. Soph. *Trach.* 205–15). Choruses were normally homogeneous in age (children, adolescents or young adults) and more often than not in sex: cf. C. Calame, *Les choeurs de jeunes filles en grèce archaique* (Rome, 1977), 62ff.

12–22. Similar dialogues with bearers of victory-news *Hcld.* 784–98, *Supp.* 634– 49, *El.* 761–73 — and of an interim report, *Pho.* 1072–89.

12–13. **trophy:** a battlefield monument declaring victory: Pritchett, *War* II.246ff. [Text, 12: Carrara's 'Do not *lament*' seems too long. μὴ δ[ῆτα' *No*, *<indeed!>*' (cf. *Or.* 1329) or μὴ τ[αῦτα '*Not <that!>*' (cf. *Ion* 1331), possible reactions to fear or despair expressed by Prax. (Collard) do not suit the traces.   13, **land:** thus both of Austin's supplements.   12–13 ends perhaps '*<with his very hand>*' (cf. *Hel.* 1380, *Ant.* F 223.9)... *over the barbarians*' (Austin); '*<with his own hand . . . >*' (Kamerbeek); '*. . . <over countless> barbarians . . .*' (Cropp); '*. . . over the barbarians <for Zeus>*' (Collard, cf. *Pho* 572); '*. . . over the barbarian <host>*' (Reeve).]

14. [Text: neither Austin's '**But who** *<was killed>* **by Ares**' nor Martínez's '*. . . who* (is the one) *<killed> . . .*' gives γε a function. τίς γὰρ εἶ 'But who are you . . . ?' might be apt (cf. Ar. *Ach.* 594 for phrasing, *Hcld.* 638, *El.* 765 for substance), but only if a subsequent line of (late) self-identification by the messenger and one containing Praxithea's question about Erectheus have been lost.]

15. With Page's supplement, '*<Eumolpus> has fallen, <struck in the liver>.*'

17. The Messenger disguises his news with euphemisms, like Talthybius on the dead Polyxena, *Tro.* 268–70. For 'blessed' dead in the classical period see Dover on Ar. *Frogs* 85 citing Pl. *Phd.* 115d4 etc.   [Text: **<and> a fortunate <man>:** JD compares the line-ending phrase 'fortunate man' in *Med.* 1228, *Antig.* F 157, noting that Austin's '*<and at the same time>* fortunate' would only be apt if 'and at the same time' were linking two *contrasted* items (cf. *Hipp.* 348, *Hec.* 810, etc.).]

18. **successful:** εὐτυχής of military (or similar) success as e.g. 58, *Hcld.* 385, 797, *El.* 889, *Pho.* 1478.   [Text: φέρει is proper for '*<bringing>*' victory; West compares LSJ VI.3 and adj. νικηφόρος.]

19. **spoils:** brought into the city for dedication, cf. *Pho.* 1474–5. The messenger mentions these to confirm a successful victory, but avoids answering Praxithea's question about Erectheus's survival; hence her agitated reaction in the next line. [Text: '*<for the gods>*' (Cropp; cf. e.g. *El.* 6–7) seems apter than '*<for the city>*' (Kamerbeek) or '(these spoils) *<alone>*' (Austin).]

21–22. The couplet must have said that those who have died nobly are more alive than those who live on ignobly (cf. F 360.30–1 n.).   [Text: in 22 Stob. transmits absurd sense. Little better are (Diels) '*. . . are, rather, alive, and those ignobly not alive*', or (Tucker) '*. . . are alive and, rather, those ignobly not alive*'. But no apt emendation has been found (τῶν βλεπόντων is metrically impossible, breaching Porson's Law).]

23–44. The lament is comparable with e.g. *And.* 1173–1230 (Peleus, Chorus).
     Metre. Lyric at least from 28; 34–44 dochmiac and syncopated iambic rhythms.

27. **falling:** the sisters throwing themselves to their deaths? Carrara compares Hygin. *Fab.* 238.2; cf. Introd., p. 151.

28. **crying out (or calling on):** Eur. uses poetic ἠπύω/ἀπύω mainly in laments (*Hec.* 154, *Supp.* 800, *Tro.* 1304).

32. [Text: Austin's reading rules out '*<to look upon your>* **countenance**' (cf. Soph. *Aj.* 70); so πρόσοψιν may mean the sad **sight** (cf. *Or.* 952) of the daughters' corpses (cf. 37–8 below).]

34. **Deo's head(?)**: Deo (also misspelled in the papyrus at 109) is an occasional name of Demeter, of disputed derivation: see Richardson on *Hom. Hymn.* 2.47. Eur. may well have written 'Deo's daughter' (JD, Collard), i.e. Persephone, recipient of the human sacrifice (cf. *Hcld.* 409, 490, 601, *HF* 1104; Introd., p. 150). **carried . . . led:** suggesting enslavement or harassment: *Tro.* 1310, LSJ ἄγω I.3.

35. **pierced:** for διέρχομαι of physical or emotional wounds cf. Collard on *Supp.* 288. [Text: διῆλθεν (Diggle) avoids repeated **you**. JD now notes the apparent lack of a subject for διῆλθε(v) and tries σὺ δ' Ἄιδα διῆλθες οἶμον, 'but you have completed the path to Hades', cf. Aesch. F 239, *AP* 7.412.8, 7.627.2, etc.]

35–42. To whom first etc.: Praxithea's uncertainty and her rhetorical questions emphasise multiple and equally pressing sorrows, as e.g. *Pho.* 1310–12 (see Mastronarde's Comm.), 1524–9 (same structure), *IT* 655–6, Soph. *Trach.* 947–9; cf. Tarrant on Sen. *Ag.* 649–50.

37. [Both text and interpretation are uncertain. Collard suggests δράμω, '(To whom first) . . . shall I run' (Subj. verb parallel to στένω 'shall I lament', 39), with line 38 parenthetic; this is attractive, but we also need a noun agreeing with '**dear**' (e.g. ξυνωρίδα 'pair' referring to the two sisters, though this would combine awkwardly with Sing. '**you**'). Austin's ἄθλι' ὧν ('or over the dear one amongst my daughters, whose wretched limbs . . .') avoids the parenthesis but requires στένω to be the verb for the whole passage (Eur. regularly makes it transitive, never with ἐπί, though cf. Soph. *Trach.* 947). Little can be done with Kamerbeek's reading ('. . . ruin/madness of my daughters, whose . . .'). **crazed:** φρενομανεῖ is supported by Aesch. *Ag.* 1140 (the adj. applied to Cassandra).]

38. **bruised:** τακερὰ, if rightly read, seems to mean 'softened', 'melted', i.e. bruised by their fall onto the rocks (cf. μαλακός 'tender' of bruising, Com. adesp. fr. 125 Kock). **a-aah!:** showing pain or revulsion (e.g. *HF* 1120), not surprise (*Mel.* F 510). [Text: Kamerbeek doubted that τακερὰ could make sense; but his 'chilly' or 'lamented (limbs)' does not fit the traces.]

40. **murderous blasts**: so Austin (comparing *Tro.* 79, [Aesch.] *PV* 1085) and subsequent commentators, taking these to be wind-gusts created by Poseidon's trident-blow/earthquake engulfing Erectheus; hence e.g. *<whom the god's>* **murderous blasts** *<destroyed>*'. A tempting alternative is Collard's 'bloody gasps', of the dying Erectheus; cf. *Pho.* 1438 (Eteocles' 'hard-dying gasp'), *IA* 1114 (sacrificial calves' 'gasping of black blood'); but the image of a dying Erec. seems not quite apt when he has presumably vanished into the earth (note '**below**', 39).

41–2. The end of 42 must have included a participle-phrase, e.g. θ[άνατον παθοῦσαν ('**who** . . . *<suffered>* **that unholy** . . . *<death>*'). That Prax. condemns the city-saving sacrifice so emphatically is surprising even in her moment of despair, but 'unholy' etc. can hardly be applied to Eumolpus (Austin and others; ἀνίερος cannot mean 'impious' or the like). JD's 'holy and unholy, hallowed and unhallowed' (supplying clear dochmiac metre and giving an ambivalent expression typical of Eur.'s style, cf. esp. *Tro.* 1315–16, *Or.* 546–7) would alleviate the difficulty. **and the height ... through deceit:** how this fits within its context is unclear; perhaps part of the sentence has been lost (Austin). [Text: Austin's 'through god-sent deceit' (cf. Aesch. *Pers.* 93) does not fit well. Correcting to ἀπάτας would give 'and the height of deceit' (cf. LSJ κορυφά II.2); the daughter was not a victim of deceit (Introd., pp. 150–1), but Prax. might suggest that she herself was deceived in allowing the sacrifice, or by her other daughters' suicide. Collard notes that κορυφὰν ἀρετᾶς 'summit of virtue' could suit the context.]

43. [Text: Austin suggests 'O *<citizens>*', Diggle the more normal 'O *<city>*' (cf. Mastronarde on *Pho.* 613) or 'O *<city of Pallas>*' (cf. *Supp.* 377, *And.* 1176).]

44. [Text: *<and>*: Cropp's ⟨θ'⟩ gives a normal link between the two adjectives.]

44–54. Poseidon's earthquake shattering the palace mirrors the royal family's ruin, while the community survives. This earthquake scene resembles *HF* 904–9 and *Bacch.* 585–603; cf. also the Zeus-sent cataclysm [Aesch.] *PV* 1080–90, and Dionysus shaking Lycurgus's palace in a surviving line from Aesch. *Edoni*, F 58. The 5ᵗʰ C. theatre could have supported such scenes with sound-effects but hardly with physical ones. In *HF* and *Bacch.* an actor's cries from within are heard by the Chorus outside the palace. Here Praxithea is with the Chorus, but 45–6 and the consequent commentary look as if they belong to the Chorus alone (Carrara).

Metre. Dochmiacs with iambics as often in agitated scenes with offstage action.

45. O Earth: invoked as a witness of horror as e.g. *Hipp.* 672, *Pho.* 1290, but also as the focus of the earthquake. [Text: perhaps 'flee *<quickly ... flee>*'.]

46. [Text, **in any way an ending:** or (Austin) 'some end'. For 'ending of troubles' cf. *Or.* 187 etc.; J. Diggle, *PCPS* 22 (1976), 44 = *Euripidea* 151.]

47–8. [Text: it is hard to reconcile]γετε (2ⁿᵈ Plur. Imper.?) with Nom. Sing. χθόνιος without punctuation:*<Flee>* **from the land!**', then perhaps (Collard) 'subterranean' referring to the earthquake's noise. Kamerbeek (App., developing Austin) took]ατας as] ἄτας and adjusted to χθονίας: '*<Flee>* the **subterranean** ruin of the land *<on maddened feet>* (or *<with maddened minds>*)'.]

48. ground ... dancing: cf. *Bacch.* 585, [Aesch.] *PV* 1081, *IT* 46.

49. [Text: '**is hurling** *<ruin>*' Austin, '*<destruction>*' Carrara, or '*<shaking>*' Diggle comparing *Tro.* 1326 and Poseidon's title Enosichthon 'Earth-shaker'.]

50. [Text: Austin's articulation gives '**which** (is/being) **most miserable** ...'.]

51. the roof is collapsing: similarly *HF* 905 (cf. 1007), *Bacch.* 587–8 (cf. 633), *IT* 48–9. [Text: '**troubles** *<for the foundations>*' (Austin) or '*<from the quake>*' (JD), both making the line an iambic trimeter, are preferable to Kamerbeek's '*<after troubles>*'.]

53. [Text: Austin's '*<he has overturned>* **everything** ...' (cf. *Bacc.* 348) may, as he notes, be too long for the space. (Kamerbeek prefers the 5ᵗʰ C. Perf. form of τρέπω, e.g. Soph. *Trach.* 1009).]

54. bacchic dancing: like Lyssa's in *HF* 896 (making Heracles 'dance' in madness, 871, 879, 889); of a palace, Aesch. F 58. **just now:** πάλαι of a recent event, e.g. *Tro.* 624, Aesch. *Ag.* 587, *PV* 845. [Text: Kamerbeek's '*<the one>* dancing ...' is apt if the previous line did not include a subject.]

55–117. Athena could be suspended on the crane above the stage-building, or stand on its roof after arriving on the crane or emerging *via* a screened trap-door. Suspension would have emphasised the goddess's detachment from the turmoil below; cf. D. Mastronarde, *CA* 9 (1990), 247–94, esp. 278–9, 284 no. 20. For her address to the unseen Poseidon cf. *IT* 1446ff. (Athena to Orestes), *Hel.* 1662ff. (Castor to Helen). Eur. was to confront Athena with Poseidon in the Prologue of *Tro.* Her speech here is divided into a short address to Poseidon (55–62) and a long address instructing Praxithea on the burial of her daughters (67–70), their deification as the Hyacinthids (71–4), their rituals and sanctuary (75–89), Erectheus's rituals and sanctuary (90–4), Praxithea's appointment as priestess of Athena (95–7), and the future foundation of the Eleusinian Mysteries (98–117) with the catasterism of the Erectheids/Hyacinthids (see 107–8 n.).

55. **I call:** αὐδῶ is poetic and elevated, a favourite of Eur., e.g. *Hipp.* 1285, *Hel.* 1662 (gods in play-closing scenes), *Bacc.* 504, *HF* 1215 (injunctions with Infin.).

56. [Text: the verb ἀναστατοῦν is otherwise unattested before the Septuagint, but appropriate. ἀνάστατον (adj.) would be awkwardly predicative 'and not to demolish my land (so that it becomes) uprooted . . .'.]

57. **demolish . . . delightful:** Athena calmly deploys elevated language. ἐρείπω is poetic but not used elsewhere by Eur., ἐπήρατος poetic but rare in Tragedy (only here and Aesch. *Eum.* 958).

58. [Text: **may < . . . > not give:** the supplement δοῖ[εν is almost inevitable. The missing subject was probably the incomplete final word of the line, e.g. Austin's '<*the gods*>'.]

59. **below the earth:** cf. 39–40, *Ion* 281–2 (Erectheus engulfed in a chasm by Poseidon's trident).

60. **gripped:** for the metaphor cf. *Alc.* 937, *Rhes.* 916 (same phrase from a goddess at play-end), Ar. *Knights* 1237 (paratragic), LSJ ἅπτω III.2.

61–2. **And after that (etc.):** surely a question, climactic after the two preceding and filling the whole couplet (not Carrara's 'And then you hesitate?'): e.g., '**And after that you are going to <***perform***> these fulfilments *for* etc.**' (or '*with* etc.': Page, Martínez). Austin (1967), 53 supplied the shape of the sentence. For κἄπειτα in indignant and dismissive questions see on *Cret.* F 472e.27; for ταῦτα δή likewise Denniston, *GP* 207–10, esp. (viii) with Soph. *El.* 385.   **fulfilments:** Eur. has τελεσφόρος 'fulfilment-bringing' *Med.* 714, *El.* 1132, *Pho.* 69, 641; here the fulfilment is of Poseidon's hatred or of an 'obligation' to the underworld powers.   The second part of 62 remains unclear; Martínez's '**if** (= because) **a goddess** (i.e. Athena) *has* <*defeated you*>' is not persuasive. JD looks for different syntax, e.g. '**to** <*give*> **these fulfilling** <*sacrifices, in addition, to the*> **goddess** <*amongst the*> **nether powers**' (i.e. Persephone).]

63. **<*Cephisus*'>:** the local river, Praxithea's father in Lycurg. *Leocr.* 98 (and *Ion* 1261?), grandfather in Apollod. 3.15.1.

64. **Hear:** Athena commands attention thus in *Supp.* 1183, 1196, *IT* 1436; Artemis in *Hipp.* 1296.   **motherless:** cf. *Pho.* 666, Aesch. *Eum.* 736. Athena's birth from Zeus's head was traditional (e.g. Hes. *Theog.* 924, *Hom. Hymn.* 28.4; cf. Hom. *Il.* 5.875–80) and featured decorously on the Parthenon's East pediment. The point may emphasise her detachment from Praxithea's familial griefs (R. Harder 342).

66. has caused to be sacrificed: Present for past action with continuing effect, cf. *Tel.* F 696.1 n. For προθύειν 'sacrifice on behalf of' cf. *Ion* 805, *Hyps.* fr. 1.iv.36; more commonly 'make a preliminary sacrifice' (97 n. below).

67–8. Bury her . . . and these sisters: 'these' does not always indicate presence on stage (cf. *Sthen.* F 665a n.), but probably does so here in view of the distinction from the sacrificed daughter. Burials, often related to a local cult-site (cf. 73–4 n.), are a regular topic in Tragic endings (e.g. *Med.* 1377–83, *HF* 1360–4, 1419–20; divinely commanded, e.g. *And.* 1239–42, *El.* 1276–80). The sisters receive the honorific burial accorded to soldiers (cf. F 360.32–3), at the site of their death as e.g. Tellus (Hdt. 1.30.5) or the dead at Marathon: cf. N. Loraux, *Tragic Ways of Killing a Woman* (Eng. tr. Chicago, 1987), 46–7.

69–70. nobility: the Greek term is conventional for this type of noble self-sacrifice, e.g. *Alc.* 742 etc., *Supp.* 1030.   **pledges:** see Introd., p. 151.

71–2. heaven: αἰθήρ is the traditional dwelling of the gods (*Mel.S.* F 487 n.) and the destination of Eur.'s deified mortals (Cropp on *El.* 991); the sisters will be the Hyades (107–8 n.). The idea of 'body to earth, spirit to heaven' is also found for ordinary mortals in Eur. and contemporary inscriptions: cf. Collard on *Supp.* 531– 6; Kannicht on *Hel.* 1013–6.

73–4. a name . . . to call them: slight pleonasm bolsters a formal announcement, e.g. *Ion* 74–5, 1594–5.   **Hyacinthids:** see Introd., p. 153 on this identification. The cult must have originated in the supposed nurture of the vegetation god Hyacinthus by a group of Maidens, *Parthenoi*. Phanodemus *FGH* 325 F 4 identified these with the Erectheids/Hyacinthids, explaining 'Hyacinthids' by the location of the sacrifice 'on the Hyacinthus hill, above the Sphendonia' (perhaps the modern 'Hill of the Nymphs', see R. Wycherley, *The Stones of Athens* (Princeton, 1978), 188; cf. Wilamowitz, *Glaube* I.104 n. 1; A. Henrichs (84–6 n. below) 98 n. 54; for Erectheids = Hyacinthids also [Dem.] 60.27). In a separate aetiology, ill suited to the 420s, the Hyacinthids were daughters of a Spartan immigrant and were sacrificed unsuccessfully to save Athens (e.g. Apollod. 3.15.8; cf. Kearns 202).

75–6. These lines probably gave an etymology of 'Hyacinthids' supporting their identification with the Erectheids and a reason for the instructions in 77–89.   **hyacinth's brightness:** a puzzle without the full context. γάνος 'brightness' or 'sheen' usually belongs to a beneficial liquid such as water, wine or honey (Fraenkel on Aesch. *Ag.* 1392, Dodds on *Bacc.* 261); but the phrase here could be merely 'bright hyacinth' (cf. Bond on *Hyps.* fr. 60.60). [Text: the (uncompelling) suggestions for 75 in App. are: 'And since she was taken away and is gone' (Kamerbeek, with 'dressed' or 'deceived' following); '. . . and the honoured/bereft/ dishonoured girl is gone' (Austin); for 76 'for the sake of benefit' (Kamerbeek).]

78–80. annual sacrifices etc.: divinely ordained commemoration validates an established local festival (cf. *Hipp.* 1423–30, *IT* 1458–61 etc.); no more is known of it. [Text, 78: P's ἐνιαυσίωι . . . χρόνωι could mean 'at annual periods', but 'not forgetting' is then too abrupt.]

79. slaughterings of _oxen_: lit. '_ox_-slaying slaughters' (cf. 94). βουκτόνος will be unique here, but cf. e.g. ταυροκτόνος 'bull-slaying' (Soph. _Phil._ 400).

81–2. Possible sense is offered by Kamerbeek (modifying Austin): '<_and on_> learn<_ing that an_> enemy <_is launching_> into battle, rous<_ing against you the_> shield <_of his_> army'). Treu suggested '<_and on_> learn<_ing when . . .'._ Diggle's suggestions would allow 'Recognis<_ing their support when_> a commander <_comes for battle and_> rouses his **shield** <_against_> you' (or '. . . rouses his **shield** <_against_> you for a **battle-**<_contest_>'). For 'shield' as 'armament' cf. _Hcld._ 932, _Pho._ 78, 'rouse one's spear' F 352 above, _And._ 607. For protection from invasions similarly envisaged cf. _Hcld._ 1034–36, _Supp._ 1208–9.

83. sacrifice preliminary to battle: πρότομα, lit. 'pre-cuttings' (of sacrificial victims), is found only here; the verb προτομίζεσθαι is known from Byzantine lexica. On such sacrifices see Wilkins on _Hcld._ 399–409 with many refs.

84–6. not touching etc.: i.e. not using vine-wood for the sacrificial fire: so J. Bingen, _Chronique d'Égypte_ 43 (1968), 156–8. Certain woods (e.g. vine, fig, myrtle) were improper for certain sacrifices; those permitted were νηφάλια ξύλα 'sober woods'. **not pouring wine:** 'sober libations' excluding wine were prescribed for many deities (e.g. the Erinyes/Eumenides: Aesch. _Eum._ 107, Soph. _OC_ 469–81). On such rules Schol. Soph. _OC_ 100 cites Polemon and Philochorus _FGH_ 328 F 12 (mentioning the Erectheids), F 194; cf. A. Henrichs, _HSCP_ 87 (1983), 87–100 (with list for Attica 96–7 and discussion of the Erectheids/Hyacinthids 98) and in _Atti del XVII Congr. Int. di Papirologia_ (Naples, 1984), 255–68; cf. Graf, _Nordion. Kulte_ 26–9. On libations in general see Burkert 70–3 with notes.

85–6. industrious bee's produce: a solemn periphrasis for honey used in libations, like _IT_ 165, 634–5, Aesch. _Pers._ 612–3, Soph. F 398.5.

87. untrodden: inaccessible (not βέβηλος) to profane visitors; cf. _Bacc._ 10 (Semele's tomb), Soph. _OC_ 10, 167–8 (the Erinyes' sanctuary), 1760ff. (Oedipus's 'tomb').

88. prevent . . . enemies etc.: enemies' offerings might pre-empt the maidens' good will. Cf. _Hcld._ 1026–44 with Wilkins' Comm. esp. on 1040–2 (Eurystheus promising benevolence to Athens and hostility to invaders prohibits libations at his tomb), Soph. _OC_ 91–3, 1520–35 (Oedipus honoured secretly at his secret death-site will protect Athens and destroy Theban invaders).

89. so as to bring: the Accusatives νίκην and πημονήν express the effect of the verb 'make offerings': on syntax and non-punctuation see Barrett on _Hipp._ 757.

90. a precinct: Erectheus's cult-site was on the Acropolis, North of the Parthenon, associated with the older Temple of Athena Polias and the site of the Mycenean palace with which Homer connects Erectheus (_Od._ 7.80; cf. _Il._ 2.549). The Erectheum (so named by Paus. 1.26.5, [Plut.] _Mor._ 843e, but in 5th C. inscriptions identified with Athena) was being or about to be built when the play was produced (see Introd., p. 155), incorporating the old cult-objects of Athena Polias, Athena's olive tree and Poseidon's salt-spring, the altars of Poseidon Erectheus, Boutes and Hephaestus, and the tomb of Cecrops. On the layout see e.g. R.J. Hopper, _The Acropolis_ (London, 1971), 97–110; J. Travlos, _Pictorial Dictionary of Ancient Athens_ (London, 1971), 213–27 (differently Kron 41).

91. stone: Eur.'s frequent use of the adj. λάϊνος (e.g. *HF* 979, 1037, 1332) is parodied in Ar. *Ach.* 449. **enclosure:** this could be anything from a simple precinct-enclosure to the marble cladding of the newly designed Erectheum. The vagueness is probably deliberate, evoking the new building while not ignoring its predecessors. Hdt. 8.55 mentions a pre-existing temple (νηός).

93–4. slaughtering ... oxen: lit. 'in ox-sacrificing slaughters' (cf. 79). Athenian sacrifices to Erectheus nursling of Athena are mentioned as early as Hom. *Il.* 2.550–1. **august:** a common epithet for gods. **Poseidon ... Erectheus** suggests a cultic identification. 'Poseidon Erectheus' appears in a dedication *IG* I² 580 (460/450 B.C.) but is understood by some as 'Poseidon <and> Erectheus'; Lacore 217–22 infers from the other sparse evidence that the identification was not established until much later (cf. Kron 48–52) and that Eur.'s assertion is speculative. Burkert, *HN* 149 on the other hand speaks of 'two names for a single god'. At any rate this cultic association of the two figures was close; they shared an altar and a priest, and Poseidon's salt-spring could be called Erectheis (Apollod. 3.14.1). Kearns 210–1 suggests that the state cult of Erectheus, and state mythology such as Eur. was formulating, tended to identify the two figures while the tribal cult tended to maintain a separate heroic identity for Erectheus.

95–7. Praxithea ... priestess: she becomes the first priestess of Athena Polias (like Iphigeneia at Brauron, *IT* 1462–3). This important office belonged in historical times to the Eteoboutad family, along with the priesthood of Poseidon Erectheus; they claimed descent from Boutes, who was sometimes defined as Erectheus's brother (Apollod. 3.15.1); cf. Kearns 152–3, Burkert, *HN* 149. Hdt. 5.82.3 links sacrifices for Erectheus with sacrifices for Athena Polias. **restored:** lit. 'set upright out (of misfortune)'. Austin compares Archil. *IEG* fr. 130.1–2 'raise (ὀρθοῦσιν) out of troubles', Soph. *OT* 46 'raise up (ἀνόρθωσον) the city', Eur. *Alc.* 1138 'you have raised up (ἀνώρθωσας) my fortunes', and contrasts ἐξανιστάναι βάθρα 'uproot foundations' *Supp.* 1198, *Hel.* 1652 (add *HF* 944–6). **for the city:** πόλει is Dat. 'of advantage' (contrast Gen. 'on behalf of the city' with προθύειν, 66). προθύειν here has its normal reference to preliminary or preparatory sacrifices: cf. Collard on *Supp.* 29.

99. judgement of Zeus: Athena has ordained cult arrangements involving members of her Athenian 'family'. Zeus's authority settles her dispute over Attica with Poseidon, and the war between their peoples. Eumolpus and his descendants are assigned their proper role in Attic history. Zeus also authorises a major new cult and the astral deification of the maidens, as he does Demeter's cult in *Hom. Hymn.* 2.325–8, 443–4, 460–2 and Helen's deification *Hel.* 1669 (cf. Treu 127–8).

100–1. In *Hom. Hymn.* 2.150–5, 473–6 Eumolpus was one of several rulers of Eleusis to whom Demeter revealed the Mysteries; in the 6ᵗʰ C. he emerged as the most significant, and was probably then defined as Poseidon's son (cf. N. Richardson, *The Homeric Hymn to Demeter* [Oxford, 1974], 9, 197–9). Here he has become a Thracian invader killed by Erectheus, so another Eumolpus must found the Mysteries. From Schol. Soph. *OC* 1053 we know of traditions making the founder a grandson of the Thracian (Istros *FGH* 334 F 22) or his great-great-great-grandson (Acestodorus, and Andron

FGH 10 F 13 naming Musaeus as the founder's father: on this see Richardson [above, 100–1 n.], 198). Eur. will have used some such scheme.   [Text: West therefore suggests 'born <*as fifth descendant*> from . . .'.]

102–4. These lines probably concerned Demeter's revelation to the later Eumolpus, and his marriage and propagation of the Eumolpid family.

105. [Text: possibly '**and one**' <*of the sisters*> . . .' (Barrett).]

107–8. Hyades . . . **stars:** the Hyades are stars in the constellation Taurus, numbered variously between two and seven in antiquity. Eur.'s ref. seems to be explained by Schol. Arat. 172 (cf. *Pha.* F 780 with n.), 'Eur. in *Erec.* said that Erectheus's three daughters became the Hyades' (though this information could be confused: cf. on *Mel.S.* F 481. 13–22). It is unclear (beyond the similarity of names) why Eur. identified Hyacinthids (73–4) with Hyads, and why he did so at this point in the speech. Kearns 61 notes their similarity as Nurses (*kourotrophoi*) of Dionysus and Hyacinthus respectively. The Boeotian Coronids/Orionids, another group of self-sacrificed and catasterised maidens, were similarly associated with Dionysus (Kearns 59–60, 62; cf. Schmitt 98).

109. Deo's: see 34 n.

110–2. not to be uttered . . .**holy:** epithets appropriate to the Eleusis rituals; cf. *Hom. Hymn.* 2.478–9 ('holy . . . which one may not voice'); Ar. *Clouds* 302 ('unutterable').

113–4. Hermes . . . **Kerykes:** the second priestly family of Eleusis, the Kerykes, claimed descent from Keryx son of Hermes (rather than Eumolpus as in some accounts) and one of Cecrops' daughters (Paus. 1.38.3 etc.; Kearns 177).

115–7. But restrain (etc.): the goddess closes by urging Praxithea to refrain from grief (cf. *And.* 1270), consoled by the rewards of the future (cf. *Ion* 1604–5).   [Text, 117: Austin's καὶ τὰ πε[ρὶ ('and the things concerning/around . . .') gives a rare resolution type (see Cropp–Fick 36). Probably we have τὰ in crasis with ἀπό or ἐπί (as prep. or prefix); so e.g. 'and now carry out the things that follow from my announcements' (Cropp); 'on those conditions' (Collard).]

118–9. Praxithea must have assented to Athena's instructions (cf. *And.* 1273–6, *Supp.* 1227, *Ion* 1606–8, *IT* 1475–6, etc.) but perhaps also reiterated her grief in '**piteous** . . .'. We are near the end of the play. Only a few lines follow the divine speech in, e.g., *And.* and *Supp.* Extended complaint and questioning as in *El.* 1293ff. are unlikely in *Erec.*

PHAETHON

Texts, testimonia. P. Oxy. 2455 fr. 14 (Hypothesis); P. Berl. 9771; Paris ms. Gr. 107B (see esp. F. Blass, *De Phaethontis Euripideae Fragmentis Claromontanis*, Kiel, 1885); *TrGF* F 771–86; Mette Nos. 1086–1103. F. Volmer, *De Euripidis fabula quae Phaethon inscribitur etc.* (Münster, 1930) is entirely superseded by J. Diggle, *Euripides. Phaethon* (Cambridge, 1970), with Pls. IV of Paris 107B and P. Berl.

Myth. Hes. *Theog.* 984–91, fr. 311; Aesch. *Heliades TrGF* III F 68–73a; Eur. *Hipp.* 737–41; Pl. *Tim.* 22c; Schol. Hom. *Od.* 17.208 (see *TrGF* III p. 185, Diggle 31); Ovid, *Met.* 1.747–79, 2.1–400; Hygin. *Fab.* 152A, 154; 'Schol. Strozziana' on Germanicus's trans. of Arat. *Phaenom.*, pp. 174.2–175.5 Breysig (see Diggle 16–17); Nonnus, *Dionys.* 38.90–434. G. Knaack, *Quaestiones Phaethonteae* (Berlin, 1886) and in Roscher III.2.2175–2202; Frazer on Apollod. 3.14.3 (Vol. II, 82 n. 2); *RE* XIX.2 (1938), 1505–15; Diggle 3–32, 'Ovid and Nonnus' 180–200 (with rev. by F. della Corte, *Maia* 23 [1971], 75–81); L. Burelli in L. Braccesi (ed.), *I Tragici Greci e l'Occidente* (Bologna, 1979), 131–9; Aélion (1983), 303–5, 308– 10; Gantz 31–4; J. Blomqvist, *Eranos* 92 (1994), 1–16.

Illustrations. Diggle 205–20 (with Pl. VI); Schefold–Jung, *Urkönige* 49–52, Pls. 41–2 and (best bibl.) nn. 111–6; *LIMC* IV 'Helios' and VII 'Phaethon'.

Main Discussions. U. von Wilamowitz, *KS* I.110–47 (= *Hermes* 18 [1883], 396–434), cf. *Sappho und Simonides* (Berlin, 1913), 37–8; H. Weil, *REG* 2 (1889), 322–8; A. Lesky, *WS* 50 (1932), 1–25 = *Ges. Schr.* 111–30; A.W. Pickard-Cambridge in Powell, *New Chapters* III.143–7; Schmid 599–603; Pohlenz I.290–1, II.123; Webster, *Euripides* (1967) 220–32; Diggle, *Phaethon* (and reviews by H. Lloyd-Jones, *CR* 21 [1971] 341–5 = *Acad. Papers* I.452–7; J. Kamerbeek, *Mnem* 24 [1971], 207–9; H. van Looy, *AC* 39 [1971], 544–8; R. Kannicht, *Gnomon* 44 [1972], 1–12; T. B. L. Webster, *AJPh* 93 [1972], 627–30; W. M. Calder, *CPh* 67 (1972], 291–3); K. J. Reckford, *TAPA* 103 (1972), 405–32; Aélion (1983) 305–11; A. Barigazzi, *Prometheus* 16 (1990), 97–110; Hose, *Chor* I.121–31; E. Contiades-Tsitsoni, *ZPE* 102 (1994), 52–60. See also Comm. on 63–101, 227–44.

Note. All references to the play text follow Diggle's continuous line numbering, sometimes indicated by 'D'. The numbers of the separate fragments in *TrGF* are given in the Greek Text, App. and Transl. but elsewhere only for special reason.

One of the more substantial fragmentary plays; but much of the content is conjectural and the general tone is hard to know. Only the major problems are discussed here.

Recovery of the fragments. Until about 1820 very few of the fifteen or so book fragments could be related confidently to a plot presumed from mythographic accounts to include Phaethon's fatal drive in the chariot of his father Helios the

Sun. Shortly before that year two leaves from a (?) 5th/6th C. A.D. parchment text of the play were found severely trimmed and reused as palimpsest in a 6th C. *Epistles of St. Paul*, now Paris, Gk. ms. 107B or 'Claromontanus' (symbol: P). Two separated spans of text, each of about 70 complete and 70 vestigial lines, could be read (for accounts of P's successive transcriptions and gradual physical deterioration see Diggle 33–4, Kannicht [bibl. above] 2). The new texts suggested that the motivation for Phaethon's drive was unexpectedly complex, and that tragic conflict continued after his death. Goethe's enthusiasm for them (p. 203 below) fired immediate and lasting interest among German-speaking scholars, an impulse strengthened when in 1907 a Berlin papyrus (P. Berl. 9771, 3rd/2nd C. B.C.: symbol Π) from a Euripidean anthology supplemented and overlapped P in the Parodos, enabling its nearly complete reconstruction (lines 63–101; *Cresph.* F 448a has a similar overlap). Then in 1962 came a small but helpful fragment from a narrative hypothesis (P. Oxy. 2455 fr. 14). The earliest surviving illustrations of the myth are late (like most of the mythographic *testimonia*); all are Roman wall-paintings and sarcophagi of the 1st–3rd C. A.D., and all are too distantly and uncertainly derivative to aid reconstruction of the play.

Wilamowitz (1883), Weil (1889), Lesky (1932) and Webster (1967) published the most important studies before Diggle produced his authoritative annotated edition (1970; to be supplemented from Kannicht's important review of 1972). Reckford (1972) has offered the only general essay subsequent to Diggle.

Outline of the action. The scene is the palace of Merops King of Ethiopia, at the eastern edge of the world bounded by the river Oceanus (109), close to the house and stables from which Helios the sun god daily drives his chariot across the heaven (1–7, 61; cf. Hypoth. 8–9). Merops is married to Clymene, daughter of Oceanus (Hypoth. 4; 281); he believes Phaethon, her son from a premarital union with Helios (45), to be his own (102–3, 117 etc.), for she has not told Merops the truth (Hypoth. 3–4, cf. 216, 275–83) — nor told the youth himself, perhaps not until the mutilated Prologue scene (45–53, cf. Hypoth. 5–6). The time is the dawn of the day (63–4) when Merops will marry Phaethon (60, 95–102, 106–18) to a goddess (241–4, cf. ?24). But Phaethon distrusts Clymene's news of his true parentage (51–3) and resists marriage (158–9, 164–7, cf. Merops at 120, ?247); he cannot however avoid discussing the marriage with Merops (59– 61), but resolves to go immediately afterwards to Helios's nearby house, to test his mother's truthfulness by using the single promise which Helios gave her at their union; she herself suggests this (45–52, cf. Hypoth. 7–9; 61–2). After the Parodos, a 'dawn song' (63–101) by the Chorus of palace servant girls (54–8), Merops, proclaimed by a herald (103, 109–18), and Phaethon come out for their discussion. The scene is vestigial in P and can only be glimpsed through five book fragments (124–6, 158–67); it seems to be a typical

Euripidean scene of antipathy and failed persuasion (Comm. on 109–57) – even if Phaethon gives token agreement; for Merops later begins the wedding celebrations in his absence (217–8). Between this fragmentary discussion in Epis. 1 and probably the start of Epis. 3, we have only two book fragments. The first is from a messenger speech, which recounts the start of Phaethon's fatal drive (168–77; Epis. 2?). The second is part of Clymene's reaction to Phaethon's death (F 786 = fr. 3 D, her grief for his untended corpse). The speech may have followed quickly upon a simulated thunder-clap when Zeus's lightning bolt hurled Phaethon to his ruin as his wild drive threatened to burn up the world (278–9, cf. Ov. *Met*. 2.210ff.: so e.g. Webster (1967) 226, Aélion 306; the nearness of Helios's stables to Merops' palace would make the quick sequence credible, cf. p. 200 below).

P resumes at 178 (until 327, the end of our continuous text) with traces of a longish dialogue between Clymene and probably the Chorus; this is already part of Epis. 3. Then, in the first complete lines again of P (214–5), Phaethon's body has been brought to them, still smouldering from the lightning-bolt. Clymene leaves in order to conceal the body from Merops, in the treasure house (216–23), for he is already approaching with a secondary chorus of maiden girls to sing a wedding hymn (218, 227–44). After it, Merops passes a command for Clymene in the palace to begin wedding dances (245–8). A servant reports smoke issuing from the treasure house and Merops hurries to discover its cause, for it threatens the day's joy (251–69). 178 to 269 are full of action, a mid-play precipitation of (further) crisis typical of Euripides; they are the end of Epis. 3. With the scene now empty, the Chorus sing their alarm that Clymene's concealment from Merops of Phaethon's parentage and now of his death may bring her execution (270–83). Merops is heard lamenting Phaethon off-stage (284–8); then P again has only line-beginnings, from a monody of grief by the re-entering Merops (289–310) and the start of his enquiry into Phaethon's death (311–27).

The missing end of the play, perhaps another and fourth Episode running into the Exodos, was probably a dangerous scene between a vengeful Merops and a defensive Clymene (frs. 4 and 1 D = 785, 783a *TrGF*); a god would have interrupted to rescue Clymene, confirming Phaethon's divine parentage and his future after death (fr. 6 D = 782 *TrGF*: on Hypoth. 16 see the Comm.).

Other fragments and ascriptions. Frs. 2 and 5 D = 783b, 783 *TrGF* are lexicographic and come without dramatic context. Other fragments sometimes attributed: 971 *TrGF* /1096 M (= 194–5 ed. Volmer), 'a young man quenched in heaven like a falling star', named for Eur. by Plut. *Mor*. 416e, 1090c and assigned to *Pha*. by S. Rau (?Messenger: Webster [1967] 226); 982 *TrGF* /1099 M (= 199 Volmer), 'many are killed by the thunderbolt's bloodless blast', named for Eur. by Plut. *Mor*. 666c (unattrib. in Theon Smyrn. p. 47.24 Hiller, with 'wound' for 'blast') and assigned to *Pha*. by S. Rau, cf. Wilamowitz 121. 971 is rejected, 982 left as unverifiable by

Diggle p. 176; *TrGF* omits both from *Pha.* F 896 *TrGF*/1219 M, about Aethiops one of the Sun's horses (cf. *Pha.* 175, a horse Sirius), is attributed to Eur. by Athenaeus 11.12, 465b and to *Pha.* by Matthiae, cf. Blass 17, Webster (1967) 226; rejected by Diggle p. 138 n. 2 and in *TrGF*. See also Comm. on 158–9.

Myth The only extant references earlier than Euripides are brief or fragmentary, in Hesiod or Aeschylus. The play left little contemporary mark (Calder, 1972) and there are very few allusions to Phaethon in the following century or two (e.g. Pl. *Tim.* 22c). Scholars have therefore tried to reassemble both the mythic background and Euripides' own version from much later sources, chiefly Ovid, Hyginus and Nonnus: all the evidence adduced, and modern literature, esp. Knaack's two long treatments, are reviewed by Diggle pp. 1–32, 180–204; cf. della Corte 76–81, Aélion 303–5, 308–9.

Hes. *Theog.* 984–9 has Eos the Dawn as Phaethon's mother and mortal Cephalus as his father; the beautiful youth is abducted by Aphrodite and made divine as her temple keeper. Hes. fr. 311 however has him as son of Helios and Clymene; he abuses his father's chariot and is felled to earth by Zeus near the river Eridanus (Italian Po), where his sisters the Heliades shed tears which turn to amber while they themselves turn into poplar trees; but fr. 311 is an unconfident reconstruction from the narratives in Hyginus and the Aratus scholia (West on *Theog.* 991 is more confident than Diggle 15–27 and e.g. della Corte 76, Aélion 303). Aeschylus's *Heliades* (F 68–73a) dealt at least with that ending of the story (reflected in Eur. *Hipp.* 737–41: see esp. Burelli 131–9); it is a reasonable guess that such an ending followed the Heliades' aid to their half-brother Phaethon in yoking their father's chariot, for which all were punished (see esp. Aélion 310).

Wilamowitz (1883, 1913) elaborated an influential view that Euripides modelled upon Hes. *Theog.* a strong role for Aphrodite as Phaethon's intended bride and as the guarantor of his immortality as a morning star, and that he borrowed from elsewhere the story of the fatal chariot drive. This theory impressed Lesky 1, 12 and, despite doubt by e.g. Pickard-Cambridge 143, also Webster (1967) 228–9 and (1972) 628–9; cf. Reckford 406, 413 etc. seeing the goddess as a 'symbolic' bride. Webster and Reckford resisted Diggle when he forcefully revived Weil's contention of 1889 that a daughter of Helios was the intended bride: Diggle 156–60 has been supported by Kamerbeek 208, van Looy 546–7, Kannicht 9, Aélion 311; Lloyd-Jones supported his rejection of Wilamowitz. All logic indeed disqualifies Aphrodite, despite Hesiod's reference to her affection for Phaethon She is a great, not a minor, goddess. No later poet could add another marriage to her famously cuckolded one with Hephaestus in Homer, *Od.* 8. 266ff., even in the play's near-fairy-tale setting (pp. 200–1 below). Mortal Merops could not 'arrange' either an actual or even a token marriage of a youth to her (despite Schmid 600). As husband himself of a god's daughter, however, Merops might reasonably claim marriage for his son to a daughter of his divine neighbour Helios.

Diggle's disconnection of Euripides' plot from Hes. *Theog.* has raised doubt (e.g. Lloyd-Jones 341–3); Hesiod indeed mentions only Phaethon's abduction by Aphrodite, not his marriage. Most critics accept that Phaethon's marriage at least is Euripides' innovation (e.g. van Looy 547, Kannicht 3), if not also (Aélion 310) the secrecy of Clymene's union with Helios and the entire role of Merops. With these elements Euripides created opportunity for wider and more sympathetic characterization in a young man who was otherwise only the victim of his own folly, and in his family.

Themes and characters. Phaethon's fall has been seen as essentially tragic: youth destroyed by its presumption (Goethe first, cf. Lesky 24 'even a god must suffer'). This is too simple. The disaster follows Clymene's revelation to him of his true identity, probably to allay his own fear to marry above him (Goethe again, cf. e.g. Lesky 5, Pohlenz I.291, Kannicht 5f.) — a fear consistent with his distrust of his mother and his immediate need to confirm her veracity. Our fragments contain no hint he might abuse his father's promise, so that the fatal drive may have been shown as no more than a straightforward test of Clymene's claim, or both that and a foolish demand. Barigazzi 97–105 uses the treatment of Phaethon by Plut. *Mor.* 498a (see App. on 159) and elsewhere to suggest that Euripides presented him as an adventurer whose own folly and the implicitly irrational course of fortune combined to destroy him. Two places in the text are said to suggest that he was temperamentally hostile to marriage (147, 158–9: Lesky 10, taken up by Webster (1967) 224; Kannicht 5: Reckford 423 — but rejected by Pohlenz II.123 as contradicting his urgent reason to confirm his parentage); then he is seen as a kind of Hippolytus figure, perhaps devoted to athleticism (see Comm. on F 785 *TrGF* = fr. 4 D) and credibly attracted by the challenge of his father's chariot.

When we do not know cause or motive, it is hard to estimate the tragedy, but we do know the approximate proportions of the play: Euripides puts the fall early, both preparing it and continuing its effects amid irony when he gives all three main persons natural desires and behaviour which work together to ruin them all. They are blindly or half-consciously at cross-purposes, not least in their incompletely revealed relationships (cf. Webster [1967] 232; Reckford 409–11; p. 200 below). The setting of the play at the border between divine and human is significant for the action's credible development (pp. 200–1), but the semi-divine Clymene and a Phaethon unconfident of his divine parentage join the mortal Merops in an action almost wholly human in expression and experience: doubt, distrust, concealment, ambition, determination, then grief and threatened retaliation; and into this action the truly divine twice enters, with the drive across the heaven and finally the rescuing and prophetic god. (Our fragments contain nothing to suggest any malignant divine intention as in *Hipp.* and *HF.*) Whatever the full anxieties of Clymene and Phaethon, Merops is humanly ambitious for his son's high marriage (106–8, 240–4, 269), but wants also to use it to secure his kingdom's future by sharing it in his old age (59–61, 136) with an heir thus connected (124–6, cf. Phaethon at 164–7). His likely retaliation upon Clymene may have been shown as angry disappointment of his hopes and trust, rather than a natural and tyrannous brutality, however wilful he is in forcing the marriage (contrast e.g. Minos's retaliation upon Pasiphae at *Cret.* F 472e.46–7, and compare Theseus's anger against Hippolytus, *Hipp.* 885ff.); and such contrived final tensions are characteristic of Euripides.

Some of the play's motifs and their development sit a little uneasily amid irony, tragedy, pathos and melodrama. They can be matched in whole or part from *Hipp.* and *Ion*, as Reckford argues, putting *Pha.* mid-way between them in both style and date. The comparisons illustrate at least the dramaturgy of *Pha.*, while they do not guide us to a convincing appreciation of its tone and direction overall (the difficulty is notorious for *Ion* itself).[1] *Hipp.* is unequivocally tragic; Reckford 413, 431–2 notes how *Pha.* similarly presents the yoke of marriage as destructive and (423) that in both plays the young man is divinely destroyed in a chariot drive. *Hipp.* has the unsuccessfully secretive Phaedra, but she dies both as a victim of her own failure and of a goddess's enmity against Hippolytus; Clymene's secrecy recoils on her too, like that of Creusa in *Ion* or Pasiphae in *Cret.*, but all three survive, with the aid of gods. Clymene suffers her real loss, her son, before her own danger appears, again like Creusa in *Ion*: and like Creusa with Apollo she at first despairs bitterly of Helios the father of her child. Phaedra's early death in *Hipp.*, like Phaethon's here, precipitates further tension. Such comparisons can be extended but do not satisfy: they may show yet again how inventively Euripides reused elements of plot and character, but we need the whole of *Pha.* to appreciate their fresh and combined interaction.

Dramaturgy: the location. In excerpting 1–5 from the Prologue Strabo 1. 2.27 noted that the nearness of Helios's stables to Ethiopian Merops's palace 'is woven into the whole play'. The geographer's literary observation illuminates both its conceptual level and its dramaturgy. Ethiopia in the 5th C. B.C. denoted

---

[1] See K. H. Lee, 'When is a Tragedy not a Tragedy?', *Arts* (Univ. of Sydney) 16 (1992–3), 70–88 and 'Shifts of Mood and Concepts of Time in Euripides' *Ion*' in M. S. Silk (ed.), *Tragedy and the Tragic* (Oxford, 1996), 85–118 (with response by W. G. Arnott).

any area S. of Egypt or in the direction of India.[2] Thus the action is at the edge of the human world and half beyond human experience ('fairy-tale' Pickard-Cambridge 143, cf. e.g. Schmid 603), however human in fact both motive and behaviour are (above, pp. 199–200). Gods and mortals live together or as neighbours (236–44 are the only place in the fragments where family relations between god and man are explicitly remarked; elsewhere they are matter-of-fact, e.g. 49–52, 61). When Phaethon is unconfident of his divine parentage, he has only a short journey to confirm it, for his father is his next neighbour (his fear of being burned by Helios, 49, is Euripides' transparent anticipation of the catastrophe). When the chariot drive takes the action into the heaven, the nearness of its start in Helios's stables to Phaethon's home is again dramatically significant, so that Zeus's lightning-bolt may be heard and Phaethon fall in ruin for his body to be brought quickly back (p. 197 above). This speed causes immediate panic (216–21) and danger for his mother there (275–83, 309), but she is still close enough to her father Oceanus's house for the Chorus to urge her to flee to it (282).

1–62, Prologue. The Prologue speech (1–7, book fragments; rest missing) was most probably given to Clymene. Aphrodite is named as its speaker by those who think she was the intended bride (p. 198 above), or had a determinative or even vengeful role (as in *Hipp.*: here, to punish Helios the Sun for betraying her adultery with Hephaestus: so e.g. Webster [1967] 221, 231, cf. [1972] 628). Aélion 305 declared identification impossible. The Prologue scene (8–62, start missing) then developed between Clymene and Phaethon after his entry: so e.g. Schmid 600, Diggle, Kannicht 4.

63–101. For the significance of a 'dawn song' as Parodos see the Comm.

168–77. The *messenger* is identified by Lesky 2 with Phaethon's Tutor whom Merops interrogates after his death (see on 311ff. below). Such a long-standing companion might well accompany the youth when he went to Helios's palace. This identification is followed by Diggle 41, della Corte 79, Kannicht 8. Thus a mortal who has watched from the ground reports words and actions apparently in the heaven, and Euripides is overriding literal implausibility for the sake of vivid description and empathy — exactly the reason for Longinus's quotation of 168–77 (see Comm.; the same overriding perhaps occurred when the messenger described Bellerophon's fall from Pegasus: see p. 100). Those who insist on a divine (or more than mortal) messenger, e.g. Wilamowitz 120, Webster (1967) 226, name one of Helios's daughters, mythological mourners of their half-brother Phaethon (p. 198 above).

217–8, 245–8, the wedding celebrations. Merops begins the wedding in his son the groom's absence with a hymn sung by maiden girls; for a single hymn by a secondary chorus see on *Staging* below. This rite belongs properly to

---

[2] See A. Lesky, *Hermes* 87 [1959], 27–38 = *Ges.Schr.* 410–21.

the household of the bride (227–44; see Comm.). This irregularity is dictated by dramatic need and effect: Merops's happiness is at once overtaken by discovery of the groom's death; such contrast is seen as a mode of the play by e.g. Webster (1967) 232, Kannicht 9, Aélion 311. Also, if the bride is a goddess, Merops must begin any mortal celebration before the groom leaves his home to fetch her: the divine bride is to live with a mortal future king as Clymene already lives with Merops. (So Thetis weds mortal Peleus in his house, *And.* 17–20, Hom. *Il.* 18.433 etc.) The fragments do not show the parting of Merops and Phaethon after their discussion, but Merops was presumably not told by Phaethon of his intended immediate journey.

311ff.: the Tutor. The person summoned by Merops (to explain Phaethon's death?) was given by the corrector of ms. P an abbreviated name, representing either 'Nurse' or 'Tutor', and is masculine in the Greek play-text at 311, perhaps also 323; cf. 308–9. Lesky 2, following von Arnim and followed by Diggle 171–2, identified him as Phaethon's Tutor and gave him also the role of the messenger (see above on 168–77). For such male 'nurses', tutors to a family's son and heir, cf. e.g. *Med.* 53, *El.* 16; for such tutors at Athens e.g. Garland, *Life* 122–4. Others, e.g. Webster (1972) 629, think that the character-identification must be interpreted as a female nurse, here Clymene's, and adduce the common role in Tragedy of such presumed sharers of their mistresses' secrets, e.g. *Hipp.* 267ff., *Cret.* F 472e.47.

The ending. Merops's attempted retaliation upon Clymene gives a two-part dramaturgy, with a mid-play catastrophe, like *Hipp., Hec.* or *HF*, all with fresh tragedy or its danger. Kannicht 9 saw such a scene as the play's climax — very probable, if Merops and Clymene had more substantial roles than the fragments themselves suggest. Clymene rescued by a god from human punishment resembles Theonoe at *Hel.* 1642, cf. *IT* 1435, *Or.* 1625 — and Creusa in *Ion* (cf. p. 200 above). Which god? Helios/Apollo seems most likely, to save the mother of his son and to vindicate himself (so e.g. Webster [1967], 230), unless he acted through another god, as through Athena at *Ion* 1557–8. Aphrodite might appear if she was as prominent in the play as has been suggested (Wilamowitz I.146, Lesky 3; West on Hes. *Theog.* 991 thinks of her giving directions for Phaethon's body to be put in her temple). Oceanus has also been suggested (to save his daughter: Webster also, cf. Diggle 44). This question remains unanswerable.

Staging. Some moments call for comment. At 54 Phaethon describes the Chorus as already entering from the palace, so that when he and Clymene go into it together at 62, there is no 'collision' at the door: see Diggle 94–5 and Kannicht 5 against Hourmouziades 22f. and Webster (1972) 628 who find the stage movements here 'awkward'. At 103 there is a theatrically impressive triple entry of

Merops, herald and Phaethon; it portends the significance of the imminent marriage and the Chorus announce the entry with untypically elevated language, 103–8 (see Taplin [1977], 241, 393), before the herald's own metrically distinctive proclamation, 109–16 (see Comm.). At 214ff. Phaethon's body is assumed to have been brought on stage earlier (where our text is defective) like any corpse whose physical presence is to focus the meaning and consequence of its death, e.g. Ajax in Sophocles, Polydorus at *Hec.* 663; but the body is said to be smoking. Any on-stage visual effect was unlikely, so that either there was a mere pretence of smoke, or the 'smoking' body was off-stage like Semele's smoking tomb at *Bacc.* 6 or Capaneus's pyre at *Supp.* 1071. At 218 Clymene sees Merops approach with the wedding chorus; they are coming by one of the theatre's side entrances, so that Clymene avoids them by entering the stage building at 226 (at 245–6 Merops assumes her to be inside the palace). They form a secondary chorus and their song starts at 227 without further announcement; when they finish at 244 Merops bids a servant take them into the palace. His commands to this man finish only at 250–1, when another servant (see Comm. on 245) brings out urgent news. The main chorus meanwhile was presumably motionless: see Webster (1967), 227; Diggle 150; Taplin (1977) 376. Other secondary choruses perform in the presence of the main Chorus at e.g. *Supp.* 1123ff., Aesch. *Eum.* 1132ff.: see Taplin (1977) 235–7, cf. Barrett on *Hipp.* 58–71.

Date. The only sure indication is the incidence of metrical resolution in the dialogue trimeters. Diggle 47–9 and Cropp–Fick 87, cf. 22, 70, agree upon 420 B.C. or soon afterwards; cf. Reckford 427ff.. Webster (1967) 5 had used the same criterion to suggest 415–409 and (220 n. 68) found confirmation in the content and metrical style of the Parodos; the latter wholly subjective criterion had brought Kranz, *Stasimon* 196, 306 to suggest 430 or a little later.

Other dramatisations; influence. For Aeschylus's earlier *Heliades* see p. 198 above. Only one other play title is certainly known, Theodorides' *Phaethon* of 363 B.C. (*TrGF* I 78a), but (JD) an Apulian crater of c. 360–350 has a scene with named characters Merops, Clymene and Melanippus (*TrGF* adesp. F 5h, cf. Trendall–Webster III.5.5). Schol. Hom. *Od.* 17.208 attributes to 'Tragedy' a version of the story which may be an uncritical combination of Aeschylus, Euripides and others: cf. Aélion 305. Our evidence for a dramatic tradition is thus scrappy, as also for a literary one until later centuries (see p. 198 above), despite the statement in Diod. Sic. 5.23.2 (1ˢᵗ C. B.C.) that the story was 'told by many poets and historians'. Ovid and Nonnus (see bibl.) stand out: see Lesky 22–4, Aélion 308–10 and esp. Diggle 205–20. Ovid above all inspired the imagination of writers and artists in the Renaissance and later: see the copious listing in *OGCMA* II.888–92. The recovery of the first major fragments in 1820 moved Goethe to translate, reconstruct and then imitate the play (p. 196 above): see Wilamowitz I.111 etc., Schmid 836, Lesky 24, Kannicht 4 n. 4.

ΦΑΕΘΩΝ

test. ii **Hypothesis** p. 53 D

an uncertain number of lines missing from the start

δ[....]σης· τ[*?fifteen letters* Μέ-]   1

ροπι δὲ μετα[*?sixteen letters* ἐγέν-]

νησεν· πάντων δὲ [π]α[τ]έρα ἔφη[σε(ν)] τ[ὸν]

κατὰ νόμους συ[νοικ]οῦντα εἶναι[·] γε-

νηθέντι δ' ἐν ἡλικίαι τῶι Φαέθοντι   5

τὴν ἀλήθειαν ἐξέφηνεν· ἀπιστοῦντι

δὲ ὥς ἐστιν Ἡλ[ί]ου παῖς προσέταξεν

ἐ[λ]θεῖν πρὸς τὰς ἱπ[ποστ]άσεις τοῦ θεο[ῦ]

γει]τνιώσας· καὶ δῶρ[ο]ν αἰτήσασθα[ι ὃ]

ἂν ἐθελ]ήση[ι]· [π]αραγενη{ι}θεὶς δὲ κ[ ]   10

three lines with only a few letters legible,   11–13

then about twenty-two lines missing,

then three lines with only a very few letters legible;   14–16

15 *begins* θ[ήσε]σθαι[, 16 *begins* ἐθ]έσπισ[εν

Prologue speech (Clymene; start missing):

771 Κλυμένη   ... Μέροπι τῆσδ' ἄνακτι γῆς,   1–5

ἣν ἐκ τεθρίππων ἁρμάτων πρώτην χθόνα

Ἥλιος ἀνίσχων χρυσέαι βάλλει φλογί.

καλοῦσι δ' αὐτὴν γείτονες μελάμβροτοι

Ἔω φαεννὰς Ἡλίου θ' ἱπποστάσεις.   5

a short gap in the speech

772 θερμὴ δ' ἄνακτος φλὸξ ὑπερτέλλουσα γῆς   6–7

καίει τὰ πόρσω, τἀγγύθεν δ' εὔκρατ' ἔχει.

*the end of the speech and the start of the following
asymmetrical dialogue between Clymene and the newly
entering Phaethon are lost*

test. ii (1086 M, p. 53 D) **Hypothesis** P. Oxy. 2455 fr. 14, cols. xv–xvi ed. Turner (1962), re-
ed. W. Luppe, *Phil.* 127 (1983), 135–9, cf. *ZPE* 52 (1983), 43–4. Supplements by Turner except
where stated   2 μετὰ [ταῦτα (Turner) γαμηθεῖσα R. Keydell, *Hermes* 102 (1974), 117

PHAETHON

test. ii   **Hypothesis**

... ; to Merops, [   ] after [   ], she *bore* [   ]; she said
that the man she was living with legally was *the father* of them
all. Once Phaethon had come of age,[5] she revealed the truth to him.
When he disbelieved he was the son of Helios, she instructed him
to go to the god's *stables* which were in the neighbourhood and to
ask for *<any>* gift *he <wished>*; once there, he[[10]

15 *would make* ...   16 *prophesied* ...

From the beginning of Clymene's Prologue speech:

771 *Clymene*   ... (I was given in marriage) to Merops the lord of   1–5
this land, which is the first earth that Helios at his rising
strikes with his golden flame from his four-horsed chariot.
The neighbouring black peoples call it the bright stables
of Eos and Helios.

a short gap in the speech

772   The god's hot flame as it rises above the earth burns the   6–7
distant parts but keeps those nearby temperate.

end of speech missing

μετ'α[ὐτὸν ?δύο θυγατέρας Luppe, *Phil.*   ἐγέν]νησεν Diggle   3 πάντως Keydell   ἔφη[σεν]
Luppe, *Phil.*   4 συ[νοικ]οῦντα edd., incl. Luppe, *Phil.* συ[μβι]οῦντα Turner   9–10 ὃ |
ἂν ἐθελ]ήσῃ[ι] Diggle   14–16 begin col. xvi acc. to Turner; new col. questioned by Luppe,
Phil., who in *ZPE* attributes 14–16 to Hypoth. *Hypsipyle*   15 θ[ήσε]σθαι Luppe, *ZPE*

Note. The continuous line numbering of the Greek text is that of Diggle's edition ('D'). For
the principal text witnesses (see Introd., pp. 195–6) this App. draws by permission on the information given in that of Diggle and uses the same symbols: **P** = Paris, Greek ms. 107B ('Claromontanus', 5th/6th C. A.D.; has lines 8–157, 178–327) ed. G. Burges, *CJ* 22 (1820), 156–71, then G.
Hermann (1821) = *Opuscula* III (1828), 1–21; see esp. Blass (bibl. in Introd. above).   **C** =
correcting hand in P.   **Π** = P. Berl. 9771 (3rd/2nd C. B.C.; has lines 63–97) ed. Wilamowitz, *BKT*
V.2 (1907), 79–84.   **[P]**, **[Π]** = P, Π defective or illegible

771/1–5 D (1087a M)   Strabo 1.2.27 'Eur. in *Pha.* says that Clymene was given ...'
4 γείτονες] οὐγγενεῖς F.W. Schmidt   5 φαεννὰς Meineke -ὰν or -ᾶς Strabo   772/6–7 D
(1088a, b M)   6 Stob. 1.25.6, attrib. Eur. *Pha.*   7 Vitruv. 9.1.13, attrib. Eur. *Pha.*   6–7 joined as
one fr. by Barnes   7 τάγγύθεν δ' εὔκρατ' restored in Vitruv.'s (garbled Greek) quotation, on
basis of his Latin paraphrase, by Valckenaer

772a *damaged ends of thirty-seven dialogue trimeters,* 8–44
in which the following final words seem certain
(‖ marks the end of a speech):

8	]αγας θεῶν	26	θεούς
9	ἐ]κπέμπων πατήρ ‖	27	ἐ]λπίσιν
10	]εις λέχος	30	φιλεῖ
13	λέχη ‖	31	γάμοι
16	ὁρῶ	35	]θων ὅτου
19	γα]μηλίους	38	]νέπουσά μοι
20	πατρί	39	πατρός
22	πατήρ ‖	41	φίλον ‖
24	θεᾶς λέχη	42	τ]ὰ φίλτατα·
25	]αεὶ λέγεις		

four dialogue trimeters missing

773 (Κλ.) μνησθεὶς ὅ μοί ποτ᾽ εἶφ᾽ ὅτ᾽ ἠυνάσθη θεὸς 45–120

αἰτοῦ τί χρήιζεις ἕν· πέρα γὰρ οὐ θέμις
λαβεῖν σε· κἂν μὲν τυγχάνηις [ὅπερ θέλεις]
θεοῦ πέφυκας· εἰ δὲ μή, ψευδὴς ἐγώ.
Φαέθων πῶς οὖν πρόσειμι δῶμα θερμὸν Ἡλίου;
Κλ.   κείνωι μελήσει σῶμα μὴ βλάπτειν τὸ σόν. 50
Φα.   εἴπερ πατὴρ πέφυκεν, οὐ κακῶς λέγεις.
Κλ.   σάφ᾽ ἴσθι· πεύσηι δ᾽ αὐτὸ τῶι χρόνωι σαφῶς.
Φα.   ἀρκεῖ· πέποιθα γάρ σε μὴ ψευδῆ λέγειν.

ἀλλ᾽ ἔρπ᾽ ἐς οἴκους· καὶ γὰρ αἵδ᾽ ἔξω δόμων
δμωιαὶ περῶσιν αἳ πατρὸς κατὰ σταθμὰ 55
σαίρουσι δῶμα καὶ δόμων κειμήλια
καθ᾽ ἡμέραν φοιβῶσι κἀπιχωρίοις
ὀσμαῖσι θυμιῶσιν εἰσόδους δόμων.
ὅταν δ᾽ ὕπνον γεραιὸς ἐκλιπὼν πατὴρ
πύλας ἀμείψηι καὶ λόγους γάμων πέρι 60
λέξηι πρὸς ἡμᾶς, Ἡλίου μολὼν δόμους
τοὺς σοὺς ἐλέγξω, μῆτερ, εἰ σαφεῖς λόγοι.

772a/**8–44** D (1089 M) P fol. 1 *verso*, col. 1, marking speech-ends with dicolon (:) after 9, ?11, 13,
17, 22, ?23, 36, 41   8 συναλλ]αγὰς θεῶν Blass   19 Wecklein   24 θεας or θεαι Diggle

772a *line-ends from the latter part of the ensuing asymmetrical* 8–44
dialogue between Clymene and the newly entering Phaethon:

8	of the gods	26	*gods*
9	father sending out	27	(?in) hopes
10	marriage	30	*he loves*
13	marriage	31	marriage
16	I see	35	whose
19	of marriage	38	(you) *telling* me
20	(to/for) father	39	(of/from) father
22	father	41	dear
24	marriage *to a goddess*	42	*those* dearest to me
25	you are always saying		

four lines missing

773 (*Cly.*) Remind the god of what he once said to me when he lay 45–120
with me,[45] and request one thing you desire; more than that
you may not rightly get. If you succeed in <*your wish*>,
you are the god's son: if you do not, I lie.

Phaethon. How then shall I approach the god's house, with its heat?

Cly. He will take care not to harm you bodily.[50]

Pha. If he is indeed my father, what you say cannot be wrong.

Cly. Be certain of it; you will learn it as certainty in time.

Pha. Enough, thank you: I believe you are telling no lie.

But come into the house, for here are the slave girls
coming out from it, who sweep the house *in* my father's
palace;[55] they cleanse the house's laid-up things daily and
fume the house-entrances with native scents. When my old
father abandons sleep and crosses through the doors for
words with us about the marriage,[60] I will go to Helios's
house and test if what you say, mother, is certain.

38 ἐν]νέπουσα Blass   42 τ]ὰ (Blass) φίλτατα· C πράγματα P   **773/45–120 D** (1089 M)
45–81 D = P fol. 1 *verso*, col. ii   45 (Κλ.) Nauck   47 [ὅπερ θέλεις] (cf. Hypoth. 10) or (by
letter) [ὅσων ἐρᾶις Diggle   49 Φα. C, marking changes of speaker until 53   55 κατὰ
σταθμὰ Diggle κατασταθμ . . C -στομ . . . . P

Choral Parodos:

ΧΟΡΟΣ ἤδη μὲν ἀρτιφανὴς   στρ. α
        Ἀὼς ἱ[ππεύει] κατὰ γᾶν,
        ὑπὲρ δ' ἐμᾶς κεφαλᾶς   65
        Πλειά[δων πέφευγε χορός],
        μέλπει δὲ δένδρεσι λε-
        πτὰν ἀηδὼν ἁρμονίαν
        ὀρθρευομένα γόοις
        Ἴτυν Ἴτυν πολύθρηνον.   70

        σύριγγας δ' οὐριβάται   ἀντ. α
        κινοῦσιν ποιμνᾶν ἐλάται,
        ἔγρονται δ' εἰς βοτάναν
        ξανθᾶν πώλων συζυγίαι·
        ἤδη δ' εἰς ἔργα κυνα-   75
        γοὶ στείχουσιν θηροφόνοι,
        παγαῖς τ' ἐπ' Ὠκεανοῦ
        μελιβόας κύκνος ἀχεῖ.

        ἄκατοι δ' ἀνάγονται ὑπ' εἰρεσίας   στρ. β
        ἀνέμων τ' εὐαέσσιν ῥοθίοις,   80
        ἀνὰ δ' ἱστία ν[αῦται] ἀειράμενοι
        ἰαχοῦσιν '["Αγ', ὦ] πότνι' αὔρ[α],
        [ἡμᾶς ὑπ'] ἀκύμονι πομπᾶι
        σιγώντων ἀνέμων
        [ποτὶ τέκνα] τε καὶ φιλίας ἀλόχους.'   85
        σινδὼν δὲ πρότονον ἐπὶ μέσον πελάζει.

        τὰ μὲν οὖν ἑτέροισι μέριμνα πέλει,   ἀντ. β
        κόσμον δ' ὑμεναίων δεσποσύνων
        ἐμὲ καὶ τὸ δίκαιον ἄγει καὶ ἔρως
        ὑμνεῖν· δμωσὶν γὰρ ἀνάκτων   90
        εὐαμερίαι προσιοῦσαι
        μολπᾶι θάρσος ἄγουσ'
        ἐπιχάρματά τ'· εἰ δὲ τύχα τι τέκοι,
        βαρὺν βαρεῖα φόβον ἔπεμψεν οἴκοις.

63–97 Π, with heading εμ Φαε[θοντι] 'in *Phaethon*'; in these lines Π has many gaps and P is
often illegible, but both fail only in 64, 66, 81–3, 85: full details in Diggle   64 Ἀὼς Morel εως P
εω[ς] Π   ἱ[ππεύει] Wilamowitz [P]   καταγαν supplied by C: [Π]   66 (e.g.) Diggle Πλειὰ[ς

Clymene and Phaethon go in. The Chorus, entering, have now reached the orchestra

Chorus. Already the newly appearing Dawn <rides> over the earth, and above my head[65] the Pleiads' <choir has fled>; in the trees the nightingale sings its subtle harmony, awake at sunrise to grieve for 'Itys, Itys' the much lamented.[70]

Drovers who walk the mountains with their flocks stir their pipes, teams of chestnut mares are roused for pasture; already huntsmen with their dogs[75] are going to their work, to kill their prey; the tuneful swan is sounding on Oceanus's streams.

Vessels put out under oar and with the winds' favouring bluster;[80] crewmen after they raise the sails cry '<Bring us>, mistress breeze, <in> smooth voyage and quiet winds <to> our beloved wives and <children>';[85] and the canvas comes close to the forestay at its middle.

Those things are others' concern; my own right and my desire bring me to sing in honour of my master's wedding. Good times approaching for their lords[90] bring confidence and joy to slaves, to their song; but if ever heavy fortune gives birth to something, it sends heavy fear upon the house.

ἐκλείπει σκοτία] Wilamowitz [P]   72 ποιμναν Π -ας P   74 ξανθαν ΠP -ων C 75 κυναγων Π   76 θ[ηροφονοι στ]ειχουσι[Π   79 ἄκατοι Dobree, Matthiae ακοντοι P [Π] ειρεσιας P (-ας C) -αις Π   80 εὐαέσσιν Bothe ευαεσιν C ευαισιν P [Π]   81 only αν[and]αειραμενοι Π, only ανα δ ιστια γ[P ν[αῦται] Krantz   82 ἀειράμενοι —85 ἀλόχους missing in P   82 ἰαχοῦσιν Diggle αχεουσιν Π ἀχοῦσιν Wilamowitz   ["Αγ', ὦ], with 83 [ἡμᾶς σὺν] (Krantz), Lloyd-Jones ["Επου]... 83 [ἡμῖν ὑπ'] Austin (ὑπ' Volmer)   85 Krantz 86–120 D = P fol. i recto, col. i   87 πελει or μελει P τα μ[ε]ν ουν ετερων ετε[ροισι μελει Π (suppl. Rubensohn)   88 κόσμον δ' ὑμεναίων Hartung κοσμειν — υμεναιων δε Π and (no dash) P   91 εὐαμερίαι M. Schmidt ε]υημεροι Π ευαμεροι C ειαμ- P   92 θαρσ[ος Π θρασος P   ἄγουσ' Burges αιους P [Π]   93 ἐπιχαρμα]τα τε Π επιχαρματα P   τεκοι C or P τεκηι Π

210　EURIPIDES

ὁρίζεται δὲ τόδε φάος γάμων τέλει,　　　　ἐπωιδ.
τὸ δή ποτ' εὐχαῖς ἐγὼ　　　　　　　　　　96
λισσομένα προσέβαν ὑμέναιον ἀεῖσαι
φίλον φίλων δεσποτᾶν·
θεὸς ἔδωκε, χρόνος ἔκρανε
λέχος ἐμοῖσιν ἀρχέταις.　　　　　　　　　100
ἴτω τελεία γάμων ἀοιδά.

Episode 1 begins:

ἀλλ' ὅδε γὰρ δὴ βασιλεὺς πρὸ δόμων
κῆρύξ θ' ἱερὸς καὶ παῖς Φαέθων
βαίνουσι τριπλοῦν ζεῦγος, ἔχειν χρὴ
στόμ' ἐν ἡσυχίαι·　　　　　　　　　　　105
περὶ γὰρ μεγάλων γνώμας δείξει
παῖδ' ὑμεναίοις ὁσίοισι θέλων
ζεῦξαι νύμφης τε λεπάδνοις.

(ΚΗΡΥΞ)　'Ωκεανοῦ πεδίων οἰκήτορες,
εὐφαμεῖτ' ὦ　　　　　　　　　　　　110
ἐκτόπιοί τε δόμων ἀπαείρετε·
ὦ ἴτε λαοί.
κηρύσσω †δ' ὁσίαν βασιλήϊον
αὐτῶι δ' αὐδὰν†
εὐτεκνίαν τε γάμοις, ὧν ἔξοδος　　　　115
ἄδ' ἔνεχ' ἥκει,
παιδὸς πατρός τε τῆιδ' ἐν ἡμέραι λέχη
κρᾶναι θελόντων· ἀλλὰ σῖγ' ἔστω λεώς.

ΜΕΡΟΨ *one and a half lines missing, then:*

　　　　　　　　εἰ γὰρ εὖ λέγω　　　　120
then five lines missing

774　*thirty-seven lines with initial letters preserved, including:* 121–57

121　ὧν δ' υ[　　123　ἐν σοὶ ν[
ναῦν τιοι μί' ἄγκυρ' οὐχ ὁμῶς σώιζειν φιλεῖ ̣　124
τῶι τρεῖς ἰαφέντι· προστάτης θ' ἁπλοῦς πόλει ̣　125
σφαλεριός, ὑπὼν δὲ κάλλος οὐ κακὸν πέλει. ̣　126

This day is marked out for the celebration of marriage,[95] the celebration which I begged for long ago in my prayers; I have come forward to sing my dear masters' own wedding hymn. God has willed, time fulfilled, marriage for my rulers.[100] Let the song begin to celebrate the marriage!

Merops and Phaethon enter, attended by a Herald

See, though, the king here before the house, coming with the holy herald and his son Phaethon, all three in company! We must hold our tongues in stillness.[105] He will show his mind on great matters, in his wish to join his son in the holy bonds of matrimony to his bride.

(Herald) Inhabitants of Oceanus's plains, keep holy silence![110] Leave your homes and come out! People there, come! I proclaim †reverence(?) in the name(?) of the king and speech for himself(?)† and fruitfulness for the marriage[115] for which this procession has come out, as son and father wish to fulfil the marriage on this day. Let the people be silent!

Merops begins a long speech to Phaethon; one-and-a-half lines missing, then:

(Merops)   . . . for if I am talking sense . . .   120

five lines missing

774 *the following words and lines are probably all from the same*   121–57
      speech:

121 (of/from) whom . . .   123 (?it rests) with you . . .
Now one anchor does not usually keep a ship safe in the same way   124–6
as the man who lets down three — and a single leader for a city is
unsafe, while a second besides in support is no bad thing.

95 τοδε C τοδ[Π το P τελει Π τελος P 96 ευχαις C ευχαι [Π ευτυχαις P 97 Π ends after λισσο . [101 ιτω C ιω P 104 διπλουν C 107 ὁσίοισι Page ωσφησι P (so read by Bekker, Diggle οισφησι Blass) θείοισι Wecklein θελων C λεγων P 108 τε C δε P 109 (ΚΗΡΥΞ) Hermann 113 θυσίαν Weil δ' ὁρτὰν Lloyd-Jones 114 αὐτῶι δ' Blass αυτω δ' P αἰτῶ δ' Hermann 115 εὐτυχίαν Wilamowitz 118 σιγ C τηδ or τηλ P 119 ΜΕΡΟΨ and end of 120: C [P] **774/121–57** D (1089 M) P fol. i *recto*, col. ii 121 ὦν, δ' υ[C ωνλυ[P 124–6 (= fr. 774 N) Stob. 4.1.3, without lemma ms. A, attached to 4.1.2 (= 160–2 D) mss. SM; separated by Gesner and identified with 124–6 in P by Blass 124 Arsenius 11.96b Leutsch, attrib. Eur. 124 ναυν .( )[P οὐχ ὁμῶς Badham οὐδαμῶς Stob., Arsenius 125 τῶι Burges ὡς Stob. ως P τρεῖς Stob. τριϛ[P 126 σφαλερ[P πέλει Barnes πόλει Stob.

212 EURIPIDES

127 ἰσχὺν ν[142 πεσων[
128 γήμας .[143 ἔχων δ[
129 γάμοις[144 κλέψει[
130 ἄλλος .[145 πολεμ[
131 δώσει[146 κῆδος[
132 νέος δ .[147 δεδοικ[
133 ἥβης .[148 ἔξεις δ' α[
136 γέρων .[149 ὅταν τε[
137 νέαι ν[150 καὶ ζῶν[
138 τοσῶιδ[ε 151 γαμεῖς[
139 δεινον[

*a gap of uncertain length; the following four book
fragments are from the end of the scene between
Merops and Phaethon which began at 119:*

775 (Φα.) ἐλεύθερος δ' ὢν δοῦλός ἐστι τοῦ λέχους,   158-9
πεπραμένον τὸ σῶμα τῆς φερνῆς ἔχων.

775a (784 N)   160-2
(Με.) ἐν τοῖσι μώροις τοῦτ' ἐγὼ κρίνω βροτῶν,
ὅστις πατρῶια παισὶ μὴ φρονοῦσιν εὖ
ἢ καὶ πολίταις παραδίδωσ' ἐξουσίαν.

777 (Φα.) ὡς πανταχοῦ γε πατρὶς ἡ βόσκουσα γῆ.   163

776 (Φα.) δεινόν γε, τοῖς πλουτοῦσι τοῦτο δ' ἔμφυτον,   164-7
σκαιοῖσιν εἶναι· τί ποτε τοῦδ' ἐπαίτιον;
ἆρ' ὄλβος αὐτοῖς ὅτι τυφλὸς συνηρετεῖ
τυφλὰς ἔχουσι τὰς φρένας †καὶ τῆς τύχης†;

130 Diggle ἄλλοις[Blass 148 P has the apostrophe 775/158–9 D (1093 M) Eustath. on
Hom. *Od*. 13.15, attrib. Eur. *Pha*. 159 Plut. *Mor*. 498a, attrib. Eur., context mutilated (Φα.)
Goethe 775a/160–2 D (784 N, 1091 M) Stob. 4.1.2, attrib. Eur. *Pha*. (cf. on 124–6) (Με.) S.
Rau 161 πατρῶια Diggle τῶν πατέρων Stob. 777/163 D (1090 M) Stob. 3.40.2, attrib.
Eur. *Pha*. (Φα.) Goethe 776/164–7 D (1092 M) Stob. 4.31.54, attrib. Eur. *Pha*.; Arsenius

127	power	142	having fallen
128	marrying	143	having
129	(in) marriage	144	will steal
130	another	145	(?) *war*
131	will give	146	anxiety
132	young		(*or* marriage connection)
133	of youth	147	(?you) fear
136	old (? man)	148	and you will have
137	young	149	and when
138	by that much	150	and (?you) living
139	dreadful	151	you will marry

*fragments from this continuing scene between Merops
and Phaethon:*

775 (*Pha.*) Although he is a free man, he is a slave to his marriage   158–9
bed, for he has sold his body for the dowry.

775a (784 N)
(*Mer.*) I judge this among men's follies,[160] if any hands over his   160–2
patrimony to his sons, or especially authority to citizens,
when they are not in their right senses.

777 (*Pha.*) The nourishing earth is a fatherland everywhere!   163

776 (*Pha.*) It's terrible, but this is in the nature of the rich, to be fool-   164–7
ish. Whatever is the cause of this?[165] Is it because wealth
is their blind partner that their wits are blind †and of
fortune†?

Leutsch, attrib. Eur.   (Φα.) Goethe   165 τοῦδ' ἐπαίτιον Wecklein   τοῦδε ταίτιον
Arsenius τοῦτο τ'αἴτιον Stob. τοῦδ' ἔστ' αἴτιον Herwerden   166 ·συνηρετεῖ Meineke
συνηρεφεῖ Stob., Arsenius   167 κοινῆι τύχηι West κὰς τὴν τύχην Collard   sentence
incomplete, Musgrave

a gap covering Stas. 1 and the start of Epis. 2 which contained the messenger speech (perhaps spoken by Phaethon's Tutor); the following book fragment is an excerpt:

779 (Τροφεύς;)

'ἔλα δὲ μήτε Λιβυκὸν αἰθέρ' εἰσβαλὼν   168–77
(κρᾶσιν γὰρ ὑγρὰν οὐκ ἔχων ἀψῖδα σὴν
κάτω διήσει). . . .   170
a short gap
ἵει δ' ἐφ' ἑπτὰ Πλειάδων ἔχων δρόμον.'
τοσαῦτ' ἀκούσας παῖς ἔμαρψεν ἡνίας·
κρούσας δὲ πλευρὰ πτεροφόρων ὀχημάτων
μεθῆκεν, αἱ δ' ἔπταντ' ἐπ' αἰθέρος πτυχάς.
πατὴρ δ' ὄπισθε νῶτα Σειρίου βεβὼς   175
ἵππευε παῖδα νουθετῶν· ''Εκεῖσ' ἔλα,
τῇδε στρέφ' ἅρμα, τῇδε...'

a gap of indeterminate length and content, containing probably the end of Epis. 2, Stas. 2, and the start of Epis. 3. Before the end of Epis. 2:

*786   Κλ.   φίλος δέ μοι   fr. 3 D
ἄλουτος ἐν φάραγξι σήπεται νέκυς.

779a   *damaged ends of thirty-six dialogue trimeters from the start*   178–213
of Episode 3; up to four final syllables are sometimes legible:

178	]ι προθυμίαι	195	πόλις
181	]δυστυχεῖς	196	νόμος
183	χθονός	197	]ς ἐπήινεσα
184	]πλοῦτον δ' ἐμῶι	198	σοφή
187	ἴχνος	199	π]ράγματα
188	]ς ἅπαντ' ἐρῶ	201	ἀμήχανοι
189	]χθονὸς σκότου	202	γὰρ αὖ πλοκή
191	τυ]ραννίδι	205	] ιτοις κακοῖς
193	ἐ]λευθεροι	206	]σκότωι
194	πλούσιον		

779/168–77 D (1094 M) [Longinus], *On The Sublime* 15.3–4 ('Helios on handing the reins to Pha. says [168–70], continuing [171–7]')   (Τροφ.) Lesky, cf. on 317   169 ἀψῖδα σὴν Faber ἀψίδας ἦν Long. ms. P   170 κάτω διήσει (Faber: δίεισι Long. ms. P) def. M.L. West, *BICS* 30 (1983), 77 καταιθαλώσει Kock καίων (Richards) διοίσει Diggle   172 παῖς Long. ms. K,

from the messenger speech, probably in the following Epis. 2:

779 *(Tutor?)* '. . . and as you drive, neither enter the Libyan heaven (for   168–77
as it has no moisture mixed in it, it will let your wheel fall down
through it)¹⁷⁰ . . . *(a short gap)* . . . but direct and hold your course
for the seven Pleiads.' So much the boy heard, and seized the reins;
he struck the winged team on their flanks and let them go, and the
mares flew to the folds of heaven. Behind him rode his father
mounted on Sirius's back¹⁷⁵ and instructing the boy, 'Drive over
there! Turn the chariot this way, this way . . . !'

*a gap covering probably the end of Epis. 2, Stas. 2, and the start
of Epis. 3; before the end of Epis. 2:*

*786 *Cly.* My dear one's corpse is rotting in a ravine, unwashed.   fr. 3 D

*Clymene's fear that Phaethon's body may not be recovered
for funeral.*

779a *words at line-end probably from a dialogue between*   178–213
Clymene and ?Chorus at the start of Episode 3:

178	(in) eagerness	195	city
181	unfortunate	196	law
183	(of/from) the land	197	I approve *(or* I thank you)
184	wealth to/for my	198	wise (woman)
187	track	199	affairs
188	*I shall say everything*	201	difficult *(or* helpless)
189	earth's darkness	202	because trickery *(or*
191	(to/for) tyranny		a lock of hair) moreover
193	free	205	the troubles
194	wealthy	206	(? in) *darkness*

Grotius τίς Long. ms. P   175 ὄπισθε (Manutius: -θεν) νῶτα Long. ms. K ὄπισθεν ὦτα ms. P
175 Σειρίου Lesky σειρίου Long.   176–7 ἔλα,Ι τῆιδε στρέφ' Portus ἐλατῆρα ἔστρεφ'
Long. ms. P   **786/fr. 3 D** (1098 M) Plut. *Mor.* 665c, citing Clymene's words about Pha.
779a/178–213 D (1101 M) P fol. ii *verso*, col. 1   184 Diggle δομῶ (i.e. δόμων) Blass
191 Blass 197 Diggle]σεπηνεσα P 199 Diggle 205 κά]πὶ τοῖς κακοῖς ('and in the face
of the troubles') Page

216 EURIPIDES

207]ποίωι τάφωι   211 νεκροί
209 δι' ἄστεως   212] ιτας τύχας
210 κ]ειμήλιον   213 πειρατέο

six lines missing, then end of a speech by Clymene:

781 (Κλ.) †πυροσθ† 'Ερινὺς ἐν †νεκροις θ ρ νυαι†   214–88
ζώσης δ' ἀνίησ' ἀτμὸν ἐμφανῆ [φλογός].   215
ἀπωλόμην· οὐκ οἴσετ' εἰς δόμους νέκυν;
πόσις πόσις μοι πλησίον γαμηλίους
μολπὰς ἀϋτεῖ παρθένοις ἡγούμενος.
οὐ θᾶσσον; οὐ σταλαγμὸν ἐξομόρξετε,
εἴ πού τίς ἐστιν αἵματος χαμαὶ πεσών;   220
ἐπείγετ' ἤδη, δμωΐδες· κρύψω δέ νιν
ξεστοῖσι θαλάμοις, ἔνθ' ἐμῶι κεῖται πόσει
χρυσός, μόνη δὲ κλῆιθρ' ἐγὼ σφραγίζομαι.
ὦ καλλιφεγγὲς "Ηλι', ὥς μ' ἀπώλεσας
καὶ τόνδ'· 'Απόλλων δ' ἐν βροτοῖς ὀρθῶς καλῆι,   225
ὅστις τὰ σιγῶντ' ὀνόματ' οἶδε δαιμόνων.

Secondary Chorus of Maiden girls:

ΠΑΡΘΕΝΟΙ   'Υμὴν 'Υμήν.   στρ.
τὰν Διὸς οὐρανίαν ἀείδομεν,
τὰν ἐρώτων πότνιαν, τὰν παρθένοις
γαμήλιον 'Αφροδίταν.   230
πότνια, σοὶ τάδ' ἐγὼ νυμφεῖ' ἀείδω,
Κύπρι θεῶν καλλίστα,
τῶι τε νεόζυγι σῶι
πώλωι τὸν ἐν αἰθέρι κρύπτεις,
σῶν γάμων γένναν·   235

781/214–327D (1101 M) 214–50 D = P fol. ii verso, col. ii   214 (Κλ.) Hermann   πυρός τ'
S. Rau πυροῦσσ' Hermann πυρσοῖς Diggle   νεκρῶι Hartung   θ ρ   νυαι P (?-νυται C)
read by Diggle, θερηνυαι by Bekker, Blass θρασύνεται Diggle κεραυνίου Hermann
215 ζώσης δ' Diggle ζωσαηδ P, interpr. as ζῶσ' ἤδ' by edd. [φλογός] S. Rau   217 γαμηλι-
ους or -οις P   218 μολπὰς Hermann -αις P   219 θᾶσσον; οὐ σταλαγμὸν Dobree
θασσεουσομολγον P   221 ἐπείγετ' ἤδη Page επειγετεα   P (-τεαια Bekker, -τεαη Blass)
224–5 Schol. Or. 1388 and (garbled) Macrob. Sat. 1.17.9–10, both attrib. Eur. Pha.   225 ὀρθῶς

207	in what kind of tomb	211	corpses
209	throughout the city	212	fortunes
210	memorial-token (*or* heirloom)	213	*must attempt*

six lines missing, then end of a speech by Clymene:

781 *(Cly.)* . . . a Fury †of ?fire† in †corpses . . .† and sends up a clear   214–88
breath of living <*flame*>.[215] It has destroyed me! (*To her women*)
Carry the body into the house, won't you? My husband, my
husband is almost here, leading the maiden girls in singing the
wedding music. Be quicker, won't you? Wipe up any drops of
blood[220] which may have fallen somewhere on the ground. Hurry
now, you women slaves! I will hide him in the dressed-stone
chamber where my husband's gold is kept but where I alone
command the doors' seal. (*The women begin to remove the body.*)
       O Helios with your lovely light, how you have destroyed me,
and the one here! 'Apollo' you are rightly called among men[225]
where any knows the silent meaning of gods' names!
       (*Clymene enters the palace*)

*A Chorus of Maiden girls enters with Merops from the side,
singing:*

Maiden girls. Hymen, Hymen! We sing to honour Zeus's daughter
in the sky, mistress of loves, wedding-maker for maiden girls,
Aphrodite.[230] Mistress, for you I sing this bridal song, Cypris most
beautiful of gods, and for your boy newly-wed whom you hide in
the heaven, offspring of your marriage;[235] you who will make the

---

Bekker -ος P   Ἀπόλλων εἰκότως (Schol. B: οὕτως εἰ. Schol. MT) κλήιζηι βροτοῖς Schol.
Or.   ὅθεν σ' Ἀπόλλων' ἐμφανῶς κλήιζει βροτός Macrob., whence καὶ τόνδ'· Ἀπόλλων'
ἐν βροτοῖς ⟨σ'⟩ ὀρθῶς καλεῖ ǀ ὅστις κτλ. D. Korzeniewski, *Hermes* 103 (1975), 375
227 ΠΑΡΘΕΝΟΙ Diggle Χο. C   228 ἀείδομεν Dobree ειδομεν P   229 παρθένοις Burges
παρθενοι P   231 νυμφεῖ' (Hermann) ἀείδω Wilamowitz νυμφα   read by Diggle, νυμφια
(or δ) αι by Blass   233 νεόζυγι σῶι Hermann νεοζυγιστω or -ιστω P   234 κρυπτεις read
in P by Bekker, now illegible   235 γένναν Hermann γενεαν P

ἃ τὸν μέγαν   ἀντ.
τᾶσδε πόλεως βασιλῆ νυμφεύσεαι
ἀστερωποῖσιν δόμοισι χρυσέοις
ἀρχὸν φίλον Ἀφροδίτα·
ὧ μάκαρ, ὧ βασιλέως μείζων ἔτ᾽ ὄλβον,   240
ὃς θεᾶι κηδεύσεις
καὶ μόνος ἀθανάτων
γαμβρὸς δι᾽ ἀπείρονα γαῖαν
θνατὸς ὑμνήσηι.

Με. χώρει σὺ καὶ τάσδ᾽ εἰς δόμους ἄγων κόρας   245
γυναῖκ᾽ ἄνωχθι πᾶσι τοῖς κατὰ σταθμὰ
θεοῖς χορεῦσαι κἀγκυκλώσασθαι δόμοις
σεμνοῖσιν ὑμεναίοισιν, Ἑστίας θ᾽ ἕδος,
ἀφ᾽ ἧς γε σώφρων πᾶς τις ἄρχεται θεοῖς
εὐχὰς πο[ιεῖσθαι   250
four lines missing
θεᾶς προσελθεῖν τέμενος ἐξ ἐμῶν δόμων.

ΘΕΡΑΠΩΝ ὧ δέσποτ᾽, ἔστρεψ᾽ ἐκ δόμων ταχὺν πόδα.
οὖ γὰρ σὺ σώιζηι σεμνὰ θησαυρίσματα
χρυσοῦ, δι᾽ ἁρμῶν ἐξαμείβεται πύλης
καπνοῦ μέλαιν᾽ ἄησις ἔνδοθεν στέγης.   255
προσθεὶς πρόσωπον φλόγα μὲν οὐχ ὁρῶ πυρός,
γέμοντα δ᾽ οἶκον μέλανος ἔνδοθεν καπνοῦ.
ἀλλ᾽ ἔσιθ᾽ ἐς οἶκον, μή τιν᾽ Ἥφαιστος χόλον
δόμοις ἐπεισφρεὶς μέλαθρα συμφλέξηι πυρὶ
ἐν τοῖσιν ἡδίστοισι Φαέθοντος γάμοις.   260
Με. πῶς φήις; ὅρα μὴ θυμάτων πυρουμένων
κατ᾽ οἶκον ἀτμὸν κεῖσ᾽ ἀποσταλέντ᾽ ἴδηις.
Θε. ἅπαντα ταῦτ᾽ ἤθρησ᾽· ἀκαπνώτως ἔχει.
Με. οἶδεν δ᾽ ἐμὴ τάδ᾽ ἢ οὐκ ἐπίσταται δάμαρ;

236–9 ἃ (Neut. Accus.) . . . νυμφεύετε . . . Ἀφροδίται Hermann ὅς . . . νυμφεύεται (P) . . .
Ἀφροδίται Lloyd-Jones   237 νυμφεύσεαι Diggle (but preferring νυμφεύεαι), Kannicht
νυμφευεται P 238 χρυσέοις Hermann -εων P 239 ἀρχὸν Hermann αρχεον P   240 ὧ
μάκαρ, ὧ βασιλέως Hermann ω μακαρων βασιλευς P   ἔτ᾽ ὄλβον Hermann ετολβο P

will make the marriage for the great king of this city, our ruler dear to the starry golden palace! Aphrodite! O blessed man, O greater still than king in your happiness![240] You will be marriage-kin to a goddess and be sung throughout the boundless earth as the only mortal father of a groom for immortals.

Mer. (to a servant) You, go and take these girls into the house;[245] order my wife to honour all the gods throughout the palace with dancing, and to circle inside the house with solemn wedding hymns, and (to) . . . the altar of Hestia, with whom every sensible man begins making his prayers to the gods . . .[250]

four lines missing

. . . to approach the goddess's precinct from my house.

the Maiden girls go in with the servant; another servant enters:

Servant. Master, I have turned my steps quickly from the house: for where you keep your majestic golden treasures, through the door's joins a black draught of smoke is issuing from inside the building.[255] I put my eye close but saw no flame of fire, only the house full of black smoke inside. But go into the house, in case Hephaestus is visiting some anger on your home and may burn the palace down with fire in the midst of Phaethon's most happy marriage.[260]

Mer. How do you mean? Be sure you may not be seeing the fumes of sacrifice burning in the house being sent in that direction.

Ser. I looked at everything there; there is no smoke.

Mer. Does my wife know of this, or is she unaware?

---

241 θεᾶι Diggle θεαν P   244 ὑμνήσηι Hermann υμνησεται P   245 Μερ. C   246 κατὰ σταθμὰ Blass καταστομα P (cf. on 55)   247 κἀγκυκλώσασθαι Headlam κανκυμωσασθαι P   249 γε Burges τι P   πᾶς τις Blaydes πασα P   θεοῖς Blass, who read θε ι in P   250 πο[P, now illegible πο[ιεῖσθαι Burges   251–88 P fol. ii *recto*, col. i   252 Θεραπ. C δεσποτα C πατερ P   253 σώιζηι Hermann ζωση P   θησαυρίσματα Burges θηραυσμιτα P   255 καπνοῦ Elmsley, Hermann καταινου P   258 ἔσιθ' Bekker εσθ P   261–6 speakers indicated by C   263 ἤθρησ'· ἀκαπνώτως Wilamowitz ηθρησεκανπωτους P

Θε.   θυηπολοῦσα θεοῖς ἐκεῖσ' ἔχει φρένας.   265
Με.   ἀλλ' εἶμ', ἐπεί τοι καὶ φιλεῖ τὰ τοιάδε
        ληφθέντα φαύλως ἐς μέγαν χειμῶν' ἄγειν.
        σὺ δ' ὦ πυρὸς δέσποινα Δήμητρος κόρη
        "Ηφαιστέ τ', εἴητ' εὐμενεῖς δόμοις ἐμοῖς.

Χο.   τάλαιν' ἐγὼ τάλαινα ποῖ   270
        πόδα πτερόεντα καταστάσω;
        ἀν' αἰθέρ' ἢ γᾶς ὑπὸ κεῦθος ἄφαν-
        τος ἐξαμαυρωθῶ;
        ἰώ μοί μοι.
        κακὰ φανήσεται·   275
        βασίλεια τάλαινα παῖς τ' ἔσω
        κρυφαῖος νέκυς,
        ὀτοτοτοῖ, κεραύνιαί τ' ἐκ Διὸς
        πυριβόλοι πλαγαὶ λέχεά θ' 'Αλίου.
        ὦ δυστάλαινα τῶν ἀμετρήτων κακῶν,   280
        'Ωκεανοῦ κόρα,
        †πατρὸς ἴθι πρόσπεσε γόνυ λιταῖς σφαγὰς
        σφαγὰς οἰκτρὰς ἀρκέσαι σᾶς δειρᾶς†.

Με.   (off-stage) ἰώ μοί μοι.
Χο.   ἠκούσατ' ἀρχὰς δεσπότου στεναγμάτων;   285
Με.   (off-stage) ἰὼ τέκνον.
Χο.   καλεῖ τὸν οὐ κλύοντα δυστυχῆ γόνον.
                          ]άτων ὁρᾶν σαφῆ.
three lines missing, then:

beginnings of twenty-two lyric lines, apparently an   289–310
astrophic monody of Merops, of which only a few
words are certainly identifiable:

(Με.)   290 ὃς ὑμεν[αι-   304 ὅστις ι.[
          291 εὐκελαδ[308 καλεῖτε[
          293 σὺ δὲ παρ[309 ὃς ἐμαν[
          296 ὑμεναι[310 κακὰ δε[

267 ἄγειν Hermann αδι P   269 τ' εἴητ' εὐμενεῖς Bekker ειητεμευμερεις P (ειηρεπ- read by
Blass) τ' εἶτε (Dindorf; ἔστε Bothe) πρευμενεῖς Burges   270 Χο. C   271 as question, most
edd.; no punctuation, Diggle   272 ἀν' αἰθέρ' Nauck τιναθερ P   ἄφαντος Heiland -ον P

Ser. She is sacrificing to the gods and has her mind on that.[265]

Mer. Then I will go; such things taken lightly do often lead to a
great storm.

Mistress of fire, Demeter's daughter, and you, Hephaestus,
may you be favourable to my house!

(Merops and the Servant leave)

Cho. Misery! Where in my misery[270] am I to set my flying feet?
Vanish utterly unseen up into heaven, or beneath the earth's
concealment?

Oh me, me! Disaster will be revealed,[275] the wretched queen
inside and her son, his hidden body – o-o-oh! – and the lightning-
strokes of Zeus hurling fire, and her union with Helios.

So cruelly wretched in your measureless tragedy,[280] daughter
of Oceanus! †Go and fall at your father's knee in prayer to him
to hold back slaughter, piteous slaughter, from your throat.†

Mer. *(off-stage)*   Oh me, me!

Cho. Did you hear the beginning of our master's lamentations?[285]

Mer. *(off-stage)*   O-oh, my child!

Cho. He calls on his ill-fated son who cannot hear him . . . clear to see.

three lines missing, then:

Merops, now on stage, singing a monody of grief;   289–310
beginnings of a few lyric lines legible:

290	who . . . marriage (-?*song*)	304	whoever . . .
291	tuneful	308	summon . . . !
293	but you	309	who . . . *my* (?*wife*)
296	marriage (-?*song*)	310	evils

κρυφεον P end: comma, Diggle; stop, edd.   279 θ' Ἀλίου Bekker ταλιου P   282 γόνυ
λιταῖς Hermann γονυται P   283 οἰκτρὰς Burges -αι P   284–327 speakers or changes
indicated by C except at 289 (Με.) Diggle   287 καλει τον P, legible only to earlier edd.
289–327 = P fol. ii *recto*, col. ii   304 ὅστις Blass οσπο P, read by Wilson in Diggle

beginnings of seventeen trimeters from a dialogue　　　　311-27
between Chorus, Merops and Tutor; most of the initial
words identifiable:

311	Χο.	ὅδ' ἐκ δό[μων	320	Με.	διπλᾶ δ[
312		παιδὸς [	321	Τρ.	τί γὰρ λε[
313	Με.	εἶέν· θυρ[	322	Με.	τίς παιδ[
314		ὡς εἰσό[μεσθα	323	Τρ.	εἰδὼς α[
315		wording unclear	324	Με.	ἵν' ἀντα[
316		θεᾶς δε[	325	Τρ.	σμικρο[
317	Τρ.	ὤμοι.	326	Με.	κρεισσ[
318	Με.	στέναζ[ε	327	Τρ.	ὃς σεθ[
319	Τρ.	αἰαῖ.			

Fragments not certainly locatable

**783a (778 N)　　　　　　　　　　　　　　　　　　　　　fr. 1 D
　　Με.　εὐδαιμονίζων ὄχλος ἐξέπληξέ ⟨με⟩

**785　　Κλ.　†μισῶ δ' εὐάγκαλον τόξον κρανείας　　　　fr. 4 D
　　　　　　　γυμνάσια δ' οἴχοιτο.†

782　　　　　　　　　　ψυκτήρια　　　　　　　　　　　fr. 6 D
　　δένδρη φίλαισιν ὠλέναισι δέξεται.

783　　　　χρυσέα βῶλος　　　　　　　　　　　　　　fr. 5 D

783b (780 N)　　τρεῖς (Ὑάδες)　　　　　　　　　　　fr. 2 D

311 Blass　314 Wecklein　317 and 319 speech-ends marked with dicolon (:) by C　327 θ[
Wilson o[Blass　**783a/fr. 1 D** (778 N, 1102 M) restored by Meineke from Plut. *Mor.* 465a,
where 'the Merops of tragedy' is apparently credited with these words　**785/fr. 4 D** (1100 M)
Plut. *Mor.* 608e, citing (textually corrupt) words of Clymene about her son　**782/fr. 6 D** (1103 M)
Athenaeus 11.109, 503c–d, attrib. Eur. *Pha.*　**783/fr. 5 D** (1097 M) Diog. Laert. 2.10, referring
to Eur. *Pha.*　**783b/fr. 2 D** (780 N, 1095 M) Schol. Arat. *Phaenom.* 172, noting the varying
number of the Hyades in different writers, incl. Eur. in *Pha.*

Phaethon's Tutor comes out; Merops begins to interrogate him:

Cho.	This man here ... from the house ... (*your*) son ...	311–2
Mer.	Well then! ... *the door* ... so *we may know* ... of the	
	goddess ...	313–6
Tut.	Oh my sorrow!	317
Mer.	Grieve ...!	
Tut.	My pain!	
Mer.	... double ...	320
Tut.	Why, what ... ?	
Mer.	Who ... (*my*) son ... ?	
Tut.	... knowing ...	
Mer.	... so that ... in return ...	
Tut.	... small ...	325
Mer.	... greater ...	
Tut.	Who ... (?) you ...	

Fragments not certainly locatable

**783a (778 N)   fr. 1 D

Mer. The crowd unhinged <*me*> with its felicitations.

Merops explains his eagerness to celebrate the marriage.

**785 *Cly.*   †I hate the cornel-bow, so easy to carry, and athletics be   fr. 4 D
damned!†

*Clymene reflects bitterly on Phaethon's athleticism which
made driving Helios's chariot a challenge.*

782   ... cooling trees will embrace him in loving arms.   fr. 6 D

*From the god's prophecy at play-end of Phaethon's future
after death.*

783   *(Euripides in the 'Phaethon' said that the sun is)*   fr. 5 D
... a golden clod ...

783b (780 N)   fr. 2 D
(Euripides in the 'Phaethon' said that there are)
... three (Hyades) ...

Commentary on *Phaethon*

Note. The assumption is made throughout that users seeking fuller discussion especially of textual and linguistic matters will turn to Diggle's edition.

test. ii **Hypothesis.** A 'narrative' hypothesis: see Gen. Introd. I (ii). Lines 1–6 give the premiss for the play's tension: Cly. has concealed from both Merops and Phaethon that the latter was her son by Helios, whether or not he was born after her marriage to Merops. 7ff. take up the action as it begins, but both Hypothesis and fragments leave it unclear whether Cly. has informed Phaethon before the play or does so only in her mutilated scene with him (8–62) preceding the Parodos. Turner assumed that 14–16 ended the Hypothesis, for 16 **prophesied** (if correctly read: doubted by Lloyd-Jones 343) suits a god at play-end. Luppe in *ZPE*, however, argues that these rather separated lines come from the Hypothesis to *Hyps.*, posited as the next play in the collection.

2 . she *bore*: a common detail of these hypotheses, e.g. *Sthen.* 3; thus Luppe's '*bore ?two daughters after Phaethon to Merops*' is preferable to Keydell's '*married after this to Merops*'.

3 . of them all: before Luppe supplemented 2, Keydell proposed 'at any rate she said . . . was (Phaethon's) father'.

4 . [Text: **was living with:** Luppe, *ZPE* shows that συνοικεῖν not συμβιοῦν is the verb used in these narratives.]

8 . *stables*: cf. *Pha.* 5 = F 771.5 'stables of Helios'.

9 – 1 0 . *any* gift: Helios's granting it would prove his fatherhood, *Pha.* 45–8.

1 – 6 2 . The Prologue scene. Cly. makes the Prologue speech (Introd., p. 201) and is then joined by Phaethon: so the scene develops unity and momentum, like *El.* 1–111 with Farmer, Electra and Orestes appearing in succession, cf. *Med.* 1–95, *Or.* 1–131 etc. Cly. gives the play's setting (1–5) and in the missing lines her own background and new predicament, her fear she may have to reveal Phaethon's true father to Merops now that he intends to marry the boy (60, cf. 9) to a goddess (?24, cf. 240–4). Mother and son discuss the marriage (10, 13 etc.) but in terms we cannot know; before the full text begins (45), Clymene may have told Phaethon for the first time that Helios, not Merops, was his father; cf. on Hypothesis above, Introd. p. 196.

1 – 5 . Strabo (see App.) shows that in line 1 Cly. completed the history of her 'official' (Hypoth. 4) marriage to Merops.

1 . this land: Ethiopia (Strabo's context: Introd., p. 200), the Sun's resting-place at day-end (Aesch. F 192) ready for the next Dawn (2–5), cf. Mimn. *IEG* fr. 12.9.

2 – 3 . Helios . . . chariot: at dawn also *Ion* 82–3, *IA* 156–9.

3 . at his rising: for this use see LSJ ἀνέχω B.I.b, Hdt. 2.136 etc.

4 . neighbouring black peoples: i.e. neighbouring to Merops, who is there-fore by implication white-skinned (cf. 7 'temperate' climate) as the putative father of Phaethon son of the god Helios and nymph Cly.: see Lesky 29. [Text: not 'neighbouring' to Helios, for that adds nothing. Schmidt's 'native black peoples' (App.), apparently favoured by Kannicht 6, needlessly emphasizes Cly.'s own differing whiteness.] **call it etc.**: a formula of prologue details, *Mel.S.* F 481. 13, *Tel.* F 696.12 etc., but always emphasizing identity; cf. e.g. *Hec.* 827 with Collard's n.

5. bright stables: transferred adj. as e.g. *And.* 1086 'bright orbits of the sun'. The stables are correspondingly dark in the evening, *Alc.* 593.   **Eos**: (goddess of the) Dawn, 64. In some versions of the myth she is Pha.'s mother (Introd., p. 198).

6, 7. Although separate in source, these two general statements suit an expository prologue and belong together (Barnes). Helios at his rising does not heat his neighbour Merops's land, the first which he strikes (2–3), as much as the more distant parts of Ethiopia later when he is higher in the sky: see Lesky, *WS* 63 (1948), 28–30 = *Ges. Schr.* 31–3; cf. Webster (1972), 628.   **god's**: lit. 'lord's', a common synonym in clear references to gods, e.g. *IT* 1270.   **temperate**: lit. 'well mixed', describing climate in Hippocr. *Airs etc.* 2.90.5 etc.; cf. the verb 'mix' F 981.2, Hdt. 3.106.1 and below, 169 n.

8–44. The dialogue 8–62 is asymmetrical (see App.), as in the prologue scenes *Med.* 49–95, *And.* 56–102, etc.   **[8.** Perhaps *<dealings>* **of the gods** (Blass), like Soph. *OT* 34.]   **9. father sending out**: Merops, in the negotiation of Phaethon's marriage (8)?   **35. whose**: almost certainly a 'prepositive' rel. pron., rare at verse-end in Eur.: see Bond on *HF* 77; Diggle, *Euripidea* 454.   **42. those dearest to me**: Phaethon himself, probably; for the Greek phrase see *Cresph.* F 458.2 n., Page on *Med.* 16.

45–6. The raping god makes a promise or reward: Apollo (identified with Helios by Cly. at 224–6, cf. 279) and Cassandra, Aesch. *Ag.* 1202ff.; Creusa had hopes of Apollo, *Ion* 965. A single (46) gift or promise by a god often recoils, as upon Cly. and Phaethon: cf. *Alc.* 11–14 (Apollo again), *Ion* 1001–5, Nessus's gift at Soph. *Trach.* 568ff.; Stith Thompson, *Motif Index* Q.115.   **remind**: meaning of the Aor. Pass. as *Med.* 933, *Or.* 579 etc.   **one thing etc.**: τί used as rel. pron.: Soph. *El.* 316 is probably parallel (Moorhouse, *Syntax* 266f.) despite the new Oxford Text.

47. <your wish>: Diggle's very probable supplement matches that in Hypoth. 9–10, 'any gift (Phaethon) *wished*; he now suggests '*<all your desires>*', like *Med.* 688. For a god's gift which must nevertheless be tested cf. *Hipp.* 887–98.

49. heat (cf. *El.* 739): anticipation of Phaethon's disaster, Introd., p. 201.

54–8. Both Blass and Diggle note the close repetition within a few lines of several synonyms for 'house', a phenomenon common enough (e.g. 257–62, *Supp.* 1095–7, *El.* 394–8) to prove it blameless, even if displeasing to us; cf. J. Jackson, *Marginalia Scaenica* (Oxford, 1955), 220–2.

53. Enough, thank you: an idiom of qualified gratitude, indicating that Phaethon's distrust will persist; cf. perhaps Medea's insincere gratitude, *Med.* 754.

54. come: lit. 'go', but Phaethon will accompany his mother. He enters with her at 62 and returns with Merops at 103; cf. Menelaus at *And.* 433, 494. For the stage movements here, the Chorus entering while Phaethon speaks, see Introd., pp. 202–3.

55.palace: σταθμά, restored here, occurs also in 246.

56-8. Merops' Ethiopians are imagined like Egyptians who customarily perfumed the house to disguise the stale overnight air, *Hel.* 866, Plu. *Mor.* 383b; Parker, *Miasma* 227-8; (JD) guest-rooms ventilated *TrGF* adesp. 90. **sweep:** slave women's work, *And.* 166, *Hec.* 363 etc. **cleanse:** φοιβᾶν is rare (Gow on Theocr. 17.134) but (JD) cf. Aesch. F 148 'uncleansed'. **laid-up things:** i.e. the permanent and valuable furnishings. At 210 the Sing. describes a permanent tomb-offering or memorial; cf. Soph. *El.* 438.

59-60. old: preparing us for Merops about to share his rule with Phaethon after the marriage, 124-6, ?136, 160-2; 'old' in relation only to Phaethon's own youth perhaps, 132-3, 136-7. **sleep** adds to this implication. The important **words . . . about marriage** are heralded at 113-9 and begin at 120. Diggle's note on 59ff. shows that 'words' here stand in a Greek idiom of neutral implication, as in a similar discussion of marriage at *IA* 1107-8; Kannicht 6 nevertheless supports Lesky 8 with the sense 'idle words', comparing e.g. *Med.* 321, i.e. Pha. will oppose his father; they rest this on the presumed tone of disagreement.

62.what you say: for λόγοι inside the subordinate clause rather than λόγους agreeing with σοὺς, cf. e.g. *HF* 840, *Hipp.* 101.

63-101. Parodos. Phaethon has already identified the entering Chorus and their purpose (54-8), so that when Eur. has them begin with an evocation of dawn we expect a significance for it beyond its mere fact (59). Only after the first strophic pair and second strophe (63-86) do the Chorus link their description of others' habitual daybreak activities with their own particular duty on this special dawn, to assist the marriage celebration: second antistrophe and epode (87-101). Such contrast is typical of Eur.'s expressive style, and 87-101 in part recapitulate but also develop the Prologue (Kannicht 6, cf. Hose I.131). There are the same abrupt, evocative start and later, thematically important change in the derived 'dawn song' forming the Parodos at Sen. *HF* 125-201: see J.G. Fitch's Commentary (Ithaca, 1987), 158-63 for comparison and bibl. At *Ion* 82-183 Ion's monody, prominently following the divine Prologue speech rather than the Parodos, describes his dawn routines which so fully reveal his characterization in the light of the later action. The similarities, but also differences, between *Pha.* 63-101 and the 'dramatic' stasimon *Rhes.* 727-56, set at first dawn but mid-way in its play, are shown by Diggle, referring to G. H. Macurdy, *AJP* 54 (1943), 408-16 and Ritchie, *Rhesus* p. 255f.; cf. also Reckford 428, n. 32.

It is false to the overall tone of this dawn picture to find in it the associations of grief common elsewhere with nightingales (68) and swans (78), as if Eur. offers a premonition of Phaethon's death on this happy day (contrast the later and deliberate premonition for Merops's ears alone 258-60). Yet dawn it is; this second and early emphasis (cf. 59) may well prompt the audience to think at once of Phaethon's imminent and fatal morning drive.

This dawn song on its discovery fired Goethe's enthusiasm and the sensibilities of later Romantics (Introd., p. 203) even before P's mutilated text was supplemented by P. Berl. Not just the choice of the successive vignettes, or their imagination and

immediacy, give this poem its strong appeal. Eur. catches the simplicity and perhaps
innocence of ordinary life outside Merops's palace (which the Chorus have just
left) — and, no doubt, outside the Athens of his audience. Pickard-Cambridge 147
wrote of its 'perfect simplicity', Barlow, *Imagery* 23f. of the 'romantic idealised
scene'. The vignettes have therefore sometimes been seen as forerunners of Hellenistic intimacy, nostalgic or escapist (e.g. Schmid 601 n. 1); but as close and empath-
etic observations they are individually no different from brief scenes of ordinary life
such as the laundress *Hipp.* 121–9 or the wife at bed-time *Hec.* 919–26. A noteworthy
feature of all the scenes here is what Eur. suggests of sound accompanying the
images: noise after silent night 67–78, bird-song 67–70, 76–7, herdsmen's pipes
71–2, horses stirring 73–4, huntsmen's dogs 75–6, wind-noise 80, sailors' cries
82–5 (cf. the use of sounds vivifying the night attack *Tro.* 522–67; Barlow, *Imagery*
30). The entire composition, small scenes collected under the title 'Now it is dawn',
resembles an active and idealised but still everyday 'landscape' of the kind animating
so many Renaissance and later paintings which have a particular incident, often
mythological, as nominal subject (for example, the elder Brueghel's *Fall of Icarus*).
The initial dawn (63–6), top-centre as it were, illuminates the rural, mountain and
river scenes mid-centre (67–78). Ships and crews (79–86) are both foreground and
end; this, the busiest scene, which includes singing, immediately precedes the
Chorus's own intended activity, the wedding songs (88–90, 97–101). In conceiving
this panorama, Eur. was perhaps conscious of the half-landscaped activities worked
by Hephaestus on Achilles' Shield, Hom. *Il.* 18.478–608, esp. 541–608: on which
scenes see M. W. Edwards, *Commentary on the Iliad* V (Cambridge, 1991), 206–9,
noting on p. 208 the inclusion of sound effects; note too the everyday scenes in
many similes, Edwards pp. 34–7. Many of the activities in Eur.'s word-landscape
characterise the landscape-frescoes said by Plin. *NH* 35.116 to have been invented by
the Augustan painter Studius; Philostratus, *Imag.* 1.12–13 (3rd C. A.D.) describes a
painting comparable in some details with Eur. *Pha.* The styles — and even the
existence in the Classical period — of Greek perspective or landscape-painting are
uncertain: see e.g. C. M. Robertson, *Shorter History of Greek Art* (Cambridge, 1981),
149–50.

   Metre. Aeolo-choriambic in the first pair (apt for the lively, everyday picture-
poem), then chiefly anapaestic metres in the second pair and a mainly iambic epode.
Altogether a very varied sequence, which as often we do not know how to interpret
aesthetically. Formal analysis of 63–78 by Kannicht 11, of the whole by Diggle.

64. Dawn <rides>: like the sun, 5, 173 n.; for the verb restored, ἱππεύειν,
cf. e.g. 176, *Ion* 41 the Sun.

66. <choir>: of stars, *El.* 467 etc; **<fled>,** of fading stars, *Ion* 84 etc. Diggle's
supplements are attractive, but Lloyd-Jones desiderates a Present tense, like
Wilamowitz's 'the Pleias *of the dark fades*'. **Pleiads:** see on 171.

67. subtle harmony: varied in melody, tone and pace, *Hec.* 337–8, Hom. *Od.*
19.521. The nightingale's song includes repeated notes expressed through
onomatopoeia in 70 'Itys, Itys', aetiologized in the myth of Procne (for which see
Cresph. F 448a.117–22 n.); but Diggle and Kannicht 7 (cf. on *Hel.* 1107–12) agree

that the emphasis here is on the bird's musicality, like *Od.* above, Ar. *Birds* 659; cf. above on 63–101. The adj. λεπτός is rarely used of sounds, e.g. *Or.* 140 a footfall; bird-song Ar. *Birds* 235, LSJ II.2, Lloyd-Jones 344.

69. awake at sunrise to grieve: the same coupling of ὀρθρεύεσθαι and instrumental Dat. γόοις at *Suppl.* 977 (a widow's grief; cf. *El.* 142 for the idea). Diggle's note on 70 documents ornithological discussion of when the nightingale sings and ceases. Bird-song at dawn, e.g. Soph. *El.* 18–19.

71–2. drovers ... mountains ... pipes: similar details of Apollo herding *Alc.* 573–7, cf. Gow on Theocr. 11.38. The pipes here (σύριγγες) are multiple or 'Pan'-pipes, the conventional instrument of the countryman; description in Gow's n. on Theocr. 1.129, cf. 1.1ff.

73–6. chestnut mares: the adj. ξανθός registers the commonest horse colour: Denniston on *El.* 477. For 'mares' see 173 n. **are roused:** by grooms, but Greek Middle 'rouse themselves' is possible, e.g. *Rhes.* 531.

77–8. swans are associated with **Oceanus** Hes. *Shield* 315–6; for the Greeks' perception of swans see W. G. Arnott, *G&R* 24 (1977), 149–53. Oceanus's **streams** border Ethiopia Hom. *Il.* 1.423, Aesch. F 192; his daughter Clymene (281) married his neighbour Merops (1), so that Merops's land is here named as that of Oceanus, 109. **is sounding:** for the verb ἀχεῖν of the swans' carrying cry cf. the agent-noun ἀχέτας *El.* 151; similarly βοᾶν 'cry' (μελιβόας here) of a bird *Tro.* 830.

79–86. The sailors first row the boats out from shore (79–80) amid lively winds, then chant their prayers for gentle breezes after raising the sails (81–5), which fill out (86). This narrative sequence is usual and begins in Homer as a 'theme' (see S. West on *Od.* 2.382ff.); *Il.* 1.477–81 prefaces it with 'Dawn appearing'. For the details cf. *Hel.* 1451–64 in Diggle's OCT, discussed in his *Euripidea* 430–6, and *Hel.* 1575, 1612.

79–80. Vessels: lit. 'skiffs', figurative; cf. *Hec.* 446 with Collard's n. **[under oar and with ... bluster:** Greek variation of Gen. (Π) with prep. followed by Dat., like *Pho.* 823–4, *Supp.* 367–8 etc. A first Dat. (εἰρεσίαις P), sharing the one prep., is less likely because of the Plur., lit. 'rowings', despite Diggle's appeal to Ap. Rhod. 1.114.]

81–5. quiet winds: but not totally silent as in *IA* 10, or no sailing can be done; cf. Diggle, *Euripidea* 430 n. 45.   **[Text:** ἰαχοῦσιν **cry** Diggle (cf. *CQ* 40 [1990], 116 for the prosody), since the verb ἠχεῖν '(re)sound' appears never to be used of articulate speech; the noun ἠχή is rare in this sense, e.g. *Pho.* 1148 a battle order. The gaps in P and Π are plausibly filled. **<Bring>** (Lloyd-Jones), controlling 85 **<to> our ... <children>,** is slightly superior to 'follow' (Austin), i.e. 'escort', for this idea appears in 82 **voyage** lit. 'sending, escort', πομπά, used of winds *IA* 352, 1324 etc.; prayers to winds *Hec.* 444ff., *Hel.* 1504f. Volmer's **<in>,** ὑπό, completes an apparent echo of a Homeric phrase *Il.* 6.171 θεῶν ὑπ' ἀμύμονι πομπᾶι, 'in the gods' blameless sending', apparently a sea voyage.]

85. wives and <children>: *Tro.* 21, the Greeks' main desire on leaving Troy, also an echo of the Homeric longing, e.g. *Od.* 13.334.

86.close to the forestay etc.: filled out by sufficient wind; the same details at *Hec.* 111, *IT* 1132–7 (also departures); cf. Diggle, *Euripidea* 435.

87–8. honour of..wedding: the expression κόσμον ὑμεναίων is traced back by Diggle to poetry's self-description as κόσμος ἐπέων Solon *IEG* fr. 1.2 etc., lit. 'honour (consisting) of poetry'.   [Text: P and Π differ considerably, but Π is overfussy, 'other men's cares belong to others'. Hartung's text restores the necessary distinction between others' daily work already in hand (87) and the Chorus's imminent work on this particular day.]

89–95. right ... desire etc.: servants identify with the joys and sorrows of their masters, *Med.* 54–5, *Hel.* 726–7 etc.

90, 92.to slaves, to their song: a free use of the grammatical construction of 'whole and part', cf. *Mel.S.* F 481.3–5 n.

91. good times: Plur. of an abstract, 'instances of . . .'; for the noun (Schmidt's correction) cf. *El.* 197 with Denniston's n.

93.joy: the compond noun ἐπίχαρμα, usually 'malignant joy', has a parallel in the verb ἐπιχαίρειν 'rejoice', Soph. *Aj.* 136. Cf. the name of the comic poet Epicharmus, 'Joyful'.

93–4. Interlacing of syntax in the Greek to place the two **heavys** side by side, a mannerism of Eur. (e.g. 98, cf. 166–7), but here very effective, like *Med.* 513: see Denniston on *El.* 337. **gives birth:** metaphor as e.g. *Hcld.* 898 (Fate). **something:** euphemistic understatement with the indef. Pron. *Alc.* 138, *And.* 1072 etc.

95. day ... marked out: the idea is emphatically repeated in 99 'time (has) fulfilled'. Metaphor from a boundary mark *IT* 979, *Antiope* F 218.2. **celebration:** τέλος 'end, completion' and so 'rite, enactment'; with γάμων **of marriage,** first at Hom. *Od.* 20.74; cf. the adj. τέλειος 101, verb τελεῖν *Cret.* F 472.12 and n.

96. which: def. art. as rel. pron., common in lyric, 234, *Alc.* 883 etc. **long ago:** word-order points to this sense of δή ποτε (Lloyd-Jones 344), not Diggle's '(I have) at last (come forward)' which conflicts with the Cho.'s desire in 89.

98.masters': perhaps a genuine rather than allusive Plur., the Cho. identifying father and son. **dear ... own:** mannered doubling of the Greek adj.: see 93–4 n.

99.God has willed, time fulfilled: the trans. reproduces the 'liturgical' parallelism of sense, syntax, sound and metre: cf. *Bacc.* 1153, Soph. *El.* 197, Aesch. *Cho.* 327, Ar. *Frogs* 1099 and commentators. The 'god' is anonymous, cf. e.g. *Tel.* F 716.3; 'fulfil', κραίνειν, of a god's higher ordinance (Fraenkel on) Aesch. *Ag.* 369, for marriage Eur. *Supp.* 1008, R. Seaford, *JHS* 107 (1987), 125 n. 193; cf. our 118 of human fulfilment.

101. Let ... begin: ἴτω of a marriage rite e.g. *Supp.* 1025. **to celebrate** (95 n.): adj. and objective Gen. *Hel.* 1081, *And.* 1194.

103. holy herald: the phrase is either a synonym for the noun ἱεροκῆρυξ, 'herald at a sacrifice etc.', e.g. [Dem]. 59.78, or the adj. ἱερός, like θεῖος describing the herald Talthybius *Il.* 4.192, registers the protection of all heralds by the gods' own herald Hermes, *Supp.* 121.

104. all three in company: lit. 'triple yoke-pair', the noun ζεῦγος used loosely of any unified group, like *Tro.* 924, *Erec.* F 357 (cf. Breitenbach 142 on this metaphor in Eur.); but the locution helps emphasize this particular ensemble and occasion (cf. 109–18 and nn.; Introd., p. 203).

106. great matters: substantival adj. μεγάλα like *And.* 387, *Supp.* 368.

107. join . . . in the holy bonds: normally the bride is joined, lit. 'yoked', to the groom, e.g. *Bacc.* 468; Kannicht 8 takes the reversal here, and the use of **bonds,** to imply that Merops will force the marriage upon Phaethon: cf. 109–57 n. **holy:** duly consecrated, *Supp.* 1027, 1028, etc. **to his bride:** objective Gen. in the Greek. [Page's correction of P's empty 'as he says' is palaeographically superior to Wecklein's of the same sense.]

109–57. The lost Epis. 1, beginning here, would have revealed the nature of Merops's persuasion and of the boy's misgivings. The fragmentary lines 127–57 show that marriage, youth contrasted with age, and the responsibilities of power were the themes; the book fragments in 158–67 show disagreement about the way a rich father (Merops? cf. 222–3!) must deal with a son unwilling to marry (the order of 158–67 varies among editors, but all put 158–9 first). We cannot know the temper or formal styling of the Episode. Was it an 'agon' (Pickard-Cambridge 146), a 'formal debate', ending typically without reconciliation (see Lloyd [1992], esp. 131–2), or something less than that, with Phaethon assenting at least verbally to the marriage and then escaping to test his parentage (cf. 59–60)? Kannicht 7–8 thinks the latter. Cf. Introd., p. 199 and on F 785 = fr. 4 D below.

109–18. Alternate dactylic and iambic lines, the dactyls suggesting solemnity; cf. the solemn proclamation Ar. *Frogs* 814–29.

109. Oceanus: see on 77.

110–4, 118. The herald's formal proclamations for public assembly and then for respectful silence resemble in wording the Cho.'s ritual summons to hear its devotional hymn in *Bacc.* 68–70.

113–5 are a textual nightmare, and translation is insecure. [The chief problems, all carefully reviewed by Diggle, are (1) to determine whether ὁσίαν is a noun (**reverence** in the trans.) or an adj. qualifying αὐδάν **speech;** (2) the grammatical congruence and the meaning of the adj. βασιλήϊον, **in the name of the king,** whether with 'reverence' or 'speech'; (3) the usage of αὐτῶι **himself** apparently taking up the identity of the king; (4) the extreme improbability of a herald's proclaiming silence and then commanding **fruitfulness** for a marriage yet to be solemnised (117–8). The App. mentions a variety of piecemeal remedies; 113 'I proclaim a royal sacrifice', Weil; '. . . festival', Lloyd-Jones (but an incongruous dialect form); 114 'I beg (speech: for the king)', Hermann; 115 'happiness' instead of 'fruitfulness', Wilamowitz. One might unconfidently add 113 βασιλήϊοις 'royal' (metrically precarious) in agreement with 115 'marriage' or posit a loss of two whole lines before 115.] **fruitfulness,** εὐτεκνία, cf. the phrase τέκνων εἰς ἔργον, English 'to make children', in marriage formulae, Aesch. *Ag.* 1207, with Fraenkel's n., cf. *Eum.* 835; παιδοποιεῖν 'make children' e.g. *Hcld.* 514.

116. procession ... out: lit. 'coming-out', ἔξοδος of a stage-entry promising significance e.g. *Hcld.* 474.

117-8. son and father etc.: as Ion and Xuthus publicly celebrate their meeting *Ion* 1122ff.

120. if ... talking sense: though Merops may seem to recognise that he will have to go cautiously about persuading Phaethon, **123** (**? it rests) with you** sounds very purposeful; but with **124-6 one anchor (etc.)** he seems to be inducing Pha. both to marry and to expect an immediate share in the kingdom (see on 160-2), for the safety of the (ship of) state. For the anchor image, and this proverb, in an Athenian forensic speech (cf. **single leader for a city**), see e.g. [*Dem.*] 56. 44; cf. Pind. *Ol.* 6.100-1, Plut. *Sol.* 19, LSJ I. Hecuba's one surviving son is her house's sole anchor, *Hec.* 80. A rash (single) sailor is **unsafe** (126 σφαλερός) as a city's captain also *Supp.* 508-9. **in support:** the verb ὑπεῖναι in a similar context *Supp.* 442. [Text: **not ... in the same way:** Stob.'s οὐδαμῶς 'in no way' gives no adequate preparatory correlation for the comparison in 125 (despite F. Maltomini, *ASNP* 7 [1977], 575-6). Burges's def. art. τῶι for Stob.'s ὡς is less certain though probable; ὁμῶς is found with a bare Dat. in comparison only in Homer (LSJ II), and with ὡς retained ἀφέντι will be a bare substantival part. as in *Pho.* 270, cf. *KG* I.609. **and:** frequent in examples juxtaposed, coordinated and implicitly compared: *Hel.* 769-71, *HF* 101-2, *Bell.* F 298.]

158-9. The antithesis free/slave is common, especially in paradoxes of male dominance restricted, e.g. *Hec.* 864-96; for this one cf. (Trag.) *Mel.?D.* F 502.4 and n., Hippothoon *TrGF* I 210 F 3.1, (Com.) Alexis fr. 264.7 *PCG*. It is usually women who lose control of their bodies when married, *Med.* 233-4, *Danae* F 318.2. A man is foolish to sell out for a dowry *Mel.* F 502, *And.* 1279-82, Menand. fr. 333.10-11 Koerte. **has sold his body:** lit. 'having his body sold', with πεπραμένον Accus. Perf. Pass. participle predicative to ἔχων, like Plut. *Anton.* 85.4 δέλτον ἔχουσα γεγραμμένην ... ἀπέστειλε 'she wrote a letter and dispatched it'. [159 App.: Diggle pp. 127-9 concluded that Plut. *Mor.* 498a probably contains no matter from *Pha.* beyond this one line; but Barigazzi 103-5 detects echoes of Eur.'s vocabulary describing Phaethon's physical distress during his fatal chariot drive: see on the messenger speech (168-77), Introd. p. 201.]

160-2. patrimony: Diggle's fine correction accommodates the clause **when ... senses** to both **sons** and **citizens**. For a father unwisely deputing to son cf. *Phoenix* F 806, Soph. F 936; for a living king ceding power (cf. 59-60 n.) *Alc.* 655, *Bacc.* 213, *Tel.* F 696.10 n. Greek τοῦτο ... ὅστις **'this (thing) ... if any (man)'** is common, cf. *Erec.* F 360.1-3 n.; ἐν with Neut. Plur. μώροις like *Alc.* 1037. The combination ἢ καί (**or especially**) insists on attention to the alternative: Willink on *Or.* 1359.

163 is a commonplace, e.g. F 1047.2. Phaethon is presumably comforting himself against exile if he refuses to marry.

164-7. Has Merops left the stage? (Webster [1967], 224 believes these lines to be a generalisation closing the Episode). If Merops is still there to hear **foolish** from Phaethon (a reference to 'follies' 160?), he will hardly show continuing enthusiasm for the marriage (217–8) but fear its wreck (cf. 266–9). **It's terrible:** an idiom of outrage, like *Hec.* 846, *Ion* 1312.   **but:** for the Greek word-order cf. Denniston, *GP* 188.   **the rich . . . foolish:** *El.* 943, *Arch.* F 235 etc. **wealth . . . blind:** proverbial. Wealth is a blind character in Comedy, e.g. Ar. *Plut.* 89, cf. Hipponax *IEG* fr. 36.1. For the doubling of 'blind' cf. 94 n.   [Text: **165. the cause:** Wecklein's correction is a little more stylish than Herwerden's of the same sense.   **166. is . . . partner:** συνηρετεῖ, lit 'row together with', if right, is found only here and Soph. *Aj.* 1329 (also conjecture) in the 5ᵗʰ C. Stob.'s συνηρεφεῖ, lit. 'roof over', cannot be stretched to mean 'cloud, befuddle'.   **167.** The end is beyond sure repair. West gives 'in common fortune', i.e. 'their wits are blind too'. Perhaps κὰς τὴν τύχην (Collard), '. . . towards fortune too', cf. *Hipp.* 701 'in relation to our fortunes', πρὸς τὰς τύχας. Musgrave may have been right in thinking the quotation incomplete.]

168–77. On the Messenger's identity, and the general character of this passage, see Introd. p. 201. Direct speech (168ff., 176–7) is frequent in messengers' reports (de Jong 131ff.); the Imperatives in asyndeton (175–6) express impatience and hint at the imminent disaster: cf. *Hipp.* 1240–1, *Bacc.* 732–3.

168. neither enter: a second prohibition, 'nor . . .', is lost after the parenthetic explanation 169–70 (for this structure cf. *Cret.* F 472e.35–9 and n.).

169–70. no moisture mixed in it: it is dry and hot (Libya also, Hdt. 2.26.1), cf. on 6–7 above, with insufficient substance to support the chariot. West (App.) 82 n. 51 defends Faber's slight correction of P to **it will let . . . fall down** by citing Pre-Socratic statements that the sun itself is supported by moist air, esp. Anaximander 12 A 27 DK (cf. Aristot. *Meteor.* 353b6), Anaxagoras 59 A 8 (Q2) DK; for Eur.'s acquaintance with the latter's theories cf. F 783 below, *Mel.S* F 484.2–6 n., Willink on *Or.* 982–3.   [Other editors have conjectured either καταιθαλώσει 'consume your wheel in fire' (Kock, cf. Lloyd-Jones 344) or καίων (Richards) διόισει 'tear your wheel apart by burning' (Diggle).]   **wheel:** lit. 'felloe', the rim, metonymic like *Hipp.* 1233, Hdt. 4.72.

171. Pleiads: the disappearance of this prominent constellation commonly signifies the dawn (e.g. *Rhes.* 529, cf. Diggle on 66, Fraenkel on *Ag.* 826): so Phaethon is to drive the new day's sun towards it.

173. The Sun's **winged team** *El.* 466, *Or.* 1001–2 etc. (cf. 64 n.): K. Schauenburg, *Helios* (Berlin, 1955), 70 n. 320 and Figs. **team:** lit. 'chariot'; the animate implication of Neut. 'team' (*Alc.* 66, *Hipp.* 1355) is continued in the Fem. pronominal article 174 (cf. KG I.55). Chariot horses collectively are usually Fem.: Barrett on *Hipp.* 231.

174. folds of heaven: i.e. clouds forming valleys like an earthly landscape, *Hel.* 44, *Mel.* F 506.4 (n.), cf. Mastronarde on *Pho.* 84.

175. Sirius: one of Helios's spare horses, perhaps named earlier in the report (Lesky 20–2).   **mounted on:** βεβώς with Acc. as *Pho.* 172, a chariot.

F 786/fr. 3 D. in a ravine, unwashed: Cly.'s distress is in immediate reaction
to the news of Phaethon's death, probably at the end of the Episode. 'Unwashed'
meant for her in that instant the denial of a mother's greatest need and grief, to
prepare her son's body for funeral, *Pho.* 1319, cf. Collard on *Hec.* 613. The belief
that the lightning-struck do not rot (Plutarch's context, cf. also *Mor.* 685c, *Qu. Nat.*
XL Sandbach [Loeb ed.]) did not go unquestioned, e.g. Sen. *Qu. Nat.* 2.31; for their
special funerals see e.g. Collard on *Supp.* 935 (Capaneus blasted by Zeus); Garland,
Death 99–100.

178–213. The theme of the discussion is Phaethon's funeral (189, 206, 207, 210,
211) after his ill fortune (181, 205, 212), without apprising Merops of the body's
presence (187, ?209, cf. 216–3): it will be difficult (201) but must be attempted
(213), perhaps by trickery under cover of dark (202, 206). All that is reasonable
speculation (Blass); but why are there apparent references to Merops's tyranny (191,
or law 196) or wealth (194)? Who or what are 'free' (193)? Are these dramatic anticipations of Merops's likely punishment of Cly. (Introd. pp. 200, 202)? Blass, cf.
Webster (1967), 227, thinks 191–6 to be the end of Cly.'s rhesis, with a sententious-
ness typical of a mourning (and angry?) mother. New evidence might show that 202
πλοκή **trickery** is rather 'lock of hair', i.e. (Diggle) perhaps a **memorial token**
(210) of Phaethon; for such locks see Cropp on *El.* 91, Richardson on Hom. *Il.*
23.127–530.

214–5. Unfortunately the damage to P denies us clear understanding of how Cly.
interprets Phaethon's still smouldering corpse. Is **of fire** (Rau, Hermann: App.)
merely figurative, or does it indicate that Phaethon's punishment is to continue in
some way, perhaps against herself (cf. 280–3, n. on 178–213)? If the latter,
'Fury' is metaphorical like *Tro.* 457, *Med.* 1260; but if the former, the image may
still connote the Fury's persecuting and purifying role: Diggle's 'Fury with its fire-
brands' (App.) makes this explicit, cf. *IT* 188, Aeschin. I.190. Here is a frustrating
impasse. **breath:** ἀτμός of flame, Aesch. F 187a; 'fume' of a burning sacrifice,
252 below. [Text: P's line-end in 214 was never certainly deciphered. If C indeed
wrote -νυται the verb intended is hard to find: perhaps συνδαίνυται 'joins in the
feast'? Fire 'feasts' on bodies *Hcld.* 914 (see Wilkins's Commentary). Diggle's
θρασύνεται 'waxes wanton' is more likely than Hermann's κεραυνίου '(fire) of
lightning'. †**corpses**† must be wrong: only one is in question (Hartung, App.),
for the Plural in 211 must be general. The identification of a verb at the end of 214
compels Diggle's simple correction at the start of 215; then Rau's supply of
<*flame*> is palmary: cf. *Bacc.* 8 'living flame', of Semele's smouldering burial
place.]

217. My husband, my husband: realistic doubling to represent panic, like *Or.*
257.

219–21. Cly.'s urgency is shown by the abruptness of her commands and the lack
of connective particles, cf. e.g. 176–7, *Med.* 808–9, *Hipp.* 353–7.   [221 text:

Page's correction is necessary: the obvious ἐπείγετ' εἶα would be against the idiom of the interjection εἶα: see Diggle.]

222. dressed-stone: implying its splendour, 253. For this adj. see on *Bell.* F 305. The attention here and 253 to Merops's wealth may reflect an issue in his debate with Phaethon: see on 109–57.   **chamber:** for Contiades-Tsitsoni the Greek noun θαλάμους, often meaning 'marriage chamber', is ironic: Phaethon's marriage led only to his death.

223. the doors' seal: not the door itself, but the means of indicating that its closure is secure and that opening by others will be detected; cf. Aesch. *Eum.* 827–8 'I (Athene) alone of the gods know the keys of the house in which (Zeus's) lightning is sealed', *Or.* 1108 Helen sealing off possessions as her own, Menand. *Shield* 358 doors with 'marks'; and on the housewife's responsibility for storing valuables, n. on *Mel.D.* F 494.9–11.

224–6. Those about to die, as Cly. fears, regularly bid farewell to the sunlight (*Alc.* 244, *Hec.* 411 etc.), but Cly. accuses Helios the Sun himself, and in his other *persona* as Apollo. This is the earliest certain identification of the two gods, for Aesch. *Supp.* 212–3, *Sept.* 858 and fr. 83 Mette (= *TrGF* III p. 158) have again been doubted by recent commentators; cf. Burkert 149 n. 55. Helios is however invoked here as Apollo rather for the etymological play which the name afforded (= 'Destroyer': see Fraenkel on *Ag.* 1081, Cassandra's denunciation of him; cf. Apollyon 'The Destroying Angel', *Revelation* 9.11). **with your lovely light:** Cly. follows this conventional praise of the god with his condemnation; similarly Creusa prefaces her abuse of Apollo with praise of his music, *Ion* 881–6, 905–12. **rightly:** the adv. and synonyms (note the variants 'naturally' in Schol. *Or.* and 'clearly' in Macrob.) are regular in such etymologies, on which see Collard on *Supp.* 497. Cly.'s ruin is emphasised in her exit lines immediately before the entry of the joyful wedding chorus, itself soon to be overtaken by disaster (for such quick contrast as a mode of the play cf. Introd. p. 201, 63–101 n.). **silent meaning:** lit. 'gods' silent names', i.e. voiceless but speaking to those who know the etymology (so Diggle, cf. Kannicht 9). On the naming of gods see A. B. Lloyd on Hdt. 2.3.2, Burkert 182f., Comm. on *Mel.D.* F 494.18; on men's power over gods through using their names see Wilamowitz, *Glaube* I.32 (our passage); S. Pulleyn, *CQ* 44 (1994), 17–25. Cf. *IT* 763 'will tell though silent' (a letter), *Hipp.* 1076 (a deed), and the equivocation whether silence speaks, speech is silent, Pl. *Euthyd.* 300bc, Aristot. *SE* 166a13. [Text: Korzeniewski reconstructs 225–6 by reconciling the differing witnesses.]

227–44. Wedding song by the secondary chorus; since it approaches from outside the palace (see Introd. pp. 202–3 on staging), it probably consists of maiden girls who do not necessarily belong to the palace. Dramatic need dictates its performance in the bridegroom's house, abnormally (Introd., pp. 201–2), rather than to accompany the bride to her new home or the bridal pair into the bedroom: see the bibl. in Diggle, p. 149 n. 1. Like the wedding songs at *Tro.* 308–41 (Cassandra's ecstatic evocation of her own 'wedding'), Ar. *Peace* 1332–57 and *Birds* 1720–65 (both hymns for 'holy marriages' at the end of comedies), it is addressed to the gods of marriage, here both Hymen (227, cf. 233–5) and Aphrodite (228–32); similarly it celebrates both the marriage itself (esp. 231) and its splendid future (236–8, 240–4). For weddings in general see Garland, *Life* 217–25, 332–3: in Tragedy R. Seaford, *JHS* 107 (1987), 106–30. Contiades-Tsitsoni 54–8 discusses the similarities between this hymn and the wedding evocations at *IA* 1036–79 and *Tro.* 308–41, noting their common irony: the audience know that Phaethon the groom is already dead; the marriages of Iphigenia and Cassandra are unreal. The happy hymn is placed between the play's two catastrophes, Phaethon's death and Merops's discoveries.   [The song throws up the play's most textual and interpretative problems, esp. that of the bride's identity: see Introd. p. 198 and below on 233–4, 236–9, 240, 241.]

Metre. Diggle and West, *Metre* 132, 134 identify dactyloepitritic, Kannicht 11 dactylo-iambic. The wedding songs cited above display differing metrical character.

228. in the sky . . . Aphrodite: Pind. fr. 122.3–5 'mother of loves in the sky . . . Aphrodite', cf. *Med.* 840–4.

229–30. wedding-maker for maiden girls: for the Greek Dat. controlled by an honorific title cf. *Pho.* 17, 88; KG I.428, n.1.

231. [**I sing:** text conjectural (Wilamowitz), but according to Diggle not inconsistent with the traces in P. A verb of singing is needed to define the substantival adj. νυμφεῖα lit. 'of the bride'; such self-reference is regular in these songs, e.g. *Tro.* 336, Ar. *Birds* 1729.]

232. Cypris most beautiful: *Hel.* 1348, *IA* 553.

233–4. your boy newly wed: Hymen(aeus), 227, in most mythological accounts son of Apollo and a Muse, in some of Venus (Aphrodite) as 235 here and Bacchus (Dionysus), e.g. Sen. *Med.* 110. All accounts have him disappearing on his wedding night, so that Aphrodite **hid** him **in the heaven:** cf. 228 n. Diggle says succinctly 'The significance . . . of Hymen's death or disappearance is transparent'. This identification of 'your boy' was made by Weil, strongly urged by Diggle pp. 155–60 (cf. *Latomus* 27 [1968], 179–80), favoured by Lloyd-Jones 342 and accepted by Kannicht 9. Much less likely interpretations (and emendations) of 233–4 had been given by Lesky 18–19 and Webster (1967), 229. **boy:** πῶλος, lit. 'colt', like *Pho.* 947; this image of the newly 'broken' or still 'unbroken', i.e. unmarried, child is common of girls e.g. Anacreon *PMG* 417.1, Eur. *Hipp.* 546. Cf. above 107 n. for 'yoking' abnormally of the male in marriage

236–9. If Weil rightly identified Phaethon's bride as a daughter of Helios (accepted at p. 198 above), Aphrodite is invoked here as patroness of the marriage, cf. 229–30. While the bridegroom must be Phaethon, only Merops can be **great king,** whether or not he intends to share power with Phaethon after the wedding (124–6 n.). Thus Aphrodite in 239 **will make the marriage for** Merops, i.e. 'vouchsafe marriage of his son for the king', consistently with the sense of 241 '(Merops) who will be marriage-kin to a goddess', i.e. a daughter of Helios: for the verb νυμφεύεσθαι 'marry (off)', Middle in the sense of the Active, cf. *Hipp.* 561.   **dear to the . . . palace:** i.e. to that of divine Helios, 5; for 'dear' (φίλος) expressing the value set on a new marriage-kinsman cf. *And.* 641, [*Hipp.*] 635.

Similar adjectives for divine abodes e.g. *HF* 406, *Ion* 459. [Text: this constitution of the text is Diggle's, approved by Kannicht 9–10 (but with an uncontracted Fut. form of the verb rather than Diggle's preferred Pres.) who notes that the metrical phrasing corresponds with that of 229–30 in the strophe. The App. records two other constitutions: 'in which (wedding, νυμφεῖα, 231) you (Plur.: Hymen and Aphrodite) make the marriage for . . . king in . . . palace, our ruler dear to Aphrodite' (Hermann) and 'who (Hymen, 234) makes (3rd Pers. Sing.) . . .', then Hermann's text (Lloyd-Jones). Very adventurous conjectures by Wilamowitz, deriving from his insistence that Phaethon's bride was Aphrodite (Introd., p. 198), were supported and developed by Lesky 15–16.]

240. **Oh blessed man:** because Aphrodite will secure the marriage; but the words echo a formula of wedding songs, addressed to groom or bride, *Tro.* 311–2, *Hel.* 375, cf. F 783a below: Seaford (227–44 n. above) 106 n. 5. **greater still than king:** because he will be famous as kin to gods, 241–4, and like the gods themselves in wealth and prosperity: *El.* 994–5, Aesch. *Pers.* 709–11 etc. **happiness:** of divine kinship, ὄλβος as *And.* 1218, *Hel.* 640 etc. [Text: see Lloyd-Jones 342 and Kannicht 10 for the cogency of Hermann's second correction, only the change to 'oh blessed man' being accepted by Diggle.]

241. goddess: 236–9 n. [Text: Diggle's hesitant conjecture of the Dat. is endorsed by Lloyd-Jones 343. For the Dat. with κηδεύειν 'contract a marriage (-relationship) with' cf. e.g. *Thyestes* F 395.3, also of gods.]

242–4. The interlacing of the Greek word-order perhaps tries to reflect the intimacy of **mortal** and **immortals.** **be sung:** Fut. Middle as Passive, *Tro.* 1139, *Bacc.* 1317, etc. **throughout the boundless earth** echoes a Homerism, *Od.* 1.198 etc. **father of a groom:** γαμβρός, most commonly 'son-in-law', is any relation by marriage, e.g. *Hipp.* 635, *And.* 641.

245. The servant here sent indoors by Merops is a stage-extra (cf. Taplin [1977], 75), not the servant who enters at 252: so Webster (1967) 231, Diggle; disputed by D. Bain, *Masters, Servants and Orders* (Manchester, 1981), 53 n. 6; cf. Introd., p. 203.

246. order my wife etc.: similar command for a wife's religious duties *Ion* 422. **honour . . . gods . . . with dancing:** χορεύειν with Dative 'of advantage' *Bacc.* 195. **throughout the palace:** at their house-altars, *Alc.* 170, *HF* 610.

247. circle inside the house: the proper place for them at a wedding, except for their wedding song (227–44 n.), for it is the house and its future which is celebrated, 248 n. Circular dance at a wedding e.g. *IA* 1055–7. [Text: Headlam's correction; the Dat. is locative, cf. Hes. *Theog.* 7, Kannicht 10.]

248. altar of Hestia: e.g. *Or.* 1442. For the hearth-goddess's prime place in all family occasions see e.g. *Alc.* 162–4, *Hom. Hymn* 29.4–6, Pl. *Crat.* 401b–d; Burkert 170. [Text: P was never clearly decipherable in 249: see Diggle. An infinitive (**to . . .**) governing **altar** stood in 250–1.]

251. goddess's precinct: probably Aphrodite's, the goddess inevitably prominent in marriage rituals (cf. 231), but possibly Artemis's: for her role in girls' preliminary marriage rites see *IA* 433, Burkert 151.

252–69. Comparably brief roles for servants etc. bringing important news e.g. Aesch. *Cho.* 875–91, Soph. *Ant.* 1277–1316.

253. majestic: σεμνός, causing awe; a palace Aesch. *Ag.* 519; the cognate verb σεβίζειν *El.* 994, of a man's wealth. Cf. 222 n.

254–7. The servant's alarm is expressed through repeated insistence on smoke and flame, and by the lack of a connective in 256. **door's joins:** either the meeting of the two leaves (*Med.* 1315) or the carpentered joints (cf. on *Cret.* F 472.8). **eye:** lit. 'face'. Diggle cites Dionys. Hal. 5.7.3 and Plut. *Alex.* 3.1 for eyes applied to door-joins.

258. Eur. sends Merops in, preparing him to find Phaethon's body off-stage, 284; he at once fears disaster, 266–9.

259. Hephaestus (also 269): fire's master-god (Burkert 168), so that its sudden appearance is presumed to be his **anger.** Phaedra's nurse assumes her dangerous passion to be Aphrodite's 'anger' *Hipp.* 438; cf. Pan's 'anger' causing an as yet unexplained fit, *Med.* 1272. **visiting:** for the morphologically puzzling verb (ἐπ)εισφρεῖν see Barrett on *Hipp.* 867.

261. Be sure you may not etc.: anxiety to disprove a fear Subj. (as 258), to confirm it Indic.: Jebb on *Phil.* 30. **seeing:** perhaps literally (Diggle), but verbs of seeing are sometimes used of general awareness, e.g. *Cyc.* 154, the bouquet of wine (see Seaford's Comm.). For ἀτμός 'fumes' see on 215.

263. [Text: **no smoke:** a certain correction (Wilamowitz) but an otherwise unattested verbal form.]

265. has her mind etc.: use of ἔχειν (πρός) as e.g. *Pho.* 360.

266. Then: ἀλλά in this exit formula 'indicates agreement' (Denniston, *GP* 16) with the servant's suggestion in 258.

267. storm: image of sudden disaster e.g. *Hcld.* 427–30, Menand. *Sam.* 207–9.

268–9. Mistress of fire: Hecate, torch-kindler and light-bearer *Tro.* 323, *Hel.* 569, *Soph.* F 535 etc.; nocturnal and underworldly, associated and here identified with **Demeter's daughter** Persephone, abducted by dark Hades: *Ion* 1048, Burkert 222. [**favourable:** text: εὐμενής (Bekker, Diggle) of Hecate *Hel.* 569, Soph. *Ant.* 1110 (of chthonian gods generally: A. Henrichs in Hofmann and Harder, *Fragmenta Dramatica* 163 n. 6), rather than πρευμενής (Burges) 'gentle'.]

270–83. Tense lyric alarm by the Cho. anticipating off-stage action (284, 286); it makes a bridge from Cly.'s fear of detection and punishment (216–23: 275–83) and Merops's fear of unknown discovery (266–9), to the realisation of both (284–7). Comparable theatrical passages are given by Collard on *Hec.* 1023–34 and Cropp on *El.* 1147–71; most, like our 270–83, are cast largely in irregular, excited dochmiacs; cf. Kannicht 11, who gives a metrical commentary; also Dale, *LM* 160–1.

270–3. A despairing or panicking Chorus regularly fantasizes escape to the sky or underworld, e.g. *Ion* 1238–9, cf. Barrett on *Hipp.* 1290, R. Padel, *CQ* 24 (1974),

225ff. Most editors punctuate as two questions (translated), Diggle as one continuous question. The former are slightly to be preferred, Kannicht 10 pointing out that **Where?** is otherwise answered within the question itself. **flying:** lit. 'winged', perhaps figurative 'frantic' like *HF* 1187, rather than a literal preparation for **up into heaven.** **vanish utterly:** the already powerful verb ἀμαυροῦν (of life obliterated *Hipp.* 816) is here intensified with Eur.'s favourite preverb ἐκ-. [Text: **unseen:** Eur.'s habit in these fantasies is to apply this adj. predicatively to the person, e.g. *Hipp.* 828, not the destination.]

275–9. Disaster will be revealed: similar wording *Supp.* 603; for such anticipations of a dramatic development by the Cho. see Collard on *Hec.* 83, Kranz, *Stasimon* 209f. **lightning-strokes of Zeus:** the Cho. know of these from the (lost) messenger's report, cf. 214–5. **union with Helios:** Clymene's, 45. The last place in the series of nouns defining (by grammatical apposition) **disaster** is given to the earliest in time, about to be revealed to Merops as the causative one and so the object of his anger. [Text: Diggle's punctuation makes the interruptive interjection emotionally realistic. Some editors put a stop before it.]

280. daughter etc.: Clymene. The Chorus apostrophize an off-stage figure (usually to re-enter, like Cly.) for whom they foresee disaster: with pity e.g. *And.* 497, *Pho.* 1533; with joy *Hec.* 1024ff., cf. *HF* 740. **throat:** as the target of punitive execution, e.g. *Bacc.* 631, *Cret.* F 472e.37; for sacrificial, usually female, throat-killings see N. Loraux, *Tragic Ways of Killing a Woman* (Cambridge, Mass., 1987), 50–2. [Text: 282–3 are obelized because metrically questionable; sense and style are sound, Hermann's λιταῖς **in prayer** being palaeographically convincing but not necessary to idiom: cf. *El.* 221 προσπίτνω σε μὴ θανεῖν.]

284, 286. Off-stage cries reacting to off-stage events, preceding entry by the crier, *HF* 885ff., *Hec.* 1035ff., etc.

287. He calls: as Alcestis's son calls vainly on his dead mother, *Alc.* 402–4.

289–310. Brief monody by the re-entering Merops, who moves apparently from grief at the happy marriage destroyed (290–1, 296) to a summons (308) to a man who will explain Cly.'s knowledge or behaviour (309).

Metre. Many lines in P are written unusually far to the left for lyric verses; Blass suggested they were dochmiac, a rhythm certainly appropriate to Merops's distress.

308. summon: an off-stage character, *IT* 1286, *Bacc.* 170 etc.

311–27. In 313–4 Merops appears to command opening the stage door, to disclose Phaethon's body 312: cf. *Med.* 1314, *Or.* 1561. When the Tutor arrives (for his identification see Introd., p. 202), he is at first very distressed; his apparently single cries of grief (317, 319) are like *Tro.* 578ff. (lyric). Then he collects himself, to ask Merops's intention (321); it is, to know 'who killed my son?' (322: so Blass).

318. Grieve: encouragement following another's grief; cf. *HF* 914, *Hipp.* 1313–4.

320. double: i.e. 'you have twice lamented', 317, 319. Cf. 'double grief' at *Hec.* 518; *Hel.* 143 with Kannicht's note.

321–7. Little can be made of the remaining part-words here.

783a (fr. 1 D). Merops is perhaps explaining to Cly. why he persisted with the marriage despite Phaethon's unwillingness.   **felicitations:** upon the marriage, perhaps an echo of the ritual 'blessing', 240 n.   **unhinged:** ἐκπλήττειν lit. 'knock off (course, out of normality)', a common word, e.g. *Supp.* 160 of others' unsettling enthusiasms, *Polyidus* F 644 their success.

785 (fr. 4 D). Plut. implies that Cly.'s grief for Phaethon was sharpened by re-calling his athleticism, including training for war or the hunt (the **bow**). Did that in itself predispose him to try driving Helios his father's chariot, or was it in his blood? (Hose I.124 compares Ion inheriting his father Apollo's archery, *Ion* 108–11, 158–74. Cf. Introd., pp. 199, 200)   **cornel-bow:** Hdt. 7.92.   **easy to carry:** adj. as [Aesch.] *PV* 350, but is it 'transferred' from the (light) wood to the product? Scorn for athletics: *Autolycus* F 282, *Antiope* F 199; Cropp on *El.* 386–90.   [Text: hopelessly corrupt and unmetrical, with two incongruent constructions joined. Speculative reconstructions reviewed by Diggle, cf. Hose above.]

782 (fr. 6 D). trees will embrace: only a god at play-end could make such a prediction (cf. Hypoth. 16 and Comm.); the reference is to Helios's daughters turned into poplars and shedding tears for Phaethon. The myth located this incident usually in the West, by the River Po (see Introd., p. 198), but Diggle pp. 45–6, 179 thinks of an Eastern location for a tree shrine to Phaethon, citing Plin. *NH* 37.2.33. **cooling:** the Eur. quotation, if sound, illustrates not the noun ψυκτήριον 'shady grove', for which Athen. gives also (correctly) Aesch. F 146, but the adj. in -ιος.

783 (fr. 5 D). Diog. Laert. in citing the fr. associates the phrase **golden clod** with Anaxagoras's prediction of a meteorite split from the sun's mass; perhaps then the messenger is describing the sun beginning to fall as Phaethon loses control of the chariot. For Eur. and Anaxagoras see also 169–70 n.   [Wilamowitz, *Glaube* II.218 n. 2 believed the ascription to Eur. wrong, thinking that he would not include in his play so plain an allusion to the Anaxagorean controversy: but see comment-ators on the 'Socratic' *Hipp.* 377ff.]

783b (fr. 2 D). (Hyades): in popular etymology both 'the rainy ones' (Greek ὕειν 'to rain'), because of their seasonal phenomena, e.g. Hes. *WD* 615, but also 'the piglets' (Greek noun ὗς 'pig'), named from proximity to the luminous star (our Aldebaran) 'the mother pig': see Owen on *Ion* 1156, *OCD* 'Hyades'. They are named in connection with the Pleiads (our 171 and n.) in *El.* 468, and as **three** apparently in *Erec.* (see F 370.107–8 n.).

WISE MELANIPPE and CAPTIVE MELANIPPE

Texts, testimonia. P. Oxy. 2455 frs. 1–2 and P. Leiden inv. 145 (Hypothesis of *Wise Mel.*); P. Berlin 9772 and P. Oxy. 1176 fr. 39 col. 11 (*Capt. Mel.*); P. Berlin 5514 (*Capt. Mel.*); P. Berlin 21144; Nauck frs. 480–514; Mette Nos. 654–687; van Looy, *Zes Tragedies* 196–304. See also App. (below) on F 494, F 495, F 511.

Myth. Dionys. Hal. *Art Rhet.* 8.10 and 9.11 (*Wise Mel.*); Hygin. *Fab.* 186 (mainly *Mel. D.*); Diod. Sic. 4.67, Strabo 6.1.15, *Anth. Pal.* 3.16, Schol. Dionys. Perieget. 461 (all *Capt. Mel.*). Roscher II.2576; Preller–Robert I.589, II.1.53; Gantz 168, 734–5. ('Melanippe' will be in *LIMC* Supplement.)

Illustrations. Wise Mel., Apulian RF krater: A. Cambitoglou and others, *Le Peintre de Darius et son milieu* (Genève, 1986), 190–9 and colour plate p. 24; A.D. Trendall, *Second Suppl. to the Red-Figured Vases of Apulia* (London, 1991: *BICS* Suppl. 60), I.162, No. 283d; Schefold–Jung, *Urkönige*, 47–8, fig. 36a. *Capt. Mel.*, lost relief (*Anth. Pal.* 3.16): Wilamowitz (below), 67–8; van Looy (above), 195–6. Etruscan Urns(?): Brunn–Koerte II.232, Plates 103.1, 104.2–3; Wilamowitz (below), 67 n. 1; Webster, *Euripides* (1967), 155; J. P. Small, *AJA* 80 (1976), 349–63, figs. 1–3; Schefold–Jung 48–9, figs. 37, 38. (*LIMC*: see above.)

Main discussions. R. Wünsch, *RhM* 49 (1894), 91–110; Wilamowitz, *KS* I.440–60 = *Sitzb. Preuss. Akad.* (1921), 63–80; Pickard-Cambridge in Powell (ed.), *New Chapters* III.113–20; Schmid 412–6; Page, *GLP* 108–13 (*Capt. Mel.*); van Looy (above); H. J. Mette, *Lustrum* 9 (1964), 72–4; Z. Vysoky, *LF* 87 (1964), 17–31 (German summ., 31–2); Webster, *Euripides* (1967), 147–57; L. Burelli in L. Braccesi (ed.), *I Tragici greci e l' Occidente* (Bologna, 1979), 160–2 (*Capt. Mel.*). (S. Auffret, *Mélanippe la philosophe* [Paris, 1981], 1–134 gives a non-classicist's view.)

The character and fate of Euripides' young and beautiful female intellectual, granddaughter of the founder of the Hellenic race and of the wise and humane centaur Cheiron, deserve to be better known. Reconstruction of his two plays is hampered by uncertainties about the plot of *Wise Mel.* and about the reliability of the indirect sources for *Capt. Mel.* More than half of the fragments (F 483, 489, 491, 493, 497–514) are not conclusively assigned to one play or the other.

In *Wise Mel.* the young Melanippe has borne twin sons by Poseidon and tried to hide them from her father Aeolus in a stable; when discovered they are taken for cow-born monsters which must be destroyed, and she tries to protect them without incriminating herself, by arguing that they must be some unknown girl's natural children. The twins Aeolus (named after his grandfather) and Boeotus survive to become the ancestors of Aeolian and Boeotian Greeks; the outcome for Melanippe is not known. The preserved Hypothesis material gives the mythical background and plot as far as the crisis. Melanippe's Prologue speech (F 481 known, in part, only since 1908) explained her ancestry, her

240

mother's transformation into a mare and (it seems) miraculous disappearance, her own union with Poseidon, and the hiding of the twins against her father's return from a temporary exile. We do not know the shape of the whole Prologue (perhaps a scene with Melanippe's Nurse followed the speech), nor of the Parodos, nor the identity of the Chorus. Melanippe's father arrived home at some early point, and Epis. 1 must have featured a herdsman bringing the infants and Aeolus deciding to consult his father Hellen. Then perhaps Stas. 1 allowed time for Hellen to arrive, Epis. 2 had the consultation and Aeolus's instruction to Melanippe to dress the infants for burning, Stas. 2 covered this process, and Melanippe returned in Epis. 3 with the infants and interceded for their lives. To this scene belong F 484, 485, probably 482, and perhaps 483, 514.

The continuation is unknown, but presumably the truth emerged (from the Nurse or Melanippe herself?), Aeolus threatened to punish her (encouraged by Hellen as Webster suggests?), and Melanippe asserted her innocence. The oath (of Melanippe?) in F 487, the demand for punishment in F 497, and two fragments about Justice (F 486, 506) fit plausibly into this scheme. F 508–510 and 500 could come from arguments between Aeolus and Hellen over the twins' or Melanippe's fate. Hygin. *Fab.* 186 (see under *Capt. Mel.* below) starts with Melanippe blinded and incarcerated by her father and the infants exposed and rescued by herdsmen. One cannot tell if this reflects the end of *Wise Mel.*, the background of *Capt. Mel.*, or both. The appearance of Melanippe's mother Hippo in the form of a horse at the end of *Wise Mel.* was inferred by Welcker from Pollux 4.141 ('Special masks: . . . Cheiron's daughter Euippe changed into a horse in Euripides'); Hippo had been transformed to prevent her prophesying divine secrets, and later deified as a constellation (see Comm. on F 481.13–22, where it is argued that the romantic account of these transformations in ancient astronomical writers is wrongly ascribed by them to Euripides). Many scholars (including Wilamowitz 74, van Looy 238, Webster 149) conclude that Hippo averted the threatened punishment of Melanippe in *Wise Mel.*, but it could be that Aeolus acted drastically against his daughter (e.g. by blinding her) and that Hippo appeared only in time to reveal his error, like Artemis in *Hipp.* or the Dioscuri in *El.* This would give a tragic twist to the ending and exhibit the suppression of Melanippe's (as of Hippo's) excessive knowledge; women in Melanippe's situation usually suffer while their sons survive (see below under *Motifs etc.*).

A fine Apulian vase, recently published, assembles the main characters of *Wise Mel.* and evokes a critical scene: an old herdsman holds the twins before the aged Hellen while Aeolus looks on from one side, Melanippe and her Nurse from the other. To the left, and not integrated in the action, is Cretheus, one of Aeolus's sons, holding a wreath over a horse. His presence does not necessarily suggest that he had a role in the play. The horse might suggest Hippo, but it is not named like the human characters and shows no sign of being a transformed human. The upper register shows Poseidon, Aphrodite and Eros, whose relevance is obvious, along with Athena, Artemis and Apollo, who can be only loosely associated with the story. (On this vase see Green, *Theatre* 54–6, and in general cf. Gen. Introd. above, pp. 3–4. The identification of Melanippe's defence speech on an Etruscan urn-relief, e.g. Schefold–Jung 48 with fig. 37, is implausible.)

Capt. Mel. was not simply a sequel to *Wise Mel.* (unless *Wise Mel.* ended with her banishment to S. Italy with the infant twins). Its key features were the rearing of the twins by a royal couple, a foiled plot by their stepmother to have them killed as they approached adulthood, and the liberation of Melanippe by her sons from the bondage which gives the play its subtitle. We have two different versions of such a story, neither directly reproducing Euripides:

In Hygin. *Fab.* 186 Melanippe, 'the very beautiful daughter of Desmontes, or of Aeolus as other poets say', is raped by Poseidon and bears Boeotus and Aeolus. 'Desmontes' blinds and imprisons her, and exposes the children who are fed by a cow. Herdsmen look after them, but when Metapontus ('king of Icaria') asks his wife Theano to bear him children or give up her royal position she acquires the twins and presents them as her own sons. Later she bears two sons of her own and in due course, since Metapontus favours the older boys, Theano prompts her own sons to kill them and secure the kingdom. They attempt this during a hunting expedition, while Metapontus is absent sacrificing to the Metapontine Artemis, but the twins receive help from Poseidon and kill Theano's sons. She commits suicide, and the twins take refuge with the herdsmen and learn from Poseidon of their real parentage and Melanippe's incarceration. They kill 'Desmontes', release their mother (her sight restored by Poseidon), take her to 'Icaria' and tell Metapontus the truth about Theano. Metapontus marries Melanippe and adopts the twins. They found communities named after themselves 'in the Propontis'.

In Diod. 4.67 the mother of Boeotus and Aeolus by Poseidon is Arne (here confusedly the daughter of Hippotas's son Aeolus and of Melanippe, and great-great-granddaughter of Aeolus son of Hellen). Arne's father gives her away during her pregnancy to Metapontius, who 'in accordance with an oracle' adopts the twins when they are born. Later they seize the kingdom during a civil conflict and kill Metapontius's wife Autolyte with whom Arne has quarrelled. To escape his wrath they sail away with Arne and a band of friends, Aeolus to settle the Aeolian Isles north of Sicily, Boeotus to succeed his grandfather in central Greece where he names his land Arne and his people the Boiotoi. (Schol. Dionys. Perieget. 461 has a variant with Metapontus ruling the Italoi and dismissing his first wife 'Siris' to the place called Siris in order to marry Arne.)

Hyginus is the closer to the Euripidean fragments, while Diodorus may help in overcoming difficulties and gaps. Hyginus's 'Desmontes' obviously results from a misunderstanding of the subtitle *Desmotis*; in Euripides' plot Melanippe's father was presumably Aeolus, and if this is still the Thessalian Aeolus the punishment of Melanippe's father which Hyginus recounts can hardly come from Euripides. Hyginus's 'Icaria' (despite the attempts of Wünsch and of J. Beloch, *Hermes* 29 [1894] 605 to associate Metapontus with the Attic deme of that name) must be 'Italia', in Euripides' time the area of Bruttium and S. Lucania (cf. e.g. Strabo 6.1.4.). The play must be sited at Metapontium, its easternmost city; this is indicated by the king's name in both versions, by Artemis's title in Hyginus, by the 'Italoi' in Schol. Dionys., by Diodorus's connection of the youngest Aeolus with the Aeolian Isles, and above all by Strabo's mention (6.1.15) of the story of 'Metapontus and Melanippe Desmotis and her son Boeotus' told at Metapontium. Schol. Dionys.'s 'Siris', the name of both a river and a Greek colony close to Metapontium (see below, p. 245) is the most likely name for Euripides' Queen in view of F 496. Concerning Melanippe, then, we need to know how she reached Italy, how she has lived while her sons have grown up, and why she is 'Captive' if an imprisonment by 'Desmontes' is discounted. Page and Webster may be right in inferring from Diodorus that Aeolus gave or sent her while pregnant to Metapontus. Then perhaps the twins were exposed or given to a herdsman who later gave them to the .Queen, or (as Vysoky infers further from Diodorus, comparing F 491) Metapontus adopted the twins at birth and was not deceived by the Queen into thinking they were his own sons. In either case Melanippe may have lived in the palace as a slave, with or without knowing her sons' identity. Her role in the action becomes suitably important if her imprisonment was imposed by the Queen during the play, to secure her silence concerning the past (Wilamowitz) or after discovering the plot against her sons (Page) or quarrelling with the Queen as in Diodorus (Vysoky). Van Looy and Webster prefer to place her imprisonment shortly before the start of the play, during the King's absence. It remains unclear whether Melanippe was blinded by her father and healed by Poseidon (as Hyginus relates), or blinded by the Queen and healed by Poseidon, or not blinded at all. The assertion in *Anth. Pal.* 3.16 that the twins rescued her from *death* might possibly reflect a threat to her life by the Queen in the play.

The fragments of *Capt. Mel.*, even with two substantial papyri, offer limited help. F 495 yields a Report scene and confirms Hyginus's ambush, but by the Queen's brothers rather than her sons. (Most scholars have concluded that in Euripides' play the Queen remained childless; Page supposes young sons with their uncles acting on their behalf, but this makes the King's position and the Queen's death problematic.) F 494 reveals a debate on misogyny to which F 493 and 498 probably belong too. The situation of Melanippe, the twins and the King and Queen must have been explained in the Prologue (probably including F 489). Early episodes are generally agreed to have included the plotting between the Queen and her brothers and (though Wünsch and van Looy place it near the end) the debate on misogyny. Opinions vary on the extent of this debate (to include marriage, cf. F 501–3, and adoption, F 491?) and on the debaters: Metapontus and Melanippe (Wünsch, Wilamowitz, van Looy), or Metapontus and the Queen (Schmid), or the twins and Melanippe in a debate on lifestyles as in *Antiope* (Webster, who adds F 492 on mirth-makers at symposia), or the Queen addressing the Chorus like Phaedra in *Hipp.* (Vysoky). Whether Melanippe was imprisoned or even appeared during the first part is unclear as noted above. After the report of the failed ambush the Queen either committed suicide (Hyginus) or was killed by the twins (Diodorus, accepted by Wilamowitz, van Looy), and the twins liberated Melanippe. Hyginus's narrative may or may not be a useful guide here. (The amount of text lost between the end of the Messenger's report and the end of the play is unknown: see Comm. on F 495.51). A final appearance of Poseidon, confirming his paternity, directing the twins' futures and probably the marriage of Melanippe and Metapontus, and referring to the naming of Siris (F 496), is widely accepted.

The identification of the Queen's suicide on a group of Etruscan urns, proposed by Brunn–Koerte and accepted by e.g. Webster (hesitantly) and Schefold–Jung, is questionable (cf. Wilamowitz 67–8, Small 353–4).

Other ascriptions. Only Hartung's ascription of F 928 to *Wise Mel.* is at all attractive (but not admitted by Kannicht), a comment on the dangers of excessive beauty like Ennius, *Mel.* fr. 118 Jocelyn. The following have little or no chance of belonging to either play: some parts of a Strasbourg papyrus (see Mette No. 1356; rejected by van Looy 187–92, 321); fr. 14 N = *TrGF* F 929b (*Capt. Mel.* No. 656 Mette); the comic P. Lit. Lond. 86 (= P. Grenf. 12, *CGFP* fr. 226, rejected by van Looy 192–4, 321); F 910; F 950; F 1004 (cf. Introd. to *Cretans*, p. 56); *TrGF* II adesp. F 510.

Myth. No coherent account of Melanippe's story survives from before the Augustan era. Her name ('Black-Mare') suggests the mythical Melanippe may have originated as an equine consort of the horse-god Poseidon (on whom see e.g. Burkert 138–9). In Euripides she is daughter of Hippo (who has been transformed into a mare) and granddaughter of the centaur Cheiron. Diod. 4.67.3 makes her the mother of Hippotas's son Aeolus who is master of the winds in Hom. *Od.* 10.2. (On the recurrence of wind- and horse-spirits in this set of myths see Wilamowitz 77–80.) Perhaps it was the conflation of the master of the winds with Aeolus son of Hellen which caused Melanippe to become an alternative to Arne as mother (usually by Poseidon) of Boeotus. Arne's name identifies her both with Arne in Thessaly where the Boeoti were supposed to have originated (Thuc. 1.12.3) and with the Boeotian place Arne of Hom. *Il.* 2. 507. Arne/Melanippe sometimes (as in Euripides) also bears an Aeolus who could be identified with Aeolian settlements abroad (perhaps for Euripides simply with the

Aeolis of NW Asia Minor). The Hesiodic *Catalogue*, however, seems not to have included her in the family of Hellen's son Aeolus and may have placed Arne and Boeotus in a separate Boeotian family (cf. West, *Catalogue* 58–69, 102).

For Melanippe in S. Italy (*Capt. Mel.*) evidence reaches us through Strabo 6.1.15: Euripides' contemporary Antiochus of Syracuse knew a colonial legend in which she was transported to Metapontus at Metapontium (both were originally called Metabos, and Metapontus was worshipped as the city's founding hero).[1] The birth and adoption of her sons there provided a link between colony and homeland, albeit entailing the oddity that Boeotus must now return to Greece to settle Boeotia. The probable identification of the unhappy wife as Siris also seems to evoke colonial history. The archaic state of Siris seems to have been formed from two Ionian colonial settlements, Polieion (early 7th C.: now the abundant archaeological site of Policoro) and Siris (mid–7th C.: on both see L. Moscati Castelnuovo, *Siris* [Brussels, 1989]). It was destroyed and annexed by Achaeans from neighbouring colonies including Metapontium in the early 6th C., and in 433 refounded as Heraclea under the influence of Thurii and Tarentum. F 496 suggests that the future of Siris, named after the dead Queen, was foretold at the end of *Capt. Mel.* (see F 496 n.). Connections have been suggested (recently by Burelli) between Euripides' use of this Metapontine legend and Athenian strategic interest in the area in his time. Tragedies were probably performed at Heraclea by the end of the 5th C. (Taplin [above, p. 3 n. 2], 16–17), and Euripides could have envisaged a production there.

Themes and characters. A royal daughter, seduced or raped by a god or hero, bears a son or sons who survive exposure to fulfil a heroic destiny; she suffers tribulations which lead sometimes to her death, sometimes to survival and reunion with her son(s). Euripides used this mythical core inventively in many plays. In its setting at the time of the sons' birth *Wise Mel.* resembles the relatively early *Danae* (the mother cast out to sea in a chest with her infant son Perseus) and *Aeolus* (where the birth of a son to Canace and her brother Macareus caused their father to drive them to suicide); also the undated *Alope* (killed by her father after bearing Hippothoon to Poseidon; the child re-exposed, at least in Hygin. *Fab.* 187) and the late *Auge* (rescued with the infant Telephus from her father's anger by her seducer Heracles, and floated to Mysia in a chest).[2]

---

[1] See esp. Wilamowitz 69. Steph. Byz., 'Metapontion', makes Metabos/Metapontus a son of Sisyphus, one of Aeolus's many sons, which could be relevant for Eur. Antiochus also quoted from the archaic epic poet Asius of Samos (*EGF* F 2) a variant version of the birth of Boeotus to Mel. There were competing accounts of the foundation of Metapontium: see Maehler's Comm. on Bacchyl. 11, esp. p. 195.

[2] See M. Huys, *SEJG* 31 (1989–90), 169–185, on *Auge* (with 172 n. 13 on *Alope*).

Capt. Mel. shares its outline — the sons grown up, rescuing their mother from tribulations and reunited with her through divine assistance — with some of Euripides' most inventive and elaborate plays. In *Antiope* the heroine has exposed her twin sons by Zeus (Amphion and Zethus), then been captured, imprisoned and persecuted by a usurping uncle Lycus and his jealous wife Dirce; Dionysus frees her to be recognised by the twins who punish Dirce (she becomes a spring) and claim their heritage. *Hypsipyle* concerned the heroine's separation from her infant sons fathered by Jason, her exile and slavery as a nursemaid in the Nemean royal household, a crisis when she faces punishment by the Queen for causing the death of the Queen's son, the twins distinguishing themselves in athletic games, and her reunion with them. *Ion* is a subtle variation: Creusa's son by Apollo is exposed, reared at Delphi, and claimed by her husband Xuthus so that Creusa becomes the jealous 'stepmother' and each almost kills the other before the recognition. *Hyps.* is surely, *Antiope* not so surely, later than *Capt. Mel.*; Wilamowitz 76 saw a model for these three in Soph. *Tyro B* (dated before 414 and deriving from Hom. *Od.* 11.235–59) where the daughter of Salmoneus and future wife of Cretheus (both sons of Aeolus) was seduced by Poseidon, bore and exposed Pelias and Neleus, and was later rescued by them from the persecution of her stepmother Sidero. The uncertainty of the chronological relationship between *Tyro B* and *Capt. Mel.* is stressed by Pohlenz I.409, van Looy 302, Webster 150.

In *Wise Mel.* Melanippe is one of Euripides' intelligent and rhetorically articulate women placed in sexually charged situations beyond their control and exposed to the inflexibilities of the surrounding male world. Melanippe is distinguished by her connection with the Centaur family and her mother's knowledge of arcane things such as pharmacy, cosmology, astrology and prophecy (F 481.16–21, 483, 484). This alien element, and her unfeminine eloquence, seem calculated to provoke an ambivalent response in Euripides' audience; Aristophanes groups Melanippe with Phaedra as a 'pernicious woman' (γυνὴ πονηρά, *Thesm.* 547). But she is both younger and more guiltless in her actions than Phaedra, Pasiphae or Medea, and may have been less interesting as a tragic character. Euripides achieved some dramatic impact through the singularity of her intellect and the peculiar situation in which she defended her children. He may have made Aeolus a more than one-dimensional figure by contrasting him (as F 500, 508–510 may suggest) with the aged and reactionary Hellen, and perhaps by playing on his recent exile for murder, a routine device in itself (see Comm. on Hypoth. 5) but capable of giving point to Melanippe's warning about inflicting 'murder' on the infants, F 485. Aeolus's relationship with the vanished Hippo might also have coloured his attitude to Melanippe's wisdom and to her illegitimate children.

Whether Melanippe had the same distinctive character in *Capt. Mel.* is unknown, and we can only guess that her role (if active at all) may have developed the pathos arising from the loss of her sons (F 505, ?507: cf. esp. Creusa in *Ion*, Hecuba in *Alex.*, Hypsipyle). The Queen may have been the more central character, locked in an unhappy marriage (F 501–3) and suffering from her childlessness like Hermione in her conflict with Andromache (*And.* 32ff., 155ff. etc.). The criticisms of misogyny would have point in her mouth, although Melanippe is at least an equally suitable proponent (cf. Wilamowitz 67, van Looy 254). It should not be assumed that the Queen was wholly unsympathetic any more than Phaedra or even Hermione or Medea. She might have been portrayed as influenced by her family, especially the brothers who are ultimately killed. Van Looy suggested plausibly, in view of F 502, 503, that Metapontus had married 'above himself' into a royal family whose superior status fuels resentment of his adoption of Melanippe's sons. (Hermione is status-conscious in *And.*, Creusa in *Ion*, Hecuba and her sons in *Alex.*, the uncles whom Telephus kills in Soph. *Aleadae.*) If F 503 closed the play (see Comm.), this points to both marriage and status as significant themes in it. The question of the status of the twins (innate nobility transcending apparently low birth as always in tales of exposed heroic children) is evident in F 495.19–23, 40–3, and perhaps F 504, 511.

Staging. No special problems arise. The unusually masked Hippo (Pollux: above, p. 241) can be compared with the cow-horned Io in [Aesch.] *PV* and (Pollux again) the transformed Actaeon in an unknown play.

Dates. Wise *Mel.* is quoted by Aristophanes in 411, and (probably) *Capt. Mel.* by Eupolis in 412 (see App. on F 482, 487, 507). The metrical evidence suggests dates between the mid-420s and these limits (though possibly biased data may make *Wise Mel.* look later than it is even if F 497, 500, 506, 508–510 are included). There are no compelling circumstantial grounds for dating either play, but the comparisons under *Themes* above and the S. Italian setting of *Capt. Mel.* encourage the hunch that *Wise Mel.* belongs to the 420s and *Capt. Mel.* closer to 412. For details and refs. see Cropp–Fick 83–4.

Other dramatisations; influence. Wise *Mel.* seems to have made the greater impression. Aristophanes exploits lines from it three times (F 481.1, 482, 487) and refers to Melanippe in it at *Thesm.* 547 (above, p. 246). Eupolis used a line probably from *Capt. Mel.* (F 507.1). Melanippe's famous speech in *Wise Mel.* was used by Aristot. *Poet.* 1454a. 22–31 to exemplify an unsuitable excess of cleverness in a woman. It was *Wise Mel.* too that Ennius chose for a Latin version, the only other known treatment. Among six short book fragments, frs. 120 and 121 Jocelyn have Hellen advising Aeolus to burn the infants, fr. 118 probably comes from a criticism of Melanippe's beauty, and fr. 119 from a wish for the future of the twins as rulers: see Jocelyn 382–7, van Looy 194–5, and Mette, *Lustrum* 9 (1964), 73–4. There seem to be no modern derivatives.

ΜΕΛΑΝΙΠΠΗ Η ΣΟΦΗ

test. i Hypothesis

ἡ δὲ τῆς σοφῆς Μελανίππης (i.e. ὑπόθεσις) αὕτη · Ἕλληνος τοῦ
Διὸς Αἴολος τεκνωθεὶς ἐκ μὲν Εὐρυδίκης ἐγέννησε Κρηθέα καὶ
Σαλμωνέα καὶ Σίσυφον, ἐκ δὲ τῆς Χείρωνος θυγατρὸς Ἵππης
κάλλει διαφέρουσαν Μελανίππην. αὐτὸς μὲν οὖν φόνον ποιήσας
ἐπ᾽ ἐνιαυτὸν ἀπῆλθε φυγάς, τὴν δὲ Μελανίππην Ποσειδῶν   5
διδύμων παίδων ἔγκυον ἐποίησεν. ἡ δὲ διὰ τὴν προσδοκίαν τῆς
τοῦ πατρὸς παρουσίας τοὺς γεννηθέντας εἰς τὴν βούστασιν
ἔδωκε τῆι τροφῶι θεῖναι κατὰ τὴν ἐντολὴν τοῦ κατασπείρ-
αντος. ὑπὸ τὴν κάθοδον δὲ τοῦ δυνάστου τὰ βρέφη τινὲς τῶν
βουκόλων φυλαττόμενα μὲν ὑπὸ τοῦ ταύρου, θηλαζόμενα δὲ   10
ὑπὸ μιᾶς τῶν βοῶν ἰδόντες, ὡς βουγενῆ τέρατα τῶι βασιλεῖ
προσήνεγκαν. ὁ δὲ τῆι τοῦ πατρὸς Ἕλληνος γνώμηι πεισθεὶς
ὁλοκαυτοῦν τὰ βρέφη κρίνας Μελανίππηι τῆι θυγατρὶ προσ-
έταξε⟨ν ἐν⟩ταφίοις αὐτὰ κοσμῆσαι. ἡ δὲ καὶ τὸν κόσμον
αὐτοῖς ἐπέθηκε καὶ λόγον εἰς παραίτησιν ἐξέθηκε φιλότιμον.   15
προλογίζει Μελανίππη καὶ λέγει ταῦτα (**F 481**) ἐν προ-
οιμίοις.

480   *See App. on F 481.1*

481 *Beginning of Melanippe's Prologue speech:*

ΜΕΛΑΝΙΠΠΗ   Ζεύς, ὡς λέλεκται τῆς ἀληθείας ὕπο,
                Ἕλλην᾽ ἔτιχθ᾽ ὃς ἐξέφυσεν Αἴολον ·
                οὗ χθών, ὅσην Πηνειὸς Ἀσωποῦ θ᾽ ὕδωρ

test. i Hypothesis (665a M) Ioannes Logothetes, Comm. on Hermogenes' Περὶ μεθόδου δεινότητος 28 (ed. H. Rabe *RhM* 63 [1908], 145); same text (to 15 φιλότιμον) with minor divergences
in Gregory of Corinth's Comm. on the same passage, *Rhet. Gr.* 7.1313 Walz (whence Nauck
p. 509f.); parts of 2–11 (ἐ]κ μὲν . . . τ[έρατα) in P. Oxy. 2455 (2ⁿᵈ C. A.D.); parts of 10–14
(θηλαζόμε]νοι *(sic)* . . . [κοσμ]ῆσαι_ or]ἡ δὲ κ[αὶ) in P. Leiden inv. 145 recto (1ˢᵗ–2ⁿᵈ C.
A.D.), ed. R. Daniel, *Papyrologica Lugduno-Batava XXV* (Leiden, 1991), 3–4 (cf. W. Luppe, *ZPE*
89 (1991), 15–17: P. Leiden's divergences negligible).   1 ⟨ὑφ᾽⟩ Ἕλληνος prob. in P. Oxy.:
Luppe, *ZPE* 73 (1988) 30   3 Ἱπποῦς von Arnim (cf. F 481.21)   13–14 προσέταξεν ἐνταφίοις
Greg.

248

THE WISE MELANIPPE

test. i   Hypothesis

The (plot) of the *Wise Melanippe* is this. Aeolus was begotten by Zeus's son Hellen. By Eurydice he fathered Cretheus, Salmoneus and Sisyphus, and by Cheiron's daughter Hippe the extraordinarily beautiful Melanippe. Now he himself went into a year's exile for committing a murder, and Melanippe was impregnated by Poseidon[5] with twin sons. In the expectation of her father's return she gave the infants when she had borne them to her nurse to place in the ox-stable, in accordance with their father's instruction. Upon the ruler's homecoming, some of the ox-herds saw the infants being watched over by the bull and suckled[10] by one of the cows. Taking them to be the monstrous progeny of the cow, they brought them to the king who, following his father Hellen's opinion, decided to burn up the infants and instructed his daughter Melanippe to furnish them with funeral apparel. Melanippe put the apparel on them, and also interceded for them with an ambitious speech.[15]

Melanippe delivers the Prologue in the play and speaks as follows (**F 481**) in her opening.

480 N   *See App. on F 481.1*

481 *Beginning of Melanippe's Prologue speech:*

Me. Zeus, as is stated by true tradition, sired Hellen who was father to Aeolus. All of the land that Peneus and the waters of Asopus

---

481 (665a–c M) Ioannes Logothetes (see under Hypothesis above): corr. by Rabe except where noted.   1–2 ἔτιχθ᾽ cited before the Hypothesis by Ioann. and Greg. (= fr. 481 N)   1 = Ar. *Frogs* 1244, attrib. Eur. *Mel.S.* by Schol. V (Eur. by Schol. R); cited by Hermog. Π. μεθ. δειν. 28, attrib. Eur.; Plut. *Mor.* 756c, attrib. Eur. *Mel.*   P. Oxy. 2455 fr. 1 has the beginning of 1 in a different form (see below).   Plut. *Mor.* 756b cites as the original first line (= **480** N/No. 665d M) Ζεύς, ⟨ὅστις ὁ Ζεύς·⟩ οὐ γὰρ οἶδα πλὴν λόγωι, 'Zeus, whoever Zeus is; for I know not but by report'; this is also cited by Ps.-Justin, *Monarch.* 5, confused and adjusted to fit with *Tro.* 886–7, all attrib. Eur. *Hec.*; and by Lucian 21 (*Zeus in Tragedy*) 41, attrib. Eur., with κλύων 'hearing' added after λόγωι in nearly all mss.; adapted in Athenagoras, *Legatio* 5, attrib. Eur.: see further Comm.   11 ἀλλ᾽ . . . λόγος = fr. 970 N (Plut. *Mor.* 390c and 431a, both attrib. Eur.)   1 Ζεὺς δε[P. Oxy.

ὑγροῖς ὁρίζων ἐντὸς ἀγκῶσι στέγει,
σκήπτρων ἀκούει πᾶσα καὶ κικλήισκεται 5
ἐπώνυμος χθὼν Αἰολὶς τοὐμοῦ πατρός.
ἐν μὲν τόδ᾽ ἐξέβλαστεν Ἕλληνος γένος·
πτόρθον δ᾽ ἀφῆκεν ἄλλον εἰς ἄλλην πόλιν
κλεινάς ⟨τ᾽⟩ Ἀθήνας Ξοῦθον, ὧι νύμφη ποτὲ
θυγάτηρ Ἐρεχθέως Κεκροπίας ἐπ᾽ αὐχένι 10
Ἴων᾽ ἔτικτεν. ἀλλ᾽ ἀνοιστέος λόγος
ὄνομά τε τοὐμὸν κεῖσ᾽ ὅθενπερ ἠρξάμην.
καλοῦσι Μελανίππην ⟨με⟩, Χείρωνος δέ με
ἔτικτε θυγάτηρ Αἰόλωι· κείνην μὲν οὖν
ξανθῆι κατεπτέρωσεν ἱππείαι τριχὶ 15
Ζεύς, οὕνεχ᾽ ὕμνους ἦιδε χρησμωιδοὺς βροτοῖς
ἄκη πόνων φράζουσα καὶ λυτήρια.
πυκνῆι θυέλληι δ᾽ αἰθέρος διώκεται
μουσεῖον ἐκλιποῦσα Κωρύκιόν τ᾽ ὄρος.
νύμφη δὲ θεσπιωιδὸς ἀνθρώπων ὕπο 20
Ἱππὼ κέκληται σώματος δι᾽ ἀλλαγάς.
μητρὸς μὲν ὧδε τῆς ἐμῆς ἔχει πέρι.

the source concludes in prose:

εἶτα λέγει καὶ ὅτι Ποσειδῶνι μιγεῖσα τέτοκε τοὺς
διδύμους παῖδας.

482 (483 N) (Με.) ἐγὼ γυνὴ μέν εἰμι, νοῦς δ᾽ ἔνεστί μοι.

483 (482 N) ἢ πρῶτα μὲν τὰ θεῖα προυμαντεύσατο
χρησμοῖσι σαφέσιν ἀστέρων ἐπ᾽ ἀντολαῖς.

---

4 ὁρίζον Rabe   8 a following line lost, Wilamowitz   9 ⟨τ᾽⟩ or ⟨δ᾽⟩ Petersen   νύμφη
Κρέουσά ποτε Ioann.   12 ἐπ᾽ ὄνομα τοὐμὸν Wilamowitz   ηὐξάμην Ioann.   19 [τ᾽] Wilamowitz, CPh 3 (1908), 225 n. 2 (later withdrawn)   21 ἱππο Ioann.; cf. App. to F 483   δι᾽ ἀλλαγάς
Brinkmann (see Rabe) διαλλαγαῖς Ioann.   **482** (483 N, 669 M) = Ar. Lys. 1124, where Schol.
attrib. 1124 or 1125 to Eur. Mel.S. (1125–7 αὐτὴ δ᾽ ἐμαυτῆς οὐ κακῶς γνώμης ἔχω·| τοὺς δ᾽
ἐκ πατρός τε καὶ γεραιτέρων λόγους | πολλοὺς ἀκούσασ᾽ οὐ μεμούσωμαι κακῶς, 'I am
not poorly equipped for myself with understanding; and having heard the discourse of my father

bound and contain in the crooks of their wet arms hearkens to
Aeolus and his rule, and it is called[5] the Aeolian land, being named
after my father. This is one line that grew from Hellen; other
branches he sent forth to other realms, <and> to glorious Athens
Xuthus, whose bride, Erectheus's daughter, bore him a son, Ion, on
Cecropia's promontory.[10]
But I must bring my tale, and my name, back to the point
whence I began. They call <me> Melanippe; Cheiron's daughter
bore me to Aeolus. Now she became plumed with tawny horse-
hair[15] by Zeus because she sang oracular songs to men, telling
them cures and deliverances from their pains. She was swept away
by a dense squall of mist, quitting her place of inspiration, the
Corycian mountain. This young prophetess is known by men[20] as
Hippo, owing to the alteration of her body. That is the story
concerning my mother.

Then she adds that she has mated with Poseidon and borne
the twin sons.

482 (483 N)

(Me.) I am a woman, but I have intelligence.

Melanippe opening her defence of the infants.

483 (482 N)

. . . who was the first to foretell divine intentions in
accurate prophecies based on the risings of the stars.

Hippo described perhaps by Melanippe.

---

and his elders in abundance, I am not poorly accomplished in the Muses' arts', may be more or
less closely derived from *Mel.S.*: Nauck)   1 μοῦσα δ' ἔνεστί Suidas μ 1304 Adler (μουσω-
θῆναι) citing *Lys.* 1124   μοῦσα δ' ἔστι μοι Porson, cf. *Med.* 1085   **483** (482 N, 666 M)
Clem. Alex. *Strom.* 1.15.73, attrib. Eur. 'about Cheiron's daughter Hippo'; similarly (but 'Hippe')
Cyril Alex., *Against Julian* 4 (Migne, *Patrol.Gr.* vol. 76, p. 705); assigned to *Mel.S.* by Valckenaer
2 χρησμοῖσιν ἢ δι' ἀστέρων ἐπανατολάς Clem. ἐπ' ἀντολαῖς· ἐπ' ἀνατολαῖς Hesych. ε
4199 Latte

484	Με.	κοὐκ ἐμὸς ὁ μῦθος, ἀλλ' ἐμῆς μητρὸς πάρα,
		ὡς οὐρανός τε γαῖά τ' ἦν μορφὴ μία·
		ἐπεὶ δ' ἐχωρίσθησαν ἀλλήλων δίχα,
		τίκτουσι πάντα κἀνέδωκαν εἰς φάος,
		δένδρη, πετεινά, θῆρας οὓς [θ'] ἅλμη τρέφει		5
		γένος τε θνητῶν.

485	*Prose paraphrase of an argument of Melanippe:*

	Με.	εἰ δὲ παρθένος φθαρεῖσα ἐξέθηκε τὰ παιδία
		καὶ φοβουμένη τὸν πατέρα, σὺ φόνον δράσεις;

486	(Χορός)	*(a)* δικαιοσύνας τὸ χρύσεον πρόσωπον

		(b) οὔθ' ἕσπερος οὔθ' ἑῷος οὕτω θαυμαστός

		(The last four words in (b) may be prose paraphrase.)

487		ὄμνυμι δ' ἱερὸν αἰθέρ', οἴκησιν Διός

488 N		*See test. v TrGF and Comm. on F 481.13–22*

Plausibly attributed to *Mel.S.*: F 497, 506, 508, 509, 510, (500?, 514?)

ΜΕΛΑΝΙΠΠΗ Η ΔΕΣΜΩΤΙΣ

*489		τὸν δ' ἀμφὶ βοῦς ῥιφέντα Βοιωτὸν καλεῖν

484 (667 M) 1–2 Dionys. Hal. *Art Rhet.* 9.11, attrib. Mel. in Eur. *Mel.S.*   1 Dionys. Hal. *Art Rhet.*
8.10, attrib. Mel. in Eur. *Mel.S.*   κοὐκ...ἀλλ(ά) adapted by Pl. *Symp.* 177a.3, attrib. 'Mel. in Eur.';
Aristid. II.132 Behr, attrib. 'Pl. making fun of Eur.'; often elsewhere without attrib.   2–6 Diod.
Sic. 1.7.7, Euseb. *Praep. Evang.* 1.7.9, both attrib. Eur. *Mel.*   2–4 Tzetzes *Exeg. Iliad.* p. 41.18
Hermann   2 οὐρανός . . . μία is inscribed with three Orphic inscriptions on a 3ʳᵈ–6ᵗʰ C. A.D.
alabaster bowl: see R. Delbrueck and W. Vollgraff, *JHS* 54 (1934), 129–39   5 θ' deleted by
Wecklein   **485** (668 M) Dionys. Hal. *Art Rhet.* 9.11, attrib. Mel. in Eur. *Mel.S.*   **486** (671 M)
(a) Anon. Comm. Aristot. *Eth.Nic.* 1129b28 (*Comm.Aristot.Gr.* XX, p. 210 Heylblut), attrib. Eur.
Mel.S.; Athen. 12.65, 546b (= Aristoxenus F 50 Wehrli; repeated by Eustath. on Hom. *Od.* 1.44),

484   *Me*. This account is not my own; I had it from my mother.
Heaven and Earth were once a single form; but when they
were separated from each other into two, they bore and
delivered into the light all things: trees, winged creatures,
beasts reared by the briny sea[5] — and the human race.

Part of Melanippe's defence of the infants.

485   *Me*. But if a girl exposed the children because she had been
raped and was in fear of her father, will you then commit
murder?

*Paraphrase of an argument of Melanippe in defence of the
infants.*

486   *(Chorus) (a)* Justice's golden countenance

(b) Neither evening- *nor morning-star is so marvellous.*

The Chorus hope for, or celebrate, Melanippe's vindication?

487   I swear by holy aether, Zeus's dwelling.

Melanippe asserting her innocence?

488 N   *See test. v* TrGF *and Comm. on F 481.13–22*

Plausibly attributed to *Wise Mel.*: F 497, 506, 508, 509, 510, (500?,
514?)

THE CAPTIVE MELANIPPE

*489   . . . and to call the one thrown amongst oxen 'Boeotus'.

Probably from the Prologue.

unattrib.   *(b)* Aristot. *Eth.Nic.* 1129b28, the first two words attrib. Eur. *Mel.S.* in the same
Comm.   There are several derivative adaptations of these phrases.   **487** (670 M) Ar.
Thesm. 272 (with τοίνυν 'now' for δ' ἱερὸν), attrib. Eur. *Mel.* by Schol.; (exactly) Schol.
Ar. *Frogs* 100 (αἰθέρα Διός δωμάτιον, 'aether, Zeus's bedroom': similarly *Frogs* 311),
attrib. Eur. *Mel.* (*Mel.S.* Bergler, cf. Schol. M); Suidas π 356 Adler (παρακεκινδυνευμέν-
ον), attrib. Eur.   **489** (657 M) Steph. Byz. *Ethn.*, 'Βοιωτία' (p. 173 Meineke), attrib. Eur.;
paraphrased by Eustath. Comm. Dionys. Perieget. 426 (*Geogr. Graec. Min.* II.296 Müller),
unattrib.; assigned to *Mel.D.* by Wilamowitz   βοῦς Meineke βοῦν Steph. βόας Eustath.

490   σὺν τῶι θεῶι χρὴ τοὺς σοφοὺς ἀναστρέφειν
       βουλεύματ' ἀεὶ πρὸς τὸ χρησιμώτερον.

491   ἴστω δ' ἄφρων ὢν ὅστις ἄτεκνος ὢν τὸ πρὶν
       παῖδας θυραίους εἰς δόμους ἐκτήσατο,
       τὴν μοῖραν εἰς τὸ μὴ χρεὼν παραστρέφων·
       ὧι γὰρ θεοὶ διδῶσι μὴ φῦναι τέκνα,
       οὐ χρὴ μάχεσθαι πρὸς τὸ θεῖον, ἀλλ' ἐᾶν.   5

492   ἀνδρῶν δὲ πολλοὶ τοῦ γέλωτος οὕνεκα
       ἀσκοῦσι χάριτας κερτόμους· ἐγὼ δέ πως
       μισῶ γελοίους, οἵτινες τήτηι σοφῶν
       ἀχάλιν' ἔχουσι στόματα, κεἰς ἀνδρῶν μὲν οὐ
       τελοῦσιν ἀριθμόν, ἐν γέλωτι δ' εὐπρεπεῖς.   5

493   ἄλγιστόν ἐστι θῆλυ μισηθὲν γένος·
       αἱ γὰρ σφαλεῖσαι ταῖσιν οὐκ ἐσφαλμέναις
       αἶσχος γυναιξί, καὶ κεκοίνωνται ψόγον
       ταῖς οὐ κακαῖσιν αἱ κακαί· τὰ δ' εἰς γάμους
       οὐδὲν δοκοῦσιν ὑγιὲς ἀνδράσιν φρονεῖν.   5

494 P. Berlin 9772 and P. Oxy. 1176 fr. 39 col. 11

   (Με.?) μάτην ἄρ' εἰς γυναῖκας ἐξ⌋ ἀνδρῶν ψιόγος
       ψάλλει κενὸν τό⌋ξευμα καὶ λέγει κα⌊κ⌋ῶς·
       αἱ δ' εἴσ' ἀμείνους⌋ αἱρσ⌊ένων. δείξω δ' ἐγώ.

490 (658 M) Orion 5.3, attrib. Eur. *Mel.D.*   1 ἀναστρέφειν Schneidewin -τρέφειν Orion
491 (663 M) Stob. 4.24.26, attrib. Eur. *Mel.*, assigned to *Mel.D.* by Matthiae   5 μάχεσθαι
Conington γλεῖσθαι Stob. mss. SM τλεῖσθαι ms. A (ἐ)γκαλεῖσθαι Trincavelli   **492** (659 M)
Athenaeus 14.2, 613d, attrib. Eur. *Mel.D.*, with F 494.9–10a subjoined   1 γέλωτος —2 κερτόμους
and 5b adapted (εὐπρεπεῖς ὄντες ἐν γέλωτι) Eustath. on Hom. *Od.* 18.35, attrib. Eur.   3 τήτηι
Wilamowitz, *Eur. Herakles* I.15 n. 23 (τήτει L. Dindorf) τι εἴ τι Ath.   **493** (661M) Stob. 4.22.
86, attrib. Eur. *Mel.*; assigned to *Mel.D.* by Nauck, cf. attribution of F 494.   **494** (660 M) P. Berl.
9772 (anthology, 2nd C. B.C.) *recto*, col. iii.4–v.1 (followed without break by *Protes*. F 657), ed.
Schubart and Wilamowitz, *BKT* V.2 (1907), 125; parts of 5–8, 16 and most of 9–15 in P. Oxy. 1176

490   The wise should always turn back counsels towards what is
more beneficial, in concord with divine influence.

Context uncertain.

491   If anyone who was childless in the first place has acquired
alien children for his house, diverting what is ordained for
him towards what is not right, he should realise he is a fool.
The man to whom the gods allot childlessness should not
fight against divine will but let it be.

Criticism of Metapontus; context uncertain.

492   Many men practise mockery as a grace, for the sake of
mirth. But I do not much like those wits who keep unbridled
mouths through want of wise things to say; they do not
count as real men, though they look good in moments of
mirth.

Context uncertain.

493   The hatred women incur is very hurtful. Those who have
fallen are a disgrace to those who have not; the bad ones
share their censure with the good. And with regard to
marriage men think that women are entirely corrupt.

Probably the same scene and speaker as the next fragment.

494 P. Berlin with P. Oxy.

A woman (Melanippe?) defends women against misogyny:

(Me.?)   Vainly, it seems, does men's censure twang an idle shaft
against women and speak badly of them. In fact they are
better than men, and I shall prove it..

(2nd C. A.D.) fr. 39 col. 11, ed. Hunt (1912), from Satyrus' *Life of Euripides* (re-ed. G. Arrighetti,
Pisa, 1964: see pp. 64–5)   1–3 = fr. **499** N (from Anon. *Life of Eur.* 6: ed. E. Schwartz, *Scholia in
Eur.*, I.6), attrib. Eur. *Mel.*   9–10 σώιζουσι wrongly subjoined to F 492 in Athenaeus 14.2, 613d,
attrib. Eur. *Mel.D.*   27–9 = fr. 494 N (Stob. 4.22.78, attrib. Eur. *Mel.*; Porphyry in Euseb. *Praep.
Evangel.* 10.3.19, attrib. Eur. *Mel.D.*)   Composite texts: A.S. Hunt, *Trag. Gr. Frag. Papyr. Nuper
Reperta* (Oxford, 1912); von Arnim; Page, *GLP* 108–15 with introd. and transl.; van Looy 256–71
with comm.   Suppl. and corr. in first ed. except where noted. ⌊ ⌋ enclose text not represented in
P. Berl.   Photograph of 11–28 (P. Berl.) in R. Seider, *Palaeogr. der gr. Papyri*, II (Stuttgart, 1970),
49–50, Pl. 5, No. 9.   2 κακῶς λέγει Anon. *Life*   3 ἐγὼ λέγω Anon. *Life*

]ι ξυμβόλαι' ἀμάρτυρα
]α κοὐκ ἀρνιοͺύμεναι   5
ͺμε . . . . . . χο . . . . . . ἀλιͺλήλας π[ό]νους
κη . . . . . . δε . . . . . . ιθ. αἰσχ[ύ]νην φέρει
. . αν σ . . . . το. ιͺωτος ἐκβαιͺλεῖͺ γυνή.
νέμουσι δ' οἴκους καὶ τὰͺ ναυστολούμενα
ἔ[σω] δόμων σώιζουσιν, οὐδ'ͺ ἐρημίαι   10
γυναικὸς οἶκος εὐπινὴς οὐδ' ὄλβιος·
    τὰ δ' ἐν θεοῖς αὖ (πρῶτα γὰρ κρίνω τάδε)
μέρος μέγιστον ἔχομεν. ἐν Φοίβου τε γὰρ
δόμοις προφητεύουσι Λοξίιοͺυ φρένα
γυναῖκες, ιͺἀμφὶͺ δ' ἀιͺγιͺνὰ Δωδώνη⟨ς⟩ βάθρα   15
φηγῶι παρ' ἱερᾶι θῆλυ τὰ[ς] Διὸς φρένας
γένος πορεύει τοῖς θέλουσιν Ἑλλάδος.
    ἃ δ' εἴς τε Μοίρας τάς τ' ἀνωνύμους θεὰς
ἱερὰ τελεῖται, ταῦτ' ἐν ἀνδράσιν μὲν οὐ⟨χ⟩
ὅσια καθέστηκ', ἐν γυναιξὶ δ' αὔξεται   20
ἅπαντα. ταύτηι τὰν θεοῖς ἔχει δίκη
θήλεια. πῶς οὖν χρὴ γυναικεῖον γένος
κακῶς ἀκούειν; οὐχὶ παύσεται ψόγος
μάταιος ἀνδρῶν †οἵ τ' ἄγαν ἡγούμενοι†
ψέγειν γυναῖκας, εἰ μί' ηὑρέθη κακή,   25
πάσας ὁμοίως; διοριῶ ιͺδὲͺ τῶ[ι] λόγωι·
τῆιςͺ μὲν κακῆς κάκιͺιοͺͺν οὐδὲν γίγνεται
γυναικός, ἐσθλῆς δ' οὐδὲν εἰς ὑπερβολὴν
πιͺέͺφυκ' ἄμεινον· διαφέρουσι δ' αἱ φύσεις.

495 P. Berlin 5514 *conclusion of a Messenger speech:*

(Ἄγγελος) τίς ἦν ὁ . .[. . . . . μ]εθεὶς ἐμοί;
          ὡς δ' οὐκ ἐφαινόμεσθα, σῖγα δ' εἴχομεν,
          πρόσω πρὸς αὐτὸν πάλιν ὑποστρέψας πόδα
          χωρεῖ δρομαίαν, θῆρ' ἑλεῖν πρόθυμος ὤν,
          βοᾶι δέ· κἂν τῶιδ' ἐξεφαινόμεσθα δή,   5

4 ταῖς μὲν γάρ ἐστ]ι Page ξυμβόλαι' ἀμάρτυρα so divided by Mekler 7 φέρει P. Berl.
ἔχε[ι P. Oxy. 9 οἰκοῦσιν οἴκους Ath. 11 εὐπινὴς οὐδ' ὄλβι[P. Oxy. [δυσ]πινὴς ὅ γε
ὄλβ[ιο]ς P. Berl. 12 ἃ δ' εἰς θεοὺς P. Berl. 14 χρησμο[ῖ]ς P. Oxy. 15]δα[ ]να δωδώνη
(or -νης with ς above line lost? Wilamowitz) βάθρα P. Berl. ἀμφὶ θ' ἁγν[ ] δωμάτων [ ]ς

<   > contracts unwitnessed <   >
and not reneging[5] <   > troubles <*to*?> one another
<   > brings disgrace<   > a woman will
expel(?) . . . They order households, and what is brought in by sea
they keep safe within their homes; nor in the absence[10] of a woman
can a house be tidy and prosperous.

Now as for our dealings with the gods, which I judge to be of
prime importance: we have a very great share in them. In
Phoebus's halls it is women who proclaim the mind of Loxias, and
around Dodona's holy foundations[15] by the sacred oak it is the
female sex that purveys the thoughts of Zeus to any Greek who
seeks them. Also those rituals which are performed for the Fates
and the Nameless Goddesses are not open to the participation of
men; they flourish in the hands of women[20] entirely. That is how
women's rights stand in our dealings with the gods.

Why then should the female sex suffer ill repute? Will it not
cease, this futile denigration from men, †and those excessively
thinking†, if just one woman is found to be bad,[25] to denigrate all
alike? But I will make a distinction in my argument: nothing
indeed is worse than a bad woman — but nothing excels a decent
one in goodness. Their natures are not all alike.

495 P. Berlin *Conclusion of a Messenger speech:*

(Messenger) . . . 'Who was it who let fly <   > at me?'
But as we *(i.e. ambushers)* kept ourselves hidden and stayed
silent, he *(i.e. a twin)* turned back in his tracks and moved forward
at a run towards him *(i.e. an ambusher)*, eager to take the beast,
and shouted out. As he did so, now we began to show ourselves,[5]

βάθρα P. Oxy. 16 φηγῶι παρ᾽ ἱερῶι P. Berl. only ηπα[at line-beg. P. Oxy. 19–20 ὅσια . . .
ἱερὰ P. Berl. 19 οὐ⟨χ⟩ Page (οὐ Wilamowitz) ευ P. Berl. 20 stop at line-end, Radermacher
21 ηπαντα P. Berl. δίκη Cropp δίκης P. Berl. δίκηι van Looy 23 λόγος Collard
24 corrupt at end, Wilamowitz 26 διοριῶ Herwerden διορίσω P. Berl. **495** (664 M)
P. Berl. 5514 (4th–5th C. A.D.), upper part of a single parchment book-page, *recto* 1–25 (then some
lines lost), *verso* 26–50, and a few letters from the attached page (51), ed. F. Blass, *RhM* 35
(1880), 290–7, cf. H. Weil, *RPh* 4 (1880), 121–4; re-ed. Nauck fr. 495; Schubart and Wilamowitz,
BKT V.2.84–7; von Arnim; Page, *GLP* 114–7; van Looy with comm. Corrections and supplements
by Blass except where noted. Photograph of 2–19: W. Schubart, *Gr. Palaeogr.* (Berl., 1925), 136–
7, Pl. 94. 40–3 Stob. 4.29.11, attrib. Eur. *Mel.* 1 τισηνω [P. Berl. ὁ [τυφλὸν τόδε βέλος
μ]εθεὶς Weil ὁ τἀ[ργὸν (etc.) Wilamowitz ὁ κ[ωφὸν (etc.) von Arnim

ὀρθοσταδὸν λόγχαισ᾽ ἐπείγοντες φόν[ον.
τὼ δ᾽ εἰσιδόντε δίπτυχον θείοιν κάρ[α
ἤσθησαν, εἶπόν θ᾽· 'Εἶα συλλάβεσθ᾽ ἄγρα[ς,
καιρὸν γὰρ ἥκετ᾽ ' — οὐδ᾽ ὑπώπτευον [δόλον
φίλων προσώπων εἰσορῶντες ὄ[μματα.   10
οἱ δ᾽ εἰς τὸν αὐτὸν πίτυλον ἤπειγ[ον δορός,
πέτροι τ᾽ ἐχώρουν χερμάδες θ᾽ ἡ[μῶν πάρα
ἐκεῖθεν, οἱ δ᾽ ἐκεῖθεν· ὡς δ᾽ ἠίε[ι μάχη
σιγή τ᾽ ἀφ᾽ ἡμῶν, γνωρίσαντ[ε δὴ τὸ πᾶν
λέγουσι· 'Μητρὸς ὦ κασίγνη[τοι φίλης,   15
τί δρᾶτ᾽; ἀποκτείνοντες ο[ὓς ἥκιστα χρῆν
φωρᾶσθε. πρὸς θεῶν δρᾶτ[ε   .᾽
   σὼ δ᾽ αὐταδέλφω χερμ[
λέγουσί θ᾽ ὡς ἔφυσα[ν
κοὐ δεῖ τυρανν[20
πρεσβεῖ᾽ ἔχοντ[ας
κἀπεὶ τάδ᾽ εἰσή[κουσαν
  υ λῆμ᾽ ἐχο[23
traces of 24–5; some lines from foot of page missing, then:
ἔσφηλέ τ᾽ εἰς γῆν τ[ὸν βίον τ᾽ ἀ]φ[εί]λετο.   26
ἡμῶν δ᾽ ἐχώρει κωφὰ πρὸς γαῖαν βέλη.
δ]υοῖν δ᾽ ἀδελφοῖν σοῖν τὸν αὖ νεώτερον
λό]γχηι πλατείαι συοφόνωι δι᾽ ἥπατος
παῖσ]ας ἔδωκε νερτέροις, καλὸν νεκρόν,   30
. . . .] ος, ὅσπερ τὸν πρὶν ἔκτεινεν βαλών.
  κἀντεῦ]θεν ἡμεῖς οἱ λελειμμένοι φίλων
κοῦφον] πόδ᾽ ἄλλος ἄλλοσ᾽ εἴχομεν φυγῆι.
εἶδον δὲ τ]ὸν μὲν ὄρεος ὑλίμωι φόβηι
κρυφθέν]τα, τὸν δὲ πευκίνων ὄζων ἔπι·   35
οἱ δ᾽ εἰς φάρ]αγγ᾽ ἔδυνον, οἱ δ᾽ ὑπ᾽ εὐσκίους
θάμνους κα]θῖζον. τὼ δ᾽ ὁρῶντ᾽ οὐκ ἠξίουν
δούλους φονε]ύειν φασγάνοις ἐλευθέροις.
  τάδ᾽ οὐκέτ᾽ ὄντων σ]ῶν κασιγνήτων κλύεις.
ἐγὼ μὲν οὖν οὐκ] οἶδ᾽ ὅτωι σκοπεῖν χρ[ε]ὼν   40

6 λόγχαισ᾽: λόγχαις P. Berl. λόγχαισι (Nauck) τείνοντες Headlam   7 δίπτυχον Weil -οιν
P. Berl.   11 δοροός Weil   13 μάχη Weil   14 [ε τὸν δόλον van Looy   16 ο[ὓς ἥκιστ᾽ ἐχρῆν
Weil χρῆν Nauck   17 δρᾶτ[ε μηδαμῶς τάδε (e.g.) Weil   18 χερμ[άδ᾽ αἴρουσιν χεροῖν

standing up straight and urging on bloodshed with our spears. But
the twins, catching sight of their two uncles, were pleased and said,
'Come on now, join in the hunt, you are just at the right moment'
— suspecting no <treachery> when they observed these friendly
faces.[10] They, however, pressed on with the same <spear>-
onslaught, and rocks and boulders flew <from our side> on either
quarter; and as <battle> and silence continued from our side, they
realised <now the whole truth> and then spoke out: 'Brothers of
<our dear> mother,[15] what are you doing? You are caught in the
act of killing those <you should least kill>. For the gods' sake, do
<   .>'
But your brothers . . . rock(s) <   > and said that they
were born <   > and it was not right . . . royal <   >,[20]
holding prerogatives <   >. And when they heard these
things <   > hav<ing . . . > spirit . . .
    (Lines 24–5 fragmentary, and several more lost)
. . . felled (him) to the ground <and> robbed him of <his life>. Our
missiles, meanwhile, kept flying vainly to the ground. And now in
his turn the younger of your two brothers was <struck> through
the liver with a thick boar-spear, and so delivered to the powers
below, a fine corpse,[30] by . . . who had hit and killed the first.
    From then on we, the remainder of their companions, headed
off <nimbly>, each fleeing in a different direction. <I saw> one
man <concealed> in the mountain-brush, another perching on
pine-branches;[35] <others> slipped <into> a ravine, and others
crouched beneath shady <bushes>. The twins could see them but
did not deign to slaughter <slaves> with free men's swords.
    <That> is my news about your brothers <who are no more>.
As for me, I do not know by what means we should examine[40]

(e.g.) Blass   19 ἔφυσα[ν ἐκ δούλης ποθέν (e.g.) Blass (νόθοι Nauck, τινος van Looy)
20 τύρανν[α σκῆπτρα καὶ θρόνους κρατεῖν (e.g.) Weil (λαβεῖν Wecklein) τυράνν[ων
σκῆπτρα τοὺς νόθους λαβεῖν (e.g.) von Arnim   21 ἔχοντ[ας δυσγενεῖς τῶν εὐγενῶν (e.g.)
Weil   22 Nauck   end οὐκ ἐδεισάτην (e.g.) von Arnim   23 λῆμμ' P. Berl.   ε]ὖ λῆμ' ἔχο[ντες
or ο]ὺ λῆμ' ἔχο[ντ' ἄθυμον (e.g.) Blass   31 Βοιω]τός Blass ἐκεῖ]νος Weil   33 Nauck
34 εἶδον Weil (-ες Blass)   τ]ὸν μὲν δρυὸς ⟨ὑφ'⟩ (or ⟨ἐν⟩) ὑλίμωι φόβηι Maas, Kl. Schr.
205 n. 4.   35 πτώσσον]τα or κεύθον]τα Weil   36]αγγ' ἔδυνον Weil]αγγας δυνον P. Berl.
37 Nauck   39 von Arnim μόρον τοιοῦτον σ]ῶν Nauck   40 so P Berl.   οὐκ οἶδ' ὅπως δὴ
Stob.   οὖν οὐκ οἶδ' ὅπως Matthiae (ὅτωι Nauck, 1856)

260 EURIPIDES

τὴν εὐγένειαν. το̣ὺς γὰρ ἀνδρείους φύσιν
καὶ τοὺς δικαίους τῶ̣ν κενῶν δοξασμάτων,
κἂν ὦσι δούλων, εὐγεν̣εστέρους λέγω.

Ends of seven more lines (44–6 Chorus?, 47ff. Queen?)   44–50
including:

44]κακοῖς κακά   45]χει δόμοις   46]ντες σέθεν
47]εν ἐλπίδων   48]ται μέγα

A few letters from the now lost next page are imprinted in
reverse at the ends of lines 31–3; a remnant of the middle
of a subsequent page (distance from the above text uncertain) includes a coronis marking the end of the play
beside the first three letters of its last line, probably part
of the formulaic Choral comment:

(Χορός) τοι[όνδ᾽ ἀπέβη τόδε πρᾶγμα.   51

496 (= test. iib)

Athenaeus reports:

ὠνομάσθη δ᾽ ἡ Σῖρις, ὡς μὲν Τίμαιός φησιν καὶ Εὐρι-
πίδης ἐν Δεσμώτιδι Μελανίππηι, ἀπὸ γυναικός τινος
Σίριδος, ὡς δ᾽ Ἀρχίλοχος, ἀπὸ ποταμοῦ.

Plausibly attributed to Mel.D.:
F 498, 501, 502, 503, 507, (504?, 505?, 511?)

ΜΕΛΑΝΙΠΠΗ

497   τείσασθε τήνδε· καὶ γὰρ ἐντεῦθεν νοσεῖ
τὰ τῶν γυναικῶν· οἱ μὲν ἢ παίδων ὕπερ
ἢ συγγενείας οὕνεκ᾽ οὐκ ἀπώλεσαν
κακὴν λαβόντες· εἶτα τοῦτο τἄδικον
πολλαῖς ὑπερρύηκε καὶ χωρεῖ πρόσω,   5
ὥστ᾽ ἐξίτηλος ἀρετὴ καθίσταται.

498   πλὴν τῆς τεκούσης θῆλυ πᾶν μισῶ γένος.

42 τέκνων Stob. (κενῶν Gesner there)   44–6 assigned to Chorus, 47ff. to Theano: Blass
496 (655d M) Athenaeus 12.25, 523d, attrib. Eur. Mel.D. (= Timaeus FGH 566 F 52, Archilochus
IEG fr. 22)   497 (679 M) Stob. 4.23.6, attrib. Eur. Mel.   1 ἐντεῦθεν Elmsley ἐνταυθοῖ Stob.

nobility. Those who are manly and just by nature, albeit from slave backgrounds, are, I declare, more noble than those who are mere empty appearances.

Ends of lines 44–6 (Chorus?) and 47–50 (Queen?) include:

44 . . . troubles (upon) troubles   45 . . . (for) the house
46 . . . (from/ of) you   47 . . . (of) hopes   48 . . . great . . .

Last line of the play (distance from the above text uncertain):

(Chorus)   Such <has been the outcome of this affair>.   51

496 (= test. iib)

> *According to Timaeus and Euripides in 'The Captive Melanippe', Siris was named after a woman called Siris; according to Archilochus, after a river .*

Plausibly attributed to *Captive Mel.*:
F 498, 501, 502, 503, 507, (504?, 505?, 511?)

MELANIPPE (WISE or CAPTIVE)

497   Make her pay! This is the source of women's corruption: some men when they find a woman is bad do not do away with her, either protecting children or because of kinship; then this wrongdoing seeps gradually into many women and advances,⁵ and so in the end the virtue they had is vanished.

Hellen to Aeolus in Wise Mel.?

498   Except for my mother I hate the whole female sex.

Part of the debate on misogyny in Capt. Mel.?

---

2 ὕπερ Herwerden πέρι Stob.   4 τοῦτο τἄδικον Porson   δ' οὐ τότ' ἄδικον Stob.   6 ὥστ' Elmsley ὡς Stob.   **498** (662 M) Stob. 4.22.146, attrib. Eur. *Mel; cf.* Menand. *Sentent.* 665 πλὴν τῆς τεκούσης μὴ φιλεῖν ἄλλην θέλε, 'Refrain from loving any woman but your mother.'

262 EURIPIDES

499 N   = F 494.1–3 above

500   ὅστις δ᾽ ἄμεικτον πατέρ᾽ ἔχει νεανίας
        στυγνόν τ᾽ ἐν οἴκοις, μεγάλα κέκτηται κακά.

501   γάμους δ᾽ ὅσοι σπεύδουσι μὴ πεπρωμένους,
        μάτην πονοῦσιν· ἡ δὲ †τῶι χρεὼν πόσει
        μένουσα† κἀσπούδαστος ἦλθεν εἰς δόμους.

502   ὅσοι γαμοῦσι δ᾽ ἢ γένει κρείσσους γάμους
        ἢ πολλὰ χρήματ᾽, οὐκ ἐπίστανται γαμεῖν·
        τὰ τῆς γυναικὸς γὰρ κρατοῦντ᾽ ἐν δώμασιν
        δουλοῖ τὸν ἄνδρα, κοὐκέτ᾽ ἔστ᾽ ἐλεύθερος.
        πλοῦτος δ᾽ ἐπακτὸς ἐκ γυναικείων γάμων   5
        ἀνόνητος· αἱ γὰρ διαλύσεις ⟨οὐ⟩ ῥάιδιαι.

503   (Χο.?)   μετρίων λέκτρων, μετρίων δὲ γάμων
        μετὰ σωφροσύνης
        κῦρσαι θνητοῖσιν ἄριστον.

504   ὦ τέκνον, ἀνθρώποισιν ἔστιν οἷς βίος
        ὁ σμικρὸς εὐκρὰς ἐγένεθ᾽, οἷς δ᾽ ὄγκος κακόν.

505   τὰ προσπεσόντα δ᾽ ὅστις εὖ φέρει βροτῶν,
        ἄριστος εἶναι σωφρονεῖν τ᾽ ἐμοὶ δοκεῖ.

506   (Με.?)   δοκεῖτε πηδᾶν τἀδικήματ᾽ εἰς θεοὺς
        πτεροῖσι, κἄπειτ᾽ ἐν Διὸς δέλτου πτυχαῖς
        γράφειν τιν᾽ αὐτά, Ζῆνα δ᾽ εἰσορῶντά νιν

500 (680 M) Stob. 4.26.3, attrib. Eur. *Mel.*   1 ἀμείλικτον Stob.   **501** (676 M) Stob. 4.22.91, attrib. Eur. *Mel.*   1 παιδεύουσι Stob. ms. A   2 ἡ δ᾽ ὅτωι Collard   3 μέλλουσα von Arnim μέλουσα M. L. West, *BICS* 30 (1983), 75   ἢ ἀσπούδαστος Stob. ms. M   γάμους Nauck (*Index* xxii)   **502** (677 M) Stob. 4.22.94, attrib. Eur. *Mel.*   1 δ᾽ ἢ Gesner δὴ Stob.   3 ἐν δώμασιν Gesner ἐν τοῖς δώμασιν Stob. ἐν τοῖς δόμοις Nauck   6 ⟨οὐ⟩ Scaliger   **503** (678 M) Stob.

499 N = *F 494.1–3 above*

500 A young man with an unsociable, sullen father at home is the possessor of many troubles.

Context uncertain. (Aeolus criticising Hellen in Wise Mel.*?)*

501 People who urgently pursue marriages that are not destined are labouring in vain; the woman †awaiting her proper husband† even(?) without urging arrives at his house.

From Capt. Mel. *with reference to Metapontus?*

502 Men who make a marriage above their rank, or marry wealth, do not know how to marry. The wife's sway in the house enslaves the husband, and he is no longer free. Imported wealth coming from marriage with a woman[5] brings no benefit; for divorces are <*not*> easy.

Context as F 501?

503 *(Cho.?)* For mortals it is best to obtain moderate unions, moderate marriages accompanied by temperance.

Closing lines of Capt. Mel.*?*

504 Child, for some people a lowly life is the right blend; for some grandeur is a bad thing.

Context uncertain: addressed to one of the twins in Capt. Mel.*?)*

505 The one who bears well the things that befall seems to me to be excellent and self-controlled.

Context uncertain: addressed to Melanippe in Capt. Mel.*?)*

506 *(Me.?)* You think that wrongdoings leap up to the gods on wings, then someone inscribes them on Zeus's folded tablet,

---

4.22.132, attrib. Eur. *Mel.* **504** (681 M) Stob. 4.31.93, attrib. Eur. *Mel.* 2 εὐκρὰς (Valckenaer) ἐγένεθ', οἷς δ' Porson (τ' Musgrave) εὔκρατος ἐγένετο δ' Stob. **505** (682 M) Stob. 4.44.55, attrib. Eur. *Mel.*; [Plut.] *Mor.* 116f, attrib. Eur. 1 τυγχάνοντα Stob. 2 σοφὸν νομίζω Stob. **506** (672 M) Stob. 1.3.14a, attrib. Eur. *Mel.*; detached by Grotius from 14b = *TrGF* II adesp. 489.

θνητοῖς δικάζειν; οὐδ' ὁ πᾶς ἂν οὐρανὸς
Διὸς γράφοντος τὰς βροτῶν ἁμαρτίας 5
ἐξαρκέσειεν οὐδ' ἐκεῖνος ἂν σκοπῶν
πέμπειν ἑκάστωι ζημίαν· ἀλλ' ἡ Δίκη
ἐνταῦθά πού 'στιν ἐγγύς, εἰ βούλεσθ' ὁρᾶν.

507   τί τοὺς θανόντας οὐκ ἐᾶις τεθνηκέναι
        καὶ τἀκχυθέντα συλλέγεις ἀλγήματα;

508   παλαιὸς αἶνος· ἔργα μὲν νεωτέρων,
        βουλαὶ δ' ἔχουσι τῶν γεραιτέρων κράτος.

509   τί δ' ἄλλο; φωνὴ καὶ σκιὰ γέρων ἀνήρ.

510   παπαῖ, νέος καὶ σκαιὸς οἷός ἐστ' ἀνήρ.

511   δοῦλον γὰρ ἐσθλὸ]ν τοι ̈]νομ' οι ̇ὺ διαφθερεῖ,
        πολλοὶ δ' ἀμείνους] εἰσὶ τῶν]ἐλευθέρων.

512   ἀργὸς πολίτης κεῖνος, ὡς κακός γ' ἀνήρ.

513   ἀλάστορας οὐκ ἐτόλμησεν κτανεῖν.

514   *Eur. is said to have mentioned in* Mel.:
        Ἀδώνιδος κῆποι

4 ὁ πᾶς ἂν Grotius ὁ πασοῦν Stob. ms. F ὁποσοῦν Stob. ms. P   6 σθένοι Nauck (*Index*, xxii)
507 (685 M)   Stob. 4.56.16, attrib. Eur. *Mel.*   1 = Eupolis, *Demes*, *PCG* fr. 99.102
508 (683 M) Stob. 4.50.12, attrib. Eur. *Mel.*   509 (684 M) Stob. 4.50.57, attrib. Eur. *Mel.*
510 (674 M) Stob. 4.11.7, attrib. Eur. *Mel.*   511 (675 M) Stob. 4.19.38, attrib. Eur. *Mel.*;
P. Berl. 21144 (Gnomology, ed. H. Maehler, *Mus.Helv.* 24 (1967) 70–3) recto 6–7, unattrib.
1 Flor. Monac. 130, unattrib.   1 διαφθερεῖ Flor. Monac. -φθείρει Stob.   512 (673 M) Stob.
3.30.11, attrib. Eur. *Mel.* perhaps κακὸς πολίτης . . . ἀργός γ' ἀνήρ Cropp   513 (686 M)
Erotian, *Hippocr. Glosses* α 47 (ἀλάστορες), p. 17 Nachmanson, attrib. Eur. *Mel.*; ἴσως
preceding ἀλάστορας is excluded from Eur.'s text by Nachmanson and by Luppe, *Philologus* 113
(1969), 277–9   ἴσως ἀλάστορ' Elmsley ἀλάστορας ⟨γὰρ⟩ or ⟨μὲν⟩ (e.g.) Luppe
514 (687 M) Identified as proverbial and said to have been recalled in Eur. *Mel.* by Schol. T
Pl. *Phaedr.* 276b3, p. 88 Greene

and Zeus looks at them and enacts justice on men? Not even the entire sky would suffice if Zeus were writing down men's sins,[5] nor he himself to examine them and send punishment to each. The fact is that Justice is somewhere here close by, if you want to see her.

Melanippe in defence of the infants, or herself, in Wise Mel.*?*

507   Why do you not let those who have died be dead? Why are you collecting griefs that are already spent?

Someone consoling Melanippe in Capt. Mel.*?*

508   It's an old saying: action belongs to the young, but the counsels of their elders are superior.

Hellen arguing with Aeolus in Wise Mel.*?*

509   What else? An old man is but a voice and a shadow.

Aeolus arguing with Hellen in Wise Mel.*?*

510   Whew, what a young, gauche kind of man he is!

Hellen arguing with Aeolus in Wise Mel.*?*

511   An honourable slave will not be corrupted by his title; many slaves are superior to free men.

*Context uncertain. (*Capt. Mel. *with reference to the Herdsman?)*

512   That man is a useless citizen, for he is a worthless man.

Context and reference uncertain.

513   He did not dare to kill murderers(?).

Context and reference uncertain.

514   *Adonis-gardens*

*Context uncertain. (*Wise Mel. *with reference to the infants?)*

Commentary on *The Wise Melanippe*

Hypothesis. See Hypoth. *Sthen.* n. on the sources.

1 . **Hellen:** ancestor of the Hellenic people, son of Pyrrha and either Deucalion or Zeus (e.g. Apollod. 1.7.2), perhaps Zeus already in the Hesiodic *Catalogue*: see West, *Catalogue* 50–6.

2 – 3 . Cretheus, Salmoneus . . . Sisyphus: the *Catalogue* (Hes. fr. 10a.25– 34) gave Aeolus five daughters and seven sons (including these three) and a very complicated set of descendants: see West 63–8, 175–6. Eur. fr. 14 N = *TrGF* F 929b includes these three and Athamas.

3 . **Hippe:** probably Hippo in Eur. A Centaur's daughter but with human form before her transformation into a mare: see below, F 481.13–22 with Comm.

5 . **a year's exile:** probably Eur.'s *ad hoc* invention here. On exiles for murderers see *Sthen.* Hypoth. 4 n.

6 . **twin sons:** a common motif with divinely sired heroes, e.g. Heracles and Iphicles, Amphion and Zethus, Romulus and Remus; cf. Introd., pp. 245–6.

10 – 11 . suckled by one of the cows: many infant heroes survive exposure through the attentions of animals. Hygin. *Fab.* 252 lists cases including Telephus, Romulus and Remus, Aegisthus, Alope's son Hippothoon.

13 . to burn up the infants: such burnings, eliminating the product of an unnatural birth and the pollution it caused, are sparsely evidenced in Greek texts: Parker, *Miasma* 221.

14–15. put the apparel on them: Melanippe must have brought the funereally clothed infants on stage like Megara, *HF* 451ff. Ino (Hygin. *Fab.* 4) was told to clothe her own children for sacrifice and clothed her rival Themisto's instead, but may not have brought them on stage (cf. Webster, *Euripides* [1967], 100).

481. About the first half of the Prologue speech. Genealogy (1–11), parentage (11–14) and a digression on her mother Hippo (14–22, preparing for Hippo's later intervention) lead towards an explanation of Melanippe's own situation. The genealogy is plainly presented as in *HF, IT, Ion* (by contrast with the later *Hel.*, *Pho., Or., Arch.*; parodies, Ar. *Frogs* 1206–44). The text up to line 22 is probably complete, although Wilamowitz posited a line lost after 8 (see 8 n.) and Luppe, *WJA* n.f. 15 (1989), 83–95 argues that lines have also been lost after 2 and 11, in the middle of 14, and perhaps around 18 (before which he would delete 16–17: see 13–22 n. Luppe's complex arguments are not all addressed here).

1 . Certainly the authentic first line of the play, said to have recurred (cf. Ioannes, Gregory) in *Pir., TrGF* I 43 (Critias) F 1.9 = Eur. fr. 591.4 N. The variance in P. Oxy. is, one hopes, a minor aberration. Plutarch's 'original first line' (fr. 480 N: see App.), replaced by Eur. 'on receiving another chorus' because it had caused a commotion, comes from parody, anecdote or simple confusion: cf. e.g. Wilamowitz on *HF* 1263. Van Looy 210–3 observes that fr. 480 N suits neither

Melanippe's character nor the opening of a play; this tells against Luppe's suggestion, *WJA* n.f. 9 (1983), 53–6, that it is the first line of *Capt. Mel.* Its ascription to *Wise Mel.*, and of our line 1 only to *Pir.*, is maintained by Schmid 413 nn. 5, 6.   **true tradition:** similar declarations with λέγειν/λόγος: *El.* 737, *HF* 25, *Hel.* 18 (cf. 21), etc.

2 . Hellen: see Hypoth. 1 n.

3 . Peneus . . . Asopus: the main rivers of N. Thessaly and S.E. Boeotia. Strabo 8.7.1 echoes this definition of Aeolus's realm.

3 – 5 . All . . . his rule: lit. 'to whom, (i.e.) his sceptre, all the land which P. and the water of A. enclose, bounding it with wet arms, hearkens . . .'. For the sentence structure cf. *IT* 5–7. οὗ is object of ἀκούει with σκήπτρων in apposition (the 'whole-and-part' figure or *schema Ionicum*: cf. *Pha.* 90–2, *HF* 162 with Wilamowitz or Bond), KG I.289.   [Text: Rabe's ὁρίζον (Neut. to agree with ὕδωρ) is not needed because 'water of Asopus' is merely a periphrasis for Masc. 'Asopus': cf. e.g. Hom. *Od.* 11.90–1, 16.476–7, *Il.* 11.690; Gildersleeve, *Syntax* §123.]

8 – 9 . other branches . . . other realms: πτόρθος of individuals as *Hec.* 20 (Polydorus); for ἄλλον εἰς ἄλλην 'one to one, another to another' see LSJ ἄλλος II.2; for πόλις 'realm' cf. e.g. *Ion* 1583, 1591. Traditionally Hellen's younger sons Dorus and Xuthus went to Doris and to Attica. Xuthus was of special interest to Eur.'s audience as father of Ion, eponym of the Ionians whose leadership Athens claimed. In his later *Ion* Eur. turned Ion into Apollo's son while (1589–94) relegating Dorus to being with Achaeus a son of Xuthus and Creusa.   [Text: Petersen's <and> is needed for the sense. Wilamowitz supposed one line lost after 8 (Luppe two, and perhaps one before) to allow an expected mention of Dorus (cf. the wording of Strabo 8.7.1 mentioned on 3 above). But Eur. may have chosen to highlight Xuthus and Ion here at the expense of Dorus and Achaeus.]

9 – 11 . Athens (etc.): Xuthus is now known to have been associated with Athens in the Hesiodic *Catalogue*, Hes. fr. 10a.20–4 (OCT ed. 2, 227–8), as husband of Erectheus's daughter Creusa and father of Achaeus and (a very probable supplement) Iaon (= Ion), and of a daughter Diomede. See also p. 181 on *Erec.* F 362.

1 0 . Cecropia's promontory: the Athenian Acropolis (cf. *El.* 1289), realm of Athens' first mythical king Cecrops: J. Diggle, *GRBS* 14 (1973), 254 = *Euripidea* 73, and *Studies* 17. Creusa gives birth there, *Ion* 7–18, 936–49. αὐχήν 'neck' is sometimes an isthmus, strait or defile (LSJ II.1–3), here the elongated Acropolis.

1 2 . point whence I began: with the line descending through Aeolus (line 2). **and my name:** i.e. '(the explanation of) my name', if the text is sound (so van Looy).   [Text: Wilamowitz's conjecture, also unconvincing, gives 'to the question of my name, to the point from which I began'. Perhaps e.g. λόγος | γένος τε τοὐμὸν (Cropp), 'my story and my family' = 'my family's story'; but the corruption of this is not likely.]

1 3 – 2 2 . This passage, with F 483 and its citation by Clement, F 484, and Pollux 4 . 141, is our main evidence for Eur.'s account of Melanippe's mother Hippo (cf. Hypoth. 3 n.; Introd., p. 241). A set of interdependent sources (ps.-Eratosth. *Catast.* 18, Schol. Arat. *Phaen.* 205, Hygin. *Astron.* 2.18, etc.: cf. fr. 488 N, *TrGF* test. vb) credits to Eur. 'in *Mel.*' the story that on bearing Melanippe Hippo was turned into a mare at her own request so as to escape detection by her father, and became the constellation Hippos ('Horse') 'owing to her and her father's piety' (Cheiron becoming the constellation Centaur). Hyginus adds that her name had been 'Thea' (but this seems to be corrupt) and attributes to writers other than Eur. the story that her transformation was due to her prophecies. There is clearly some confusion here, for the girl transformed at her own request on giving birth to Melanippe is hardly compatible with the sage and prophetess, teacher of Aeolus and Melanippe, transformed to put an end to her prophesying, whom we meet in this Prologue and in the texts and citations of F 483–4. Wilamowitz 74 n. 3 and van Looy 207–9 do not resolve the conflict by ascribing to Eur. all of the astronomical sources' story *except* for the catasterism. Nor does Luppe (*WJA* cited above, and *SEJG* 31 [1989/90], 257–70), ascribing even their account of the catasterism to Eur. and deleting lines 16–17 so as to alleviate the contradiction. Probably the astronomical sources are wrong in ascribing their romantic story to Eur. The vagueness of 18–19 (see below) may however mean that only Hippo's disappearance, and not her catasterism, was known to the human characters at the play's start.

1 5 . plumed: deliberately misused (*catachresis*) for 'covered with hair': cf. Eur. *El.* 530 βοστρύχους ὁμοπτέρους 'similarly-feathered locks' (recalling Aesch. *Cho.* 174–5), *Hel.* 632–3. **horse-hair:** θρίξ of a horse's mane: Soph. F 475.

1 6 . oracular: lit. 'oracle-chanting' (cf. Soph. F 573 'oracle-chanting utterance'); the second element of the adj. duplicates the sense of the noun as often in Eur. (Collard on *Supp.* 400–1).

1 7 . cures . . . deliverances: probably medical (ἄκη) and ritual (λυτήρια); the two go hand in hand, e.g., Pind. *Pyth.* 3.45–53, Aesch. *Supp.* 268 (similar phrase), Pl. *Charm.* 155e5; cf. *Bell.* F 286b.4ff. n. Hippo was an *iatromantis*, 'healer-seer' (see Parker, *Miasma* 207ff.) like e.g. Apollo (Aesch. *Eum.* 62, Ar. *Plut.* 11), Apis (Aesch. *Supp.* 263); cf. Prometheus's gifts, [Aesch.] *PV* 476ff.

1 8 . a dense squall of mist: θυέλληι 'squall' suggests a divinely managed disappearance: cf. *Supp.* 830 with Collard's n., Hom. *Od.* 20.63 and 66, *Il.* 6.346, *Hom. Hymn.* 5.208, Soph. *OC* 1659–60, *Kings* II.2.1–2 (Elijah taken up in a fiery chariot by a whirlwind). Aether here is a damp, misty substance (cf. e.g. *Tro.* 79 δνοφώδη τ' αἰθέρος φυσήματα 'murky blasts of aether', *Danae* F 330.4, *Ion* 796, *Bacch.* 865, Soph. *OC* 1081), 'dense' (πυκνή) like e.g. 'dense cloud' Hom. *Il.* 5.751, Hes. *WD* 553. Jesus ascends in a cloud, *Acts* 1.9. **she was swept away:** διώκεται historic Pres.; for the sense cf. Hom. *Od.* 5.332 (wind driving ships), LSJ III; but the clause ends abruptly, and a line elaborating it may be lost.

1 9 . her place of inspiration, the Corycian mountain: i.e. Mt. Parnassus (cf. *Bacc.* 559), with ref. to the Corycian Cave high above Delphi, sacred to the Nymphs: sources in *RE* XI.1448–50, XVIII.2.1590–2; descriptions in Frazer on Paus. 10.32.2, J. Fontenrose, *Python* (Berkeley, 1959), 409–12 (suggesting the Cave was an oracular site before Delphi itself, 412–9); P.-Y. Péchoux and others, *L'Antre Corycien* I (Paris, 1981: *BCH* Supp. 7), 1–24. For the Greek phrasing with 'and' linking the second, defining ('epexegetic') phrase to the first cf. e.g. Aesch.

Ag. 9–10, Eur. *HF* 15 with commentators and (though not all his examples are apt) Denniston, *GP* 502, cf. 291. Cf. also *Hel.* 1107 μουσεῖα καὶ θάκους 'seats of inspiration', Pl. *Phdr.* 278b9 τὸ Νυμφῶν νᾶμά τε καὶ μουσεῖον 'the Nymphs' inspiring stream'. [Text: τ(ε) need not be deleted (Wilamowitz 1908) nor translated as if μουσεῖον refers to a second mountain, Helicon (Wilamowitz 1921, van Looy). JD would prefer γ(ε) (also used epexegetically: Denniston 138–9).]
2 1 . Hippo: Rabe so corrected ms. ἵππο since Clement gives 'Hippo' in citing F 483 (see App. there); everywhere else she is 'Hippe'.

482 (483 N). Ar. *Lys.* 1124 is probably the fr. indicated by Schol. Ar. *Lys.* (so e.g. Henderson there, Rau 201). *Lys.* 1125–7 (cited in App.) are Tragic in tone but 1126 as it stands hardly suits Melanippe (educated by her mother, F 484) and 1125 seems coherent with 1126–7 (native wit *vs.* education). The context is generally agreed to be the start of Melanippe's defence speech. *Med.* 1081–9 is a more elaborate female defensive claim to wisdom; *And.* 364–5, *Or.* 1204 are comments on female displays of cleverness. [Text: μοῦσα 'muse' in Suidas is surely a mistake due to the subject of the citation, not evidence for Eur.'s text as Porson supposed.]

483 (482 N). Clement (App.) says Hippo 'cohabited with Aeolus and taught him natural science (φυσικὴ θεωρία), her father's knowledge'; presumably this too depends on the play. This fr. is amongst a very few late 5ᵗʰ C. Greek refs. to astrology, the Babylonian science which became influential with Greeks in the Hellenistic period; cf. T. Barton, *Ancient Astrology* (London, 1994), 21–3 (not mentioning our fr.). Earlier refs. relate seasons and weather with astronomical phenomena for cultural and nautical purposes: Hes. *WD* 383–7, 414–22 etc. (cf. D. R. Dicks, *Early Greek Astronomy to Aristotle* [London, 1970], 34–8), the ps.-Hesiodic *Astronomy* (frs. 288–93), Thales 11 B1 DK; Prometheus is made the author of this knowledge, [Aesch.] *PV* 457–8. **divine intentions** and **accurate prophecies** go beyond this (although Wilamowitz 74 n. 2 limited the ref. to 'weather prognoses'). **risings of the stars:** cf. Aesch. *Ag.* 7, *PV* 457–8 "stars' risings . . . and settings"; specific examples in Hes. *WD* (above).

4 8 4 . The citations in Dionys. Hal. show that this was part of Melanippe's defence of the babies, supporting her argument that their birth must have been natural.
1. not my own: an appeal to authority (cf. *Hel.* 513); Dionys. says Hippo's being Melanippe's mother helped Melanippe's 'philosophising' carry conviction.
2–6. For the association of cosmogonical with magical/healing knowledge (F 481.16–17, 483) see W. Burkert in J. Bremmer (ed.), *Interpretations of Greek Mythology* (London, 1987), 24. Heaven and Earth *(a)* were once one form, then separated from each other, *(b)* are parents of all natural animal and plant life. *(a)* is the ancient mythical conception found in the Babylonian *Enuma Elish*, Tablet 4.135–46 (Pritchard, *ANET* p. 67), in Hes. *Theog.* 154–210 (cf. West's Comm.), and in early Orphic theogonies (West, *The Orphic Poems* [Oxford, 1983], 104). *(b)* is also mythical, cf. Aesch. F 44 imitated by Eur. F 898 (Aphrodite prompts Sky to

fertilise Earth), Eur. F 839 (Aether and Earth generate and recycle all life; cf. F 1023). *(a)* and *(b)* together are found in Ap. Rhod. 1.496–502, the cosmogonical song of Orpheus, and are associated with Orphic tenets on the bowl cited in App.; the combination need not have been specifically 'Orphic' for Eur., although Hippo's cosmogony, astrology and healing practices together do have an exotic character. There is no reason to trace here a reflection of 5th C. philosophical/scientific accounts of the generation of life-forms by 'separation' from a common source (e.g. Anaxagoras 59 B1, Archelaus 60 A4, Diogenes Ap. 64 B2, all DK) as Dionys. and Diod. did with ref. to Anaxagoras in citing our fr. For such accounts see W. K. C. Guthrie, *In the Beginning* (London, 1957), 29–45; Guthrie is sceptical about Eur. as 'pupil' of Anaxagoras, *HGPh* II.323–5 (cf. *Pha.* 169–70 n.). [Text: **5. beasts reared by the briny sea:** better (JD) than the transmitted 'beasts, and those reared by the briny sea'. Wecklein's alteration gives a tripartite expression with one item from each of the elements earth, air and water.]

485. Cited by Dionys. Hal. (cf. on F 484) as one of Melanippe's arguments 'in rehearsing all the reasons for preserving the children'. There is no point in trying to reconstruct Eur.'s exact words (sample efforts in van Looy 233).

486. The sources make it clear that both phrases refer to Justice. In *(b)* Eur.'s wording probably goes at least as far as 'morning-star'. Probably the Chorus demand or (Wünsch, van Looy) acknowledge Melanippe's vindication as a triumph of Justice (cf. F 506 n.). They maintain a more traditional view of Justice as a divine personality than Melanippe in F 506. **Justice's:** the personification of Dikaiosyné rather than Diké is unusual; cf. *AP* 9.164. **golden countenance:** cf. Soph. F 12 'Justice's golden eye has observed' (cited by Aristoxenus along with our fr.). 'Eye' or 'countenance' is applied to the Sun in Soph. *Ant.* 103, *Trach.* 102 (see Davies), the Moon in Aesch. *Sept.* 390, the 'face' of the heaven itself in daylight or darkness e.g. *El.* 102, *Pho.* 543; cf. LSJ ὄμμα II, ὀφθαλμός III. Justice's divine light 'has shone out', *TrGF* II F adesp. 500.

Metre: dactylo-epitrite.

487. Generally assigned to Melanippe and connected with the emergence of the truth. **holy aether, Zeus's dwelling:** ἱερὸν 'holy' of aether as F 985. Zeus's dwelling in aether is traditional, esp. when he is called on as a witness looking down from the heaven: cf. Hom. *Il.* 2.412, 4.166, Hes. *WD* 18, Eur. *Tro.* 1079 (cf. *Pho.* 84) and (gods in general) *Bacc.* 393, *Or.* 1636; cf. *Erec.* F 370.72 n. More surprising (though cf. [Aesch.] *PV* 88) is aether itself as a witness like more traditionally 'divine' phenomena (Sun, Sky etc.). This and Eur.'s *identifications* of aether with Zeus or divinity (F 877, 941; Cropp on *El.* 991) in accord with newfangled 'philosophy' (esp. Diogenes of Apollonia 64 B4–5 DK; cf. Guthrie, *HGPh* II.364–9, III.232) may account for Aristophanes' parody. οἴκησιν 'dwelling', a pedestrian word, may also have attracted attention (hence Ar. *Frogs* 100 and 311 'Aether, Zeus's bedroom').

Commentary on *The Captive Melanippe*

489. Attributed to *Capt. Mel.* Prologue by Wilamowitz 67; this is widely accepted, but van Looy 238–9 shows that the ending of *Wise Mel.* is at least equally possible. An explanation of Aeolus's name preceded. For names derived from circumstances of birth or discovery cf. *Antiope* F 181–2, *Ion* 661–3; on Eur.'s etymologising of names in general see *Pha.* 224–6 n.

490. The terminology suggests not personal opportunism (Webster, ascribing the fr. to the plotting Queen) but political responsibility, perhaps even public counsel regarded as a duty (rare in 5th C. sources: Collard, cited below). The speaker might be the King planning his future at the end (Hartung, van Looy). **turn:** cf. *Supp.* 413 στρέφει 'directs (the city)', F 491.3 παραστρέφων 'diverting'. **beneficial:** a political label: cf. e.g. *Or.* 909–11 'those who ... give good counsel (χρηστὰ βουλεύουσι) ... are ... beneficial (χρήσιμοι) to the city', Collard on *Supp.* 439, *Ion* 598–9 (Diggle's text), Ar. *Birds* 372–3, *Lys.* 639, Eupolis *PCG* V fr. 129.2. **in concord with divine influence:** lit. 'with the god'; cf. Jebb on Soph. *Aj.* 383, τὸ θεῖον 'divine will' in F 491.5; elsewhere 'with the gods', e.g. *Erec.* F 352.

491. The attribution to *Capt. Mel.* with ref. to Metapontus is universally accepted; spoken by the Queen? *Erec.* F 359 criticises adoption on different grounds. For adoption as a tragic motif cf. *Ion* 591–2, *Hipp.* 305–10. **3. not right:** μὴ (not οὐ) is generic or categorising, cf. e.g. *HF* 311, *Bacc.* 515. [**5.** Text: Trincavelli's 'to complain' is neat but not quite the right sense.]

492. Cited in a discussion of mirth-makers (on whom cf. *Erec.* F 362.22); it is hard to see how the irrelevant F 494.9–10a became attached, but the attribution to *Capt. Mel.* need not be doubted (as by Wilamowitz and van Looy, who like Schmid oddly suppose that Eur. is 'replying' to Aristophanes and other comic critics). Hartung and Webster guess that one of the twins is preferring hunting to the symposium. **2. mockery as a grace:** lit. 'taunting gratifications' (but *Alc.* 1125 κέρτομος ... χαρά mocking joy'). **3. wise things:** σοφῶν Neuter substantive like *Med.* 298 (cf. Ar. *Thesm.* 1130), *Supp.* 294, *Bacc.* 480. **4. unbridled mouths:** cf. *Bacc.* 386. **5. look good:** cf. *Tro.* 951, LSJ εὐπρεπής I.3; this contrasts well with what precedes (they *look* like proper men, but only at the symposium; cf. *Erec.* F 362.22 'notable only for raising laughs'.). **5. count:** metaphor from tax-qualification like *Bacc.* 822, Soph. *OT* 222: LSJ τελέω II.3. [Text: in 3 Ath.'s reading is nonsense. Neither τήτη nor τῆτος is found outside the lexicographers (Hesych., Phot.); Wilamowitz preferred the -η form comparing the verb τητάομαι (Eur. *Or.* 1084 etc.) For the rare οὐ at line-end in a continuing sentence see West, *Metre* 83. The fr. ends abruptly and may be incomplete, perhaps because of the textual confusion noted above (van Looy).]

493. Stob.'s subsection 'Marriage suitable for some but not for others' also includes F 494.27–9, *Hec.* 1183–6, *Alcm.* F 78 etc. See further on F 494 and F 498. The idea that isolated instances of 'badness' in women (i.e. sexual misconduct, cf. *Sthen.* F 661.29 n.) tend to corrupt them all is expressed in F 497 (cf. *Hipp.* 407–12), and rejected (as here) in F 494.24–6; *Ion* 1090–8 is another rejection of women's reputation for adultery. See further Barrett on *Hipp.* 405–12. **1. The hatred women incur:** lit. 'the female species having become hated' (Aor. part.). **5. (are) entirely corrupt:** lit. '(think) nothing healthy'; probably colloquial, frequent in Eur.; cf. Stevens on *And.* 448–9; F 497 n.

494. A rebuttal of misogyny which found its way into anthologies such as the Berlin papyrus and Stob. (see previous n.), and into the biographers' fiction (Satyrus etc., inspired esp. by Ar. *Thesm.*) that Eur. composed the speech to mollify women outraged by his insulting portrayals of them in other plays. The parabasis of Ar. *Thesm.* (785–845) is a comic version of such a defence. For possible contexts and speakers in *Capt. Mel.* see Introd., pp. 243–4. The defence rests on points where women excel or are distinct from men: honesty in returning loans (4–5), (sharing work or troubles with each other, and modesty, 6–8?), domestic economy (9–11), and special religious roles (12–21).
2. twang an idle shaft: with no effect but noise; cf. Pind. *Isthm.* 5.47 'my ready tongue has many shafts (τοξεύματα) to sing about them', *Anth.Plan.* 4.211 'twanging an arrow' (LSJ ψάλλω).
3. [Text: Anon. *Life*'s 'I say' was substituted when 1–3 were cited in isolation.]
4–5. contracts unwitnessed ... not reneging: Page suggests '<*they have*> unwitnessed contracts . . .'. Wilamowitz, *BKT* compared Ar. *Eccl.* 446–50, Praxagora's claim that women make loans to each other 'one on one, not in the presence of witnesses, and give everything back without filching'. Such informal borrowing between neighbours was not confined to women (see P. Millett, *Lending and Borrowing in Ancient Athens* [Cambridge, 1991], 37–9, 145), but the formalisation of loans was a matter of public (male) life.
8. expel(?): ἐκβάλλειν has several possibly relevant meanings.   [Text: P. Oxy. 'has' for 'brings'.]
9–11. The wife's sphere is defined as the house, as e.g. *El.* 73–6 (and limited to it, cf. *Meleag.* F 521, F 927 compared by van Looy); the classic statement of her domestic duties with similar emphasis on organisation, storage and safe keeping (cf. *Pha.* 223 n.) is Xen. *Oec.* 7.18–9.19.   **sea:** sea trade is a typical (male) mode of gathering wealth, e.g. Solon *IEG* fr. 13.41–6.   [Text: in 9 Ath.'s verb (same sense) is a trivialisation. In 11 P. Berl. seems to give (feebly) '. . . in the absence of a woman that prosperous house is dirty.']
12–22. dealings with the gods (etc.): women had a distinct and indispensable role in Greek religious practice, complementing that of men albeit within a male-supervised framework; see in general L. Bruit Zaidman in P. Schmitt Pantel (ed.), *A History of Women in the Western World*, vol. 1 (Cambridge, Mass., 1992), 338–78 (on priestesses and prophetesses, 372–7). Athens had many priestesses;

the examples here concentrate on communication with deities who ordain and enforce 'what is to be', a matter of fundamental importance for men and women alike.
12. [Text: **as for . . . :** P. Oxy. is preferable and consistent with the recapitulation in 21 (cf. also F 493.4); P. Berl. gives 'as for what . . .', but no following verb (contrast 18–19, *Med.* 453, *Pal.* F 578.8).]

13–14. Phoebus's halls: Apollo's temple at Delphi where the Pythia was his prophetess; for brief description of sanctuary and rituals see Burkert 115–6 with bibl. 394, nn. 63, 65. [Text: 'halls' rather than P. Oxy.'s 'oracles' are in apt contrast with the topography of Dodona which follows.]

14. mind: i.e. 'intentions' here and in 16, cf. *Ion* 1271, *Hec.* 746; LSJ 4.
Loxias: a name of uncertain etymology, often used in refs. to Apollo's oracular function and suggesting 'oblique', 'ambiguous' (λοξός).

15. Dodona: the ancient oracular sanctuary of Zeus in Epirus (see further on 16–17). **holy foundations:** i.e. the stone bases of the sacred altar, buildings and monuments. Eur. uses βάθρα 'foundations' to the point of cliché in such evocative descriptions: *Pho.* 982 'Dodona's august foundations', *IA* 1263 'Troy's famed foundations', etc.; cf. *Arch.* F 228a.20 'Dodona's holy vales'. [Text: P. Oxy. has unmetrical 'foundations of the house <of . . . >'. If P. Berl. δ' is right against P. Oxy. θ' in 15, it adds a nuance of contrast to the second example: cf. Denniston, *GP* 513.]

16. sacred oak: the focal point of the sanctuary; the rustling of its leaves was thought to indicate Zeus's intentions.

16–17. the female sex: the Greek phrasing emphatically separates 'female' from 'sex' and juxtaposes it with 'Zeus'. At least from the 5th C. three prophetic priestesses known as 'Doves' delivered the oracles: see Burkert 114 and (bibl.) 393 nn. 46–51; on Dodona in 5th C. authors, H. W. Parke, *The Oracles of Zeus* (Oxford, 1967), 51–81; A. B. Lloyd on Hdt. 2.55. See also on *Erec.* F 367–8.

18. Fates . . . Nameless Goddesses: the latter (so described at *IT* 944, cf. Soph. *OC* 128–9) are the avenging spirits often called Erinyes (Avengers, Furies) or Poinai (Punishers), euphemistically Semnai (August Ones) or Eumenides (Benevolent Ones), occasionally Keres (Spirits of Death): see West on Hes. *Th.* 217 (Fates and avenging Keres amongst the daughters of Night); cf. Aesch. *Eum.* 962, and on their parentage Podlecki on *Eum.* 321. For Fates together with Erinyes see Fraenkel on Aesch. *Ag.* 1535–6, A. Henrichs in Hofmann and Harder, *Fragmenta Dramatica* 175 n. 28. Henrichs (169–79) argues that Erinyes and the like were not so much 'nameless' as 'not to be named' because of their threatening nature, and discusses the strategies for naming them safely. Wilamowitz in *BKT* referred our passage to domestic cult (cf. e.g. Aesch. *Eum.* 106–9, 964), Henrichs to the cult of the Semnai Theai (the 'nameless goddesses' of *IT* 944) on the Areopagus at Athens; but the setting of the play and the generality of Melanippe's claim do not encourage any specificity. On cults of the Erinyes, *RE* Supp. 8 (1956), 128–36.

19–20. open: approachable without ritual offence: cf. *Cresph.* F 448a.116–7 n. [Text: the changes are needed for sense. Negative at line-end: cf. F 492.4.]

21. [Text: Cropp's δίκη could give 'Thus a female right maintains our dealings with the gods', but better the translation printed, with τὰν θεοῖς Acc. of respect (so JD,

cf. Soph. *Phil.* 1336 ταῦτα τῆιδ' ἔχοντα 'these things standing thus', *Or.* 427 τὰ
πρὸς πόλιν ... πῶς ἔχεις 'how do you stand in relation to the city?'). P. Berl.'s
wording barely makes sense. Gen. δίκης cannot mean 'with rightness' and can
hardly depend on ταύτηι ('in this manner of rightness'). θήλεια can hardly mean
'women': we would need Fem. Plur. as in *Supp.* 294, *Pho.* 198, *Tro.* 651. Van
Looy's δίκηι 'with right, rightly' does not solve the second problem.]

23. [Text: Collard's λόγος 'talk' would remove the slightly awkward repetition
'denigration (21) ... denigrate (25)'; he compares the textual corruption in *Bell.*
F 297.5. Eur. elsewhere has (Plural) 'futile words' (*And.* 692, *Hipp.* 450, *Supp.*
583, *Dictys* F 334.3.]

24. [Text: no plausible correction has been found for the obelised words. Page took
ἡγούμενοι as = ἡγούμενοι δεῖν ('those excessively thinking it necessary'); but
the parallels are textually suspect (*Or.* 555–6, Thuc. 2.42.4) or open to different
interpretation (Pl. *Prot.* 346d6; constructions such as *Cret.* F 472e.3 'take thought
(so as) to ...' are a different matter); and there are still awkwardnesses of syntax
('this futile denigration ... and those who ...') and sense ('excessively thinking'.]

24–6. All women unfairly blamed for the 'badness' of one or a few: F 493 n.

26. [Text: (δι)ὁριῶ is the Attic Future form of (δι)ὁρίζω: see LSJ.]

27–9. Women (wives) either extremely bad or extremely good: Hes. *WD* 702–3,
imitated by Semonides *IEG* fr. 6, Soph. *Ant.* 650–1, Theogn. 1225; see also on
F 493, and on F 498 for the negative side.

27. [Metre: the line-end does not break Porson's law: West, *Metre* 85.]

28–9. excels ... in ... : lit. 'is better, to excess, than ...': cf. μᾶλλον with
compar., e.g. 'more easier' (LSJ μάλα II.2). Eur. elsewhere uses εἰς ὑπερβολήν
with compar. Gen., 'to excess (over)', *Hipp.* 939, *Autolycus* F 282.6.)

495. P. Berl. spans the last 50–60 lines of the Report speech (a member of the
ambush party reporting to the Queen: 18, 28, 39) and the next 7 lines of the scene.
Judging from the roughly contemporary *El.*, *HF*, *Ion*, *IT* and *Hel.*, the speech will
have occupied 80–110 lines. The lost part will have included the two hunting
parties setting out, the locale and ambush described, the twins' hunt in progress
and interrupted. In the extant narrative Poseidon's protection of the twins,
mentioned by Hyginus, is not evident; the Messenger could not know of it, but it
could have been implied by observations such as line 26, to be clarified by
Poseidon himself in the play's final scene.

1. Weil's '**Who was it** *let fly* <*this unseen missile*> **at me**?' must give the
general sense, but his τυφλὸν 'blind' (cf. *HF* 199) does not fit the traces according
to Wilamowitz who suggested 'idle' (cf. *Pho.* 1387); von Arnim 'ineffective'
(cf. below, 27).

3. **him:** probably not his brother (Blass), nor a boar (Wecklein, van Looy), but one
of the ambushers who, it seems, are spread out or in two groups; the twins have
advanced on some of them thinking they are finding a boar; a missile flies at them
from the side provoking their complaint; getting no response, they press on
towards their original objective and the ambushers then reveal themselves.

4. at a run: δρομαίαν is internal Acc. with e.g. ὁδόν understood, 'a running (path)'; cf. Page on *Med.* 384, Denniston on *El.* 1046, KG I.313 n. 12.

5. now: δή marks a climactic verb: cf. Denniston, *GP* 214–5.

6. [Text: adding an apostrophe to P. Berl.'s λόγχαις gives a caesura common enough in Eur.: cf. esp. *Hec.* 1159, *Bacc.* 1125; J. Diggle, *GRBS* 14 (1973) 263–4 = *Euripidea* 82–3 (further, 473 n. 151); West, *Metre* 82–3 with n. 18. Headlam's 'aiming murder' (cf. *Hec.* 263, Collard on *Supp.* 672) was designed to give a commoner 4ᵗʰ-foot caesura. A few mid-line caesuras are accepted by some in Eur.'s text as deliberate special effects: cf. Collard on *Supp.* 699.]

7. their two uncles: lit. 'the twofold head of their uncles' (Weil's improvement on P's 'head of their twofold uncles'). For the slight illogicality cf. Soph. *Ant.* 14.

9. just at the right moment: καιρόν is adverbial Acc., cf. e.g. *Hel.* 479, *Hyps.* fr. 60.27; LSJ III.1.b.

11.<spear>-onslaught: πίτυλος 'denotes a regularly repeated movement' (Barrett on *Hipp.* 1464) and here suggests the relentlessness of the onslaught. [Text supplement: *HF* 816 is similarly phrased. Weil's δορός '*spear*-' is modelled on *Hcld.* 834 πίτυλος . . . δορός ('insistent spear-thrusting').]

12. flew: for χωρέω of missiles cf. 27 below, *And.* 1134.

14. [Text: for δή see on 5 above; for τὸ πᾶν with verbs of learning, revealing etc. cf. [Aesch.] *PV* 273, Soph. *Phil.* 241 ('now you know the whole truth'), *Trach.* 369, 1134, etc. Van Looy's alternative is 'recognising the treachery'.]

16.those <*you should least kill*>: i.e. your relatives; cf. *El.* 1012, *Bacc.* 26, *IA* 487.

17–20. The supplements of Weil and Blass are no doubt on the right lines: '. . . do <*not do this by any means*'. But your brothers <*lifted (each) a*> rock <*in his hands*> and said that the twins were born <*from a slave woman somewhere*> (or *as bastards from a slave woman*, Nauck; *from some slave woman*, van Looy), and <*that they*> ought not <*to control a*> royal <*sceptre and throne*> (or <*bastards*> ought not <*to take the sceptres*> *of kings*, von Arnim following Nauck). In favour of <*from a slave woman somewhere*> in 19 cf. *Hec.* 365 'a purchased slave from somewhere'. [Text: in 18 some form of χερμαδ- 'rock' seems necessary since Blass read χερμ- confidently.]

21.'<*the low-born*> holding prerogatives <*belonging to the high-born*>' according to Weil's supplement; πρεσβεῖα may be inherited rights (cf. Soph. F 24.2) or specifically rights of primogeniture (so van Looy; cf. LSJ 3).

22–3. With the correction and supplements in App., '**And when they heard these things** <*they were not dismayed,*> holding their **spirit** well . . . (or *not having a dejected spirit* . . .)'. [Text: λῆμμ(α) 'receipt, gain', hardly fits the context and is used only once in Tragedy, Soph. *Ant.* 313.]

24ff. The missing text described the resumption of the conflict and one of the twins confronting the elder of the Queen's brothers, who falls in 26.

30.delivered . . . a fine corpse: a macabre use of sacrificial language, as if an offering to the dead had been made. For δίδωμι so used see LSJ I.2; for καλός 'fine' of auspicious victims LSJ II.2. At *HF* 454 Megara and her children led out for execution are 'an unlovely group of corpses' (ζεῦγος οὐ καλὸν νεκρῶν).

31. by *<Boeotus>* (Blass), printed by most editors, is a convenient but hardly certain supplement. Weil's *<that man>* is plausible but less consistent with the traces reported by Blass.

34. mountain-brush: lit. 'mountain's brush-outgrowth' like *Bacc.* 1138 ὕλης ἐν βαθυξύλωι φόβηι 'in the wood's deep-timber outgrowth'. One man hides in the brush clothing the mountainside, another (35) climbs a tree. [Text: this takes ὑλιμός as 'brush-' rather than 'forest-' (cf. LSJ ὕλη). Maas's 'under the forest-foliage of an oak' providing a contrast between two types of tree is hardly needed.]

35. [Text, *<concealed>*: cf. *Bacc.* 723, 954–51 and (for the line-end) 1070. Weil's 'cowering', 'lurking' are rarer words, the latter not otherwise intrans. in Eur.]

37–8. did not deign: killing mere slaves is beneath their dignity: cf. Orestes with the effeminate Phrygian, *Or.* 1127–8. This leads towards the messenger's concluding reflection on the innate nobility of the twins (41–3).

39. about: simple Gen. with verbs of hearing, e.g. *El.* 1124; KG I.360 n. 9b. [Text: von Arnim's supplement is more apt than Nauck's 'such is the fate . . .']

40–3. I do not know etc.: on such gnomic conclusions in Eur.'s messenger speeches see de Jong 191–2. This one contrasts appearances and reality; cf. *Med.* 1224–30, *Hcld.* 863–6. The unpredictability of human worth, multiplicity of standards of 'nobility', and natural equality of human potential are common topics in Eur.: cf. esp. *El.* 367–85 with Cropp's n., and for background Guthrie, *HGPh* III.155–60, Kannicht on *Hel.* 726–33. For slaves equalling or excelling free men in nobility cf. also F 511 below, *Ion* 854–6, etc. (and for the converse in unsympathetic mouths e.g. *Alex.* F 49, *Alcmaeon* F 86). **empty appearances:** this phrase at *El.* 383 means 'vain estimations', here the objects of such estim-ations like δοκήματα, *Erec.* F 359.2. [Text: the correction of Stob.'s wording (for metre) at the start of 40 is partially confirmed by P, whose **'by what means'** is more likely to have been corrupted than Stob.'s 'in what way'.]

44ff. A Chorus comment normally follows Eur.'s messenger speeches, even those addressed to an individual. The Queen begins to speak of her lost hopes at 47.

51. This remnant appears on a scrap of the page which was originally the other half of the surviving sheet of the Parchment. Wilamowitz, *BKT* V.2.87 inferred that the codex originally had four sides of text (one folded sheet) interposed, say 120–60 lines. He later estimated twelve sides lost out of a quaternion, or some 350 lines (*Sitzb.Pr.Akad.* 66 = *KS* 443). The sides lost might in fact be four, eight or twelve; and the number of lines per page is unknown. The gap between lines 50 and 51 might be anything between 140 and 500 lines or more.

496 (= test. iib). On Siris see Introd., p. 245. As Moscati Castelnuovo (cited there), 46 notes, Athenaeus does not state that Siris was the Queen in Eur.'s play, nor that she appeared in it at all. But the appearance of Siris as Metapontus's first wife in Schol. Dionys. Perieget. 461 (see p. 242 above) supports the identificat-ion. Siris was also the name of the river beside which the colony Siris was placed.

Melanippe (Wise or Captive)

497. Corruption of women by the sexual misconduct of a few: see on F 493 above. For **corruption** (1 νοσεῖ) and **bad** (4 κακήν) referring to sexual misconduct cf. F 493.4–5 and *Sthen.* F 661.6, 29 nn. Probably this fr. refers to Melanippe in *Wise Mel.* (e.g. Wünsch, Wilamowitz 75) rather than the Queen in *Capt. Mel.* (von Arnim, van Looy); Webster persuasively suggests Hellen rather than Aeolus as speaker. **2. women's:** τὰ τῶν γυναικῶν is virtually 'women', perhaps contemptuously as *Hel.* 276 (barbarians); cf. Gildersleeve §581, Stevens on *And.* 713. **5. seeps gradually (etc.):** metaphor from flooding; see LSJ ὑπορρέω II.1, esp. Pl. *Rep.* 424d8 of lawlessness seeping throughout the attitudes and behaviour of the young. [Text: In **2**, Herwerden's ὕπερ rather than Stob.'s πέρι gives the needed sense: cf. Dale on *Alc.* 178 (*And.* 713 cited by van Looy is not parallel).]

498. Usually assigned to the debate on misogyny in *Capt. Mel.* with F 494 and F 493. Other attacks on women cited by Stob. include *Hec.* 1178–82, *Hipp.* 616ff., 664–8, *Sthen.* F 666 (where see Comm.) etc.

500. More likely Aeolus criticising Hellen in *Wise Mel.* (Wilamowitz, Webster) than Hippo criticising Aeolus as a father at the end (van Looy: why then 'young man'?) or in *Capt. Mel.* Metapontus criticised by his wife (Hartung) or himself (von Arnim).

501. Usually assigned with F 502, 503 to *Capt. Mel.*, and perhaps to be associated with the frs. about misogyny (493, 494, 498). The thought is unusual, its implications unclear without a context. For the idea of a 'destined' husband cf. Hom. *Od.* 16.392. **3. arrives:** probably gnomic Aor. though Wünsch and van Looy place the fr. near the end of the play and see a past-tense ref. to Melanippe's union with Metapontus. [Text, **2–3**. †awaiting her proper husband†: χρεών as adj. 'proper' is unparalleled, as is the Dat. τῶι . . . πόσει as object of μένουσα (van Looy takes it with ἦλθεν εἰς δόμους, 'comes to the house of the proper husband', but it belongs in the participial phrase ἡ . . . μένουσα). Von Arnim's μέλλουσα 'intended for' would have an unparalleled Dat. object. West's μέλουσα is no solution in itself but with Collard's ἡ δ' ὅτωι could give tolerable sense, 'the woman who is a concern to the man to whom she should be . . .'.]

502. Grouped by Stob. with F 501, and usually assigned with it to *Mel.D*: see previous note. This fr. suggests that Metapontus owed his status to his wife: see Introd., p. 247. The topic of marrying above oneself is common in Eur. (e.g. *And.* 1279–82, *El.* 930–7 with Cropp's Comm., [1097–9] = *Cret.W.* F 464.3–5) and elsewhere (e.g. Menand. fr. 579, 581–2): see also on *Pha.* 158–9. **3. the wife's sway:** τὰ τῆς γυναικός is virtually 'the wife'; cf. F 497.2 n. **4. enslaves:** cf. *Pha.* 158–9. **6. divorces . . . <not> easy:** the wife's ability to take her dowry with her (e.g. Isaeus 3.28; Lacey, *Family* 107–10) is a discouragement.

503. Usually assigned to the Chorus in *Capt. Mel.* and associated with F 501, 502, but metre, the flat gnomic generality (**For mortals it is best**) and banal anaphora (**moderate . . . moderate**) suggest these may be amongst the final lines of the play (so Wünsch) like *El.* 1357–9, Soph. *Ant.* 1347–53; on similar grounds *Arch.* F 264 and Soph. *Tereus* F 590 are regarded as play-ends. Cf. D. H. Roberts, *CQ* 37 (1987), 51–64, esp. 58–60 and n. 28 on gnomic content. **moderate:** probably not emotionally (van Looy comparing *Hipp.* 253, *Hel.* 1105, etc.) but socially/materially. **temperance**, then, is avoidance of the excessive behaviour which wealth and power encourage (cf. *Med.* 125–8), and the thought is complementary to F 502. If this is the Chorus's final word on events in the play, it is typically reductive (cf. Roberts 59–60). *Metre:* anapaests, apparently recitative.

504. Various contexts have been suggested, e.g. in *Capt. Mel.* the herdsman or Melanippe to one of the sons (von Arnim; cf. Webster), or less attractively in *Wise Mel.* Hellen to Aeolus (Wilamowitz) or Hippo to Melanippe (van Looy). **Child:** cf. *Cresph.* F 457 n. **a lowly life:** cf. *El.* 407, 1098, LSJ I.3. For the position of the article, rare in Prose, see Gildersleeve, *Syntax* §609, 612. **right blend:** metaph. from climate; cf. n. on *Pha.* 7 'temperate'. **grandeur:** lit. 'bulk', metaph. in Eur. *And.* 320, *Tro.* 108 etc. [Text: for the accent in εὐκράς see Kambitsis on *Antiope* fr. XIII = F 197. Musgrave's τ' giving 'and grandeur a bad thing' is hardly necessary.]

505. A consolatory commonplace (cf. e.g. *Alkmene* F 98, *Oenomaus* F 572, *Hel.* 253–4, Bond on *HF* 1228). A connection with F 507 with ref. to Melanippe in *Capt. Mel.* seems possible. **self-controlled:** accepting human limitations; cf. e.g. *Med.* 1018, *HF* 1320–1. [Text: Stob.'s variants are weak banalisations.]

506. The ascription to *Wise Mel.* is widely accepted, Melanippe the probable speaker in view of the religious sophistication. Many (e.g. van Looy, Webster) have thought of the defence of the twins and rejection of monstrous portents as a context; but Justice may be a topic near the end of the play too (cf. F 486), in Melanippe's mouth or (Wilamowitz 75) Hippo's. The statement rejects, not divine Justice, but an understanding of this in terms of a limited anthropomorphic deity; this is in the tradition of Empedocles (31 B 134 DK) and Xenophanes (e.g. 21 A 28, 31, 32, B 14–16 DK); cf. Guthrie, *HGPh* I.370–3, II.256–7. Its enunciation by a great-granddaughter of Zeus is paradoxical, like Heracles' Xenophanean denial of divine immorality, *HF* 1341–6.

1–2. wrongdoings leap up etc.: in Hes. *WD* 220–4 Justice herself is in the world, complaining and causing retribution when mishandled. In *WD* 248–62 three myriads of immortal watchers observe men's wrongs while Justice brings complaints to Zeus and persuades him to punish them. The idea that wrongs themselves are winged spirits is not found elsewhere, but cf. the personification of Prayers for retribution (albeit as daughters of Zeus) in Hom. *Il.* 9. 502–12. West on *WD* 259 lists examples of servants reporting misdeeds to gods; cf. E. Fraenkel, *CQ* 36 (1942), 10–14 on Plaut. *Rud.* 9–16.

2 . folded tablet: lit. 'tablet-folds'; cf. *IT* 760, *IA* 98. The idea of a divine written record of men's deeds (as also of a divinely written plan for the world) is almost as old as the use of writing for administrative record-keeping in the ancient Near East. For Mesopotamian, Egyptian and Persian sources and the Old Testament (e.g. *Jeremiah* 17.1) see L. Koep in *RAC* II.725–32. For actual (Persian) royal practice van Looy compares Thuc. 1.129.3, *Esther* 6.2. The idea's currency in archaic Greece cannot be traced (cf. van Looy's discussion, 227–32, with later examples from lexica and proverbs, 230 with notes 3, 5; also Babrius 127, Lucian 36.12, Hesych. σ 1190 Schmidt [σκυτάλαι]), but in Aesch. F 281a Justice rewards the just and the unjust, writing the latter's transgressions 'on Zeus's tablet' and opening the record on the due day, and in Aesch. *Eum.* 273–5 Hades observes men's wrongs with 'tablet-writing mind' so as to call them to account.

4 . the entire sky: the sky's serving as a huge book is fanciful, perhaps suggested by its having πτυχαί 'folds' = 'recesses' (cf. *Pha.* 174 n.) and ἀναπτυχαί 'unfoldings' = 'expanses' (*Ion* 1445, Soph. F 956). Van Looy compares *Isaiah* 34.4, the sky as book-roll (cf. *Rev.* 6.14).

6 . [Text: Nauck's '(nor would he) have the strength (to send punishment)' loses the balance between Zeus's *writing* (5) and his *examining* (6).]

7–8 . Justice is . . . close by: not, surely, in Hesiod's traditional sense (1–2 n. above, cf. *Andromeda* F 151, *Arch.* F 255 etc.) but in the sense that recognising and enacting justice lie within human power. In Menand. *Epitrep.* 1084–99 a similar argument makes character the guardian of morality.

8 . if you want to see her: a challenge to understanding; cf. Xenophanes 21 B18 DK, 'the gods have not shown everything to mortals from the outset, but in time, by searching, they discover what is better.'

507 . Cited as a consolatory saying. The appearance of line 1 in Eupolis's *Demes* (produced in 412) is relevant to dating. Generally assigned to *Capt. Mel.*, and plausibly (since it refers to griefs of long standing) to an early scene with a sympathiser or the Chorus consoling Melanippe over her supposedly dead sons.   **1.** Cf. *Alc.* 541 (Admetus) 'those who have died are dead'.   **2. spent:** lit. 'poured out' (hence **collecting**), cf. *Phil.* F 789, LSJ ἐκχέω II.2.

508 . Assigned by Wilamowitz 75 and Webster to an argument between Hellen and Aeolus (*Wise Mel.*) with other frs. on fathers, old age and youth (F 500, 509, 510; Wilamowitz added F 504); less attractively by von Arnim and van Looy with F 509 to an argument between Herdsman and Twins (*Capt. Mel.*) For the sentiment cf. *Bell.* F 291 n.   **an old saying:** cf. *Aeolus* F 25.1 = *Dictys* F 333.1; Moschion *TrGF* I 97 F 8.1 ('a true saying'). Other appeals to proverbial wisdom *Sthen.* F 668.1, *Bell.* F 285.1. Cf. Davies on Soph. *Trach.* 1.

509 . Citation and attributions as F 508. Old men as **voice**, **shadow** etc. *And.* 745– 6, *HF* 111–2 (Bond notes similar images of humans in general), 229, *Aeolus* F 25. **What else** (is he?): colloquial, cf. *Or.* 188, Ar. *Clouds* 1088.

5 1 0 . Perhaps Hellen criticising Aeolus in *Wise Mel*. (so e.g. Wilamowitz, Webster, van Looy). **Whew:** παπαῖ shows (here sarcastic) surprise (cf. *Cyc*. 110, Soph. F 153, LSJ II) rather than anguish (LSJ I, Bond on *HF* 1120); οἷος is rel. with the exclamation, cf. e.g. *HF* 1120, Hom. *Od*. 1.32: KG II.439, Fraenkel on Aesch. *Ag*. 1256f. **gauche:** for possible connotations (intellectual, moral, social) see Bond on *HF* 283. Foolishness associated with youth: *Hipp*. 119–20, *Supp*. 250 etc.

5 1 1 . Perhaps from *Capt. Mel*. with ref. to the Herdsman (e.g. von Arnim, Webster, van Looy). For birth or status *vs*. moral worth see on F 495.40–3 and Introd., p. 247. **not . . . corrupted by his title**: name *vs*. moral substance in slaves: *Ion* 854–5, *Hel*. 730–1, *Phrix*. F 831; in low-born men, *Meleag*. F 526; in bastards, *Eurysth*. F 377. On real contemporary attitudes see Dover, *GPM* 115.

5 1 2 . **useless:** ἀργός is usually 'idle' with ref. to people but sometimes 'ineffectual' (though recognised by LSJ only for things); cf. *Antiope* F 187, 'A man who has a good living but neglects his domestic affairs . . . will become useless to home and city . . .'; also *Ion* 337. ἀργία was an indictable offence at Athens: see A. R. W. Harrison, *The Law of Athens: family and property* (Oxford, 1968), 79. Domestic ἀργία leads to political turmoil: *HF* 588–92. 'Uselessness' in the city is harmful to it: Collard on *Supp*. 238–9. The topic might be related with the political exhortation in F 490 where 'beneficial' is the opposite of 'useless' here.   [Text: probably sound, but the sentence may be incompletely cited and there is some temptation to invert the adjectives: 'That man is a bad citizen, for he is an idle man'. ὡς 'inasmuch as' . . . γε (pointing the explanation): Denniston, *GP* 143.]

5 1 3 . Erotian cites an earlier writer as taking ἀλάστορες in Eur.'s phrase to mean **murderers**. Normally ἀλάστωρ is an 'avenging spirit' or a person who is (lit. or metaph.) a 'plague' because he carries some pollution (cf. Parker, *Miasma* 108–9, 224 n. 92). Perhaps to murderers (as to Orestes at Aesch. *Eum*. 236) is misrepresented by Erotian or his source. Such a description might fit the Queen's brothers or Melanippe's sons in *Capt. Mel*., or perhaps Aeolus and Hellen in *Wise Mel*. (cf. F 485). [Text: if ἴσως belongs to Eur.'s words it means 'perhaps'; if to the context, Luppe suggests 'similarly' (i.e. in meaning to another use of the word), but this is not a normal sense for ἴσως. The conjectures in App. provide iambic rhythm; the citation suggests ἀλάστορ(ε) dual rather than singular ἀλάστορ(α).]

5 1 4 . *Adonis-gardens:* plants (wheat, lettuce, etc.) sown in pots and allowed to die before reaching maturity, to honour the young dying god Adonis (at Athens, in the autumn festival of the Adonia); so proverbial for 'the untimely, shortlived and unrooted' (Schol. Pl. *Phaedr*.: see App.) or 'the superficial and vain' (Suidas): cf. Gow on Theocritus 15. 113; L. Deubner, *Attische Feste* (Berlin, ed. 2, 1966), 220–2 with Pl. 25; M. Détienne, *The Gardens of Adonis* (Eng. tr., 1977), esp. 65–6, 99–122. The fr. may be from *Wise Mel*., Melanippe faced with the burning of her children (Hartung, van Looy, Webster).

ADDENDA TO VOLUME I

We reproduce here the Addenda *printed in Vol. 2 (2004), pp. 363–9, omitting a few items now included in the corrected main text. The* Addenda *originally printed on p. 78 (*Cretans*) and p. 239 (*Phaethon*) have been added, as well as a few essential more recent items. We have not attempted to take into account the wealth of relevant material in Kannicht's* TrGF 5 *(see note below on p. 5), and as before we regret that much other work can only be mentioned summarily here.*

General Introduction

p. 1. In I.(i) we ought not to have omitted the still useful appreciation of 'fragmentary' transmission by A. C. Pearson, *The Fragments of Sophocles* (Cambridge, 1917), I.xiii–xciv. C. Collard's 'Euripidean Fragmentary Plays' in F. McHardy and others, *Lost Dramas of Classical Athens. Greek Tragic Fragments* (Exeter, 2005), 49–62 discusses the uneven contribution of papyri to reconstruction, chiefly for *Cretan Women* and *Oedipus.* For Euripidean citations in Stobaeus see R. M. Piccione, *RFIC* 122 (1994), 175–218.

p. 2, n. 1. The two kinds of hypothesis continue to receive attention: see especially M. Huys, *APF* 42 (1996), 168–78 and 43 (1997), 11–30 dissociating Hyginus' *Fabulae* from the 'narrative' kind, and van Rossum-Steenbeek 1–36 endorsing Huys; also W. Luppe, 'Zur 'Lebensdauer' der Euripides-Hypotheseis', *Philologus* 140 (1996), 213–24. In G. Bastianini and A. Casanova, *Euripide e i papiri* (Florence, 2005), 27–67 J. Diggle documents the use of rhetorical clausulae in the narrative hypotheses, offers textual comments and suggestions, and observes that the prose style of these hypotheses tells against an author so early as Dicaearchus.

p. 3, n. 2. L. Todisco and others, *La ceramica figurata a soggetto tragico in Magna Grecia e Sicilia* (Rome, 2003) provides a comprehensive survey of both Attic and locally produced vases found in southern Italy and Sicily, with a catalogue, bibliographies, indexes and photographs.

p. 4, n. 3. R. Kassel's essay in *Fragmenta Dramatica* is translated as 'Fragments and their Collectors' in *Lost Dramas of Classical Athens* (see above), 8–20. See also D. Harvey, 'Tragic Thrausmatology: the study of the Fragments of Greek Tragedy in the Nineteenth and Twentieth Centuries' in the same volume, 21–48.

p. 5, line 12. On the Budé edition of F. Jouan and H. Van Looy see this vol., p. ix.

p. 5, end of section (i). On *TrGF* V *Euripides* see this vol., p. ix. Kannicht discusses the historical and practical problems of identifying and collecting fragments, and in particular his own task as editor, in ΛΗΝΑΙΚΑ. *Festschrift für C. W. Müller* (Stuttgart, 1996), 21–31, and in G. W. Most (ed.), *Collecting Fragments: Fragmente Sammeln* (Göttingen, 1997), 67–77.

p. 6, n. 5. See also R. Kannicht, 'Scheiben von den grossen Mahlzeiten Homers: Euripides und der Troische Epenkreis', in A. Bierl and others, *Antike Literatur in neuer Deutung* (Munich, 2004), 185–201.

Bibliography

p. 13. K. Matthiessen, *Die Tragödien des Euripides* (Munich, 2002: surveys the main fragmentary plays, pp. 250–76).

Telephus

p. 17, Texts etc. Add Diggle, *TrGFS* 132–4 (F 696, 727a); van Rossum-Steenbeek 218 (Hypoth.); C. Preiser, *Euripides: Telephos* (Hildesheim, 2000: a very full edition with commentary, to be consulted on all points; for notable features see review by M. Cropp, *Gnomon* 75 [2003], 253–6); F. Jouan, ed. Budé VIII.3 (2002), 91–132.

pp. 17, 22, Myth. To the early sources for Telephus' routing of the Achaeans in Mysia add the new fragment of Archilochus (mid-7th C.), P. Oxy. 4708 fr. 1 (ed. D. Obbink, 2005), with analyses in *ZPE* 156 (2006), 1–9 (D. Obbink) and 11–17 (M. West), 157 (2006), 15–18 (P. Mayer), and 158 (2006), 1–7 (H. Bernsdorff). E. Pellizer, *EL* (1998), 43–55 discusses historicizing uses of the Telephus myth, and M. Davies, *ZPE* 133 (2000), 7–10 possible folktale origins.

p. 19, line 10. H. P. Foley's *JHS* article was reprinted in briefer form in R. Scodel (ed.), *Theater and Society in Ancient Greece* (Ann Arbor, 1993), 119–38. On the paratragedy in Ar. *Ach.* see also F. Jouan, *CGITA* 5 (1989), 17–28. The problems of disentangling history from comedy and paratragedy in Ar.'s scene are discussed by C. Pelling, *Literary Texts and the Greek Historian* (London, 2000), 141–63.

pp. 19–20, and Comm. on F 699, F 727. Against the relevance of the sacrifice of Iphigenia in *Tel.* see C. Preiser, *WJA* 24 (2000), 29–35 (as well as in her commentary).

pp. 23–4. On the characterization of Achilles in *Tel.* see P. Michelakis, *Achilles in Greek Tragedy* (Oxford, 2002), 182–4.

p. 25. W. Stockert in S. Faller and G. Manuwald, *Accius und seine Zeit* (Würzburg, 2002) doubts that Ennius and Accius both used the same Greek original.

p. 26, App., Hypothesis. Add van Rossum-Steenbeek, 218.

p. 27, App., F 696. Add Diggle, *TrGFS* 132–3. Diggle, Preiser and Kannicht in *TrGF* adopt H. Maehler's reading ἐπ[ι]στρωφῶν πατεῖ in v. 16 of the papyrus. Similar phrasing in v. 21 of the new Archilochus (see above on *Myth*).

p. 43. The text problem in F 696.14 is discussed at length by Preiser in her commentary and by M. Magnani, *AUFL* n.s. 2 (2001), 35–46.

p. 51. On F 724 and the method of Telephus' healing see C. Preiser, *RhM* 144 (2001), 277–86 (as well as in her commentary).

Cretans

p. 53, Texts etc. Add Diggle, *TrGFS* 115–9 (F 472, 472b, 472e); H. Van Looy, ed. Budé VIII.2 (2000), 303–32; A.-T. Cozzoli, *Euripide: Cretesi* (Pisa and Rome, 2001: full edition with commentary, rev. V. Di Benedetto, *RFIC* 129 [2003], 210–30).

p. 53, Myth. For Malalas see now pp. 33.52ff., 62.58ff., 280.73ff. Thurn, and §§ 2.8, 4.21, 14.12 Jeffreys. At end add *LIMC* VI 'Minotauros' and VII 'Pasiphae'.

pp. 53, 56, Myth, Illustrations. M. Schmidt in H. Froning and others, *Kotinos: Festschrift für Erika Simon* (Mainz, 1992), 306–11 and Pl. 59 publishes a very fragmentary 4ᵗʰ C. B.C. Apulian calyx-crater with a composite scene perhaps suggested by our play. Daedalus, in artisan's costume and named, sits despondently beside a frightened youth, presumably Icarus, below an unidentifiable structure (an altar?, the labyrinth?) on which a woman's lower half (Pasiphae?) is seated. An elderly woman (Nurse?) stands between these figures and an elderly, bearded and gesticulating male (Minos?). If the identification is correct, the scene may give a general impression of the crisis for Pasiphae — and for Daedalus (but all these persons would not have been on the stage together); and it perhaps strengthens the view that Icarus was a stage character (cf. p. 55). A separate, upper fragment has Athena and Zeus; again, this may help to confirm a role on- or off-stage for Athena (p. 55). A mosaic of the Pasiphae story uncovered during the excavation at Zeugma in Syria has been published by C. Abadie-Reynal, *CRAI* (Avr.–Juin 2002), 743–71, at 751–3 with Fig. 6; it is not clear whether it relates to Euripides' play.

p. 55. Van Looy 316–7 is guarded about a full role for Daedalus and Icarus (with a monologue); he hesitantly includes F 988 *if* there was a debate between Minos and Daedalus, and F 912 as uncertain (p. 315; cf. our *Other ascriptions*). M. Huys, *APF* 43 (1997), 13–14 also expresses doubts.

p. 58. Van Looy accepts Collard's placing of F 472f.

pp. 58, 60. F 472.4–15 are extensively reedited, on the basis of P. Oxy. and new editions of Porphyry and Erotian, by Cozzoli and Di Benedetto, who return largely to Porphyry's text and add valuable interpretative matter. Another reedition with very detailed commentary (but with bibl. only to 1995) is provided by A. Bernabé in J. A. López Férez, *La tragedia griega en sus textos* (Madrid, 2004), 257–86.

p. 62, F 472b–c.31. Diggle conjectures φορεῖ at line-end, accepted by Van Looy.

p. 62, F 472b–c.38. Diggle and Van Looy print Luppe's more recent conjecture μ]αστ[ῶι] δὲ [μ]ητρὸς ἢ βοὸς θ[ηλάζεται 'And *is it suckled>* by a mother's breast or a cow's (udder)?' Diggle and Luppe read θ[at the end of the line, Di Benedetto reverts to ed. pr.'s σ[, conjecturing σ[φ' οὖθαρ τρέφει 'And *does* a mother's breast or a cow's *<udder nourish it>*?'; but οὖθαρ is not Euripidean, and if the sigma is correct, a possible alternative would be σ[παργῶν τρέφει 'Does a mother's *<swelling>* breast or a cow's (swelling udder) *<nourish it>*?'; for σπαργῶν μαστός of an animal cf. *Bacc.*70.

p. 63, F 472e.1–3. The attribution to Minos and Chorus is accepted by Van Looy 313, 329 app.; 1–3 given to Chorus by Diggle (entertained by Cozzoli 104).

p. 63, line 2 of App. for F 472e. Cozzoli 41–3 reports that P. Berlin 13217 has been rediscovered in Warsaw; public access is not yet permitted. She republishes the original photographs of about 1905 (see her p. 43), not clear for confident reading.

p. 64, F 472e.23. ὅνπερ ηὔ]ξατο now Diggle, '*<the very>* bull *<that>* he vowed.'

p. 64, F 472e.27. For the anaphoric and emphatic pronoun 'you!' Diggle cites KG I.656–7 (some Sophoclean examples, mainly lyric).

p. 66, F 472e.51. Diggle cites Collard's subsequent conjecture θερ]μός 'hot-tempered'.

p. 66, lines 6–7 of Comm. on F 472f. R. Scodel, *Phoenix* 51 (1997), 226 cites S. *Phil.* 461 Ποίαντος τέκνον for a younger person's respectful address of an older.

p. 68, on F 472.3, Crete of the hundred cities: for Homer see Pearson on Soph. F 899.

p. 73, Comm. on F 472e.4–41. Detailed rhetorical analysis of vv. 4–20 by G. Paduano in *Euripide e i papiri* (cited above for p. 2 n. 1), 127–44.a

p. 75, on F 472e.19. For φύτωρ with short first vowel see Jebb on S. *Trach.* 1032 (conjectured by Dindorf).

p. 76, on F 472e.29–30 'hid', 31–33 'proclaim'. Cf. *Cret.W.* F 460.2–3, *Oed.* F 553.2. Concealing marital infidelity: Men. *Sam.* 507–13 with J. Roy, *Greece & Rome* 44 (1997), 11–22.

p. 78, on F 988 at end. Daedalus' automata: S. Morris, *Daedalus and the Origins of Greek Art* (Princeton, 1992), 215ff.; N. Spivey on 'Bionic Statues' in A. Powell (ed.), *The Greek World* (London, 1995), 446–8.

Stheneboea.

p. 79, Texts etc. Add van Rossum-Steenbeek 209–11 (Hypotheses, reporting on p. 22 that an unpublished Michigan papyrus has parts of a hypothesis); Diggle, *TrGFS* 128–31 (Hypothesis, F 661, 670); F. Jouan, ed. Budé VIII.3 (2002), 1–27.

p. 79, Discussions. Add J. Pòrtulas in F. de Martino and C. Morenilla, *El caliu de l'oikos* (Bari, 2004), 503–22 [not seen: cf. *APh* 75 (2004), 216].

p. 80, mid-page. Jouan 8–10 reluctantly abandons Murray's view that Bellerophon at the start of the play is already returning from killing the Chimaera; on 16–18 he has a good review of the two long time-interruptions, showing that Eur. here cleverly and uniquely pushed the limits of one play to an extreme.

p. 81, lines 5ff. and pp. 84–5, Hypoth. 14. Diggle rejects Rabe's παρά του 'by someone' because of the hiatus, and prints Wilamowitz's παρ' αὐτῆς 'by her'.

p. 81, Other ascriptions. Jouan p. 13 n. 28 and p. 27 tentatively admits adesp. F 292 as his fr. *10, placing it before F 670. At p. 13 n. 27 he rejects adesp. F 60.

p. 83, lines 3–7. For 'Potiphar's wife' see also J. Bremmer, *Greek Religion* (Oxford, 1994), 57–8 with n. 20 (bibl.), and S. R. Cavan in *Celebratio. Thirtieth Anniversary Essays at Trent University* (Peterborough, Ontario, 1998), 29–41 (bibl.).

p. 83, Date. On the probable significance of Eupolis, *Prospaltioi* F 259.126 see now I. Storey, *Eupolis* (Oxford, 2003), 231, 233.

p. 84, Hypothesis 6–7. For ἐπιθυμημάτων and deletion of ἐκείνηι see Diggle (cited above for p. 2 n. 1), 54.

p. 86, F 661.15. Diggle prints von Arnim's Ζηνὸς ἱκεσίου '(reverence for) the laws of Zeus the god of suppliants'.

p. 86, F 661.22–5 and App. Diggle deletes all four lines (22–3 Wilamowitz, 24–5 Holford-Strevens).

p. 90, on Hypoth. 3. Diggle would have expected the children's names to be given.

Bellerophon

 p. 98, Texts etc. Add van Rossum-Steenbeek 191–3 (Hypotheses); Diggle, *TrGFS* 98–100 (F 285, 286, 292); F. Jouan, ed. Budé VIII.2 (2000), 1–35; M. Curnis, *Il Bellerofonte di Euripide* (Turin, 2003), an exhaustive and well-balanced commentary (review: D. Milo, *Vichiana* 6.2 (2004), 304–11).

 p. 98, Illustrations. Add *LIMC* VII.1.241–30 with VII.2.142–71 ('Bellerophon': C. Lochin, 1994).

 pp. 98–9. On *Bellerophon* and Bellerophon in Comedy see G. Dobrov, *Figures of Play* (Oxford, 2001), 89–104 etc.

 pp. 99, 110, 119: F 304a. Jouan 14 accepts the fr. for *Bell.* and thinks of a scene with Megapenthes.

 p. 100. Jouan 9–10, 14 rejects a single '*agon* scene'.

 p. 101, Themes and characters. 'Atheism' is rare in surviving literature; cf. esp. Critias, *TrGF* 43 F 19 (*Sisyphus*) and a few Presocratics cited by H. Yunis, *A New Creed* (Göttingen, 1988), 60 n. 2. For Euripides see M. Fusillo, *Poetica* 24 (1992), 270–99.

 p. 101, Date. Curnis (cf. Milo 303–8) relates F 286.10 πόλεις . . . μικρὰς to the siege of Plataea in 429–7, and dates the play to that period.

 pp. 102–4, F 285.13–14: {ἐστίν} ἔνδοθεν δ' ἀλγύνεται | φρενῶν Curnis ({ἐστίν} ἔνδοθεν δ' accepted by Milo).

 p. 103, App. for F 285.13, with Comm. pp. 113–4. Diggle cites F. W. Schmidt's ἦ ν ἀλγύνεται φέρων '(poverty) which he endures with pain'.

 p. 104, F 286b.5. Diggle obelizes ἀλλὰ τῶι νόμωι.

 p. 104, App. for F 286b.6, with Comm. p. 116. Müller reaffirms his lacuna in K. Gärtner, H.-H. Krummacher (eds.), *Zur Ueberlieferung, Kritik und Edition alter und neuerer Texte* (Stuttgart, 2000), 95–7; he reports a suggestion of R. Kannicht that 1–6a may be a digression in Bellerophon's speech, and 6b the resumption of the main theme. W. Luppe in *Dissertationes Criticae. Festschrift G. Hansen* (Würzburg, 1998), 123–6 prefers a lacuna at the end of 5. A long discussion also by Jouan 26 n. 57.

 p. 108, F 297.2, with Comm. p. 117. Jouan conjectures μεῖω 'less (pay)', making the contrast plain (with Buecheler).

 p. 110, App. for F 304.2, with Comm. p. 118 on 2–3. Jouan conjectures ἁλὸς '(deep) of the ocean'.

 p. 117, on F 298. Compare *Antigone* F 176.3–5: 'Who is going to inflict pain on a rocky crag by wounding it with a spear, and who on corpses by outraging them, if they feel nothing of the injuries?'

 pp. 119–20. On F 306, 308, 311 see M. Paterlini, *Sileno* 19 (1990), 513–23, and on F 304a/68 N (to be assigned to *Bell.*) A. Carlini, *Studi . . . Privitera* (Naples, 2001), 179–84.

 p. 120, on F 309a. Cf. perhaps *Hipp.* 1030 (earth and sea refusing welcome), *HF* 1295–6 (earth and sea forbidding human passage).

p. 120, on F 312. J. R. Porter in his *EMC* review rightly objects that ὑφ' ἅρματ' ἐλθών does imply yoking, citing the Homeric formula at *Od.* 3.476, 15.47.

Cresphontes

p. 121, Texts etc. Add Diggle, *TrGFS* 111–4 (F 448a, 449, 453); H. van Looy, ed. Budé VIII.2 (2000), 257–88.

pp. 121, 123–4, Myth. Add J. N. Bremmer, *ZPE* 117 (1997), 13–17 (Euripidean invention of plot and main characters; 4th C. political exploitation of the myth); N. Luraghi in H.-J. Gehrke (ed.), *Geschichtsbilder und Gründungsmythen* (Würzburg, 2001), 37–63 (political aspects of the myth of the division of the Peloponnese, especially the elder Cresphontes' role).

p. 125, Date; p. 139, Comm. on F 448a.83–109. E. Medda, *Eikasmos* 13 (2002), 67–84 compares F 448a.83ff. with other monologues addressed to the heart, and suggests Ar. *Ach.* 480–8 is modeled on it, with implications for the dating of *Cresph.*

pp. 132–4, F 453 (with Comm., p. 144): P. Köln 398 (ed. M. Gronewald, 2003) provides a partial text of F 453 with fourteen additional verses preceding and four following: see *TrGF* 5, pp. 1161–2. The preceding verses are the end of a speech of Cresphontes as he exits to confront Polyphontes, The choral song of yearning for Peace thus marked this moment of political crisis.

pp. 134–5, 156: F 456 text. Collard suggests τῷ νερτέρῳ, 'it is to you who are below that I give this blow myself', i.e. to her supposedly dead son as an act of vengeance when in fact she about to kill him: *AC* 75 (2006), 161–3.

pp. 140–1, on F 448a.110–28 Metre. Diggle in *TrGFS* app. suggests the text in P. Mich. is written as prose.

Erectheus

p. 148, Texts etc. Add Diggle, *TrGFS* 101–10 (F 360, 362, 369, 370); F. Jouan, ed. Budé VIII.2 (2000), 95–132.

pp. 148 and 153, Myth. See further M. Lacore, *Kentron* 11 (1995–6), 89–107 on the deification of Erechtheus' daughters, and M. Christopoulos in R. Hägg (ed.), *Ancient Greek Cult Practices from the Epigraphical Evidence* (Stockholm, 1994), 123–30 on the cult of Poseidon Erechtheus.

pp. 153–4, Illustrations. J. Breton Connelly's suggestion concerning the Parthenon Frieze was published in *AJA* 100 (1996), 53–80. For E. Harrison's response (to the conference paper) see J. Neils (ed.), *Worshipping Athena: Panathenaia and Parthenon* (Madison, 1996), 202–6; in her view the scene shows the Archon Basileus handing Athena's new peplos to a boy temple servant. Weidauer's interpretation of the Lucanian vase is rejected by K. Clinton, *Myth and Cult: the Iconography of the Eleusinian Mysteries* (Stockholm, 1992), 77, who connects it with the contest of Athena and Poseidon.

pp. 158, 177, text of F 358. Separation of vv. 2–3 from v. 1 is indicated by punctuation in ms. V of Orion: see M. Haffner, *Das Florilegium des Orion* (Stuttgart, 2001), 117, 250.

p. 159, transl. of F 360.6. For λαβεῖν = 'find' see Diggle, *CQ* 47 (1997), 103–4; cf. also *El.* 70 and Ellendt, *Lexicon Sophocleum* 'λαμβάνω' II §5.

p. 167, line 1 of App. Add Diggle, *TrGFS* 106–10; Jouan, ed. Budé VIII.2.126–30.

pp. 168–73, text and App. for F 370, with Comm. pp. 187–91. The conjectures of Diggle mentioned on lines 17, 34, 41, 51 are discussed by him in *CQ* 47 (1997), 103–7; that in 62 is mentioned in his *TrGFS* app. In *CQ* he also suggests in 35 σὺ δ' ''Αιδα διῆλθες οἶμον 'but you have completed the path to Hades' (addressed to one of the daughters), and in 42 e.g. θ[άνατον (qualified by the preceding adjectives). His *TrGFS* app. includes a further conjecture: 37–8 φρενομανὴς ἀφῶ δάκρυα '. . . shall I, distraught in mind, release my tears'. New readings by M. Fassino in the Sorbonne papyrus (vv. 17, 19, 32, 36a, 41, 54, 58, 61, 98, 108) are listed by Kannicht in *TrGF* 5, p. 1161.

p. 169, App. for F 370.22. C. Austin notes (by letter) that κοὐ (Diels) was also proposed by W. Headlam, *JPh* 23 (1895), 276–7, comparing Soph. F 837 for the evaluation of life (ζῆν) after death; he thinks the papyrus might have (accordingly)]μαλλον καιου[.

pp. 170, 174, F 370.34 and 109 text: J. N. Bremmer, *ZPE* 158 (2006), 27 points out that the papyrus' spelling Δηιοῦς is confirmed in col. 22.12 of the Derveni papyrus.

p. 176, on F 350, 'moons'. Cf. E. Kearns, 'Cakes in Greek sacrifice regulations', in R. Hägg (ed.), *Ancient Greek Cult Practices etc.* (cited above), 65–70.

p. 176, on F 352. Cf. Xen. *Cyrop.* 1.5.14, 1.6.44.

p. 177, on F 358, 'Love'. 'Love' (ἔρως) of *polis* also in Pericles' Funeral Speech, Thuc. 2.43.1.

pp. 182–3, on F 362.18–20. For dismissals of discourse aimed 'at gratification (χάρις) and pleasure (ἡδονή)' cf. Critias *TrGF* 43 F 23, Isocr. 8.10, 12.271, Plut. *Mor.* 55e. In Pl. *Laws* 694b the good ruler profits from the intelligence and good counsel of those around him, allows *parrhesia*, and does not show *phthonos*. Xen. *Cyr.* 5.4.36 has *ponêroi* in an exactly similar context. *Ponêroi* natural associates of tyrants: Xen. *Hiero* 5.1–2 (cited by Collard on *Supp.* 444–6).

p. 184, on F 365. On good and bad *aidôs* see also Bernard Williams, *Shame and Necessity* (Berkeley, 1993), 225–30.

p. 190, on 55–117. Athena's speech is discussed by F. Jouan, cited in the Comm. on *Antiope* F 223.67 in this volume, p. 319.

p. 191, on 73–4. See also M. Lacore, cited above for pp. 148, 153.

pp. 192–3, on 90. The identification of the Erechtheum is now debated. For a brief introduction to the problem see J. Hurwit, *The Athenian Acropolis* (Cambridge, 1999), with refs. in note 114; cf. N. Robertson in Neils, ed. (cited above), 37–44.

p. 193, on 93–4. See also M. Christopoulos, cited above for pp. 148, 153.

p. 194, on F 370.107–8. On Hyacinthides and Hyades see T. Hadzisteliou-Price, *Kourotrophos* (Leiden, 1978), 127.

Phaethon

p. 195, Texts etc. Add van Rossum-Steenbeek 222–3 (P. Oxy. 2455 Hypothesis); Diggle, *TrGFS* 150–60 (Hypothesis and lines 1–7, 45–126, 158–77, 214–88) with J. Diggle, 'Epilegomena Phaethontea', *AC* 65 (1996), 189–99; H. Van Looy, ed. Budé VIII.3 (2002), 225–68.

p. 195, Illustrations. Add *LIMC* VIII.1.350–4 with VIII.2.311–13 ('Phaethon': F. Baratte, 1997).

p. 196, top. On the study of P see Diggle, 'Epilegomena' (above), 190–1.

p. 198, Myth. Concerning the origin of the myth, Blomqvist (see Bibl., *Myth*) speculatively associates Phaethon's blazing fall with that of a large meteorite in the Baltic (source of amber, location of 'Eridanus') dated 4,000–3,000 B.C. Cf. Comm. on F 782, 783.   A. Debiasi, *Anemos* 2 (2001), 285–319 at 316–9 discusses Hes. *Theog.* 984–91 in relation to *Phaethon*, line 241, and the views of Wilamowitz and Diggle.

p. 202, on the ending. Van Looy 243 is categoric that Oceanus is the god, for he not only 'saves his daughter but restores order': a good point.

pp. 208, 227–8, line 67. Diggle now prefers δ' ἐ⟨ν⟩ δένδρεσι (Burges) instead of a bare locative Dative; for the assonance δεν/δεν cf. his *Euripidea* 32–3.

p. 218, line 238. Diggle (and Van Looy) now prints Willink's metrical improvement δόμοις χρυσέ⟨οις θε⟩ῶν 'starry golden palace of the gods'.

pp. 220, 237, line 273. Diggle still prefers ἄφαντον, the idea of disappearance being adequately given by the verb ἐξαμαυρωθῶ and the adj. adding to κεῦθος, 'unseen concealment', as in the comparable fantasy *Ion* 1238–9, 'beneath the earth's dark recesses'.

p. 218, line 240. Diggle now accepts Hermann's conjectures (printed by us).

p. 222, F 783a = fr. 1 D. Van Looy 265 n. 94 notes Meziriac's supplement (in Plut.) ⟨σε⟩, 'unhinged ⟨you⟩' (i.e., Phaethon speaks ironically to Merops during their discussion of marriage).

p. 226, on 59–60. Diggle, 'Epilegomena' (above) has more on λόγοι here.

p. 226, on 63–101, para. 1. For dawn pictures add Hollis on Callim. *Hecale* 74.23ff.

pp. 227–8, on 67. Diggle, 'Epilegomena' has further notes on nightingales.

p. 231, on 158–9. The construction of Acc. part. with ἔχω occurs 15 times in Herodotus (see J. E. Powell, *Lexicon to Herodotus*), once in Thucydides (1.144.3).

p. 232, on 168. Cf. Nestor's instructions to Antilochus on how to drive, Hom. *Il.* 23.306ff.

p. 233, on 217. Copious illustration of such doubling by Diggle, 'Epilegomena'.

pp. 234–5, on 227–44. J. R. Porter in his *EMC* review observes that if Merops is an *ersatz* bridegroom the difficulty of 241 is resolved.

p. 235 Comm. Diggle, 'Epilegomena' gives many examples of a word or name in corresponding places in strophe and antistrophe, as Aphrodite here in 230 and 239.

Wise Melanippe, Captive Melanippe

p. 240, Texts etc. Add Diggle, *TrGFS* 120–7 (*Mel.S.* Hypoth., F 481; *Mel.D.* F 494, 495; *Mel.* F 506); H. van Looy, ed. Budé VIII.2 (2000), 347–96.

pp. 240, 245, Myth. Political aspects of the foundation myths of Metapontium are discussed by D. Giacometti, *Annali della Fac. di Lett. e Filosofia* . . . *Perugia* 28 (1990–1), 277–96 and M. Nafissi, *Ostraka* 6 (1997), 337–57.

p. 248, App. for test. i, Hypothesis. Add van Rossum-Steenbeek 199 (P. Leiden), 206–7 (P. Oxy.); Diggle, *TrGFS* 120; ed. Budé VIII.3.356–7.

p. 250, text of F 481, with Comm. p. 266. The integrity of the transmitted text is defended further by S. Cives, *RCCM* 40 (1998), 45–53, who notes that a date for *Mel.S.* about 413 would help to explain the omission of Dorus and his descendants from the narrative. Both Diggle and van Looy print a lacuna after line 8, allowing for mention of Dorus. In 12 Diggle obelizes ὄνομά τε τοὐμόν, while Luppe (personal correspondence) suggests the text in 11–12 may have been disrupted (ἀλλ' ἀνοιστέος λόγος Ι ⟨ x – ◡ – x ⟩ κεῖσ' ὅθενπερ ἠρξάμην, Ι ὄνομά τε τοὐμόν ⟨ – ◡ – x – ◡ – ⟩).

p. 255, App. for F 494. Add Diggle, *TrGFS* 123–4; ed. Budé VIII.3.385–7.

p. 256, text of F 494.25. Diggle in *TrGFS* prints his conjecture ἦν μί' εὑρεθῆι ('if ever' rather than just 'if').

p. 257, App. for F 495. Add Diggle, *TrGFS* 124–6; ed. Budé VIII.3.389–91.

p. 259, App. for F 495 with Comm., pp. 275–6. J. Diggle, *Analecta Papyrologica* 7 (1995), 11–13 proposes in line 18 χερμ[άδων ἔσχον βολάς, 'your brothers put a stop to the rock-throwing', and in 30–1 ἄλλον νεκρὸν [παῖς αὐ]τὸς 'another corpse, by the same youth . . .' (both printed in *TrGFS*); in 39 he rejects von Arnim, preferring (in *TrGFS* app.) Nauck's τύχην τοιαύτην or μόρον τοιοῦτον ('such is the fortune/death of your brothers that I tell you of'). In *TrGFS* app. he proposes in 23–4 ο]ὐ λῆμ' ἔχο[ντες δοῦλον ἀλλ' ἐλεύθερον Ι ἧιξαν π]ρὸς ἀ[λκήν, 'having a temper not slavish but free, (the twins) leapt to their own defence'.

p. 272, on F 494. J. Butrica, *CQ* 51 (2001), 610–3 sees arguments from this speech reflected in Ar. *Eccl.* 441–54, and suggests a 'Socratic' source for them.

pp. 272–3, on F 494.12–22. L. Maurizio, *JHS* 105 (1995), 85 discusses this passage in a study of the Pythia's prophetic role at Delphi. On women's religious roles see also M. Lefkowitz in Neils (ed.), *Worshipping Athena* (see above for p. 154), 78–91.

p. 279, line 7. At end of sentence add M. L. West, *The East Face of Helicon* (Oxford, 1997), 561–2.